MORRIS AUTOMATED INFORMATION NETWORK

0 1006 0171179 7

JUN 0 2 2006

Chester
Library

DISCARD

250 West Main Street
Chester, NJ 07930

D1248230

North Sea

North Sea

Amsterdam ✷

NETHERLANDS

Bremen

Rhine

GERMANY

Zeebrugge
Ostend
Calais
ARTOIS
FLANDERS
Yser
oulogne
Ypres
Ghent
BELGIUM
Antwerp

Brussels ✷

Liège
Cologne

Namur
Meuse
Mons
Neuve-Chapelle
Lille
Loos
Lens
Koblenz
Vimy
Arras
Cambrai
Charleroi
Sambre
Rhine
Bapaume
Le Cateau
ARDENNES
Mosel
Frankfurt
Albert
St. Quentin
Somme
Amiens
Péronne
ICARDY
Mondidier
Noyon
CHEMIN
DES DAMES
Sedan
ARGONNE
Luxembourg ✷
Compiègne
Aisne
Soissons
Reims
Longwy
Oise
Ourq
Meuse
Verdun
Metz
Chantilly
Marne
CHAMPAGNE
Troyon
Chateau-
Thierry
St. Mihiel
Paris ✷
Seine
Seine
Yonne
Orléans
Loire
Belfort
Basel
Saône
SWITZERLAND

© 2005 Jeffrey L. Ward

A WORLD
UNDONE

✠

Also by G. J. Meyer

The Memphis Murders
Executive Blues

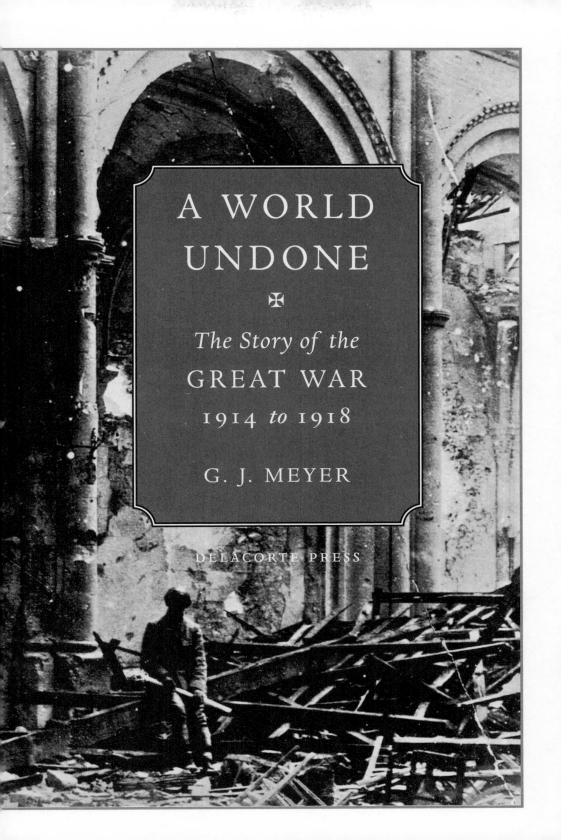

A WORLD UNDONE

✠

The Story of the GREAT WAR
1914 *to* 1918

G. J. MEYER

DELACORTE PRESS

A WORLD UNDONE
A Delacorte Press Book / June 2006

Published by Bantam Dell
A Division of Random House, Inc.
New York, New York

All rights reserved
Copyright © 2006 by G. J. Meyer
Maps by Jeffrey L. Ward

Book design by Virginia Norey

Delacorte Press is a registered trademark of Random House, Inc.,
and the colophon is a trademark of Random House, Inc.

Library of Congress Cataloging in Publication Data

Meyer, G.J.
A world undone: the story of the Great War, 1914–1918 / G. J. Meyer
p. cm.
ISBN-10: 0-553-80354-9
ISBN-13: 978-0-553-80354-9
1. World War I, 1914–1918. I. Title

D521 .M56 2006   2005058966
940.3 22

Printed in the United States of America
Published simultaneously in Canada

www.bantamdell.com

BVG   10 9 8 7 6 5 4 3 2 1

Dedicated to the memory of my parents,
Cornelia E. and Justin G. Meyer

Contents

List of Maps

List of Illustrations

Abbreviations

CNP   *Collier's New Photographic History of the World's War* (New York, 1918)

CPE   *Collier's Photographic History of the European War* (New York, 1918)

GW   *The Great World War: A History,* edited by Frank A. Mumby (Gresham Publishing Company, five volumes 1915–1917)

HW   *History of the World War* by Francis A. March (Philadelphia, 1918)

IWM   Imperial War Museum

NA   National Archives

NW   *The Nations at War* by Willis John Abbot (New York, 1917)

WW   *Liberty's Victorious Conflict: A Photographic History of the World War* (Woman's Weekly, Chicago, 1918)

A Chronology of the Great War

1914

June 28:	Archduke Franz Ferdinand is assassinated at Sarajevo.
July 5:	Kaiser Wilhelm II gives "blank check" to Austria-Hungary.
July 23:	Austria-Hungary delivers ultimatum to Serbia.
July 25:	Serbia responds to ultimatum and mobilizes. Russia declares Period Preparatory to War.
July 28:	Austria-Hungary declares war on Serbia.
July 30:	Russia and Austria-Hungary order general mobilization.
July 31:	Germany issues "double ultimatum" to France and Russia.
August 1:	France orders general mobilization. Germany mobilizes, declares state of war with Russia.
August 2:	German troops enter Luxembourg.
August 3:	Germany declares war on France. Britain orders general mobilization.
August 4:	Germany declares war on Belgium. Britain declares war on Germany.
August 5:	Austria-Hungary declares war on Russia.
August 6:	Serbia declares war on Germany.
August 7:	French troops invade Alsace.
August 10:	France declares war on Austria-Hungary. Austria-Hungary invades Serbia.
August 12:	Britain declares war on Austria-Hungary.
August 16:	Russian troops invade East Prussia.
August 23:	Germans and British meet in Battle of Mons in Belgium.
August 26:	Battle of Le Cateau.
August 28:	Russian Second Army is destroyed at Tannenberg.
September 3–11:	Russians force Austro-Hungarians out of Lemberg, drive them back to Carpathian Mountains.

September 5:   French-British counterattack opens Battle of the Marne.

September 9:   German withdrawal marks end of Schlieffen Plan offensive.

September
9–14:   Germans defeat Russians in Battle of Masurian Lakes.

October 6:   Belgian troops abandon Antwerp to Germans.

October 19:   Opening of First Battle of Ypres.

October 29:   Turkey enters war on side of Austria-Hungary and Germany.

November 5:   Austria-Hungary invades Serbia.

December 14:   French and British launch general offensive all along Western Front.

1915

January 24:   British-German warships meet at Dogger Bank in North Sea.

February
7–22:   German victory over Russians in Second Battle of Masurian Lakes.

March 10–13:   Battle of Neuve Chapelle in France's Artois region.

March 18:   British-French naval task force fails to force open the Dardanelles.

April 22:   Second Battle of Ypres begins with German offensive.

April 25:   British and French forces land on Gallipoli Peninsula.

May 1:   German offensive at Gorlice and Tarnow in Galicia.

May 9:   British attack Aubers Ridge; French begin Second Battle of Artois.

May 23:   Italy declares war on Austria-Hungary.

June 23:   Italian attack opens First Battle of the Isonzo.

August 5:   German forces occupy Warsaw, climaxing an offensive that began on July 13.

August 6:   British forces land at Suvla Bay in Gallipoli.

September 25:   Massive French offensive begins Second Battle of Champagne and Third Battle of Artois while British attack at Loos.

October 6:   Germans and Austro-Hungarians invade Serbia.

October 14:   Bulgaria and Serbia declare war on each other.

December 17:   Douglas Haig replaces John French as commander of British Expeditionary Force.

1916

January 8:	British complete evacuation of Gallipoli peninsula.
February 21:	Germans open offensive at Verdun.
March 18:	Russians attack German defenders at Lake Naroch.
May 5:	Beginning of Arab revolt against Ottoman Empire.
May 31:	The Battle of Jutland in the North Sea.
June 4:	Russians begin the Brusilov offensive in Austria and Poland.
July 1:	British and French begin the Battle of the Somme.
August 27:	Romania declares war on Austria-Hungary.
August 29:	Hindenburg replaces Falkenhayn as chief of German General Staff.
September 1:	Bulgaria declares war on Romania.
September 3:	German-Bulgarian-Turkish force invades Romania.
October 24:	French launch counteroffensive at Verdun.
November 23:	Provisional Greek government declares war on Germany and Bulgaria.
December 5:	David Lloyd George replaces H. H. Asquith as British prime minister.
December 6:	German troops enter Bucharest, Romania.
December 12:	Joseph Joffre is replaced by Robert Nivelle as commander of French forces on the Western Front.

1917

January 31:	Germany announces resumption of unrestricted submarine warfare.
February 3:	United States ends diplomatic relations with Germany.
February 23:	Germans begin withdrawal to Hindenburg Line on Western Front.
March 1:	Contents of Zimmermann telegram are made public.
March 15:	Tsar Nicholas II abdicates.
April 6:	United States declares war.
April 9:	British attack opens Battle of Arras.
April 16:	Nivelle offensive begins with French attack at the Chemin des Dames.
April 17:	First outbreak of mutiny among French troops on Western Front.

May 12:	John J. Pershing is appointed commander of American Expeditionary Force.
May 15:	Nivelle is replaced by Henri-Philippe Pétain as French commander in chief.
June 7:	British offensive at Messines Ridge in Flanders.
July 1:	Russians launch Kerensky offensive.
July 31:	British attack opens Third Battle of Ypres (Passchendaele).
October 24:	Austro-Hungarian forces open Battle of Caporetto on Italian front.
November 6:	Passchendaele falls to Canadian Corps, ending Third Battle of Ypres. Bolsheviks under Lenin and Trotsky overthrow Russian government.
November 20:	British attack with tanks at Cambrai.

1918

January 8:	Woodrow Wilson presents Fourteen Points peace program to Congress.
March 3:	Russians accept German peace terms at Brest-Litovsk.
March 21:	Germans launch Operation Michael on Western Front.
March 28:	General Pershing invites Foch to use U.S. troops against German offensive.
April 9:	Germans launch Operation Georgette.
April 14:	Ferdinand Foch is named General in Chief of the Allied Armies.
May 27:	Germans launch offensive at the Chemin des Dames and the River Aisne.
June 9:	Germans attack at the River Matz.
July 15:	Germans open final offensive in Champagne along the River Marne.
July 18:	British and French counterattack to begin the Second Battle of the Marne, forcing German withdrawal.
August 8:	British launch Amiens offensive, "the Black Day of the German Army."
August 21:	Germans begin withdrawal back to Hindenburg Line.
September 8:	Germans begin withdrawal from St. Mihiel salient.
September 15:	Allied Army of the Orient moves out of Salonika against Bulgaria.

September 16:   Americans launch Meuse-Argonne offensive north of Verdun.

September 30:   Bulgaria agrees to an armistice—in effect a surrender.

October 1:   Allied forces enter Damascus.

October 14:   Italian offensive launches Battle of Vittorio Veneto.

October 26:   Erich Ludendorff resigns as Quartermaster General of the German Army.

October 29:   German sailors mutiny at Kiel naval base.

October 30:   New Turkish government agrees to armistice.

November 4:   Austro-Hungarian government agrees to armistice.

November 8:   German delegation meets with Allied leaders in Compiègne to discuss armistice terms.

November 9:   Kaiser Wilhelm II, having abdicated, goes into exile in Holland.

November 11:   Armistice terms accepted by Germans become effective at eleven A.M.

Major Characters

Albert I. King of Belgium; commander of Belgian forces during the war

Alexandra. Tsarina of Russia; wife of Nicholas II

Alexeyev, Mikhail. Chief of staff to Nicholas II; commander in chief of Russian armies following the tsar's abdication

Asquith, Herbert Henry. British prime minister, 1908–16

Balfour, Arthur. British Conservative leader; succeeded Churchill as First Lord of the Admiralty in May 1915; succeeded Grey as foreign secretary December 1916

Below, Otto von. German general holding major commands on the Eastern, Western, and Italian Fronts and in the Balkans

Berchtold, Leopold von. Austro-Hungarian foreign minister, 1912–15

Bernstorff, Johann von. German ambassador to the U.S. 1908–17

Bethmann Hollweg, Theobold von. Chancellor of Germany, 1909–17

Bonar Law, Andrew. British Conservative and Unionist leader; chancellor of the exchequer, 1916–18

Briand, Aristide. French politician; succeeded Viviani as premier, October 1915; headed government until March 1917

Bruchmüller, Georg. German artillerist; originator of brilliantly innovative offensive tactics

Brusilov, Alexei. Russian army and army group commander; leader of the 1916 offensive that bears his name

Bülow, Karl von. Commander of German Second Army at the start of the war

Byng, Julian. Commander of British Third Army in 1917 and 1918

Cadorna, Luigi. Chief of general staff of the Italian army, July 1914–November 1917

Caillaux, Joseph. Leader of French political opposition in 1914; arrested by Clemenceau government in 1918

Carden, Sackville. British admiral; commander of Royal Navy forces involved in the start of the Dardanelles offensive

Castelnau, Noël-Edouard de. French army and army group commander

Churchill, Winston. Britain's First Lord of the Admiralty, 1911–15; minister of munitions, 1917–18

Clemenceau, Georges. "The Tiger"; French premier from November 1917

Conrad von Hötzendorf, Franz. Austro-Hungarian field marshal; army chief of staff to March 1917

Currie, Arthur. Commander of Canadian army corps on the Western Front, 1917–18

De Robeck, John. British admiral; second commander of Royal Navy forces at the Dardanelles

Driant, Émile. French politician, writer, and lieutenant colonel; killed in opening fighting at Verdun

Enver Pasha. Turkish general; leading member of the Young Turks; minister of war 1914–18, commanding troops in the Caucasus and Middle East

Evert, Alexei. Commander of Russia's Western Army Group from September 1915

Falkenhayn, Erich von. Prussian war minister, 1913–15; army chief of staff, September 1914–August 1916

Fisher, John. British admiral; first sea lord, October 1914–May 1915

Foch, Ferdinand. French general; appointed Allied supreme commander, April 1918

Franchet d'Esperey, Louis. French army and army group commander on the Western Front and, from mid-1918, in Salonika and the Balkans

Franz Ferdinand. Archduke; heir to the throne of Austria-Hungary; assassinated in Sarajevo, June 28, 1915

Franz Joseph. Emperor of Austria and King of Hungary, 1848–1916

French, John. Commander of British Expeditionary Force, August 1914–December 1915

Gallieni, Joseph. French general; key figure in First Battle of the Marne; minister of war, 1915–16

George V. King of Great Britain

Gough, Hubert. British division, corps, and army commander; removed after defeat of his Fifth Army in the German offensive of 1918

Grey, Edward. British foreign secretary, 1905–16

Gröner, Wilhelm. German staff officer and administrator; succeeded Ludendorff as Hindenburg's chief of staff, October 1918

Haig, Douglas. Senior general with British Expeditionary Force from August 1914; commander in chief from December 1915

Hamilton, Ian. British general; commander of Entente forces at Gallipoli, March–October 1915

Hertling, Georg von. German chancellor, November 1917–October 1918

Hindenburg, Paul von Beneckendorff und von. German field marshal; army chief of staff from August 1916

Hoffmann, Max. Key German military planner and leader on the Eastern Front

Holtzendorff, Henning von. Chief of staff of the German navy, 1915–18

Horne, Henry. Commander of British First Army, 1916–18

House, "Colonel" Edward. American president Woodrow Wilson's principal adviser on foreign affairs

Hutier, Oskar von. German corps and army commander on Eastern Front, 1915–17; introduced innovative offensive tactics that came to bear his name; commander of Eighteenth Army on the Western Front, 1918

Jagow, Gottlieb von. German foreign minister to March 1917

Jellicoe, John. Commander of Britain's High Seas Fleet, 1914–16; first sea lord, 1916–17

Joffre, Joseph. Chief of French general staff, 1911–16

Karl I. Emperor of Austria and King of Hungary from 1916

Kemal, Mustafa. Turkish division commander at Gallipoli; later served in the Caucasus and Middle East

Kerensky, Alexander. Russian social democratic leader; prime minister, July–November 1917

Kitchener, Horatio. British war minister, August 1914–June 1916

Kluck, Alexander von. Commander of the German First Army at the start of the war

Kühlmann, Richard von. German foreign minister, August 1917–July 1918

Lanrezac, Charles. Commander of the French Fifth Army at the start of the war

Lansing, Robert. U.S. secretary of state, 1915–20

Lawrence, T. E. "Lawrence of Arabia"; planner and leader of Arab revolt, 1917–18

Leman, Gérard. Commander of Belgian defenders at Liège, 1914

Lenin, Vladimir Ilyich. Leader of the Bolshevik faction of the Russian Communist Party; head of the government from late 1917

Lichnowsky, Karl Max. German ambassador to Britain

Lloyd George, David. British chancellor of the exchequer, 1908–15; minister of munitions, 1915–16; war minister, 1916; prime minister from December 1916

Ludendorff, Erich. German general; chief of staff to Hindenburg, August 1914–August 1916; quartermaster general of the German army, 1916–18; effectively dictator of Germany from mid–1917

Mackensen, August von. German field marshal holding important commands on the Eastern Front, 1914–18

Mangin, Charles. French general; prominent at Charleroi, Verdun, the Chemin des Dames, and the Second Battle of the Marne

Marwitz, Georg von der. Commander of the German Second Army at Cambrai in 1917 and in the 1918 offensive

Max of Baden, Prince. German chancellor, October–November 1918

Michaelis, Georg. German chancellor, July–October 1917

Millerand, Alexandre. French minister of war, August 1914–October 1915

Milner, Alfred. Member of Lloyd George's War Council, 1916–18; minister of war from April 1918.

Moltke, Helmuth von. Chief of staff of German army, 1906–September 1914

Monash, John. Commander of Australian Army Corps on the Western Front from May 1918

Nicholas, Grand Duke. Cousin of Nicholas II; Russian general; commander in chief, August 1914–September 1915; then served in the Caucasus

Nicholas II. Tsar of Russia, 1894–1917; executed, 1918

Nivelle, Robert. Commander in chief of the French armies, December 1916–May 1917

Painlevé, Paul. French minister of war from March 1917; premier, September–November 1917

Paléologue, Maurice. French ambassador to Russia, 1914–17

Pasic, Nikola. Prime Minister of Serbia

Pershing, John J. Commander in chief of the American Expeditionary Force from May 1917

Pétain, Henri-Philippe. French general; army commander in chief from May 1917

Plumer, Herbert. British corps and army commander, responsible for sector around Ypres

Poincaré, Raymond. President of France, 1913–20

Polivanov, Alexei. Russian general; succeeded Sukhomlinov as war minister, June 1915; dismissed, March 1916

Pourtalès, Friedrich von. German ambassador to Russia

Prittwitz, Max von. Commander of German Eighth Army in August 1914

Putnik, Radomir. Serbian field marshal, war minister, and army chief of staff until 1916

Rasputin, Grigori. Russian monk, mystic, and intimate of the tsar's family

Rawlinson, Henry. British general, serving primarily as commander of the Fourth Army

Rennenkampf, Pavel von. Commander of Russian First Army at Tannenberg, August 1914

Robertson, William. British general; chief of the imperial general staff, December 1915–March 1918

Rupprecht, Crown Prince. Heir to the throne of Bavaria; commander of a German army from August 1914; of an army group from July 1916

Samsonov, Alexander. Commander of Russian Second Army at Tannenberg, August 1914

Sanders, Otto Liman von. German general, commander of Turkish defenses at Gallipoli

Sarrail, Maurice. Commander of French Third Army, 1914–15; Army of the Orient at Salonika, 1916–17

Sazonov, Sergei. Russian foreign minister, 1910–16

Smith-Dorrien, Horace. Corps and army commander with British Expeditionary Force, August 1914–May 1915

Stopford, Frederick. Commander of the landing force at Suvla Bay, Gallipoli, August 1915

Stürmer, Boris. Russian prime minister, February–November 1916; also served as interior minister and foreign minister

Sukhomlinov, Vladimir. Russian war minister, 1909–15

Tirpitz, Alfred von. Prussian naval minister, 1897–1916

Tisza, István. Prime Minister of Hungary, 1913–17

Trotsky, Leon. Leading member of Bolsheviks; principal political adviser to Lenin; head of Russian delegation to Brest-Litovsk negotiations

Viviani, René. Premier of France, June 1914–October 1915

Wilhelm, Crown Prince. Eldest son and heir of Wilhelm II; commander of the German Fifth Army from August 1914 and of an army group from September 1916

Wilhelm II. Emperor of Germany and King of Prussia, 1888–1918

Wilson, Henry. Britain's military liaison with France; chief of the imperial general staff from March 1918

Wilson, Woodrow. U.S. president, 1913–21

Zimmermann, Arthur. German deputy foreign minister

Introduction

This book is a labor of love. It has grown out of a lifelong fascination with the war that George F. Kennan called "the great seminal catastrophe"—the one out of which a century of catastrophes arose.

My fascination began when, as a boy of twelve or thirteen, I came into possession of a paperback copy of Erich Maria Remarque's *All Quiet on the Western Front*. I remember being unable to put it down—even taking it with me to the ballfield, where I could return to it on the bench when my side was at bat. I remember reading some of its more lurid descriptions of life in the trenches aloud to my pals and then to my mother, who, horrified, ordered me to stop.

It was not until twenty years later, when I made two long camping trips through Europe, that the immensity of the tragedy that was the Great War became clear to me. Nearly every village and church in Austria, Britain, France, and Germany has its First World War memorial, and their lists of the dead seem impossibly long. Everywhere I went the question was the same: how could so small a place have lost so many boys and men? My curiosity grew. My reading, untainted by any thought that I might one day undertake to write about what I was learning, broadened.

Years passed, and I gradually became aware that I had never found a one-volume history of the war that seemed to me entirely satisfactory. It hardly need be said that the number of fine works on the subject is very, very large. Among these works are brilliant scholarly accounts of how the war erupted when it did in spite of the fact that almost no one wanted it, why it went on year after year as European civilization slipped toward collapse, just how vast a calamity it was, and the terrible things that came in its wake. Some of these books are almost above criticism. Few of them even attempt to appeal to the general reader.

There are also, of course, many admirable popular histories. Some are about specific aspects of the war (one of its years, fronts, battles); some embrace the entire conflict. That even the broadest leave out important things is not only unsurprising but inevitable—no one knows better than I now do that no narration confined within a single pair of covers can deal with *everything*. Still, I never found a work without gaps that struck me as unnecessary and regrettable, or whose narrative seemed quite as fully rounded as it could and should have been.

And so, no doubt presumptuously, nearly four years ago I embarked on the writing of this book. From the start my objective was to weave together all of the story's most compelling elements—the strange way in which it began more than a month after the assassination that supposedly was its cause; the mysterious way in which the successes and failures of both sides balanced so perfectly as to produce years of bloody deadlock; the leading personalities; the astonishing extent to which the leadership of every belligerent nation was divided against itself; the appalling blunders; the incredible (and now largely forgotten) carnage—while at the same time filling in as much as possible of the historical background. And I use the word *weave* advisedly. An early decision was to intertwine the stories of the war's major fronts rather than dealing with them separately in the usual way, and to mix foreground, background, and sidelights in such a way as to make their interconnections plain. I continue to think that such an approach is essential to showing how the many elements that made up the Great War affected one another and deepened the disaster.

It has long seemed to me that practically all popular histories of the Great War assume too much, expect too much of the reader, and therefore leave too much unexplained. In dealing with Hohenzollern Germany, for example, they commonly presume that today's reading public knows more than a little about who the Hohenzollerns were, where they came from, and why they mattered. Authors are right, of course, in making mention of the decadence of the Ottoman Empire, the frailty of the Austro-Hungarian Empire, the backwardness of the Russian Empire—of all the elements that gave rise to the war and that the war destroyed. The recurrent mistake, it seems to me, has been to *only* make mention of such things, thereby diluting the story. I believe that this volume, whether or not it has any other distinction, is unique in the extent to which it attempts to restore parts of the story that have almost always been missing. I hope that it captures at least some of the multidimensional richness of one of the most epic tragedies in the history of the world.

My final objective, and not the least of my objectives, has been to offer this story in the most *readable* form possible and thereby to do justice to its inherent drama. Candidly, this has never seemed a singularly daunting challenge. Mark Twain said it isn't hard to be funny: one need only tell the truth. Something similar can be said about my subject: to make a great drama of the Great War, one need only be clear and careful and thorough in telling it as it was.

The war is unique in the number of questions about it that remain unsettled. Who caused it—if it can be said that anyone did? Should Germany have won it in 1914—and need Germany have lost it in 1918? Could it have ended earlier if only a few things had gone just a little differently at Gallipoli, or on the Marne, or at

Ypres? Was Douglas Haig—or Erich Ludendorff, or Conrad von Hötzendorf—a great commander, or a disastrously bad one, or something in between? Could the conflict have been brought to a negotiated conclusion before it did so much damage to so much of the world? After ninety years, scholars remain divided on such questions. It seems likely that they always will. I do not claim to have the answers—am not sure that answers are possible, which is part of what makes the questions so interesting. I hope I have provided enough information to allow readers to understand why the questions persist, and perhaps in some cases to arrive at conclusions of their own.

It is testimony to the power of the story that in all these years of learning about it and developing my own account of it, I have not had one boring day. If I have succeeded in making the reader understand and perhaps even share my fascination, I will regard my labors as rewarded fully. Among the many people to whom I am grateful as this project comes to completion, I must mention my agent, Judith Riven, and my editor, John Flicker, both of whom have been indispensable and endlessly supportive. I am grateful both to and for my children, Eric, Ellen, and Sarah, and I will never forget how Paul Wagman, that best of friends, saved the whole project from a very early death.

Finally, I must try to express my admiration for and gratitude to those scholars and researchers—among whom I cannot claim to be numbered—who for nearly a century have been devoting their lives to unearthing the buried secrets of the Great War. Without their labors and achievements, works like this one would be impossible.

G. J. Meyer
New York City
January 2006

A WORLD
UNDONE

✠

PART ONE

July 1914

✠

Into the Abyss

Franz Ferdinand and Sophie minutes before their assassination.

Chapter 1

✠

June 28:
The Black Hand Descends

"It's nothing. It's nothing."

—ARCHDUKE FRANZ FERDINAND

Thirty-four long, sweet summer days separated the morning of June 28, when the heir to the Austro-Hungarian Empire was shot to death, from the evening of August 1, when Russia's foreign minister and Germany's ambassador to Russia fell weeping into each other's arms and what is rightly called the Great War began.

On the morning when the drama opened, Archduke Franz Ferdinand was making an official visit to the city of Sarajevo in the province of Bosnia, at the southernmost tip of the Austro-Hungarian domains. He was a big, beefy man, a career soldier whose intelligence and strong will usually lay concealed behind blunt, impassive features and eyes that, at least in his photographs, often seemed cold and strangely empty. He was also the eldest nephew of the Hapsburg emperor Franz Joseph and therefore—the emperor's only son having committed suicide—heir to the imperial crown. He had come to Bosnia in his capacity as inspector general of the Austro-Hungarian armies, to observe the summer military exercises, and he had brought his wife, Sophie, with him. The two would be observing their fourteenth wedding anniversary later in the week, and Franz Ferdinand was using this visit to put Sophie at the center of things, to give her a little of the recognition she was usually denied.

Back in the Hapsburg capital of Vienna, Sophie was, for the wife of a prospective emperor, improbably close to being a nonperson. At the turn of the century the emperor had forbidden Franz Ferdinand to marry her. She was not of royal lineage, was in fact a mere countess, the daughter of a noble but impoverished Czech family. As a young woman, she had been reduced by financial need to accepting employment as lady-in-waiting to an Austrian archduchess who entertained hopes of marrying her own daughter to Franz Ferdinand. All these things made Sophie, according to the rigid protocols of the Hapsburg court, unworthy to be an emperor's consort or a progenitor of future rulers. The accidental discovery that she and Franz Ferdinand were conducting a secret if chaste romance—that he had been regularly visiting the archduchess's palace not to court her daughter but to see a lowly and thirtyish member of the household staff—sparked outrage, and Sophie had to leave her post. But Franz Ferdinand continued to pursue her. In his youth he had had a long struggle with tuberculosis, and perhaps his survival had left him determined to live his private life on his own terms. Uninterested in any of the young women who possessed the credentials to become his bride, he had remained single into his late thirties. The last two years of his bachelorhood turned into a battle of wills with his uncle the emperor over the subject of Sophie Chotek.

Franz Joseph finally tired of the deadlock and gave his consent. What he consented to, however, was a morganatic marriage, one that would exclude Sophie's descendants from the succession. And so on June 28, 1900, fourteen years to the day before his visit to Sarajevo, Franz Ferdinand appeared as ordered in the Hapsburg monarchy's Secret Council Chamber. In the presence of the emperor, the Cardinal Archbishop of Vienna, the Primate of Hungary, all the government's principal ministers, and all the other Hapsburg archdukes, he solemnly renounced the Austro-Hungarian throne on behalf of any children that he and Sophie might have and any descendants of those children. (Sophie was thirty-two, which in those days made her an all but hopeless spinster.) When the wedding took place three days later, only Franz Ferdinand's mother and sister, out of the whole huge Hapsburg family, attended. Even Franz Ferdinand's brothers, the eldest of whom was a notorious libertine, self-righteously stayed away. The marriage turned out to be a happy one all the same, in short order producing a daughter and two sons whom the usually stiff Franz Ferdinand loved so unreservedly that he would play with them on the floor in the presence of astonished visitors. But at court Sophie was relentlessly snubbed. She was not permitted to ride with her husband in royal processions or to sit near him at state dinners. She could not even join him in his box at the opera. When he, as heir, led the procession at court balls, she was kept far back, behind the lowest ranking of the truly royal ladies.

But here in Bosnia, a turbulent border province, the rules of Vienna could be set aside. Here in Sarajevo, Franz Ferdinand and Sophie could appear together in public as royal husband and wife. It was a rare experience, and they were enjoying it as much as any pair of small-town shopkeepers on their first vacation in years. They were staying in the nearby seaside resort town of

Franz Ferdinand,
his wife Sophie, and
two of their children
*"Sophie dear, don't die! Live
for our children!"*

Bad Ilidz, and on Saturday they had browsed the local antique markets. They had started Sunday with mass in an improvised chapel at their hotel, after which the archduke sent a telegram to the children, Sophie, Max, and Ernst. Momma and Poppa were well, the wire said. Momma and Poppa were looking forward to getting home on Tuesday.

And now on this brilliant morning, the air crisp and clear after a week of rain and chill, the streets lined with people some of whom cheered and some of whom merely looked on in silence, Sophie was seated beside the archduke in an open car as they rode toward the town hall. They looked less imperial than like characters out of a comic opera: an overweight middle-aged pair, Franz Ferdinand faintly ridiculous in an ornate military headpiece and a field marshal's tunic that stretched too tight across his ample torso, Sophie's plump face smiling cheerily under a broad bonnet and the dainty parasol that, even in the moving car, she held above her head.

Suddenly there was a loud crack: the sound, as police investigators would later determine, of the percussion cap on a Serbian-made pocket bomb being struck against a lamppost. A small dark object was seen flying through the air: the bomb, thrown by someone in the crowd. It was on target, but the driver of the royal car saw it coming and accelerated, so that it fell inches behind the archduke and his wife. Franz Ferdinand too saw it, swung at it with his arm, and deflected it farther to the rear. It exploded with a shattering noise as the car sped off, damaging the next vehicle in the procession and injuring several people. A tiny fragment of shrapnel grazed Sophie's neck.

In the crowds along the route of the motorcade that day were six young men who had traveled to Sarajevo for the purpose of killing the archduke. Five of them, including the one who had thrown the bomb, were Bosnian Serb teenagers—youths born and raised in Bosnia but of Serbian descent. All five were sick with tuberculosis, curiously enough, and all were members of Young Bosnia, a radical patriotic organization linked to and supported by a deeply secret Serb nationalist group formally called Union or Death but known to its members as the Black Hand. Though the Black Hand had been active for years, Austria-Hungary's intelligence services still knew nothing of its existence. Its purpose was the expansion of the Kingdom of Serbia, a smallish and ambitious young country adjacent to Bosnia, so that all the Serbs of the Balkans could be united. Its ultimate goal was the creation of a Greater Serbia that would include Bosnia, and its members were prepared to use terrorism to achieve that goal. The assassins of June 28 had been assembled just across the border in the Serbian capital of Belgrade, armed with bombs and Belgian revolvers, and slipped into Sarajevo well in advance of the archduke's arrival.

June 28, as it happened, was an awkward day for a Hapsburg to be visiting Bosnia. It was St. Vitus Day, which for more than five hundred years had been an occasion of mourning for the Serbs. On St. Vitus Day in 1389 a Serbian kingdom that had flourished through the Middle Ages was defeated by the Ottoman Turks at the Battle of Kosovo, on the so-called Field of Blackbirds. The Serb army was not merely vanquished but slaughtered. Soon afterward the kingdom ceased to exist. The Serbs became subjects—slaves, really—of their savagely harsh Turkish conquerors. Kosovo was avenged in 1912, when the Turks were driven out of the Balkans at last, but it would never be forgotten—certainly not while so many Serbs were still under alien rule. There could be no better day than this one to strike a blow against the oppressors—which now meant a blow against the Hapsburgs, the Turks being gone from the scene.

Between the throwing of the bomb and the motorcade's arrival at the town hall, the car carrying Franz Ferdinand and Sophie drove past three more members of the gang. They were armed but did nothing. Later two of them, after being arrested, made excuses for their failure to act. The third, probably the most truthful, said he had lost his nerve.

After a standard ceremonial welcome—the mayor, absurdly, didn't deviate from a script declaring that everyone in Sarajevo honored the archduke and was delighted by this visit—Franz Ferdinand announced a change in his itinerary. He insisted on going to the hospital where the people injured by the bomb had been taken. It was the right Hapsburg gesture, a demonstration of concern for servants of the crown. Franz Ferdinand asked Sophie to stay behind, out of any possible danger. She refused, saying that her place was with him. This did not seem reckless. The military governor of Bosnia, who was riding in the same car with the couple that morning, had already declared his confidence that there would be no further trouble. If he knew anything about the Serb fanatics, he said, it was that they were capable of only one assassination attempt per day.

The motorcade set out once again. The route originally planned by the authorities was still cleared of traffic, and the lead driver mistakenly took it rather than the road to the hospital. The others followed. They passed still another would-be assassin, but he too did nothing. When the governor, seated in front of Franz Ferdinand and Sophie, discovered that they were going the wrong way, he ordered their driver to stop. The driver brought the car to a halt, shifted gears, and prepared to turn around. By a coincidence that has reverberated down the decades, he had stopped less than five feet from Gavrilo Princip, nineteen years old, the one remaining member of the assassination gang and its leader. Princip pulled out his revolver, pointed it at the stopped car, and fired twice.

Husband and wife remained upright and calm in their seats. The governor, seeing no signs of injury and thinking that they must have escaped harm, shouted again at the driver, telling him to turn around.

Suddenly a thin stream of blood came spurting out of Franz Ferdinand's mouth.

"For heaven's sake!" cried Sophie. "What's happened to you?" Then she slumped over, her head falling between her husband's knees. The military governor thought she had fainted, but somehow the archduke knew better. "Sophie dear, Sophie dear, don't die!" he called. "Stay alive for our children!" Other members of the party surrounded him, struggling to open his tunic to see where he had been shot. "It's nothing," he told them weakly. "It's nothing."

Gavrilo Princip meanwhile tried to shoot himself in the head but was stopped by a member of the crowd. In the struggle that followed, he managed to swallow his vial of the cyanide that all the members of the gang had been given. The cyanide was old: it would make him vomit but not kill him. He was quickly captured.

Within minutes Franz Ferdinand and Sophie were both dead. (Princip, in prison, would express regret at Sophie's death, which he had not intended; the bullet that killed her had passed through the door of the car before striking her in the groin and severing an artery.) The news caused a sensation, of course, but there was little sense of crisis. In Vienna the eighty-three-year-old emperor, Franz Joseph, seemed almost grateful when he heard. He had long regarded Franz Ferdinand as a nuisance, not only because of the marriage problem but also because of the archduke's unpleasantly advanced ideas. (He had even wanted, ironically, to give the Hapsburgs' Slavic subjects, the Bosnian Serbs included, a voice in the governance of the empire.) Apparently Franz Joseph believed at first that the Sarajevo murders had simplified things, had even put them right. "A higher power," his private secretary would remember him saying, "has re-established the order which I, alas, could not preserve."

Germany's Kaiser Wilhelm II, when he learned of the assassination, ended his sailing vacation off the coast of Norway and headed for home. He did so more because he and the archduke had been friends than because he foresaw an emergency; he and his wife had been guests at Franz Ferdinand and Sophie's country estate just weeks before.

From his royal yacht the *Standart*, Tsar Nicholas II of Russia declared three weeks of mourning in honor of the slain archduke. Beyond that he showed little interest; he had other things on his mind. His ten-year-old only son had a few days earlier twisted his ankle in jumping aboard the *Standart* for a family cruise in the Gulf of Finland. The injury activated the hemophilia that the boy had inherited from his mother, who in turn had inherited it from her grandmother, Queen Victoria of England. By June 28 he was in intense pain from internal bleeding. His parents, not for the first time and not for the last, feared for his survival.

The murders aroused little interest in Britain and France. Both countries were focused on other stories, London on a crisis over Ireland, Paris on a sensational murder trial that combined sex with political scandal. And assassinations were not unusual in those days. In the two decades before 1914, presidents of the United States, France, Mexico, Guatemala, Uruguay, and the Dominican Republic had been murdered. So had prime ministers of Russia, Spain, Greece, Bulgaria, Persia, and Egypt, and kings, queens, and empresses of Austria, Italy, Serbia, Portugal, and Greece. People had grown accustomed to such things and to expecting that their consequences would not be terribly serious.

Across the Atlantic in the United States, yet another killing of people no one had ever heard of in a place no one had ever heard of could hardly have seemed less important. President Woodrow Wilson had only somewhat more interest in European affairs than most of his fellow citizens, though he was inclined to believe that he might be the man to enlighten the Old World and save it from its foolish ways. During the summer his personal emissary, a Texan who styled himself "Colonel" Edward House despite never having served in any military capacity, spent two months visiting the capitals of the great powers and conferring with some of their most important men. "My purpose," House confided to his diary, perhaps somewhat smugly, "was to

Col. Edward House,
confidant to Woodrow Wilson
*"There is some day to be
an awful cataclysm."*

plant the seeds of peace." What he found, he reported to Wilson, was "militarism run stark mad. Unless someone acting for you [it is not difficult to guess who he thought that someone might be] can bring about a different understanding, there is some day to be an awful cataclysm."

House would depart for home having accomplished essentially nothing. He returned to an America that appeared to be on the verge of war with Mexico (U.S. troops had forcibly occupied the coastal town of Veracruz in April), was embroiled in violent labor disputes (also in April, Wilson had sent troops to Colorado to crush a strike by coal miners), but was as confident as the president of its uniquely virtuous, uniquely pacific role in the world. William Jennings Bryan, Wilson's secretary of state, saw it as "the imperative duty of the United States...to set a shining example of disarmament." In January the influential *Review of Reviews* had confidently told its readers that "the world is moving away from military ideals; and a period of peace, industry and world-wide friendship is dawning," while statesman and Nobel Peace Prize winner Elihu Root wrote unhappily that, even for educated Americans, "international law was regarded as a rather antiquated branch of useless learning, diplomacy as a foolish mystery and the foreign service as a superfluous expense."

None of these people had even the faintest idea, as June ended, of what lay just head. But they are hardly to be blamed. What was coming was unlike anything anyone had ever seen.

THE SERBS

NO ONE COULD HAVE BEEN SURPRISED THAT TROUBLE had broken out in the southeastern corner of Europe, or that the Serbs were at the center of that trouble. In 1914, as before and since, the Balkan Peninsula was the most unstable region in Europe, a jumble of ill-defined small nations, violently shifting borders, and intermingled ethnic groups filled with hatred for one another and convinced of their right to expand. By 1914 the Balkans were exploding annually. The little Kingdom of Serbia, seething with resentment and ambition, was never not involved.

The roots of the trouble went deep. Almost two millennia ago the dividing line between the Eastern and Western Roman Empires ran through the Balkans, and so the dividing line between the Catholic and Orthodox worlds has run through the region ever since. Later, after the Turks forced their way into Europe, the Balkans became another of the things it continues to be today: the home of Europe's only indigenous Muslim population, the point where European Christendom ends and Islam begins. Through many generations the Balkans were a prize fought over by Muslim Turkey, Catholic Austria, and Orthodox Russia. By 1914, Turkey having been pushed almost entirely out of the region, the contest was between Russia and Austria-Hungary only, with Turkey waiting on the sidelines in hope of recovering some part of what it had lost.

The Russians wanted Constantinople above all. In pre-Christian times it had been the Greek city of Byzantium, and it then became the Eastern Roman capital until falling to the Turks. It dominated the long chain of waterways—the Dardanelles, the Sea of Marmara, the Bosporus—that linked Russia's Black Sea ports to the Mediterranean. Possession of Constantinople would make the *tsar*—the word means "caesar" in Russian, as does *kaiser* in German—what Russia's rulers had long claimed to be: rightful leader of the whole Orthodox world, rightful heir to the old eastern empire. It was largely with Constantinople in mind that the Russians anointed themselves patrons and protectors of the Slavic and Orthodox populations in the Balkans, the Serbs included. As the nineteenth century unfolded and the Turkish empire entered a terminal state of decay, it was mainly Britain that

kept the Russians from seizing Constantinople. The British were motivated
not by any affection for the Turks but by simple self-interest. They feared
that Russian expansion to the south would threaten their own position in
the Middle East and ultimately their control of India.

The Serbs had been part of a wave of so-called South Slavs (Yugoslavs,
in their language) that moved into the Balkan region during the seventh
century, when the Eastern Roman Empire was beginning to totter (Rome
itself had collapsed much earlier) and many tribal groups were on the
move. In the centuries that followed, the Serbs built a miniature empire
under their own tsar. For a time it was uncertain whether all the Serbs
would be Orthodox or some would be Roman Catholic, but eventually
they settled into the Orthodox faith. Thereby they helped to ensure that a
thousand years hence their descendants would identify themselves with
the greatest of Slavic and Orthodox nations, Russia, and would look to the
Russians for protection. They assured also that religious differences would
contribute to separating them from Catholic Austria and from the Magyars
(many of them Calvinist Protestants) who dominated Hungary.

From the late Middle Ages, in the aftermath of their defeat at Kosovo,
the Serbs were trapped inside the empire of the Ottoman Turks. By the
eighteenth century the Turks, the Austrians, and the Russians were entangled in what would turn into two hundred years of bloody conflict in and
over the Balkans. In 1829 a Russian victory over the increasingly incompetent and helpless Turks made possible the emergence of a new princi-
pality that was, if almost invisibly tiny, the first Serbian state in almost half
a millennium and a rallying point for Serbian nationalism. In the 1870s
another Russo-Turkish war broke out, with Serbia fighting actively on
the side of Russia this time and gaining more territory as a result. Now
there was once again a Kingdom of Serbia, a rugged, mountainous, and
landlocked little country surrounded by the whole boiling ethnic stew of
the Balkans. Its neighbors were Europe's only Muslims, Catholics, and
Orthodox Christians some of whom thought of themselves as Serbs and
some of whom did not. Among those neighbors were Magyars, Bulgars,
Croats, Albanians, Macedonians, Romanians, Montenegrans, Greeks,
and—just across the border in Bosnia—brother Serbs suffering the indignity of not living in Serbia. Despite the inconvenient fact that Serbs were
only a minority of the Bosnian population (fully a third were Muslims, and
one in five was Croatian and therefore Roman Catholic), the incorporation
of Bosnia into an Orthodox and Slavic Greater Serbia became an integral
part of the Serbs' national dream. The fact that under international law
Bosnia was the possession of two of the great powers—officially of the

Ottomans but actually of the Austrians in recent years—mattered to Serbia not at all.

As the years passed, trouble erupted with increasing frequency, and sometimes with shocking brutality. At the start of the twentieth century Serbia had a king and queen who were friendly to Hapsburg Vienna. In 1903 a group of disgruntled army officers staged a coup, shot the royal pair to death, threw their naked bodies out the windows of their Belgrade palace, and replaced them with a dynasty loyal to Russia.

In 1908 Austria-Hungary enraged Serbia by annexing Bosnia and the adjacent little district of Herzegovina, taking them from the Ottoman Turks and making them full and presumably permanent provinces of the Hapsburg empire. Serbia turned to Russia for help. The Russians, however, were still recovering from a 1905 war with Japan in which total and humiliating defeat had exposed the incompetence of both their army and their navy, forced the abandonment of their ambitions in the Far East, and ignited a revolution at home. As a result—and to its further humiliation—the Russian government felt incapable of doing anything to support the Serbs.

In 1911 the same conspirators who had murdered Serbia's royal family founded Union or Death, the Black Hand. Then in 1912 came the First Balkan War. Serbia joined with several of its neighbors to drive the Turks all the way back to Istanbul. The victory doubled the kingdom's size and raised its population to four and a half million. A year later, in the Second Balkan War, Serbia defeated its neighbor and onetime ally Bulgaria. Again it grew larger, briefly seizing part of the Dalmatian coast but being forced to withdraw when the Austrians threatened to invade. Serbia was still getting not nearly as much support as it wanted from Russia, but France, seeing a strategic opportunity in the Balkans, was now providing money, arms, and training to the Serbian army. France's motives were transparent: to make Serbia strong enough to tie up a substantial part of the Austro-Hungarian army in case of war, so that France and its ally Russia (and Britain too, if everything went perfectly) would be free to deal with Germany alone.

To what extent did the government of Serbia know in advance of the plot to kill Franz Ferdinand? To what extent could Belgrade therefore be held responsible? As with many parts of this story, the answer is neither clear nor simple. Prime Minister Nikola Pasic, a shrewd old man with a majestic white beard, did hear about the plot weeks before the shooting, but he emphatically disapproved. He put out the word on the Belgrade grapevine that the plot should be called off. On the other hand, Serbian officialdom was not entirely innocent. The leader of the Black Hand was the country's chief of military intelligence, one Colonel Dragutin Dimitrijevic, a monomaniacally dedicated Pan-Serb nationalist whose physical strength had caused him to be nicknamed "Apis" after a divine bull in ancient Egyptian mythology. Apis had been the mastermind behind the strategy that led to Serbia's successes in the Balkan wars. Now, in 1914, he was the mastermind behind the plot to kill Franz Ferdinand. But there has never been any evidence that Pasic's cabinet was involved.

Serbian Prime Minister Nikola Pasic
"Our cause is just. God will help us."

On the contrary, Apis and his allies in the Black Hand and the military saw Pasic as an obstacle, even as an enemy. The prime minister's lack of enthusiasm for extreme measures, for another round of war, was contemptible in their eyes. Pasic was so unacceptable to the Serbian army's high command that in June 1914 the generals forced him out of office. He was almost immediately restored, but only at the insistence of the Russians and the French, who regarded him as sane and sensible and therefore as a badly needed man in the Balkans. Pasic's return to office was a defeat for Apis, an indication that his influence was waning. Apis may have seen the assassination of Franz Ferdinand as a way of precipitating a crisis that would cause Pasic's government to fall, and if the crisis led to war, he would not have been likely to regard that as too high a price to pay. Pasic, on the other hand, understood that Serbia was physically and financially exhausted after two wars in as many years—its casualties had totaled ninety thousand, an immense number for such a small country—and that the army was in no condition to challenge the Austrians. In case of war, Serbia would be able to muster only eleven badly equipped divisions against Vienna's forty-eight. And of course Pasic was mindful of Russia's failure to come to Serbia's aid in 1908, in 1912, and again in 1913.

Why didn't Pasic intervene more actively to stop the assassination? Actually, he went so far in that direction as to put himself at risk. He sent out an order that the three conspirators whose names had become known to him should be stopped from crossing the border into Bosnia. But the answer came back that he was too late—the three were already across. He then directed his ambassador in Vienna to deliver an oral warning. But this ambassador, himself an ardent Serb nationalist, had no great enthusiasm for such a mission. He met with Austria's finance minister rather than with someone better positioned to take action on such a matter. He expressed himself so vaguely—he said he was concerned that "some young Serb might put a live rather than a blank cartridge in his gun, and fire it," never indicating that Belgrade had knowledge of an actual plot and even knew the names of conspirators already in Sarajevo—that the finance minister could see no reason for alarm and was given no basis on which to do anything. It must have seemed to Pasic, who could have known nothing of how his warning had been diluted, that there was nothing more he could do. That summer Serbia was in the midst of an election. The result would decide whether Pasic remained as prime minister. It would have been suicide, certainly politically and perhaps literally, for him to become known as the enemy—the betrayer, even—of the most violently passionate patriots in the kingdom.

By then no one but the assassins themselves could have stopped the assassination. Not even the Black Hand, not even Apis himself, was now in control. On June 14 Apis told a meeting of the Black Hand executive committee of his plans for Sarajevo in two more weeks. The committee's members did not react as he expected. They voted that the plot must be called off. Like Pasic, they realized that the assassination could lead to war with the empire next door, and undoubtedly they understood that the prime minister had reason to be opposed. Apis, through a chain of intermediaries, managed to get word to the assassination gang to abandon its plot. Now it was his turn to be ignored. Gavrilo Princip, in an interview with a psychiatrist as he lay dying of tuberculosis in an Austrian prison midway through the war (an interview in which, strangely, he often spoke of himself in the third person), would say that in going to Sarajevo "he only wanted to die for his ideals." He had been happy to accept the Black Hand's weapons but unwilling to obey when instructed not to use them.

Chapter 2

✠

Never Again

*"In 1908–1909 we would have been playing cards up,
in 1912–1913 we still had a clear chance,
now we have to go for all or nothing."*
—AUSTRIAN FIELD MARSHAL FRANZ CONRAD

Leopold von Berchtold and Franz Conrad were polar opposites as men, and over the years they had often been at odds over how Austria-Hungary should deal with its Serbian problem. But in the days following the assassination, their differences disappeared and they became partners. To understand how this happened is to understand much about the origins of the war.

Conrad (Conrad von Hötzendorf was his full family name, but the *von* part was an addition, an honorific that had come with his grandfather's elevation to the nobility) was a soldier to the marrow of his bones, sometimes even a rather fanatical one. His father had been an officer; he himself began his military training at age eleven, and he became chief of the Austro-Hungarian general staff in 1906 at the age of fifty-four. He looked the part: a compact, tidy figure with a fierce mustache that turned up at the corners and pale hair cut in a brush. He was an almost neurotically hard worker, intent upon trying to turn the hodgepodge Austro-Hungarian armies into a modern and effective fighting force, constantly drawing up and issuing new orders and war plans, painfully conscious that the empire was militarily weak and its status among Europe's great powers no longer assured. He was certain that the empire could save itself only by asserting itself in the Balkans—above all by eliminating Serbia's endless subversion and, if possible, by eliminating Serbia. Time after time, until Emperor Franz Joseph grew sick of hearing it, he had urged attacks on the Serb kingdom. At times he even wanted to attack the recently created Kingdom of Italy, which officially was Austria's ally but

Conrad von Hötzendorf
Chief of Staff of
Austro-Hungarian Army
Frustrated by Austria's
passivity during the
two Balkan Wars.

had taken over a great expanse of what had previously been Hapsburg territory and was obviously hungry for more. In 1911 Conrad had been dismissed from his position as chief of staff because of his obsessive aggressiveness. But a year later war in the Balkans made his talents and his energy seem indispensable. And so he was recalled to duty and showed himself to be no less bellicose than before. In the course of 1913 he made no fewer than twenty-five proposals for war on Serbia.

Count Berchtold, by contrast, was an enormously wealthy, deeply cultivated, pleasure-loving aristocrat of ancient family. And he too looked the part: polished, serenely self-assured, a vision of elegance in spotless collars and cuffs and diamond stickpins. He spoke German, French, Hungarian, Czech, and Slovak, and he had married a Hungarian heiress. (Unusually, he held both Austrian and Hungarian citizenships, and when asked his nationality, he said he was "Viennese.") He owned a racing stable and was famous for his charm and his success with women. He was also widely regarded as weak, lazy, frivolous, and unreliable. He had spent much of his early career as a diplomat in Paris and London, splendid places for a wealthy young nobleman eager to indulge his many appetites. He became the Austro-Hungarian ambassador to Russia in 1907 and was appointed foreign minister in 1912, when he was fifty years old. His conduct in the Balkan crises of that year and 1913, when Serbia enlarged itself at the expense of the Turks and the Bulgarians while Vienna stood by watching, had cemented his reputation for passivity and vacillation. Conrad among others came to be convinced that Berchtold lacked the backbone to protect Hapsburg interests in the slippery world of great power diplomacy. Berchtold himself was well aware by then that important people regarded him as unworthy to be foreign minister and that he needed to repair his reputation. He was ready to believe what Conrad had always believed: that the monarchy had squandered too many opportunities in its area of greatest vulnerability, the Balkans. He expected good opportunities to be far less plentiful in the years ahead, now that Serbia had grown bigger and Russia was recovering its strength, and he was as determined as Conrad not to let the next one slip away. He had become, in short, dangerous: a weak man determined to appear strong. Within forty-eight hours of the assassination he was calling for "a final and fundamental reckoning with Serbia."

Austria-Hungary in 1914 was a second-rate and declining empire trying desperately to hang on to its traditional place among the nations that recognized one another as Europe's leading powers. In the half-century leading up to the Sarajevo assassinations, it had been displaced as leader of the German states—had been, in effect, evicted from Germany—by Otto von Bismarck, Prussia's great chancellor and the creator of the new German Empire. Then it had lost great hunks of territory—Tuscany, Lombardy—to a new Kingdom of Italy that, although also militarily weak, was supported in its expansion by France. Austria-Hungary had become a paradox, simultaneously obsolete and ahead of its time. In an era of nationalism run rampant, it was not a nation at all but a cobbled-together assortment of thirteen nationalities that spoke sixteen languages, belonged to five major religions, and were organized into seventeen "lands" served by twenty parliaments. But it had the potential to provide a model for a Europe in which diverse peoples could live together in peace and might even, one day, think of uniting. Archduke Franz Ferdinand, as much as Franz Joseph disliked him, had appeared to understand that potential. His murder left the empire without the one man who might possibly have been strong and canny enough to lead it through the crisis of 1914. The archduke had always disliked Conrad's lust for military adventures and almost certainly would have restrained him. He was "a man," as Berchtold would observe sadly amid the ruins of postwar Europe, whom "the monarchy needed."

Just across Hungary's southernmost border was the nightmare Kingdom of Serbia, stirring unrest whenever it could. For many Austrians, and not only for such hawks as Field Marshal Conrad, the empire faced a simple choice: it could maintain a strong position in the Balkans, or it could allow itself to be gradually undone by implacably hostile, Russian-sponsored Balkan troublemakers. The threat was not only external—every new Serbian success seemed an incitement for the many ethnic minorities inside Austria-Hungary to seek either independence or union with whatever Balkan nation they felt themselves to be linked to by culture, religion, blood, and geography. The situation was a recipe for trouble, and throughout the decade leading up to 1914, one development after another added new poisons to the mix.

The first of these developments, when it came in 1906, was a Gilbert and Sullivan–style affair that came to be known, in suitably comic fashion, as the Pig War. Serbia was still a tiny country at that time, but its position on Bosnia's border gave it opportunities for mischief that the expansionists were delighted to exploit. Exasperated officials in Vienna, almost desperate to find some way to strike back, decided that they could punish and perhaps even subdue Serbia economically by refusing to import its livestock, pigs included. They enacted an embargo that went on for five years and accomplished nothing except to make Vienna look ridiculous. The Serbs were able to find so many new markets for their animals that their exports increased. They learned—or thought they learned, which came down to the same thing—that they could defy the mighty Hapsburgs and pay no price for doing so.

Things turned in a more serious direction in 1908. Austria, having had no success in stopping Serbia from making trouble in Bosnia and Herzegovina, became increasingly concerned about the fact that, in strict legal terms, these two southernmost pieces of its empire didn't belong to it at all. According to international law, they were still provinces of the Ottoman Empire, though Austria had occupied and administered them since 1878, when the Turks had been forced to withdraw after suffering another in their seemingly endless series of defeats. Vienna saw that it had good reason to fear the consequences if somehow this territory ever became part of Serbia. And the aggressiveness of the Serbs, coupled with the increasingly decrepit state of the Ottoman Empire, made such a development far from unimaginable. So Vienna announced that it was annexing Bosnia and Herzegovina into the Austro-Hungarian Empire. Serbia, predictably, howled in protest and appealed to Russia. But Russia was still recovering from its disastrous war with Japan and the revolution that followed and therefore was powerless to intervene.

Conrad, who was by then entering his third year as the Austrian army's chief of staff, wanted to send his troops into Serbia and regarded victory as assured. He had at his disposal a standing army of more than three hundred and sixty thousand men, while Serbia at this point had fewer than twenty thousand. Even more important, he had the full support of the Germans, who understood the extent of Russia's impotence and were increasingly worried about Austria's slow decline. The time seemed right for eviscerating Serbia, perhaps for partitioning her out of existence. Characteristically, Conrad started saying that scores might be settled with other neighbors too: with tiny Montenegro, for example, another Balkan nuisance and an ally of Serbia's. And perhaps even with Italy, which had its own territorial ambitions in the Balkans but would have been hopelessly outmatched in a war with Austria.

Not everyone in Austria and Berlin wanted war. Emperor Franz Joseph, in his sixtieth year on the throne by then, had experienced far more military humiliations than triumphs in the course of his long life and had little appetite for a new adventure. The Hungarians were always opposed to any move that might disturb the status quo. They feared that a military victory that brought still more Serbs into the empire would dilute their influence by turning the dual monarchy into a three-cornered system with the Slavs as equal partners. This was not an idle idea: it had powerful advocates in Vienna. People who knew Franz Ferdinand well were convinced that he planned to bring the Slavs into a triple monarchy upon succeeding to the throne.

Germany ended the crisis by issuing an ultimatum: unless the Russians approved the annexation, Germany would regard Vienna as justified in moving against Serbia. Resentfully, Russia yielded. It had no choice.

Supposedly this was a great diplomatic victory. Conrad, however, regarded it as a disaster. Others agreed, among them some of Germany's leading generals. And they had persuasive arguments on their side. Austria had come out of the crisis without acquiring one inch of territory and without having done anything to weaken Serbia. The annexation had, on the other hand, infuriated both the Kingdom of Serbia and those Serb nationalists living in Bosnia. It had subjected Russia to a fresh humiliation—this was the first time in its history that Russia had had to yield to the demands of another European nation. It showed Russia the importance of building up its army as quickly as possible, clinging to its alliance with France, and becoming capable of demonstrating that it was not a useless ally.

Three years after the annexation crisis, the Balkans began to convulse. It is a measure of just how far the decay of the Ottoman Empire had advanced that in 1912 the minuscule nation of Montenegro launched an attack on the once-invincible Turks. Serbia, Bulgaria, and Greece all joined in, and in a single stunning month the Turks were driven from a region they had dominated for more than five hundred years. The map of the Balkans was redrawn. Immediately the victors doubled in size. Serbia was now big enough to be, not a major power certainly, but a real military problem for Austria.

This First Balkan War began and ended before Austria was able to mobilize its army and become involved. Thereafter the balance of power shifted significantly not only in the Balkans but in Europe as a whole, and in ways that were not at all to Vienna's advantage. No longer was there an Ottoman presence in the Balkans to balance Russia's, and Russia's Balkan allies had grown more powerful than ever. Again there had been demands in Vienna for military action, and of course Conrad had been in favor. Berchtold, now the foreign minister, had opposed him. So had Franz Ferdinand, who was shrewd enough to understand that making war on Slav neighbors was no way to win the loyalty of Vienna's tens of million of restive Slavic subjects. Once again nothing was done. One reason for Vienna's failure to act was the mobilization, by a Russia that was nonetheless extremely fearful of war, of many thousands of troops. Another was a conspicuous absence of support from Berlin. The kaiser's government told the Austrians that there was no popular support in Germany for a war in the Balkans, so that hostilities were politically impossible.

One of the winners of the 1912 war, Bulgaria, was a rival of Serbia's and therefore a potential ally for Austria: this was a world in which the enemy of your enemy was sometimes your only friend. Bulgaria was not satisfied with its gains in the war, and in 1913, less than a month after the finalization of the peace agreement, it launched a surprise attack on Serbia. Greece and Montenegro both came to Serbia's aid. So did Romania, which had not been involved in 1912. Even Turkey, hoping to recoup some of its losses, came in against Bulgaria, which quickly went down to defeat. It was all over before Austria could even ready its army for action. Serbia's gains this time included part of the Adriatic coast—like Bosnia and Herzegovina, one of the prime objectives of the Serb expansionists. When peace was restored, Vienna insisted that Serbia withdraw from the coast. Serbia refused. Austria, almost petulantly determined to stop Serbia from getting *everything* it wanted, issued an ultimatum: If Serbia didn't get out of Albania, it would be attacked. Again Serbia turned to Russia for help, and again the Russians showed themselves to be reluctant. Finding that even Britain and France opposed their occupation of the coast, and infuriated despite their other gains, the Serbs pulled back. The area they gave up became the new nation of Albania.

By the summer of 1914 the Balkans were a region in which nobody was satisfied and everyone found reason to be angry and afraid. The Turks had lost almost everything they had ever possessed in the region; Bulgaria had lost much of its spoils from 1913; and although Greece had kept its gains, it did not think it had been given enough. The region was as unstable as it had ever been.

Russia and Austria both were aggrieved as well: Russia because it was seen as having failed the states whose patron it wanted to be; Austria because, only five years after it let slip its best opportunity to crush Serbia, it had been able to do nothing while the part of the world where it felt most threatened was reshaped to Serbia's advantage. Certain that their credibility would be destroyed if they permitted any such thing to recur, both empires resolved never to be so weak and passive again.

The Austrians concluded also that the international conferences that ended both Balkan wars had done them no good. Only their ultimatum to Serbia, their direct threat of war, had made a difference. They had learned to regard peace conferences as traps.

Finally, the Austrians were disgusted by Germany's failure to support them. Germany knew this; it was something that Berlin now had to take into account. Feeble though it might be, Austria-Hungary was the only even marginally dependable ally that Germany had in all of Europe. If the Germans again failed to support Austria-Hungary in a crisis, if they lost their junior partner as a result, they would be alone and surrounded by enemies. The conclusion, for Berlin, was obvious. Never again must Vienna have reason to doubt the value of its alliance with Germany.

Never again. For three weeks and more following the assassination of Franz Ferdinand, that was the German position.

THE HAPSBURGS

IN 1914 EMPEROR FRANZ JOSEPH WAS IN HIS SIXTY-SIXTH year at the head of the most successful family in the history of Europe. He ruled an empire that extended from what is now the Czech Republic and deep inside what is now Poland to the Italian port city of Trieste. He did so from grand palaces in and near Vienna, a city as cosmopolitan, as culturally rich, and as beautiful as any in the world. He had been doing so since he was eighteen years old, which made him one of the longest-reigning monarchs in the history of the world.

He was not only very old, however, but also sad, tired, lonely, and profoundly bored with life. He had always been the most conscientious of autocrats; even at eighty-four he rose daily before dawn, was at his desk by five A.M. after saying his morning prayers on his knees, and worked around the clock. And what he had to look back on, after so many decades of dull toil, was enough disappointment and failure to blight any three lives. Little wonder that he spoke, in unguarded moments, of yearning for death. It was almost as if he knew that his dynasty was now near the end of its thousand-year run.

But what a run it had been. The Hapsburgs had been kings of Austria and other places (Bohemia, Germany, Hungary, and Spain, to name just some) for six and a half centuries. With minor interruptions, they had been emperors for more than four and a half centuries. At their apex in the 1500s they had dominated Europe and the New World as no family has done before or since.

The name of the first member of the line to appear in recorded history, one Guntram the Rich, makes clear that even in his time, a century before the Norman conquest of England, the family was prospering to a far-from-common degree. In 1273 a descendant of Guntram's became the first Hapsburg monarch, King Rudolf I of Germany. One of Rudolf's sons succeeded him on the German throne, and another became King of Austria. Thereafter the Hapsburgs were never less than royal; the only question, from then on, was how many kingdoms the family would rule at any given time.

From the year 800, when the barbarian chief of a Germanic tribe called

Emperor Franz Joseph
"All are dying,
only I can't die."

the Franks went to Rome and had himself crowned Emperor Charles (we remember him as Charlemagne, the Germans as Karl der Grosse), the rulers of Germany had fancied themselves successors to the ancient emperors of Rome. As a result of their ancestors' success in overrunning the Roman Empire in the fourth and fifth centuries, they controlled much of Italy. They did so through the Dark and Middle Ages and on through the Renaissance into modern times. The highest possible honor for a German was to become Holy Roman emperor, a title that continued to represent supremacy over the fragmented German states even when the men who held it no longer controlled Rome. The last German emperor to be crowned in Rome was a member of the Hapsburg family's Austrian branch. He became Emperor Frederick III in 1440, and though the throne was "elective" (the only voters were the hereditary rulers of major German states, including Austria), from that point on the Hapsburgs had so much wealth and power that until 1711 not a single non-Hapsburg was elected to it.

Apparently thanks to his mother, Frederick III was the first member of the line to display the famous "Hapsburg lip," a sometimes grotesque protuberance of the lower lip and jaw that became a mark of the family as its members had increasing difficulty finding spouses worthy of their exalted status and so, increasingly, married one another. He was also distinguished by his success in raising the Hapsburg practice of making advantageous marriages to a level never equaled. The Hapsburgs were not warriors or adventurers; rather, they were congenitally risk-averse. They expanded their holdings less by the sword than by matrimony. In the days when every educated European knew Latin, a saying about the Hapsburgs became famous: *Bella gerant alii, tu felix Austria nube.* "Let others wage wars; you, happy Austria, marry."

First Frederick III married his son Maximilian to the heiress to the Netherlands, Luxembourg, and the Artois and Burgundy regions that are now parts of France. Then, a generation later, he married Maximilian's son Philip to the eldest daughter and heir of Ferdinand and Isabella of Spain. By this marriage the family acquired not only Spain, not only the kingdoms of Naples and Sicily and Sardinia, but all of Spain's vast possessions in the New World. That Philip's Spanish bride happened to be insane scarcely seemed to matter.

All this was inherited by Philip's son, Emperor Charles V, who thereby ruled more of the world than any man ever had and along the way added the kingdoms of Portugal and Milan to his domain. Charles ultimately found his possessions to be more than one man could manage, so he divided them. His son Philip II was based near Madrid as King of Spain (and was married for a time to Mary Tudor, the queen of England called Bloody Mary, failing however to produce a child with her and thereby to secure that promising little realm for the Hapsburgs). Charles's brother Ferdinand became Holy Roman emperor and took charge of the eastern, German branch of the family business.

It was downhill from there. The Spanish line of the Hapsburgs died out after a few generations, evidently the victim of inbreeding (a practice that also weakened the German line, though not to the point of extinction) and of the insanity brought into the family through the marriage that had given it Spain in the first place. The last Hapsburg king of Spain, Charles II, married three times but failed to reproduce. The Austrian line was more vigorous but beset with problems. France under Louis XIV seized all of the Hapsburgs' possessions west of the Rhine, including the provinces of Alsace and Lorraine. The Ottoman Turks invaded Europe, conquered most of the Balkans, and twice reached the gates of Vienna before being turned back. The Reformation cast Catholic Austria into the role of enemy in newly Protestant northern Germany. This was particularly convenient for Prussia, the leading Protestant state on the continent, which grabbed important pieces of the Hapsburg inheritance. Finally there came the rise of Napoleon Bonaparte. He occupied Vienna twice, stripped away many of the Hapsburgs' southern possessions, and, determined to produce an heir, took a juicy little Hapsburg princess (the grandniece of Marie Antoinette, also a member of the family) as his bride.

Napoleon ended the fiction of the Holy Roman Empire, and from that point forward the Hapsburg monarchs bore the humbler title of hereditary emperors of Austria. The Congress of Vienna that followed the fall of Napoleon, as part of its program of restoring the old order across Europe, returned to the Hapsburgs some of their most important southern holdings, including northern Italy. After that things remained relatively tranquil for more than thirty years.

Then came the Revolution of 1848, an upheaval in which, from France to Russia, people demanding reform rose up against their rulers. Most of the major cities of the Hapsburg empire revolted, and for a time the survival of the dynasty was in question. The childless emperor at the time abdicated, and a younger brother was passed over in favor of his son Franz Joseph. The royalists hoped that this attractive boy, tall, vigorous, and only eighteen years old, could win the loyalty of his subjects. Their hopes were fulfilled. Franz Joseph, born during the presidency of Andrew Jackson and crowned twelve years before the election of Abraham Lincoln, was still on the throne when Woodrow Wilson moved into the White House.

Both personally and politically, however, Franz Joseph's reign was almost as sorrowful as it was long. Everything went wrong for him in the end. As a young man, he married the most beautiful princess in Europe, Elizabeth of Bavaria, but after six happy years and four children he passed on to her the gonorrhea that he had contracted on one of his disastrous Italian campaigns. Formalities aside, that was the end of the marriage.

In 1859 Austria was driven out of Lombardy in northern Italy by the rising forces of Italian nationalism. Shortly thereafter it lost Tuscany and Modena as well.

In 1866 Prussia defeated Austria and forced it to abandon its ancient claim to leadership over Germany. At this point, fearful of further losses, Franz Joseph entered into a compact under which Hungary became not merely one of the empire's possessions but an equal partner in a new and peculiar kind of dual monarchy. The ruler would be not only emperor of Austria but also "apostolic king" of Hungary. Austria and Hungary each would have its own prime minister and parliament, though the war, finance, and foreign affairs ministries would be centralized in Vienna. This arrangement was successful insofar as it gave the Magyars, who dominated Hungary, a more powerful and secure position in European politics than they could possibly have had otherwise. It gave them a reason to want the empire to survive. But it also created problems. It greatly complicated the process of making policy: all the most important decisions had to be approved not only in Vienna but in the Hungarian capital of Budapest as well. It also gave Hungary reason to oppose anything that might weaken its position within the empire. Thus Hungary would resist the transformation of the dual monarchy into a three-cornered arrangement that included the Slavs. It would do so despite the fact that by 1914 fully three-fifths of the empire's subjects were Slavic: Poles, Czechs, Slovaks, Ukrainians, Serbs, and others.

In 1867 Franz Joseph's younger brother Maximilian, who three years earlier had quixotically accepted an invitation to go to Mexico and become its emperor, was shot to death there by a firing squad.

In 1870, with Austria on the sidelines looking on, Prussia led a confederation of German states in a swift and stunning victory over France. The Franco-Prussian War led to the creation of a new German Empire in which the King of Prussia was elevated to kaiser and from which Austria was excluded. From this point Vienna could not hope to be more than the distinctly junior partner of a Berlin that had risen to first place among the continental powers.

In 1889 Archduke Rudolf, Franz Joseph's only son, intelligent and talented but also frustrated, rebellious, neurotic, a drug addict, and syphilitic (he not only followed his father in infecting his wife with venereal disease but sterilized the lady in the process), committed suicide with his teenage mistress, leaving no male heir.

Nine years later Empress Elizabeth was stabbed to death by an Italian anarchist who had hoped to kill King Umberto I of Italy but, unable to raise the train fare to Rome, settled for her.

Two years after that came the refusal of Archduke Franz Ferdinand, the soldierly nephew who had become heir after Rudolf's death, not to marry Countess Sophie Chotek, mere lady-in-waiting to a Hapsburg cousin.

In his seemingly endless old age Franz Joseph was a kindly but inflexible man, devoted to preserving the traditions of his ancestors, ardently hoping to live out his remaining days in peace. He remained doggedly faithful to his responsibilities if only because they were his heritage and he had no one to share them with. Once, reminiscing with Field Marshal Conrad about a general both of them had known, he said plaintively that "all are dying, only I *can't* die." When Conrad offered a courtly response, expressing gratitude for the emperor's long life, Franz Joseph replied, "Yes, yes, but one is *so* alone then."

Chapter 3

✠

Setting Fire to Europe

"I don't believe we are heading for a great war.
France and Russia are not ready for war."
—KAISER WILHELM II

On the day after the assassination, crowds of non-Serb Bosnians, mainly the Muslims and Catholic Croats who together made up a majority of Bosnia's population, marched through the streets of Sarajevo holding up black-draped Austro-Hungarian flags and pictures of the slain archduke and his wife. Gangs of hooligans attacked buildings housing the institutions of the Bosnian Serb community—vandalizing schools, newspaper offices, and a hotel, breaking windows at the residence of the city's leading Orthodox priest. Some fifty people were injured, and one was killed. There were demonstrations in other cities of the dual monarchy, and in Munich and Berlin as well, but they were smaller and nonviolent and quickly subsided.

In the Serbian capital of Belgrade, the uproar was more intense. An Austrian diplomat reported that the Serbs were falling "into one another's arms in delight." Disorderly crowds roamed the city, and as news arrived of the disturbances in Sarajevo, their jubilation was laced with anger. Belgrade's newspapers fueled the fires, "behaving shamefully" according to a British diplomat on the scene, telling their readers that ten thousand of the Serbs living in Austria-Hungary had been injured or killed and that Serbian women were being subjected to outrages. (This was all untrue.)

It is easy to make too much of all this. Even in Sarajevo the demonstrations came to an end after a few hours, and in Vienna the government promptly announced that victims would be compensated for their losses. The Serbian government conducted itself responsibly, attempting to discourage the demonstrations. In Vienna life quickly returned to normal. The slain archduke had been too cold and stiff a public figure ever to become popular, and there were few signs that his death was mourned. "The event almost failed to make any impression whatever," said one observer. "On Sunday and Monday, the crowds in Vienna listened to music and drank wine as if nothing had happened." Franz Ferdinand and Sophie were interred at their country estate with so little fanfare that the late archduke's friends were offended and the emperor found it necessary to explain his failure to do more.

The Austro-Hungarian leadership, though determined to take action against Serbia, was not yet ready to do so. The forty-eight hours after the assassination brought meeting after meeting—Foreign Minister Berchtold, Field Marshal Conrad, Hungarian prime minister István Tisza, Emperor Franz Joseph, and others conferred and dispersed in a continuous round robin, but no consensus emerged. Berchtold and Conrad wanted an attack on Serbia, and they wanted it to happen speedily. The emperor was uncertain; Tisza was opposed. The one point on which they agreed was that nothing could be decided until certain preliminaries had been attended to.

First, the support of Germany had to be made certain. Nothing would be possible without it. Any Austrian action against Serbia was sure to be of concern to Russia, and Vienna alone was not nearly powerful enough to deter the Russians from intervening or to deal with their enormous army if they did intervene.

It was just as essential to get Hungary on board, and that was likely to be at least as difficult. Under the clumsy arrangements of the Hapsburg system, Vienna could not make war without the consent of Budapest, and the Hungarians were sure to have little interest. Failure in such a war would be a disaster, obviously, but from the Hungarian perspective even success could be regrettable.

Finally, no action would be possible until the Austrian army had been mobilized. Mobilization in 1914 was a cumbersome, difficult, expensive undertaking. It required calling up and organizing hundreds of thousands of reserve troops, commandeering entire national railroad systems for the movement of soldiers and supplies, and getting the most enormous and mechanized military machines the world had ever seen into motion according to timetables so intricate that years had been required for their development. Either of the Austro-Hungarian mobilization plans (Vienna was unusual in having two such plans, one for war against Serbia only and the other for war in conjunction with Germany against Serbia and Russia) would take weeks to implement. Part of the problem was that many thousands of soldiers had been sent home, as was customary each summer before the mechanization of agriculture, to help bring in the harvest. Conrad feared that calling them back to their units earlier than planned would alert Serbia and Russia to what was in process.

Further complicating the situation—and a particularly exasperating complication because it was sheer bad luck—was the fact that the President of
France, Raymond Poincaré, was going to be paying a state visit to the Russian
capital, St. Petersburg, from Monday, July 20, to Thursday, July 23. If Austria-
Hungary took any steps against Serbia before the end of that visit, if it mobilized before then or even signaled that it intended to mobilize, the leaders of
France and Russia would be given a unique opportunity to coordinate their
response and cement their alliance at the moment of decision. Thus, mobilization being the unavoidably slow process that it was in Austria-Hungary,
the army could not be ready for action until mid-August, a month and a half
after the assassination. By that time whatever sympathy the assassination had
generated for Austria would be largely dissipated.

There was no need for delay, however, in securing Germany's support, and
soon there seemed no need for concern about the extent of that support.
Kaiser Wilhelm had liked and admired Archduke Franz Ferdinand, who
understood the dangers of the Balkans and had been more restrained, more
thoughtful, than Conrad. The kaiser and the men around him needed no
reminding that, with Russia and France allied against them and Britain leaning the same way, Germany needed Austria and needed to help Austria
defend itself against the centrifugal force that was Balkan nationalism. The
Germans were far more ready to support Austria-Hungary than they had
been during the Balkan wars of the preceding two years, more conscious of
being surrounded by enemies who were growing in strength.

Wilhelm had been racing his new sailboat, the *Meteor V,* off the coast of
Norway when word reached him of the assassination. Returning almost
immediately to his palace at Potsdam outside Berlin, he began to monitor
events. There was not much to monitor, actually—not a great deal was happening in Vienna or elsewhere once the initial disturbances had played themselves out. As it became clear that the assassins were Bosnian Serbs who had
been prepared for their mission in Belgrade, Wilhelm went into one of his
belligerent moods. It was his practice to write in the margins of diplomatic
dispatches as he read them, and his comments were often wildly dramatic; it
was a way of blustering, of playing his beloved role of All-High Warlord, and
also of letting the foreign office know where he stood. "Then he's a false rascal!" he would soon be saying of Britain's foreign secretary in one such note.
"He lies!" "Rot!" When at the beginning of July he received a wire in which
the German ambassador in Vienna reported having urged the Austrians not
to be too quick in moving against Serbia, Wilhelm exploded. "Who authorized him to act that way?" he wrote. "Serbia must be disposed of, and that
right soon!"

Word of this reaction soon spread and reached official Vienna. The Austrians, of course, were delighted, especially as Berlin was sending similarly strong signals of support through other channels. The German ambassador, Heinrich von Tschirschky, had been shown the error of his ways: he knew now that the kaiser wanted him to be tough and to urge the Austrians to be tough as well. Tschirschky welcomed the lesson, actually. He was one of the many members of the old Prussian aristocracy who believed that Germany's position in Europe was rapidly becoming unsafe. He feared that Austria-Hungary was weakening almost to the point of collapse. "How often have I asked myself," he had lamented in one of his dispatches, "whether it really is worthwhile to commit ourselves to this state, creaking in all its joints, and to continue the dreary work of dragging it along."

On July 5 and 6 Wilhelm and Germany's deputy foreign minister, Arthur Zimmermann, met separately with emissaries from Vienna. Wilhelm made no effort to tell the Austrians what to do. What he did tell them, emphatically, was what they wanted to hear: that this time something had to be done about Serbia, that action should be taken *soon,* and that the Austrians could count on Germany's support whatever they decided. "It was his opinion that this action must not be delayed," the Austrian ambassador said of Wilhelm II immediately after their meeting. "Russia's attitude will no doubt be hostile, but for this he [Wilhelm] had been for years prepared, and should a war between Austria-Hungary and Russia be unavoidable, we might be convinced that Germany, our old faithful ally, would stand at our side. Russia at the present time was in no way prepared for war, and would think twice before it appealed to arms." This report became famous as the "blank check"—the promise that Berlin would be with Vienna no matter what.

Apparently the Austrians had made no effort to explain what exactly they intended to do, or when. It is unlikely that they could have done so if asked; not yet having come to an agreement with Hungary, they had no settled policy or plan. Neither the kaiser nor Zimmermann took the trouble to ask— one indication among many that at this point the Germans did not regard the situation as being serious enough to require much thought or care. War Minister Erich von Falkenhayn, after being briefed on the meetings and the contents of a letter from Franz Joseph and an accompanying memorandum from Berchtold (these dealt less with the Sarajevo crisis than with Vienna's long-term plans for changing the balance of power in the Balkans through alliance with Bulgaria), said that what he had learned "did not succeed in convincing me that the Vienna Government had taken any firm resolution." Like a number of his colleagues, Falkenhayn thought it likely that the Austrians were going to have to be prodded into action.

The Austrians, armed with the kaiser's unqualified promise of support, would from this point feel free to proceed autonomously. They would be slow at best in telling Berlin of their plans. The Germans, for their part, would continue to be slow to ask. The Austrian envoys to Berlin hadn't even explained that they regarded any action as impossible until after the French visit to St. Petersburg. The Germans continued to assume that Austria intended to proceed without delay to strike at Serbia, after which it would be free to move almost all of its forces to its border with Russia.

Everything known about Kaiser Wilhelm and his closest associates indicates that in early July they saw little possibility of a general European war. Falkenhayn's skepticism about whether Vienna would in the end actually do anything reflected widespread German doubt, based on much experience, about the Hapsburg empire's ability to take action to save itself. Recent experience also encouraged the Germans to be equally skeptical—scornful, perhaps—about Russia. Evidently it was all but inconceivable to them that this time, unlike 1908 or 1912 or 1913, the Russians would feel not only capable of taking military action but compelled to do so. Almost immediately after his talks with the Austrians, when Falkenhayn asked the kaiser if military preparations were necessary, Wilhelm said no. He soon returned to his boat-racing vacation off Norway, telling one of his admirals before departing that "I don't believe we are headed for a great war. In this case the tsar's views would not be on the side of the prince's [Franz Ferdinand's] murderer. Besides this, France and Russia are not ready for war."

German chancellor Theobold von Bethmann Hollweg, an intelligent and conscientious servant of the crown but a statesman of limited vision, also went on vacation. Army Chief of Staff Helmuth von Moltke had not even been called back from the spa where he was recovering from a bronchial infection, and the head of the German navy went off to a spa of his own. Thus scattered, the principal figures in the German government and military were incapable of making or coordinating plans, of responding to anything done by other countries, or even of staying abreast of developments. At the July 5–6 meetings they had shown less interest in the Serbian problem than in Berchtold's arcane scheme for using Bulgaria as a lever to pry Romania out of its alliance with Russia.

In Vienna, where Germany's promise of support was received as the best possible news, attention swung next to the Hungarians. At center stage now was Hungary's prime minister, Count Tisza, a gruff but politically adroit man who cared little about the Hapsburg empire except insofar as its existence benefited the Hungarians. Tisza was so absolutely opposed to any Austro-Hungarian expansion into Serbia that he had once warned Emperor Franz Joseph that any effort in that direction would ignite civil war in Hungary.

Hungarian Prime Minister
István Tisza
*"Our exactions may be hard,
but not such that they cannot
be complied with."*

(Conrad, always ready for a fight, reacted by saying that after thrashing Serbia, Austria would probably have to thrash the Hungarians as well.)

On July 7 Austria-Hungary's council of ministers was assembled by Berchtold to discuss measures to "put an end to Serbia's intrigues once and for all" and, he hoped, to approve a course of action. Tisza surprised no one when he showed himself willing to do little. He tried to divert attention to Berchtold's plans for Bulgaria and Romania. (Such diplomatic intrigues, typical of eastern Europe in the years before the war, are almost impossible to explain briefly.) When he saw that everyone had lost interest in such long-term speculative ventures, that nothing short of a showdown with Serbia would satisfy the Austrians, Tisza groped for ways to slow things down. He insisted that nothing be done until he had an opportunity to prepare a memo explaining his objections to Franz Joseph, who was away at his summer retreat. Berchtold and the council had no choice but to agree. Tisza was, after all, the head of the Hungarian government and not to be ignored.

Much of the discussion focused on the idea, with which none of the council members disagreed, that Serbia should be presented with a set of demands. At issue was whether these demands should be framed in such a way that Serbia could reasonably be expected to accept and act on them. Again Tisza was alone: "Our exactions may be hard," he said, "but not such that they cannot be complied with. If Serbia accepted them, we should have a splendid diplomatic success." Such a success, he added, "would decidedly improve our situation and give a chance of initiating an advantageous policy in the Balkans." A failure to limit the conflict to diplomatic measures, he warned, could lead to "the terrible calamity of a European war."

No one had any interest in going along with what Tisza proposed. The Austro-Hungarian war minister responded that "a diplomatic success would be of no use at all" and would be "interpreted as weakness." According to a summary of the proceedings, everyone except Tisza agreed that "a purely diplomatic success, even if it ended with a glaring humiliation of Serbia, would be worthless." It was finally decided, therefore, that "such stringent demands must be addressed to Serbia" that refusal would be "almost certain."

Implicit in all this was the assumption that an Austro-Hungarian invasion would lead without complications to the defeat of Serbia. This led to the question of Serbia's fate after it was defeated. Tisza's position was that "by a war we could reduce the size of Serbia, but we could not completely annihilate it." Here he carried the council with him, probably because of the reason he offered: "Russia would fight to the death before allowing this." But all agreed that Serbia was to be made smaller. Parts of it were to be given to Bulgaria, Greece, and Albania. What remained, though formally an autonomous state, was to be an Austro-Hungarian satellite. In this way Berchtold— always too clever by half—thought that he could proceed with the destruction of Serbia while promising Russia and the world that Vienna did not want an inch of Serbian territory.

The summary of the council's proceedings makes plain the near-desperation of the men participating. They were genuinely afraid of Serbia—convinced that, if Serbia were not crushed, it would be impossible to keep their South Slav subjects from fighting to break free of Hapsburg control. Another striking aspect of the discussion is the attention *not* given to how the other great powers—even Germany—might react to what was being planned. At the opening of the meeting, Berchtold had acknowledged that a "decisive stroke" of the kind he and Conrad wanted "cannot be dealt without previous diplomatic preparation." But by this he meant only that Vienna could not proceed without an assurance of German support, and he had already been given that assurance. The council did not recognize the advisability of keeping Germany informed. Nor, beyond assuming that Russia would not intervene unless Vienna tried to absorb Serbia, did the ministers pay the slightest attention to the need to try to prepare Russia for what lay ahead. The emphasis, instead, was on secrecy. On secrecy, and on surprise, and on deceit: in the weeks to follow not even the Germans would be told of the council's decision to dismember Serbia after taking it by force. To the contrary, all the great powers would be assured—falsely but repeatedly—that Austria had no territorial aspirations where Serbia was concerned. Even Tisza appears to have decided in the end to go along with this approach. Late in the meeting he told the council that he "was anxious to meet the others halfway and was prepared to concede that the demands addressed to Serbia should be hard indeed, but not such as to make our intention of raising unacceptable terms clear to everybody else." The shift in his tone is striking. Tisza was no longer insisting that the demands be acceptable, only that Vienna's real intent be concealed from *everybody else*. In the case of Germany, the results of this secrecy would be unfortunate. They would keep the Berlin government from understanding what Vienna was doing until it was very nearly too late. In the case of Russia, the results would be disastrous. The Austrians' duplicity assured that, when their intentions became clear at last, the Russians would be shocked, panicked, and—not without reason—convinced that they had been betrayed.

This meeting was followed by a period of quiet waiting. For the sake of secrecy, and to Conrad's consternation, little could be done to ready the Austro-Hungarian army for action. Tisza remained nettlesome. On the day after the council meeting he wrote to Franz Joseph, warning that an attack on Serbia "would, as far as can humanly be foreseen, lead to an intervention by Russia and hence to a world war." He reverted to his original position that the demands to be made of Serbia should be "stiff but not impossible to meet, and that further action should be taken only if Serbia refuses." Berchtold, occupied with drafting the demands, paid him no attention.

By July 13 Vienna's ambassador in Berlin was reporting that the Germans were growing nervous about Vienna's failure to act. Berchtold ignored this report too. A day later, when Tisza pointedly objected to the use of the term *ultimatum* in connection with the demands, Berchtold cheerfully offered a compromise. The document he was drafting would be a "note with time limit," not an ultimatum. It was a distinction without a difference, and it cost Berchtold nothing. Serbia would be given forty-eight hours to respond and would be told nothing about what Vienna intended to do if the response proved unsatisfactory. Austria's ambassadors were under instructions to assure Russia and even Germany that Vienna was planning nothing that would cause concern. Again Berchtold was being too clever, deceiving friends and prospective enemies alike.

On July 19 the council of ministers met again in Vienna. Members reviewed Berchtold's draft note and gave their approval. It included ten demands. At least half were entirely reasonable. A few, however, were susceptible to being interpreted as requiring Serbia to compromise its sovereignty. The most objectionable called for direct Austrian involvement in Serbia's handling of the assassination investigation and related internal matters. Its rejection was, in practical terms, nearly inevitable. The council agreed that Berchtold should have the note delivered to the Prime Minister of Serbia in Belgrade on July 23, immediately after the departure of France's President Poincaré from St. Petersburg. Tisza was no longer objecting. Germany's promise of support had neutralized his warnings, and on top of that (the complexities of the Balkans being almost infinite) he was beginning to see

Serbia—specifically, Serbia's friendly relations with Romania—as a threat to Hungary's control of Transylvania, which had a large Romanian population increasingly restless for union with what it saw as its true homeland.

The delivery of the note to Serbia, when the evening of Thursday, July 23, finally arrived, was a sad little comedy of errors. Prime Minister Pasic had— not necessarily by coincidence, as he had been alerted that a communication from Vienna was coming—left Belgrade on an electioneering trip into Serbia's newest provinces. His foreign minister, when told to expect an important visit by the Austrian ambassador at six P.M., tried to contact Pasic by telegram but got no answer.

Vienna's ambassador to Belgrade, another of the many Austrian officials who had long regarded war with Serbia as not only inevitable but desirable, was a baron with the interesting name Giesl von Gieslingen. Upon arriving, he was taken to see the foreign minister. An interpreter was on hand because the minister spoke neither German nor French. Giesl began to read his government's note, a lengthy document that opened with a preamble complaining that the behavior of Serbia had been intolerable and would in fact no longer be tolerated. He read slowly, with frequent pauses for the benefit of the interpreter. The foreign minister, more and more alarmed by what he was hearing, began to interrupt. Again and again he complained through the interpreter that he could not accept a communication this important, that only Pasic could do so. Giesl, out of patience, said that in that case he could only leave the note and go. In departing he said that no response other than unconditional acceptance would satisfy Austria, and that Serbia's response was required by six P.M. on Saturday.

News of the Austrian demands had little impact except in Russia. The government of faraway Britain, ensnared in a violent crisis having to do with Irish Home Rule, had scant attention to spare for the Balkans. The London newspapers, never friendly toward Serbia, dealt generously with Austria's demands, in most cases describing them as appropriate and responsible. The British foreign secretary, Sir Edward Grey, suggested only that Austria's deadline ought to be extended.

There was even less interest in France. President Poincaré, having completed his visit with Tsar Nicholas and his ministers, was at sea, somewhere between St. Petersburg and home. In Paris the public and even the government were fixated on a scandal that had erupted when the wife of a former prime minister shot and killed a newspaper editor.

Berlin too was quiet. Kaiser Wilhelm, back to his customary weeks of summertime sailing, didn't learn about the Austrian note until news of it reached him through the Norwegian newspapers. He was, understandably, angry at not having been informed by his own foreign office. For the first time he showed signs of serious concern. He proposed canceling a planned visit of the German High Seas Fleet to Scandinavia but was dissuaded. Chancellor Bethmann Hollweg urged him not to interrupt his vacation a second time. Wilhelm refused and started for home.

At this point Wilhelm still knew nearly nothing about what the Austrian note said. Requests for a copy had gone out from Berlin, but when a copy reached Foreign Minister Gottlieb von Jagow on the evening of July 22—less than twenty-four hours before the delivery to Serbia—it proved to be incomplete and unaccompanied by any indication that the Austrians were determined to reject the Serbian response. Bethmann didn't bother to read it. Vienna had not consulted Berlin, now virtually no time remained for questions or objections, and the man whose questions would have mattered most—Kaiser Wilhelm—knew less than anyone. Berchtold, almost certainly, had planned things this way. Having succeeded in getting his government to commit to action despite Tisza's initial resistance and the deadly inertia of the dual monarchy's dual bureaucracy, he was determined to make further complications impossible. Thus he compounded his earlier mistakes. Not only had he left the Russian government completely unprepared for the harshness of his note, he had actively encouraged the Russians to expect something very different. He had done nothing to help newspapers across Europe, and thereby the European public, understand why Austria was taking action at last. Little had been disclosed, and less had been publicized, about Vienna's success in tracing the assassination plot back to Belgrade and establishing the likelihood that officials of the Kingdom of Serbia had been involved. Vienna had made no public complaints about Belgrade's failure to investigate the assassination. Thus the news of Vienna's note, when it flashed across the continent, came as more of a surprise than an invasion of Serbia might have done in the immediate aftermath of the Sarajevo shootings. By July 23 the assassination was three and a half weeks in the past. Tempers had cooled, and people in cities far from Sarajevo had moved on to other things. They were no longer disposed to regard the murder of the archduke and his wife as such an outrage as to require a military response.

In St. Petersburg, Russia's foreign minister, the mercurial Sergei Sazonov, went into a rage when he learned of the Austrian note. He complained that he had been deceived, that Russia couldn't possibly stand by while Serbia was humiliated or worse, that Austria couldn't possibly have sent such a note without the knowledge and approval of Germany, and that both countries must be plotting to drive Russia out of the Balkans. "You are setting fire to Europe!" Sazonov told the Austrian ambassador. The Prince Regent of Serbia, meanwhile, was sending wires to Tsar Nicholas asking for help.

How could Russia *not* help Serbia? Nicholas was being told that his people

Russian Foreign Minister
Sergei Sazonov
*"The curses of the nations
will be upon you."*

would not tolerate another abandonment of their brothers, the South Slavs. Russia would be disgraced, would have no more friends in the Balkans, no respect in Europe. A failure of such magnitude might trigger a revolution worse than the one in 1905.

One solution suggested itself. If Russia showed enough firmness, perhaps Austria would hold back. By Friday, July 24, the day after the delivery of Austria's note, the day before Serbia was supposed to reply, Sazonov was telling the Russian army's chief of staff to get ready for mobilization.

It was at this point that the Balkan crisis became a European one.

THE HOHENZOLLERNS

THE FLAMBOYANT AND ERRATIC KAISER WILHELM II OWNED
and loved to show off more than three hundred military dress uniforms. He
would cheerfully change his costume a dozen or more times daily. One of
the jokes that made the rounds in Berlin was that the kaiser wouldn't visit
an aquarium without first putting on admiral's regalia, or eat a plum pud-
ding without dressing as a British field marshal. He really could be almost
that childish, even in 1914, when he was in his early fifties and had ruled
Germany for a quarter of a century. Not surprisingly, many of the men who
were sworn to serve him regarded him not just as immature but as mentally
unstable.

Wilhelm was only the third member of the Hohenzollern family to
occupy the throne of Imperial Germany; the second had been kaiser for
only months. The Hohenzollerns, unlike the Hapsburgs, were in 1914 a
still-rising family at the top of a rising nation. Despite interruptions that at
times had brought them to the brink of ruin, they had been rising for five
hundred years, slowly emerging from obscurity in the late Middle Ages and
eventually surpassing all the older and grander dynasties of Europe. They
had always been more vigorous than the Hapsburgs, more warlike, rising through conquest and ingenuity rather than through matrimony. They
had a remarkable history not just of ruling countries but of *inventing* the
countries they wanted to rule. It is scarcely going too far to say that the
Hohenzollerns—assisted, of course, by their brilliant servant Otto von
Bismarck—invented modern Germany. Centuries earlier they had invented
Prussia, a country so completely artificial that at the end of World War II
it would simply and forever cease to exist.

The first Hohenzollern of note was one Count Friedrich, a member of
the minor nobility who in the early fifteenth century somehow got the Holy
Roman emperor to appoint him Margrave of Brandenburg, an area centered on Berlin in northeastern Germany. In his new position Friedrich was
an elector, one of the hereditary magnates entitled to choose new emperors. His descendants increased their holdings during the next century and
a half, expanding to the east by getting possession of a wild and backward
territory called Prussia.

Kaiser Wilhelm II
Still immature after a quarter-century on the throne.

Inhabited originally by Slavs rather than by Germans, Prussia had been conquered and Christianized in the 1200s by a military religious order (there were such things in those hard days) called the Teutonic Knights. It happened that, when the Protestant Reformation swept across northern Germany, the head of the Teutonic Knights was a member of the Hohenzollern family, one Albert by name. In 1525 this Albert did what most of the nobles in that part of Europe were doing at the time: he declared himself a Protestant. Simultaneously he declared that Prussia was now a duchy, and that he—surprise—was its duke. This Albert of Hohenzollern's little dynasty died out in the male line after only two generations, at which point a marriage was arranged between the female heir and her cousin, the Hohenzollern elector of Brandenburg. (The Hapsburgs must have nodded in approval.)

The first half of the seventeenth century was a low point for the family: Brandenburg found itself on the losing side in a North European war and for a while was occupied by Sweden. Better times returned with Friedrich Wilhelm, called the Great Elector, who was margrave from 1640 to 1688 and originated the superbly trained army that forever after would be the Hohenzollern trademark and would cause Napoleon to say that Prussia had been hatched out of a cannonball. Friedrich Wilhelm made Brandenburg the most powerful of Germany's Protestant states, second only to Catholic Austria to the south.

In 1701 the Hapsburg Holy Roman emperor found himself in a struggle over who would inherit the throne of Spain. He needed help—he needed the tough little army of Brandenburg. The Hohenzollern elector of the time, another Friedrich (the Hohenzollerns rarely went far afield in naming their sons), wanted something in return: he wanted to be a king. This presented difficulties, but the emperor's need was real and so things were worked out. He decided that Friedrich could have a kingdom, in a way, but that the intricate rules of imperial governance required calling it Prussia rather than Brandenburg. The rules required also that, although Friedrich could not be king *of* Prussia, it would be acceptable for him to style himself king *in* Prussia. This was nearly the feeblest way imaginable of being a king, one that made Friedrich's new status seem faintly ridiculous. But it was a step toward real kingship, and Friedrich settled for it. He became King Friedrich I, the first Hohenzollern to be a monarch, if only in a way.

It was not until two generations later that the Hohenzollerns became kings *of* Prussia. This happened during one of the most remarkable reigns in European history, that of Friedrich II, who by the age of thirty-three was known to all of Europe as Frederick the Great.

Frederick the Great is too big a subject to be dealt with in a few paragraphs. Suffice it to say that he was a writer, a composer of music that is still performed today, and a "philosopher king" according to no less a judge than Voltaire (who became his house guest and stayed so long that the two ended up despising each other). He was the first monarch in all of Europe to abolish religious discrimination, press censorship, and judicial torture. He was also a ruthless adventurer all too eager for glory, and he and his kingdom would have been destroyed except for the lucky fact that, in addition to all his other gifts, Frederick happened to be a military genius. In the course of his long life he teetered more than once on the brink of total failure—at one point he was at war with Austria, France, Russia, and

Sweden simultaneously—but after any number of hair-raising escapes he raised Prussia to the ranks of Europe's leading powers. He made the Hohenzollerns one of the leading dynasties of Europe despite never having—and giving no evidence of ever wanting—children of his own. When he died in 1786, just before the French Revolution, the crown passed to an untalented nephew.

The wars of Napoleon undid all of Frederick's achievements. They reduced Prussia first to a state of collapse, then to submissive vassalage to France. By piling humiliations upon all the German states, however, Napoleon ignited German nationalism. This led to an uprising after Napoleon's disastrous invasion of Russia. The Prussian army, lethal as always, contributed significantly to the defeat of the French first at Leipzig and finally at Waterloo. Hohenzollern princes were conspicuous on the field of battle; one of them was killed leading a cavalry charge. In 1815 the Congress of Vienna restored Prussia to major power status but in a new way: some of the kingdom's easternmost holdings were given to Russia and Austria and replaced with others in the west. Prussia thus became the only major power almost all of whose subjects were German. This was important at a time when nationalism was starting to be a powerful political force, and when Germans everywhere were beginning to talk of unification. The big question was whether there would be a Greater Germany led by Austria or a Lesser Germany from which Austria, with its millions of non-German subjects, would be excluded.

The century following the defeat of Napoleon brought triumph after triumph to the Hohenzollerns. In 1864, guided by Bismarck, Prussia took the disputed but largely German provinces of Schleswig and Holstein from Denmark. Two years after that it fought Austria and won so conclusively as to put its claim to leadership among the German states beyond challenge. The Hohenzollern realm now stretched across northern Germany all the way to the border with France and included two-thirds of the population of non-Austrian Germany. In 1870 the French emperor Napoleon III, in trouble politically and desperate to find some way of reversing his fortunes, was seduced by Bismarck into committing the folly of declaring war. Prussia and the German states allied with it—Austria emphatically not included—were more than ready. They astonished the world by demolishing the French army at the Battle of Sedan. In the Hall of Mirrors at the Palace of Versailles, the assembled German princes declared the creation of a new German empire, a federation within which such states as Baden, Bavaria, Saxony, and Württemberg would continue to have their own kings but over which there would now be a Hohenzollern emperor.

As part of the spoils of war, the German princes wanted to take from

France—to take *back* from France, they would have said—the province of Alsace and part of the province of Lorraine. This territory was not of tremendous importance economically or in any other real way, but many Germans believed it had been stolen by Louis XIV two centuries before and was German rather than French. Bismarck, architect of everything Prussia had achieved over the preceding decade, foresaw that France would never forgive the loss. He predicted that to keep what it had won, Germany would have to fight another war after a half-century had passed. He was right, as usual, but made no serious effort to block the annexation.

The first ruler of the newly united Germany, King Wilhelm I of Prussia, proved to be surprisingly unhappy about his elevation, even sullen. In his opinion being King of Prussia was as great an honor as any man could ever want. But an empire required an emperor, and he had no choice but to agree. He remained King of Prussia while assuming his new title, however, and Prussia continued to be a distinct state with its own government and military administration. It continued to be dominated by a centuries-old Prussian elite, the Junkers, whose sons went into the army and the civil administration and swore loyalty not to their country but to its king.

At that point, 1871, the Hohenzollerns stood at the pinnacle of Europe. Kaiser Wilhelm I, a man so stolid and methodical that the people of Berlin learned to set their watches by his appearances at his window, ruled what was unquestionably the most powerful and vigorous country in Europe. And he had a worthy heir: his son, Crown Prince Frederick, an able, conscientious, and loyal young man who in the centuries-old tradition of his family had led armies through all the great campaigns leading up to the creation of the empire and had been rewarded with the Iron Cross and a field marshal's baton. The crown prince was happily married to the eldest and best-loved daughter of England's Queen Victoria. She was a serious-minded young woman who had won her husband over to the idea of one day, after they had inherited the throne, transforming Germany into a democratic monarchy on the British model. Together, meanwhile, they were producing yet another generation of Hohenzollerns. Their eldest child was a boy who bore his grandfather's name. He had a withered, useless left arm—a troubling defect in the heir to a line of warrior-kings—but he was healthy otherwise and not unintelligent. When his grandfather became emperor, the boy Wilhelm was twelve years old, his father barely forty. But only seventeen years later, filled with insecurities but determined to prove himself a mighty leader, a worthy All-High Warlord, this same boy would ascend to the throne as Wilhelm II.

Chapter 4

✠

July 25 to 28:
Secrets and Lies

"This was more than one could have expected.
A great moral victory for Vienna!"
—Kaiser Wilhelm II

As the details of Austria's demands became known, three and a half weeks of drift came abruptly to an end. Actions and reactions began to follow one another at an accelerating pace. The possibility of war became increasingly real. Not only in Vienna, Berlin, and St. Petersburg but also in London, Rome, and Paris, awareness dawned that this was a genuinely dangerous crisis.

Men with the power to decide the fate of Europe did the things that brought the war on and failed to do the things that might have kept the war from happening. They told lies, made mistakes, and missed opportunities. With few if any exceptions they were decent, well-intended men, and almost always they acted for what they thought were the best of reasons. But little of what they did produced the results they intended.

Saturday, July 25
Measured by the headlines that it generated, this was an extraordinary day. The Kingdom of Serbia, forty-eight hours almost to the minute after receiving Austria-Hungary's demands, presented its response. It agreed outright to only half of the ten demands. The Austro-Hungarian ambassador to Serbia, Baron Giesl, followed his instructions to find this unacceptable and broke off diplomatic relations immediately. His bags had been packed in advance, and in less than half an hour he was on a train. Less than ten minutes later the train crossed the border into Hungary.

Both countries announced that they were mobilizing. (Serbia had started mobilizing hours before delivering its response.) Russia then declared what its military planners called a Period Preparatory to War—not yet mobilizing but moving ominously in that direction. Army units on summer maneuvers were returned to their barracks, officers on leave were recalled, and the military districts of Kazan, Kiev, Moscow, and Odessa were ordered to make ready. More secretly, preparations also began in the Warsaw, Vilna, and St. Petersburg districts. The last development was particularly dangerous, as those three districts threatened Germany directly.

But there was even more to July 25 than that.

The Serbian response to Austria's demands, far from being defiant, was actually conciliatory, respectful, and at times almost submissive in tone. But it was also long, and its language was artfully oblique. ("The most brilliant example of diplomatic skill I have ever known," an annoyed Berchtold called it.) It explained that while Serbia could agree unconditionally to a number of the demands, it had questions about several others—not objections, just questions—and was unable to accept only one: predictably, the one that would have involved Austria directly in Belgrade's search for and prosecution of the assassination plotters. But even here the wording was far from bellicose. "The Royal Government cannot accept such an arrangement, as it would be a violation of the Constitution and the law of criminal procedure," it stated. "Nevertheless, in concrete cases communications as to the results of the investigation in question might be given to the Austro-Hungarian agents."

As positive as it was in many ways, and as clever as it may have been as an attempt to hold off the Austrians while impressing the rest of the world with Serbia's willingness to cooperate, the response can fairly be regarded as one of the mistakes that led to war. By declining to yield, the Serbs gave Berchtold, Conrad, and their cohorts the one thing they wanted: an excuse for military action. Worse, they did this unnecessarily. They might have responded differently—not more shrewdly, their document being nothing if not shrewd, but more effectively—had they not been receiving reports about how Russia wanted them to stand firm. These reports were wishful thinking on the part of Serbia's combative ambassador to Russia, who was being manipulated by France's ambassador in St. Petersburg, Maurice Paléologue. They certainly were not in accord with the thinking of Russian officialdom. Tsar Nicholas was leery of a major war because he was fearful of its likely consequences—social and economic strains so severe that they could spark revolution. So was Foreign Minister Sazonov. Both men believed that Russia was years from being ready to fight the Germans. Though Russia was greatly expanding its already huge army and was also, with the help of France, building a new network of railroads designed to improve its ability to wage war, such projects would not be completed until 1917 at the earliest. But Sazonov especially believed that Austria-Hungary was acting not independently but as the tool of Berlin, that the Germans were determined to precipitate a preventive war, and that Russia could protect itself only by reacting forcefully and quickly.

The Serbian response also might have been different if someone other than Nikola Pasic had been responsible for preparing it. Because of his prior knowledge of the Black Hand's plot, and also because of the efforts he had made to stop the assassination, Serbia's prime minister had abundant reasons for not wanting Austria-Hungary to become involved in any investigation. It would be bad for him, and probably bad for Serbia, if Austria discovered how much he had known and started asking why he had not done more. It might be even worse for him if the Black Hand learned that, in attempting to stop the assassination, he had actually tried to alert the Austrians. To all this was added Pasic's need to show himself willing to stand up to the Austrians in the run-up to the Serbian election.

The Austrian mobilization that followed put into motion a plan for assembling twenty divisions—some three hundred thousand troops—just a few miles from Belgrade. In deploying his forces in this way, Conrad left himself with only twenty-eight divisions for Galicia to the north, where Austria-Hungary would have to face much larger numbers if Russia went to war. This alarmed the German general staff when it became known in Berlin. It meant—contrary to what Conrad had indicated in earlier consultations with the German high command—that the German army in the east would have painfully limited Austrian support in case of a Russian attack. It showed Conrad's blind determination to believe that Russia was going to stay out, and that he was therefore free to give the Serbs the thrashing that he had been wanting to give them for years.

Russia, in declaring its Period Preparatory to War, took the steps that would enable it to get its troops into action more quickly if it too mobilized. And if its actions were "preparatory," they were far from trivial. They involved the mustering of 1.1 million troops in the four districts nearest to Austria-Hungary. Serbia's mobilization, necessarily much smaller, was based on the mistaken but eminently rational assumption that Austria was preparing to attack within a few days. The same assumption prompted the Serbs to begin moving their government out of Belgrade and away from the border.

Mobilization, a momentous word in those days, meant something short of—but not always a great deal short of—declaring and going to war. The degree of difference varied from nation to nation, and in this fact lay a world of trouble. For Russia, geographically vast and systemically inefficient, mobilization was an almost glacial affair. It was a matter of calling up reserves (no simple matter where railways were few and men reporting for duty might have to travel hundreds of miles), assembling divisions and armies in their assigned positions, and getting them ready to advance against the enemy or face an enemy advance. Crucially, an invasion of enemy territory was not integral to Russia's mobilization arrangements; that was to be decided according to circumstances. Even after mobilization, the Russian leadership would continue to have options. Its mobilized armies could be kept in place on Russian soil without disruption of their ability to act.

The sprawling Austro-Hungarian Empire faced transport problems similar to, though not quite so serious as, those of Russia. And again like St. Petersburg's, Vienna's mobilization plans gave it a measure of flexibility. Conrad had divided his forces into three groups: one for use against Serbia, one for Galicia and engagement of the Russians, and a third to be deployed to either front depending on need. It was by deciding to send his third group to the south that Conrad was able to assemble twenty divisions for an attack on Serbia.

Germany, in 1914 the most modern and efficient of Europe's industrial giants, could mobilize with a speed that was dazzling by comparison with either Russia or Austria-Hungary. Its planners were convinced that in case of war the country's survival would depend on that speed. Ever since 1894, when France and Russia had first become allies, the Germans had been faced with the likelihood that war with either would entail war with both. They also assumed—this was arguable but not unreasonable—that they could not expect to win a protracted war against both. For this reason their mobilization plan was focused on a single overriding objective: to knock France out of action in the west in no more than six weeks, before Russia could launch a major attack from the east. Germany's plans, therefore, included the start of a drive on Paris. Once started, such a drive would be nearly impossible to stop or even significantly modify without reducing all the arrangements to chaos. For Germany alone, mobilization equaled war.

But mobilization was bound to be dangerous, regardless of which power undertook it. It was inherently threatening. Even if undertaken by Austria-Hungary, the least of the great powers, and even if directed at a mere Balkan kingdom, it was certain to draw some kind of response.

The start of Austria-Hungary's mobilization caught the chief of the Serbian army, the aged Field Marshal Radomir Putnik, on his way home from a summer vacation in the Austrian province of Bohemia. The authorities in Budapest detained him. But Emperor Franz Joseph demanded not only that Putnik be allowed to proceed but that a special train be made available to return him to Belgrade. It was a charming gesture of Old World courtliness, one that the new world of industrialized warfare would soon render obsolete. As Putnik took charge of the Serbian defenses, Conrad and his troops would have reason to regret their emperor's chivalry.

Sunday, July 26

This was a day when no headlines were made, a day when little, supposedly, was happening. Again, however, things were less simple than they appeared, particularly in Austria and Russia, whose leaders were now putting their military machines in motion and hoping that the other powers would understand their actions as they wanted them to be understood.

Austria mobilized in part to start the clock ticking on a process that would require sixteen days to bring the army to readiness. But it also wanted to demonstrate that the situation was serious, that if France and Britain wanted to avoid something worse than a localized Balkan problem, they had better restrain Russia. France mattered even at this early stage because it was Russia's one powerful ally, and because everyone understood that without French support the Russians would be reluctant, probably even unwilling, to risk war with an Austria-Hungary acting with German support. Britain mattered because it was powerful despite having only a small army, because it had allied itself with France and Russia in a loose and informal way, and because it was certain to want to avoid a general war.

The second of Vienna's purposes could not possibly be achieved. France's President Poincaré was still at sea. With wireless communications still primitive (and with Germany attempting to jam radio transmissions), he was nearly incommunicado. Britain's foreign secretary, Sir Edward Grey, was both cautious by nature and paralyzed by divisions within the government of which he was a member. In the near term, no one in Paris or London was going to be pressuring St. Petersburg—or Berlin or Vienna for that matter—to do anything. Grey's own position, which he expressed within the cabinet only, was that the greatest threat to British security was German dominance in Europe. He believed that if war were to break out between Austria and Russia and lead to war between Germany and France, Britain would have to side with France. This did not mean, however, that he wanted war.

On July 26 Grey felt that the most he could do was communicate his concerns to the German ambassador in London, Prince Karl Lichnowsky, and suggest a conference of Britain, France, Germany, and Italy as a means of resolving the crisis. Lichnowsky, whose position in London permitted him to see almost from the start that Grey and other British leaders were likely to oppose Germany in a showdown, seized on this suggestion. "I would like to call your attention to the significance of Grey's proposal of a mediation *à quatre* between Austria and Russia," he said in a telegram to Berlin. "I see in it the only possibility of avoiding a world war, in which for us there would be everything to lose and nothing to gain."

Russia's declaration of a Period Preparatory to War had a less subtle purpose than the Austrian mobilization. Its goal was, simply, to make the Austrians reconsider. St. Petersburg was also eager to make Berlin believe that it was not being threatened, but German intelligence soon learned that the Russian military was doing much more than it would admit to. Its secret preparations in the military districts closest to Germany reflected the Russian government's fear that, as Foreign Minister Sazonov told Tsar Nicholas, it faced not just a dispute over Serbia but "a question of the balance of power in Europe, which is seriously threatened." But they also bore an uncomfortably close resemblance to an undeclared mobilization. When the German military attaché in St. Petersburg made inquiries, however, he was given lies in response. As more was learned about how much the Russians were doing, and as the Russians continued to pretend that they were doing very little, Berlin grew increasingly nervous. It became progressively less willing to accept the assurances of goodwill coming from St. Petersburg.

Maurice Paléologue, France's ambassador in St. Petersburg, was able to keep himself informed of the extent of Russia's preparations. The Russians had a responsibility under their Entente with France to tell Paris in advance of any mobilization plans, but Paléologue did not remind them of this fact. He appears to have been unwilling to do anything that might discourage them from proceeding. He did not even tell his own government what he knew; he didn't want anyone in Paris to restrain the Russians either. A similar game was being played in Vienna by Germany's Ambassador Tschirschky, a onetime foreign minister who had decided that it was his duty to encourage Austrian aggressiveness without doing so openly.

It happened that Kaiser Wilhelm's younger brother, Prince Heinrich of Prussia, was in England on this Sunday, attending the annual yacht races at Cowes and lunching as the guest of his first cousin, King George V. Afterward—heedless of the fact that the king had little voice in foreign policy—Heinrich sent a message to Berlin reporting that "Georgie" had given him the impression that London wanted to stay neutral. The prince, a naval officer by profession, had already earned a reputation as a not entirely reliable reporter, and his message contradicted warnings being sent by Ambassador Lichnowsky. The German foreign ministry, however, had never taken Lichnowsky seriously. Its leading figures saw him as a gullible Anglophile, a wealthy dilettante who owed his position to his long friendship with the kaiser. They were predisposed to find the views of Prince Heinrich more credible because they were so very much more pleasing.

And so the final week of peace had begun with Austria mobilizing while sending signals that no one was available to receive; with Russia in the first stages of mobilizing while pretending not to be; with Germany beginning to feel directly threatened; and with France's ambassador urging the Russians as well as the Serbians on. Britain was sending ambiguous signals that the continental powers were free to interpret as they wished. Berlin and Paris were both, for the time being, effectively leaderless. Nothing irreversible had happened, but neither was anyone quite in control.

Monday, July 27

This was yet another day when, so far as the public knew, nothing much of importance was happening.

But in fact it was the day when the Austro-Hungarian Council of Ministers met in secret and voted to declare war on Serbia. This was a strange because utterly unnecessary decision. Even Conrad, eager as he was for action, questioned it. He couldn't see the point of declaring war more than two weeks in advance of the completion of Austria's mobilization. But Berchtold, determined to commit the dual monarchy to military action before Germany's position softened or the mediation proposals coming out of Britain could have an effect, brought Conrad around.

The declaration of war was to be announced on Tuesday and required the approval of Franz Joseph. When Berchtold and Conrad went to see him, he proved to be reluctant. They told him lies about Serbian attacks. Actually there had been nothing more than a brief and meaningless exchange of gunfire at an insignificant border town. Persuaded by this tale that war had begun and that Serbia was responsible, the emperor signed. In preparing to do so, he trembled so badly that he had difficulty putting on his glasses.

In London, Grey read the text of Serbia's response to the ultimatum and found it promising. He met with Lichnowsky and repeated his suggestion of a conference of the powers. Lichnowsky again relayed the suggestion to Berlin, urging that it be pursued. Chancellor Bethmann Hollweg, who disliked the proposal but didn't want to offend the British, indicated by return wire that he was forwarding it to Vienna. But he explained to Austria's ambassador in Berlin "in the most decided way" that the German government wanted nothing to do with Grey's ideas, "that on the contrary it advises to disregard them, but that it must pass them on to satisfy the English." The Germans and Austrians had reason to be skeptical about the proposed conference. At least two of the four countries that would participate, France and Italy, would have little reason to look sympathetically on Austria's grievances. A third, Britain, seemed unlikely to do anything to damage its relations with France and Russia. At best, the Germans and Austrians believed, a conference would substitute talk for action, degenerating into a sterile debate over the wording of the Austrian note and Serbia's response. In the end, they feared,

Serbia would dance away scot-free, with Austria-Hungary looking on as help-lessly as in 1912 and 1913. Serb activists both within and outside the Hapsburg empire would be encouraged to continue making trouble, and Austria-Hungary's other minorities would be encouraged to do the same.

The Austrians had financial reasons too for resisting mediation. Theirs was a financially starved administration—Conrad had never been given enough money to keep the armies of Vienna competitive with the other great pow-ers in size, equipment, or technology—and the mobilizations during the two Balkan wars had been as costly as they had been fruitless. By 1914 all the great powers, but Austria-Hungary especially, were creaking under the weight of an arms race that was becoming constantly more onerous as the machinery of war grew more massive and complex. Vienna could not afford to be mobi-lizing year after year. It wanted to be sure that this time it got something for its money.

In the afternoon Kaiser Wilhelm arrived home from his vacation cruise. Chancellor Bethmann and Gottlieb von Jagow, the head of the German for-eign ministry, were not delighted by his return. They had urged him to stay away, telling him that a premature end to his vacation might alarm the other

German Foreign Minister
Gottlieb von Jagow
*"Nothing has helped.
I am appointed."*

powers. What they really feared, probably, was that the unpredictable kaiser would interfere in their handling of the crisis.

With or without the kaiser's presence, Bethmann and Jagow were not an ideal pair to be steering the most powerful state in Europe through such difficult straits. Bethmann was a tall, dour career civil servant who five years earlier had been raised to the chancellorship despite having no experience in foreign affairs and despite being disliked by the kaiser. ("He was always lecturing me," Wilhelm complained, "and pretends to know everything.") Like many Germans in high places, he was terrified by the presence of unfriendly powers to the east and west and convinced that Germany could only grow more vulnerable with the passage of time. Jagow was a frail hypochondriac who had used an elder brother's connections to get into the foreign service and had then successfully leveraged those same connections to get a series of plush and undemanding assignments in Rome and elsewhere. When summoned home to head the foreign ministry, he had pulled every string he could reach in a futile effort to escape. "Nothing has helped," he had said despairingly at last. "I am appointed."

Late in the night Vienna sent word to Berlin of its decision to declare war. When the message reached Bethmann and Jagow, they were not astonished. The Austrians were doing at last what Berlin had been urging from the start: they were taking action. No effort was made to inform the kaiser. This was, after all, exactly what he too had demanded at the start.

Tuesday, July 28

Wilhelm II was back in his office, seated in his saddle chair. (Wanting no doubt to be the perfect Hohenzollern warrior-king, and proud no doubt of the agonies he had endured in boyhood to become a skillful horseman in spite of his crippled arm, he claimed to be more comfortable in a saddle than in a conventional chair.) He had much work to catch up on. First he read the most recent wire from Lichnowsky in London: it quoted Sir Edward Grey as saying that an Austrian attack on Serbia would have disastrous consequences, but that the Serbian response to Austria appeared to provide a basis for negotiations. Then he read the Serbian response itself. Perhaps in part because he had just seen Grey's thoughts on the subject—Wilhelm was one of those men who tend to agree with whoever talked with them last—his reaction was much the same as Grey's. "This was more than one could have expected," he declared. "A great moral victory for Vienna; but with it every reason for war drops away, and Giesl might have remained quietly in Belgrade. On the strength of this I"—he underlined the pronoun, implicitly rebuking the Austrians—"should never have ordered mobilization!"

Seeing an opportunity and eager to seize it, Wilhelm sent a handwritten note to Jagow declaring the Serbian response "a capitulation of the most humiliating kind," so that *"every cause for war* falls to the ground!" He instructed the foreign ministry to prepare a message to go out over his name informing Vienna that a basis now existed for resolving the crisis through mediation, and that he was prepared to help. He added an idea that a member of his military staff had suggested to him at the start of the day. Because the Serbs could not be trusted ("Orientals," Wilhelm called them, "therefore liars, tricksters and masters of evasion"), Austria should send its army across the border and occupy Belgrade but then go no farther. In possession of Serbia's capital, the Austrians would be in a position of strength as mediation proceeded. This would come to be called the Stop-in-Belgrade proposal, and soon Grey too would be suggesting it. It offered a solution much like the one that ended the Franco-Prussian War in 1871. The German armies had remained in France until Berlin's terms were met—the payment of immense reparations plus the surrender of Alsace and Lorraine—then paraded through the streets of Paris and gone home.

Bethmann and Jagow, incredibly, had still not told Wilhelm that an Austrian declaration of war was only hours away. The kaiser assumed that such a declaration would not come for another two weeks if at all. Just as incredibly, Bethmann and Jagow prepared the kaiser's message to Vienna as instructed but surreptitiously delayed its transmission for twelve hours, making certain that it wouldn't be received until after the Austrians issued their declaration.

Though Bethmann and Jagow had deceived the kaiser, depriving him of any chance of intervening before Austria declared war, their motives may well have been good. As clumsy as their behavior had been at a crucial juncture where nothing less than brilliance was required, they knew Wilhelm all too well—his childish arrogance, his unpredictability, his history of reversing himself and even breaking down in the midst of a crisis. (He had done so in 1908, 1911, and again early in 1914, sinking so low that he had to be talked out of abdicating.) No doubt they thought they had a better grasp of the situation than he. Having been in Berlin while he was still away, they definitely were better informed, if only because they had gone to such lengths to keep him uninformed. And they had reason to think that, in their support of the Austrians, they had been carrying out the kaiser's wishes. They must have felt that involving him more directly at this late hour could only complicate an already confusing situation.

The Austrian declaration, issued in the middle of the afternoon, changed everything. It was one of the two or three most important blunders committed by any of the great powers during the days leading up to war. And, as with the delivery of the Austrian note to Serbia five days earlier, there was a farcical aspect to how it happened. Berchtold, knowing that the Serbian government had withdrawn from Belgrade to the interior and not knowing how to make contact with that government wherever it now was, sent a telegram, uncoded and in French, informing Prime Minister Pasic that a state of war now existed between their two countries. He addressed this message to Pasic via Serbian army headquarters. Shortly thereafter, in an abundance of caution, he sent a second, identical telegram via the Serbian foreign ministry. The two messages reached Pasic separately after being routed through Romania. The first was handed to him as he was having lunch at a provincial hotel. After reading it he got to his feet and addressed the room. "Austria has declared war on us," he said gravely. "Our cause is just. God will help us." When the second telegram arrived a short time later, Pasic became suspicious. Never having heard of one nation declaring war on another in such a manner, he began to think that the whole thing might be a hoax. The German ambassador, when asked, replied that he knew nothing about a declaration of war. (He was being truthful; not even the kaiser, as we have seen, was informed in advance of Austria's declaration.) The authenticity of the telegrams was confirmed soon enough. News of the declaration sparked anti-Serbian demonstrations in Vienna and even in Berlin, but there was no movement of Austrian troops. Conrad merely began shelling Belgrade from the Bosnian side of the border.

The kaiser met with Bethmann after learning the truth. The chancellor, a visibly unhappy man afterward, immediately began steering a new course. He composed a long telegram to Tschirschky in Vienna, complaining that the Austro-Hungarian government "has left us in the dark concerning its intentions, despite repeated interrogations" and that its declaration of war had put Germany in "an extraordinarily difficult position" that could cause it to "incur the odium of having been responsible for a world war." He instructed Tschirschky to urge the Austrians to respond positively to what was now Grey's, not just the kaiser's, Stop-in-Belgrade proposal. No doubt Tschirschky, who shortly after the assassination had been rebuked for urging caution on the Austrians, was taken aback. Berchtold was more than taken aback. For three weeks the Germans had been prodding him to act. Now at last he was taking action—and suddenly the Germans wanted him to stop.

The day brought one additional misfortune, and a serious one. Russia's ambassador to Austria, having been kept waiting since Monday, finally was allowed to meet with Berchtold. He wanted to discuss a number of ideas that were being passed around among the various capitals: a suggestion by Sazonov that he and Vienna's ambassador to St. Petersburg should review the original Austrian note to see if it might be modified enough for Serbia to accept it, for example, and Sir Edward Grey's proposal that the Serbian reply be used as a starting point for negotiations rather than a reason for war.

Everyone was distracted by the rush of events, however, and Berchtold and his visitor apparently lost track of exactly which idea they were discussing at various points in the conversation. The result was misunderstanding. Berchtold, when the meeting was over, believed that he had made it clear that while he would not negotiate with Serbia, he was prepared to do so with Russia. But the ambassador came away with a distinctly different impression. He reported to Sazonov that Berchtold was not willing to negotiate even with Russia. Probably for no other reason than that both parties had too much on their minds and were approaching exhaustion, an important door had been inadvertently closed.

So Tuesday ended badly. Vienna, with its declaration of war, had convinced Sazonov in St. Petersburg that it was mobilizing not merely to underscore its grievances but to destroy Serbia (which was, in fact, not far from the truth where Berchtold and Conrad were concerned). The Russians had accelerated their preparations for war, Sazonov had been told that it was not even possible to talk with Vienna, and he took this as further evidence that war had become inevitable. Meanwhile he was also being told by France's Ambassador Paléologue that Paris wanted him to stand firm, by Germany's Ambassador Friedrich von Pourtalès that if Russia proceeded with its military preparations Germany would have to mobilize as well, by Serbia's ambassador that the Austrians were bombarding Belgrade, and by Russia's generals that Germany was preparing for war and they must do the same. In important ways, Sazonov was being deceived. French prime minister René Viviani, from the ship on which he and President Poincaré were returning from St. Petersburg, had sent a telegram urging Paléologue to do everything possible to resolve the crisis without war. Paléologue, so determined to encourage Russian belligerence that he was in effect creating his own foreign policy, instead told Sazonov of the "complete readiness of France to fulfill her obligations as an ally in case of necessity."

Paléologue's motivation in all this is clear enough. Notoriously excitable, so inclined to take the darkest possible view of every situation that he was widely distrusted (he owed his appointment to a lifelong friendship with Poincaré), he had been warning even before the July crisis that a European war was inevitable by year-end. Among the terrors that tormented him was the thought that, if France failed to demonstrate a willingness to support Russia almost unreservedly, St. Petersburg would abandon the Entente and seek to ally itself with Berlin. Thus he saw himself as preventing the collapse of France's entire foreign policy, and therefore of France's security.

THE ROMANOVS

IN 1914 THE ROMANOV FAMILY HAD JUST COMPLETED THE celebration of its three hundredth year on the Russian throne. It had been a turbulent, often bizarre three centuries. Geniuses and degenerates had worn the crown by turns, amazingly strong women succeeded by alarmingly weak men. There had been royal murders and assassinations, questions about whether a tsar who was presumably dead and buried had actually died at all, and enough sexual irregularity to make it uncertain whether the Romanovs of the twentieth century were even related to the founders of the dynasty. By fits and starts Russia had changed from a remote and exotic eastern kingdom into one of Europe's dominating powers—still only half modern, still not entirely European, but an empire of immense wealth reaching from Poland to the Pacific Ocean. By 1914 the Romanovs had been, by the standards of Russian history, stable and respectable for five generations. The reigning tsar, Nicholas II, was a far more virtuous man than many of his predecessors. He was also, unfortunately, far weaker and less capable than the best of them.

The first Romanov tsar was Michael, crowned in 1613 when he was sixteen years old. He was given the crown because Russia's previous royal family had died out; because after fifteen years of leaderless disorder the country's most powerful factions were desperate for stability; and because no better choice was available. If Michael's blood was not quite royal, it was nearly so: his aunt Anastasia, his father's sister, had been the beloved first wife of Ivan the Terrible and the mother of the last tsar in Ivan's line. Grief over her death is supposed to have been a factor in Ivan's transformation into a homicidal maniac of almost inconceivable savagery.

The Romanovs did not burst upon the European scene until almost a century later, when Peter I, Peter the Great, became tsar. He was a gigantic figure in every sense: more than six and a half feet tall, immensely strong, infinitely energetic, violent, a reformer of everything and at the same time a ruthless tyrant. He was so determined to force Russia into the modern Western world that he moved its capital from Moscow to a swampy piece of wilderness on the coast of the Baltic Sea. Here he built a magnificent new city that was laced with canals and became known as the Venice of the North. He named it St. Petersburg because that was more Western than the Russian equivalent, Petrograd. There was nothing that he wasn't determined to change, and when his ministers weren't quick enough in doing what he wanted, he would lash even the most exalted of them with his stick. He forced the men of Russia to shave their beards and adopt Western dress; the traditionalists were scandalized. He modernized the government and the military. He conquered and developed seaports not only on the Baltic but on the Black Sea, beginning the long process of pushing the Ottoman Turks southward back toward their capital of Constantinople. By the time of his death in 1725, he had transformed Russia into a major player among the nations of the world.

As a young man Peter had married a woman from the Russian nobility, but he soon found her tedious and eventually sent her to a convent. He replaced her with a mistress, a Lutheran girl named Marta who had begun her life as a humbly born orphan in Latvia. She had become a prisoner when an invading Russian army captured her hometown, was given to a man who happened to be close to Peter, and so was taken back to St. Petersburg, where she was discovered by the tsar. Marta and Peter had twelve children together (only two, both of them daughters, survived to adulthood), and she came to be the one person in whom he had complete

The Russian royal family: Nicholas, Alexandra, their four daughters and son

confidence. She was rechristened in the Orthodox faith and given the baptismal name Catherine, and was married to Peter in 1712, when she was twenty-eight and he fifty. He had her crowned his empress consort in 1724 (Peter was the first tsar to call himself emperor), and upon Peter's death she was proclaimed Empress Catherine I in her own right. Her career has to be considered among the more remarkable in history.

The story becomes fuzzy in the years following Catherine's death. The Romanovs became extinct in the male line (Peter had his heir, a son by his first wife, tortured until he died), and in time the crown went to an obscure German princeling whose mother had been Peter's and Catherine's daughter. This new tsar, Peter III, was a drunkard, a fool, probably sexually impotent, and an ardent admirer of Russia's enemy Frederick the Great of Prussia. Not surprisingly, the Russian nobility despised him. He matters in history for one reason only: before becoming tsar, he had married a fifteen-year-old German princess—another Catherine, as it happened—who quickly succeeded him on the throne. (Plotters from the army, in collusion with this second Catherine, murdered him less than a year after his coronation.) She became Catherine the Great, the second monumental figure of the Romanov era.

She was a physically tiny woman whose appetites and ambitions equaled those of Peter the Great. She became more Russian than the Russians, and during her thirty-four-year reign the empire expanded tremendously and again was prodded along the road to modernization. Like Peter the Great, she reached out to the West. She corresponded with such Enlightenment giants as Voltaire and Diderot. She brought John Paul Jones from the New World to take command of her Black Sea Fleet and use it against the Turks. It was with Catherine that the Russians began to aspire seriously to the role of patron of the Christian peoples of the Balkans. And under Catherine they first dreamed of driving the Turks out of Constantinople, the ancient and holy imperial city of the East.

Like Peter the Great before her and like many of her own descendants, Catherine was a perplexing mixture of reformer and tyrant. She was also a woman of great intellect and cultivation, as well as a libertine. She had multiple lovers before her husband's death, and it is at best questionable whether her son and heir, Paul, was actually the son of Peter III. Her long string of handsome young lovers, most of them playthings whom she was far too shrewd to take seriously except in the boudoir, continued until her death of a stroke at sixty-seven. Unprovable stories about her sexual encounters with a horse have come down to the twenty-first century.

Catherine had no confidence in her son Paul; in fact, she despised him. She took charge of the upbringing of Paul's sons, especially the eldest,

Alexander. She carefully supervised his preparation for the throne. When she died, Paul succeeded. But he was soon murdered, just as his father had been—assuming that Peter III was in fact his father. He was then succeeded, as Catherine had intended, by the tall, handsome, and intelligent young Alexander I.

In what would become something of a Romanov pattern, Tsar Alexander began his reign as a reformer of whom great things were expected, then took alarm at the forces of change all around him, and finally turned into the most iron-handed kind of reactionary. His first fifteen years on the throne were turbulent in the extreme, with Napoleon marching his armies up and down Europe and finally occupying and burning Moscow. It fell to Alexander to save Russia and his dynasty, and he succeeded brilliantly. In the end he outwaited and outwitted the French emperor. At one point he even pretended to consider offering his sister to Napoleon, though in fact giving a Romanov princess to such an upstart was unthinkable. After Napoleon took an Austrian bride instead (even the mighty Hapsburgs turned out to be more submissive than Alexander) and finally was driven into exile, Alexander was more influential than any other monarch in restoring the old order.

Intriguing questions hang over the end of Alexander's life. In 1825, childless but at the peak of his power, he was suddenly reported to have died in a town where he had been staying far from the capital. When his coffin arrived in St. Petersburg, his brothers refused to have it opened. There were rumors that he had not died at all but had done something that he had long talked yearningly of doing—withdrawn into a monastery in Siberia to spend the rest of his life in contemplation. Nothing of the sort was ever proved. But toward the end of the twentieth century, when his coffin was finally opened in St. Petersburg's Peter and Paul Fortress, it was found to be empty.

Alexander's heir was his brother Constantine, but because this archduke refused the crown, it was passed to a third and much younger brother who thereby became Nicholas I. This Nicholas, lacking even ephemeral reforming instincts, was a reactionary in all ways from the start. When he died in 1855, he was called the man who had frozen Russia for thirty years.

His son Alexander II was also conservative but more intelligent and therefore able to understand the need for change. He began his career as a reformer and even something of an idealist, abolishing the serfdom that had long been the shame of Russia. Gradually he too turned in the direction of reaction and repression, taking such severe measures against a movement of young reformers that some became bomb-throwing radicals.

In the last years of his reign there were repeated attempts on his life, but Alexander never completely abandoned his efforts to move Russia closer to if not quite into the modern world. In 1881, shortly after he had approved the creation of a parliamentlike body that was to be allowed to advise on legislation without actually passing laws, a bomb thrown by a young Pole blew him apart.

Still alive but oozing blood from every part of his body, one leg gone and the other shredded, his torso torn open and his face disfigured, the tsar was carried to his palace. There he died, horribly, in the presence of his family, including his eldest son, who then became Alexander III, and the latter's eldest son, thirteen-year-old Nicholas. He was the third tsar to be murdered in six generations.

Alexander III was a huge and bearlike man, powerful enough to bend a poker and roll pieces of silverware into balls with his bare hands. On succeeding to the throne he declared his "faith in the power and right of autocracy," and he was as good as his word. He dedicated himself unreservedly to reversing as many of his father's reforms as possible (a restoration of serfdom was not among the possibilities), refusing any innovations that might reduce the power of the Romanovs, and clamping down in almost totalitarian fashion on every form of dissent. Newspapers were not even allowed to print the word *constitution*.

Alexander III's son Nicholas was improbably unlike his father in almost every respect: physically slight, something of a playboy in his youth though in fairly innocent ways, and utterly lacking in self-confidence. He was, however, given the same tutor who had taught his father, an archconservative named Constantine Pobedonostsev, known as the High Priest of Social Stagnation. "Among the falsest of political principles is the principle of the sovereignty of the people," Pobedonostsev taught. "It is terrible to think of our condition if destiny had sent us the fatal gift—an all-Russia Parliament. But that will never be." Young Nicholas listened, and like his father he believed. He learned that it was not only the tsar's right but his sacred duty to be a strong father to all the Russians, to yield power to no one. But he had a clear sense of his own limits, knew that he could never be like his father, and had absolutely no wish to succeed him.

There appeared to be no cause for worry on that score. In 1894, with Nicholas in his mid-twenties and preparing to marry Princess Alix of Hesse-Darmstadt (his parents were not at all happy about the match, though the bride was a granddaughter of Queen Victoria of Britain and therefore Wilhelm II's first cousin), Alexander III was not yet fifty and a fountain of vitality. It seemed likely that he would rule for another twenty years or more, and his own expectation that this would be so was reflected in his failure to do anything to prepare his heir for the responsibilities of government. (Nicholas himself demonstrated no wish to learn.) But then, abruptly, he went into a swift decline—the problem was diagnosed as nephritis—and soon died. His heir was shattered, and not only because he had lost the father he idolized.

"What am I going to do?" he asked. "I am not prepared to be a tsar. I never wanted to become one. I know nothing of the business of ruling. I have no idea of even how to talk to the ministers."

Chapter 5

✠

July 29 to 31:
Fear Is a Bad Counselor

"Think of the responsibility which you are advising me
to take! Think of the thousands and thousands of men
who will be sent to their death!"
—TSAR NICHOLAS II

Wednesday, July 29

At one o'clock in the morning Tsar Nicholas sent a telegram to Kaiser Wilhelm. It was signed "Nicky," and it expressed indignation that an "ignoble war has been declared on a weak country." It asked the kaiser "in the name of our old friendship to do what you can to stop your allies from going too far." While this wire was making its way to Potsdam, Wilhelm sent one of his own to the tsar. It was signed "your very sincere and devoted friend and cousin, Willy." In it the kaiser declared his hopes for peace and said, "I am exerting my utmost influence to induce the Austrians to deal straightly to arrive to [*sic*] a satisfactory understanding with you."

This exchange was promising, though in his marginal scribblings the kaiser dismissed Tsar Nicholas's message as "a confession of his own weakness, and an attempt to put the responsibility on my own shoulders." The two monarchs wrote to each other in English, a language in which they could not have been more fluent if born and raised in London. In any case, like every glimmer of hope during this exhausting and interminable week, the exchange would soon be submerged in the rush of events. The tsar's foreign minister, Sazonov, continued to be under intense pressure from all sides. He needed little persuading when, later in the morning, War Minister Vladimir Sukhomlinov and the army's chief of staff came to him with their solution to the crisis: mobilization. Mobilizing the army, they said, would put Austria-

Hungary on notice in the strongest possible way. Not mobilizing, on the other hand, would leave the army unable to respond if Austria's troops entered Serbia. In case of a wider war, the army would be totally unprepared. Sazonov was quick to agree.

The chief of staff then took the train to Tsar Nicholas's summer palace (the tsar, capable of a strange degree of detachment when terrible things were happening around him, had not visited the capital once since Franz Ferdinand's assassination) and got his signature on two decrees. One ordered the mobilization of twelve army corps, fifty-five divisions, in the four military districts where secret preparations were already most advanced. This was a massive force, bigger than the entire Austro-Hungarian army, but it would include less than half of Russia's troops and so was not intended as a threat to Germany. The other decree would put in motion a general mobilization involving all districts including those nearest Germany and thereby drastically escalate the crisis. Nicholas believed he was merely putting in place the paperwork necessary for possible action later. He told his visitor that neither order was to be executed without specific authorization from him. That night army headquarters was preparing for execution of the general mobilization—and Sazonov was telling lies to the British ambassador, assuring him that Russia was considering no action that could possibly distress the Germans—when the tsar sent word that he had made a decision. Only a partial mobilization, he said, would be allowed; there must be no move against Germany. Nicholas was continuing to exchange telegrams with "Willy," who was continuing to assure him—truthfully—that he was trying to slow the Austrians down.

On this same day President Poincaré of France and Prime Minister Viviani landed at Dunkirk and hurried to Paris by train. They were surprised to learn

Raymond Poincaré
President of France
*Determined to bring
Britain into the war.*

that Austria had declared war, surprised too by the crowds that had gathered to greet them and were shouting "To Berlin!" Here as in other capitals, the man in the street was giving every appearance of being eager for the fighting to begin. Crowds were gathering in Vienna too and in Berlin and Hamburg and London, where a young bank clerk returning from vacation observed that the city was in "a state of hysteria." The enthusiasm was not universal, however. Bertrand Russell, also in London, said he "discovered to my horror that average men and women were delighted at the prospect of war." Across Europe Socialist leaders were mustering their followers in opposition to the impending conflict. Even among the political and military elites, the mood was generally grim. Sir Edward Grey, from his office at the foreign ministry, made his famous comment that "the lamps are going out all over Europe. We shall not see them lit again in our lifetime." (Ironically, long before the war's end Grey would have to retire from public life because he was going blind.) Poincaré, though touched by the fervor of the Paris crowds and determined to give the Russians no reason to doubt his government's support, was equally determined to avert hostilities if possible. He and Viviani sent a telegram to St. Petersburg urging that the Russians do nothing that might provoke a German mobilization; this arrived, however, after the tsar's approval of partial mobilization.

Among the holders of high office, one man at least did not share the sense of glum foreboding: the ebullient—sometimes excessively ebullient—young Winston Churchill. "I think a curse should rest on me," he wrote to Prime Minister Asquith's wife, obviously believing nothing of the kind, "because I *love* this war. I know it's smashing & shattering the lives of thousands every moment—& yet—I *can't* help it—I enjoy every second of it."

Churchill was still a little premature in writing of "this war." As Wednesday ended, the outlook appeared to be slightly less dark, the likelihood of war diminishing if only slightly. The kaiser and the tsar were not only communicating but cooperating in an attempt to impose restraint. Only two things now seemed necessary for a resolution of the crisis to remain possible. Russia must refrain from general mobilization; the kaiser seemed willing to accept, temporarily, limited Russian measures that did not threaten Germany directly. And Austria must agree to something akin to the Stop-in-Belgrade plan. This second condition was likely to be met eventually, simply because Germany wanted it to happen; Austria would find it difficult to proceed without Berlin's support. It all came down, therefore, to the question of whether the Russians would mobilize and stampede the Germans into doing likewise. The German military authorities remained divided. War Minister Erich von Falkenhayn, frightened by the dangers of allowing a Russian mobilization to go unanswered, was urging preliminary steps toward mobilization. But for Chief of Staff Moltke (sometimes accused, unjustifiably, of having plotted from the start to provoke a preventive war), the greatest fear at this point was of doing anything that might cause the Russians to mobilize. In a memorandum dated July 29 he told Chancellor Bethmann Hollweg that if war came, "the leading nations of Europe would tear one another limb from limb... in a struggle that would destroy the culture of almost all of Europe for decades to come." Bethmann, who needed no persuading, sent an evening telegram instructing Ambassador Pourtalès to "kindly impress upon M. Sazonov very seriously that further progress of Russian mobilization measures would compel us to mobilize and that then European war could scarcely be prevented."

Thursday, July 30

The European public was now fully awake to the possibility of war. Runs on banks were becoming widespread. Austria, Germany, and Russia were all withdrawing their reserves from foreign banks. The financial markets in Berlin and Brussels had to be shut down because of panic selling.

Even the Nicky-Willy telegrams were beginning to go wrong. In one of his middle-of-the-night messages, in a maladroit attempt to assure the kaiser that Russia had no hostile intentions where Germany was concerned, Tsar Nicholas told him that "the military measures which have now come into force were decided on five days ago for reasons of defense on account of Austria's preparations." Wilhelm concluded from this that Russia "is almost a week ahead of us," and that "that means I have got to mobilize as well."

In the morning the leaders of the Russian general staff came back to Sazonov with bad news. They said there was no acceptable way of executing the kind of partial mobilization that the tsar had approved, one supposedly directed at Austria-Hungary alone. Any such mobilization would have to be done off the cuff and would throw Russia's armed forces into a state of confusion that might leave them helpless in case of a German attack. In practical terms only general mobilization was possible, and it must be postponed no longer. When Sazonov accepted this argument—its validity has been a bone of contention ever since—the chief of the general staff telephoned the tsar and again asked him to approve a general mobilization. Nicholas refused, saying that the question was closed. He was persuaded, grudgingly, to meet with Sazonov at three P.M. Sazonov was soon on his way.

The meeting was a long one, with the foreign minister arguing the generals' case. Austria, Sazonov said, was preparing to destroy Serbia and refusing to talk. Germany was playing a double game, appearing to restrain the Austrians but really just trying to buy time for its own preparations: Germany was far along with an undeclared mobilization of its own. Russia could not afford not to respond. Russia also could not mobilize in any way short of fully—the result of trying such a thing could be disastrous. Sazonov was wrong about almost everything except Austria's determination to attack Serbia. He was not lying, but he was dangerously misinformed.

Nicholas continued to refuse, and Sazonov continued to plead. The tsar, conscious of the magnitude of what he was being asked, agonized aloud. "Think of the responsibility which you are asking me to take!" he declared. "Think of the thousands and thousands of men who will be sent to their death!"

Finally, probably inevitably, Nicholas was worn down. He was a stubborn but not a strong man, and even the strongest of men would have found it difficult to resist when being told that war could no longer be avoided regardless of what they did and that nothing less than national survival was at stake. Perhaps Sazonov's most powerful argument—another falsehood that he believed to be true—was that a general mobilization would not necessarily drive Germany to war. What neither Sazonov nor Nicholas understood was that Russia's mobilization would arouse in Germany's generals a panic indistinguishable from the fears driving the Russians, and that those generals would demand a German response. Far worse, neither of them had any way of knowing how fast the Germans would be able to mobilize, or how inflexible and therefore dangerous the German mobilization plan was. Not even Kaiser Wilhelm or Chancellor Bethmann Hollweg understood clearly at this point that Germany was literally incapable of mobilizing without invading its neighbors to the west and thereby igniting the continental war that all of them dreaded. The final tragedy is that the tsar's decision was based largely on the things that Sazonov told him about Germany's preparations for war, when in fact Germany remained the only one of the continental powers to have taken no military action at all.

Russia's general mobilization, decided just a little more than forty-eight hours after Austria's declaration of war on Serbia, added nine hundred thousand active-duty troops to the number that would have been affected by partial mobilization. It also called up the Russian reserves—a staggering total of four million men, enough to frighten any nation on earth. By making German mobilization—and therefore war—a near-certainty, it drastically reduced the possibility that the Willy-Nicky telegrams or any of the other increasingly desperate efforts to defuse the situation (cables were flying among the capital cities around the clock) could produce results before it was too late. It all but ended the hope of negotiations, or of a compromise based on Stop-in-Belgrade.

Tragically, Russia's mobilization, while dictated by military considerations, was not only militarily unnecessary but counterproductive. Tactically it was a gift to the Austrians (or would have been, if Conrad had taken advantage of it), relieving them of the anguish of not knowing whether they needed to prepare to fight the Russians or were free to focus on Serbia alone. Strategically it was an act of high folly. In no real sense had the security of Russia ever been threatened by the July crisis. Even the destruction of Serbia—something that certainly could have been averted without resorting to war—would have had little impact on Russia's strategic position. Russia would still have had the biggest army in the world by a huge margin, and it would still have been in the beginning stages of a program aimed at expanding that army by 40 percent within three years.

Tsar Nicholas was shown a telegram that the monk Rasputin had sent to Tsarina Alexandra. Rasputin, who had maneuvered himself into being almost a member of the imperial family, was at his home village deep in the interior of Russia, just beginning to recover from a stab wound that had nearly taken his life. Because of his distance from the capital and the state of his health, he could not possibly have known what was happening in St. Petersburg or Vienna or elsewhere. Thus his telegram, like so many other things about this strange and sinister man, continues to mystify even today. "Let Papa [Rasputin's name for Nicholas] not plan war," the telegram said. "With war will come the end of Russia and yourselves, and you will lose to the last man." The tsar read it and tore it into pieces.

British foreign secretary Sir Edward Grey, alarmed by the deepening seriousness of the crisis, finally stopped being so diplomatic as to be nearly incapable of saying anything. Speaking without the knowledge of the British cabinet, he told Germany's Ambassador Lichnowsky that in his opinion, quite unofficially, "unless Austria is willing to enter upon a discussion of the Serbian question, a world war is inevitable," and that he would expect such a war to bring Britain in on the side of France and Russia. When the kaiser and Bethmann Hollweg learned of this, they abandoned any lingering hopes that war if it came could be a "local" one involving only Austria-Hungary and Serbia, and they intensified their attempts to restrain the Austrians. If Grey had been this forthright just a few days earlier, Berlin almost certainly would have changed its position more quickly and firmly. Austria might then have deferred its declaration of war, and Russia would have had little reason to mobilize. Now, however, it was all but too late. Also too late, Bethmann awakened to the fact that the Russians were laboring under a misunderstanding about Vienna's willingness to talk. He cleared this up by having Tschirschky alert Berchtold to the problem, but with things now happening so fast and diplomacy being submerged under the concerns of the generals, there was little chance that talks could be got under way in time to avoid disaster.

Bethmann was peppering Tschirschky with telegrams, each one more urgent and exasperated than the last. In one he instructed the ambassador to make clear to Berchtold that any Austro-Hungarian refusal to negotiate with Russia would be not only a "serious error" but "a direct provocation of Russia's armed intervention." "We are, of course, ready to fulfill the obligations of our alliance," he said in another, "but must decline to be drawn wantonly into a world conflagration by Vienna, without having any regard paid to our counsel." But here again the remedies were coming too late—all the more so because Berchtold had withdrawn into an almost total silence. He was bent on war and wanted no discussion.

The tension continued to increase. President Poincaré, concerned about jeopardizing France's alliance with Russia, sent assurances to St. Petersburg through Ambassador Paléologue that Russia could depend on France. Paléologue hurried to tell Sazonov. Not yet knowing that Russia had already mobilized (if Paléologue knew, he did not deign to inform Paris), Poincaré also told his ambassador to urge the Russians to proceed cautiously. This Paléologue had no interest in doing.

Paris and St. Petersburg continued to receive reports of extensive military preparations within Germany, reports that continued to be untrue. France was beginning to prepare, but it was doing so extremely tentatively, to avoid alarming the Germans or, what Poincaré cared about even more at this point, giving the British any cause to see France as an aggressor. No reserves were called up, and no movement of troops by train was permitted. Determined to bring Britain to France's assistance if war started, and mindful that this would require casting Germany in the role of aggressor, Poincaré ordered that all troops be kept six miles back from the border. When the French commander in chief, General Joseph Joffre, requested permission to mobilize, he was refused. Even limited movements of troops toward the six-mile limit were not permitted—until Joffre, later in the day, threatened to resign.

Poincaré summoned the British ambassador to his office. He asked for a firmer line in London. He said that if Britain would declare its intention to support France, Germany might be deterred and war averted. The ambassador, aware of how divided the government in London remained, was able to say nothing more than "how difficult it would be for His Majesty's government to make such a statement."

General Helmuth von Moltke, chief of the German general staff, checked on the status of Austria's mobilization. When he learned that Conrad was still deploying unnecessarily large numbers of his mobilized troops to the south—the field marshal continued to be unable to put aside his dream of invading Serbia—Moltke panicked. As things stood, the Austrian troops on the Russian border would, if fighting began, be outnumbered by two to one. Moltke sent a wire to Conrad, urging him to shift his main force to the north—to mobilize against Russia, in effect. Unless Conrad did so, Germany, in beginning a war against France, would be unprotected in its rear. Getting into matters that were not supposed to be the business of generals, Moltke also warned Conrad that Vienna must refuse to be drawn into the Stop-in-Belgrade proposal. That proposal, of course, was exactly what Bethmann Hollweg had been pushing Berchtold to accept. "What a joke!" Berchtold exclaimed when he learned of Moltke's warning. "Who's in charge in Berlin?"

At nine P.M. Moltke took Erich von Falkenhayn, the war minister, with him to the chancellor's office. The two generals told Bethmann that German mobilization had become imperative, that a postponement would put the country at risk, and that at a minimum a State of Imminent War (Germany's equivalent of Russia's Period Preparatory to War) must be declared. Bethmann, reluctant to commit to military action but equally unwilling to assume responsibility for leaving Germany undefended, promised a decision by noon on Friday. He too was coming to regard war as inevitable, and his focus was shifting from preserving the peace to preparing for hostilities. Knowing that Conrad had declared Stop-in-Belgrade to be infeasible and was supported in this by Berchtold, he, like Moltke, was yielding to a fatalistic acceptance of the notion that if Germany's enemies were determined to make war, now was better than later.

Friday, July 31

When they learned of Russia's mobilization—unofficial reports reached Berlin almost immediately—the German generals intensified their demands. Germany continued to be the only European power not to have undertaken any military preparations at all, and the situation was becoming intolerable. Even Britain was on the move, First Lord of the Admiralty Churchill having ordered the Grand Fleet to take up a position in the North Sea from which it could respond quickly to any forays by the German High Seas Fleet and protect France's Channel ports.

Holes were appearing in Germany's war plans. No one had foreseen a situation in which Russia mobilized without declaring war, or in which war erupted between Germany and Russia with France waiting on the sidelines. No one was sure what to do. The generals, of course—Chief of Staff Moltke included—were all but howling for action. Germany, they argued, was in a better position to win a two-front war now than it would be after a few more years of French and Russian military buildup, and with every day of delay it was being drawn deeper into a death trap. Kaiser Wilhelm refused mobilization but agreed to declare a State of Impending War, which put in motion a variety of measures (securing borders, railways, and Germany's postal, telephone, and telegraph systems, and recalling soldiers on leave) in the expectation that mobilization would follow within forty-eight hours. He did so with the same deep reluctance shown by Franz Joseph when asked to declare war on Serbia, and by Tsar Nicholas when begged for mobilization. Like his fellow emperors, he yielded only because the military men, now taking charge in Berlin, St. Petersburg, and Vienna, were insisting that there was no alternative. Bethmann too, desperately worried about keeping Britain out of any war and bringing Italy in on the side of Germany and Austria-Hungary, agreed only when, minutes before noon, the earlier reports of Russia's mobilization were confirmed.

Berlin continued to ask Vienna to demonstrate some willingness to negotiate on the basis of various proposals being offered by London and St. Petersburg (such proposals had become numerous and complex), but Berchtold maintained his silence. Short-circuiting diplomatic channels, Wilhelm sent a telegram directly to Franz Joseph, requesting his intervention. After conferring with Berchtold and Conrad, the Hapsburg emperor replied that Vienna could not do more than it had already done. He did not explain that Austria-Hungary too was now caught in the snares of its own military planning. Just as Russia had been unable to limit its mobilization to Austria because (as the generals claimed) it had no plan that would permit it to do so, and just as Germany had no way of mobilizing without attacking its neighbors, Austria had no plan that would send its army into Belgrade but no farther. Conrad feared, as the Russian generals had feared before their mobilization and as Germany's generals would soon be fearing with equally fateful consequences, that attempting to change his arrangements could lead only to disorder. Vienna could not regard this as a tolerable option with Serbia mobilizing and the Russians assembling immense forces along their common border. In important regards, however, Conrad was not in touch with reality. Even as war with Russia became likely, he remained obsessed with punishing Serbia. Just as foolishly, he clung to the delusion that Italy would be entering the war on the side of the Central Powers, providing hundreds of thousands of additional troops.

All options except the military ones were shutting down. Power was moving into the hands of the soldiers and away from the diplomats and politicians. The soldiers were motivated mainly by fear. And as the Austrian ambassador to France had observed on Thursday in a message to Berchtold, "Fear is a bad counselor."

In a display of German diplomacy at its ham-handed worst, Berlin informed London that if Britain remained neutral, Germany would promise to restore the borders of both France and Belgium (though not any overseas colonies that Germany might seize) at the end of whatever war might ensue. This was ominous—no one had even mentioned Belgium until now. Grey, an English gentleman of the old school whose passions were fly-fishing (he had written a book on the subject) and bird-watching, saw the offer as nothing better than a crude attempt at bribery, an insult to be rejected out of hand. His anger is transparent in his instructions to the British ambassador in Berlin:

"You must inform German Chancellor that his proposal that we should bind ourselves to neutrality on such terms cannot for a moment be entertained. He asks us in effect to engage to stand by while French colonies are taken and France is beaten so long as Germany does not take French territory as distinct from the colonies. From the material point of view such a proposal is unacceptable, for France could be so crushed as to lose her position as a Great Power, and become subordinate to German policy without further territory in Europe being taken from her. But apart from that, for us to make this bargain with Germany at the expense of France would be a disgrace from which the good name of this country would never recover."

To this warning he added assurances that German assistance in averting war would be rewarded. "If the peace of Europe can be preserved and this crisis be safely passed," he said, "my own effort would be to promote some arrangement to which Germany could be a party, by which she could be assured that no hostile or aggressive policy would be pursued against her or her allies by France, Russia and ourselves, jointly or separately." He appeared to be pointing toward fundamental changes in the overall system of European alliances, changes calculated to make this the last crisis of its kind. The implication was that until now Grey had not understood the intensity of Germany's fear of encirclement, but that his eyes had been opened.

Grey next took a step that would give Bethmann much reason to regret having broached the question of Belgium. With the approval of the cabinet, he asked France and Germany to declare their intention to respect Belgian neutrality in case of war. France was able to agree without difficulty. Its plans for an offensive against Germany were focused far to the south of Belgium in the area of Alsace-Lorraine, and Poincaré understood that British support in case of war would be infinitely more valuable than any possible use of Belgian territory. Germany, trapped by the inflexibility of its mobilization plan, was unable to respond at all. Thus was the first major step taken toward Britain's entry into the war.

Germany now sent what would become known as its double ultimatum to France and Russia. This was a message warning that German mobilization "must follow in case Russia does not suspend every war measure against Austria-Hungary and ourselves within twelve hours." France was asked for a declaration of neutrality. The deadline for responses was Saturday afternoon.

The double ultimatum was in part Berlin's desperate final effort to escape mobilization and in part an effort to precipitate a breakdown in diplomatic relations to help justify the westward invasion that must follow mobilization. As directed to Russia, it was a straightforward request for cooperation. As directed to France, it was a kind of wild theatrical gesture aimed at making clear to the world that if war with Russia came, Germany and France would be at war also. It was intended to explain, in the court of public opinion, a German attack on France. What it actually looked like was overbearing German bluster. The likelihood that Berlin never expected Paris to accept it is supported by the outrageous additional demand that the German ambassador to France was instructed to make in case of acceptance: France's temporary surrender of its great fortresses at Verdun and Toul, in return for a promise that they would be returned at the end of Germany's fight with Russia. Bethmann would intimate as much in his memoirs. "If France had actually declared her neutrality," he wrote, "we should have had to sit by while the French army, under the protection of a specious neutrality, made all its preparations to attack us while we were busy in the East."

There came a final flurry of Nicky-Willy telegrams. The kaiser told the tsar that he was continuing to try to mediate in Vienna, and that "the peace of Europe may still be maintained by you, if Russia will agree to stop the military measures which must threaten Germany and Austria-Hungary."

Once again, messages between the two emperors crossed in midair. Nicholas told Wilhelm that it was "technically impossible" to stop Russia's mobilization but that Russia did not want war and still did not see war as unavoidable. "So long as the negotiations with Austria on Serbia's account are taking place, my troops shall not take any provocative action. I give you my solemn word for this. I put all my trust in God's mercy and hope in your successful mediation in Vienna for the welfare of our countries and for the peace of Europe."

As soon as the kaiser's message reached the tsar, Nicholas sent back an answer. He said he understood that Russian mobilization might require Germany to mobilize as well. He said he accepted this, but it need not mean war. He asked Wilhelm for "the same guarantee from you as I gave you, that these measures do not mean war and that we shall continue negotiating for the benefit of our countries and universal peace dear to all our hearts. Our long proved friendship must succeed, with God's help, in avoiding bloodshed. Anxiously, full of confidence await your answer."

It was obviously heartfelt and must have seemed the richest of opportunities. But nothing would come of it. Because of all that had already happened, nothing could.

THE OTTOMAN TURKS

IT IS ONE OF HISTORY'S LITTLE JOKES, SURELY, THAT TURKEY and the Ottoman Empire that it ruled had no part to play in the July crisis that brought on the Great War. For the crisis could never have unfolded as it did if not for the profound impact that the empire of the Turks had had on the development of eastern Europe. And no one would be affected by the war itself more profoundly than the Turks and the many peoples who, century after century, had been their unhappy subjects.

Without the decline of the Ottoman Empire, the Hapsburgs would not have been in Bosnia at all, and there could have been no Kingdom of Serbia. There would have been no power vacuum in the Balkans. Russia and Austria-Hungary could never have been pulled into that vacuum or into such dangerous conflict with each other.

To go back further, without the *rise* of the Ottomans the whole bitter saga of the Balkans would have been unimaginably different. The Turks had ruled the peninsula for five hundred years, reaching at their height westward into Italy, northward into Austria, Hungary, and Russia, and all the way around the Black Sea. For a time they seemed destined to conquer the whole eastern half of Europe, if not the entire continent. When the Great War began, their empire, while maintaining only a toehold in Europe proper, still extended across the Middle East to the Arabian Peninsula.

The empire reached its pinnacle, and its decline began, with the life of a single man, Sultan Suleiman the Magnificent. (That was what Christian Europe called him—to his own people he was Suleiman the Lawmaker.) He ruled from 1520 to 1566 and led the Ottomans to their zenith both culturally and geographically. He was ten generations removed from the Turkish-Mongol chieftain named Osman who had founded the dynasty three hundred years before and given it his name. In every one of those ten generations, in an unbroken sequence of achievement that no other family has ever approached, the Ottoman Turks were led by yet another dynamic, heroic, conquering figure. Generation after generation, starting where Osman had first emerged from obscurity in what is now eastern Turkey and from there moving outward in all directions, the dynasty took control of more and more of the world around it. The sultans forced their way into Europe for the first time in 1354, and ninety-nine years later they captured Constantinople, the heart of the Byzantine Empire. From then on Constantinople was their home. Its mighty basilica of Hagia Sophia, perhaps the greatest architectural achievement of the Roman era, became an Islamic mosque.

The Ottomans continued their expansion for another century after taking Constantinople, conquering among other places all of eastern Europe south of the Danube. Suleiman's father, Selim I, doubled the size of the empire by winning a single battle that made him the master of Syria, Palestine, Egypt, and Algeria. The domain that he passed on to Suleiman included among its major cities Alexandria, Algiers, Athens, Baghdad, Cairo, Damascus, Jerusalem, and Smyrna. The Ottomans had become not only the political and military masters of the Islamic world but also—what put their supremacy beyond challenge—the custodians of Mecca and Medina and the other holy places associated with the Prophet Muhammad.

As its power increased, the dynasty evolved into something that was not a family in any ordinary sense of the term but a chain of fathers and sons who never married. Instead of taking wives, the sultans kept scores and even hundreds of women who were property rather than spouses. These women lived as prisoners in a harem. They were allowed contact with no men except the rulers who owned them and an army of custodians, many of them black Africans, whose sexual organs had been surgically removed.

Suleiman, a contemporary of Henry VIII of England, took this strange heritage to a peak of vitality. Like his forebears, he was a warrior, personally leading his army in thirteen campaigns. He pushed deeper into Europe, capturing Belgrade and Budapest and completing the conquest of the Balkans. He besieged Vienna, the keystone of central Europe, and would have captured it too if torrents of rain had not made it impossible for him to bring his heavy guns north. He was a poet, a student of the works of Aristotle, and a builder who made Constantinople grander and more beautiful than it had ever been. The opulence of life in his Topkapi Palace beggars the imagination.

Suleiman had some three hundred concubines, as well as a promising young son and heir named Mustafa, when he was given a red-haired Russian girl named Ghowrem, who came to be known as Roxelana. She came into his harem as part of his share of the booty from a slave-gathering raid into what is now Poland, and she must have been a remarkable creature. (Not surprisingly, in light of the power she acquired in Constantinople, she eventually won a second new name: "the witch.") Almost from the day of her arrival, Suleiman never slept with another woman. Eventually and amazingly, he did something that no sultan had done in centuries: he married. Their love story would have been one of the great ones if it hadn't ended up taking the dynasty and the empire in such a sordid direction.

Mustafa gave every indication of developing into yet another mighty branch on the family tree. At an early age he showed himself a bold military leader adored by his troops, a capable provincial governor, and a popular hero. But he stood in the way of the son whom Roxelana had borne to (presumably) Suleiman, and so he was doomed. Working her wiles, Roxelana persuaded Suleiman that Mustafa was plotting against him. (He was doing nothing of the kind.) With his father looking on, Mustafa was overpowered and strangled by five professional executioners whose tongues had been slit and eardrums broken so that they would hear no secrets and could never speak of what they saw. And so when Suleiman died some years later, master of an empire of almost incredible size and power, he was succeeded by Roxelana's son, Selim II. Nothing was ever the same again.

Selim the Sot was short and fat and a drunk. He never saw a battlefield and died after eight years on the throne by falling down and fracturing his skull in his marble bath. His son, Murad III, was also a drunk and an opium addict as well; during a reign of twenty years he sired 103 children and apparently did little else. His heir, Mahomet III, began his reign by ordering all of his many brothers, the youngest of them mere children, put to death, thereby introducing that custom into Ottoman royal culture. Having done so he followed his father in devoting the rest of his life to copulation. And so it went. Every sultan from Roxelana's son forward was a monster of degeneracy or a repulsive weakling or both. The abruptness and permanence of the change, the sharpness of the contrast between the murdered Mustafa and his half-brother Selim II, has given rise to speculation that perhaps Roxelana's son was not Suleiman's son at all.

In the post-Suleiman empire, a new breed of craven sultans came to live in terror of being overthrown by rivals from within the dynasty. Appalling new traditions emerged, to be observed whenever one of them died. All the women of the deceased sultan would be moved to a distant place and kept in even deeper solitude for the rest of their miserable lives. Any who happened to be pregnant would be murdered (generally by being bundled in sacks and drowned), and the younger brothers and half-brothers of the new monarch (often a large number of men, boys, and infants) were murdered as well (generally by strangulation).

The rulers erected a windowless building called the Cage in which their heirs were confined from early childhood until they died or were put to death or, having been taught nothing about anything, were released to take their turns on the throne. The result was as inevitable as it was monstrous:

an empire ruled year after year and finally century after century by utterly ignorant, utterly incompetent, sometimes half-imbecilic, half-mad men, some of whom spent decades in the Cage before their release and all of whom, after their release, were free to do absolutely anything they wanted, no matter how vicious, for as long as they remained alive. They commonly indulged their freedom to kill or maim anyone they wished to kill or maim for any reason—for playing the wrong music or for smoking, for example— or for no reason at all.

Throughout the three and a half centuries from the death of Suleiman until the Great War, only one sultan displayed some of the fire and strength of the men who had built the empire. This was Murad IV, who reigned from 1623 to 1640. He became sultan when he was only ten years old— too young to have been incapacitated by the Cage—and he grew into a man of immense courage and physical power. He was the first sultan since Suleiman to be a soldier, leading his army into Persia, where he savagely put down an uprising. He was also even more insanely cruel than most sultans. In just one year of his reign, 1637, some twenty-five thousand of the empire's subjects were executed, many of them by Murad's own hand. He claimed the right to kill ten innocent people per day, and occasionally he would sit on the wall of his palace shooting randomly at passersby. At night he would make incognito visits to the taverns of Constantinople, where anyone found smoking would be executed on the spot. "Wherever the sultan went," says Noel Barber in his book *The Sultans,* "he was followed by his chief executioner, Kara Ali, whose belt bulged with nails and gimlets, clubs for breaking hands and feet, and cannisters containing different kinds of powder for blinding."

Almost uniquely among the Ottomans, Murad produced no children, and on his deathbed he ordered the death of his brother and heir, Ibrahim, who had been living in the Cage from the age of two. This order was not obeyed, Ibrahim being the last living member of the dynasty, but from that point there were few further signs of vitality in the Ottoman line. Ibrahim devoted himself to building up a harem of 280 beautiful young women. Then, acting on a dubious report that one of these women (no one could say which one) had become romantically involved with a eunuch, he had all of them drowned. And so it continued.

Not surprisingly, the empire rotted from within under this kind of leadership and became an increasingly inviting target. Young General Napoleon Bonaparte first showed Europe just how impotent the Ottomans had become when, in 1798, he invaded and almost effortlessly conquered Egypt. Also suggestive of what lay ahead was the fact that Napoleon was driven out of Egypt not by the Turks or their Egyptian subjects but by the

British navy. From then on, and increasingly, the survival of the sultans and their decaying empire depended less on themselves than on the jealousies and rivalries of the European powers. The Ottomans hung on through the nineteenth century less through any acts of their own than because Britain and France blocked Russia from finishing them off.

Even so, the hundred years leading up to 1914 brought uninterrupted losing wars: with the empire's own Turkish satraps as they tried for autonomy in Egypt, Syria, and elsewhere; with Arab chieftains seeking independence; with Persia; with the Christian peoples of the Balkans; and—four times between 1806 and 1878—with a Russia hungering for Constantinople.

In 1830 the French seized control of Algeria in North Africa. At about that same time the British began building a power base in Arabia and the Persian Gulf. In 1853 Russia, tempted by what appeared to be easy pickings, invaded the Ottoman provinces south of the Danube. The Ottoman presence in Europe might have come to an end then if not for the Crimean War, in which Britain and France intervened to stop the Russians.

Britain, fearful that its position in the eastern Mediterranean and control of India might be lost if Russia broke through to the south, saved the Ottomans from destruction yet again in 1878. But by that time several European countries, Britain included, were feasting on the Turkish empire's extremities. Austria-Hungary took possession of Bosnia and Herzegovina, literally preparing the ground for the Sarajevo assassination. France, with British support and in the face of such strong German opposition that for a time the issue threatened to spark a war, took Tunisia and Morocco in North Africa. Britain took Egypt and Cyprus, and finally even Italy reached across the Mediterranean to grab Tripoli (today's Libya), along with islands in the Aegean and Mediterranean. Germany meanwhile, having arrived too late to share in this plunder, focused on building ties with the Turks. It began work on a Berlin-to-Baghdad railway, and Kaiser Wilhelm II paid a state visit to Constantinople and Jerusalem.

In 1908, the year when Austria-Hungary formally annexed Bosnia and Herzegovina, a group of would-be reformers called the Young Turks (their leader, an army officer named Enver Pasha, was only twenty-seven years old) seized control of the government in Constantinople and introduced a constitution. In 1912 the First Balkan War drove the Turks almost entirely out of the Balkans. This, and the failure of the Constantinople regime to deliver the reforms expected of it or to stop the disintegration of the empire, gravely damaged the prestige of the ruling faction, which was replaced by nationalist extremists once again led by Enver. Some of it was regained the following year, however, when the Second Balkan War led to Turkey's recovery of the city of Adrianople on the European mainland. The

Enver Pasha
War Minister
and Young Turk
Eager to recoup the
Ottoman Empire's
humiliating losses
in the Balkans
and elsewhere.

sultan was at least as ridiculous a figure as the sorriest of his predecessors. (He had been deemed a safe choice for the throne after boasting that he had not read a newspaper in more than thirty years.) No one even pretended that he mattered. In January 1914, Enver Pasha left the army to become minister of war, and in July he took his empire into a secret defensive alliance with Germany.

Astonishingly in light of all the humiliations it had experienced, the Ottoman Empire of July 1914 was still bigger geographically than France, Germany, and Austria-Hungary combined. It still ruled Arabia, which soon would emerge as the world's greatest source of oil. If war did erupt, no one knew if the empire would enter it or, if so, on which side. It would be a coveted ally—or a rich, probably easy conquest.

Chapter 6

✠

Saturday, August 1:
Leaping into the Dark

"If his majesty insisted on leading the army eastwards,
he would have a confused mass of disorderly
armed men."

—Helmuth von Moltke

Why didn't the Germans seize upon Tsar Nicholas's eleventh-hour offer? Why didn't they agree to do as the Russians were doing, mobilize their forces but at the same time pledge not to attack? Why didn't they wait, pressuring Austria-Hungary to be sensible while Russia put pressure on Serbia and some sort of settlement was worked out? It was a splendid opportunity. Seizing it could have put Germany in a solid bargaining position.

It all came to nothing in part because of the unmanageable difficulties that mobilizing and then waiting would have created for Germany and Germany alone. An open-ended postponement of hostilities after the great powers had mobilized would have destroyed Germany's chances of defeating France before having to fight Russia. It would have given Russia especially, but France as well, an advantage that could only grow as time passed. The high command of the German army would, understandably, have called any such postponement an act of madness. When the kaiser suggested something like it, Army Chief of Staff Helmuth von Moltke came close to calling the idea insane.

Ever since becoming chief of staff, Moltke had been developing a highly secret plan for fighting a two-front war. This came to be called the Schlieffen Plan, after the general who first conceived and proposed it, but it was Moltke who made it Germany's only military option. By 1914 he had spent a decade immersed in it, tinkering with it, torturing himself about how to make it work. No matter how often or in how many ways he introduced new refinements, the plan continued to have one unchanging thesis at its center: speed was everything. Anything that slowed the Germans down, anything that might allow Russia to get into a war before France had been taken out, was regarded as likely to be fatal.

For this reason the tsar's promise to "take no provocative action" while mobilizing was, from the German perspective, nonsense. General mobilization meant, by definition, that Russia was marshaling its forces for an attack on Germany. Every day of mobilization brought Russia closer to being ready to strike at Germany from the east as soon as Germany was ready to engage France in the west. Viewed from Berlin, Russian mobilization *was* a provocative action of the most serious kind. It was inherently threatening to an extent that the tsar and his advisers could not possibly have understood. And while the Russians hoped that mobilization, by demonstrating the gravity of the situation, would increase the willingness of the Central Powers to negotiate, actually it worked in the opposite direction. The Germans—fearful like all the great powers of appearing weak—were unwilling to give the appearance of having been forced to negotiate by the threat of Russian action.

But Germany's mobilization problems went even deeper. Moltke, over the years, had transformed Schlieffen's idea for a lightning-fast attack on France from an option into an inevitability in case of war. Any delay after mobilization had gone from being a danger into being an impossibility. Moltke and his staff gradually lost the ability to imagine situations in which delay might become advisable. Their planning became so rigid that it left Germany—today this can seem almost impossible to believe—with no way of mobilizing without invading Luxembourg and Belgium en route to invading France.

This was the self-created trap that the Germans found themselves in on August 1—a trap that gave the army's high command no choice except to tell the kaiser that Tsar Nicholas was asking Germany to do the one thing that Germany absolutely could not do. Only Russia could now prevent war, the generals told Wilhelm, and Russia could do so only by agreeing to the terms of the double ultimatum.

At midday on the fifth Saturday since the murder of Franz Ferdinand, the deadline for the double ultimatum arrived without an answer from Russia or France. Kaiser Wilhelm, at the urging of Moltke and Falkenhayn and with the reluctant agreement of Chancellor Bethmann Hollweg, approved a declaration stating that because of St. Petersburg's continued mobilization a state of war now existed between the two empires. This declaration was wired to Friedrich von Pourtalès, Berlin's ambassador to Russia, with instructions to deliver it at six P.M. (It would not reach Pourtalès until five-forty-five, and he had to decode it before taking it to Sazonov.)

Later in the afternoon, when the German ambassador in Paris called on

Viviani and asked for his government's response to the ultimatum, he was told icily that "France will have to regard her own interests." An hour later the French government declared a general mobilization—General Joffre, chief of the French general staff, was warning that every twenty-four hours of delay would cost ten or twelve miles of territory when the fighting began—and fifteen minutes after that Kaiser Wilhelm agreed to mobilization as well.

The German mobilization order was made public at five P.M. The kaiser had made its signing a solemn and, in an improvised way, a formal occasion, inviting Bethmann Hollweg and a number of Germany's most senior military officials to serve as witnesses. After handshakes and words of firm resolution by men with tears in their eyes, they remained together to wait for word from Pourtalès. Their conversation turned into a discussion of what should be done next, which soon became a heated and somewhat confused argument. Long-bearded old Admiral Alfred von Tirpitz, father of the High Seas Fleet that had poisoned relations with Britain, said that neither mobilization nor a war declaration was needed at this point—that all reasonable possibilities of a negotiated settlement should be allowed to play out. Almost everyone except the kaiser, who appeared to be uncertain, disagreed with Tirpitz, but not always in the same way or for the same reasons. Moltke and Falkenhayn remained firm on the need for mobilization without delay. Bethmann, who never would have assented to mobilization if Russia's earlier mobilization had not been confirmed without possibility of doubt, said that a formal declaration of war was what was needed now.

The dispute was interrupted by the arrival of Gottlieb von Jagow, the head of the foreign office. Bursting into the room, he announced that a message had just arrived from Ambassador Lichnowsky in London. It was still being decoded but would be ready in minutes. It appeared to be important.

It was a good reason to delay the mobilization, said Tirpitz, at least until they knew what it was all about.

Rubbish, said Moltke and Falkenhayn, and they departed. They were off to oversee the mobilization.

The message from London proved to be not just important but astonishing. Lichnowsky reported that the British foreign secretary, Sir Edward Grey, had just telephoned him with a momentous question. Grey wanted to know, the ambassador said, "if I thought I could assure him that in case France should remain neutral in a Russo-German war, we would not attack the French." The question had come just in advance of a meeting of the British cabinet, and Lichnowsky had assured Grey "that I could take responsibility for such a guaranty, and he is to use this assurance at today's cabinet session."

The kaiser, when he had absorbed this, was almost beside himself with joy. So was Bethmann: it seemed almost too good to be true. It placed at Germany's feet an historic diplomatic victory. The Germans were now free to bring Russia to heel virtually without risk and to restore Austria-Hungary's position among the powers.

Moltke and Falkenhayn were intercepted and summoned back to the palace. The message from London was read to them. Then the kaiser gave new orders to Moltke:

"We shall simply march the whole army east!"

These words came as a blow to Moltke. He was the nephew and namesake of Field Marshal Helmuth von Moltke, one of the greatest figures in German military history. The elder Moltke had led the Prussian army to victory over Austria in 1866, thereby establishing Prussia as the leader of the German states. He had then, in 1870, led the armies of Prussia and the German states allied with it in the defeat of France. His nephew had always enjoyed a special place in the army simply because of his name. It was almost certainly his name, in fact, that had propelled him to the top of the general staff. He was a stolid, insecure man, gloomy and filled with fear of the future, convinced that Germany's enemies were growing stronger so rapidly that within not many more years the empire's position would be hopeless. This fear had caused him to toy with the idea of preventive war (an idea that Bismarck had ridiculed as "committing suicide out of fear of death"), though he had never actually advocated or prepared for such a war. He was sixty-seven years old in 1914, with heavy jowls and too much flesh on what had once been his impressively martial frame, a weary man recovering from a bronchial infection, devoid of the slightest trace of charisma. No one had ever mistaken him for a military genius.

All the same he was a competent, conscientious, experienced soldier. And now he could scarcely believe what the kaiser was telling him. Stop this enormous army? Smash all the clockwork plans for transporting it and feeding it and making certain that at every point it would have what it needed to fight? Turn it around? March it *east?* Call off the great wheeling movement to the west that was the whole and only point of German mobilization and almost certainly Germany's sole hope of victory?

Moltke collected his wits and began to speak. "I assured his Majesty," he would write later, "that this wasn't possible. The deployment of an army of a million men was not a matter of improvisation. It was the product of a whole year's work—of timetables that once worked out could not be changed. If his Majesty insisted on leading the whole army eastwards, he would not have an army ready to strike, he would have a confused mass of disorderly armed men without commissariat." Not only would his army be a confused and disorderly mass of troops, he added, but once facing eastward it would have at its back sixty-two French army divisions ready for action and equipped with their own carefully developed plans for the conquest of Germany. How could Britain, how could anyone, guarantee that France would not seize such an opportunity?

The kaiser, his withered left arm tight against his side as usual, the waxed points of his great hornlike mustache reaching upward almost to his eyes, answered Moltke in the most wounding way possible.

"Your uncle," he said, "would have given me a different answer."

"This pained me a good deal," Moltke would recall, "for I have never pretended to be the equal of the great Field Marshal." He tried to explain that once the mobilization plan had been executed, it would become possible to start moving troops to the east, adding that he could not accept responsibility for the military consequences of halting its execution. Bethmann interrupted in a way that Moltke could not have welcomed, saying that he could not accept political responsibility for a failure to respond positively to Britain's remarkable offer. Finally and with difficulty, a compromise was worked out. Falkenhayn took Moltke into a side room and quietly argued that some slowing of the mobilization process had to be possible. The invasion force could be stopped at least briefly at the Luxembourg border, surely. Moltke gave in. This could work for a while—for hours, though not for days.

Before the slowdown could create serious problems, causing troops and trains that were supposed to be advancing to back up on one another and wreck all the timetables, Berlin learned that what is usually true of things that seem too good to be true applied in this case: the message from London was the result of a tangle of misunderstandings. The origins of these misunderstandings remain hard to unravel even today. It seems certain that Grey, in raising the question of possible French and British neutrality, had not regarded himself as offering anything like a formal proposal. But he like everyone else had been willing to clutch at straws by this point, and apparently he had tossed out an idle thought to see what kind of response it might draw. Perhaps, enmeshed as he was in the struggle going on within the British government and exhausted by long days and nights of searching for a resolution to the continental crisis, he had been less than clear in what he said. Certainly it could never have occurred to him that his idea would be seized by the Germans as an opportunity to delay fighting with France in order to crush Russia first; what he probably had in mind, rather, was an arrangement in which Germany would stand on the defensive on both fronts while the Austro-Russian dispute was worked out.

Perhaps Lichnowsky, who throughout the crisis had displayed exceptional understanding of its dangers and exceptional courage in telling his government truths that it did not want to hear, had been too eager to believe that

Grey was telling him what he most wanted to hear. As early as 1912, even before taking up his post in London, he had told the kaiser that "it is understandable that each increase in Serbian power and her expansion towards the sea is regarded with alarm by the Austrian statesmen; but it would be incomprehensible if we should run even the faintest risk of becoming involved in a war for such a cause." His feelings on the matter were even stronger in 1914, and he never hesitated to say so.

For a few blissful hours an exultant Kaiser Wilhelm was able to occupy himself with grandiose new schemes. The German foreign ministry cabled Lichnowsky that Britain would be required to *guarantee* French neutrality, that it had until seven P.M. on Monday to make the necessary arrangements,

German Ambassador Lichnowsky making his last call on
the British Foreign Office

and that until then Germany would refrain from attacking. Finally, all such fantasies were brought crashing down by another message from London. Lichnowsky reported that Grey, after meeting with the cabinet, had told him that a German violation of Belgian neutrality "would make it difficult for the Government here to adopt an attitude of friendly neutrality." Germany's failure to promise that it would not enter Belgium, Grey had added, "has caused an unfavorable impression." He had again raised the question of whether it might be possible for France and Germany "to remain facing each other under arms, without attacking each other, in the event of a Russian war," but there was no further suggestion that Britain was promising neutrality in return.

Grey was offering, in a word, nothing. Obliquely but clearly enough, he was indicating that Britain would likely join with France in case of war—especially a war that took German troops into Belgium. The kaiser, after venting his rage about the deceitful English (his feelings about Britain had always been a mess of admiration, envy, and resentment), put everything back on track. Moltke was told that the mobilization could go forward as originally intended. Later, in making his marginal comments on Lichnowsky's last message, the kaiser gave particular attention to Grey's mention of an "unfavorable impression" having been created in London. "My impression," he wrote, "is that Mr. Grey is a false dog who is afraid of his own meanness and false policy, but who will not come out in the open against us, preferring to let himself be forced by us to do it." His childish language aside, the kaiser did have a point.

Shortly after seven P.M. in St. Petersburg, Germany's Ambassador Pourtalès was admitted to the office of Foreign Minister Sazonov. The two men were friends, though throughout July their meetings had sometimes been volcanic. Pourtalès had been in St. Petersburg for seven years and had developed an affection for Russia. Like diplomats and politicians in all the capital cities, he had had almost no sleep in days. He was an old man, already preparing for retirement when the crisis began, and by Saturday he was approaching collapse. Quietly, he asked Sazonov if Russia was prepared to answer the double ultimatum.

Sazonov, exhausted himself, overwrought, and a volatile personality under the best of circumstances, had just come from a meeting at which he had been trying to assure the British ambassador that Russia's mobilization did not necessarily mean war. He answered Pourtalès by echoing what the tsar had earlier told the kaiser: although it was not possible to stop mobilization, Russia wanted to continue negotiations. Russia remained hopeful of avoiding war.

Pourtalès took from his pocket a copy of Germany's ultimatum, read it aloud, and added that the consequences of a negative reply would be grave.

Sazonov repeated his first answer.

Pourtalès too repeated himself: the consequences would be grave.

"I have no other reply to give you," said Sazonov.

Pourtalès took out more papers. "In that case, sir, I am instructed by my government to hand you this note." In his hands he held two messages, both of them declarations of war. One was for use if Russia gave no answer to the ultimatum, the other a reply to a negative answer. In his distress and confusion he pressed both on Sazonov and burst into tears.

Or so Sazonov wrote years later in his memoirs. Pourtalès's recollection was that Sazonov wept first. Whatever the sequence, apparently both men cried. They embraced, then pulled apart and began to exchange accusations.

"This was a criminal act of yours," Sazonov said. "The curses of the nations will be upon you."

"We were defending our honor."

"Your honor was not involved."

Finally they parted forever, Sazonov helping the distraught Pourtalès to the door.

PART TWO

August–December 1914

✠

Racing to Deadlock

*Bound for glory: the troops of imperial Germany,
adorned with the* pickelhaube *headgear that will soon be
replaced with more practical steel helmets, marching off
to start the war.*

Chapter 7

The Iron Dice Roll

"If the iron dice roll, may God help us."
CHANCELLOR THEOBOLD VON BETHMANN HOLLWEG

Before every commander of the armies that went to war in August 1914 there lay the possibility of becoming a hero, a giant, a deliverer of his people. Likewise there lay before every one of them the very real possibility of everlasting disgrace.

This was nowhere more true than in the case of Helmuth von Moltke, who as the war began was sixty-six years old, in questionable health, and approaching the ninth anniversary of his appointment as head of the German high command. His long service as chief meant that he was responsible not only for winning the war but for the plans—the inconceivably intricate plans, including among much else the timetables of the eleven thousand trains that would have to be moved to complete German mobilization—according to which the war was to be prosecuted. All of it was on his shoulders. And Moltke went to war without a trace of Napoleonic zest. Throughout most of the July crisis he had been a voice for restraint. Though Russia's mobilization turned him into a strident advocate of military action, even then he was motivated not by any hunger for conquest or expectation of victory but by fear of a kind that was far from uncommon in the upper reaches of the German civil and military administration. This fear rose out of the belief, the conviction, that Germany was encircled by enemies who were growing stronger at an alarming rate, and that if the showdown were delayed just a few years more there might be no possibility of victory, even of survival. Far from looking forward to a quick and easy victory, Moltke said that if war came it would be "a long weary struggle with a country that will not acknowledge defeat until

Helmuth von Moltke
*"Too reflective, too scrupulous,
and too conscientious."*

the whole strength of its people is broken, a war that even if we should be the victors will push our own people, too, to the limits of exhaustion."

This prognosis was consistent with Moltke's innate pessimism; he was so notorious for his gloomy outlook that the kaiser had long made a joke of it. His pessimism even extended, and always had, to his own abilities; in 1905, when it was beginning to appear that he would be promoted to head of the general staff over capable and more experienced rivals, Moltke had confided to the German chancellor of the time that he regarded himself as "too reflective, too scrupulous, and, if you like, too conscientious for such a post." He said he did not possess "the capacity for risking all on a single throw" that marked great commanders. About that he appears to have been right; he was less a man of action than an intellectual and aesthete, more cultivated than Prussian generals were expected to be. "Art is the only thing I live for," he once commented, revealing just how remote his values were from those of the Junkers whose sons made up Germany's military elite. But he was also right about what lay ahead. The accuracy of his dark prophecy reflected not only his disposition but his acumen, his grasp of the realities of twentieth-century warfare.

It is not only ironic but mystifying, in light of what he foresaw, that Moltke had committed himself and his nation to a strategy focused exclusively on the achievement of a lightning-fast victory over France. This strategy was embedded in the deeply secret Schlieffen Plan, originally the work of Field Marshal Count Alfred von Schlieffen, Moltke's predecessor as chief of the general staff. He had developed it before his retirement in 1905 in response to the formation of the Franco-Russian Entente and the resulting likelihood that, if war came, Germany was going to find itself fighting on two fronts. He based it on simple assumptions: that even with Austria-Hungary on its side Germany could not expect to win a protracted war against both France and Russia; that Russia would be unable to mobilize rapidly; and that the immense size of the Russian empire meant that any invader looking for a quick and decisive victory was likely to be as disappointed as Napoleon had been after capturing Moscow in 1812. Out of these assumptions rose the conclusion that Germany had to crush France before Russia became capable of mounting an offensive. It could then shift its forces to the east and crush Russia in its turn.

Moltke had adopted the plan upon succeeding Schlieffen, and in the years that followed he changed it substantially. As a result of his changes, and ultimately as a result of the failure of the altered plan to deliver Paris into German hands within the forty days that Schlieffen had set as his deadline, Moltke's assigned place in history has generally been among the fools and weaklings. Schlieffen, by contrast, has been enshrined as a strategist of much brilliance, the creator of a key to glory that Moltke proved incapable of using. If such judgments are not flagrantly unfair, they are at a minimum arguable. It would be absurd to think that Moltke should have regarded the plan he received from Schlieffen as too sacred to be altered as circumstances changed. Schlieffen had handed his ideas over to Moltke at a point when Russia was weaker than it had been in generations. It had just lost its war with Japan and was faced with a popular uprising that had shaken the Romanov regime. Schlieffen had good reason to assume that Russia might be unable to put an effective army into the field at all, never mind speedily.

By 1914 the situation had changed. For five years the Russian government had been spending a third of its revenues on its army and navy. The so-called Grand Program, initiated in 1913, provided for the addition of 585,000 men to the tsar's armies annually, with each recruit to remain on active duty for at least three years. By 1914, 1.4 million Russian troops were in uniform, with several million more reservists available in case of mobilization—enough to form as many as 150 divisions. Russia had also made great strides in industrializing, French capital was financing a radical improvement of the Russian rail system in ways directly threatening to Germany, and France itself was growing both in strength and in confidence. Moltke would have had to be a fool not to fear that the Russians might be capable of fighting their way to Berlin before the Germans reached Paris.

Moltke's uncle and namesake, the architect of Germany's victories over Austria and France almost half a century earlier, had seen things very differently from Schlieffen. In his last years he came to believe that in a two-front war Germany should stand on the defensive in the west, attack in the east just enough to drive the Russians out of Poland, and then allow its enemies to wreck their armies by hurling them against walls of fire and steel. He believed that such a war would end not in victory but in a negotiated peace with exhausted but undefeated foes—and that that was all Germany should hope for. "We should exploit in the West the great advantages which the Rhine and our powerful fortifications offer to the defensive," he had said as early as 1879, "and should apply all the fighting forces which are not absolutely indispensable for an imposing offensive against the east." This remained German doctrine until Schlieffen, an austere and solitary man with few interests outside military history and strategy, became head of the army and gradually set Moltke's thinking aside.

The validity of the new strategy was, however, something less than self-evident, as Schlieffen himself acknowledged. His commentaries, which he continued to produce and share with the general staff throughout the years after his retirement, make clear that he was far from certain that it could succeed. It bet everything on an overwhelming right wing made up of seven out of every eight soldiers available for the fight with France. This massed force was to punch like a fist through three neutral countries—Holland, Belgium, and tiny Luxembourg—on its way into France. It would swing counterclockwise in a great wheeling motion, first to the west and then southward into France, overrunning whatever enemy forces confronted it, encircling and cutting off Paris, and finally swinging back to the east to take whatever remained of the French army in the rear and destroy it.

The plan was majestic in conception and breathtakingly bold but also fraught with problems not all of which were military. From a narrowly military standpoint the invasion of the three neutral countries was sensible: it would enable the Germans to move across northern Europe's flat and open coastal plain, avoiding the powerful fortresses that the French had constructed in the rough hill country just west of their long border with Germany. In terms of grand strategy and international politics, however, it was dangerous in the extreme. It gave no weight to the possibility that a violation of the treaties guaranteeing the neutrality of Belgium and Holland might provoke Britain to intervene. If Schlieffen considered the possibility of British intervention, he obviously regarded it as an acceptable risk. Britain's army was small (Bismarck had joked that if it ever invaded Germany, he would have it arrested). If Germany could wrap up the war in the west on Schlieffen's timetable, the British would have little opportunity to become a factor.

The French general staff was equally alert to the attractions of Belgium as a route into its enemy's heartland. But it did not have the autonomy that allowed Schlieffen and then the younger Moltke to consult with no one; hard experience with two Bonapartist empires had made republican France wary of placing too much authority over strategy in the hands of the military. As late as 1913 the French Supreme War Council was exploring a possible invasion of Germany through Belgium, but it was obliged to keep the Paris government informed as it did so. By this time the French and British were well along in planning joint operations, and the French government was determined to bring the British in on its side in case of war. Therefore Paris checked with London about the War Council's idea and was sternly warned off. Any such move, France's friends on the British general staff said, would destroy even the possibility of support from Britain. And so the council stopped all work in that direction.

In Germany no such course correction was, in practical terms, even possible. No German chancellor since the young Wilhelm II's dismissal of Bismarck in 1890 had ever attempted to question, never mind challenge, the war planning of the general staff. As Bethmann Hollweg wrote in self-defense after the war, "for the civilian side to have tried to foil a thoroughly thought-out military plan described as absolutely essential would have entailed an intolerable responsibility. In the event of a subsequent failure, such a policy would have been considered its sole cause." Bethmann's administration was afraid to interfere with the army's plans even when those plans entailed terrible political risks. There is no better example of how the governmental machinery created by Bismarck proved inadequate to deal with the dangers and complexities of the twentieth century, when Bismarck's strong hand and towering intellect no longer controlled the levers of power.

In his splendid isolation Schlieffen assumed that Germany's enemies were intent not just on her defeat but on her destruction, and that as a result she was justified in doing things that under less harrowing circumstances would not have been thinkable. The seizure of the Dutch and Belgian roads and railways became not only desirable but imperative. Nothing less could save Germany, and anything else would increase Germany's peril. "If we were to attack along the entire Belfort-Montmédy front [along the line of French fortresses] with blind faith in the sanctity of neutrality," Schlieffen wrote, "we would soon be effectively enveloped on our right flank by a realistic and unscrupulous enemy advancing through southern Belgium and Luxembourg." The "unscrupulous enemy" was, of course, France. Schlieffen's guiding principle was that if Germany declined the benefits of violating the neutrality of its neighbors, France would happily seize them.

If Schlieffen had few concerns about the price of invading Belgium and Holland, he had many about whether his plan was militarily feasible. The outer edge of his right wing, in sweeping toward Paris, would have to advance more than two hundred miles through enemy territory in no more than forty days, defeating whatever enemies it encountered along the way. The infantry would have to do this mainly on foot, each soldier carrying seventy or more pounds of equipment every step of the way. If the horse-drawn artillery failed to keep up, if the huge amounts of food and fodder and ammunition and replacements needed by all these hundreds of thousands of men and their scores of thousands of horses were not always near at hand, if good order was not maintained, the entire venture would collapse of its own weight under the guns of the enemy.

Schlieffen calculated that the German army would need ninety divisions to execute his plan. (It had only about sixty in 1905.) He concluded that if the right wing did manage to reach Paris, the effort would likely drain it of the strength and mobility needed for a final swing to the east and the climactic battle that was the plan's whole point. "Before the Germans reach the Somme or the Oise," he wrote when his plan was still in gestation, "they will have realized, like other conquerors before them, that they are too weak for the whole enterprise." Even after his retirement, Schlieffen never stopped tormenting himself with such questions. Part of his legend is that in January 1913, as he lay dying, he became conscious just long enough to say, "It must come to a fight. Only keep the right wing strong!"

The younger Moltke, like Schlieffen a bookish and introspective man, unlike Schlieffen a man with many nonmilitary interests (he was an accomplished cellist, followed his wife into occult religious practices, and raised Prussian eyebrows by taking books by Goethe on maneuvers), inherited not only the plan but his predecessor's obsession with it. By 1911 he decided that it would be unnecessary and unwise to invade Holland; the Germans could neither take the time to defeat the Dutch army before advancing on France nor allow that army to stand undefeated and hostile on the northern edge of the route to Paris. Moltke said, too, that Germany would need neutral Holland as a "windpipe" through which to get access to supplies. In doing so he again exposed his doubts about the plausibility of the entire plan: a campaign that ended in victory after six weeks would have no need for a windpipe.

The most challenging aspect of Moltke's change was that it would crowd the armies of the Schlieffen right wing—more than half a million men with all their artillery and support—into a twelve-mile-wide passage south of Holland and north of the Ardennes Forest. This would give them far fewer roads and rail lines to use—no small complication when hundreds of thousands of troops and their supply trains had to be moved great distances as rapidly as possible. It also meant that the Germans would be unable to go around, but would have to attack and destroy, the powerful network of fortresses that the Belgians had constructed at Liège just inside their border with Germany. For this reason German mobilization required an immediate invasion of Belgium: Moltke's entire strategy would collapse if the Belgians were given time to ready their Liège defenses. The Schlieffen Plan itself, Moltke had said, "will hardly be possible unless Liège is in our hands. The fortress must therefore be taken at once . . . the possession of Liège is the *sine qua non* of our advance."

Moltke came to believe that Germany could not afford to concentrate such an overwhelmingly large part of its forces in the attacking right wing. As the years passed, he altered the distribution of his troops so that the right wing would be only three times the size of the left, not seven as Schlieffen had prescribed. In its 1914 iteration the plan entailed positioning fifty-five divisions north of the fortified city of Metz, which lay directly to the east of Paris, with twenty-three divisions in a defensive posture farther south. Schlieffen, with fewer divisions to deploy, had assigned fifty-nine to the north and only nine to the left. This change, though controversial ever since, was certainly rational; after 1910 the French army, like the Russian, had become much more formidable than it had been in Schlieffen's day. It was bigger, better trained, better equipped, better led, and more professional overall. It was sure to be ready with an offensive of its own, and Moltke and his staff guessed rightly that its attack force would be concentrated somewhere south of Belgium and therefore opposite the relatively weak German left wing. If the French broke through into Germany, they might then be able to swing to the north, cut the German right wing off from its home base, and achieve their own quick victory.

But in broad terms, and without any apparent enthusiasm or even anything approaching real confidence, Moltke embraced Schlieffen's approach. There is no evidence that he ever seriously considered *not* keeping it—that he ever thought through, for example, the potentially immense advantages of reverting to his uncle's idea and standing on the defensive in the west at least for a while, forcing the French to attack him if they wanted a war. In 1913 he abandoned an alternative plan that his staff had until then been updating regularly and keeping ready for use—one for directing Germany's offensive capabilities toward Russia. When the crisis came, therefore, he *had* no alternative.

Perhaps he was unable to think through the ramifications of the strategic situation in Europe (one such ramification being the certain fact that Britain would never have gone to war if France had attacked Germany rather than vice versa). More likely he was in the grip of a fever that infected all the military planners of Europe in the years leading up to 1914, the French especially but the Germans and others to a more limited extent. This was "the cult of the offensive"—the belief that the only way to succeed in war was to attack your enemy as quickly as possible and then stay on the attack regardless of the consequences. This belief was rooted in what everyone took to be the lessons of the Franco-Prussian War, in which many of the most senior generals of 1914 had taken part at the beginning of their careers. In that war the forces of Napoleon III had allowed the Prussians to seize and keep the initiative, and the results had been disastrous. Probably this idea played some part in Molke's strategic decisions. It is also possibly true, for all that even Moltke's severest critics really know, that no alternative to his final version of the Schlieffen Plan could have produced better results.

In the thirty days following the start of the war, mobilization increased the German army from its peacetime strength of seven hundred and sixty-one thousand men to slightly more than two million. This ocean of humanity was organized into eighty-seven infantry divisions averaging some eighteen thousand men each, plus another eleven cavalry divisions. These divisions formed eight field armies, each commanded by a full general. Seven took up positions along Germany's western border, and the last stood alone in faraway East Prussia with responsibility for holding off whatever Russia threw at it. To the south of East Prussia, separated from it by Russian Poland, was Austria-Hungary, with an initial mobilized force of 1.3 million men—forty-nine infantry and eleven cavalry divisions under Conrad von Hötzendorf. Farther south still was Serbia, with a tough, experienced, and almost fanatically dedicated army of some two hundred and fifty thousand troops making up twelve and a half divisions. Also opposing Germany and Austria was a Russian army whose three and a half million troops were organized into 114 infantry and thirty-six cavalry divisions and had the potential, given Russia's immense population, to grow much larger. This was "the Russian steamroller," the sheer size of which made it a chilling threat for the German and Austrian planners. To the west, thirty days after mobilization, France had 1.8 million men under arms (all the numbers given here would soon be dwarfed by floods of new volunteers and conscripts) and organized into ninety divisions—eighty infantry and ten cavalry.

Even without possible British and Belgian involvement, therefore, the

Germans and Austrians began at an overwhelming manpower disadvantage in the east. In the west the German armies were at best equal in size to those of the French. In their advance on Paris they would be facing the only military organization in the world that was comparable to theirs not only in manpower but in fighting capability as well—a huge modern army whose generals had a secret plan of their own for swift and conclusive victory.

PARIS IN 1914

THE START OF THE WAR CAME AS A FAR GREATER SHOCK
to Paris than to Berlin, Budapest, St. Petersburg, or Vienna. Until almost the
end of the July crisis, the French paid it little attention. They, and the newspapers they read, were focused instead on a lady named Henriette Caillaux.

Not that the lady and the war are entirely unrelated. Among the what-
ifs of 1914 is the intriguing possibility—remote to be sure, but real
nonetheless—that the war might have been averted if not for six pistol
shots fired by Madame Caillaux 101 days before the assassination of Franz
Ferdinand.

Madame Caillaux was the wife—the second wife, importantly, just as
he was her second husband—of Joseph Caillaux, a former French premier
who in early 1914 was making a serious bid to become once again the
head of the government. In arm's-length partnership with a brilliant and
charismatic Socialist leader named Jean Jaurès, Caillaux was campaigning
to displace the men who, a year earlier, had enacted a controversial measure aimed at improving France's readiness for war. This measure was a
requirement, demanded by President Poincaré and the leadership of the
army, that every military conscript (and France was drafting 80 percent of
its eligible men by that time, as opposed to 56 percent in Germany) must
spend three years on active service, rather than two as in the recent past.
The change had been one expression of a surge of patriotic fervor that
arose in the wake of a French-German showdown over control of Morocco
in 1911 and swept Poincaré into the presidency two years later. (When the
Germans ended that showdown by backing down, in large part because
Britain was siding with France, it seemed proof that France's long period
of weakness on the international stage had ended at last.) Supporters of the
extension were convinced that unless France maintained its credibility as
a military power, it would lose the confidence of its Russian ally and be
left to face Germany alone. Jaurès was insistent that the European arms
race was madness, that a general war would be ruinous for everyone
involved no matter who won, that it was ridiculous for the only republic
in Europe to tie itself to a regime as antediluvian as tsarist Russia, and that
it was not impossible for France and Germany to come to an understand-

ing. Though Caillaux had not pledged himself to repeal the extension, the conservatives convinced themselves that he would do so if given the opportunity. They did everything in their power to turn him into what the writer-politician Maurice Barrès said he already was: "the most hated man in France."

A national election was scheduled for early summer. It would decide the membership of the Chamber of Deputies, which in turn would choose the next premier. (The premiership, a position analogous to that of British prime minister, changed hands more or less annually as shifting coalitions of France's many factions caused governments to rise and fall. It is not to be confused with the presidency, an elective office with a fixed six-year term and roughly comparable to Britain's monarch.) The election became a referendum on the three-year-service question and, by implication, on France's place in the European balance of power.

Joseph Caillaux, the leading opponent of the Poincaré camp, was an interesting figure if not an altogether appealing human being. Trained in accounting and as an auditor, meticulous as only a dedicated accountant can be, he had followed his father into politics and had risen to cabinet rank on the basis of hard work and his knowledge (unusual in the Chamber of Deputies) of the intricacies of budgeting, taxation, and finance. At an early age he became minister of finance, an office to which his unrivaled competency would cause him to be returned repeatedly over the years. Haughty to the point of insufferable arrogance, rich, impeccably honest and therefore able to survive the numberless accusations hurled at him over the years, he remained throughout his career the very picture of stuffy, almost comic *haut bourgeois* respectability.

Paradoxically, by 1914 Caillaux had moved about as far to the left as it was possible for a French politician to move in those days and still be a contender for the highest offices of government. This had happened gradually, as a result of his mastery of finance. He had conducted a study of the tax system and, offended by its inadequacy to the needs of a modern state, had proposed an income tax. The idea horrified the conservatives, who predictably had no interest in surrendering their exemption from being taxed. But it won Caillaux so many new friends in the so-called Radical faction (which in fact was not radical at all but barely left of center) that he became for a time premier.

Caillaux's tenure as premier included the 1911 Moroccan crisis, and he had been firm and effective in negotiating a settlement with the Germans. Though his enemies accused him, inevitably, of bending under German pressure, he had won for France the colony of Morocco at the lowest price Berlin was prepared to accept short of war. It was also during Caillaux's premiership that General Joseph Joffre was made head of the French general staff, which meant that, in the years just before the war, the army had a commander who insisted on better training, better equipment, and promotion on the basis of ability and performance. Even in his skepticism about the military service extension, Caillaux never challenged the idea that France should be militarily strong. His questions were about how strength could best be achieved. Keeping many thousands of men on active duty for an additional year required heavy spending for barracks and other facilities, but it did little to increase the size of the army upon mobilization. Caillaux wanted to invest in artillery (in which France was seriously deficient) and innovations such as aircraft.

One other thing was paradoxical about Joseph Caillaux. Behind his invincible facade of fashionable propriety, behind his cold and eccentric public persona, he was an adventurous womanizer. He did not marry until he was into middle age. When he did, his choice was a divorcée older than himself who had been his mistress for some years. Not long afterward he entered into an affair with a married woman, Madame Henriette Claretie. Their liaison was not frivolous. With some difficulty the two divorced their spouses and were married.

All these currents—hatred for Caillaux's taxation proposals, conservative belief that the future of the nation hinged on the service extension, questions about the alliance with Russia, and the support given to Caillaux by Jaurès and the Socialists—came together in the 1914 election. In the words of Barrès, Caillaux was a menace because he was the one man who could "bring Jaurès's pacifist dream down from the clouds, to make the theories of working-class internationalism and the fraternity of all people both practical and realizable."

The campaign was more than spirited. As a Caillaux victory loomed, his enemies cast aside what little restraint was customary in the politics of France. The conservative press attacked him relentlessly. Characteristically, Caillaux disdained to reply; he would coolly assert his innocence of whatever the latest charge happened to be but go no further. He was coasting toward a victory that would lead to a reappraisal of national policy and possibly to the resignation of Poincaré (who threatened just such a step). But then his private life was brought into the political arena, and everything changed.

Caillaux's first wife, a woman spurned and vengeful, made available to Gaston Calmette, the editor of the conservative publication *Le Figaro,* letters that Caillaux had sent to her in 1901 when she was still his mistress and married to another man. Calmette, who had been attacking Caillaux viciously, now promised his readers a "comic interlude" that he opened by printing one of the letters. Its content was not scandalous in any sexual sense; Caillaux had boasted of appearing to fight for his income tax proposal while actually assuring that it could not pass. This raised questions about possible duplicity on his part (unless of course he was simply trying to impress his paramour), but it was hardly a smoking gun. Much was made of the fact that Caillaux signed himself *Ton Jo*, "Your Joe." The *ton* was inappropriately intimate when used by a gentleman in addressing a married lady, but even by the standards of its day it was something less than outrageous.

The second Madame Caillaux, however, was not amused. Despite her affair and divorce and remarriage, Henriette cared greatly about her reputation and place in society. She hated the world of politics and the abuse to which it exposed her husband. Lately, when in public, she had found herself hissed and laughed at when people learned that she was the spouse of that traitor to his class, the man who wanted to tax incomes. She complained of being unable to eat or sleep, and when she tried to talk with her husband about what was happening, he (as he ruefully acknowledged later) did not take her seriously.

What terrified Henriette about the publication of the letter, apparently, was the possibility that it would be followed by love letters that she and Caillaux had exchanged while still married to other people. There was gossip to the effect that these letters too had been given to *Le Figaro.*

On the afternoon of March 16 she dressed elegantly, went by chauffeured auto to the shop of a Paris gun dealer, and there purchased a small Browning automatic pistol. The dealer took her to his basement for instruction in the pistol's use. From there she went to the offices of *Le Figaro,* where, her hands and her weapon concealed in a fur muff, she created consternation by identifying herself and asking to see Calmette. The editor was out, as it happened, and she had to wait hours for his return. When at last he arrived through a rear entrance, he was told of his visitor and urged not to see her. He gallantly replied that he would not deny a lady. Upon being admitted to his office, Henriette asked Calmette if he knew why she wanted to see him. When he replied that he did not and offered her a chair, she took out her pistol and squeezed the trigger until its six bullets had been discharged. Calmette was hit four times and killed. Later Henriette testified that, intending only to frighten him, she had closed her eyes before firing and pointed the pistol at the floor. Calmette, unfortunately for both of them, had fallen to the floor as soon as he saw the gun and so put himself in the line of fire. When members of the *Figaro* staff came running into the office, Henriette surrendered her weapon but imperiously maintained her dignity. "Do not touch me," she declared. "I am a lady." When the police were preparing to take her to jail, she refused to enter their wagon. She had a vehicle suitable to her station, she said, and would travel in it. The police agreed.

It was the most sensational story in years, one that combined murder and sex with wild speculation about what had motivated Henriette and what further scandals might be revealed. It monopolized the attention of the Paris newspapers all that spring and summer. Its first effect was to side-line Caillaux politically: he immediately resigned from the cabinet and announced (he would later change his mind) that his political career was over.

In spite of the scandal, the election turned out to be a disaster for Poincaré and the conservatives and a triumph for Caillaux's Radicals and their Socialist allies. Under ordinary circumstances, Caillaux would have become premier. But now someone else had to be found for the job, and with Caillaux out of the running, no one was holding Poincaré to his threat to resign. For two weeks, as the formidable Poincaré used his constitutional authority to block a succession of candidates who were opposed to the service extension, France remained without a government. Finally, grudgingly, Poincaré agreed to the appointment of René Viviani, a onetime socialist and a rising but inexperienced political star who in 1913 had voted against the extension but now promised to withdraw his opposition. In the weeks ahead Viviani would show himself to be emotionally fragile (his career would end in insanity) and willing to follow Poincaré's guidance in dealing with the July crisis.

Henriette's trial, from its start early in July, was an early specimen of full-bore media circus, obsessing press and public alike, making the news about yet another crisis in the distant Balkans seem dreary and pointless by comparison, and constantly giving rise to new sensations. (One of the trial judges challenged another to a duel.) Then came the state visit that Poincaré paid to St. Petersburg, taking Viviani with him and using the long days at sea to instruct the new premier in the importance of military readiness and the alliance with Russia.

Even if there had been no trial and no voyage to Russia, French passivity throughout the crisis undoubtedly would have been to Poincaré's liking. The president was the closest thing to a true master of French politics to have emerged in decades. He had begun his career as the youngest lawyer in the country, became the youngest member of the Chamber of Deputies at twenty-six, was elected premier in his forties, and in 1913, at age fifty-two, became both the youngest president in the nation's history and the first to be elected while serving as premier. In 1914 he was mindful of what General Joffre had told him: that France was now strong enough to win a war with Germany if Serbia tied up a substantial part of the Austro-Hungarian army, Russia took the field against the Germans, and Britain too came in on France's side. The British factor made it essential that France stand aside during the diplomatic crisis. Paris could have changed the outcome of the crisis only by discouraging the Russians from being so quick to mobilize. Caillaux, as premier, almost certainly would have done this. The tsar's reluctance to mobilize makes it at least possible that Caillaux could have succeeded.

The magnitude of the international crisis finally came crashing in on Paris on Wednesday, July 29. A chivalrous jury found Madame Caillaux not guilty, and France's newspapers awoke from their trance to discover that Europe was on the brink of war. Poincaré and Viviani returned to Paris, finding the capital burning with war fever. July 29 was also the day on which Tsar Nicholas first ordered and then temporarily canceled general mobilization. Thanks to the scheming Ambassador Paléologue, Paris had only limited knowledge of what was happening in St. Petersburg, and the Russians had no reason to think that the French government was not enthusiastic about their mobilization. By Friday full mobilization was under way in Russia, but no word of it appeared in the Paris newspapers. The papers were, however, carrying excited and unfounded reports that Germany was mobilizing secretly. Joffre was demanding French mobilization.

With Caillaux out of the picture and the final slide into war under way, there was in all of France only one man of importance who not only thought that war might be prevented but was committed to preventing it if he could. This was Jean Jaurès, whose gifts were so prodigious that it seemed briefly possible that even now, far into the eleventh hour, he might make a difference.

As a leader, a thinker, and simply as a human being, Jaurès stood out like a giant in the summer of 1914. Like Caillaux he was widely hated, but only for the most honorable of reasons: he had dedicated his life to the achievement of democracy and genuine peace not only in France but across the continent. But he was respected too—respected and loved to an extent remarkable for a man whose socialist convictions had put him permanently outside the boundaries of political respectability. Everyone who knew him and has left a record of the experience tells of a sunny, selfless, brilliant personality, bearded and bearlike and utterly careless of his appearance, indifferent to personal success or failure but passionately dedicated to his vision of a better, saner world.

Born in provincial obscurity, he had been sent to Paris on scholarship and excelled at the most elite schools to be found there. He had gone first into an academic career and then into politics, earning a doctorate along the way. Drawn by his sense of the injustices of industrial society into the Socialist Party, he soon became its dominant figure and a practical, non-dogmatic adapter of Marxist thought. He was opposed to imperialism, colonialism, and militarism, all of which he saw as a waste of resources that could be used for better purposes. But he was not opposed to nationalism, envisioning a Europe of autonomous democracies working together for a prosperity in which the poor and the powerless could share. He believed that political liberty was meaningless without economic liberty, that the power of the industrialists, banks, big landowners, and church must be curtailed, and that small family businesses and farms must be preserved. An anticlerical, he nevertheless opposed the efforts of his associates to bar Catholics from teaching in the universities. Above all he was opposed to the secret alliances of the great powers, France included. He foresaw how disastrous a general war would be with a clarity that can still astonish anyone who reads the things he wrote and said. He was widely regarded as the greatest orator of his time, and by consistently demonstrating his integrity and indifference to personal advantage, he had unified France's leftist factions and made the Socialist Party a force in national politics. By late July France appeared to be divided into two camps: one that regarded Jaurès as a public danger, another that was ready to follow him. In the midst of mounting hysteria he was the one prominent figure calling for restraint, deliberation, and a search for a way out of war—for *sangfroid.* "The danger is great but not insuperable if we keep our clearness of mind and strength of will," he wrote in his last newspaper column, which appeared on Friday, July 31, "if we show the heroism of patience as well as the heroism of action."

France's conservative voices, meanwhile, were anything but calm. "We have no wish to incite anyone to political assassination," the newspaper *Action Française* had declared on July 23 in what was becoming the characteristic tone of Jaurès's enemies, "but M. Jean Jaurès may well shake in his shoes! His words may perhaps give some fanatic the desire to settle by the experimental method the question of whether anything would be changed in the invincible order of things if M. Jean Jaurès were to suffer the fate of M. Calmette." Another paper told its readers that "if on the eve of war a General were to detail half a dozen men and a Corporal to put Citizen Jaurès against a wall and to pump the lead he needs into his brain at point-blank range—do you think that General would be doing anything but his elementary duty?"

On the evening of July 31, just back from a hurried trip to Brussels where he had addressed an emergency meeting of Socialists from several countries, including Germany, Jaurès and a small group of his associates went to the foreign ministry, where they met with vice minister Abel Ferry and demanded every possible effort to keep Russia from mobilizing. By this time the government not only knew of the Russian mobilization but had received, via the German ambassador, Berlin's warning that it too would mobilize if the Russians did not reverse course. Viviani, after consultation with Poincaré, had given the Germans his promise of an answer by one P.M. tomorrow, Saturday. Now Ferry simply told Jaurès that it was too late, that "everything is finished, there is nothing left to do."

"To the very end," Jaurès answered angrily, "we will continue to struggle against war."

"No," Ferry replied. "You won't be able to continue. You will be assassinated on the nearest street corner."

Two hours later a twenty-nine-year-old man named Raoul Villain, well educated but aimless, confused, and unemployed, was walking along the Rue Montmartre when he saw several men enter the Café du Croissant. Among them was Jaurès, and Villain recognized him. As he watched, Jaurès took a seat with his back to an open window. For half an hour, while Jaurès ate his dinner and conferred with the editors of his newspaper, *L'Humanité,* about what should be said in the Saturday edition, Villain paced outside. He was armed; inflamed by the hysteria all around him, he had been planning to travel to Germany and shoot the kaiser. Here, suddenly, was an opportunity to demonstrate his patriotism and strike a blow for France right at home.

Inside the restaurant a man rose from his place at another table and approached the Jaurès group. He was a friend of one of Jaurès's companions, and he wanted to show off a photo of his baby daughter.

"May I see?" Jaurès asked. He examined the picture, smiled, asked the child's age, and offered congratulations. At that instant Villain, standing just outside the window, fired two shots into the back of his head. Jaurès was dead before the police arrived, and the next day France and Germany mobilized. The Socialists in both countries, now without anyone capable of bringing them together, supported the move to war.

Chapter 8

✠

First Blood

*"All the courage in the world cannot
prevail against gunfire."*
—Captain Charles de Gaulle

The war began in earnest on August 2, when an advance force of German cavalry moved into Luxembourg to seize its network of railways. That same day Germany delivered an ultimatum to Belgium, demanding unobstructed passage for its armies. Young King Albert refused. His little army, which could put only seven divisions totaling one hundred and seventeen thousand troops into the field, began blowing up bridges and rail lines leading into Belgium from Germany. Suddenly the little city of Liège, always locally important as a center of road, rail, and water transportation, became the most important place on the continent. Its defenses, on high bluffs looming over the River Meuse, dominated the narrow passage through which the Schlieffen right wing had to pass on its way westward. Unless these defenses were overcome, and quickly, the German advance would be blocked almost at its starting point and the entire offensive reduced to a shambles.

Liège was no ordinary city but a ring of twelve massive forts that together made it one of the most formidable military strongpoints in the world. Each of these forts contained eight or nine big guns under armored turrets, and each was built of reinforced concrete and designed to withstand direct hits from the heaviest artillery then in existence. General Gérard Leman, the elderly Belgian commander at Liège, had some eight thousand troops inside the forts plus, as a mobile force, a division of twenty-four thousand infantry, five hundred cavalry, and seventy-two field guns. The Germans, as part of their mobilization plan, had formed, trained, and stationed near the border a special strike force of thirty thousand men plus mobile field artillery whose sole mission was to attack and neutralize the forts. When the lead elements of this force moved on Liège from the south on August 4, they were greatly outnumbered by the defenders but immediately launched a night assault. They met ferocious fire and were thrown back. They quickly attacked again and were again repulsed. This put the Germans in a desperate situation.

Leman, ordered by King Albert to hold his position at all costs (a term meaning death before surrender or retreat), learned of the appearance of German cavalry to his north and concluded that he would soon be surrounded. To keep his mobile force from capture, he sent it off to join the main Belgian army. This removed almost a quarter of Belgium's total fighting forces from danger of encirclement and capture, but at a price: it ended any possibility that Leman would have enough troops to keep the Germans at a distance from which their guns would be unable to do their worst.

There now arrived on the scene, and on the world stage, an obscure German officer who quickly established himself as the hero of the siege and with startling speed would become one of the most important men in the German army. This was Erich Ludendorff. (Note the absence of a *von* in the name—he was not a member of Prussia's Junker aristocracy.) Recently promoted to major general, a tall, portly, double-chinned forty-nine-year-old, Ludendorff was on temporary assignment as liaison between the Liège assault force and the German Second Army, which was still assembling on the German side of the border. There had been good reason for giving Ludendorff this assignment: a few years earlier, as a key member of Moltke's staff, he had developed the plans for the reduction of the Liège fortifications. (With typical thoroughness, he had once spent a vacation in Belgium in order to examine the defenses at first hand.) In the German army, unlike the French, it was customary to send staff officers into the field, into combat, where they could observe their plans in action, assist in making adjustments when reality began to intrude, and learn from the experience. But Ludendorff was constitutionally incapable of remaining a mere observer or adviser. It was he who had sent the cavalry that, by showing itself north of Liège, had caused Leman to send most of his troops away. Then, coming upon a brigade whose commander had been killed in one of the early attacks, he put himself in charge. Bringing howitzers forward and directing their fire on the Belgian defenses, he led an assault that gave him possession of an expanse of high ground from which the city and its central citadel were clearly visible.

When he could see no sign of activity around the citadel (Leman had moved to one of the outlying forts), Ludendorff drove to it. He shouted a demand for surrender while pounding on the gate with the pommel of his sword. Astoundingly, he was obeyed in spite of being greatly outnumbered. Thus the centerpiece of the Liège defenses fell into German hands almost without effort. Though the circle of forts was still intact, all were now isolated and without any support except what they could give one another. Ludendorff then hurried back into Germany to see to it that more and bigger guns were brought forward without delay.

Moltke's seven western armies, meanwhile, were forming up on a north-south line just inside the German border south of Holland. Picture a clock with Paris at its center. The line of armies was in the upper-right portion of the clock's face, extending, roughly, from one to three o'clock. The biggest and northernmost of these armies, positioned to the north and east of Liège, was commanded by General Alexander von Kluck, tough, aggressive, irascible, and sixty-eight years old, a hardened infantryman who had begun life as a commoner and had been elevated to the nobility in reward for decades of distinguished service. Remarkably for a high-ranking German officer, Kluck had never had a tour of duty on the high command's headquarters staff. His First Army, almost a third of a million men strong, was assigned to be the outer edge of the right wing. It would have the longest distance to travel as it moved westward across Belgium and then looped toward the southwest. If things went perfectly it would, on its way to Paris, move around and past the westernmost end of the French defensive line. It would then continue southward, circle all the way around Paris, and move back to the east. Finally it would hit the French line from the rear, pushing it into other German armies positioned at two and three o'clock and crushing it in a great vise.

The Germans did students of the war a lasting favor by arranging their armies in numerical order. Next to Kluck, immediately to his south during the mobilization (later to his east, as the Schlieffen wheel made its great turn), was the Second Army under General Karl von Bülow, a member of the high Prussian aristocracy who also was in his late sixties. Then came the Third Army, the Fourth, and so on down to the Seventh, which was almost as far south as Paris and had the Swiss border on its left. The first three of these armies made up the right wing, and though that wing no longer included as big a part of the German army as Schlieffen had intended, it was still an awesome force of seven hundred and fifty thousand troops. This was war on a truly new scale; the army with which Wellington defeated Napoleon at Waterloo had totaled sixty thousand men.

The First, Second, and Third Armies would be side by side as they drove forward. Their left would be protected by the rest of the German line. Though their right would be exposed, this would be no problem if Kluck could get around the equally exposed French left. His primary assignment, until he had circled Paris, was not to engage the enemy but to *keep moving*. If circumstances developed in such a way as to permit him to strike at the flank of the French left as he advanced, perhaps crippling it, so much the better. That would be secondary, however. The goal was Paris.

King Albert of Belgium

GERMAN ADVANCE *of 1914*

ENGLAND

North Sea

Amsterdam ⊛

NETHERLANDS

GERMANY

• Antwerp

FLANDERS

BELGIUM

Cologne •

• Calais

Ypres •

Brussels ⊛

GERMAN 1st

• Aachen

Lille •

Mons •

Charleroi

Meuse

Liège •

GERMAN 2nd

Rhine

Sambre

Namur •

Koblenz •

Le Cateau •

Maubeuge •

GERMAN 3rd

Mosel

Somme

GERMAN 4th

Amiens •

• Guise

Ardennes Forest

LUXEMBOURG

PICARDY

Noyon •

Oise

Aisne

Meuse

• Luxembourg

FRANCE

Soissons •

Reims •

Argonne Forest

GERMAN 5th

Seine

Château Thierry •

Marne

Verdun •

• Metz

Ourq

Épernay •

St. Mihiel •

GERMAN 6th

FRENCH 6th

Petit Morin

Marsh of St. Gond

FRENCH 3rd

Nancy •

GERMAN 7th

Paris ⊛

Grand Morin

FRENCH 4th

Toul •

Strasbourg •

BRITISH

FRENCH 9th

FRENCH 2nd

Moselle

Rhine

FRENCH 5th

Aube

Épinal •

Mülhausen

FRENCH 1st

Belfort •

SWITZERLAND

	Front Line September 5, 1914
	Front Line September 14, 1914

0   Miles   25   50   75

0   Kilometers   50   75

© 2005 Jeffrey L. Ward

The Armies and Their Commanders:

BRITISH EXPEDITIONARY FORCE—John French

France at start of war:
FIRST ARMY—Auguste Dubail
SECOND ARMY—Noël de Castelnau
THIRD ARMY—Pierre-Xavier Ruffey
FOURTH ARMY—Fernand de Langle de Cary
FIFTH ARMY—Charles Lanrezac

Organized during the Battle of the Marne:
SIXTH ARMY—Michel Maunoury
NINTH ARMY—Ferdinand Foch

Germany
FIRST ARMY—Alexander von Kluck
SECOND ARMY—Karl von Bülow
THIRD ARMY—Max Klemens von Hausen
FOURTH ARMY—Albrecht, Duke of Württemberg
FIFTH ARMY—Crown Prince Wilhelm of Germany
SIXTH ARMY—Crown Prince Rupprecht of Bavaria
SEVENTH ARMY—Josias von Heeringen

The two armies on the German left, the Sixth and the Seventh, were not intended to be an attack force. Their role was to absorb an expected advance by the French into Alsace and Lorraine, stopping the invaders from breaking through while keeping them too fully engaged to spare troops for the defense of Paris. Between the three armies of the right wing and the two on the left were the Fourth and Fifth Armies, the latter commanded by Imperial Crown Prince Wilhelm, the kaiser's eldest son. They were to provide a connecting link between the defensive force in the south and the right wing, keeping the line continuous and free of gaps. They would be the hub of the wheel on which the right wing was moving, and they would not have to move either far or fast. They would be an anchor, a pivot point, for the entire campaign. Ultimately they were to become the killing machine into which Kluck was to drive the French after his swing around Paris.

French General Joffre, for his part, had his million-plus frontline troops organized into five armies. They too were forming up in a line and were in numerical order, with the First on the right just above Switzerland. The French Second Army was immediately to its north, the Third above it, and so on northward and westward in a great arc that ended approximately midway between Paris and the starting point of Kluck's army. Joffre's First, Second, and Third Armies, as they took up their positions, faced eastward toward Alsace and Lorraine with their backs to the chain of superfortresses (Verdun, Toul, Épinal, and Belfort) that France had constructed between Switzerland and Belgium. The Fourth and Fifth, being to the north and west of these forts, had no such strongpoints to fall back on. The position of the Fifth, commanded by Joffre's friend and protégé Charles Lanrezac, was problematic. It was the end of the French line in exactly the same way that Kluck's army was the end of the German, with no significant French forces to its north or west. Its left flank ended, as tacticians say, "up in the air"—out on a limb. This position carried within it the danger that the Germans might get around Lanrezac's left, exposing him to attack in the flank or from the rear. In the opening days of the war, however, this danger seemed so hypothetical to Joffre as to be unworthy of concern.

Neither Lanrezac nor Joffre had any real way of knowing what the Germans were going to do. Aerial reconnaissance, like military aviation generally, was barely in its infancy in the summer of 1914. Until mobilization was completed, it would not be possible to make much use of the cavalry that was supposed to function as the eyes of the army. The commanders on both sides could do little more than make educated guesses, using whatever information came in from spies or could be gleaned from the questioning of captured soldiers. The sheer size of their armies and of the theater of operations, and the unavoidable remoteness from the front lines of headquarters responsible for the movements of hundreds of thousands of men, compounded the intelligence problem.

The individual armies, too, would be half-blind as they went into action. And they would be far more vulnerable than their size would suggest. A mass of infantry on the move is like nothing else in the world, but it may usefully be thought of as an immensely long and cumbersome caterpillar with the head of a nearsighted tiger. (The monstrousness of the image is not inappropriate.) It is structured to make its head as lethal as possible, ready at all times to come to grips with whatever enemy comes into its path. A big part of an army commander's job is to make certain that it is in fact the head that meets the enemy, so that the tiger's teeth—men armed with guns and blades and whatever other implements of destruction are available to them—can either attack the enemy or fend off the enemy's attack as circumstances require.

An advancing army's worst vulnerability lies in the long caterpillar body behind the head. (*Long* is an inadequate word in the context of 1914: a single corps of two divisions included thirty thousand or more men at full strength and stretched over fifteen miles of road when on the march.) Great battles can be won when a tiger's head eludes or even accidentally misses the head of its enemy and makes contact with its body instead. When this happens the enemy is "taken in the flank," and if an attacking head has sufficient weight it can quickly tear the enemy's body apart, finally reducing even the head to an isolated, enfeebled remnant. Much the same can happen when an army on the move is taken in the rear, or surrounded and cut off from its lines of supply. Hence the importance that Moltke and Joffre attached to arranging their armies in an unbroken line, so that each could protect the flanks of its neighbors. Hence too the dangers inherent in the fact that both generals would begin the war with one end of their lines unprotected.

Joffre, like Moltke, was intent upon taking the offensive. His master plan, approved in 1913, reflected the French government's refusal to permit any move into neutral territory. It assumed that the Germans too would stay out of Belgium and Luxembourg, and so it assumed further that the first great clash of the war would take place on the French-German border, somewhere between Verdun to the north and the fortress of Belfort to the south. Joffre's five armies were more than sufficient to maintain a solid line while attacking from one end of that border to the other, and so he saw no reason to be concerned about Lanrezac's left, which would be anchored on Luxembourg.

Joffre's advantage was that he was not irrevocably committed to attacking at any specific place or time or even to attacking at all. Unlike Moltke he had options—he could change his plans and the disposition of his armies according to how the situation developed. This ability quickly proved important:

when the Germans moved into Luxembourg and then on to Liège, Joffre was able to order the Fourth and Fifth Armies to shift around and face northward. He now expected the Germans to come from the northeast, through Belgium's Ardennes Forest toward the French city of Sedan. His left wing would move north to meet them.

Lanrezac was not so sure. As word reached him of the intensifying assault on Liège, he could think of no reason for it unless the Germans needed to clear a path to the west. As early as July 31—before war was declared—he had sent a message to Joffre expressing concern about what would happen if the Germans advanced westward while his army stayed south of the Belgian border or moved east to join in the French offensive. "In such a case," he warned, "the Fifth Army . . . could do nothing to prevent a possible encircling movement against our left wing." Joffre did not respond; he was certain that no such thing would happen. A week later, with the Germans continuing to concentrate troops opposite Liège, Lanrezac sent another appeal. "This time there can be no doubt," he said. "They are planning a wide encircling movement through Belgium. I ask permission to change the direction of the Fifth Army toward the north." He had it exactly right, but Joffre remained unpersuaded, confident that whatever was happening around Liège must be a German feint intended to lure his forces out of position. His attention was focused on launching an attack by his right wing into Alsace and Lorraine—the capture of France's lost provinces would be a tremendous symbolic triumph. As a precaution, though, he did send cavalry on a scouting expedition into Belgium. When this foray found no evidence of German activity—inevitably, the Germans not yet having moved beyond Liège—Joffre felt free to proceed with his own plans. His First Army began crossing into Alsace as early as August 7, the day Ludendorff captured the Liège citadel, and it made good progress. Another week passed, and the direction of the German right wing became undeniable, before Joffre at last responded to Lanrezac's warnings, telling him almost laconically that "I see no objection (to the contrary) to your considering the movement that you propose." Even then he added, with thinly veiled annoyance, that "the threat is as yet only a long-term possibility and we are not absolutely certain that it actually exists." Lanrezac started northward, not knowing that it was already too late for him to escape being outflanked in exactly the way he had feared from the start.

The Germans, by this time, had hauled into Belgium the weapons that would decide the fate of Liège, two new kinds of monster artillery: 305mm Skoda siege mortars borrowed from Austria, plus an almost unimaginably huge 420mm howitzer secretly developed and produced by Germany's Krupp steelworks. Neither gun had ever been used in combat. The bigger of

the two weighed seventy-five tons and had to be transported by rail in five
sections and set in concrete before going into action. It could fire up to ten
2,200-pound projectiles per hour, each shell carrying a hardened head and a
delayed-action fuse so that it penetrated its target before exploding. It had a
range of nine miles, its projectiles following such a high trajectory that they
came down almost vertically. It had to be fired electrically so that the two-
hundred-man crew operating it, their heads covered with protective padding,

The Austrian 305mm Skoda siege mortar
One of the weapons that broke the defenses of Liège.

could move three hundred yards away and lie down on the ground before detonation. Once "registered"—its elevation and direction set so that every round landed on target—it was a hellishly destructive weapon, capable of breaking apart even the strongest of the Liège forts and vaporizing the men inside. It was a fitting opening act for a hellishly destructive war.

The big guns arrived at Liège on August 10, but two days more were needed to get them in place. By this time, off to the south, Joffre's Alsace offensive had captured several towns, but on August 11 the Germans counterattacked and brought the advance to a stop. The day after that Austria's Field Marshal Conrad, launching the punitive campaign that he had so long

craved, sent three armies totaling four hundred and sixty thousand men into Serbia, where they soon were moving rapidly across easy terrain toward the mountains to the east.

On August 13, after taking several shattering hits, Fort Chaudfontaine at the southeastern corner of the Liège circle surrendered, with only seventy-six of the 408 members of its garrison still alive. Later on the same day two more of the forts, similarly devastated, also surrendered. On August 15 Fort Lonçin ceased to exist when the twenty-third 420mm shell fired at it penetrated its ammunition stores and set them off. Taking possession, the Germans found Belgian General Leman lying in the wreckage. As he was being carried away, he opened his eyes. "I ask you to bear witness," he said to the German commander, "that you found me unconscious." Though a few of the forts had not yet surrendered or been destroyed, their ability to interfere with the German advance was at an end. Moltke's armies were ready, the road to the west was open, and the right wing went into motion almost exactly on Schlieffen's schedule. German engineers hurried to repair rail lines destroyed by the Belgians, and trains rolled forward one after another, carrying the mountains of supplies needed to support the offensive. More than five hundred trains were crossing the Rhine every twenty-four hours; in the first sixteen days after troop movements began, 2,150 trains crossed a single bridge at Cologne—one every ten minutes. And with good reason. Kluck's First Army alone required five hundred and fifty tons of food every day. Its eighty-four thousand horses consumed eight hundred and forty tons of fodder daily.

Things now started happening at an accelerating pace and on an expanding scale, and it became uncommon for anything to happen as anyone had expected or intended. By August 16, in a heroically speedy if tragically premature response to the French government's calls for the opening of a second front, Russia inserted its First Army into East Prussia. This move was far in advance of what the Germans had thought possible; obviously other Russian armies would be arriving soon, and so Moltke was faced with a possible disaster in the east long before the fight in the west could be decided. That same day a Serbian counterattack stopped the Austrians and threw them back in disorder. Suddenly major developments were occurring daily.

August 17: A collision of German and Russian troops at Stallupönen in East Prussia ends inconclusively; the Germans are forced into a retreat that disrupts their plans, but they take three thousand prisoners with them.

August 18: Joffre broadens his eastward offensive by sending the French Second Army into Lorraine. The invasion makes good progress, but only because Moltke has ordered the German Sixth Army to fall back. He too has a plan for Lorraine: to allow the French to advance until they are between his

Fifth Army to the north and Seventh Army to the south. Then they can be hit on both flanks and destroyed. This trap, if successful, could produce a victory on the German left so decisive that the success of the Schlieffen right wing might become unnecessary. The Austrians are hit again in Serbia and suffer another severe defeat. Four Russian armies enter Galicia, the Austrian part of Poland (there being no country of Poland in those days—it was long ago divided among Russia, Germany, and Austria). The Austrians are not nearly as prepared as they should be for this offensive because of Conrad's decision to invade Serbia.

August 19: The French continue to advance in Lorraine.

August 20: Crown Prince Rupprecht of Bavaria, commander of the German Sixth Army in Lorraine and temporarily in command of the Seventh Army as well, watches as the French offensive overextends itself and runs out of momentum. Unable to resist so tempting a target ("We cannot ask our Bavarian soldiers to retreat again," he complains, "just when they feel absolute superiority over the enemy facing them"), he orders a counterattack that proves to be brilliantly successful, inflicting tremendous casualties on the French and driving them back across the border to the city of Nancy. Even Nancy is nearly abandoned. It is saved by a defense and counterattack organized by a corps commander named Ferdinand Foch, another sudden hero who will loom ever larger in the years of war to come (and will receive word this very week that his son-in-law and only son have been killed in combat). Rupprecht's counterattack, for all its success, is a serious mistake. It neither destroys the French Sixth Army nor captures anything of strategic importance. Instead it pushes the French backward out of Moltke's trap, returning them to their line of fortresses. The latest developments in technology have, as time will prove, made these fortresses capable of standing up even under the kinds of guns that broke Liège, and in the weeks ahead their strength will permit Joffre to shift troops from his right wing to his imperiled left. The Germans' chances of achieving a breakthrough are vanishingly small, but Rupprecht thinks otherwise. Wanting to press his advantage, he asks—all but demands—that Moltke send him more troops. Moltke, in one of his departures from a Schlieffen Plan in which all possible manpower was supposed to be concentrated in the right wing, agrees.

On this same day the Austrian invasion of Serbia is transformed from a failure into a humiliating rout: the Austrian forces take fifty thousand casualties, including six thousand men killed, and flee back across the border. The Russians and Germans collide again in East Prussia, this time at a place called Gumbinnen, and again the fighting is bloody but inconclusive. The Germans pull back, but the Russians do not pursue. The commander of the Eighth

Army, Max von Prittwitz, telephones Moltke and reports that he is in trouble and needs to withdraw from East Prussia. This is disastrous news tactically, strategically, and in terms of morale. East Prussia is the homeland of the Junkers, Prussia's hereditary elite, and as such it is the cradle of Germany's general staff. The thought of the Junker farms being left to the mercies of rampaging Cossack horsemen is horrifying. But once again, as with Rupprecht, Moltke decides that he is too far from the action and too lacking in reliable information to disagree. He does not challenge Prittwitz's decision, does not tell him to stand and fight.

In Belgium, meanwhile, things continued to go well for the Germans. Having done their work at Liège, the big guns were quickly moved westward to Namur, a cluster of nine forts nearly as strong as Liège and a junction of six rail lines. Namur surrendered after five days of shelling. The Germans, however, had something to regret: their failure to cut off and destroy the Belgian army before it slipped off to Antwerp, near the coast. Now Kluck had to reduce his army by two corps in order to keep the Belgians from coming back south and threatening his lines of communication. But the French and Belgians had made an equally serious mistake in failing to send troops to Namur while it still might have provided them with a fortified base from which to block the German advance. Such a move, with enough troops involved, would have had a good chance of succeeding. Now, with that opportunity gone, Lanrezac was going to have to find a way to stop the Germans in open country.

As the Germans took possession of Brussels, they paused to give themselves a parade—the first such celebration since the Franco-Prussian War. From there, while continuing westward, they began to bend their route toward the south, toward Paris. In their wake they were leaving a trail of killings that, even after the truth was separated from the exaggerations of propaganda, would disgrace them in the eyes of the world, give their enemies reason to argue that this was a war for civilization, and begin the long process that would end with the United States entering the war against them. They destroyed towns. They took civilian hostages, including women and children. They killed many of these hostages—in some cases machine-gunning them by the score. They killed priests simply because they were priests (while claiming that they were leaders of a guerrilla resistance). They destroyed the storybook city of Louvain, with its exquisite medieval university and irreplaceable library.

To the extent that such acts can be explained—not excused, but explained—they had tangled origins. In the Franco-Prussian War the Germans had suffered significant casualties at the hands of *franc-tireurs,* civilian snipers and guerrillas, some of whom were urged on by French priests. They were determined not to have a repeat. When they encountered guerrillas in Belgium, they lashed out viciously. The German newspapers carried sensational accounts of German soldiers being mutilated and killed by Belgian townsfolk. These stories were read by the troops, angering and frightening them and causing them to respond with further violence. And senior officers were fixated on the same idea that had made the violation of Belgian neutrality possible in the first place—the idea that Germany was in a life-or-death struggle and so had no choice but to take extreme measures. "Our advance in Belgium is certainly brutal," Moltke observed. "But we are fighting for our lives and all who get in the way must take the consequences."

Wherever enemy armies were believed to be approaching, in Belgium and in France, in southwestern Germany and in East Prussia, in Serbia and in Poland, the civilian populations fled by the hundreds of thousands in whatever way they could. Roads became clogged with refugees and their livestock and whatever possessions they could load onto wagons and carts. Whenever armies wanted to use those same roads, the civilians had to make for the fields and woods.

But Europe was focused on the fortunes of the armies, not the savagery

Belgian civilians, displaced by war, crowd the docks of Antwerp
waiting for passage to Britain.

and suffering that the war was already visiting on the innocent, as the middle of August passed. By August 21 things seemed to be moving rapidly to a climax. On that day a second Russian army entered East Prussia and began taking town after town. The Russians' plan was obvious: their two armies would converge on Germany's one eastern army, which they vastly outnumbered, and obliterate it. The road to Berlin would then be open, and the Germans would have no way of saving themselves except by pulling apart their long wall of armies in the west. Kaiser Wilhelm was almost unhinged by the news from East Prussia. After nervously pacing the garden outside his headquarters, he seated himself on a bench and told his companions—the heads of his military and naval cabinets—to sit down as well. The two men, no doubt trying to be properly deferential to their emperor, pulled up a second bench and sat on it. "Do you already hold me in such contempt that none will sit beside me?" the kaiser cried. It was an early sign, the first of many, that he was not going to stand up well under the strain of war.

It was on August 21, too, that Joffre launched a new offensive, sending the Third and Fourth Armies that formed the center of his line northward into the Ardennes. By now it had become obvious that the Germans' main attack would not be coming from that direction, and Joffre guessed that their center couldn't possibly be very strong. His intelligence bureau had estimated that the Germans would begin the war with sixty-eight combat-ready divisions in the west—not seventy-eight infantry and ten cavalry divisions plus fourteen brigades of territorial militia, as was actually the case. It assumed incorrectly that the Germans would, like the French, regard their newly mobilized reserve troops as too green for action on the front lines. Joffre therefore reasoned that if the Germans had enough strength on their left to push back his offensive in Alsace-Lorraine and enough on their right for a drive across Belgium, the center had to be vulnerable. By thrusting upward into southeastern Belgium, he thought, he could penetrate far enough to strike the German right wing in its flank and separate it from its sources of supply and reinforcement.

The fourteen French divisions sent into the Ardennes ran head-on into exactly fourteen German divisions that found strong defensive positions in the region's rough wooded hills and were well equipped with machine guns and artillery. The French attacked and attacked again under increasingly hopeless conditions until finally, weakened by appalling casualties, they had no choice but to stop. The fight at the town of Rossignol was sadly typical: of the fourteen thousand crack colonial troops thrown at the Germans there, nearly a third were shot dead. Lanrezac's Fifth Army might have been mangled in this offensive as well, if not for his warnings and appeals and Joffre's grudging decision to allow him to stay farther west.

Now the Fifth was the only French army not fully engaged. And by now it was clear that Lanrezac had been right all along: the main German invasion force was to his north, moving through Belgium virtually unopposed. A seventy-five-mile shift had taken Lanrezac's left to a point across the River Sambre from the town of Charleroi. Lanrezac didn't know where the Germans were and had little in the way of instructions from Joffre, and so he did something that was extremely unfashionable in the French army of 1914: he had his troops take up defensive positions. It was fortunate that he did. The next day his army was hit by advance units of Bülow's Second Army coming out of the east. The striking fact here is that Lanrezac, at the far left end of the French line, had met not the end of the German right wing under Kluck but the army on Kluck's left. Important as Lanrezac's move to the north was, it had not reached far enough to intercept the outer edge of the German right. All five French armies were now locked in combat, but this was true of only six of Germany's. Kluck's army was out somewhere to the north and west, beyond Lanrezac's reach and meeting no serious resistance as it plowed its way forward.

By this point all of Joffre's offensives had been beaten back, several of them ending in severe disorder. French casualties for the war's first month are believed to have totaled two hundred sixty thousand, of whom seventy-five thousand were killed (twenty-seven thousand on August 22 alone).* Among the dead were more than ten percent of France's regular and reserve officers. The cult of the offensive was not delivering its promised results. As a young French captain named Charles De Gaulle would say of the fight in which he was wounded and had his eyes opened, "In a moment it is clear that all the courage in the world cannot prevail against gunfire."

The Germans, except on their right where continued movement was essential, tended to rely on their artillery and let the French attack first. In this way they held their own at worst and took significantly fewer casualties overall: eighteen thousand of their troops were killed on the Western Front in August, a fraction of the French and British total.

And Kluck, with Bülow keeping pace on his left and the German line unbroken all the way to Switzerland, was pounding to the southwest on schedule. The Schlieffen Plan was being achieved. It was actually happening.

---

*Historians of a statistical bent have been moving the Great War's casualty figures upward and downward for generations. In many cases definitive information is not available. France never specified its losses for August 1914; the records of Austria-Hungary, Russia, and Turkey are often disorderly or worse; some archives are lost, and those that survive sometimes conflict. Anything approaching exactness, especially for whole nations and whole years, is in many cases forever unattainable.

The stage was set for Kluck to swing around Lanrezac and continue on to Paris.

Or so it seemed until Sunday, August 23. Then, suddenly, Kluck crashed into a mass of dug-in riflemen freshly arrived from England. It must have been a shock. Kluck hadn't known that British troops were in the neighborhood. He hadn't even known, until the day before, that they were in France in sufficient numbers to take the field.

LONDON IN 1914

FOR ALEXANDER VON KLUCK, THE UNEXPECTED COLLI-sion with British troops on August 23 was not a great deal more than a serious inconvenience. The men of the British Expeditionary Force were some of the world's best soldiers, hardened in their empire's colonial wars, but there were simply not enough of them to stop the avalanchelike advance of Kluck's First Army.

For the French, politicians and generals alike, the very fact that Britain was in the war was a dream come true, something toward which they had been bending national policy for years. It meant that, if the war turned out to be a long one, they would have on their side the richest nation in Europe and the world's greatest navy.

For the British themselves, both those in favor of war and those opposed, the whole thing must have seemed strangely improbable. Nothing had been less inevitable, as Berlin and Paris and St. Petersburg and Vienna stumbled toward catastrophe in July 1914, than that London would be drawn in as well.

Though Sir Edward Grey's foreign office had involved itself in the crisis from the start, its efforts had been directed at preserving the peace. To that end it had maintained a posture of almost excessive impartiality, doing nothing to inflame public opinion. The attention of the public, and of most of the government in London, had been focused meanwhile on a crisis closer to home—one that involved Ireland, the nearest and most troublesome part of the British Empire.

Legally, officially, Ireland was no longer a British possession at all, no longer a colony but rather as integral a part of the United Kingdom as Scotland and Wales. Its elected representatives sat in Parliament. They were numerous enough not only to influence policy but, when the House of Commons was narrowly divided, to cause governments to rise and fall. For the mainly Catholic nationalists of Ireland, such power was not nearly enough. They argued, and not implausibly, that in reality their homeland was still what it had been for centuries: conquered and oppressed. They wanted their own parliament and government—Home Rule. But for the Ulstermen of northern Ireland, descendants of the Protestants transplanted from Scotland by Oliver Cromwell two and a half centuries earlier when to be a Catholic was a crime, Home Rule meant subjection to the pope in Rome. They—the Unionists—were prepared to fight Home Rule to the death.

By the summer of 1914 the Liberal Party had been in power in London for more than eight years. Its popularity had, inevitably, been worn down by year after year of struggle and crisis and controversy, by the things it had done as well as by those it had failed to do. It was, compared with its Conservative or Tory rivals, a reformist government, the champion of such things as national health insurance and a government system of old age pensions. Governments in Britain fall and are replaced when they can no longer command a majority of the votes in Commons, and by 1914 the Liberals were dependent for their majority on a bloc of thirty Irish nationalists.

The price for this support was Home Rule, and the nationalists, aware of how essential they had become to the government, were demanding to be paid now. Prime Minister Herbert Henry Asquith and his cabinet knew that they had to deliver or be replaced. Thus they were moving a Home Rule bill through Parliament. This bill was passionately opposed by the Conservatives, who were passionately supported by the Unionists. Compromise seemed impossible, so that the struggle became increasingly dangerous. Weapons were being smuggled into northern Ireland, where the Unionists were organizing a hundred thousand Ulstermen into militias with the threat that they would rise in armed rebellion rather than become an impotent minority in an autonomous Ireland.

Tensions rose as the Home Rule bill moved toward passage, and the

Prime Minister
Herbert Henry Asquith
"How one loathes such levity."

dangers of the situation were multiplied by the fact that much of the army's leadership was Anglo-Irish, Unionist, and implacably opposed to the Asquith government. As it became clear that implementation of Home Rule was likely to require military suppression of a Unionist rebellion, the crisis began to boil over. In the spring the war office had announced that no British officers whose family homes were in Ireland would be required to participate in putting down a Protestant rebellion. All others would be expected to follow whatever orders they were given. Any who found this policy unacceptable were to state their objections and expect to be discharged.

This sparked what was called the Curragh Mutiny. A number of the army's senior officers openly declared that they supported the Unionists, that the Unionists' only crime was their loyalty to the United Kingdom, and that portraying the Unionists as disloyal was an outrage. Fifty-seven of the seventy officers of a cavalry brigade based at Curragh in Ireland, their commanding general among them, announced that they would prefer dismissal to waging war against Ulster.

Things rapidly went from bad to worse. The secretary of state for war attempted to defuse the situation by offering assurances that there would be no armed suppression of the Protestants. When the prime minister repudiated these assurances, Field Marshal Sir John French resigned as chief of the imperial general staff. Other senior officers resigned also. The king found it necessary to intervene, and leaders on both sides began to step back gingerly from the edge of chaos. By the end of May it was widely accepted that, in spite of the objections of the nationalists, Ireland was going to have to be partitioned. Some part of the North would be retained as part of the U.K. This situation continued to absorb the government in the weeks following the assassination of Franz Ferdinand. The day when Vienna delivered its ultimatum to Serbia was also the day when a Buckingham Palace conference on how to partition Ireland—a conference called by King George himself—ended in failure. On Sunday, July 26, six days before the French and Germans mobilized, British troops fired on a crowd of demonstrators in Dublin. Civil war seemed imminent.

Meanwhile, and with the public barely noticing, Britain was slowly being drawn into the European crisis. London had long based its foreign policy on maintenance of a balance of power on the continent, its aim being to ensure that no country or alliance could become dominant enough to threaten British security. Throughout all the generations when France was the most powerful nation in Europe, it was also, almost automatically, Britain's enemy. After the fall of Napoleon, when Russia rose for a time to preeminence, relations between it and Britain became so badly strained that in the 1850s the two went to war against each other in the Crimea—with France now on Britain's side. Prussia had often been England's ally, but after 1870 the emergence of the German Empire and the corresponding decline of France changed that too. Suddenly the Germans, who for centuries had been too fragmented and backward to threaten anyone, appeared to have become the leading threat to an evenly divided and therefore (from the British perspective) safe Europe. London's concerns were intensified when Kaiser Wilhelm II made it his goal to build a High Seas Fleet big and modern enough to challenge the Royal Navy. This more than any other factor implanted in many British minds the belief that the next war was likely to be with Germany, and that, in order to keep the Germans from ruling Europe, it was going to be necessary to keep them from overwhelming France.

This kind of thinking was conspicuous at the headquarters of the British army, especially among those Unionist officers who thought (rightly, as it turned out) that British involvement in a European war would mean the death of the Home Rule bill. For years before 1914 British general staff planners had been meeting secretly with their French counterparts to plan a joint war against Germany. (Asquith, it might be noted, got little thanks for allowing these talks.) The chief military liaison to Paris, General Sir Henry Wilson, was an almost violently passionate Unionist. He was heard to say that his loyalty to Ulster transcended his loyalty to Britain. His contempt for Asquith, whom he called "Squiff" in his diary, and for Asquith's "filthy cabinet," was only a somewhat extreme example of the prevailing army attitude.

Wilson's talks with the French led gradually to the development of detailed plans for the movement of a British Expeditionary Force to France in the event of war. Only the "imperialist" minority in the Asquith cabinet was allowed to know the details of this planning, however. When other members asked for information, Grey would assure them that they need not be concerned, that nothing had been done to commit Britain. The skeptical majority was not reassured when, early in the summer, it was revealed (in German newspapers) that British military and naval authorities were now also engaged in secret talks with Russia. Grey publicly denied that any such talks had taken place, but he was lying. Here as in the July crisis that followed the assassination of Franz Ferdinand, his position was excruciatingly difficult. He had agreed to talks with the Russians only out of fear that without evidence of British interest—of *possible* British support in case of war—the Russians might abandon their Entente with France. Some influential Russians thought it absurd that the Romanov regime should be allied with republican France. Nor, such men thought, did it make sense for Russia to be allied with Britain, which to protect its overseas interests had consistently blocked Russian expansion to the south. More than a few British, by the same token, were scornful of a possible alliance with the autocratic, repressive court of St. Petersburg. An agreement worked out with Russia in 1907 was basically, as London saw it, a way of relieving pressure on an empire that had grown too big for even the Royal Navy to defend. It was a quid pro quo affair: a willingness to be friendly toward Russia on the continent of Europe in return for Russia's willingness not to threaten India, Britain's portion of Persia (Iran to us), or Afghanistan.

Only gradually was the attention of Asquith's government drawn from the Irish problem to the worsening crisis in Europe. The cabinet was divided, with a solid majority opposed to involvement in a war that now seemed increasingly likely. The men who made up this majority had varied motives. Some believed that Britain should be allied with Germany, not France or Russia, and that the anti-German bias of the imperialists was irrational and sure to lead to trouble. Some warned that, instead of ensuring a balance of power, the defeat of Germany would make tsarist Russia dominant in Europe—an unappealing prospect to say the least. Some were simply convinced that there was no justification for going to war, that saving France was not Britain's business, and that the human and material costs would far outweigh any possible gain.

A cabinet meeting on Saturday, July 25, showed plainly that the antiwar majority would resign rather than approve any declaration of war. Such resignations would mean the end of the Asquith government, its near-certain replacement by a Conservative government under the dour Unionist Andrew Bonar Law, and the undoing of everything the Liberals had achieved or expected to achieve in Ireland and at home. It would also mean war, because the Conservatives wanted war, and not incidentally it would mean the loss of every cabinet member's job. Not even the most vociferous members of the majority were eager to bring the government down.

It would be unfair to say that the cabinet's imperialist minority actively wanted war. Such an accusation might have some plausibility if directed at the flamboyantly adventurous young Winston Churchill, who as First Lord of the Admiralty had responsibility for the Royal Navy and admitted to being thrilled by the prospect of a fight. Asquith and Grey were more sober in their views. Both agreed that war, if it came, was likely to be a disaster for winners and losers alike, though they remained convinced that allowing Germany to crush France would be an even more terrible disaster. Russia mattered only as one of the means by which France could be saved. If a successful war increased Russia's size and power, that would be regrettable.

The problem of finding a way through all these complexities fell most heavily on the thin shoulders of Sir Edward Grey, and it presented him with two distinct dilemmas. The first was an immediate one: he had to try to use the influence of the British Empire to avert war while not saying or doing more than the cabinet's majority would tolerate and thereby triggering resignations. In this he failed, though his failure was not his fault. The divisions of the cabinet made it impossible for him to intervene in ways that might have made a difference. Grey's other dilemma had to do with persuading both the cabinet and the House of Commons—it too was mainly against war as August came to an end—to agree to intervention *if* the continental powers went to war. In this he was ultimately successful, but his success like his failure rose out of factors beyond his control. It was made possible by an issue that emerged abruptly, as if out of nowhere (actually it was Kaiser Wilhelm who brought it to light), and ultimately swept the opposition aside.

Grey, fifty-two years old in 1914, was the very model of what an Englishman was supposed to be at the zenith of the British Empire. Quiet and refined, intelligent and aristocratic and splendidly well educated, he had the requisite country estate to which he loved to retreat on weekends. He also had the requisite firm belief that Britain was at least one large

British Foreign Secretary
Sir Edward Grey
*"The lamps are going out
all over Europe. We shall not
see them lit again
in our lifetime."*

notch above the Europeans in the realm of morals and ethics, and that in serving the interests of the empire he was serving civilization. He was a lonely man—his wife had been killed when her pony cart overturned on a country lane in 1906, three years before he took charge of the foreign office—whose life was dominated by work. Work was becoming difficult for him because his eyesight was failing.

Prime Minister Asquith was more than content to leave the hard work of diplomacy in Grey's hands. A cautious, cunning lawyer of middle-class origins, Asquith was sixty-one in 1914. He had been in Parliament for three decades and had survived at the head of the Liberal government through six eventful years. Though he was not without principles, he appears to have been dedicated above all other things to staying in power without exerting himself overmuch—without having to give up the pleasures of society, his nightly game of bridge, or the pursuit of desirable women. Staying in power meant holding together his increasingly fragile Liberal majority, a combustible coalition that ranged from the Irish nationalists to the fiery Welsh reformer David Lloyd George, from near-pacifists to the bellicose Churchill. Accomplishing this in July 1914 required skills of the highest order.

From Saturday July 25 on, the cabinet met almost daily, and it remained clear that any attempt to bring a majority around to the support of France could lead to nothing but the end of the government. Asquith and Grey could do little more than hang on and wait. By Monday it was obvious that Grey's proposal for referring the Austro-Serbian dispute to a conference of Britain, France, Germany, and Italy was not going to work. The proposal itself had been naïve, doomed by the fact that the London Conference of 1913 had settled the Second Balkan War in a way that Austria-Hungary and Germany found thoroughly unsatisfactory. By using the London Conference to their own advantage, the other powers had destroyed the potential of conferences generally.

On Wednesday members of the cabinet's majority suggested a resolution by which Britain would declare itself to be unconditionally neutral in case of war. Grey told his fellow ministers that he was not the man to implement such a resolution, and that if it were approved he would resign. When Asquith supported him, the majority drew back. Everything remained unresolved. The pressure on the government—on Grey in particular—was intense and coming from many directions. General Wilson, the Asquith-hating director of military operations, was demanding that the army be mobilized. The French were doing everything possible to persuade the British to support them, while German ambassador Lichnowsky was virtually begging Grey to remain neutral and trying to persuade him that

Germany neither wanted war nor had hostile intentions where British interests were concerned. The position that Grey and Asquith had taken with the cabinet might have had a powerful impact if the Germans had learned of it, but it remained secret.

General Wilson began insisting with almost hysterical fervor that the government had a moral obligation to stand with France—that the years of military consultation justified the French in expecting nothing less. He pointed out that France had demonstrated its trust in Britain by agreeing to move its navy to the Mediterranean, leaving the defense of northern waters to the Royal Navy. The antiwar ministers, annoyed, replied that over the years they had repeatedly expressed concern that joint military planning would draw Britain into commitments to France, and that they had been assured that such concerns were unfounded.

Thursday was the day when Tsar Nicholas consented to mobilization. Grey, to his credit, had been urging the Russians to delay, but he and his ambassador in St. Petersburg had less influence there than France's Ambassador Paléologue, who from the start had been urging action. This was also the day when French President Poincaré sent word to Grey that he believed Britain could stop the slide to war if it warned Berlin that it was prepared to support France. Grey, clinging to his pose of impartiality, responded in almost the feeblest way imaginable, saying only that he doubted Britain's ability to make that big a difference. Privately, he now took a step for which he did not have cabinet approval. He told Lichnowsky, whom he knew to regard the prospect of a war between their two countries with horror, that in his opinion a German war with France would mean war with Britain as well.

By Friday, with everyone's options narrowing and the cabinet's majority still against war, Grey pressed upon Lichnowsky his Stop-in-Belgrade idea. When Vienna rejected the proposal despite Kaiser Wilhelm's endorsement, that option too was at an end. It was then that the kaiser, desperate for a way out, instructed Lichnowsky to promise Grey that if Britain would remain neutral, Germany would pledge itself to restore the borders of France and Belgium if war came and Germany won.

Belgium: Germany's raising of this subject introduced an explosive new element into the drama. Even the antiwar ministers saw immediately that this was a momentous question. The cabinet authorized Grey to ask France and Germany for an explicit guarantee of Belgium's neutrality and autonomy. The inability of the Germans to respond said everything.

And so, in a matter of hours, the question of British intervention was cast in an entirely new context. The issue was no longer whether Britain should go to war in support of France and Russia—of whether the British public could possibly be brought to support such a war. Now it was a question of whether Britain would compromise its own interests by allowing a small but strategically important neutral nation, a nation whose neutrality Britain had pledged to uphold, to be invaded. This was something that the public would have no difficulty understanding.

On the last weekend of peace, the weekend when Germany and France both mobilized, the cabinet remained divided with eight members favoring war if Germany invaded Belgium and eleven opposed. Churchill, Grey, and the prime minister were in favor. The most prominent figure on the other side—but careful not to allow himself to be positioned as the leader of the antiwar group, which would destroy his freedom to maneuver—was the chancellor of the exchequer, David Lloyd George. Though the opponents of intervention had maintained their majority, several were no longer firm. Asquith and Grey had deftly softened the ground on which their opponents stood by misleading them into thinking—by allowing them to hope, at a minimum—that Britain's role in the coming war would be a strictly naval one and therefore relatively low in risk and cost. The situation was moving away from the antiwar faction, and few still believed that resignations could make a difference.

Some of the most senior members of the antiwar faction saw the whole matter as a kind of bait-and-switch ruse. Lord John Morley, an aging bulwark of the Liberal Party and one of the small number of cabinet members who in the end did resign rather than assent to war, said "the precipitate and peremptory blaze about Belgium was due less to indignation at the violation of a Treaty than to natural perception of the plea that it would furnish for intervention on behalf of France, for expeditionary force, and all the rest of it." This resentful view would be supported years later by the woman who served as Lloyd George's private secretary (and mistress) in 1914, saw him swing around to support a declaration of war early in August, and later became his wife. "My own opinion," wrote Frances Stevenson Lloyd George more than forty years later, "is that L.G.'s mind was really made up from the first, that he knew we would have to go in, and that the invasion of Belgium was, to be cynical, a heaven-sent excuse for supporting a declaration of war."

On Sunday, August 2, things still hung in the balance. "I suppose," Asquith wrote that day to the young woman with whom he was conducting his own romantic intrigue, "that a good three-fourths of our own party in the House of Commons are for absolute non-interference at any price." But as he wrote, the Germans were moving their army into Luxembourg and launching small raids into France. In the evening Berlin sent its ultimatum to Belgium, lamely stating that it had to invade Belgium before

France could do so and demanding unobstructed passage for its troops. The French meanwhile were still holding their forces back from the borders, doing everything possible to make certain that Britain and the world would see the Germans as the aggressors.

Early on Monday King Albert of Belgium issued his refusal of Germany's demands. Later in the day Germany declared war on France. Grey, the eyes of Europe on him, addressed the House of Commons. He spoke for an hour, putting all of his emphasis on the government's efforts to keep the war from happening, on the threat that a violation of Belgium would be to Britain itself, and on his conviction that Britain must respond or surrender its honor. He kept his arguments on a high moral plane, artfully avoiding less lofty subjects such as the continental balance of power.

Not everyone was persuaded. "The Liberals, very few of them, cheered at all," one member of the House noted. But the Conservatives "shouted with delight." In any case a majority of the Commons was won over, and so was the public. The sole remaining questions were whether the Germans were going to pass through only a small corner of Belgium or move into its heartland, and whether the Belgians were going to resist. (The Germans, in demanding free passage through Belgium, had promised to pay for all damage done by their army.)

Tuesday brought the answers. Masses of German troops began crossing the border into Belgium and moved on Liège. King Albert made it clear that he and his countrymen intended to fight.

It was done. Before midnight Britain and Germany were at war. Some members of the cabinet resigned, but only a few, and they knew that no one cared. The pretense that only the Royal Navy would be involved was quickly forgotten. The British army prepared to fight in western Europe for the first time in exactly one hundred years.

Lloyd George, having maneuvered in such a way as to keep his position in the government without seeming to compromise the principles that had long since made him a prominent anti-imperialist, found himself cheered on August 3 as he rode through London. "This is not my crowd," he said to his companions. "I never want to be cheered by a war crowd."

"It is curious," wrote Asquith, "how, going to and from the House, we are now always surrounded and escorted by cheering crowds of loafers and holiday makers. I have never before been a popular character with 'the man in the street,' and in all this dark and dangerous business it gives me scant pleasure. How one loathes such levity."

Chapter 9

✠

A Perfect Balance

"The most terrible August in the history of the world."
—Sir Arthur Conan Doyle

T he commander of the British Expeditionary Force, Sir John French, had arrived in France with little knowledge of where the Germans were or what they were doing or even what he was supposed to do when he found them.

French—the same Sir John French who had resigned as chief of the imperial general staff at the time of the Curragh Mutiny—carried with him written instructions from the new secretary of state for war, the formidable Field Marshal Earl Kitchener of Khartoum. These instructions were not, however, what a man in his position might have expected. They did not urge him to pursue and engage the invading Germans with all possible vigor, to remember that England expected victory, or even to support his French allies to the fullest possible extent in their hour of desperate need.

In fact, he found himself under orders to do very nearly the opposite of these things. He was to remember that his little command—a mere five divisions, four of infantry and one of cavalry—included most of Britain's regular army and could not be spared.

"It will be obvious that the greatest care must be exercised towards a minimum of loss and wastage," Kitchener had written. "I wish you to distinctly understand that your force is an entirely independent one and you will in no case come under the orders of any Allied general." In other words, French was not to risk his army and was not to regard himself as subordinate to Joffre or Lanrezac or any other French general. In taking this approach, Kitchener created an abundance of problems.

Certainly the BEF, compared with the vast forces that France and Germany had already sent to the Western Front, seemed so small as to risk being trampled. Kaiser Wilhelm, drawing upon his deep reserves of foolishness in exhorting his troops to victory, had called it Britain's "contemptibly little army." But man for man the BEF was as good as any fighting force in the world: well trained and disciplined, accustomed to being sent out to the far corners of the world whenever the empire's great navy was not enough. The BEF was also an appealingly human, high-spirited army. Even the rank and file were career soldiers for the most part, volunteers drawn mainly from Britain's urban poor and working classes, more loyal to their regiments and to one another than to any sentimental notions of imperial glory, and ready to make a joke of anything. When they learned what the kaiser had said about them, they began to call themselves "the Old Contemptibles." When the first shiploads of them crossed from Southampton to Le Havre, they found the harbor jammed with crowds who burst into the French national anthem, "La Marseillaise." The thousands of British troops—Tommies, they were called at home—responded by bursting spontaneously not into "God Save the King" but into one of the indelicate music hall songs with which they entertained themselves while on the march. The French watched and listened reverently, some with their hands on their hearts, not understanding a word and thinking that this must be the anthem of the United Kingdom.

The BEF moved first to an assembly point just south of Belgium, and on August 20 began moving north to link up with Lanrezac's Fifth Army and extend the French left wing. They were still en route when, on August 21, the units that Lanrezac had positioned near Charleroi on the River Sambre were struck by Bülow's German Second Army. Sir John French, when he learned of this encounter, ordered his First Corps (two divisions commanded by Sir Horace Smith-Dorrien) to move up toward the town of Mons, about eight miles west of Charleroi. From there, it was to cover Lanrezac's flank.

On the next day, with the Germans and French alternately attacking each other on the Sambre (Ludendorff, who happened to be in the area as a member of Bülow's staff, organized the seizure of the bridges across the river), a scouting party of British cavalry encountered German cavalry coming out of the north. The Germans withdrew. The British, savvy veterans that they were, dismounted and began using their trenching tools to throw up earthwork defenses while Smith-Dorrien's infantry came up from behind and joined them. They didn't know what to expect when the sun rose, but they intended to be as ready as it was possible for men armed with little more than rifles to be.

Ahead of them in the darkness was the entire German First Army. Its commander, Kluck (it was a gift to the amateur songwriters of the BEF that his name rhymed with their favorite word), knew nothing except that his scouts had run into armed horsemen, and that they claimed those horsemen were British. It did not sound serious; Kluck's intelligence indicated that the main British force was either not yet in France or, at worst, still a good many miles away. There seemed no need to mount an immediate attack.

Kluck at this point was an angry, frustrated man who didn't want to be where he was and in fact shouldn't have been there. He had recently been put under the orders of the more cautious Bülow, whose army was on his left. The Germans, like the French, were still in the early stages of learning to manage warfare on this scale, and they had not yet seen the value of creating a new level of command to direct forces as large as their right wing. Neither side had yet seen that when two or three armies are operating together and need to be coordinated, the answer is not to put the leader of one of those armies in charge of the others. It is almost inevitable, human nature being what it is, that a commander made first among equals in this way will give too much weight to the objectives and needs of his own army.

This is exactly what happened between the rough-hewn Kluck and the careful, highborn Bülow. Kluck had wanted to swing wide to the right, well clear of the French. Bülow insisted that he stay close, so that their two armies—plus Max von Hausen's Third Army on his left—would be able to deal with Lanrezac together. Kluck protested, but to no effect. Bülow was a solid

General Alexander von Kluck
Commander,
German First Army
*An angry, frustrated man—
and eager for a fight.*

General Otto von Bülow
Commander, German Second Army
Favored direct attack rather than encirclement.

professional who had long held senior positions in the German army, and a decade earlier he had been a leading candidate to succeed Schlieffen as head of the general staff, losing out to Moltke largely because he favored a direct attack on the French in case of war, rather than envelopment. His approach in August 1914 was conventional military practice; if his army locked head to head with Lanrezac's, Kluck and Hausen would be able to protect his flanks and then try to work around Lanrezac's flanks and surround him. But Bülow's orthodoxy (obviously the war would have opened in an entirely different way if he rather than Moltke had been in charge of planning since 1905) cost the Germans a huge opportunity. Left free to go where he wished, Kluck would have looped around not only the French but also the forward elements of the BEF. He then could have taken Smith-Dorrien's corps in the flank, broken it up, and pushed its disordered fragments into Lanrezac's flank. The possible consequences were incalculable; the destruction of Lanrezac's army—of any of the armies in the long French line—could have led to a quick end to the war in the west. Continuing to protest, appealing to Moltke but finding no support there, Kluck had no choice but to follow orders. Doing so caused him to run directly into the head of the British forces, engage them where they were strongest instead of weakest, and give them a night to consolidate their defenses because he didn't know he was faced with anything more dangerous than a roving cavalry detachment.

On the morning of August 23 (a day marked by Japan's declaration of war on Germany), Kluck ordered an artillery bombardment of the enemy positions in his path. When this ended at nine-thirty, thinking that the defenders must now be in disarray, his troops attacked—and were quickly shot to pieces in a field of fire so devastating that many of them thought they must be facing an army of machine guns. They attacked repeatedly and were cut down every time. What they were up against was the fruit of years of emphasis on what the British still called musketry. Every private in the BEF carried a .303 Lee Enfield rifle fitted with easily changed ten-round magazines and had been trained to hit a target fifteen times a minute at a range of three hundred yards. Most could do better than that. Every soldier was routinely given all the ammunition he wanted for practice, and high scores were rewarded with cash. These practices had been put in place after the South African War at the turn of the century, when the Tommies had found themselves outgunned by Boer farmers fighting as guerrillas, and this was the payoff.

But as the day wore on, hour by hour and yard by bloody yard, the persistence of the Germans and the sheer weight of their numbers forced the British back. When the day ended, more than sixteen hundred of Smith-Dorrien's men had been killed, and the Germans had lost at least five thousand. Kluck and his army had been stopped for a full day. In itself, one day meant little. But if the Germans could be stopped for another day and another after that, Moltke's entire campaign would begin to fall to pieces.

After sundown, the BEF's Second Corps under Sir Douglas Haig having come forward to join Smith-Dorrien's, the British again went to work on their defenses. But during the night an English liaison officer arrived at French's headquarters with stunning news: Lanrezac, rather than holding his ground at Charleroi, was pulling back. This exposed the British right and gave them no choice but to pull back as well. French reacted bitterly. He regarded Lanrezac's withdrawal—which probably saved his army and was conducted with great skill under difficult circumstances—as unnecessary. He had entered the war with a very British disdain for the French. That disdain now began to turn into entirely unjustified contempt.

There arose in the aftermath of this battle the strangest and most beautiful legend of the war. It was said that, when the British peril was at its height, a majestic figure had appeared high in the sky with arm upraised. Some said it had been pointing to victory, others that it held back the Germans as the

Tommies got away. It came to be known as the Angel of Mons. Even more colorful was the simultaneous legend of the Archers of Agincourt. In the late Middle Ages at Agincourt—not a great distance from Mons—English yeomen armed with longbows had won a great victory over a much bigger force of mounted and armored French knights. Four hundred and ninety-nine years later there were stories of German soldiers found dead at Mons with arrows through their bodies.

It was all nonsense. The disappointing truth, established beyond doubt by postwar investigations, is that the legends were journalistic inventions, and that they first emerged long after the battle. No one ever found a witness who had personally seen an angel, arrows, or anything of the kind.

When the Germans resumed their attack on the morning of August 24, braced this time for tough resistance, they found nothing in front of them but abandoned entrenchments. They got back on the road, caught up with the BEF after two days of hard pursuit, and on August 26 hit Smith-Dorrien's corps at Le Cateau. Under severe pressure, his men exhausted, Smith-Dorrien found it impossible to disengage and resume his retreat when ordered to do so by French. He was the proverbial man with a wolf by the ears, unable to take the initiative and unable to escape. He organized a rear guard that managed by the narrowest of margins to fight off envelopment. Le Cateau turned into a bigger, bloodier fight than the one at Mons, with fifty-five thousand British desperately holding off one hundred and forty thousand Germans. Ultimately, when the Germans found it necessary to pull back and regroup, the British were able to resume their retreat. They had taken some eight thousand casualties (more than Wellington's at Waterloo) and lost thirty-six pieces of artillery. And already-strained relationships within the BEF command were worsened. French, who had disliked Smith-Dorrien for years and had not wanted him in his command, refused to believe that he had not been willfully disobedient. Smith-Dorrien, for his part, thought that Haig had been too slow in entering the fights both at Mons and at Le Cateau. It is a mark of how desperate the British were for something to feed into their propaganda machine that Le Cateau was celebrated, at the time and long afterward, as a British triumph. The only thing to celebrate was that the BEF was still intact when it made its escape.

Elsewhere along the Western Front the Germans were scoring victory after victory. They were turning back French assaults, achieving a high rate of success with their own offensives, and usually losing far fewer men. The reason is not to be found in numbers; as we have seen, the two sides were numerically just about equal. Even the German right wing had no consistent manpower advantage. A French counterattack that marked the climax of the Charleroi fight, for example, ended with three German divisions not only stopping nine of Lanrezac's divisions but ultimately driving them back seven miles—even though the French force included ten regiments of elite colonial troops, veterans akin to the men of the BEF. Clearly the Germans were doing something right, or the French were doing something wrong, or both.

The answer is "both." In the face of repeated bad results, generals throughout the French army threw their infantry against the Germans whatever the circumstances and kept doing so no matter how grisly the results. Lanrezac was a rare exception; he had been reluctant to attack at Charleroi, doing so only because two of his corps commanders insisted. Joffre's other commanders believed that French troops were supposed to charge, not crawl in the earth like worms. They were to win at the point of their bayonets, not by firing steel-clad packets of high explosives into the sky. The Germans, by contrast, quickly became adroit, upon making contact with the enemy, at digging in, waiting to be attacked, and mowing down the attackers with rifle fire, machine guns capable of firing up to six hundred heavy-caliber rounds per minute, and above all artillery. (From the start of the war to the end, cannon would account for most of the killing.) When the attackers fell back, the Germans would continue punishing them with their field artillery, firing shrapnel and high explosives. Then they would come out of their holes and keep the fleeing enemy on the move. From the start they were even better than the British at creating defenses for themselves with the trenching tools every man carried plus picks and shovels brought forward by combat engineers. The difference in the tactics of the two sides explains why, despite the lives they squandered at Mons and Le Cateau and later in other, bigger fights, the Germans had significantly lower casualties on the Western Front in 1914 than the French and British.

But as French casualties climbed without producing a single victory of consequence—it was "the most terrible August in the history of the world," said British author Sir Arthur Conan Doyle—Joffre found it necessary to conclude that the French army's "cult of the offensive" had to be abandoned. On August 24 he unhappily announced that the armies of France were for the time being "forced to take defensive action based on our fortified positions and on the strong natural obstacles provided by the terrain, so as to hold on as long as possible, taking, meanwhile, all steps to wear down the enemy's strength and resume the offensive in due course." He ordered his left wing—his Third, Fourth, and Fifth Armies—to begin what would come to be known as the Great Retreat. Day after day, in relentless heat, weary French soldiers in their hundreds of thousands trudged farther and farther south. The BEF marched with them, covering more than a hundred and ninety miles in thirteen days. One of its battalions retreated fifty-five miles in thirty-six hours.

Joffre also ordered the creation of a new army to lengthen his left. This

Sixth Army was to be "capable of taking up the offensive again while the other armies contained the enemy's effort for the requisite period," Joffre said, but its position near Paris obviously had defensive implications. The Germans' continued pursuit of Lanrezac's army after the defeat at Le Cateau had awakened the government to the fact that Paris was in jeopardy. Minister of War Adolphe Messimy examined the city's defenses and was alarmed by what he found. They were in a sorry state of neglect, at least in part because the army's fixation on the offensive had caused it to give little attention to defenses of any kind.

Messimy turned not to Joffre but to General Joseph Gallieni for help, asking him to become military governor of Paris and offering him near-dictatorial powers to organize a defense of the city. Gallieni, who had been in semiretirement at the start of the war, agreed on one condition. He said he would need not only the garrison forces inside the city walls but a substantial mobile force capable of engaging the Germans as they approached. At least six corps would be needed for this purpose, he said. (A corps was usually made up of two, sometimes three divisions of nearly twenty thousand men each.) Messimy agreed without hesitation, but in fact he had no authority to fulfill his pledge. It was Joffre alone who decided the deployment of troops, and Joffre showed no interest in assisting, or even consulting with, either Gallieni or the government.

Nevertheless, Gallieni set to work immediately to ready Paris for a siege, bringing herds of livestock inside the walls to provide a supply of food, installing new lines of trenches, positioning artillery, and demolishing buildings to give the guns a clear line of fire. As this work proceeded, a political crisis erupted over the city's failure to start preparing earlier, the government fell, and Messimy was displaced (in part, ironically, for refusing to agree to the dismissal of Joffre). He took up his reserve army commission and went off to the front as a major. When Gallieni finally got his mobile force, it came to him in the form of Joffre's new Sixth Army, which was still in the early stages of being assembled. The first elements of this army, many of them brought in by train from stabilizing sectors at the eastern end of the front, were moved inside the Paris defensive perimeter as part of the Great Retreat. They were completely out of touch with Lanrezac and the BEF and not nearly ready for action in any case. Joffre evidently decided that he might as well let Gallieni have them, if only temporarily and if only to quiet the complaints coming from the government.

Behind the retreating French armies, sometimes even beside them in the spreading confusion, marched masses of Germans, tired but energized by the thought that they had the enemy on the run, that victory lay ahead. Joffre's plan was to pull back only as far as a line along the east-west course of the River Somme, call a halt there and, when circumstances were right, counterattack. This plan proved infeasible; when the French got to the Somme, the enemy was still right behind them. They had no choice but to cross the river and keep going.

Nobody, not even the high generals in their headquarters, had a detailed understanding of what was happening along the front. British and French newspapers carried hair-raising but inspiring stories of how the Germans, the Huns, were committing mass suicide in throwing themselves against the guns and bayonets of the valiant defenders of civilization. In the German papers it was civilization's defenders who were advancing victoriously, moving constantly forward on the soil of a nation that had conspired to destroy their homeland. On both sides, anything that wasn't an outright defeat was made a cause for celebration, and every setback was either treated as a canny tactical adjustment or, more commonly, ignored. Journalists were kept far from the action. Even the senior commanders, flooded with reports some of which were accurate and many of which were not, could have little confidence that they knew what the enemy was doing or which side was doing more killing.

With the BEF and Lanrezac's army in almost headlong flight, it seemed to many on Moltke's staff that the Germans had already won in the west; "complete victories" were being declared. Belgium was firmly in hand, and the right wing was in France and staying on Schlieffen's schedule. The German Fourth and Fifth Armies had broken the back of the French offensive in the Ardennes, and in the southeast Crown Prince Rupprecht of Bavaria continued to report that he was gaining ground, taking thousands of prisoners and capturing guns. Rupprecht was also continuing to badger Moltke for more troops with which to press his advantage. Moltke agreed. He also decided to send three infantry corps and a cavalry division to East Prussia. These were fateful moves. Combined with Moltke's earlier adjustments—the use of two corps to besiege Antwerp, and of another to besiege a French stronghold at Maubeuge—they would reduce his right wing from seventeen corps to fewer than twelve. This was a reduction of two hundred and seventy-five thousand men, and it was in addition to the Germans' battlefield losses. The hammer upon which Schlieffen had wanted to bet everything thus shrank by nearly a third. Meanwhile Joffre was doing the opposite, using his rail lines to transfer increasing numbers of troops from his right to his left. Even as the Germans continued their advance, in terms of manpower the balance at the western end of the front was gradually shifting in France's favor.

Moltke's decision to dispatch troops to East Prussia has been much criticized but is easy to understand. He had good reason to be alarmed not only by the situation in East Prussia but by what was happening all across the eastern theater. He knew that the Austrian invasion of Serbia—an invasion he had opposed, arguing rightly that all of the Hapsburg empire's available troops were needed against Russia—had ended in total defeat. He knew too that massive Russian forces were engaging the Austrians on the Galician plain to the north of Serbia, and that if this too ended badly, Conrad's position would become desperate. And his own commander in East Prussia had told Moltke that the German position there was already desperate. That commander, the fat and elderly Max von Prittwitz, an intelligent enough general but one with no combat experience, had at his disposal a single army of some one hundred and thirty-five thousand men—eleven undermanned divisions of infantry and one of cavalry, barely one-tenth of Germany's available total. Moving against this Eighth Army, a small one by the standards of 1914, were two exceptionally large Russian armies that outnumbered it by a huge margin. The Russian First Army, commanded by General Pavel von Rennenkampf (German surnames were not uncommon in the Russian aristocracy and senior officer corps), had been first to cross the border into German territory, approaching from the east. Thereafter it had continued to move forward, capturing towns, burning the farms of the Junkers, and clashing with elements of Prittwitz's army first at Stallupönen and then at Gumbinnen. It was shortly after the Gumbinnen fight, and upon learning that the Russian Second Army under General Alexander Samsonov was entering East Prussia from the south with fourteen and a half infantry divisions, four divisions of cavalry, and 1,160 guns, that Prittwitz had telephoned Moltke and told him that he had to abandon East Prussia. He was afraid that if he stayed where he was, Samsonov would soon be behind him and able to block his escape. The situation was ripe for an encirclement that would end in the destruction of the Eighth Army and leave Germany defenseless in the East. There was no alternative to withdrawing behind the north-south Vistula River, Prittwitz said. Moltke did not demur. Giving up the Prussian homeland was an intolerable thought, but everything being accomplished in France would become meaningless if the Eighth Army were lost.

That Prussian homeland was already involved in the war more directly than any other part of Germany, with the invaders inevitably clashing with the inhabitants and outrages being committed on both sides. An Englishman, John Morse, was serving among the Russian troops, and he later wrote of the brutalities he witnessed. "The Cossack has a strong disinclination to be taken prisoner," he observed, "and I knew of several of them sacrificing their lives rather than fall into the hands of the Germans, who heartily detest these men, and usually murdered such as they succeeded in catching—and murdered them after preliminary tortures, according to reports which reached us. The country people certainly showed no mercy to stragglers falling into their hands. They usually pitch-forked them to death; and this lethal weapon was a favorite with the ladies on both sides of the border, many a fine Teuton meeting his end by thrusts from this implement."

Members of Moltke's staff began telephoning the commanders of the four corps that made up the Eighth Army. The technology of the day made this a laborious process, requiring much waiting for connections, much shouting into receivers, much uncertainty about what the faint and fuzzy voice on the other end of the line was saying. Moltke's men had one question: was a retreat really necessary? The answer was unanimously negative: the Eighth Army need not, must not, fall back. This was reported to Moltke, who concluded that Prittwitz had lost his nerve and could not be left in command.

Prittwitz himself, however, was having his mind changed too. This was accomplished by a new member of his staff, the tall, chubby, hard-drinking, and colorfully un-Prussian Lieutenant Colonel Max Hoffmann, who had been sent from Alsace to join the Eighth Army when mobilization was declared and now took the first of the steps by which he would establish himself as one of the war's master tacticians. Using a map and compass, Hoffmann showed Prittwitz that Samsonov's army was already closer to the Vistula River than the main German force, so that a clean escape was no longer possible. He outlined a plan aimed not only at making withdrawal unnecessary but at defeating both Russian armies. First the Germans would strike again at Rennenkampf, who was still at Gumbinnen, apparently regrouping after the clash there. Finishing off Rennenkampf, Hoffmann calculated, would take only a few days; at a minimum his army could be rendered incapable of pursuit. The Germans would then be free to deal with Samsonov.

His composure restored, Prittwitz agreed that there need be no retreat. He did not, however, accept Hoffmann's plan without amendment. He decided to go after Samsonov without first attacking Rennenkampf. Speed was essential—everything depended on wrecking one of the invading armies before the two of them could combine into a single force too big to be coped with. Expecting his troops to deal with two big armies in just a few days, Prittwitz wisely decided, would be asking too much.

But in the excited rush to prepare, Prittwitz made two mistakes. He neglected to tell Hoffmann or anyone else on his staff of his conversation with Moltke—his announcement of a retreat—and after changing his mind he failed to inform Moltke that he had done so. Moltke continued to believe that the Eighth Army was beginning to withdraw.

Fearful of the consequences if the Eighth Army did not stand and fight,

Moltke looked about for a solution. And he thought of Erich Ludendorff, who had been an important member of his planning staff until 1913 and was now the hero of Liège. "I know of no other man in whom I have such absolute trust," Moltke said. He sent orders for Ludendorff to join the Eighth Army not as commanding officer—he was too young for that, too junior in rank, and definitely too much the parvenu commoner—but as chief of staff.

On his way east Ludendorff stopped at Koblenz to confer with Moltke, and the two agreed that the situation in East Prussia was not yet hopeless. When Ludendorff suggested attacking the Russian armies one by one before they could combine, Moltke agreed. That Hoffmann and Ludendorff came up with exactly the same idea, and that they had no difficulty in winning over Prittwitz and Moltke, is not as astonishing as it may seem. The German general staff had given much thought to the defense of East Prussia, had anticipated the arrival of Russian forces from two directions, and had planned accordingly. Ludendorff and Hoffmann were simply drawing upon established doctrine in making their proposals, and in giving their assent Moltke and Prittwitz were simply endorsing that same doctrine.

Before departing Koblenz, Ludendorff was taken to see Kaiser Wilhelm, receiving from him the Pour le Mérite (Germany's highest military honor, higher than the Iron Cross, created and named by the Francophile Frederick the Great) and learning that a new commanding general of the Eighth Army had just been appointed. This was the sixty-seven-year-old Paul von Beneckendorff und von Hindenburg, who was being called out of retirement because of his reputation for steadiness and the fact that he, like Ludendorff, knew the complicated East Prussian terrain. Then Ludendorff was again on his way east, traveling in a special train, stopping along the way to pick up his wife so that she could join him for part of the trip. Hindenburg, dressed in the outdated uniform in which he had ended his long career two years earlier, came aboard at Hanover at four A.M. They talked briefly—Ludendorff outlined the plan he had discussed with Moltke—and retired for a few hours' sleep.

Upon their arrival in East Prussia the next morning, they had much to do. Hindenburg had to tell Prittwitz, who happened to be his wife's cousin, that he was being put on the army's inactive list effective immediately. Ludendorff meanwhile got a staff briefing. When Hoffmann outlined his plan and explained that it was already being put in motion, Ludendorff of course approved it without change. The two knew each other well—had even lived in the same quarters for four years earlier in their careers. Despite being very different kinds of men, they respected each other's abilities. From the start they were able to work together easily.

The situation was challenging in the extreme, requiring the Eighth Army to fight its own two-front war. Its complications began with the landscape of East Prussia, a region pocked with lakes and marshes and studded with woods and low hills, difficult for large armies to maneuver in, especially in the sectors nearest to Russia. Running north-south was a jumble of irregular-shaped bodies of water known as the Masurian Lakes. Rennenkampf's army was north of the lakes, Samsonov's south. They would have to move westward in order to unite. Between them were the Germans, already west of the lakes and in a position from which they could attack in either direction. They also had the advantage of knowing the terrain intimately—it was often the setting for their annual maneuvers. And they had installed the rail lines needed for the execution of their plans.

It was obvious that the Russians should converge without delay. If they did so, the Eighth Army was doomed. It was equally obvious that the Germans must proceed with extreme caution. If they attacked one of the Russian armies, they would have to leave enough troops behind to protect themselves from an advance by the other. It was far from clear that they had enough troops to do both things.

At this point—August 25, the same day on which the British fell back from Mons and Kluck resumed his march toward Paris—there occurred one of those small, strange events that sometimes alter the fates of nations. This one was weirdly like what had happened, in the American Civil War, the first time Robert E. Lee invaded the north: a copy of Lee's orders was found in a Maryland road wrapped around a packet of cigars. The discovery led directly to a stinging Confederate defeat and the end of Lee's offensive. The East Prussian counterpart to this incident was the discovery, on the body of a Russian officer killed in a skirmish, of the plans for both Russian armies. It seemed too good to be true, but the plans' authenticity was soon corroborated by uncoded Russian radio messages intercepted by the Germans.

The intelligence that the Germans now had in their hands indicated that Samsonov intended to continue moving westward, which would increase the distance between the two Russian armies unless Rennenkampf moved too. What the Germans didn't know was that Samsonov was being drawn forward by a glimpse that his troops had caught of the backward movement of a German infantry corps. This move had been nothing more than a minor tactical adjustment: the commander of the corps was shifting to a ridge stronger than his original position. But Samsonov leaped to the conclusion that the Germans were in retreat. He intended to press forward, keep the Germans moving, try to overrun them. A radio message sent from his headquarters, when intercepted, told the Germans exactly what direction he intended to take and what timetable he intended to follow. It stated also, not surprisingly, that he wanted Rennenkampf to come forward to join him.

Rennenkampf's messages indicated that he had other things in mind. He didn't know what had happened to the German force that had attacked him at Gumbinnen, and so, like Rennenkampf, he guessed. His guess was that the Germans had decided to withdraw to the north, toward or even into the coastal fortress of Königsberg ("kingstown," the principal city of East Prussia and the place where the rulers of Prussia had always been crowned). Focusing his attention in that direction, he could see no need to move toward Samsonov; he didn't suspect that the main German force might be between them. If he laid siege to Königsberg and bottled up the Eighth Army inside it, all the rest of East Prussia would be undefended. He was in no hurry, however, because there was no way of being sure how far the Germans had moved. He had no way of knowing (but might have guessed, the reasons being so obvious) that allowing himself to be trapped inside Königsberg was the one thing Moltke had ordered Prittwitz *not* to do.

For the Germans, the situation really did seem too good to be true. By continuing to move forward alone, Samsonov was practically inviting the Germans to lay a trap. By declining to come forward, Rennenkampf was making certain that his army would be unable to rescue Samsonov from that trap. Together they were eliminating the need for the Germans to proceed cautiously. They were freeing the Germans to throw everything into their attack on Samsonov.

Hoffmann had received the Russian messages after his initial meeting with Ludendorff, who had departed by car with Hindenburg. He showed them to the Eighth Army's quartermaster general, a Major General Grünert, offering them as confirmation that the entire Eighth Army could safely be sent against Samsonov. Grünert was skeptical; what seems too good to be true, after all, usually is. It seemed inconceivable to him that the Russian commanders would violate one of the fundamentals of military doctrine by keeping their forces divided in the presence of the enemy.

Max Hoffmann may have been the only man on earth who was junior to Grünert in rank and yet able to win him over at this critical juncture. Hoffmann was one of Germany's experts on the Russian army, and a decade earlier he had been sent as an observer to the Russo-Japanese War. There he had observed Samsonov and Rennenkampf in action. One of the war's minor legends is that, by an astonishing coincidence, Hoffmann had been present when the two Russian generals literally came to blows at a train station in Manchuria. Though it is now regarded as unlikely that anything of the kind actually happened, Hoffmann did know that Rennenkampf and Samsonov belonged to rival factions of the Russian general staff and disliked

General Pavel
von Rennenkampf
Commander,
Russian First Army
*Failed to respond
to Samsonov's
pleas for help.*

each other intensely. He was convinced that neither would exert himself to help the other. When he explained this history, Grünert was persuaded. The two got into a staff car and sped off, catching up with Hindenburg and Ludendorff and showing them the intercepted messages. All reservations about risking everything were immediately dissolved.

Risking everything meant exactly that: the Germans posted only a single division of cavalry opposite Rennenkampf's army. This was not a serious blocking force but merely a screen; its only function was to keep the Russians from seeing that nothing was behind it. All the rest of the Eighth Army was moved south and west into Samsonov's path. Many of the troops were sent by rail and thus were able to move a hundred miles overnight. Nine divisions were formed into an arc that was open to the southeast and sixty miles across. This arc was intentionally weak in the center but had two strong wings. The idea was for Samsonov, as he continued forward, to strike the center, find himself able to drive it backward, and thus be encouraged to keep moving. When he had gone far enough, the wings would move in on him from both sides.

The very fact that they had two armies inside East Prussia by this date was, for the Russians, a great achievement. The Germans had hoped that Russian mobilization would take six weeks, and they had not given sufficient weight to the fact that two-fifths of Russia's regular army was stationed in Poland when the war began and so was near East Prussia and nearly ready for action. The result had been Rennenkampf's arrival in East Prussia in just over two weeks, with Samsonov close behind. This much speed was also, however, an act of folly: the Russians had begun their advance without adequate provision for supplying their troops, for dealing with the wounded, or for communicating. (Hence the uncoded radio messages that proved such a boon to the Germans.) Some of their soldiers were without shoes, marching with their feet wrapped in rags. Some had no rifles. They were worn out long before making contact with the enemy. Rennenkampf's troops had been on the march for a week by the time they crossed into East Prussia, and their supply system was already failing badly.

These problems were the work of General Yakov Zhilinski, commander of the Russian North-West Front and therefore in charge of the two invading armies. Two years earlier, while serving as chief of the Russian general staff, Zhilinski had promised the French that he could have his forces in the field fifteen days after mobilization. Now he was keeping his promise. Far to the rear—his headquarters were more than one hundred and fifty miles from the showdown that was now taking place—he thought he was masterminding a historic victory.

On August 26, fearing a possible sudden forward lunge by Rennenkampf and unsettled by rumors of substantial Russian forces arriving from Rennenkampf's direction, a nervous Ludendorff tried to spring the trap on Samsonov. When he ordered an attack, however, the usually aggressive General Hermann von François (whose name derived from the fact that his ancestors had migrated to Prussia to escape France's persecution of Protestants in the seventeenth century) curtly refused. His troops were still detraining. They did not yet have their ammunition, their heavy artillery, or all of their field artillery. If they attacked, he said, they would have to do so with bayonets. When Ludendorff repeated his order, François went through the motions of complying but limited himself to occupying an uncontested ridge. In yet another of the odd and unintended twists in this oddest of battles, his failure to strike worked to the Germans' advantage. It allowed Samsonov to continue to believe that he was in contact with a weak enemy force and so to continue pushing forward into the trap. Both of his flanks were encountering German troops and being badly mauled, but his communications were so faulty and he had moved the divisions that formed those flanks so far out from his center that throughout most of the day he knew almost nothing of this. The Germans, meanwhile, were eager to engage him. Much of the Eighth Army was made up of East Prussians, men with personal reasons for wanting to clear the region of invaders. One officer, on August

26, found himself directing artillery fire on his own house after the Russians took possession of it.

Zhilinski continued to prod Samsonov to keep moving and to stay on his present course. When the scanty intelligence reaching Samsonov began to indicate that worrisome numbers of German troops were on his left, he sent a message to Zhilinski suggesting that perhaps he should confront this enemy force—whatever it was—by turning toward it. "I will not allow General Samsonov to play the coward," Zhilinski imperiously replied. "I insist that he continue the offensive."

Samsonov followed orders, but by the end of the day he understood that he was in serious trouble. A cautious withdrawal would have been the right next step. But perhaps because of Zhilinski's rebuke, he decided not to pull back, or even to stay where he was while watching the situation develop, but to continue moving forward. Though his flanks were in increasing disarray, and though his troops had no food and were low on ammunition, his center remained intact. That night he sent plaintive messages asking for confirmation that Rennenkampf was coming to join him. There was no answer.

Rennenkampf's failure to move need not be attributed to any hatred for Samsonov. He had lost seventeen thousand men in the Gumbinnen fight, thousands more before that at Stallupönen. He still thought that much or even most of the Eighth Army was to his north, near Königsberg, and that if he moved westward it could fall on his flank. He feared also that a pursuit of the Germans might hurry them across the Vistula before Samsonov could cut them off. Within the limits of the information available, he was thinking rationally if too cautiously.

At this point Moltke, never having been informed that the situation of the Eighth Army was not nearly as alarming as he and Ludendorff had believed when they met in Koblenz, had his chief of staff telephone Ludendorff and announce that three infantry corps were being detached from the right wing in France and sent by rail to East Prussia. Ludendorff replied that reinforcements were not needed. He did not, however, state categorically that they should not be sent. Moltke ultimately decided to send two corps instead of three, and Ludendorff would find plenty of use for them after their arrival.

At four A.M. on August 27, ready for action at last, François opened an artillery barrage that devastated Samsonov's left wing. Confused and starving Russian soldiers, exhausted after having marched ten and twelve hours daily for a week, broke and ran. François sent his troops forward in what he intended to be an encircling maneuver, but this was blocked. Samsonov, almost incredibly, then resumed the advance of his center. He advanced so aggressively that Ludendorff began to worry that the Russians were going to break through and out of the trap. He decided to call François's corps back to reinforce the center—a move that would have made an encirclement impossible. Hindenburg gently overruled him.

At dawn on August 28 François again attacked and discovered that the Russian left had evaporated. Its troops had had enough and fled en masse into the nearby woods. Everything began to fall into place for the Germans. François, meeting almost no resistance, swung his corps around to the south and cut off Samsonov's escape. Other elements of the Eighth Army converged from the nooks and crannies of the East Prussian landscape. A corps hit Samsonov from the west. A division emerged from the northwest and attacked the Russians there. When a corps that had been stationed to the northeast in case Rennenkampf showed up finally turned around and also marched toward Samsonov, the trap was complete. Samsonov, saying that he had failed the tsar and could not go home, walked off alone into the woods and shot himself.

It was now just a matter of mopping up. But still Ludendorff was tortured, his judgment distorted by his fears. When he learned that François had spread his corps in a thin line along thirty-five miles of road southeast of the encircled Russians, he ordered him to pull it together more compactly. François ignored him; he had witnessed the disintegration of Samsonov's army and knew that the only remaining need was to intercept the bewildered and demoralized enemy soldiers as they came stumbling toward Poland. In the course of the next three days, François's thin net hauled in sixty thousand prisoners. Overall the Germans captured ninety-two thousand Russians. Total casualties were two hundred and fifty thousand for the Russians, about thirty-seven thousand for the Germans. The Germans decided to call what had just happened the Battle of Tannenberg because a nearby town of that name had been the site of a terrible German defeat at the hands of the Poles hundreds of years before. Hindenburg's ancestors had taken part in that battle.

On the same day that Samsonov's left collapsed, a very different story was unfolding to the south. Conrad's Austro-Hungarian armies, having launched an offensive against superior Russian forces in Galicia, were suffering a defeat even worse than the one inflicted on them earlier by the Serbs. Conrad never should have attacked (the Russians outnumbered him by an immense margin, and he had the Carpathian Mountains in which to stand on the defensive), but the fact that he did was not entirely his fault. Moltke, fearing that if Conrad did not engage the Russians they would send more of their armies into East Prussia, had demanded action. Promising to send help within six weeks, as soon as France had been defeated, he tried to ease Conrad's reservations by assuring him that "the fate of Russia will be decided not on the

Bug [a Galician river] but on the Seine." In other words, defeating the Russians was for the moment less important than simply keeping them occupied.

In fact, Conrad's offensive may have contributed to making Tannenberg possible. It not only kept Russia's Galician forces in Galicia but drew out of Poland reserves that otherwise might have gone to East Prussia. But the long-term results would be disastrous. Austria's ability to deal with the Russians, to provide Germany with a strong ally, was going up in flames.

And at that same time, almost within sight of Paris, the war in the west was suddenly and decisively changing. Across Europe a mixture of successes and failures was emerging on both sides, a balance so perfect as to seem almost mysterious. It would make victory impossible for either side and ensure that the terrible carnage of the war's first month was barely the beginning.

THE JUNKERS

IT IS PART OF THE STRANGE DARK POETRY OF THE GREAT
War that the Battle of Tannenberg, the most dramatic and complete victory
achieved by either side in more than four years of bloody struggle, was
fought in East Prussia.

This was sacred ground. Though the most remote and least developed
region of the German federation—so remote that in 1914 it lay north of
Russian Poland and today it is part of Poland—East Prussia was in a sense
the heart of the Hohenzollern empire. It was the ancient home of a collection of families who were neither conspicuously wealthy nor particularly
distinguished in any other way but regarded themselves as Germany's
rightful leaders and were regarded as such by their king.

Hindenburg himself was a son of one of those families, which for him
made the victory exquisitely sweet. He had saved the tabernacle from violation, overnight turning himself into a national idol. He had kept alive not
only Germany's hopes of winning the war but his kinsmen's hopes that
their privileged place in the life of Germany would not be lost, and that
the weaknesses and contradictions of that special place—its absurdities,
even—could continue to be ignored.

The Germany that Hindenburg and his kind dominated had come a
long way since the Franco-Prussian War. Long regarded as the land of
musicians and dreamy philosophers and Black Forest elves, by 1914 it was
the most modern, efficient, innovative, and powerful economy in Europe.
Not only in industrial output but in science, even in the arts, Germany was
a powerhouse. Militarily it was so strong that Britain, France, and Russia
had good reason to fear that even in combination they might not be able
to stand up against it.

Politically, though, Germany was a kind of Rube Goldberg device. Its
system of government had not evolved like those of Britain and France,
had not been passed down from time immemorial like Russia's or gradually improvised like Vienna's. Instead it was the creation of one man, Otto
von Bismarck. He had designed it not so much to help Germany become
a modern state as to keep modernity at bay—while, not incidentally, concentrating as much power as possible in his own hands. Its deficiencies

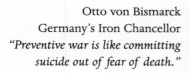

Otto von Bismarck
Germany's Iron Chancellor
*"Preventive war is like committing
suicide out of fear of death."*

had been serious from the start, and they grew more serious as the years passed, the world changed, and the Bismarckian system failed to keep pace. By the second decade of the twentieth century, with Bismarck long dead, those deficiencies had become dangerous. Ultimately they would render the system incapable of functioning under the strain of the Great War.

The root of the problem was that the empire, when it was declared in the Hall of Mirrors at the Palace of Versailles in 1871, was completely dominated by Prussia, the most powerful of the German states and the one that had led the others to victory over France. Prussia's king, Wilhelm I, was proclaimed the first kaiser by a jubilant crowd of sword-brandishing princes and generals. It is not possible to understand the peculiar nature of Prussia, or why Prussia would ultimately not only fail but pass out of existence, without understanding what Wilhelm meant when he said that the creation of the new empire felt like a kind of death—that the day it happened was the most miserable of his life.

What he feared was the disappearance of "the old Prussia," a thing that since the Middle Ages had come to be holy not only to his Hohenzollern ancestors but to the kingdom's landholding gentry. The old Prussia was a place like no other in Europe, and its people were like no other. It arose in what is now northern Poland, east of where the Vistula River runs northward into the Baltic Sea, and originally it was the homeland not of Germans but of Slavs. In the thirteenth century the Teutonic Knights, an order of religious warriors created to participate in the Crusades, were invited to help ambitious German nobles seize the territories around the

Vistula. The area east of the river was taken from a Slavic tribe called the Prussians, who disappeared from history but left their name to be picked up by the early Hohenzollerns when they needed something to call the insignificant little quasi-kingdom that the Holy Roman emperor permitted them to establish on the outermost fringe of the German world.

Though the Teutonic Knights tried to recruit Germans to settle east of the Vistula, the soil was too poor and the climate too dank to be powerfully attractive. The Slavs were permitted to remain if they converted to Christianity. Gradually, as the generations passed, German and Slavic families intermarried and gave rise to an ethnically mixed local aristocracy that came to be known as the Junkers. The irony is that when Prussia became dominant in Germany and Prussia's military might made Germany one of the great powers of Europe, the world saw this half-Slavic Junker elite as the most Germanic of Germans. Some of the most Prussian of the Prussians—for example, Karl von Clausewitz, who wrote the classic *On War*—bore names that were Slavic in origin.

The Junkers were not, as a group, rich, and their estates were not large. Life was often almost hardscrabble, requiring much labor and generating barely enough income to sustain a marginally aristocratic way of life. The people who grew up on those estates were, as a rule, neither particularly well educated nor particularly sophisticated. They were pious and provincial Lutherans, upright and sober, hardworking and hardheaded and often hard-hearted, with a deeply ingrained reverence for the law, for property rights, and for the class structure atop which they sat. What came to distinguish them above all was their almost mystic bond not to Prussia as a nation but to the Hohenzollern dynasty. This bond developed slowly, and what made it develop was the advantage it offered the Junkers. In return for their loyalty, they were assured nearly exclusive access to the more coveted positions in the Prussian army and civil service—opportunities for their sons to win a measure of power, snatches of glory, and sometimes, though not commonly, real wealth. The Junkers evolved into Prussia's hereditary military elite. A culture emerged that was unlike any other in Europe, an army, it was said, that happened to have a country attached to it. This arrangement was threatened by the Napoleonic wars at the start of the nineteenth century and by the revolution that shook Europe in 1848. (Prussian king Frederick William IV horrified the Junkers by granting the revolutionaries a constitution, though this was rescinded at the first opportunity.) Having barely survived these upheavals, the Junkers emerged more conservative than ever, their hatred of change in any form deeply ingrained.

Kaiser Wilhelm I was not a man of great intellect, but it was perceptive of him to find little to celebrate in the creation of his empire. In the most visible ways, the empire was a glorious achievement, one that put him at the pinnacle not only of Germany but of Europe and appeared to multiply the opportunities available to the Junker elite. But on a deeper level the new situation was fraught with difficulties, especially for the Junkers. First among the problems was the question of legitimacy. The Junkers were determined to maintain their special connection to the crown and the prerogatives that came with it. The Hohenzollern dynasty wanted much the same thing. But if the Junkers had been a small slice of the population of Prussia, they were an even smaller part of the empire. In the new world of giant industries and great cities, they remained a tribe of provincial farmers without real economic power.

Inevitably, the Junkers came to seem an anachronism to the increasing numbers of Germans who knew how different things were in America, Britain, and France. As agriculture became a less important element in the economy, what little prosperity the Junkers traditionally had came under threat. The richer and more educated the German nation grew, the more prominent among the peoples of the world, the odder it seemed that East Prussia should dominate as it did.

What is most odd is how little resistance to Junker privilege other Germans displayed during the half century that the empire existed. Bismarck, again, made this possible. Though he had deep roots in Junkerdom and for much of his early adulthood had worked a family farm, Bismarck was never entirely trusted or accepted by his own class. (His mother, an outsider from the professional classes, had given young Otto an education that made him more cosmopolitan than was considered quite proper.) He was permitted to create the empire only on the basis of certain understandings. He made it not a centralized country but a federation in which Bavaria, Baden, Württemberg, and other states were allowed semi-autonomy under their ruling families while Prussia stood supreme. He fashioned a constitution that concentrated nearly all political power in the hands of the monarch (who remained King of Prussia in addition to being kaiser) and the officials he appointed. He did so with the tacit understanding that the Junkers would continue to be specially favored. And so they were. Though it would have been politically awkward to fill every important chair with Junker bottoms, the Junkers could always be confident of getting more than their statistically fair share. Bismarck's system made ample room for economic liberalism—that was good for revenues and so for the army—but made political liberalism, and above all democracy, impossible.

This was not a system well equipped to deal with the tensions of a modern capitalist and industrial society, and even Bismarck had trouble

making it work. After he passed from the scene, his successors were sometimes barely able to keep its wheels turning. In a free market for agricultural products, the Junker estates would have sunk into bankruptcy; to save
them, the government enacted so many tariffs on food imports that
Germany became what has been described as "a welfare agency for needy
landowners." There was a legislature, the Reichstag, but it had little power.
As men infected with democratic and even socialist notions became
increasingly common within the Reichstag, the Junkers kept them in check
by joining forces with industrial interests in what came to be called the
alliance of iron and rye. They were greatly helped by an electoral system
that gave more votes to people with land and money.

In consequence, thousands of Germans of professional attainment,
people with education and talent, had no real voice in public affairs. The
political life of the nation remained in an atrophied state. The Reichstag,
though it did have a role in budget-making, was otherwise little more than
a debating society. In England and France the members of the legislature—
the House of Commons and the Chamber of Deputies—chose the prime
minister. Thus they, and the people who elected them, had a real connection to the levers of power and could regard themselves as a kind of ultimate authority. Their counterparts in Germany were essentially impotent.
Their parties, instead of being contenders for control of the government,
were held at arm's length by a government that remained very nearly what
it had been in feudal times: a collection of Junkers chosen by their king.
The result, in the short term, was widespread public indifference to politics. In tougher times it was a recipe for alienation.

The problem of how the Junkers were going to keep intact what
remained of the old Prussia extended into the army. With all their limita-
tions and faults, the Junkers were never expansionist imperialists. They
were not even German nationalists; many of them cared little about
Germany except as an extension of Prussian power. What they wanted was
the little world of their forebears, and every new stage of growth, of expansion, made that world less sustainable. Even the expansion of the army,
unavoidable in the arms race that gripped the great powers of Europe at
the start of the twentieth century, deeply troubled many traditionalists. Just
as for a good Junker the only thoroughly acceptable army officer was an
East Prussian of acceptable family background, so too the only dependable
recruit was an ignorant and docile East Prussian farm boy. The increasing
numbers of alternatives—growing hordes of city dwellers and factory
workers, many of them infected with modern notions—were aliens and
not to be trusted.

Tensions associated with such questions cost Erich Ludendorff, himself an upstart whose father had sold insurance, his place on Moltke's planning staff just a year before the start of the Great War. He had become convinced that a larger army was essential if the Schlieffen Plan was to remain practicable in the face of increasing French and Russian strength, and he began pressing for the creation of six new army corps. When only half this total was approved, he continued to demand more. After being told to keep silent but refusing, he was banished from the staff. This was a blow; it meant that, in case of war, Ludendorff would not become Moltke's chief of operations. He had brought this punishment down on himself by touching two sets of raw nerves. The government and the army did not want to stir up resistance in the Reichstag by asking for too big an increase in military spending too quickly. And many influential Junkers knew that it would not be possible to find nearly enough young aristocrats to fill the officer billets in six new corps. Outsiders in large numbers would have to be given commissions. The biggest army that Germany was capable of mustering was not likely to be the kind of army that the Junkers could continue to control.

While Ludendorff departed Berlin for Düsseldorf and command of a nonelite regiment (his not being given a unit of the Prussian Guard was seen as another rebuke), the man who would become his archenemy was rising almost effortlessly. Four years older than Ludendorff, Erich von Falkenhayn had been a favorite of Kaiser Wilhelm's since 1911, the year he had become a regimental commander in the guard. Just a year after that he was made a major general, and in 1913 he was promoted again and made minister of war. Though surprising even to his fellow generals, this rapid ascent (and the still greater promotion that would soon follow) is

Erich von Falkenhayn
A model Junker
*Described the German army
as "a broken instrument"
at the end of 1914.*

explicable in terms of Falkenhayn's background. He was very nearly the ideal Junker. Tall and slender, haughtily elegant in bearing, he had been raised on a modest farm in easternmost East Prussia to a family that traced itself back to the twelfth century and the Teutonic Knights and had produced one of Frederick the Great's generals.

He was a pure product of the old Prussia, and Ludendorff's opposite in far too many ways.

Chapter 10

✠

To the Marne

"We must not deceive ourselves.
We have had successes, but we have not had victory."
—CHIEF OF STAFF HELMUTH VON MOLTKE

As big and confused and drawn out as it was, the Battle of Tannenberg was a model of clarity and simplicity compared with the more famous Battle of the Marne, which has come down to us in history as the fight that saved Paris but in fact was settled by one side's decision not to fight.

Far more than Tannenberg, "First Marne" (there would be another huge and crucial encounter in almost exactly the same place four long years later) was not a single great encounter but a weeks-long series of maneuvers punctuated with bursts of ferocious combat. It involved millions rather than mere hundreds of thousands of troops, and they were stretched out over vast expanses of territory. Its starting date is hard to pinpoint; traditionally it has been placed on or about September 5, but events began flowing toward it during the closing days of August, at the time when the Germans were destroying the Russian Second Army in East Prussia.

All the French and German forces, as August ended, were still arranged in the order in which they had begun the war. Kluck's First Army was still the outer edge of the Schlieffen right wing, but now it was well south of Belgium, setting the pace for the rest of the German line as it swung down toward Paris like a great hour hand in counterclockwise motion.

South of Verdun, the German left was also pushing toward Paris but making much slower progress. In place after place there, in woods and fields and on stony hilltops, men were dying by the thousands in savage, obscure fights the names of which are almost completely forgotten today.

Movement had always been most pronounced at the other end of the line, where Lanrezac and the British Expeditionary Force were no longer even attempting to turn and fight. The situation north of Paris had become almost surreal: hundreds of thousands of weary French and British doggedly trudging southward, hundreds of thousands of equally weary Germans following in their tracks, and almost none of them doing any actual fighting. Looming over all was the idea of Paris, the supreme symbolic prize but also a great if dubiously prepared fortress with a sixty-mile perimeter of defensive walls and artillery emplacements. Bülow, when he got there, was supposed to besiege it while Kluck went around. One question was whether Bülow could get there. Another was whether, having arrived, he could take the city. The Germans had encircled Paris in the Franco-Prussian War but failed to get inside.

Schlieffen had predicted that a decisive battle would take place on or about the fortieth day after mobilization. As the twenty-fifth day arrived, then the thirtieth, mounting tension and the increasing exhaustion of the troops as they drew closer to Paris made it seem that a climax of some kind had to be imminent.

The commanders on both sides had little reason to feel that they were in charge of, rather than reacting to, events. At German supreme headquarters, which had been moving westward in cautious steps from Berlin to Koblenz and then on to Luxembourg, the continuing progress of Kluck and Bülow was igniting celebration. Moltke did not join in. As his armies penetrated deeper into France, clashing with or pursuing the French according to what Joffre was ordering his generals to do on any given day, his contact with them became increasingly tenuous. (Radio was still a new and highly unreliable medium.) Keenly aware of his own blindness, under no illusions about his ability to direct the campaign with so little knowledge of what was happening at the front, Moltke became unwilling to issue orders. Expectations became cloudy, prediction impossible, every shred of information precious. Would Kluck, his army worn down and outrunning its lines of supply, really be able to circle all the way around Paris and still remain capable of attacking the French? Or might the best chances now be in Alsace and Lorraine, where the French defenses were reported to be vulnerable?

Joffre, even as he surrendered great expanses of countryside, was accomplishing important things. He was making it impossible for the Germans to close with his left and force it into a fight it had little chance of winning. And he was maintaining good order: his armies remained fully under control in conditions that could easily have produced chaos. They were staying in formation and following routes and timetables worked out by headquarters, their every move planned, coordinated, and carefully directed.

But this couldn't continue. Unless they were going to march past Paris and leave it to the Germans, at some point soon the French, and presumably the

British, were going to have to stop and make a stand. When this was going to be possible, or where or even whether, remained unclear. The sphinxlike Joffre was sharing his plans, if at this point he had any, with no one.

Lanrezac was daily more pessimistic. Sir John French, thinking it likely that France had already lost the war, was talking of saving his little army by pulling it out of the line, perhaps even taking it back to England. The only really aggressive commander remaining in the area was Kluck, but his aggressiveness was taking a heavy toll on his troops. They were now advancing an average of more than twenty miles daily, each man burdened with his ten-pound rifle and his sixty or more pounds of gear as the hot dry summer of 1914 blazed on. Often, at the end of a long day on the march, the men had to spread out across the countryside and forage for meat and the vegetables that were, providentially, being harvested in abundance at summer's end. As they moved sixty and then eighty miles beyond the farthest points that their railway support could reach and their horses began to collapse, the problem of supply threatened to become unmanageable.

The German cavalry had difficulty operating in this country; rivers, canals, woods, and other obstructions slowed and complicated every foray. When horsemen closed with enemy troops, they found themselves no match for machine guns and magazine-fed rifles. The labor of constantly moving the artillery, and with it thousands of shells, was terrible and endless.

Things were little better for the French and British, but as they drew closer to Paris they were moving toward rather than away from supplies and reinforcements. They were able to make increased use of the railroad network centered on the capital.

The city was seized with fear. Politicians asked if Joffre intended to retreat forever, got no answer, and called for his dismissal.

On Lanrezac's left the British were retreating so fast—the infantry given only four hours' rest in twenty-four, the cavalry even less—that the Germans no longer knew where they were or if they remained a factor that had to be reckoned with. In his haste, French left Lanrezac's flank once again exposed. But the Germans too were having a hard time keeping their armies aligned. Kluck was outrunning Bülow and beginning to realize that somewhere out in front of him—a juicily tempting target—was Lanrezac's naked flank. On August 27 he had received fresh instructions from Moltke reiterating that his mission continued to be what it had been from the beginning: to march around Paris and proceed from there to the east. By this time, however, Moltke was receiving sketchy reports of a buildup of forces near Paris. The activity being reported was the birth of the French Sixth Army, which Joffre had let General Gallieni have for the defense of the capital. Moltke saw these new forces, correctly, as a threat to his right wing.

Accordingly, on August 28 he sent new instructions. Kluck was to stay not just in line with Bülow but slightly behind him—"in echelon" is the military term. But he neglected to say anything about the new threat from the direction of Paris, thus making it impossible for the First Army's commander to see how these new orders were necessary or even made sense. To put himself in echelon with Bülow, Kluck would have had to stop his advance for a day or more, perhaps even turn around. In doing so he would have thrown away his chance to hit Lanrezac, perhaps to start the unraveling of the French left, and possibly to win the war. He decided that if he continued to move forward but shifted toward the southeast, he could fulfill the letter of his new orders, bring his army closer to where Bülow was heading if not literally to Bülow's side, and continue his pursuit. Destroying Lanrezac's army, or at a minimum pushing it eastward out of Bülow's path and away from Paris, would surely satisfy the spirit of his instructions even if it violated their letter. And so Kluck crossed the River Marne on September 3 and pushed on. He felt free to do so because he was ignorant of one important fact and wrong about another: ignorant of the new French army taking shape to the west, wrong in believing that the mysterious disappearance of the British meant that the BEF was no longer an effective fighting force.

Among Joffre's problems, at this point, was getting the BEF back into the war. He needed the cooperation of Sir John French—something easier said than done, the British commander having decided that his allies were not only unreliable but doomed. Joffre hoped that he could restore French's confidence, and make a try at blocking the German advance in the process, by having Lanrezac attack Bülow's army near the towns of St. Quentin and Guise. Learning that Lanrezac was unwilling, Joffre went to Fifth Army headquarters and confronted his old friend in person. When Lanrezac continued to resist, Joffre threatened to dismiss him. "If you refuse to carry out my orders," Joffre was reported to have said, "I'll have you shot!"

Joffre went next to the BEF's headquarters at Compiègne. There, in the grand château that had become a base of operations for the BEF's staff, he all but begged French to turn his army around, assuring him that in doing so he would be protected by Lanrezac on his right and by the new Sixth Army on his left. French refused. He said that the sorry state of his army left him with no choice but to take it south of Paris for at least ten days of refitting and recuperation.

Lanrezac's attack had begun, meanwhile, and quickly developed into a hard fight. The French were soundly whipped on their left; Lanrezac had again been correct in warning that the German Second Army would overwhelm them there. But on the right, at Guise, the battle seesawed inconclusively and the French were able to hold. At one critical point their position was saved when the dashing General Louis Franchet d'Esperey, a flamboyant character whom the admiring British troops called Desperate Frankie, led an almost theatrical counterattack on horseback, his sword held aloft, accompanied by unfurled regimental banners and a band playing "La Marseillaise." The other side had its moment of glory after the Prussian First Foot Guards, as elite a unit as any in the armies of Germany, was thrown back and seemed in danger of falling apart. Prince Eitel Friedrich, the second of Kaiser Wilhelm's six sons, took command. Beating on a drum, he rallied the troops and led them forward in a successful counterattack. The prince survived, but the son of the commander of the guards corps was killed. Most of the generals on both sides were men in their fifties and sixties, and many had sons in uniform. As the fighting went on and losses continued to be heavy among junior officers responsible for leading attacks and organizing defenses, news that yet another general's son had been killed became almost commonplace.

At Guise, Lanrezac found himself with both flanks so dangerously exposed that he had no choice but to withdraw. Bülow, though he declared victory in reporting to Moltke, had taken heavy casualties. He decided that he had to stop for a day. He asked Kluck to move closer—farther east—to support him. Kluck, hungrier than ever for Lanrezac's flank, agreed. Joffre had had no choice but to accept Lanrezac's decision to resume his retreat. Without the BEF he lacked the manpower to make a stand, as desperately necessary as a stand of some kind was beginning to be.

French, no doubt, was guided in his obstinacy by the instructions he had received from Kitchener before leaving England: to regard his army as independent of the French and to protect it from destruction. Despite his concerns, however, the condition of the BEF was something short of desperate. The corps commanded by Smith-Dorrien, having borne the brunt at Mons and Le Cateau, was indeed no longer fully functional. But the other corps, the one commanded by Haig, had still seen little hard fighting. Haig had, in fact, agreed to an appeal from Lanrezac to move his corps north to join in the fight at Guise, but before he could act he was countermanded by French. This had deepened Lanrezac's sense of betrayal.

In his reports to London, the BEF's commander had much to say about his lack of confidence in the French but little about his own movements and plans. It was only obliquely, from other sources, that the cabinet learned that he had denied Joffre's urgent request for help, that he had decided to move behind Paris, and that he was even considering a withdrawal to the coast. Kitchener sent a wire asking him to explain. When French replied that he was indeed withdrawing south of the River Seine and that "my confidence in the

ability of the leaders of the French Army to carry this campaign to a successful conclusion is fast waning," Kitchener shot back another message informing him that he was expected to "as far as possible conform to the plans of
General Joffre for the conduct of the campaign." In response, French again
gave vent to his disdain for his allies and emphasized how unready the BEF
was to withstand further combat. It may have been the haughtiness of his
tone—"I think you had better trust me to watch the situation and act according to circumstances"—that prompted Kitchener to don his field marshal's
uniform and cross the Channel by destroyer that night.

The next afternoon Kitchener, French, and Joffre met at the British embassy
in Paris. Joffre told the Englishmen that with trainloads of troops pouring in
from the east, he now had two armies in formation—not only the Sixth at
Paris but also a new Eighth, which was to be inserted immediately east of the
Fifth. The Germans, he said, were probably unaware of these new units, and
almost certainly could not know that a new French army now lay on their
right. Thus it might now be possible to turn the tables—*if* the BEF would
come forward. French argued, complained, and resisted. As he would acknowledge in his postwar memoir, he not only had no confidence in his allies
but was deeply offended by Kitchener's sudden appearance in France. He
thought that His Lordship was undercutting him with the impossible French
and insulting him by wearing his uniform rather than attire appropriate to
what he now was: a representative not of His Majesty's army but of the government. Kitchener took French into a separate room. It is not clear what
was said there. French's account states that he put Kitchener in his place in
no uncertain terms, but the aftermath of the conversation makes that
unlikely. When the two men emerged, there was no further need for discussion. French was prepared to take the BEF north.

Joffre went to Fifth Army headquarters, took his old friend Lanrezac off
for a stroll in a nearby schoolyard, and there relieved him of his command.
Lanrezac may have saved France by being first to understand what the
Germans were planning in Belgium, by putting his army in the path of the
Schlieffen right wing, and by being the only army commander unwilling to
sacrifice his troops in futile attacks. He had absorbed blow after blow from
the invaders, performing well at Charleroi and Guise and keeping his army
in good order through its long retreat. But now he had become expendable.
Was he, as Joffre would claim, too worn down to remain capable of acting
decisively? Or was Joffre unable to forgive subordinates who disagreed with
him and turned out to be right? It hardly mattered. What did matter was that
Lanrezac hated Sir John French and French hated him. Joffre was determined
to do everything possible to satisfy the British. Lanrezac's successor was obvious: Franchet d'Esperey, Desperate Frankie, a particular favorite of the BEF.

Farther to the east, the front was aflame. Moltke was hurling his Third, Fourth, Fifth, Sixth, and Seventh Armies against the French Fourth, Third, Second, and First. The Germans were repulsed, fell back, and were counterattacked in their turn. Joffre by this point was firing generals almost wholesale; by September 6 he would replace the commanders of two of his original five armies, seven corps, and twenty infantry and four cavalry divisions. Other officers were rising to fill the vacancies. Ferdinand Foch, after performing well as a corps commander in Lorraine at the start of the war and heroically during the retreat that followed, was promoted to command of the new Ninth Army. Henri Philippe Pétain, whose brigade had distinguished itself as part of Lanrezac's command in early fighting in Belgium, was given a division.

Uncertainty gave way to panic. The government left Paris for Bordeaux on the Atlantic coast. But in the midst of it all Joffre remained impassive, maddeningly silent, *calm*. No matter how alarming the situation, how terrible the

General Joseph Joffre
"If you refuse to carry out my orders, I'll have you shot!"

emergency, the tall and rotund generalissimo never seemed disturbed. He became famous for the care he took always to have a good lunch followed by a nap, end the day with a good dinner, and always get a full night's sleep (in bed at nine, back at work at five). Even when things seemed to be at their worst, he made his staff understand that under no circumstances was his rest to be disturbed. But between mealtimes and bedtimes he was steadily on the move, using a big touring car driven by a Grand Prix racing champion to make repeated visits to his generals, especially those on the left. Thus he was able to keep himself in touch with events and observe his subordinates in action. He said so little during these visits, had so little to say even when told of shocking events or asked for guidance, that some of the men who dealt with him decided that he was little better than a stately idiot and that his principal contribution was his tranquilizing example. He has also been described as viciously political and self-serving behind his rocklike exterior. He has been accused of dismissing subordinates not so much for failure to perform as for becoming potential rivals or, worst of all, for showing their chief to have been wrong.

But fools rarely succeed under the kinds of circumstances confronting Joffre, and it was not by accident that things began to turn his way. The decision to strip troops from his embattled right wing and send them west by rail was his, and the consequences could not have been more important. The number of divisions facing the German right, seventeen and a half on August 23, rose to forty-one by September 6. In this way, gradually, Joffre gave himself one of the greatest advantages a general can have: superior mass. He magnified the significance of what has to be considered Moltke's most grievous mistake: his incremental removal of nearly a quarter of a million men from the right wing, which was left without enough divisions to do all the things needing to be done. Thus the great strike force that had obsessed Schlieffen literally to his dying breath found itself outnumbered. It was also enfeebled: bone tired, short of supplies, and increasingly without food. It is possible that Moltke's greatest mistake was in sending reinforcements to his left, which was in no danger, and accomplishing little of importance, instead of to Kluck and Bülow, where they might have made all the difference. Apparently he was discouraged from doing so by the Belgians' destruction of key railways.

The French, in contast to the Germans, were reaping all the benefits of fighting on home ground with interior lines of communication. Every twenty-four hours another thirty-two trains arrived at the capital loaded with troops and guns from the east.

Even now, however, Joffre could find no way of stopping the Great Retreat. He continued to wait and watch. "A natural reluctance to abandon even provisionally more of our national territory," he wrote to the minister of war as late as September 3, "must not make us engage too early in a general battle that might be launched in unpropitious circumstances."

Moltke now made a change of strategy so far-reaching that it amounted to the end of the Schlieffen Plan. Kluck and Bülow were told to halt their advance. They were to stand in place and face west against whatever forces the enemy was mustering near Paris. All the other German armies were to return to the attack. The Third Army was to fight its way southward to the River Seine. The Fourth and Fifth were to advance west of Verdun, the Sixth and Seventh to force a crossing of the Moselle River. The goal of this last two pairs of armies was to break through on their respective fronts, link up, and so encircle the entire French right in the area around Verdun. Never in history had there been an encirclement on such a scale; it would dwarf Tannenberg. There was no way of being confident that such a thing was possible. The irony of this sudden and drastic shift was that its success would depend on the ability of the German left wing to get past the very fortifications whose strength had made the Schlieffen Plan seem necessary in the first place.

It is difficult to judge whether Moltke's change of thinking was rooted in a genuine expectation of success or a desperate sense that his right wing was doomed to failure. It is certain that he did not believe the triumphal reports that continued to arrive at his headquarters and cause his staff to rejoice. "We must not deceive ourselves," he told a member of the German government. "We have had successes, but we have not had victory. Victory means annihilation of the enemy's power of resistance. When armies of millions of men are opposed, the victor has prisoners. Where are ours? . . . The relatively small number of captured guns shows me that the French have withdrawn in good order and according to plan. The hardest work is still to be done."

As remote as he was from the action, as inadequate as knowledge of the situation on the ground was, his intuition was sound.

THE FRENCH COMMANDERS

IT MAY SEEM ODD, AT FIRST, THAT ALMOST NO STUDY OF the French army at the start of the Great War fails to discuss Louis Loyzeau de Grandmaison. Though a professional soldier, Grandmaison never achieved high rank, and he did nothing of importance in the war before being killed in combat (a fate his critics could consider poetic justice) in 1915.

Still, he deserves the attention. Three years before the war began, as a lieutenant colonel in the Operations Bureau at army headquarters, Grandmaison delivered a pair of lectures that thrilled the generals in his audience. He heaped scorn on French military doctrine since the Franco-Prussian War, laying out a new approach that soon came to dominate the nation's military thinking.

His doctrine, remembered today as "the cult of the offensive," was rooted in the idea of all-out, nothing-held-back aggressiveness as the key to success in battle. And the word *cult* really does apply; by 1914 any French officer who failed to embrace it would find himself out of favor, suspect, and professionally sidetracked.

The consequences were fateful, almost fatal. Faith in the offensive, in the power of men wielding bayonets to overcome any enemy, caused Joffre's generals to send their troops against German machine guns and artillery again and again in the war's opening months, and to persist even as casualties rose to horrifying levels.

Such thinking had been in the air of France in the prewar years. Philosopher Henri Bergson, later a Nobel Prize winner, was preaching that *élan vital,* the life force, had a mystic power that if harnessed could enable the nation to defeat even the richer, more populous Germany next door. Also preaching was Ferdinand Foch, the gifted strategist and military theorist who in 1908 became director of the War College in Paris. He declared in his books and lectures that "the will to conquer is the first condition of victory." Grandmaison, enrolled at the college during Foch's tenure, became his disciple. Within a few years he was carrying belief in *l'offensive à l'outrance,* in aggressiveness without restraint, far beyond what even Foch had intended. His words were received with relief and gratitude by an officer corps tired of being told that the best France could hope for was to defend itself against the German military machine. Grandmaison's insistence that the generals should expect to *conquer* sounded to them like music.

The triumph of the new doctrine came in 1911. That July, six months after Grandmaison's electrifying lectures, a showdown over strategy erupted in France's Supreme War Council. The newly appointed commander in chief, a certain General Victor Michel, put before the council his ideas on how to prepare for war with Germany. He had based his proposals on a concept called offense-in-defense: if war broke out, he said, France's armies should be arrayed at varying distances from the nation's eastern borders, where they would wait for the Germans to make the first move (impressively, Michel foresaw their invasion of Belgium) before deciding where and how to strike back. There were advantages to such an approach. It would enable the French to know where the enemy forces were situated and where they were going before deciding how best to move against them. It could require the Germans to commit themselves, perhaps overcommit themselves, and wear themselves down on the offensive while all French options remained open. But to the believers in *offensive à l'outrance,* such thinking was heresy and not to be endured. It rejected what Grandmaison had taught them: that "for the attack only two things are necessary. To know where the enemy is and to decide what to do. What the enemy intends to do is of no consequence." Such words imply a willful blindness to the realities of the battlefield, but the beliefs on which they were based prevailed. Michel found it necessary to resign, and the Grandmaisonites became not just popular but the dominant faction in French planning.

It now became necessary to find a replacement for Michel, and the same General Joseph Gallieni who in 1914 would become military governor of Paris emerged as the pivotal figure. He had opposed Michel's proposals, but less on grounds of theory than because of concerns about Michel's personal capabilities and his intention, in case of war, to use reserves as frontline troops (something that the French generals abhorred but the Germans would do with significant success).

Minister of War Adolphe Messimy offered the job to Gallieni himself, who was respected on all sides, and Gallieni declined. Asked to take a few days to reconsider, the general again immediately said no. He explained that he regarded himself as too old; he was sixty-two at the time, in uncertain health, and within two years of retirement. He said also that he had too little experience in the command of large armies, and that—what was most important to Gallieni himself, and most reflective of his integrity—he could not honorably assume an office that he had caused to become vacant by failing to support Michel. Asked to suggest someone else, Gallieni offered the name of Paul-Marie Pau, a respected senior officer who had lost an arm in the Franco-Prussian War. Pau however was politically unacceptable, a practicing Catholic at a time when republican France suspected Catholics of seeking a restoration of the monarchy. (Foch, educated by the Jesuits and brother of a Jesuit priest, carried the same liability.) Gallieni's second suggestion, Joseph Joffre, presented no such difficulties. He was solidly republican but beyond that a man of no politics. Though he enthusiastically accepted the doctrines of Grandmaison, he was no ideologue and in fact displayed little interest in ideas of any kind. He had never attended any of the higher staff schools, had only limited experience in the command of large numbers of troops, and had never attempted to school himself in higher strategy. Because of the gaps in his experience, his appointment surprised many people. Gallieni, however, knew what he was doing—he knew Joffre well.

Gallieni (his family, like the Bonapartes, were of Italian origin and had come to France from Corsica) was twenty-one years old when, on the very day in 1870 that France declared war on the Germans to start the Franco-Prussian War, he graduated from the St. Cyr military academy. He was commissioned in the marine infantry, a branch that destined him for service in the network of colonies that France was establishing around the world. After the war, in which he became a prisoner of the Germans, he went on to assignments in West Africa, the Caribbean, and Tonkin (Vietnam). Responsibility came easily to him, and with responsibility came promotion. By the time he was forty he was governor of French Sudan, and for nine years beginning in 1896 he was governor general and commander

General Joseph Gallieni
*Prepared the way for the
Battle of the Marne.*

in chief of the new colony of Madagascar in the Indian Ocean. After putting down a rebellion there, he introduced an administration that made Madagascar not only peaceful but prosperous.

One of the needs at Madagascar was a system of fortifications for the colony's new naval base, and in 1896 an army engineer less than three years younger than Gallieni joined his staff and took charge of construction. This was Joffre, who had started life as the eldest of eleven children of a village barrel-maker in southern France, won a scholarship to Paris's elite École Polytechnique, interrupted his education to participate in the defense of the city when the Germans besieged it, and upon graduation took an army commission after failing to land the civilian job that was his first choice. He married young, but when his wife died he volunteered for foreign assignments. By 1885 he was chief engineer in Hanoi, and in 1893 in Africa he won his first moment of fame and promotion to lieutenant colonel by successfully taking command of an expedition to Timbuktu after his commanding officer was killed by rebellious tribesmen. He was recalled to France in 1900, Gallieni five years later, and by 1911 the two were among the army's highest-ranking generals.

Joffre did not disappoint as commander in chief. He upgraded the army's training and equipment and reformed the promotion system, giving more weight to ability and performance than to political connections or ideological correctness. (He insisted, as a condition of his appointment, on being allowed to select an aristocratic Catholic, the talented General Noël de Castelnau, as his chief of staff.) He was content to leave the Operations Bureau, where strategies were hatched, in possession of Grandmaison and his followers. Under their influence, investment in artillery, especially heavy artillery, was seriously neglected. The reasons were obvious: bayonets, not big guns, were the supreme weapon.

In May 1913 the bureau issued two sets of new field regulations. One was for corps and armies, and the other for units of division size and smaller. Both were saturated with the Grandmaison doctrine. "Battles are beyond everything else struggles of morale," they declared. "Defeat is inevitable as soon as the hope of conquering ceases to exist. Success comes not to him who has suffered the least but to him whose will is firmest and morale strongest." Grandmaison's staff also drafted Plan 17, which discarded the Michel approach and was duly approved by Joffre as the definitive statement of how his armies would be deployed when war came. The French equivalent of the Schlieffen Plan, Plan 17 disregarded even the possibility of a German move into western Belgium, an inexplicable decision in light of what Michel had concluded years earlier. Though Plan 17 was more flexible than the Schlieffen Plan, leaving Joffre free to decide where and when to attack, that he would attack was beyond question.

Adherents of the cult of the offensive did very well during these prewar years. Foch, who could have claimed to be the cult's grandfather, was given command of a division in 1911 and of a corps just one year after that. That at the beginning of the war he was not given an army is surprising; the religious factor is likely the reason. Grandmaison was promoted to brigadier general and did not long survive.

Those deemed to have insufficient faith in the offensive did not prosper. One such officer was Henri Philippe Pétain, who as a lowly assistant professor of infantry tactics at the École de Guerre had attracted unfavorable attention by persistently warning of the vulnerability of flesh and bone when confronted with twentieth-century firepower. In July 1914 he was, as a result, a mere colonel of fifty-eight, an obscure outsider expecting to be retired soon. Even mobilization and the start of the war brought no advancement. When the French Fifth Army assembled (its commander, Lanrezac, was only four years older than Pétain), Pétain commanded a regiment and was still a colonel.

Gallieni had sunk into what appeared likely to be terminal obscurity. Before the start of the war, he had come around to Michel's view that if Germany invaded France, it would do so through Belgium. He had tried to explain his concerns to Joffre and the deep thinkers of the Operations Bureau but was ignored. Relieved by Joffre of responsibility for anything, he retreated to his country home and a kind of preretirement limbo. In July his wife died, and on the last day of the month he was informed by Messimy that, in case of mobilization, he would be named Joffre's principal deputy and successor if the need for succession arose. When mobilization came, he was given the promised title but no staff, no duties, no information about what was happening, and no access to the man whose chief support he was supposed to be. Joffre evidently regarded him as a rival and wanted to give him no opportunities to be seen or heard. Thus Gallieni, a thin and almost comically homely man with tiny eyeglasses and a flamboyantly bushy mustache, spent the opening days of the war alone. He followed the opening movements of the armies on his maps and worried.

He was unresentful. As the danger to Paris increased and alarmed members of the government began to complain of Joffre's retreat and talk of replacing him, it was Gallieni, to whom the politicians would cheerfully have given the supreme command, who urged patience.

Chapter 11

✠

Back from the Marne

"Attack, whatever happens! The Germans are at the extreme limit of their efforts... Victory will come to the side that outlasts the other."

—FERDINAND FOCH

Fears that war would mean a continent in flames had literally come true by early September. The entire Western Front from Paris to the Alps had turned into a vast bloody slugfest in which more than a dozen armies were fully and simultaneously engaged. In the east, Galicia was the scene of a massive running battle between the Russians and the Austro-Hungarian forces of Field Marshal Conrad. In East Prussia the German Eighth Army was following up its victory at Tannenberg with a pursuit aimed at the destruction of Rennenkampf's Russian Second Army near the Masurian Lakes.

Nothing was more critical than the point where the German right met Joffre's left. Still unaware of the existence of a new French army at Paris, seeing no reason to halt as Moltke had ordered, Kluck continued to plunge southward in search of the French Fifth Army's flank or, failing that, whatever remained of the BEF. But his army was in danger of crumbling even as it advanced. "Our soldiers are worn out," a member of Kluck's staff was recording as early as September 2. "For four days they have been marching forty kilometers a day. The ground is difficult, the roads are torn up, trees felled, the fields pitted by shells like strainers. The soldiers stagger at every step, their faces are plastered with dust, their uniforms are in rags; one might call them living rag-bags. They march with closed eyes, and sing in chorus to keep from falling asleep as they march. The certainty of victory close at hand and of their triumphal entry into Paris sustains them and whips up their enthusiasm. Without this certainty of victory they would fall exhausted. They would lie down where they are, to sleep at last, no matter where, no matter how. And, to give their bodies a drunkenness like that of their souls, they drink enormously. But this drunkenness also helps to keep them up. Today, after an inspection, the General [Kluck] was furiously angry. He wanted to put an end to this collective debauch. We have just persuaded him not to give severe orders. It is better not to be too strict, otherwise the army could not go on at all. For this abnormal weariness abnormal stimulants are needed. In Paris we shall remedy all this."

And Paris still seemed an achievable goal. The British, despite Sir John French's promise to rejoin the fight, were continuing to withdraw. (French would later explain this as an effort to connect as quickly as possible with reinforcements and supplies before turning north.)

Then everything changed. Intercepted German radio messages, some of them not in code, informed the French that Kluck was now heading not toward Paris but southeast. Papers found on a German officer who had taken a wrong turn and been shot dead by a French patrol indicated the same thing—showed not only where the various parts of Kluck's army were but where they had been ordered to go. Joseph Gallieni, quickly grasping the implications, assembled a small group of reconnaissance pilots and told them where he wanted them to fly the next morning and what he wanted them to look for. They returned with the news he wanted: Kluck's army, formed into six thick columns, was indeed moving to the southeast. In doing so it was exposing its right flank to Gallieni's new Sixth Army. The opportunity for a counterattack appeared to have come at last.

Gallieni ordered the Sixth Army, still only half-organized and made up largely of inexperienced reserve troops, to get ready to move. Then he took off by car to visit British headquarters and get Sir John French to join in the attack. French was away when Gallieni arrived, and the staff officers who received this unexpected visitor did so with amused and barely concealed contempt. One of them said later that Gallieni, ungainly and unkempt in his high laced-up black boots and yellow leggings, looked like "a comedian," like somebody "no British officer would be seen talking to."

After three hours of waiting, having extracted from his hosts nothing better than a promise that someone would telephone him after French's return, Gallieni departed. The promised call, when it finally came, informed him that the BEF would be continuing its move to the south; the British had checked with Joffre and received no encouragement to cooperate with Gallieni. Wherever he turned, Gallieni found little cooperation. Joffre, though he approved Gallieni's attack, said he wanted it launched from south rather than north of the Marne. This would blunt its impact, Gallieni thought, and he spent long minutes on the telephone changing Joffre's mind. Worse, Joffre was reluctant to send the additional troops needed for hitting the Germans hard. Worst, when he understood just how rich in opportunity this situation was, how laden with potential glory, Joffre took the Sixth Army back from Gallieni, who then returned to Paris.

Kluck was too good a soldier to offer quite as fat a target as Gallieni hoped. Though he continued his advance, he did not leave his flank uncovered. He moved one corps—two infantry divisions plus artillery—to the River Ourcq to his west, where it took up defensive positions facing Paris and was directly in the path of the French Sixth Army as it began moving eastward. This corps, though made up of reserve units, was commanded by a capable officer, a General von Grönau. Grönau moved his troops onto high ground, had them dig in, and used his artillery to tear at the French as they began arriving on the scene. The result was a battle so singularly uneven that it proved to be the undoing of any hopes for the quick destruction of Kluck's army. On the German side, success gave a last burst of life to Kluck's hopes of breaking the Entente left.

On September 5 France, Great Britain, and Russia entered into the Treaty of London, by which they formalized their Triple Entente and pledged that none of them would enter into a separate peace with Germany. On the same day a member of Moltke's staff, Lieutenant Colonel Richard Hentsch, arrived at Kluck's headquarters to alert him to the existence and probable approach of a French force in the west. While he was there, a report arrived from Grönau stating that he was under attack (by that same French force) and needed help. Kluck was not alarmed. He assumed that this was less a serious French assault than an attempt to trick him into halting the First Army's advance. But he did the prudent thing and detached another corps to go back to support Grönau. He also sent a message to Bülow, asking for the return of two corps that he had earlier made available to the Second Army. Bülow was reluctant to comply, knowing that doing so would weaken his own depleted right wing. If he had known that the BEF was now moving northward in his direction—French had turned around at last—he might not have agreed. But under the circumstances, with Kluck under attack and no one currently attacking him, Bülow had little choice. Though Kluck's reinforcement of Grönau was a turning point, the first backward movement by a sizable unit of the German right wing, it did not mark the end of the offensive. Kluck was still bent on victory.

He was no longer defining victory as Paris, however, and that became a problem in terms of troop morale. For the soldiers of Kluck's army, arrival at Paris meant an end to their long ordeal. This is clear in a German officer's account of an episode on September 3. "One of our battalions was marching wearily forward," he wrote. "All at once, while passing a crossroad, they discovered a signpost, on which they read: Paris, thirty-seven kilometers [twenty-three miles]. It was the first signpost that had not been erased. On seeing it, the battalion was as though shaken up by an electric current. The word Paris, which they have just read, drives them crazy. Some of them embrace the wretched signpost, others dance around it. Cries, yells of enthusiasm, accompany these mad actions. This signpost is their evidence that we are near Paris, that, without doubt, we shall soon be really there. This notice board has had a miraculous effect. Faces light up, weariness seems to disappear, the march is resumed, alert, cadenced, in spite of the abominable ground in this forest. Songs burst forth louder." But now, with Kluck's shift to the southeast and the move back to the Ourcq, the dream of Paris had to be let go.

The Germans were not, however, out of fight. By nightfall on September 5, Grönau's artillery had badly disordered the advance of the French Sixth Army, which was growing rapidly as reinforcements continued to arrive. At one point, when the French appeared to be on the verge of panic, a dashingly aggressive officer named Colonel Robert Nivelle, a man who like Pétain had nearly reached retirement age without achieving the rank of general, led a heroic intervention with field artillery. Rolling his guns through the French infantry to where they could fire point-blank, he drove the Germans back.

After dark, judging correctly that he was badly outnumbered and that his stand had given Kluck sufficient time to adjust, Grönau pulled back from the Ourcq. In doing so he probably saved his corps. The Sixth Army attacked by moonlight but found the Germans gone. Kluck, understanding now that the threat from the west was a serious one, marched his entire army back across the Marne toward the Ourcq. As always, he was thinking aggressively, looking not just to defend himself but to encircle and destroy his enemy.

But by now Kluck was laden with problems. He was no longer engaged with the main line of French armies, no longer in position to contribute to the decision that appeared to be approaching along that line. In pulling back to the Ourcq, he had opened a thirty-five-mile gap between his army and Bülow's, and in the next few days this gap would grow even wider. Between Kluck's and Bülow's armies were only two divisions of cavalry and a few units of light infantry—not nearly enough to hold off a significant enemy advance. The exploitation of such gaps had been the key to many of Napoleon's victories.

"Kluck marched his entire army back across the Marne to the Ourcq" is far too simple a statement to reflect what was happening that day. Every such movement meant yet another long and hurried trek, to be followed by yet another firefight, for men who had been marching and fighting for weeks. Kluck's men had been issued no rations in five days. They rarely got more than a few hours of sleep. Their uniforms were in tatters, and their boots were falling off their feet as they struggled to drag with them the cannon and shells without which they could neither attack nor defend themselves. And they were now outnumbered.

The French Sixth Army, though fresh, was still too raw and unorganized to be a match for Kluck's now-hardened veterans. When it renewed its attack on September 6, it again ran headlong into waiting German artillery. The result was another disaster—not merely a failure to dislodge Kluck's troops from their hastily improvised defenses but a debacle that left the French units shattered. Kluck's hopes of finishing off the Sixth Army began to look more plausible.

Off to the east, the French were falling back in several places. The anchoring strongpoint of their line, the great fortress of Verdun, was in deepening jeopardy. By September 6 it appeared possible that the entire line from Verdun southward might begin to come apart. Moltke's new plan, dual breakthroughs leading to a grand climactic encirclement, also was beginning to seem plausible.

The hour of decision had arrived, and everyone knew it.

The BEF was feeling its way northward in company with a corps of French cavalry and making extremely slow progress. More by happenstance than design, it inched into the gap between Kluck and Bülow. This was a frightening and exciting development. If the two German armies converged, the BEF would be crushed. If the British pushed forward swiftly, on the other hand, they might break through to the German rear and create havoc there.

They did not move swiftly. In part this was because of mistakes: one British division spent an entire day moving in a confused circle, so that at nightfall its lead units ran into the supply train that formed its own tail end. But it was also an understandable reaction to having enormous enemy forces on both of its flanks. What the British didn't know was that neither Kluck nor Bülow was in any position to turn on them. Kluck, on their left, was occupied with the French Sixth Army. Bülow—now at the end of the continuous German line, with his own flank bare—was in a hard fight with Franchet d'Esperey's Fifth Army. Because of his return of two corps to Kluck, Bülow was weak on his right. He was being hammered there by a division commanded by the recently promoted Brigadier General Pétain, and his troops were being pushed back and out of position. Kluck and Bülow were alarmed when they learned that the British were now between them, and both reacted characteristically. Kluck swung some of his troops around to face a possible advance by the British but continued to batter away with his main force at the French. Bülow began to plan a withdrawal in which both his army and Kluck's would pull back at least ten miles and reconnect north of the British.

The fighting intensified all along the line. The French were on the defensive everywhere but on their left; on the right the need was to hold the line against German armies trying to deliver the breakthrough that Moltke had ordered. Gallieni began filling Paris taxicabs with soldiers and sending them out to swell the ranks of the army that Joffre had taken from him. His energy, despite so many reasons to be grudging, caused the Sixth Army to keep growing hour by hour.

The madness rose to its climax on September 8 and 9. The outcome would depend on whether any of the German armies in the east could crack the French line or, alternatively, whether the German First Army or the French Sixth could destroy its opponent. The Battle of the Marne became a series of crises following one after another until finally something broke down.

September 7 had ended with Foch's new army separated from General von Hausen's German Third Army by a treacherously soggy expanse of territory called the Marais (the Marsh) of Saint-Gond. Foch, determined as always to carry the fight to his enemy but naturally assuming that advance across a swamp was not feasible, had launched an attack around both sides. Both wings of this attack ran into strong German defenses and were thrown back with heavy loss of life. Hausen's staff, meanwhile, had been exploring the interior of the Marais and discovering that it was not at all as impassable as its name indicated. Early the next morning the Germans moved across it without the kind of artillery preparation that would have alerted the French, mounted a dawn charge that caught Foch's center unprepared, and forced it out of its defenses. Though this clash was a defeat for the French, it added to Foch's growing reputation. "Attack, whatever happens!" he had said at Saint-Gond. "The Germans are at the extreme limit of their efforts. Victory will come to the side that outlasts the other!" He had been pushed back, but his line had not snapped. The Germans still did not have the breakthrough on which all their hopes depended.

Not only at Saint-Gond but at many places along the front, the French, like the Germans, were near the end of their resources. "For my part I preserve only a confused and burning recollection of the days of 6th and 7th September," a cavalryman would observe afterward. "The heat was suffocating. The exhausted troops, covered with a layer of black dust sticking to their sweat, looked like devils. The tired horses, no longer off-saddled, had large open sores on their backs. The heat was burning, thirst intolerable...we knew nothing, and we continued our march as in a dream, under the scorching sun, gnawed by hunger, parched with thirst, and so exhausted by fatigue that I could see my comrades stiffen in the saddle to keep themselves from falling." A French general painted an even darker picture. "What a mess!" he

exclaimed. "What a shambles! It was a terrifying sight...no order in the ranks...
straggling along...Men emaciated, in rags and tatters, most without haver-
sacks, many without rifles, some marching painfully, leaning on sticks and
looking as though they were about to fall asleep."

Moltke, a hundred and seventy miles to the north at his headquarters in
Luxembourg, was getting almost no reports from Kluck or Bülow. Kaiser
Wilhelm was in Luxembourg also, complete with an enormous staff of his
own and advisory groups that also had staffs. This may be one reason why
Moltke, unlike Joffre, never ventured out to see for himself what was happening at the front. He had reason to fear that in his absence the kaiser, hungry
for a great victory and (as Moltke told his wife in the deeply gloomy letters
he sent home every day) incapable of understanding the dangers of the situation, would take personal command and do something disastrous.

While Hausen was attacking Foch across the Marais de Saint-Gond,
Moltke again sent Colonel Hentsch, the trusted head of his intelligence staff,
off to the front by car. Hentsch's instructions—oral rather than written, so
that whether he ultimately exceeded his authority can never be conclusively
answered—were to visit the commanders of all but the two southernmost
German armies, determine whether they were or were not in trouble, and
send reports back to Moltke.

Hentsch worked his way westward along the front, visiting the headquarters of the Fifth Army of Crown Prince Wilhelm, the Fourth Army of Duke
Albrecht of Württemberg, and Hausen's Third Army. He found the situation
of each of these armies acceptable, with no reason for alarm, and informed
Moltke accordingly. It was evening when he got to Bülow's Second Army, and
there the picture began to darken. Bülow had Franchet d'Esperey's battered
but hard-fighting army in front of him, and between himself and Kluck to
the west was a gap that now stretched for as much as fifty miles and had been
penetrated by the BEF. A shaken Bülow told Hentsch that only a "voluntary
concentric retreat" by his army and Kluck's could avert disaster. This was not
a loss of nerve on Bülow's part. His position was dangerously weak. Pétain's
attacks had captured tactically important terrain, so that Bülow's right was
continuing to be pushed back into an increasingly awkward position.

And this was only one of many emergencies. At the eastern end of the
front, the French First and Second Armies were holding high ground near the
Alsace border and repelling repeated attacks. The commander of the Second
Army, Castelnau, absorbing news of the death in combat of his son (he
would lose two more sons before the war ended), reported to Joffre that he
had to withdraw from Nancy or risk the loss of his entire force. Joffre told
him to hold where he was at all costs for at least another twenty-four hours.
To Castelnau's north, around Verdun, the French Third Army was hanging

on to rubble that once had been stout French fortifications and slaughtering the oncoming Germans.

Far away in East Prussia, at the Masurian Lakes, Hindenburg's Eighth Army was closing in on Rennenkampf's retreating Russians. Even that wasn't the end of it: in Galicia, the main forces of the Austro-Hungarian army were engaged with more than two million Russian troops in yet another series of battles that were as confusing as they were bloody but in the end would prove little less important than Tannenberg and the Marne.

The only truly fluid sector of the Western Front remained as before the front's western extreme. An incident of September 8 indicates just how confused the situation was, with large and small French, German, and British units in motion all over the landscape. In the afternoon a detachment of French cavalry suddenly came upon a caravan of three German automobiles. When the horsemen started toward them at a gallop, the drivers quickly turned and sped off. In one of the cars was Kluck, moving among the dispersed units of his army. Still tirelessly combative despite his sixty-eight years, Kluck remained confident of his chances. For three days the French had been throwing themselves at his position on the Ourcq. Having withstood these attacks and worn the French down, he now saw an opportunity to finish them off before some other enemy force—possibly the BEF—could fall on him from the rear. He ordered an attack. The goal this time would be an encirclement of the Sixth Army from the north. The assault would be led by a corps of infantry under General Ferdinand von Quast. This was one of the corps that Kluck had lent to Bülow and then taken back. It had crossed Belgium and France with Kluck, had fought at Mons, had been in the thick of things all through the campaign, and was very nearly spent. At the end of the day Kluck said in a message to his army that "the decision will be decided tomorrow by an enveloping attack."

Early on the morning of Wednesday, September 9, Hentsch set out to find Kluck. The roads were jammed with soldiers and equipment moving eastward. This was Kluck's shift of part of his army to positions from which it could protect its rear, along with the usual pathetic streams of refugees. The direction of the flow gave the appearance of an army in retreat. It appeared to support Bülow's appeal for a general pullback. It took Hentsch five hours to cover fifty miles, and during those hours Quast unleashed his attack. The Sixth Army didn't simply retreat—it fell apart. French troops fled in all directions.

In East Prussia, Rennenkampf was still withdrawing, trying to escape destruction at the hands of a German force that was smaller than his but brimming with confidence in the aftermath of Tannenberg. Desperate, he sent two of his divisions in a heroic, suicidal attack on the advancing German center. Both divisions were destroyed, but they accomplished their purpose. The Germans were stopped, and what remained of Rennenkampf's army got away.

On the plains of Galicia, Conrad's long fight with the Russians was ending in disastrous—in almost final—defeat. He had moved against the Russians despite being grossly outnumbered, despite learning that the Germans would not be able to support him, and despite the disappointment of learning that Romania with its army of six hundred thousand men would not be joining the Central Powers as hoped. He had sent thirty-one divisions against the Russians' forty-five infantry and eighteen cavalry divisions, and the results were inevitable. The Austrians were driven back a hundred and fifty miles to the Carpathian Mountains. Conrad had lost more than four hundred thousand men—one hundred thousand killed, an equal number taken prisoner, two hundred and twenty thousand wounded—plus 216 pieces of artillery and a thousand locomotives. He had lost more than a fourth of the manpower with which he had begun the war, and among that fourth were insupportably large numbers of Austria-Hungary's commissioned and non-commissioned officers. Less than a month and a half into the war, his capacity for dealing effectively not just with the Russians but even with smaller enemies was nearly exhausted. From now on Vienna would be not so much Berlin's junior partner as a weak and burdensome appendage. The Germans would grow fond of saying that being allied with the Hapsburg empire was like being "shackled to a corpse."

Conrad himself shared in a personal way in the immensity of the tragedy. "I have one of my sons seriously ill," he lamented, "and the son that I idolized in a mound of corpses at Ravaruska."

Around Verdun, where the French were hanging on by such a thin thread that Joffre twice authorized the commander of his Third Army to retreat if necessary, September 9 brought a final, convulsive German assault. The French had no reserves left, no way to seal up any holes in their front. They did, however, have the remains of their immensely strong defenses. In the years leading up to 1914 the main Verdun forts had been greatly improved, with deep sand and loose rock piled onto the original masonry and reinforced concrete as a top shell. Heavy artillery had been installed within armored retractable turrets. As a result, these forts could withstand direct hits even by the kinds of monster guns that had wrecked Liège and Namur, and they could also keep attackers under continuous fire. The rough terrain stiffened French resistance by making retreat almost impossible. At the same time it worked against the Germans by compounding the difficulties of bringing in artillery. The French not only kept their line intact but butchered the attackers as they themselves had been butchered in their earlier offensives. On the night of

September 9 the Germans made a last effort to punch through, but in the darkness they ended up blasting away at one another.

When Hentsch arrived at First Army headquarters at last, Kluck was away, keeping a close eye on the victory unfolding at the Ourcq. Hentsch talked with Kluck's chief of staff, explaining that the BEF was now north of the Marne, that Bülow was planning to withdraw, and that there was no alternative to Kluck's withdrawal as well. While they were talking, a message arrived from Bülow reporting that he was starting his retreat. This left nothing to discuss or decide, so Hentsch departed. When Kluck learned of Hentsch's visit and the plans for a retreat, his first reaction was to resist, to insist as always on pushing forward. When he learned that Bülow was already withdrawing, however, he had no choice but to yield. With Bülow moving north, his army was so vulnerable that nothing except retreat could possibly save it.

From the German perspective, the story of the Schlieffen right wing had a melancholy final chapter. At almost the same moment when Kluck was accepting the necessity of retreat, Quast's corps was tearing apart the last of the disintegrating French defenses. Nothing lay between it and Paris but thirty miles of open, undefended ground. It must have been like having an impossible dream come true: all they had to do was keep marching. But then new orders arrived from Kluck: Quast was to call off his attack and turn back. The First Army was retreating.

It was over. Quast's men had more marching to do, but now they would be heading back in the direction from which they had come.

No one felt the melancholy more deeply than Moltke. "I cannot find words to describe the crushing responsibility that has weighed upon my shoulders during the last few days and still weighs on me today," he wrote his wife. "The appalling difficulties of our present situation hang before my eyes like a dark curtain through which I can see nothing."

THE BRITISH COMMANDERS

ON AUGUST 3, 1914, WHEN *THE TIMES* OF LONDON REPORT-
ed that Field Marshal Sir John French had been chosen to lead the British
Expeditionary Force to France and the war, it was eager to make its readers understand that this was the best of all possible appointments in the
best of all possible armies.

"There was not a moment's hesitation," the newspaper said of French's
selection. "No painful canvassing of candidates, no acrimonious discussion, no odious comparison of the merits of respective generals, no hint of
favoritism, of Party intrigue."

This happy state of affairs was possible, it explained, because French
"surrounds himself with capable leaders and staff officers, and not only
brings his troops to a high degree of efficiency, but also makes his officers
a band of brothers, and establishes a good comradeship between all arms
and all ranks."

As an early exercise in wartime propaganda, in helping the public take
pride in its armed forces and the men chosen to lead them, this report was
exemplary. As a reflection of the truth, it did not fall far short of absurd. In
the art of generalship, French was rarely better than ordinary. An ability to
identify and make use of the best available men was not among his talents,
and no knowledgeable observer would credit him with displaying, or raising the forces under his command to, impressive levels of efficiency.

As for the officer corps being free of acrimony or favoritism or "party
intrigue," *The Times* could hardly have departed more shamelessly from
the truth.

The British army of 1914 was a considerably more effective military
instrument than it had been at the start of the century, when it experienced
great difficulty (and had to resort to savagely brutal methods) in defeating
a ragtag collection of guerrilla-farmers in South Africa's Boer War. Since
then it had improved its training, started at least to modernize its equipment, and established a general staff on the Prussian model. But in many
ways—in its leadership above all—it remained stubbornly in the past. It
was the army of a predemocratic culture in which a majority of the population was poor and powerless, the benefits of empire were reserved for a

tiny elite, and people at every level of society were expected to accept the status quo as the natural order of things.

Britain was changing, however, and slowly the army, heels dug in, was being pulled along. At the start of the 1870s the government had ended the time-honored system by which officers bought their commissions and promotions, often paying fortunes to rise to the senior ranks. Even after this reform, however, only gentlemen were regarded as suitable candidates for the officer corps. The term *gentleman* applied only to individuals with the right family antecedents, and not even gentlemen found it possible to survive as junior officers without private sources of income. Late in the nineteenth century, when an outstanding young sergeant named William Robertson was offered the rare opportunity to accept a commission, he was unable to do so because his expenses as a junior lieutenant (everything from uniforms to mess fees to a share in supporting the regimental band) would have been at least four times his salary of £100. When they did somehow manage to become officers, "rankers" were commonly shunned and even viciously hazed by gentlemen unwilling to accept them.

This was the system that had produced Sir John French and the other generals at the head of the BEF. They were gentlemen almost to a man, the only exception being the aforementioned William Robertson, who by then had risen, almost miraculously, to major general. (He had taken a commission in the Army of India, where expenses were lower, and his tailor father made his uniforms.) As gentlemen they adhered to a code that elevated amateurism in all things to a supreme virtue. Hunting, shooting, polo, and weekend gatherings at country estates were proper activities. Too much seriousness—for example, too much reading even about military history and strategy—definitely was not. The kinds of disputes over theory that racked the French officer corps were unimaginable north of the Channel, where nobody in uniform cared about theories. The right connections, and a proper degree of aristocratic insouciance, were highways to advancement. They made the army an especially attractive career for the less intelligent sons of the very best families.

French himself, sixty-one years old in August 1914, was the son of a naval officer and had begun by entering the Royal Navy at age fourteen. At twenty-two he had switched to the cavalry, the most elite (and expensive) branch of the army, and thereafter he advanced with the help of impressive social skills and his dash as a horseman. In 1899, freshly promoted to major general, he went out to South Africa as commander of a cavalry division, and there he won fame for his boldness while learning to hate, and coming to be hated by, the famous and powerful Lord Horatio

Field Marshal Sir John French
*"My confidence in the ability of
the leaders of the French Army...
is fast waning."*

Kitchener. In 1912 he reached the summit, becoming chief of the imperial general staff, and though he resigned at the time of the Curragh Mutiny, this was such a respectable, gentlemanly act of disloyalty that it proved no obstacle to his later selection as head of the BEF. By the time he went to France he was a stocky, almost dumpy-looking man in late middle age, stolid, unimaginative, and sour. Kitchener still regarded him as reckless, and so ordered him in writing to do nothing that would put his army at risk.

French's chief of staff in the Boer War had been a young colonel named Douglas Haig, who as a lieutenant general became commanding officer of one of the BEF's two corps. A member of the whiskey-making Haig family of the Scottish borderlands, regarded by the true aristocrats as unworthy of admission to one of the elite cavalry regiments at the start of his career, Haig was not noticeably more intelligent than French but was gifted at acquiring influential patrons. He entered the military academy at Sandhurst at an unusually late age, having first attended Oxford, where he spent the standard three years but failed to earn a degree. Early in his career he failed the examination for entry to the army staff college but was rescued by his connections. His sister, married to a member of the Jameson whiskey dynasty who held the honorary position of keeper of the Prince of Wales's racing yachts, got the Duke of Cambridge (an aged member of the royal family) to have the entry requirements waived on Haig's behalf.

In the Boer War he attracted the favorable attention of Lord Kitchener while building a friendship with French. Haig was handsome and unmarried and outspoken about his disdain for women, and the lifelong bachelor Kitchener always approved of officers of that type. Haig won French's gratitude by lending him the immense sum of £2,000, which French needed to extract himself from woman trouble. After South Africa Haig was made aide-de-camp to King Edward VII, a position that provided visibility in the loftiest circles. In 1905 he married the Honorable Dorothy Vivian, favorite maid of honor to the queen. The Haigs were the first nonroyal couple ever to be married in the chapel at Buckingham Palace; he had proposed seventy-two hours after meeting the lady, and one wonders what his bride thought when he wrote that "I have often made up my mind on more important problems than that of my own marriage in much less time." Within a year of his marriage, when the British army entered the modern world by creating a general staff for the first time, Haig's friends in government and at court campaigned to have him made its chief. This proved impossible, the candidate being only forty-four and never having held a major command, but afterward he never stopped angling for the job. He was still angling even as the BEF prepared for deployment, whispering his doubts about French's abilities to everyone who would listen from his friend King George down, rarely failing to add that of course he was prepared to serve wherever needed. He always got a respectful hearing despite being wrong on a wide range of subjects: before the war he had pontificated that "the role of cavalry on the battlefield will always go on increasing" and "artillery only seems likely to be effective against raw troops." It was typical of Haig that he was able to maintain a good relationship with French while despising him and trying to undermine him. Haig despised almost every one of his brother officers except his own subordinates—so long as those subordinates were sufficiently submissive. Almost paranoid in his belief that he was constantly being conspired against, he responded with endless intrigues of his own.

The other of the two corps with which the BEF began the war was supposed to be headed by James Grierson, but he dropped dead of a heart attack upon arriving in France. This was a stroke of luck for Haig. Grierson was a gifted infantry commander who, in the summer war games of 1912, had defeated Haig so completely, so humiliatingly, that the whole operation was brought to a stop ahead of schedule. Sir John French asked for Herbert Plumer as replacement for Grierson, but Kitchener sent Horace Smith-Dorrien instead. Again Haig was lucky. Plumer, like Grierson, was not only a very senior lieutenant general but an extremely capable one. He would have been a formidable rival, not only because Kitchener liked him but because years earlier, as an examiner at the staff college, he had expressed a scaldingly negative opinion of his student Haig. But he arrived in France under a tremendous handicap: French's intense dislike. He was under a microscope from the start, his every decision questioned.

French's deputy chief of staff was the BEF's archschemer, the wily Henry Wilson, who as director of military operations during the Curragh Mutiny had served as the Unionists' spy inside the general staff and was described by Haig as "such a terrible intriguer, and sure to make mischief." As Britain's primary liaison to the French general staff before the war, Wilson had made important friends in Paris, and almost from the start of the war he was trying to use them to get himself promoted to chief of staff. He and French were united by their hatred of Kitchener, whom Wilson called "as much an enemy of England as Moltke."

When French's chief of staff was replaced, the job went not to Wilson but to "Wully" Robertson, who had performed brilliantly as the BEF's quartermaster general in the opening weeks of the war. He was not French's choice—Kitchener had blocked Wilson's appointment—and not for the first time he paid the price of being up from the ranks. French regularly dined with Wilson while excluding Robertson. Haig was more careful in showing his disdain. "He means well and will succeed, I feel sure," he wrote of Robertson. "How much easier though it is to work with a *gentleman.*"

At the top of this dysfunctional brotherhood stood the stern and iron-willed Kitchener. Like Joffre and Gallieni, he had spent most of his life in far-flung colonial outposts. At age twenty he had interrupted his training to serve as a volunteer on the French side in the Franco-Prussian War, and soon thereafter he was sent to the Middle East with the Royal Engineers. From then on his career was the stuff of legend. By 1886, when he was thirty-six, he was governor of Britain's Red Sea territories. He became commander of the Egyptian army in 1892, a baron after putting down a rebellion in the Sudan in 1898, and Viscount Kitchener of Khartoum after leading the British forces to victory in the South African War (burning the farms of the Boers and herding their wives and children into concentration camps, where they died by the thousands). He was commander in chief in India from 1902 to 1909, battling endlessly with the viceroy, and from 1911 he ruled Egypt and the Sudan as British proconsul. By 1914 he had little knowledge of English society or politics and was so accustomed to being in charge of everyone and everything around him that he had virtually lost the ability to cooperate or delegate.

He happened to be in England during the crisis of August 1914. (He had been invited to come home to be made an earl.) When the war began, he

Lord Kitchener of Khartoum
"This is not war!"

was on a ship preparing to return to Egypt. Asquith called him back to London, asking him to join the cabinet as secretary of state for war. He agreed but without enthusiasm; his sole remaining ambition was to become Viceroy of India, and until that became possible, he preferred to remain in Cairo. In his new post (he did not relinquish his commission as the army's senior field marshal, or the salary that went with it) he was the first serving officer to hold a British cabinet post since the 1600s. He was a hard and shrewd man and a living legend, as familiar a symbol of the empire as the King. Other members of the government and the army were skeptical when he predicted that the main German invasion force would cross Belgium before entering France, incredulous when he warned that the war was going to last three years at least and that Britain would have to build an army of a million men. He was right on all points. In the end not a million but five and a half million men would serve in His Majesty's armed forces.

Chapter 12

✠

Flanders Fields

*"The enemy fought desperately for
every heap of stones and every pile of bricks."*
—OFFICIAL GERMAN ACCOUNT OF FIRST YPRES

The French and British, though jubilant at and in many cases astonished by the German withdrawal from the Marne, were badly battered, worn out, and running low on essential equipment. Many were almost too exhausted to move. "After five days and nights of fighting," one English soldier wrote, "decimated, spent and hungry, we are lying on the bare earth, with only one desire in our hearts—to get ourselves killed." And they were short of shells for their artillery. It is one measure of the sustained intensity of this new kind of warfare that the French faced critical shortages of ammunition for the 75mm cannon, their most effective field artillery piece, because only ten thousand rounds were being produced per *day*. This was barely 20 percent of the need.

For any number of such reasons, the armies of the Entente failed to close with the retreating Germans or exploit the huge gap that had prompted their withdrawal. They did not attack in force until after the German First, Second, and Third Armies had settled into fortified positions on high ground north of the Aisne, the next east-west river north of the Marne. By then it was too late. The fighting was ferocious, with the British especially taking heavy losses in trying to force the Germans out of their defenses, but it accomplished essentially nothing. "Three days ago our division took possession of these heights and dug itself in," a German officer wrote his parents. "Two days ago, early in the morning, we were attacked by an immensely superior English force, one brigade and two battalions, and were turned out of our positions. The fellows took five guns from us. It was a tremendous hand-to-hand fight. How I escaped myself I am not clear. I then had to bring up supports on foot... and with the help of the artillery we drove the fellows out of the position again. Our machine guns did excellent work; the English fell in heaps... During the first two days of the battle I had only one piece of bread and no water. I spent the night in the rain without my overcoat. The rest of my kit was on the horses which had been left behind with the baggage and which cannot come up into the battle because as soon as you put your nose up from behind cover the bullets whistle. War is terrible. We are all hoping that a decisive battle will end the war."

The fighting was anything but decisive, however, and the British and French had lost whatever opportunity they might have had to force the Germans into a Great Retreat of their own. Some of France's richest mining and industrial areas remained in German hands.

The Germans made a final unsuccessful effort to capture Verdun, which if taken would have given them an anchoring strongpoint from which to keep their armies on the Marne. Without Verdun, the Marne line was untenable. In pulling back, the Germans had to abandon valuable real estate—notably the rail junctions of Reims, Amiens, and Arras.

British and French headquarters bubbled with optimism, with Sir John French predicting that his troops would be in Berlin within six weeks. Erich von Falkenhayn, the fifty-three-year-old general and former war minister who replaced a bitterly disappointed Moltke as head of the German general staff (illness was given as the excuse for Moltke's reassignment), was quicker to see that the war was now likely to be a long one. He encouraged Chancellor Bethmann Hollweg to pursue a negotiated settlement on either the Eastern or Western Front—perhaps a negotiated peace with Russia that would persuade the French too to come to terms. Woodrow Wilson's government in Washington had already offered its services as a mediator, and soon Denmark would do the same. It was already too late, however, for such overtures to bear fruit. None of the warring governments thought they could possibly accept a settlement in which they did not *win* something that would justify all the deaths. The war had become self-perpetuating and self-justifying.

Though not as ebullient as French and Joffre, Falkenhayn believed that a decision in the field was still possible. Within days of taking command he was developing plans for a fresh offensive, and before the end of September he was putting those plans in motion. He had two primary aims: The first was to correct the Germans' single greatest vulnerability, their exposed right wing, which came to an unprotected end north of Paris. The other was to capture Antwerp, the last stronghold of the Belgian army, the greatest port on the north coast and, so long as it remained in enemy hands, a redoubt from which the Belgians and British could strike at Germany's lines of supply.

Falkenhayn could have solved the problem of his exposed right wing by pulling back still farther—by withdrawing, for example, to a line running from the Aisne to Brussels or even east of Antwerp. But this would have surrendered most of the gains of Moltke's offensive, demoralizing the armies and outraging all of Germany. Instead, he took an aggressive approach, deciding to extend his line westward along the River Somme all the way to the Atlantic. Such a move was feasible only if the French failed to defend the region northwest of Paris, but if it succeeded the Germans would control all of northern France, the ports on the English Channel included. They would be positioned to resume the move on Paris from both the east and the west.

Like Kluck and Moltke before him, however, Falkenhayn was trying to do too much with the resources at hand. To strengthen his right, he ordered the transfer of the Sixth and Seventh Armies from Alsace and Lorraine (where they would be replaced by two of the several new armies now being formed). This was not easily accomplished; the movement of a single army required 140 trains, and only one rail line connected the German right more or less directly with the left. Partly because of the resulting delays, Falkenhayn's offensive westward along the Somme was not as strong as it should have been; it ran into a new French Tenth Army and was stopped. That left Antwerp, which though more strongly fortified than even Liège (it was surrounded by nineteen large, state-of-the-art, powerfully armed forts plus a number of smaller ones, and defended by nearly a hundred thousand troops) seemed a more achievable objective.

Before the Germans began hauling their siege guns to Antwerp, General Sir Henry Wilson, the BEF's deputy chief of staff, suggested transferring the BEF from France, where it was tucked between two French armies on the Aisne, to its original position beyond the end of the French left. This meant, as the line now stood, moving the British troops to the Flanders region of western Belgium. Such a change, Wilson said, would put the BEF where it logically ought to be: close to the ports from which it drew its supplies, reinforcements, and communications. Sir John French was reluctant at first, thinking no doubt of the advantages of having one of Joffre's armies on each of his flanks. But when Winston Churchill pointed out that, if the BEF were in Flanders, the guns of the Royal Navy would be able to support it from the Channel, he changed his mind. A career cavalryman, French began to see the flat terrain of Flanders as a place where his mounted troops could prove their value at last, spearheading a plunge eastward into central Belgium and from there to Germany.

Now it was Joffre's turn to be reluctant. He feared that if the BEF again got into trouble, and if French started thinking again of taking his army back to England, a position on the coast would make withdrawal all too easy.

When French announced that he was moving north with or without Joffre's assent, Joffre urged him to proceed slowly and cautiously. French instead moved so swiftly that soon Joffre was blaming his haste for the success of German attacks along the Aisne and blaming his commandeering of scarce railcars for the Germans' capture of the industrial city of Lille. Falkenhayn's movement of troops and guns toward Antwerp had by this time awakened Joffre to the danger on his left. He moved his Second Army, which Foch now commanded, north into Flanders along with the British. The BEF's destination was west of Ypres, a lace-manufacturing center endowed with treasures of medieval architecture and suddenly important as the nexus of roads leading eastward into central Belgium and westward toward France and the Channel ports.

When the Germans began systematically crushing Antwerp's fortresses with their artillery, the British were more alarmed than the French. For a major port so close to England to fall into the hands of an enemy possessing a navy as substantial as Germany's would be no trivial matter. Winston Churchill hurried a small force of marines—all that were available—to help with the Belgians' defense. Churchill himself went with it, met with Belgium's king and queen, conferred with the Belgian commanders, and involved himself in the search for some way to hold the Germans off. He sent a telegram to the government in London, proposing that he be appointed British military commander in Antwerp and replaced as First Lord of the Admiralty. Members of the cabinet were said to have laughed when they read this message; it seemed typical Winston, too eager for adventure, constantly hatching wild ideas, always thinking himself capable of anything. Kitchener, not only the secretary of state for war but the living symbol of the British military (it was his face that fiercely told young Englishmen that "Your Country Wants You!" on the recruiting posters), did not regard Churchill's suggestion as ridiculous at all. He knew the first lord fairly well and had apparently been impressed. He knew that Churchill had been almost alone in recognizing the importance of the Channel ports even before the turnaround at the Marne and in urging that something be done to secure them. (Nothing had been.) Kitchener proposed that Churchill be made a lieutenant general on the spot. The prime minister did not agree.

By October 6 the Belgians themselves, staggered by round-the-clock German shelling, decided that Antwerp could not be saved and that giving it up was the only way to save their army. Churchill departed for home, and a day later sixty thousand Belgian troops under the command of their king left the city. Demoralized, nerves stretched, they hurried west until they were almost in France, arranging themselves in a defensive line north of Ypres behind the barrier that the River Yser forms as it flows to the sea. There they waited while Foch's army began to extend their line to the south and British troops filed into Ypres from the west. The Germans, meanwhile, took possession of Antwerp. The end of resistance there freed four German corps, most of an army, for other uses. Whole corps of new, barely trained reserves, many of them student volunteers, were arriving in Belgium from Germany.

As commander of all German forces, Falkenhayn faced far broader problems than did French or even Joffre. He had the vast war in the east to deal with—a war that now stretched across five hundred miles of front and in which his forces and those of the Austrians continued to be outnumbered by frightening margins. The heroes of Tannenberg—Hindenburg and Ludendorff—were scrambling to cope with the Russian threat not only to East Prussia but to Silesia to its south and, farther south still, to the badly shaken armies of Vienna. Two things were imperative. The Germans had to move south to connect with the Austrian left, shoring up Conrad's armies before they were overrun. And, not having enough troops to defend at every threatened point, they had to go on the offensive. They had to strike a blow that would stop the Russian juggernaut before it became unstoppable.

Hindenburg, Ludendorff, and their operations chief, Max Hoffmann, decided that they could satisfy both imperatives simultaneously by taking a newly formed Ninth Army south by rail to the vicinity of Warsaw, a key base of operations for the Russians. There they could link up with the Austrian left and join it in a move against the four armies that the commander in chief of the Russian forces, the tsar's cousin Grand Duke Nicholas Romanov, was sending toward Silesia. The Eighth Army would remain behind to guard East Prussia. Ludendorff, bold as usual, wanted to take part of it south too, but Falkenhayn rejected this proposal as too risky.

These movements set the stage for the First Battle of Warsaw, in which eighteen German and Austrian divisions found themselves in the path of sixty Russian divisions advancing on a 250-mile front. Conrad's assignment was to break the Russian line in the south by moving forward across the River San in Galicia, but his attempts to do so failed. Farther north, the German right and center made swift progress at first but then were slowed by days of torrential rain. "From Czestochowa we advanced in forced marches," an officer in charge of munitions transport wrote. "During the first two days roads were passable, but after that they became terrible, as it rained every day. In some places there were no roads left, nothing but mud and swamps. Once it took us a full hour to move one wagon, loaded with munitions and drawn by fifteen horses, a distance of only fifteen yards... Horses sank into the mud up to their bodies and wagons up to their axles... One night we reached a spot which was absolutely impassable. The only way to get around it was through a dense forest, but before we could get through there it was necessary to cut an opening through the trees. For the next few hours we felled trees for a distance of over five hundred yards...For the past eight days we have been on the go almost every night, and once I stayed in my saddle for thirty consecutive hours. During all that time we had no real rest. Either we did not reach our quarters until early in the morning or late at night. We consider ourselves lucky if we have one room and straw on the floor for the seven of us. For ten days I have not been out of my clothes. And when we do get a little sleep it is almost invariably necessary to start off again at once...Long ago we saw the last of butter, sausages, or similar delicacies. We are glad if we have bread and some lard."

As the Germans struggled forward, the Russians had time to assemble a mass of forces and counterattack. The German left was gradually bent back under the weight of repeated assaults until it faced northward instead of eastward and appeared to be on the verge of disintegrating.

By October 17 the Germans saw that they had to withdraw or be destroyed. The Ninth Army retreated sixty miles in six days, and by the time it was free of the Russians, it had lost forty thousand men. Overall the campaign had cost Germany a hundred thousand casualties, including thirty-six thousand men killed, the Austrians between forty and fifty thousand. The Russians pulled their guns out of the slime, and Grand Duke Nicholas began reassembling his sodden forces for a resumption of their advance.

By the start of the German retreat from Warsaw, Sir John French was beginning to move some of his forces eastward in Flanders. Falkenhayn, at almost exactly the same time, was setting in motion a westward offensive over adjacent ground. Until hours before their armies crashed into each other, neither was expecting to encounter an enemy in force. Both commanders were after territory: French's goal was Brussels by way of Ghent, while Falkenhayn wanted the area directly west of Belgium and the port towns that would come with it. Each was eagerly aware that, if he could advance far enough, he might then be in position to turn away from the sea and encircle his enemy. Glory seemed just over the horizon.

Almost immediately, both sides encountered immovable resistance. A joint French-British thrust toward Ghent ran into Falkenhayn's main force and was thrown back. The Germans tried to tear through the Belgian line at the Yser, but they too were stopped. Thus was set in motion the month of carnage called the First Battle of Ypres.

The nightmare was nowhere more hellish than where the Germans met the remains of the Belgian army. The suffering was magnified for the Belgians by the impossibility of digging in the waterlogged ground of the Flemish lowlands; for the Germans by the terrors of trying to cross a river under infantry fire while British navy shells screamed down on them from the nearby Channel; for both sides by the approach of winter and the new experience of being not only wet but half-frozen day after day and night after night.

King Albert rallied the Belgian troops. He was a competent soldier and a young man of considerable courage. He was also motivated: Foch had sternly warned him that if he failed to hold this last sliver of Belgium, he could not expect to retain his throne after the war. His Majesty positioned noncommissioned officers behind his line with orders to shoot any man who tried to retreat.

After days of murderous German shellfire that killed or wounded more than a third of the Belgians and effectively ended their ability to stand their ground, Albert played his last trump card. He ordered the opening (in some places the process required dynamite) of sluice gates in the dikes holding back the sea. The Germans, who were getting more and more men across the Yser and sensed that victory was near, could not understand what was happening. In the morning the ground was covered with ankle-deep water. Assuming that this was the result of the continuing rains, the Germans slogged on. By midnight, the water was knee-deep and still rising. The Germans not only had to give up any hope of continuing their offensive but spent a difficult night getting their troops back to dry land. Soon they were separated from the Belgians by a five-mile-wide, shoulder-deep lake, and that part of the fight was at an end. The German troops who had been attacking across the Yser were sent south to join in the fight around Ypres. They found themselves in a terrible struggle, often hand to hand, for the villages atop the low ridge that circled around Ypres to the north, east, and south. The German objective was to break through the Entente line on that ridge and close in on Ypres itself.

At one of the villages, Wytschaete, there was hard fighting a day after the opening of the dikes. A unit of Bavarians had tried to take Wytschaete and failed, and in the aftermath of the attack a captain named Hoffman lay badly wounded between his troops and the French defenders. One of Hoffman's men moved out of a protected position and, under enemy fire, picked him up and carried him to safety. The rescue accomplished nothing—the captain soon died of his wounds. But his rescuer would claim years later, in a notorious book, that his escape without a scratch was his first intimation that he was being spared for some great future. In the nearer term he was decorated for bravery. It was just a few days after Adolf Hitler's exploit that Kaiser Wilhelm pinned the Iron Cross Second Class on his tunic.

The Germans found progress against the British and French as hard as it had been against the Belgians. But when the BEF and Foch launched their own attacks, they too were quickly thwarted. Along this part of the line, however, there were no dikes to be opened, so that the opposing forces could be separated and their misery brought to an end. The fighting continued day and night, the two sides taking turns on the offensive, and as the casualties mounted companies were reduced to the size of platoons and the tattered remnants of units were mixed together helter-skelter. Officers were all but annihilated, so that young lieutenants found themselves in command of what remained of battalions and regiments.

The rain continued, the nights grew colder, men lay on the surface of the earth because any holes they dug immediately filled with water, and still somehow the fighting went on. The landscape, though almost uniformly flat, was broken by villages and patches of woodland and by rivers and canals and hedgerows and fences extending in every direction. This was far better for defense than offense, and practically impossible for cavalry (which in any case was proving to be helpless against machine guns). The British were often out-numbered, sometimes by margins that seemed impossible, but time after time they held off attacks or came back to recapture lost ground. One thing that saved them was the skill of their cavalry, acquired in the guerrilla fight-ing of the Boer War, in dismounting and fighting as infantry. What ultimately saved them, at Ypres as earlier at Mons and Le Cateau, was the accuracy and speed (and of course the courage) of the ordinary British rifleman. Here again the fire laid down by the Tommies was often intense enough to con-vince the Germans that they were advancing not against rifles but against machine guns.

The devastating effectiveness of the British fire, coupled with the inexpe-rience of some of the German reserves thrown into the Ypres meat-grinder, led to perhaps the most poignant of the many butcheries of late 1914. Thou-sands of schoolboy recruits, many of them as young as sixteen, followed almost equally inexperienced reserve sergeants and officers in heavily massed formations directly at the waiting BEF. They formed a wall of flesh—British soldiers recalled them advancing arm in arm, singing as they came, wearing their fraternity caps and carrying flowers—that blind men could hardly have missed. They were mowed down in rows. Where they somehow succeeded in driving back their enemies, they often didn't know what to do next and so milled around aimlessly until hit with a counterattack. Many thousands of these youngsters lie in a single mass grave a short distance north of Ypres. At the site is a sculpture, the figures of a pair of parents kneeling in grief, cre-ated after the war by the mother of one of them.

Flanders was disaster after disaster for both sides, and horror after horror. One evening, at the end of a day of murderous infantry gunfights under con-stant artillery fire, one of the German reserve units managed at tremendous cost to drive the British out of the village of Bixshoote. Later they received word that they were to be relieved overnight. In their lack of experience they assembled and marched away before their relief arrived. Observing this, the British moved in and again took possession. In the following two weeks the Germans would try again and again to retake what they had given away, failing repeatedly and always with even more casualties than before.

Losses were no less shocking on the other side. When Scotland's Second Highland Light Infantry Battalion was taken out of action, only about thirty men remained of the thousand-plus who had come to France at the start of the war. The BEF was moving toward annihilation. In some places along the line the British were stretched so thin that the Germans, observing, outsmarted themselves. They decided not to attack at those points, thinking that such a tempting target must be a decoy behind which lay masses of British or French reserves. There were no such reserves.

Somehow, the Germans and British again launched simultaneous attacks on October 30, and again they ran head-on into each other and grappled in a struggle in which the losses were almost insupportable on both sides. The next day the Germans alone were still attacking, and this time, at the village of Gheluvelt, another of their green reserve units broke through the defensive ring. Nothing lay between them and Ypres, but this sudden success after so much failure apparently was more than they could believe. While they waited for instructions, a British brigadier general found the only troops in the vicinity, the seven officers and 357 enlisted men who remained of the Second Worcester Regiment, and ordered them to retake Gheluvelt. To get to the village, these men had to cross a thousand yards of open ground, and during the crossing a hundred of them were cut down. The survivors, when they reached the edge of the village, darted into a grove of trees, fixed their bayonets, and attacked. Twelve hundred confused and frightened German soldiers, thinking that this ragged little gang must be the advance of some powerful force, ran for their lives. The Worcesters, with nothing between them and Ypres but open country, had sealed the hole.

That night Falkenhayn called a halt. He had no idea that the BEF was at the point of breakdown—out of reserves, nearly out of ammunition, at the limits of endurance. He still thought that a breakthrough was possible, but he wanted to assemble more trained and experienced troops before trying again.

Things became briefly quiet both in Flanders and in Poland in the early days of November, but almost daily the war continued to grow in size and change in shape. The first Canadian troops were in England now, being readied to cross the Channel and link up with the British. An entire corps of Indian troops, tough Gurkha units among them, was with the BEF in Flanders, and black troops from France's African colonies were arriving at the front as well. In the east, Hindenburg was named commander in chief of all German forces on the Russian front. Ludendorff continued as his chief of staff, and Hoffmann stayed with him as well. When word came from Istanbul that the Ottoman Empire was entering the war on the side of the Central Powers, in Berlin and Vienna it must have sounded like a gift from heaven.

Before November was a week old, the Eastern and Western Fronts were heating up again. Grand Duke Nicholas put two armies on the march through Poland toward Silesia, and other Russian armies were moving southwest-ward to the Carpathians. And Falkenhayn was almost ready to try again to take Ypres. The kaiser was still at Supreme Headquarters, and his presence was as big a headache for Falkenhayn as it had been for Moltke. Wilhelm was constantly demanding a victory, a reason to don one of his most gorgeous uniforms and be paraded in triumph through some conquered city. In his protracted disappointment he was like a petulant adolescent, and no more useful.

During the lull in the Flanders struggle, Falkenhayn received a hurried visit from Ludendorff. As usual, and with Hoffmann's help as always, Ludendorff had an ambitious plan ready for execution. Also as usual, his plan was aimed not just at stopping the Russian armies advancing into Poland but at destroying them. He proposed to do this by allowing the Russians to advance beyond the railheads that were their source of support until they ran out of momentum. Then the Germans would descend on them from the north, taking them in the flank and rear, cutting them off from Warsaw and safety. But more troops were needed. This was what Ludendorff had come for: reinforcements. Falkenhayn refused; he had been assembling all the divi-sions he could find for the new attack in Flanders, and the kaiser was hound-ing him. Ludendorff departed in a fury. Another war, this one within the German general staff, began at about this time. It was between Falkenhayn and the Hindenburg-Ludendorff team, and it was over the question of whether the Germans' best hope of victory lay in the west or the east.

Denied the manpower their original plan required, Hindenburg, Ludendorff, and Hoffmann did not give up. They moved their Ninth Army, the one that had had such a narrow escape from the Russians near Warsaw, back into East Prussia by train. There they combined it with the Eighth Army to form a mass of troops extending across seventy miles. They then waited as the Russians moved across Poland toward the west. When, as expected, the advance began to show signs of bogging down under its own tremendous weight and the dif-ficulties of resupply, they sent their two armies down on it like a hammer. At the main point of contact the Germans actually had a numerical advantage, and the Russians were staggered. After four days of hard fighting they began to retreat. The Germans pursued, hitting at the Russians repeatedly.

Falkenhayn was attacking again in Flanders, this time using more experienced troops and limiting himself to a narrower front. What he got was not victory but another series of inconclusive battles all along the ridge outside Ypres, which was slowly being destroyed as the Germans shelled the ancient towers being used by the defenders as observation posts. Large and small groups of soldiers dashed from village to woodland, from canal to hedgerow, settling into firefights, advancing with bayonets, being thrown back and counterattacking while artillery from both sides rained shrapnel and high explosives down on every target their spotters could find. The nature of the struggle is captured in the official account of First Ypres later prepared for the German general staff:

> The enemy turned every house, every wood and every wall into a strong point, and each of them had to be stormed by our men with heavy loss. Even when the first line of these fortifications had been taken they were confronted by a second one immediately behind it; for the enemy showed great skill in taking every advantage of the ground, unfavorable in any case to the attacker. To the east and south-east of Ypres, even more developed than in the north, there were thick hedges, wire fences and broad dikes. Numerous woods also of all sizes with dense undergrowth made the country almost impassable and most difficult for observation purposes. Our movements were constantly being limited to the roads which were swept by the enemy's machine-guns. Owing to the preparatory artillery bombardments the villages were mostly in ruins by the time the infantry reached them, but the enemy fought desperately for every heap of stones and every pile of bricks before abandoning them. In the few village streets that remained worthy of the name the fighting generally developed into isolated individual combats, and no description can do adequate justice to the bravery of the German troops on such occasions.

Nor, of course, is it possible to do justice to—perhaps even to understand—the bravery of the British and French troops who were defending those piles of stones and bricks. Even the barest chronology of how the villages near Ypres were taken and surrendered and taken again is enough to show why, in the end, hardly a stone was left standing upon a stone. Lombartzyde was captured by the Germans on October 23, retaken by the French a day later, recaptured by the Germans on October 28, taken yet again by the British and French on November 4, recaptured by the Germans on November 7, only to change hands twice more before finally and permanently ending up in the possession of the Germans.

Gradually, village by village, the Germans managed to inch forward and tighten their grip on the Ypres Salient, the semicircle held by the French and British east of the town. But time after time they failed to break through. On several occasions various French and British generals suggested that a retreat might be in order. Always it was Foch who refused. Before the war he had written that an army is never defeated until it believes itself to be defeated. Now, with considerable help from the Tommies, he appeared to be proving his point.

The German offensive crested on November 11 when the most elite unit in the entire German army, the First Guards Regiment led by the kaiser's son Prince Eitel Friedrich, drove the British troops out of Nonnebosschen. It was a repeat of Gheluvelt. Once again nothing separated the Germans from Ypres, and once again a ragtag assortment of the only British soldiers in the neighborhood (not combat troops at all but cooks, drivers, staff officers— anyone who could pick up a rifle) mounted a seemingly hopeless counterattack. Once again the Germans thought that the mysteriously absent Entente reserves must be moving into action at last and fled. That turned out to be the last time the Germans came close to breaking through.

The fighting went on until November 22, with more attacks, but increasingly it was an obviously futile struggle in rain and cold mud by half-crazed and hungry men desperate for rest. Even the old lion Kitchener was horrified. "This," he exclaimed, "is not war!" Whatever it was, it finally came to an end when the rains turned to snow and the mud froze hard and the impossibility of achieving anything became too obvious to be ignored. Both sides claimed victory, the Entente because they had held on to Ypres and kept the Germans from reaching the Channel ports, the Germans not only because they had kept the enemy from breaking through but because by the end they had captured so many of the strongpoints around the destroyed town that the British and French no longer had an adequate base from which to launch new offensives.

By the time the Flanders front shut down for the winter, the British had taken fifty thousand casualties there. More than half of the one hundred and sixty thousand men that Britain had by then sent to France were dead or wounded. France's Ypres losses are believed to exceed fifty thousand, Germany's at least one hundred thousand. *Burke's Peerage*, the registry of Britain's noble families, had to postpone publication of its latest edition to make the editorial changes required by the death in combat of sixty-six peers, ninety-five sons of peers, sixteen baronets, eighty-two sons of baronets, and six knights.

The Russian retreat across Poland continued, with the Germans in pursuit. First the Russians tried to withdraw behind an expanse of wet lowland marshes, but the Germans drove them out. Then they tried to make a stand at the city of Lodz, but on December 6 they were again forced to move on. They had lost another ninety thousand men at Lodz, the Germans thirty-five thousand. The Germans were thirty miles east of Lodz, and in possession of a hundred and thirty-six thousand Russian prisoners, when their drive finally came to a stop. Winter made the stop necessary—the killing Russian winter. "Only about half had overcoats," an English war correspondent observed of German soldiers captured in a Russian counterattack. "And these were made of a thin, shoddy material that is about as much protection as paper against the Russian wind. When you know that the prison camps are all in Siberia, try and think of the lot of prisoners. Yet for the moment the Germans were content. They were allowed to sleep. This is the boon that the man fresh from the trenches asks above all things. His days and nights have been one constant strain of alertness. His brain has been racked with the roar of cannon and his nerves frayed by the irregular bursting of shell. His mind is chaos...But when a soldier is once captured he feels that this responsibility of holding back the enemy is no longer his. He has failed. Well, he can sleep in peace now."

Both sides settled down to hacking makeshift defenses out of the frozen earth. The Germans had lost a hundred thousand men in this last 1914 campaign while inflicting the astounding total of five hundred and thirty thousand casualties on the Russians. Their success, however, was of discouragingly limited value. As winter arrived, the Russians had 120 divisions on the front, and each division included twelve battalions. The Germans and Austrians together could muster only sixty divisions of eight battalions each.

For Conrad and his armies, December was a month of high drama, of brief glory followed by final humiliation. As it opened, one of the Russian armies advancing against the Carpathians had taken possession of a mountain pass that gave it a gateway into Hungary. The commander of this Russian Eighth Army, a talented general named Alexei Brusilov, was in position to advance on Budapest and begin the conquest of the Hapsburg homeland. But at just this moment Conrad tried something that worked. He learned of a gap between Brusilov and the Russian army on its right, assembled an attack force, and on December 3 drove it into the gap. The Russians were thrown off balance. In four days Conrad drove them back forty miles. Though the masses of reinforcements sent forward out of the Russian reserve brought him to a halt by December 10, the victory was an important one. It spoiled the Russians' hopes of crossing the Carpathians. It also rendered them incapable of executing a newly hatched plan to send a force from Krakow toward Germany. In combination with Hindenburg's and Ludendorff's November successes in Poland, it left the Russians bogged for the winter far from Berlin, Budapest, and Vienna.

Conrad poisoned his own hour of triumph by launching a year-end invasion of Serbia, his third since the start of the war. This newest incursion started as promisingly as the others, with the Austrians quickly taking possession of much of the Serbian interior along with Belgrade. Just one day after the fall of Belgrade, however, in a moment of Balkan high drama, the mustachioed King Peter of Serbia, rifle in hand, announced to his soldiers that he was releasing them from their pledge to fight for him and the homeland but that he for one was going to the front, alone if necessary. This gesture rallied every doubting patriot to the cause. A counterattack organized by Serbian General Radomir Putnik—the same old soldier who had been caught vacationing in Austrian territory when the war began but was allowed to return home in an act of almost medieval courtesy by Emperor Franz Joseph—sent two hundred thousand Serb troops down on the overextended Austrians. The Austrians, who had gone days without food and were freezing in summer uniforms, fled back across the border. Again their losses were outlandish: twenty-eight thousand dead, a hundred and twenty thousand wounded, seventy-six thousand taken prisoner. The Serbs too had been badly hurt, with twenty-two thousand killed, ninety-two thousand wounded, nine thousand captured or missing, and the survivors ravaged by dysentery and cholera.

Never again, in the years of fighting that lay ahead, would the Austro-Hungarians be involved in a major offensive as anything more than adjuncts to the Germans. Never again would they win a major victory they could call their own. With the war scarcely begun, they were a spent force. With almost four years of war remaining, nearly two hundred thousand of Vienna's best troops—including ruinous numbers of its experienced officers and noncoms—were dead. Almost half a million had been wounded, and some one hundred and eighty thousand were prisoners of the Russians.

There was fighting elsewhere as the year drew to a close. Even after the last assault at Ypres, the Western Front was never entirely quiet. Joffre kept ordering attacks wherever he thought the enemy wall might be weak. "Nibbling," he called it, but its cost in lives was high. By March it would add another hundred thousand casualties to the French total.

People were becoming accustomed to the term *world war.* Since August there had been naval battles, some of them high in drama but none terribly important, all around the globe. There was bloodshed in Africa as the police and small military forces of the various European colonies jockeyed for advantage and the indigenous populations became involved, and in the Far East Japan helped itself to Germany's scattered holdings.

The Middle East was being drawn in as well. The newest member of the Central Powers, Turkey, sent troops based in Syria into Persia. After so many years of watching the Europeans feast on its crumbling empire, the government in Constantinople was eager to recover some of its losses at last.

The British, in particular, were disturbed. When Russia suggested that a show of force near Istanbul might frighten the Turks and cause them to pull back from Persia, London found the idea attractive. A battleship was dispatched to the mouth of the Dardanelles, the narrow channel leading from the northeastern Mediterranean to Constantinople, the Black Sea, and Russia beyond.

Upon arrival, the ship began shelling one of the outermost forts guarding the Dardanelles. Within half an hour the fort was totally wrecked, incapable of defending itself or the sea route to Constantinople.

The battleship, never threatened while it did its work, steamed serenely away. The whole thing had been so *easy*. First Lord of the Admiralty Churchill began to wonder: might the entire passage up to Constantinople be that easily taken?

In Flanders, where there had been so much horror, 1914 ended with a strange spontaneous eruption of fellow feeling. On Christmas morning, in their trenches opposite the British near Ypres, German troops began singing carols and displaying bits of evergreen decorated in observance of the occasion. The Tommies too began to sing. Cautiously, unarmed Germans began showing themselves atop their defenses. Some of the British did the same. Step by step this led to a gathering in no-man's-land of soldiers from both sides, to exchanges of food and cigarettes, even to games of soccer.

This was the Christmas Truce of 1914, and in places it continued for more than a day. The generals, indignant when they learned of it, made certain that nothing of the kind would happen again.

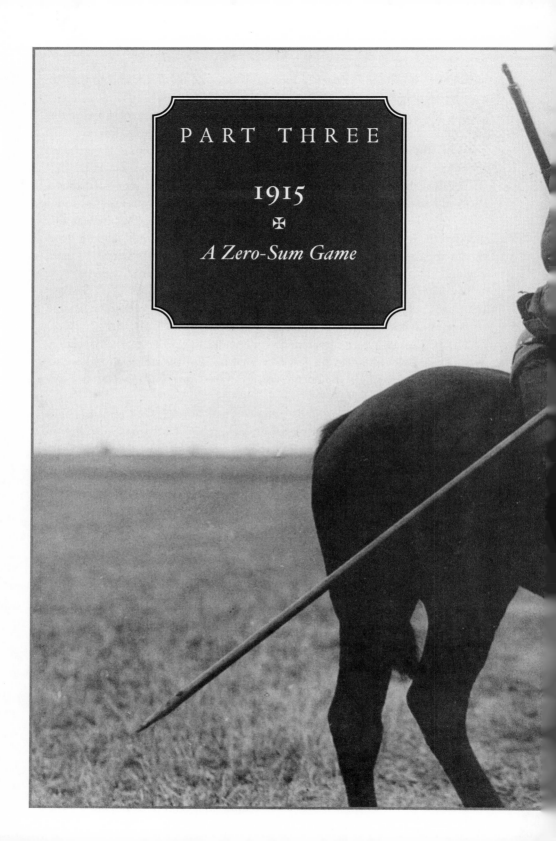

PART THREE

1915
✠
A Zero-Sum Game

The new face of war: a German Uhlan, or lancer, could seem a figure out of ancient legend except for the mask that protects him from poison gas.

Chapter 13

✠

The Search for Elsewhere

*"I can only love and hate,
and I hate General Falkenhayn."*

—Erich von Ludendorff

Nineteen-fifteen opened repetitiously and prophetically, which is to say that it opened with lethal violence on the grand scale. On New Year's Day, in the English Channel, a German submarine fired a torpedo into the hull of the British battleship *Formidable* and sent 546 seamen to their deaths. On the continent the French were on the offensive, or trying to be, all along their long front: in Flanders, the Argonne, Alsace and, most bloodily of all, the Champagne region west of Verdun. In the east, under appalling winter conditions that were causing hundreds of men nightly to freeze to death in their sleep, the Russians were slowly forcing the armies of Austria-Hungary back into the Carpathian passes that separated the plains of Galicia from the Hapsburg homeland. Beyond Europe, on the ice-packed heights of the Caucasus Mountains, the Russians and the weather together were destroying a badly led and ill-equipped army of Turks. There was bloodshed in Africa, in Asia, in the South Pacific, and in the South Atlantic—in improbable places all around the world.

All the belligerents were locked in a situation for which they were woefully unprepared. In the last five months of 1914 more than eight hundred thousand Germans had become casualties, and more than a hundred thousand of them were dead. French and Austro-Hungarian casualties were in the million-man range, Russia's total approached twice that, hundreds of thousands of Frenchmen were listed as dead or missing, and more than half of the Tommies who had come over in August were dead or injured. In every country the shock was numbing. A monument in a single Parisian church, Notre

Dame des Victoires, displays the names of eighty parishioners killed in battle between August and December.

The worst of it was that this carnage had not come close to producing a decision. In every country shattered armies had to be rebuilt and expanded and sent out to do it all again. Some of the leaders—none more than Joffre of France and Britain's Sir John French—continued to believe that victory lay just ahead and could be achieved with one or two more effusions of sacrificial blood. Others—Falkenhayn in Germany, Kitchener in Britain—were able to see that a long and terrible struggle lay ahead. For all of them, optimists and pessimists alike, one question had become paramount:

What do we do now?

All the camps but two, France and Austria-Hungary, were deeply divided over how to answer. In Paris the dominating fact was German occupation of a huge expanse of the French homeland: regions that included 14 percent of the nation's industrial workforce, two-thirds of its steel production, 90 percent of its iron mines, and 40 percent of its sugar refineries, along with substantial parts of its coal, wool, and chemical output. This made it easy for the French to agree on one great goal: to drive the Germans out, blast them out, burn them out, break their defensive line by any means possible and throw them back across the Rhine. More than in any of the other warring nations, only one man's opinion mattered. That man was "Papa" Joffre. Exclusive authority over questions of strategy had been in Joffre's hands from the start. If some were skeptical about the wisdom of trusting Joffre to such an extent, if calls for his removal had erupted during the weeks when his armies were in seemingly endless retreat, the Marne had silenced the doubters even if it had not entirely removed their doubts. Ambiguous as the victory may have been in terms of who had actually made it possible and what it meant for the long term, the simple fact that Joffre had been in command elevated his prestige to a level at which it was, and would long remain, above challenge. As shocking as Joffre's losses continued to be, his appetite for more of the same was undiminished. He remained certain that the war could still be a fairly short and glorious one, and he was determined to make it so.

A similar absence of disagreement pervaded official Vienna, but not because of any such high expectations. Austria-Hungary was forced into near-unanimity by sheer desperation. Its losses were particularly serious because the dual monarchy had less than a third of Russia's manpower to draw upon in trying to make whole its ravaged armies. Field Marshal Conrad's offensives into Galicia and Serbia had literally wiped out some of his most elite units, demoralized many of the survivors, and multiplied the difficulties of maintaining the enthusiasm of the empire's non-German majority. With Serbia unbeaten, with Russia continuing to advance, and with Italy's possible entry into the war on the side of the Entente, Austria-Hungary had only one possible first priority: to somehow keep the Russians from getting through the Carpathians. Achieving this goal was almost certain to require help from the Germans. The Austrians were already incapable of accomplishing anything of consequence without Berlin's assistance.

Conrad, rarely reluctant to engage the enemy, announced plans for a winter campaign aimed at driving the Russians back from the Carpathians and relieving the besieged fortress of Przemysl. He hoped, through a persuasive show of force, to discourage Italy, Romania, and Bulgaria (all of which were eager for a share in the spoils of war but uncertain of which side could make the best offer) from joining the Entente. He asked the Germans to contribute four divisions—upward of sixty thousand troops—to this offensive. In doing so he put his allies on the spot. Nobody in the German high command supposed that Conrad was capable of moving effectively against the Russians without assistance, and nobody was confident that he could succeed even if his request was granted. On the other hand his plan was far from pointless; if he did nothing but wait for the Russians to attack, the results could be disastrous. Falkenhayn had at his disposal four new corps, more than a hundred thousand well-equipped recruits led by experienced officers and noncoms. A struggle immediately erupted over how and where to use them.

What to do about Austria—the question that was, as Ludendorff told Falkenhayn, Germany's "great incalculable"—was only one of the puzzles facing the Germans as the winter deepened. They had not only the entire Western Front to deal with, the relentlessly growing French and British armies, but also a Russian steamroller that despite its huge losses continued to outnumber the German and Austrian forces in the east by overwhelming margins and was obviously preparing to resume the offensive. The Germans had no simple or obviously right way to balance these dangers and distribute the available resources—no clear way to victory on either front, never mind both. Nor were the leaders of the government or army agreed on what should be done. Their differences were so fundamental that they threatened the entire German war effort with paralysis.

Falkenhayn, the handsomely youthful-looking Junker who was now both chief of the general staff and war minister, appeared to have all the power needed to decide questions of strategy. And he knew what he wanted to do. Alarmed by the losses of 1914—he described his army as "a broken instrument"—he was convinced that Germany had no chance of defeating all the forces arrayed against it. A negotiated peace on one front or the other was therefore necessary. In the west, Falkenhayn believed, an acceptable peace could never be achieved without British acquiescence; the English Channel made Britain unconquerable, and the only way to bring it around was to take one of its allies out of the war. As for the east, the size of the front and of the Russian armies made victory improbable within a tolerable period of time. The answer, Falkenhayn thought, was to punish the Russians enough to make them receptive to an eventual settlement while focusing all possible force on the defeat of the French, whom he described as a sword in the hand of the British. "If we succeed in bringing Russia to terms," he said, "we could then deal France and England so crushing a blow that we could dictate peace terms."

He was unwilling to send to the east any troops that might usefully be used in the west, and he was similarly unwilling to thin his forces in East Prussia for the benefit of Conrad. This put him at odds with Hindenburg and Ludendorff. Both men—Ludendorff most importantly, because he and Max Hoffmann were the brains of the team—saw opportunities to crush the Russians. Whether out of strategic conviction or jealousy or some mixture of the two, both were contemptuous of Falkenhayn. And though Falkenhayn's two offices made him doubly the superior of Hindenburg and Ludendorff and every other member of the German high command, his credibility had been damaged by his failure to break through at Ypres even after expending so many lives. Tannenberg and the Masurian Lakes had raised Hindenburg to heights of popular adulation comparable to those occupied by Joffre in France. He was not inclined to use his prestige to help or support Falkenhayn. Prodded by Ludendorff, he undercut Falkenhayn at every opportunity, spoke openly of Falkenhayn's unfitness for the positions he occupied, and encouraged his admirers at court and in the government to do likewise. Falkenhayn, not surprisingly, responded in kind.

Things should have been simpler for the Russians because they, like the French and British, had only one truly dangerous enemy to contend with. But they too were divided and uncertain. The chief of the Russian general staff, the tsar's six-foot-six and stick-figure-thin cousin and namesake the Grand Duke Nicholas Romanov, was a competent commander. He was also aggressive and determined to use the massive forces at his disposal to invade Germany and win the war in the east. But his political position was not strong. He despised the monk Rasputin, once informing him that if he visited army headquarters he would be hanged on the spot, and partly for this reason he was distrusted and feared by the Tsarina Alexandra, who had convinced herself that the grand duke coveted the imperial throne. Though Russia could have only one prime objective in 1915—to throw the Germans into terminal disarray—the question of how to accomplish this was anything but settled. Powerful members of the general staff wanted to strike directly at central Germany. Another faction wanted to complete the penetration of the Carpathians and finish off Austria-Hungary as a prelude to Germany's

Field Marshal Paul von Hindenburg
*Germany's national idol—but increasingly
a mere figurehead as the war continued.*

destruction. The grand duke, lacking clear guidance or firm support from Tsar Nicholas, was not well positioned to resolve such questions and lacked firm convictions. His inclination was to try to satisfy everyone.

A new reality facing all the combatants was Turkey's entry into the war— a strange and unnecessary development. Backward and corrupt, economically and militarily feeble, the Ottoman Empire of 1914 was in no position to compete effectively with the great powers of Europe or even to function as a true partner of any of them. And it had much to lose by going to war with any of them. But to the Young Turks who had seized control in Constantinople in 1908 and clung to power in spite of their country's losses in the Balkan wars, Europe's August crisis had the appearance of a heaven-sent opportunity. Suddenly the Europeans coveted the Turks as potential allies. This change was as surprising as it was abrupt.

For years—for generations, actually—none of the great powers had wanted a formal connection with Constantinople. Turkey was "the sick man of Europe," slowly disintegrating, relentlessly dying. Its demise had been averted only by jealous disagreements among the powers over who should reap the benefits when it finally collapsed. Russia was prevented from taking possession of Constantinople only by Britain's and France's insistence that such a conquest would not be tolerated—that they would fight rather than let it happen. But becoming Turkey's actual *ally* was a different matter. To do that would be to incur obligations to an empire that had little to offer in return. And no ally of Turkey's would be free, precisely because it was an ally, to snatch up fragments of the empire as opportunities arose. So Turkey remained alone as Greece and Serbia and Bulgaria and Romania all broke away, as Britain grabbed Egypt and Cyprus, France took Algeria, Greece took Crete, and Austria-Hungary absorbed Bosnia-Herzegovina. Turkey and its rulers lived in a state of apparently irreversible fear and humiliation.

The two powers with which Turkey had the closest relationships were Britain, its chief protector against Russian expansion, and Germany, which had increasingly substantial economic interests in the Middle East, including a Berlin-to-Baghdad railway. Prussia had been given responsibility for training the Turkish army as early as 1822. In 1913, when German General Otto Liman von Sanders arrived in Constantinople as head of his country's military mission, he found himself also named inspector of the Turkish army—chief of staff, in effect. As a balancing measure, the Young Turks invited Britain to take charge of upgrading their navy. They placed an order for two new dreadnoughts to be built in England at the cost of £11 million—a colossal sum for an empire that had been financially ruined by the Balkan wars. This purchase was so popular with the people of Turkey that much of the necessary money was raised through public fund-raising drives.

The outbreak of the war meant the end of Turkey's long isolation—if Turkey chose to end it. What was not at all clear was which side it would embrace, or whether it should embrace either. It came down, in the end, to a matter of ships, and of British blundering, and of German bullying. When the summer crisis of 1914 rose to its climax, a crew of Turkish seamen was in Britain, ready to take possession of the first of the new dreadnoughts. First Lord of the Admiralty Winston Churchill announced that his country was confiscating both ships. He did so on July 28, the day Austria-Hungary declared war on Serbia, and his act was understandable as a way of assuring that two of the world's newest and most potent warships would not fall into enemy hands. The matter could have been handled more delicately, however. It appears not to have occurred to the British government to negotiate with Turkey—to offer to release the ships in return for an alliance that at least some of the Young Turks would have welcomed. Churchill's announcement provoked outrage in Constantinople. At the beginning of August, with the start of the war only hours away, the Turkish government proposed a formal alliance with Germany.

Berlin, as it happened, already had a draft of such an alliance ready for use and eagerly wired it to Constantinople. It would require Turkey to enter any war in which Germany became involved. The Young Turks, unprepared for such a drastic commitment, made excuses for not signing. Meanwhile they were secretly approaching Russia about a possible alliance in that direction. The Russians, confident at this early stage of the Entente's ability to overwhelm the Central Powers, brushed this overture aside. To them it seemed little more than a pathetic request that they refrain from seizing Constantinople.

While the Turks dawdled, two swift and powerful German warships, the *Göben* and the *Breslau,* were playing a game of hide-and-seek across the

Mediterranean with the British and French fleets. On August 10, pursued by their enemies after shelling the coast of Algeria, the two vessels arrived at the entrance to the Dardanelles and requested permission to enter. Enver Pasha, Turkey's thirty-four-year-old minister of war and a dominant figure among the Young Turks, found himself under intense pressure from all sides. His German advisers insisted that he admit the ships. British and French diplomats demanded a refusal. He tried to delay, but when the Germans insisted on an immediate decision, he yielded. The *Göben* and the *Breslau* were allowed to steam north to Constantinople. Later, when their pursuers arrived at the straits, they were turned away. The Dardanelles were thus sealed, with three hundred and fifty thousand tons of Russian exports suddenly unable to reach the Mediterranean from the Black Sea.

Even that did not settle the matter. Even when the Germans presented the *Göben* and *Breslau* as a gift to the Turkish government (it was an empty gesture: the ships were given Turkish names but retained their German crews and continued to take their orders from Berlin), the Turks declined to commit. Everything remained unresolved until the end of September, when, for the precise purpose of precipitating a crisis, the two German ships steamed up the Bosporus strait into the Black Sea. Flying the Turkish flag, they shelled the Russian cities of Feodosiya, Odessa, and Sebastopol. The Young Turks, as alarmed as the Russians by news of this attack, hastened to assure St. Petersburg that they remained neutral, that the attack had been a *German* act. The Russians replied that the Turks could prove their good faith by expelling the Germans. This they were powerless to do. On November 30, after an Entente ultimatum went unanswered, Russia declared war on Turkey. Britain and France did the same a few days later.

Though Turkey's alliance with the Central Powers was a serious setback for the Entente, some of Britain's leaders thought it opened new options. Being invulnerable to invasion, the British—unlike the French and Russians—had never been required to commit themselves to any theater of operations. By early 1915, thanks to the arrival of units of the regular army from distant parts of the empire and of colonial forces from India, Canada, Australia, and New Zealand, Sir John French had more than three hundred thousand troops under his command. Hundreds of thousands more, the "Kitchener's armies" made up of men who had flocked to recruiting centers at the start of the war, were in training back in England. The question was what to *do* with all this power. The answer was obvious to many senior members of the army and the cabinet, but they were far from united on exactly what they thought was so obvious.

French himself, despite the horrors of Ypres, was as convinced as Joffre that the German defenses could be cracked open, and he was as eager as Joffre to prove it. Consistent exaggeration of German casualties had helped to persuade him that the enemy must be approaching exhaustion. Entente propagandists depicted almost every fight in the West as a slaughter of Germans mounting robotlike suicide attacks, when in fact German losses were often markedly lower than those of the Entente. Back in London, the army's director of military operations produced an analysis supposedly demonstrating that Germany was going to run out of men "a few months hence." (This hopeful myth was slow to die. Before June 1915 another operations director would predict that if Britain would "keep hammering away . . . we shall wear Germany out and the war will be over in six months.") Though French like Joffre wanted to stay on the offensive, he remained unwilling to do so under Joffre and even reluctant to do so *with* Joffre. He continued to demand the freedom to operate independently. There was one final point, however, on which Joffre and French were in complete agreement: every available British soldier, they insisted, should be sent to the Western Front at the earliest possible moment.

Early in January, French went to London and met with the British War Council, a new planning body whose seven members included Asquith, Kitchener, Churchill, Grey, and Chancellor of the Exchequer David Lloyd George. He proposed a new offensive that would follow the coast and be aimed at recapturing the Belgian Channel ports. Churchill supported this idea, seeing in it a way to bring neutral Holland into the war on the Entente side and, by drawing more German troops to the west, to prepare the way for a landing of troops on Germany's Baltic coast. At first the council turned French's proposal down. Most members regarded it as too risky to justify the possible gains and also as contrary to the wishes of Joffre, who wanted the British to attack not along the coast but, again, near Ypres. Days later the idea was brought back to life, not as an approved plan but as a possibility to be kept under consideration. Asquith was unfriendly to the idea. Kitchener was absolutely opposed. What he wanted—it was not a thing to be talked about openly—was to keep Britain's new armies at home until the French and Germans had exhausted each other. Then London could send masses of fresh troops across the Channel and decisively tip the scales. "The German armies in France may be looked upon as a fortress that cannot be carried by assault," Kitchener told French. The British lines, he added, "may be held by an investing force while operations proceed elsewhere."

Elsewhere. For Kitchener and Churchill and others, that became a kind of dream. Shaken by the destruction of the BEF's first divisions and hoping to avoid a repeat, they began looking for less painful ways to prosecute the war.

Grand Duke Nicholas was encouraging their search by sending telegrams to Kitchener, asking him to make a show of force in the Middle East and thereby oblige the Turks to suspend their offensives in Persia and the Caucasus. A campaign in Syria was one idea; by drawing the Turks from the north, it could free Russian troops for the Eastern Front. A Baltic landing was another option; the navy was building a fleet of six hundred motor barges and other craft for an invasion (by *Russian* troops, though St. Petersburg had not been informed) of Germany's Pomeranian coast. Still another possibility, one less fraught with risk than the Baltic scheme, was the landing of an Entente force at the port of Salonika, in northwestern Greece. Greece was not even in the war (it was one of the several neutral states being courted by both sides), but the council hoped that the injection of Entente troops into the southern Balkans might win over not only Greece but Romania, Bulgaria, and Italy. An army moving northward out of Salonika could secure Serbia. Then, reinforced, it might be able to invade Austria-Hungary. Kitchener liked this idea. So did Lloyd George, who as chancellor of the exchequer was not necessarily a central figure in Britain's military planning but was making himself one by sheer force of will.

Finally there were the Dardanelles, which had already been briefly attacked by a British ship at the end of 1914 and had demonstrated no ability to resist. Renewed action there in greater force could create problems for all the Central Powers. Churchill sent a telegram asking the commander of the British fleet in the eastern Mediterranean if a naval force could fight its way through the Dardanelles to Constantinople. When the admiral replied that this might be accomplished "by extended operations with a large number of ships," Churchill was satisfied. He instructed the admiral to submit a detailed plan for such an operation.

The Dardanelles were becoming *elsewhere.*

Just a week into the new year, two offensives that Joffre had put in motion in France's Champagne and Artois regions were essentially at an end. The French advanced only five hundred yards in three weeks and by January 8, with the Germans launching counterattacks, had added tens of thousands of casualties to their dizzily rising total. The Champagne operation alone, by the time it was shut down, had cost ninety thousand French casualties. Even then Joffre did not give up. He would try again in February and yet again in March, continuing to think that he was on the verge of a breakthrough. The British War Council felt confirmed in its skepticism about the Western Front and about Sir John French's promises of success.

The Germans, while successful in holding their line against this endless hammering, were still divided on strategy. No mechanism existed by which

Germany's competing strategists could discuss their differences in any systematic way. The kaiser, the "All-High Warlord," rarely attempted to bring them together, and as a result the rivalries within the high command could only fester. Clear policy formulation was replaced by backstabbing and bickering. Those who wanted to concentrate on the Western Front tried in childish ways to undercut and discredit their rivals. (Falkenhayn, for example, deleted the names of Hindenburg and Ludendorff from reports of success in the east.) The "easterners" not only responded in kind but plotted to have Falkenhayn dismissed. The kaiser, meanwhile, neither led nor allowed anyone else to do so. A crisis was inevitable. But instead of experiencing *a* leadership crisis, the high command went through a series of such crises that lasted a year and a half.

Falkenhayn's position remained ambiguous in the extreme. He wanted to win the war in the west, but also to make the Russians willing to negotiate. When he refused Conrad's request for help in a winter offensive, then refused again when Hindenburg demanded that his unassigned new corps be sent to the east, Hindenburg and Ludendorff announced that they were detaching three and a half divisions from their own Ninth Army and sending them to Conrad. In any army this would have bordered on insubordination. By the traditions and standards of the Prussian army, it was little short of shocking. Falkenhayn protested to the kaiser. Hindenburg responded with an appeal of his own for the kaiser's support. The battle for control over German strategy was joined.

Falkenhayn's next move was clever but certain to enrage his rivals. He used his double-barreled authority as head of the general staff and war minister to declare that the troops being sent from Hindenburg's army to Conrad would become the core of a new Army of the South. This army would be commanded by General Alexander von Linsingen, a protégé of Falkenhayn's, who would report not to Hindenburg but to Falkenhayn himself. Ludendorff was named Linsingen's chief of staff. With this move, Falkenhayn dissolved the team that had given Germany its only victories and diminished the authority of its leading members.

Refusal to obey was out of the question, and Ludendorff prepared to go south. Before departing, he joined Hindenburg in drafting—essentially dictated for the old man's signature—a telegram to the kaiser. "I have grown into close union with my Chief of Staff," it said. "He has become to me a true helper and friend, irreplaceable by any other, one on whom I bestow my fullest confidence. Your majesty knows from the history of war how important such a happy relationship is for the conduct of affairs and the well-being of the troops." Edging closer to direct criticism of what Falkenhayn was doing, the telegram added that Ludendorff's "new and so much smaller sphere of action does not do justice to the General's comprehensive ability and great capacity." It ended on a groveling note: "I venture most respectfully to beg that my war comrade may graciously be restored to me as soon as the operation in the south is under way."

The telegram sent, Ludendorff departed. Within hours he was in the south, involved with Linsingen and Conrad in finalizing arrangements for an advance out of the Carpathians. Even when he was deeply embroiled in military politics at their most vicious, even when he was using every trick at his disposal against his rivals, Ludendorff remained a resourceful, focused, and indefatigable strategist. He had added a team of talented code-breakers to his staff, and thanks to their work he knew what Grand Duke Nicholas was planning. Conrad had been right in expecting a new Russian attack through the Carpathians, but decoded messages showed that this was not all the Russians had in mind. Simultaneously they were planning to renew operations in East Prussia, and still other Russian armies were to drive through Poland into the German heartland. Ludendorff's response was exactly as it had been when he was faced with apparently overwhelming odds in 1914. Instead of allowing the enemy to take the initiative, he would strike first. Again he saw an opportunity not just to hold off the Russians but, with coordinated attacks in the north and south, to cripple them.

Falkenhayn, in the aftermath of his restructuring of German forces in the east, was drawn into the planning of this campaign. On January 11 he met with Conrad, Linsingen, and Ludendorff at Breslau. Their talks were polite if not cordial. Falkenhayn thought it was little better than madness to launch an offensive against superior forces in mountain country in midwinter, and he said so. Conrad replied coolly that he knew the country in question and knew what he was doing. On the following day, at Posen, Falkenhayn met with the old Tannenberg team of Hindenburg, Ludendorff, and Hoffmann. This more private gathering was not a happy one; the pent-up resentments of the past months boiled over. By all accounts, Hindenburg and his lieutenants treated their commanding general with open contempt. Hindenburg told Falkenhayn that he did not have the confidence of the men under his command and should resign. After Falkenhayn's departure, Ludendorff and Hoffmann talked Hindenburg into sending another telegram to the kaiser. This one was not at all groveling. It demanded the dismissal of Falkenhayn, the dispatch of the four new corps to the east, and the return of Ludendorff to Hindenburg's staff. Behind it lay the unmistakable threat that Hindenburg was prepared to resign.

The showdown appeared to be at hand. The kaiser, offended by Hindenburg's presumption and regarding Ludendorff as "a dubious character devoured by personal ambition," declared that he wanted them both court-martialed. Chancellor Bethmann Hollweg, ordinarily all too willing to stay out of military affairs, was horrified. He replied that public punishment of the hero of Tannenberg was unthinkable, that it was Falkenhayn who should be dismissed. Almost the entire imperial court was drawn into the struggle. Falkenhayn's enemies, influenced negatively by his warnings of a long war and positively by Hindenburg's and Ludendorff's assurances that the war need not be long at all, were numerous and influential. The kaiser's wife, Empress Augusta Victoria, was active among them. So was Crown Prince Wilhelm. Even Moltke, encouraged by Bethmann to hope that Falkenhayn's fall might restore him to leadership, said Falkenhayn must go. But Falkenhayn retained the support that at this point still mattered most: that of Kaiser Wilhelm, who acted at last. Falkenhayn would remain at the head of the general staff, the kaiser announced, but would give up the war ministry. The contested army corps would be sent to the east, which the kaiser now declared the "theater of decision." Ludendorff, as soon as he could be spared in the south, would return to Hindenburg's staff.

Not nearly enough had been settled, and much damage had been done. Falkenhayn's authority had been irretrievably compromised: his subordinates had defied him and won much of what they demanded. Falkenhayn's removal from the war ministry was in all likelihood a mistake: he had proved to be a capable administrator, doing much to prepare not only the army but the German economy for a long struggle. The kaiser too had been damaged; his credibility as a commander, never strong, was wearing thin. Wilhelm was showing increasing signs of psychological fragility. Almost completely withdrawn from the real work of planning and conducting the war, he would relieve himself of nervous energy by cutting wood for hours. Unable to sleep, he would pass his nights reading popular novels. In the end he had to beg Hindenburg to accept the new arrangement rather than resign.

The confusion seemed boundless. At one point it was suggested that Falkenhayn should leave the army and replace Bethmann Hollweg as chancellor. Falkenhayn refused out of fear it would leave Ludendorff in effective charge of the army. Yet somehow these men were supposed to work together to save their country from destruction. The prospects were not encouraging. "I can only love and hate, and I hate General Falkenhayn," Ludendorff declared. "It is impossible for me to work together with him." Even Hoffmann, whose temperament was far better balanced than Ludendorff's, told his staff that Falkenhayn was "the fatherland's evil angel."

But for now, for all of them, it was back to the war that was fought with guns. Conrad's offensive began on January 23, when the forty-one divisions of a combined Austro-Hungarian and German force set out to expel forty-two Russian divisions from the Carpathians and proceed to the recovery of

Galicia and the relief of Przemysl. This last objective was crucial to the Austrians both strategically and symbolically. Przemysl was the biggest, stoutest fortress in the Austro-Hungarian Empire, the center from which Vienna had long dominated Galicia and its Polish-Ukrainian population. The Russian advance of 1914 had left it surrounded, with a hundred and fifty thousand troops and civilians trapped inside and running out of food and supplies. Conrad was desperate to break through before its surrender became unavoidable.

The campaign stalled almost as soon as it began. The problem was less the Russian defenders than the nightmarish difficulties of mountain warfare in winter—the need not just to attack but to climb up ice-bound passes. There were successes, but they were more than balanced by the failures. While one Austrian army captured the city of Czernowitz and sixty thousand Russians with it, another lost eighty-nine thousand men in two weeks. The morning discovery that entire encampments had frozen to death in their sleep became commonplace. Conrad, meanwhile, remained at his headquarters far from the action—an exceptionally comfortable headquarters where the generals lived with their wives in private villas.

Five days after the start of this offensive, Ludendorff, once again at Hindenburg's headquarters, kicked off an attack in the north. In doing so he introduced something new in warfare: gas. The Germans began their assault

The Eastern Front in winter
The cold ruined plans and took countless lives.

by opening eighteen thousand canisters of xylyl bromide, a kind of tear gas that was supposed to be carried by the wind into the Russian lines and incapacitate the defenders without killing them. They had not understood, however, that xylyl bromide is ineffective in freezing temperatures. Thus it had so little impact that the Russians scarcely noticed it—never told the British and French of having encountered it. The advance by the German infantry, when it came, made modest initial gains and then was stopped by stiff resistance. Ludendorff, sensibly, called it off. He had accomplished his objective, which was simply to keep the Russians engaged while preparations were finalized for a more important effort on another part of the northeastern front. Engaged they certainly were. Counterattacks by eleven Russian divisions took back all the ground that Ludendorff's offensive had gained—ground of no importance—at a cost of forty thousand casualties in three days. German losses were light: their infantry conducted an orderly retreat while the artillery tore chunks out of the tightly massed Russian formations.

In a month of struggle Conrad barely managed to take the objectives he had planned to reach the first day. Przemysl remained out of reach. Soon it was the Russians who were advancing, managing for a while to push back the Austrians and Germans but at last being stopped by the same impossible weather that had ruined Conrad's plans. But Ludendorff, in the north, was just getting started. He had positioned the German Tenth Army north of the Masurian Lakes, the Eighth to the south, and on February 5 he was ready to unleash a campaign aimed at encircling and destroying virtually all the Russian forces in the region. Though exceedingly ambitious, this plan was rendered almost feasible by the way Grand Duke Nicholas, under conflicting pressures from the generals commanding his northern and southern sectors, had deployed the Russian armies. Russia, at this time, had approximately a hundred divisions on the Eastern Front with others moving forward to join them. They also had, as the failure of Conrad's offensive showed, a strong defensive position in Galicia. The Central Powers, by contrast, had only eighty-three divisions in the east, half of them Austro-Hungarian, many of those of questionable reliability. It is at least possible that the grand duke, by concentrating most of his forces in the north, could have overwhelmed Hindenburg and Ludendorff. But such an approach would have required forcing the generals in the south to spare troops for the fight in the north. This the grand duke would not or could not do.

Just as Ludendorff was ready to move, heavy snow began to fall. It fell for two days, accumulating to a depth of five feet as temperatures fell to forty degrees below zero. The Germans attacked anyway. Even more incredibly, they made good progress, taking the Russians by surprise and driving them out of their defenses. Again, winter gave the fighting a specially hellish quality, made all the worse by a sudden thaw that on February 14 turned ice to ice water and frozen earth to mud. Earlier the Germans had needed as many as eighteen horses to move each of their guns forward through the snow. Now, with the guns sinking into the ground, no number of horses could move them. Soldiers became drenched with snowmelt and their own sweat, and as night fell their clothing froze hard. As in the Carpathians, men froze to death almost as often as they were shot. The battle turned into a race in which all the competitors were painfully handicapped, the Germans struggling forward to get around the Russians and encircle them, the Russians struggling to escape and abandoning trainloads of supplies.

Things moved to a climax on February 18, when a German corps managed to fight its way through deep snow around the Forest of Augustow and seal a Russian corps inside it. The trapped Russians put up a heroic defense through three long days, allowing other units to escape, but finally they were forced to surrender. The day after that some of the escaped Russian forces, having caught their breath, managed to mount a counterattack that captured no ground of consequence but brought the German advance to an end.

The German propagandists declared Augustow a great victory, one of Tannenbergian proportions. Ludendorff claimed that a hundred thousand soldiers and three hundred pieces of artillery had been captured. Though Russian casualties of all kinds were actually about fifty-six thousand and the number of guns taken was 185, this was a substantial success all the same. The Russians had been pushed back seventy miles. What mattered more, Grand Duke Nicholas's plans for a springtime attack in the northeast had been wrecked beyond possibility of recovery. Hindenburg was once again Germany's hero. The Berlin press declared him a genius, invincible, an almost godlike figure.

But the Russian forces in the north had not been destroyed as Ludendorff had said they would be. And although in the west a penetration of seventy miles would have been an immense achievement, in the vast reaches of the east it had little importance. Even Hindenburg admitted that "we failed strategically." In the south there was no basis upon which even to pretend that anything had been accomplished. On February 17 Conrad had tried to restart his offensive, and the result was more pointless carnage. The winter campaign, by the time it ended, added eight hundred thousand Austrian casualties to the million of 1914. In attempting to relieve Przemysl, Conrad had lost six or more times the number of men trapped there. By April, even after rushing the recruits of 1914 into the field, Austria would have only about half a million men available for the front. It was a pathetically small number for an army at war with Russia.

Aside from all the lives lost or ruined, very little had changed. For

Falkenhayn, Conrad's campaign and the Second Battle of the Masurian Lakes (the name given to Ludendorff's offensive) seemed a vindication. As far as he was concerned, the two ventures had proved him right not only about the folly of winter offensives but about the impossibility of defeating Russia. Every one of his warnings had turned out to be well founded. Understandably, he decided that his western strategy too would turn out to be the right one.

THE MACHINERY OF DEATH

THE GREAT WAR DID NOT END IN 1914—OR IN 1915, 1916, or 1917 for that matter—in large part because of the state of technology in the second decade of the twentieth century. The war had broken out at the end of almost a century of dizzily accelerating advances in metallurgy, chemistry, and high-precision mass production, at a moment in history when weaponry was immeasurably more advanced than it had been a few generations before. And the war itself accelerated everything still further. The nations involved were not only the world's military giants but its industrial leaders as well. They rolled out one innovation after another year after year; whenever one side produced an implement of destruction that promised to tip the scales, the other came up with a way to preserve the deadlock.

The armies that mustered after Sarajevo did not understand the potential of the weapons they already possessed, did not know that the tactics they had learned in school were obsolete. The stalemate could not be broken until two things happened: the generals figured out what to do with the power that the industrial revolution had placed in their hands, and they found solutions to such innovations as the machine gun and the submarine.

It takes effort to recall, after a century that included both Kitty Hawk and men on the moon, just how slowly military technology evolved through most of human history. There was no such a thing as an effective sword until the first production of iron implements around 1200 B.C. (weaponry was pretty much a matter of clubs and spears until then), horsemen didn't have the stirrup or the bit until the seventh century A.D., and only in the ninth century did some tinkerer in China learn to combine saltpeter, charcoal, and sulfur in proportions that turned it into a substance that exploded when touched by fire. Gunpowder didn't reach Europe until the thirteenth century—it was brought by Mongol invaders—and the process by which it came to be used effectively was glacially slow. The first muskets were markedly inferior to the longbow in range, in rapidity of fire, and in accuracy and killing power. They replaced the bow only because they required much less strength and skill and so could be used by almost anyone after hours instead of years of training. Napoleon's cannons fired balls of solid iron that were not fundamentally different from the rounded chunks of stone used by Europe's first gunners centuries before. Rifled artillery—big guns with enough range and accuracy to render obsolete the kinds of fortresses that soldiers had been building for millennia—did not appear on the scene until the time of the American Civil War.

That—the middle of the nineteenth century—was when everything really began to change. New machine tools and new ways of casting metal made possible the manufacture of identical parts in practically infinite numbers, and so the way was cleared for the locomotive, truly modern firearms, and the internal combustion engine—for total war. The chemical industry was being born too, its pioneers discovering things that further changed the face of war. They learned that when cotton is soaked in nitric acid and allowed to dry, the result is a smokeless gunpowder far cleaner and three times more powerful than the Chinese concoction. That when nitroglycerin is mixed with absorbent earth, dynamite results. That some of the gases being synthesized for peaceful purposes were deadly when inhaled.

From the start of hostilities in 1914, it became obvious that the very nature of combat had forever changed. The new artillery, equipped with hydraulic mechanisms for absorbing recoil, no longer had to be repositioned after every round. The "shells" fed into it, combining propellant, warhead, and a timing device in a single easily handled cylinder, could be rained down on the enemy more rapidly, more accurately, at greater range and for longer periods of time than anything seen before. For the first time in history, and from the beginning of the war to the end, artillery dominated. It did more killing between 1914 and 1918 than any other weapon.

But it was an entirely new weapon, the machine gun, that turned the Western Front into a prolonged siege. It was invented in 1884 by an American named Hiram Maxim, whose key achievement was using the force that smokeless powder puts into a gun's recoil and gas discharge to eject spent cartridges, reload the empty chamber, and fire again in potentially endless sequence. Maxim's gun could pour out six hundred rounds per minute. It was a simple, sturdy mechanism that, with its barrel cooled by water, could fire at that rate for hours. Batteries of machine guns could and did turn infantry attacks into mass suicides. Their weight made the early models impractical as offensive weapons (those in use at the start of the war required crews of from three to six men), which gave an almost insuperable advantage to the defense.

Even the rifles carried by the soldiers of the Great War were astonishing weapons in comparison with anything previously available. They varied little from country to country: the German Mauser, French Lebel, British Lee-Enfield, Austrian Männlicher, and Italian Männlicher-Carcano all were about four feet long, weighed less than ten pounds, were equipped with bolt actions, and fired metal cartridges of approximately thirty caliber fed from magazines containing between five and ten rounds. All were capable of putting bullet after bullet into a bull's-eye at a range of hundreds of yards. In the hands of a platoon of well-trained infantry, they could put up a field of fire as lethal as any produced by a machine gun.

Simpler innovations, some of them almost crude in technological terms, also proved to be important. Barbed wire, developed in the United States to keep cattle from breaking through fences, became an essential. On the Western Front especially, every trenchline was protected with coils of barbed wire strung between wooden uprights. Unless cleared away in advance of infantry attacks (shrapnel was the standard way of destroying wire), these coils became traps, entangling their victims within point-blank range of enemy guns.

Rudimentary methods of underground tunneling—methods brought to the war by the coal miners of every country, and by the builders of big-city subway systems—added another dimension. Eventually scores of thousands of men on both sides would be engaged in digging under enemy defenses, either to create passageways for sneak attacks or to blow up the men, weapons, and fortifications on the surface above. Inevitably the diggers on one side, accidentally or by design, would sometimes break into the tunnels of their foes. The resulting battles under the earth, often illuminated by nothing but the flash of gunfire, were as ugly and terrifying and secret as the aircraft engagements above the earth were visible, romantic, and admired.

Humblest of all was the lowly mortar. A kind of simple miniature howitzer capable of throwing a charge of explosives a short distance on a high trajectory, the mortar had fallen out of favor in the years before the war. The Germans had a version they called the *Minenwerfer* (mine thrower), but the other armies had few and the British began with none. Mortars proved to be effective in the static fighting of the Western Front—a way of lobbing an unpleasant surprise into an enemy trench—and soon the Tommies were fashioning them out of empty shells. In 1915 an Englishman named Frederick Stokes developed a more sophisticated production model, one whose teardrop-shaped projectile was equipped with stabilizing fins. In short order the "Stokes bomb" became an integral element in every company's inventory of weapons.

Some new things were more horrifying than effective. Poison gas, introduced by the Germans early in 1915 and thereafter used by both sides,

Flamethrowers: terrifying, but of limited effectiveness

killed thousands and left thousands disabled. It was "improved" as the war went on, chlorine being succeeded by phosgene and phosgene by mustard, but it never produced or even contributed significantly to a major victory on any front. Its deficiencies came to be so universally recognized that not even the Nazis would use it in World War II. Much the same happened with the flamethrower, introduced experimentally in 1914 and soon a standard weapon. Using pressurized gas from one tank to propel an ignited jet of oil from a second tank outward in a plume of fire as much as forty yards long, the flamethrower was terrifying in combat but otherwise of limited effectiveness. It was almost useless when used at any distance against entrenchments. And it was dangerous for its users. Operators would be engulfed in fire if a bullet penetrated both of the tanks strapped to their backs. Caught in an agonized dance of death, they might then helplessly spray fire in all directions, incinerating their own comrades.

A war that introduced so many new weapons naturally brought others to an end. It reduced the bayonet, long the infantry's signature weapon, to being a nearly obsolete romantic symbol. The foot soldiers of the Great War often did affix bayonets to their rifles before attacking, even to the end of the war. But they did so because they had been trained to do so and were ordered to do so; it became a largely ceremonial gesture. Men equipped with repeating rifles and face-to-face with armed enemies preferred to shoot before they got close enough to use their bayonets. They also preferred to throw grenades. When it came down to hand-to-hand combat in its most brutish form, they were more likely to use the hand-made clubs they had learned to carry with them, or trenching tools with sharpened edges, or even blackjacks or brass knuckles. The number of men killed by bayonets in the war was, on the whole, very small.

Most dramatically, the Great War brought the end of cavalry. Mounted soldiers had been a central element in offensive warfare since before the time of Alexander the Great. As a way of delivering a decisive shock to an enemy, they dominated European battlefields from the Middle Ages to the nineteenth century. All the armies that went to war in 1914 included huge numbers of troops on horseback—the Russians put more than a million in the field, many of them Cossacks—despite the fact that the decline in their value had begun to be apparent as early as the Civil War. On the Western Front especially, the cavalry were from the start more a burden than an asset, difficult to support and transport, and helpless when confronted with modern gunnery.

What is shocking is the persistence with which the British general staff, far more than the Germans or the French, refused to reduce the size of their cavalry. Right through to the end of the war, Douglas Haig clung to the conviction that horsemen were going to be the key to exploiting infantry breakthroughs (whenever they were achieved) and that under the right circumstances (whatever they might be) his cavalry would prove a match for machine guns. It never happened.

Chapter 14

✠

The Dardanelles

"To attack Turkey would be to play the German game,
and to bring about the end which Germany had in
mind when she induced Turkey to join the war."
—FIELD MARSHAL SIR JOHN FRENCH

In February the Twenty-ninth Infantry Division became the most important unit in the British army, not because it was the last of the prewar
regular divisions to have escaped being sent to the war and wrecked there—
though it was that—but because it was still in England, not committed to any
theater of operations, and therefore *available*. It became the symbol of, and
the immediate prize in, an epic tug-of-war over the direction of Britain's war
strategy.

The struggle began with the fact that Sir John French, though his command continued to grow, was not satisfied. His certainty that the German
lines opposite the BEF had to be ripe for conquest made him urgently hungry for more men. He wanted the Twenty-ninth, wanted it without delay,
and could see no reason why he should be denied. He was supported by
Joffre, who agreed with French about everything except how the British
forces on the Western Front should be used and who should make the decision.

Authority for the deployment of British troops lay not with French but
with the war minister, Lord Kitchener. Kitchener had severely narrow ideas
about what kinds of divisions should be fed into the meat-grinder of the
Western Front. The so-called territorial units, which before the war had
made up a kind of national guard, he regarded as third rate and parted with
more or less willingly. It was the same with the colonials arriving from
distant parts of the empire: Indians, Canadians, Australians, and the like.
Kitchener was fiercely protective, however, of the new, still-raw divisions

formed out of the men and boys who had volunteered in the first months of the conflict, and he was no less protective of the Twenty-ninth. After six months of war a division that was both intact and made up of experienced professional soldiers was a rare and precious asset. More than enough such divisions had been ravaged at Mons, Le Cateau, and Ypres, and on the Aisne.

The Twenty-ninth could become especially important if Britain opened a theater of operations somewhere other than in western Europe, and by February the search for such an opportunity was far along. It appeared, in fact, that the choice had been made: the new theater would be Salonika, the Greek port city that lay, like the Dardanelles but west of them, on the north coast of the Aegean Sea, which separates Greece from Turkey. Salonika was the recommendation of a committee that the War Council had created in January to evaluate possible new fronts. Because of its potential as a base from which to inject troops into the Balkans, thereby threatening both Turkey and Austria-Hungary, it quickly received enthusiastic support, especially from David Lloyd George. The government of Greece, though still officially neutral, was indicating that it would not be unfriendly to a landing in Salonika. Support for the project grew stronger when, early in February, an attack force of five thousand Turks led by a German lieutenant colonel crossed the Sinai Desert and reached the Suez Canal in British-controlled Egypt before being driven back. This alarming development threatened Britain's connection to India. Taking some kind of action in response to Grand Duke Nicholas's appeals for support in the Middle East seemed increasingly necessary. It also dovetailed nicely with the wish for a way to use Britain's manpower more productively than in Flanders.

Early in February, when Lloyd George traveled to Paris for a meeting on financial matters, he brought the idea of a Salonika expedition to the attention of the French. Though Joffre replied, predictably, that he had no troops to spare for such an adventure, Minister of War Alexandre Millerand was more receptive. Days later, it was learned that Bulgaria, one of the neutral Balkan states that both sides were courting, had accepted a large loan from Germany and appeared likely to throw in with the Central Powers. That settled the question: the War Council approved the Salonika proposal. Kitchener, among the strongest supporters of the idea, thereupon ordered the Twenty-ninth Division to move to the Aegean island of Lemnos. The Greeks had agreed to make the island available to Britain. From there, as soon as everything was in readiness, the Twenty-ninth could be quickly transferred to Salonika.

Sir John French, when he learned of this development, declared that without the Twenty-ninth he was not going to be able to fulfill a promise made earlier to take over part of the French line near Ypres and launch an attack in support of Joffre's next offensive. Nor was Joffre pleased. He joined French in protesting, and together the two brought so much pressure to bear on London that Kitchener called off the Twenty-ninth's deployment. The division would, for the time being, remain in England. Green Australian and New Zealand troops being trained in Egypt were ordered to Lemnos in its stead.

Many of the British leaders who supported the Salonika landing looked favorably also on the preparations being made for a naval incursion against the Dardanelles. There seemed no reason why both ventures could not be undertaken at the same time. Both were made possible by Britain's naval superiority, which was all the more overwhelming in the Mediterranean because France's naval forces were concentrated there as well. The two ventures would not compete for the same resources. Salonika was to be an excursion of ground troops; ships would be needed only to ferry those forces to their starting point and keep them supplied. The Dardanelles initiative, by contrast, was to be a naval operation exclusively. A fleet made up of some of the biggest warships that Britain and France had available—and the two countries had plenty—would blast its way northward to Constantinople. Churchill's enthusiasm for the project was rooted in what the commander of the British naval squadron in the eastern Mediterranean had reported at the start of the year. With a fleet of warships and enough minesweepers to clear the way, Vice Admiral Sackville Carden said, he could reach Constantinople in thirty days. Substantial army involvement would not be required.

Little was necessary except to assemble ships that were already in the Mediterranean and send them into action. On February 19, when Carden steamed up to the entry to the strait and began shelling the forts there, he had under his command the most potent fleet ever assembled in that part of the world. It included twelve British and four French battleships (second only to dreadnoughts among the world's biggest, most heavily armed vessels), fourteen British and six French destroyers (much smaller, unarmored vessels, built for speed and firepower), an assortment of cruisers (midway in size between battleships and destroyers), plus—rather an oddity—thirty-five fishing trawlers that had been brought from the North Sea with their civilian crews for use as minesweepers. Most of the battleships were old to the point of being obsolete, but they carried heavy guns capable of doing tremendous damage at long range. And among them was the crown jewel of the Royal Navy: His Majesty's Ship *Queen Elizabeth,* the newest of Britain's state-of-the-art superdreadnoughts. She had just been launched and happened to be in the Mediterranean for her sea trials when orders went out for the Dardanelles task force to be assembled.

The key to success was obvious: the fleet had to attack quickly, clearing away the mines that the Turks were known to have laid in the Dardanelles, using shellfire to destroy the artillery on the high ground on both sides of the strait, and then pushing through into the open waters of the Sea of Marmara, at the far end of which lay Constantinople. The Turks, and their German military advisers, had been expecting an attempt of this kind. Their defenses, however, were woefully thin; they had only about a hundred pieces of artillery on the heights and very few troops with which to fend off landing parties. The Germans calculated that if the invaders were prepared to lose ten ships, it would be impossible to stop them. The Turkish government was so pessimistic that it began preparations to flee Constantinople for the interior.

Naval commanders, however, are not easily persuaded to risk ships and their crews. On this first foray Carden never seriously tested the strength of the defenses. A cautious man with no experience commanding large forces, he made no effort to move his ships into or even near the two-and-a-half-mile-wide entry to the strait. Instead he stood off in the distance, shelling the forts from three miles away, and at sunset he brought the attack to an end. His second in command, Vice Admiral John de Robeck, asked permission to continue firing but was refused. Carden intended to resume the next day, but the weather turned foul and spoiled visibility. The fleet waited far offshore while the defenders, having been alerted to the fact that a major assault was imminent, hurried to fortify their positions.

The ships returned on February 25 with De Robeck commanding, possibly because Carden's health was not good. Again they brought the forts under fire, and this time they put ashore raiding parties that encountered almost no resistance. Within twenty-four hours all the outer forts were neutralized, their garrisons either dead or in flight. Some of the big ships moved just inside the entry to the Dardanelles, but they dared not venture farther. To the north were other forts, most menacingly at a point where the channel was only a mile wide. Even worse, the strait was known to be heavily mined.

Clearing away the mines had turned into the navy's first major headache. The civilian crews of the improvised minesweepers had refused to proceed when they came under fire. The navy crews who replaced them proved to be inexperienced in handling both the trawlers and their complicated minesweeping gear. When a miniature flotilla of seven trawlers made its most aggressive probe, moving beyond the entry to the strait after dark, the Turks turned spotlights on them, brought them under heavy fire, sank one and put the others to flight. That was not the only problem. The British and French lacked adequate aerial reconnaissance, and the Turks' howitzers, lobbing shells from behind the ridges that lined the strait, could not be reached by the flat trajectories of the naval guns. And so De Robeck, like Carden before him, thought it imprudent to proceed. He withdrew, the days began to slip by, and the Germans and Turks continued to build their defenses. Churchill, too far away to appreciate the difficulties of the situation, sent message after message demanding that Carden *move*.

An interesting sidelight, considering that the campaign had been undertaken largely to help the Russians, is Russia's noninvolvement. Russia had substantial forces not a great distance to the north (including warships in the Black Sea), and the campaign's ultimate target was the city, Constantinople, that the tsars had been coveting for centuries. Sergei Sazonov, foreign minister at the St. Petersburg court, was unenthusiastic about the naval assault for much the same reason that, the previous August, he had spurned an offer of alliance from Turkey. With Turkey as her ally, Russia would have been barred from seizing Constantinople and other pieces of the Ottoman Empire. Similarly, it was improbable that Britain and France, having taken possession of Constantinople, would then hand it over to their ally. If the city could not be captured by Russia alone, it should not be captured at all. "I intensely disliked the thought that the Straits and Constantinople might be taken by our Allies," Sazonov said later. "When the Gallipoli expedition was finally decided upon by our Allies...I had difficulty in concealing from them how painfully the news had affected me."

Russian nonparticipation was not the worst of it. On March 1, in what should have been a triumphant achievement for the Entente, the same Greek government that was encouraging Britain and France to send troops to Salonika and Lemnos offered three divisions of infantry for use at the Dardanelles—thereby proposing to end its neutrality. Italy, Bulgaria, Romania—all might be influenced to follow Greece's lead to get their share of the booty as Austria-Hungary and Turkey went down to defeat. The possible benefits of landing troops at the Dardanelles were brought into high relief: by clearing out the Turkish forts, they could reduce the dangers to the naval force to the vanishing point. And Joffre and Sir John French would have no reason to object.

But Samsonov was unwilling to allow Greek involvement. A British-French move on Constantinople was deplorable enough; involvement by Greece, a potential challenger to Russia's postwar dominance of the Balkans, was out of the question. And so the Russian government said no. In a message to Athens, Sazonov declared that "in no circumstances can we allow Greek forces to participate in the Allied attack on Constantinople." Sir Edward Grey intervened in an effort to save the situation, promising the Russians that at war's end they could have Constantinople and territories around it. He was too late. News of the Greek offer and Russia's rejection, when it became widely known, threw Athens into turmoil. The Greeks amended their offer, making it contingent upon Bulgaria too joining the Dardanelles operation. The Greeks feared, the Balkans being the Balkans, that if they sent a substan-

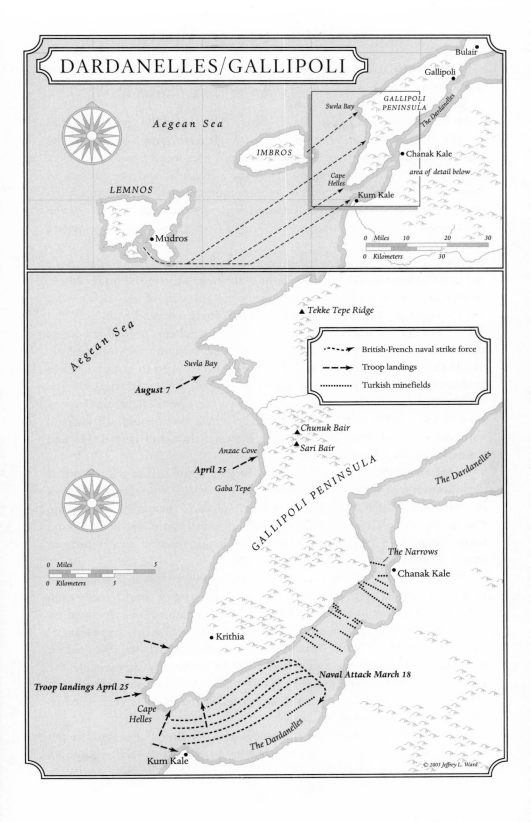

DARDANELLES/GALLIPOLI

Bulair

Gallipoli

Aegean Sea

GALLIPOLI
PENINSULA

Suvla Bay

The Dardanelles

IMBROS

Chanak Kale

area of detail below

Cape
Helles

LEMNOS

Kum Kale

Mudros

0	Miles	10	20	30

0	Kilometers		30

▲ Tekke Tepe Ridge

Aegean Sea

Suvla Bay

August 7

- - - → British-French naval strike force

- - → Troop landings

········· Turkish minefields

▲ Chunuk Bair
▲ Sari Bair

Anzac Cove

April 25

Gaba Tepe

GALLIPOLI PENINSULA

The Dardanelles

The Narrows

Chanak Kale

0	Miles	5

0	Kilometers	5

● Krithia

Naval Attack March 18

Troop landings April 25

Cape
Helles

The Dardanelles

Kum Kale

© 2005 Jeffrey L. Ward

tial part of their army to the other side of the Aegean, the Bulgarians would attack them. There was no possibility of drawing Bulgaria in, and so the negotiations limped to a sorry end.

The consequences were far-reaching. Three Greek divisions could have been invaluable at a time when (as the Turkish army's history of the Dardanelles campaign would state) "it would have been possible to effect a landing successfully at any point on the peninsula, and the capture of the straits by land forces would have been comparatively easy." Instead, the Greek government fell. It was replaced by a government friendly to the Germans, which did not displease the King of Greece, whose wife was Kaiser Wilhelm's sister.

As the political complexities multiplied and Admiral Carden waited for the strait to be cleared of mines, fissures appeared among the leadership in London. Churchill, emerging as the principal advocate of the Dardanelles incursion, demanded that Carden and De Robeck proceed. Admiral John Fisher, as lofty a symbol of the Royal Navy as Kitchener was of the army and a close ally of Churchill's since the latter had brought him out of retirement at the start of the war, was skeptical. He continued to favor what was undoubtedly the riskiest idea that anyone had come up with thus far, the landing of troops on Germany's Baltic coast. He saw the Dardanelles as a threat to that venture and insisted that an attack there could not succeed without the landing of as many as a hundred thousand troops. He and Churchill began to draw apart.

Sir John French, to complicate things further, continued to complain that a commitment of troops anywhere except on the Western Front would be a monumental mistake. "To attack Turkey," he said, "would be to play the German game, and to bring about the end which Germany had in mind when she induced Turkey to join the war—namely, to draw off troops from the decisive spot, which is Germany herself."

Churchill, seeing no need for troops and therefore not in conflict with French, impressed upon Carden that a successful assault would justify even serious costs. "The unavoidable losses must be accepted," he declared by telegram. "The enemy is harassed and anxious now. The time is precious." Kitchener was firmly with Churchill, saying that Britain "having entered on the project of forcing the straits, there can be no idea of abandoning the scheme." (Lloyd George, though without military experience, observed that continuing an offensive that has already proved unsuccessful has rarely in history turned out to be a good idea.)

Again Kitchener released the Twenty-ninth Division for service in the Aegean. This time, however, it was to be used—if needed—not at Salonika but at the Dardanelles. It was to become part of a new expeditionary force along with the Australian and New Zealand troops being transferred from Egypt. This force was put under the command of a longtime friend and protégé of Kitchener's, General Sir Ian Hamilton, a lanky sixty-two-year-old veteran who had served with distinction in India and the Boer War, had been a British observer in the Russo-Japanese War, and had a reputation for fearlessness under fire. Hamilton left England immediately, without specific orders and without a staff appropriate to his new responsibilities. He was to be rushed to the Mediterranean by train, put aboard a fast ship, and delivered to the Aegean in a matter of a few days. Once there, he was to take stock of the situation and decide what should be done. The French, meanwhile, had assembled a new infantry division for service in the Dardanelles and, in spite of Joffre's reluctance, started it for the Aegean. What was still supposed to be a naval operation, therefore, had by now come to involve almost eighty thousand troops. Russia too, Sazonov's concerns having been put to rest by Grey's grandiose offer of Constantinople, was promising a corps. It would go into action as soon as—no small condition—the British and French broke through to the Sea of Marmara.

Carden and De Robeck continued their preparations. Progress was being made in clearing the mines beyond the mouth of the strait. Weather permitting, the attack was only days away. Carden, however, was finding it impossible to eat or sleep. On March 13 he suddenly declared that he was unable to continue and would have to resign. De Robeck attempted to dissuade him—surrender of the Dardanelles command would mean the end of Carden's career—but was unsuccessful. A doctor examined Carden, declared him to be on the verge of nervous collapse, and advised him to start for home without delay. De Robeck took command.

Neither De Robeck nor anyone in his fleet knew of something that had happened on the night of March 8 inside the strait in waters that the British had earlier cleared of mines. The *Nousret,* a little steamer that the Turks had converted into a minelayer, had slipped past the destroyers guarding the cleared sector. There, parallel to the shore, it had silently deposited a line of twenty mines. It had then made its escape undetected. The mines hung motionless just beneath the surface of the water.

On March 10, the same day that Kitchener released the Twenty-ninth Division for the Dardanelles, Sir John French began at the Belgian village of Neuve Chapelle his first offensive since the onset of stalemate on the Western Front. It is perhaps no coincidence that the two things happened simultaneously. French was motivated, in part at least, by a determination to demonstrate that Britain's available troops would be better used on the

Vice Admiral Sackville Carden
*Said a British and French naval force
could reach Constantinople in
thirty days.*

Western Front than in some distant corner of the Mediterranean. It would
not be strange if Kitchener had decided to get the Twenty-ninth away from
Europe before the pressure to send it to Flanders became irresistible.

Just as French had been angling to have the Twenty-ninth added to the
BEF, Joffre had been angling to get the British to take over the portions of the
front that his troops were manning north of Ypres. What he wanted was reasonable: the patchwork character of the front, French then British then
French again, created endless logistical problems. Joffre also wanted to free
his troops for fresh offensives he was planning in Artois and Champagne. In
mid-February, when Kitchener made the first of his decisions to send off the
Twenty-ninth and French retaliated by announcing that this would leave him
without the resources to do as Joffre wished—extend his line or support
Joffre's latest offensive with an attack of his own—Joffre had called off the
part of his plans that was to have been conducted in coordination with the
British. He had begun complaining both to London and to his own government in Paris.

French and Douglas Haig feared that if Joffre got his way, the BEF would
be consigned permanently to a supportive role. They wanted a different kind

of role—they wanted *British* victories, and with them a full share of the glory. As it happened, Haig had a plan for producing victory: an artillery barrage of unprecedented ferocity to be followed by an infantry advance onto the ground cleared by the guns. He chose Neuve Chapelle because the Germans, who were thinning out their defenses in order to send troops to the more turbulent east, were known to have made especially severe cuts there. His objectives were to capture the Aubers Ridge, a long stretch of high ground a mile east of Neuve Chapelle, threaten Lille, and cut the rail line on which the Germans were shuttling troops and guns between Antwerp and Alsace-Lorraine.

French assented to Haig's plan. He wanted the attack to happen as soon as possible, before the politicians decided to give the BEF piecemeal to Joffre and independent action became impossible. March 10 became the chosen date despite the fact that the ground at Neuve Chapelle was always water-logged in springtime and would not be suitable for infantry operations until April at the earliest. Joffre, asked to mount a supporting attack at Arras on the same date, waited until March 7 to take his revenge by replying that the British failure to take over his line near the coast had left him without enough manpower to help. The British decided to proceed anyway.

Weather aside, Haig had chosen his battleground well. The sector that he had targeted was a bulge in the German line, a salient exposed to fire from three directions. It was defended by only fourteen hundred Germans equipped with only a dozen machine guns, with few reserves nearby. The wetness of the ground made entrenchment impossible, so that the Germans were up on the surface, behind sandbag barriers that provided scant protection against artillery. Haig had forty thousand men, many of them Indian colonials, to throw into the attack. Their way would be cleared by fire from a concentration of artillery that would not be equaled until 1917: one field gun for every five yards of front, one heavier piece for every nineteen.

All these weapons opened fire at seven-thirty A.M., and for thirty-five minutes they turned the German line and the areas immediately behind it into an inferno where almost nothing could survive. Then they stopped, and the infantry, bayonets fixed, began their advance. Taught by experience to expect the worst, the troops at the center of the British line instead found almost no resistance. The defenders, everywhere except on the outer edges of the barrage, had been virtually annihilated. What was supposed to be the second line of defense was unoccupied and, when the British reached it, gave no evidence of having been occupied in months. When the Tommies moved through wrecked and abandoned Neuve Chapelle to yet another German line, it too proved to be empty. Only an hour and a half after setting out, they had reached their objective for the day. Ahead was empty territory, open and undefended. Haig had broken completely through—the first of only three times in the entire war that the German line would be torn open in this way. And only about a thousand German reserves were near enough to join the survivors within the next twelve hours. The gate to a tremendous victory stood wide open.

The story of how this triumphant beginning came to nothing is a chronology of mistakes, confusion, and leadership so deficient that it explains why Max Hoffmann, when Ludendorff later in the war exclaimed that British soldiers fought like lions, replied that fortunately for Germany they were "led by donkeys." Haig had limited his attack to a front only two thousand yards wide. This was not only unnecessary in light of the thinness of the German defenses—which the British were aware of—but too narrow an opening for such a large force to pass through efficiently. But when questions had been raised by Edmund Allenby, a cavalry commander who later would win fame in the Arabian Desert, Haig swept them aside with the observation that Allenby knew nothing about handling such large numbers of troops. Another difficulty was that a four-hundred-yard-wide sector at the northern end of the German line had not been shelled according to plan and was still intact when the advance came. Although the guns responsible for bombarding the sector in question had not arrived until the night of March 9 and therefore could not be ready for action the next morning (platforms had to be built, telephone lines installed), nothing was done to assign the sector to other batteries. The result was a pocket of German defenders who, untouched by the bombardment, were able to bring machine-gun fire to bear on the attackers both directly ahead of them and to their south. This fire need not have been enough to stop the main offensive, but it and a similar problem at the other end of the attack zone caused the officers on the scene to order a halt until the machine guns could be dealt with.

There followed a series of almost inexplicable delays, most painfully at the center, the point of breakthrough, where the colonel in charge requested permission to continue his advance but received no answer. Behind him tens of thousands of troops and support units found themselves jammed together at the too-narrow hole in the line, barely able to move and not knowing what they were expected to do. Meanwhile small German units began to arrive from all directions, and though they were pitifully few they brought machine guns and light artillery with them and quickly threw together new defenses. When the attack finally resumed at the end of the afternoon, the opportunity was gone.

Haig tried again the next day and yet again on March 12, but the Germans were growing stronger by the hour and soon were counterattacking. When Haig finally gave up, his gains included little beyond the ghost town of Neuve

Chapelle. He had lost 11,600 men, the Germans 8,600—the numbers being mere abstractions that, as always, veil thousands of stories of lives lost and wrecked. The recollections of one British veteran of Neuve Chapelle provides a peek behind the veil. "I was wounded in the battle and taken to a casualty clearing station," said Cavalryman Walter Becklade. "I was beside a fellow who had got his arms bandaged up—I'd simply got my right arm bandaged. He was trying to light his pipe but couldn't get on very well so I offered to fill and light it for him. But when I'd lit it I suddenly realized he had nowhere to put it, as he'd had his lower jaw blown away. So I smoked the pipe and he smelt the tobacco, that was all the poor chap could have."

Lessons had been learned on both sides. The Germans acquired new confidence in their ability to hold off attacks even when outnumbered, and Falkenhayn became less reluctant to spare troops for the east. The British, on the other hand, learned a tragically false lesson. French and Haig concluded that Neuve Chapelle had failed because the opening artillery barrage had been too short. Henceforth they would insist on whole days of bombardment at the start of any offensive.

On March 13, the day after Haig ended his attacks, General Sir Ian Hamilton left London to take command of the not-yet-existent Mediterranean Expeditionary Force (which Kitchener had been calling the Constantinople Expeditionary Force until Hamilton suggested such a name might tempt the fates). He arrived in the northern Aegean just hours before the start of Admiral De Robeck's March 18 attempt to force the Dardanelles and was able to witness its climax.

The fleet that De Robeck took into the strait that morning was awesome: sixteen battleships—four French and the rest British—most of them old but every one of them enormous, heavily armored, massively armed. At the head of the formation, steaming abreast, were De Robeck's flagship *Queen Elizabeth* (which carried a dozen guns that fired shells fifteen inches in diameter) and three British battleships. About a mile astern of this vanguard, also abreast, were the four French vessels, commanded by a French admiral eager for combat and cheerful about following the orders of the British. Four other battleships guarded the flanks of these two groups while the others waited outside the mouth of the strait.

The only Turkish guns heavy enough to penetrate battleship armor were more than ten miles north at a place called the Narrows, where the sea-lane is only a mile wide. If these guns could be silenced, and if the mines that were known to lie in the Narrows could be removed, nothing could stop De Robeck from reaching the Sea of Marmara.

Once inside the strait De Robeck stopped the *Queen Elizabeth* and her three sister ships at a point where their biggest guns could fire on the Narrows.

They were out of range of the Turks' heaviest guns (which were manned by both Turkish and German crews), and the guns that could reach them were too light to be more than a nuisance. For half an hour the four lead ships poured high explosives on the gun emplacements at the Narrows, knowing they had to be doing tremendous damage but unable to tell if their targets were being destroyed. Then De Robeck began the second phase of his attack, signaling for the four French ships to move past him deeper into the strait. This was a courtesy to the French commander, who had requested the honor of a prominent part in the offensive, and once his ships were north of De Robeck's line, they too began firing and coming under fire themselves. The clash continued for another two hours, with the fire from the Turks growing noticeably less frequent and less accurate, until De Robeck ordered the French ships to retire to the south and the ships that had not yet been engaged to come forward. Up to this point everything had gone perfectly.

Having completed U-turns to starboard, the French battleships were moving toward the rear in single file when suddenly the second vessel in line, the *Bouvet*, blew up. She sank with stunning speed, disappearing in less than two minutes and taking almost her entire crew of more than six hundred with her. No one knew what had happened; the general assumption was that either a lucky Turkish shell had somehow penetrated one of the *Bouvet*'s shell storage compartments or an enemy submarine had entered the strait. It was in any case an isolated disaster, and otherwise everything continued to go well. The surviving French ships completed their withdrawal and were replaced by six British battleships that had not yet seen action; they moved even farther north than had the French, and for another two hours all the ships continued to fire. By late afternoon the return fire from the Narrows

Rear Admiral John De Robeck
Changed his mind about naval assault,
dashing Churchill's hopes.

had almost ended. De Robeck, moving to the next phase of his plan, called the minesweepers into action.

The trawler-minesweepers came under heavy fire from the howitzers in the hills and soon turned and fled. Minutes later the battleship *Inflexible,* which had been firing her guns all afternoon despite substantial damage to her superstructure and was now near the place where the *Bouvet* had sunk, was seen to heel over sharply to starboard. Her captain sent up signal flags indicating that she had hit a mine and began steering for the exit from the strait. Minutes later exactly the same thing happened to HMS *Irresistible,* which was so completely disabled that De Robeck dispatched a destroyer to take off her crew. In the disorder that followed, as De Robeck withdrew his gunships and sent destroyers back into the strait to tow the *Irresistible* to safety or sink her if necessary to keep her from falling into Turkish hands, yet another British battleship was hit and went to the bottom.

This sudden turn of fortune had been costly—two battleships lost, two gravely damaged—but not ruinous. De Robeck at first was despondent, certain that his losses would prompt his dismissal. Instead, he received word from Churchill that four British battleships and a French replacement for the *Bouvet* were already on their way to join him. The minesweeping problem was quickly if belatedly remedied: the trawlers were replaced with destroyers fitted with minesweeping equipment. De Robeck, his confidence restored, telegraphed his eagerness to return to the strait and finish the job. Back in London, Churchill was delighted. Even "Jackie" Fisher, his doubts temporarily dissolved by De Robeck's expressions of confidence, was pleased.

But then, slowly, the tide of opinion began to turn. General Hamilton, troubled by what he had witnessed, wired Kitchener as he had been instructed to do. His message was not optimistic. "I am being most reluctantly driven towards the conclusion that the Dardanelles are less likely to be forced by battleships than at one time seemed probable," he reported, "and that if the Army is to participate, its operations will not assume the subsidiary form anticipated." In other words, troops were likely to be essential—troops in large numbers. An army was going to have to be landed, Hamilton said, and this "must be a deliberate and prepared military operation, carried out at full strength, so as to open a passage for the Navy." Kitchener agreed, declaring that it was now his opinion that the next phase "must be a deliberate and prepared military operation"—not, that is, an assault by ships alone.

By March 22, four days after the loss of the ships, De Robeck was brought around to Hamilton's way of thinking. When he reported to London that he too was now skeptical of clearing the strait with his battleships, even the navy and army staffs became internally divided. No one, however, suggested calling the whole thing off. The fruits of success were too tempting: Turkey

General Ian Hamilton
*"The Dardanelles are less likely
to be forced by battleships than
at one time seemed probable."*

out of the war, Bulgaria, Greece, and Romania all in on the Entente side. Failure, on the other hand, might induce the Balkan states not only to remain neutral but possibly to join the Central Powers.

At the center of the struggle, still determined to resume the naval attack, stood Churchill. He prepared a telegram ordering De Robeck to take his fleet back into the strait at the first opportunity. But when he showed his draft to several senior admirals, most of them—Fisher included—refused to endorse it. They told Churchill that it was unthinkable for London to insist on an action that the responsible admiral on the scene did not himself support. Churchill tried again to get De Robeck to change his mind—De Robeck's own chief of staff was also arguing that a resumption of the attack was certain to succeed—but could not do so. The prime minister thought Churchill was probably right but found it impossible to countermand Fisher and so many other admirals. Finally Churchill had to accept that he was beaten.

It is entirely possible that De Robeck would have succeeded if he had promptly returned to the strait. The Turkish and German defenders were amazed when he failed to do so, and they were not hopeful of stopping him if he did. Though most of their guns remained operable and the worst damage at the Narrows was soon repaired, their stocks of ammunition were dangerously low (a fact that was known to the British), and they had no way of resupplying. All along the strait, they had fewer than thirty armor-piercing shells. Their supplies of mines were likewise nearly exhausted. Officials in Constantinople were hurrying their families out of the city and preparing the government for flight.

The Turks were no better prepared to deal with a military landing, but the British and French were unprepared to land. Ian Hamilton was still waiting for most of his troops, and those that had arrived were not at all ready to undertake a vastly complicated amphibious operation. Lemnos, the island being used as the British base, lacked enough fresh water for all the troops pouring in. Hamilton decided that he was going to have to transfer the troopships to Egypt, where they could be unloaded and then reloaded in proper fashion. He would have to decide where to land his forces, and how.

In one sense at least, Hamilton now seemed to have time to spare. The Russians, with the Eastern Front stabilized, were no longer quite so desperate for relief. Their defeat at Second Masurian Lakes was now weeks in the past and had done little lasting damage. In the south, in and around the Carpathians, they were by late March again on the attack. On March 22, Przemysl had fallen after a siege of 194 days. The siege had been a nightmare for most of the starving people sealed up inside—a nightmare made all the more intolerable by the fact that the fortress's top military officers and their mistresses had lived in luxury throughout the ordeal, waxing fat on secretly hoarded foodstuffs. In the hours before surrendering to the Russians outside, the Austrian commanders blew up their remaining supplies of shells. "The first ammunition dump exploded with a terrifying boom, the ground shook and the glass fell out of all the windows," a Polish woman who had gone to Przemysl in an effort to save her family's house wrote. "Clouds of ash cascaded from chimneys and stoves, and chunks of plaster fell from the walls and ceilings. There was soon a second boom. As the day dawned the town looked like a glowing, smoking crater with pink flames glowing from below and morning mist floating above—an amazing, menacing sight. These hours were perhaps the only hours like this in the whole history of the world. Countless people died of nervous convulsions last night, without any physical injuries or illnesses. By the time the sun climbed into the sky everything was still. Soldiers knelt on their balconies, praying . . . There is a corpse in our house, on the floor above the Litwinskis'. The man seems to have died of fear. I have to do something about him, but nobody wants to get involved, they are all leaving it to me. I persuaded one of the workmen to go down to the army hospital to ask what to do . . . he was told they would deal with it tomorrow, they've got too many corpses today as it is, littering the streets awaiting collection."

With Przemysl the Russians had captured a hundred and twenty thousand troops, nine generals, and hundreds of guns—all of which reduced Emperor Franz Joseph to fits of weeping. The surrender of Przemysl freed three Russian army corps to join a spring offensive that looked increasingly promising.

The Russians still were unable to move their accumulating surplus grain from the Black Sea to the Mediterranean and so get urgently needed currency for it. Nor could the British and French send supplies to the Russians via the Black Sea ports. But the Dardanelles campaign, if successful, would solve that problem permanently.

The suspension of the naval offensive at the Dardanelles, and the delay in getting an army offensive under way, were a huge boon to the Turks and their German advisers. They were still badly equipped and widely dispersed, but gradually, ever so slowly, they were managing to pull together a defense that just might, with much luck, be adequate to fend off Hamilton's attack whenever it came.

THE SEA WAR

THE DARDANELLES EXPEDITION WAS BY NO MEANS THE Great War's first demonstration of British naval power. From the start of the conflict, under the aggressive leadership of Winston Churchill, the Royal Navy had asserted control of sea-lanes around the world and denied the Central Powers access to them. But not until 1915, when the likelihood of a long war had become clear to everyone, did the importance of sea power grow equally clear.

In a short war, one in which the Schlieffen Plan succeeded and was followed by the defeat of Russia, the United Kingdom's great navy would have mattered even less than its little prewar army. But in the siege that the Western Front became, all the combatant powers desperately needed access to the outside world. Few of them, the island nation of Britain least of all, produced enough food to support their populations. None could keep their war machines in operation without imported raw materials.

Britain, by 1914, had enjoyed unchallenged naval supremacy for a century. The Royal Navy provided the sinews that held the empire together. The government in London adhered to a policy of spending whatever was needed to keep the navy bigger and more potent than any other two navies in the world.

This policy was no great burden for the United Kingdom, and it posed no great problem for the other Great Powers, from Lord Nelson's destruction of the French and Spanish fleets at Trafalgar in 1805 on through the rest of the nineteenth century. But in the 1890s the young Kaiser Wilhelm II, eager to make his empire not only a continental but a global power, was persuaded by the ambitious Admiral Alfred von Tirpitz that Germany's growing world trade and colonial possessions required a first-class navy. By the start of the new century Berlin was expending enormous sums to build warships that rivaled Britain's.

The consequences were profound. Until the kaiser began his shipbuilding program, Britain and Germany had seemed designed by destiny not to conflict. Britain had the world's greatest collection of colonies and greatest fleet of warships, but only a small and widely dispersed army and no ambitions on the European mainland. Germany's overseas possessions were small by comparison, and it had no navy at all beyond a tiny coastal defense force. Both nations were focused on France, which for generations had been the most powerful country on the continent (it had taken Britain, Prussia, Russia, Austria, and Spain together to bring Napoleon down) and Britain's great rival in North America and the Caribbean, Africa, the Middle East, and elsewhere.

Even after the Franco-Prussian War, which established the newly unified Germany as Europe's leading power, Britain saw little reason to be concerned. She and Germany continued to regard each other as natural allies and old and good friends—a relationship personalized in the happy marriage of Queen Victoria's daughter and the first kaiser's son and heir. After 1890, when Russia and France became allies, whatever worries London might have had about Germany disrupting the European balance of power were temporarily put to rest.

But when Wilhelm II and Tirpitz embarked upon the building of a navy that they hoped to make as powerful as Britain's, they threatened the foundations of British security. From the perspective of London, Germany was no longer a friend but a rival at best and a serious danger at worst. (The kaiser neither intended nor foresaw this change. At once jealous and admiring of a United Kingdom ruled in succession by his grandmother, his uncle, and his cousin, he entertained fantasies in which Britain would embrace Germany as its equal on a world stage that the two would govern to the benefit of everyone, including the "natives" of backward and faraway lands.)

The German navy was born in 1898, when legislation financed the construction of seven state-of-the-art battleships immediately and fourteen more over the next five years. This ignited an enormously costly arms race. Britain was able to pay for its shipbuilding with tax revenues, but the Germans, already spending heavily to keep their army competitive with those of France and Russia combined, had to borrow heavily. (Members of the Reichstag objected, but they had no authority over the naval budget.) Further naval construction bills were enacted in Berlin in 1900, 1906, 1908, and 1912, each one more costly than the last. In 1898 Germany's annual naval spending had been barely one-fifth of the army budget. By 1911, with the army much bigger and more expensively equipped, the navy was costing more than half as much.

The result, for a nation with little in the way of a maritime tradition, was a surprisingly excellent navy, one whose ships and crews were by every measure at least equal in quality to those of the British. But London had done, and spent, still more. Admiral Sir John Arbuthnot Fisher—"Jacky" Fisher, the brilliant, dynamic, and strangely Asian-looking little first sea

Admiral Lord John Fisher
*"Damn the Dardanelles—
they will be our grave!"*

lord—radically reformed and upgraded the Royal Navy to trump the German challenge. Thanks largely to Fisher, in 1906 Britain launched a monster ship that revolutionized naval warfare: HMS *Dreadnought,* which at 21,845 tons was more than a fourth bigger than any battleship then in service, was sheathed in eleven inches of steel armor, carried ten twelve-inch guns capable of firing huge projectiles more than ten miles, and in spite of its size and weight could achieve a speed of twenty-one knots. When the Germans then built dreadnoughts of their own, the British responded by building still more, making them even bigger and arming them with fifteen-inch guns. It was a race the Germans could not win, but it went on.

Germany began the war with fifteen *Dreadnought*-class warships, each fitted with a suite of luxury quarters for the exclusive use of the kaiser, and five under construction. The British had twenty-nine and were building another thirteen. With France's ten heaviest warships added to the equation, the Entente had an insuperable advantage. Neither side was willing to risk its best ships in all-out battle, the Germans because they were outgunned and the British because the loss of their fleet would mean ruin. And so the first months of war saw a distinctly limited naval conflict in which no dreadnoughts were involved.

That war was a costly one despite its limits. It showed the Germans that their High Seas Fleet was not big enough to compete, and the British that they could keep that fleet bottled up in port but not destroy it. On August 28 a British foray at Helgoland Bight in the North Sea turned into the war's first naval battle; three German cruisers and one destroyer were sunk. On

September 3, north of Holland, a single German submarine sank three antiquated British cruisers, fourteen hundred of whose crewmen were lost. On November 1 five German cruisers commanded by Admiral Maximilian von Spee met and defeated the Royal Navy's South American squadron off the coast of Chile, sinking two cruisers and badly damaging a third. Fisher, retired in 1910, had been called back to active duty by Churchill after war hysteria forced Prince Louis Battenberg to retire as first sea lord because of his German antecedents. (The family soon changed its name to Mountbatten.) Dispatching a task force of two battle cruisers (smaller than dreadnoughts and battleships), three armored cruisers (smaller still), and two light cruisers to South America, Fisher ordered Admiral Sir Frederick Sturdee not to return until Spee and his ships had been destroyed. On December 8 Spee raided Port Stanley in the Falkland Islands and was surprised to find Sturdee already there, taking on coal. Spee fled and Sturdee pursued, catching up with the slower German ships and sinking all but one. Spee went to the bottom with his flagship and his two sons.

Later that month German battle cruisers shelled three towns on England's east coast, killing a number of civilians. In January British and German ships clashed inconclusively—there were no sinkings—at Dogger Bank in the North Sea. Surface combat then came to an end, the British satisfied to keep the Germans in port and Kaiser Wilhelm, in the face of protests from Tirpitz, unwilling to send his fleet out to engage them.

The Royal Navy had by this time clamped down a naval blockade that cut off most of Germany's imports. In violation of international agreements, the Asquith government declared that the entire North Sea was a war zone in which not only German but neutral ships would be boarded, searched, and prevented from delivering cargo of any kind (food and medicine included) to places from which it might be forwarded to the Central Powers. Even neutral ports were blockaded, with most of Germany's merchant fleet interned therein. The British and French, meanwhile, were using their control of the world's oceans to move troops and supplies wherever they chose—to Europe from India, Africa, Australia, Canada, and the Middle East, and from Europe to the Mediterranean.

Berlin responded with a new and still-primitive weapon that was the only kind of ship it could send into open waters with any hope of survival. On February 4, though they had fewer than twenty seaworthy submarines (Britain and France each had more, Fisher having insisted on adding them to the Royal Navy during his first tenure as sea lord), Germany declared that the waters around Britain and Ireland were to be regarded as a war zone in which all ships, merchantmen included, would be fair game.

Like poison gas and the machine gun, like the airplane and the tank, the submarine was something new in warfare. Both sides needed time to adapt to it. Only the Germans went after commercial shipping, because there was no German commercial shipping for the Entente's submarines to sink. At first they observed traditional "prize rules," according to which naval vessels were supposed to identify themselves (which in the case of the submarines meant surfacing) before attacking nonmilitary ships and allow passengers and crews to depart by lifeboat before torpedoes were fired. Such practices proved dangerous for the tiny, fragile, slow-moving and slow-submerging U-boats. They became suicidal when the British began not only to mount guns on merchantmen but to disguise warships as cargo vessels in order to lure submarines to the surface. The prize rules were soon abandoned.

The U-boats (*Unterseebooten*) sank hundreds of thousand of tons of British shipping, suffering heavy losses themselves in the process. They were, however, of little real value. At its peak their campaign was stopping less than four percent of British traffic but was arousing a ferociously negative response not only in Britain but in the United States. The German foreign office, fearful of American intervention, tried to persuade the kaiser that the U-boats' successes were not nearly worth the risk. Most leaders of the German army and navy demanded that the campaign continue.

On May 1 the German consulate in New York ran newspaper advertise-

The "auxiliary cruiser" *Lusitania* embarking from
New York Harbor on her last Atlantic crossing

ments warning readers of the dangers of sailing on the *Lusitania,* a British Cunard steamship famous as the biggest, fastest liner in Atlantic service. Less known was the *Lusitania*'s status as an "auxiliary cruiser" of the Royal Navy. Its construction had been subsidized by the government, which equipped it with concealed guns, and it almost certainly had American-manufactured guns and ammunition as part of its cargo for the May crossing.

On May 7, passing close to Ireland as it neared the end of its voyage, the *Lusitania* turned directly into the path of the patrolling submarine *U-20* and was torpedoed. It sank in twenty minutes after a massive second explosion that soon would be attributed to the German commander's gratuitous firing of a second torpedo into the mortally wounded ship but has since been traced to an ignition of coal dust in empty fuel bunkers. Some twelve hundred passengers and crew drowned, 124 Americans among them, and the United States erupted in indignation. German diplomats warned with new urgency that the U-boat attacks must stop, and on June 5 an order went out from Berlin calling a halt to the torpedoing of passenger liners on sight.

Chapter 15

✠

Ypres Again

"Out of approximately 19,500 square miles
of France and Belgium in German hands,
we have recovered about eight."
—WINSTON CHURCHILL

As March turned to April the leaders of the Entente had reason to be satisfied with how the war was going for them in the East. The Russian
offensive against Austria-Hungary in Galicia and the Carpathians—the same
offensive that had taken Przemysl—continued to make headway despite lingering winter weather and chronic shortages of weapons and ammunition.
(Ludendorff wrote admiringly of how the Russian soldiers, attacking uphill
and armed only with bayonets, displayed a "supreme contempt for death.")
The Russian Eighth Army, commanded by the able and aggressive General
Alexei Brusilov, was capturing miles of the Carpathian crest and the passes
leading to the Danube River valley. Russian control of Galicia was so secure
that the tsar himself visited the conquered city of Lemberg (Lvov to the
Russians, now Lviv in Ukraine), where he had the satisfaction of sleeping in
the suite that until then only Emperor Franz Joseph had been allowed to use.
A massive Russian move beyond the Carpathians seemed inevitable by spring
or early summer. The Austrians, frightened, knew that they had little hope of
fending it off. The Russians were so confident of their prospects that they no
longer saw any need to offer a rich share of their anticipated postwar spoils
in order to draw Italy into the war. And they were being successful enough
against the Turks in the Caucasus to make a Dardanelles campaign seem no
longer imperative or even particularly desirable except in connection with a
Russian advance on Constantinople.

On the other side, Conrad saw that his armies were on the verge of collapse and was begging the Germans for more help. Falkenhayn remained

reluctant to comply, though increasingly he was of two minds on the question. His reluctance was fortified by the obvious intention of the French and British to continue their attacks on the Western Front, and by his belief that the war was going to have to be decided there. A complicating factor was the willingness of the Italian government, which until August 1914 had been joined to Germany and Austria-Hungary in what was called the Triple Alliance, to put itself on the auction block and see which side could offer the best terms.

Rome had been excluded from the July 1914 crisis by its putative but distrustful allies in Vienna and Berlin. This suited Italy's astute foreign minister, Antonio di San Giuliano, who wanted nothing to do with any of it. He saw Austria's behavior toward Serbia as aggressive and provocative, and he accused Germany and Austria of violating the terms of the alliance by failing to confer. Their actions, he said, relieved Italy of any obligation to go to war.

San Giuliano died in October, and Italy's foreign affairs were taken over by the prime minister, Antonio Salandra, a future fascist who regarded his country's neutrality not as a gift to be treasured but as a negotiable asset to be sold to the highest bidder. He put Italy up for sale, and because he claimed to have

Antonio Salandra
Prime Minister of Italy
*Put his nation and its army
on the auction block.*

a ready army of almost a million men, the bidding was intense. The Entente and the Central Powers both thought it likely that the war would be decided by what Italy did. By spring, with the situation of the Entente so promising overall, it seemed almost impossible that the Central Powers would not collapse if a million fresh troops were thrown into the scales against them.

Britain made extravagant offers. It enjoyed the advantage of not having to promise anything that it, or France, possessed or wanted. Everything to be given to Italy (the port city of Trieste, lands from the crest of the Alps southward, islands in the Aegean, pieces of the Balkans and Asia Minor and Africa) could be extracted from the Austro-Hungarian and Ottoman Empires at the end of the war. The Russians were less forthcoming. Confident at this point of defeating Austria, they wanted to promise nothing that might compromise their postwar dominance in the Balkans and points farther east. To win the acquiescence of the Russians, Sir Edward Grey promised them Constantinople and other parts of the Ottoman Empire—thus reversing what had long been an essential element of Britain's Middle East policy.

The ability of the Central Powers to bargain was limited: much of what Italy wanted belonged to or was coveted by Vienna. The Germans, accordingly, hoped for nothing more than to keep Italy neutral, but they were willing to pay a high price to achieve this goal. Chancellor Bethmann Hollweg went so far as to float the idea of giving part of Silesia to Austria-Hungary in compensation for its concessions to Italy. The proposal was shunned in Berlin; Silesia had been the single most highly prized conquest of Frederick the Great of Prussia.

The intrigues were endless. In Vienna the desperate Conrad and Berchtold came up with a scheme for getting Italy to mediate a general eastern settlement. Italy's reward would be the South Tyrol, part of Austria-Hungary's Alpine domain. Russia would be won over with offers of part of Galicia, Constantinople, and the whole chain of waterways from the Dardanelles to the Black Sea. That these plans would have been a flagrant betrayal of the Turks and likely would have been seen as a betrayal of the Germans as well appears to have been of no concern to either Conrad or Berchtold. Emperor Franz Joseph, when he learned of the idea, dismissed Berchtold. Thus the man most responsible for the war departed the stage before the conflict was a year old.

To Salandra, the bargaining appears to have been a game in which he had nothing to lose. It was obvious that he could do best by siding with the Entente. He merely went through the motions of bargaining with Germany to force the Entente partners to improve their offer. A decision could not be delayed indefinitely, however. If the Russians broke through the Carpathians, Italy's market value would plummet.

Meanwhile the French general staff had turned its attention to the St. Mihiel salient, a forward bulge in the German line south of Verdun (which was itself a French salient extending like a spear point into German-held territory). The plan was typical: by breaking the line on both sides of St. Mihiel, the French could either cut the Germans off or force them to withdraw. In so doing they would straighten and shorten their line and reduce Verdun's vulnerability. If fully successful, they would capture the railway lines extending westward from the German-held city of Metz and force an even more extensive withdrawal. These goals were, as always, deliciously attractive. The only question was, as always, their feasibility.

The offensive began on April 5. Fourteen French divisions supported by three hundred and sixty heavy guns—fully half of the total number of such guns possessed by the French army—attacked on a front almost fifty miles wide. The weather was terrible, the ground muddy, and visibility spoiled by fog, rain, and snow. French security was so lax, with French officers talking of what was coming in the cafés of Paris and towns nearer the front, that the Germans knew of the attack well before it began. Though most of the defenders were reservists, German combat engineers had been installing strong defenses since the capture of St. Mihiel in the fall, and the salient was rich in artillery. The fight quickly degenerated into prototypical Western Front warfare: bloody and sterile French assaults across the Woëvre plateau on the north side of the salient, withering fire from German machine guns and cannon. When Joffre finally allowed what came to be called the Battle of the Woëvre to gutter out, it had cost him sixty-two thousand men. But the relentless commander in chief, convinced yet again that he had come tantalizingly close to success, immediately set his staff to work on plans for another, bigger, two-pronged offensive north of St. Mihiel and in the Artois region to the west. All Europe settled down to a brief period of relative quiet. Even the Russians, their troops and supplies exhausted, had found it necessary to suspend—temporarily, they expected—their attacks in the Carpathians.

No one on the Entente side was comfortable with the lull. Joffre wanted another attack by the British, to keep the Germans occupied in Belgium. Sir John French, eager as ever to demonstrate that London should let him have more troops, was willing to cooperate. Falkenhayn meanwhile, unable to ignore a cacophony of warnings about danger in the east, continued to thin his lines in Belgium and France. He wanted, naturally, to keep these withdrawals secret from the French and British. To this end he was preparing a series of diversionary offensives. The first and most important would be at Ypres, where France too was preparing to take the initiative.

The Second Battle of Ypres, which introduced a horrifying new element into the history of warfare, had a suitably novel and horrendous prologue.

For weeks British miners operating crude foot-powered devices called "clay-kickers" had been digging a tunnel from behind their lines into German territory. Their destination was Hill 60, the highest point on the Messines Ridge that overlooked much of the Ypres salient. The hill had been a key strongpoint and artillery observation post for the Germans since the autumn, when they first captured it. Once under Hill 60 (so named because it was sixty meters high, having been created years before with earth removed for construction of a railway), the tunnelers scooped out an underground chamber and packed it with explosives. When this cache was detonated at seven P.M. on April 17, it blew much of the hill hundreds of feet into the air, the German defenders and their weaponry and bunkers with it. The explosion was followed by an infantry attack that captured what remained of the hill at a cost of exactly seven casualties. An estimated one thousand Germans had died, with perhaps a hundred surviving. Hill 60 proved to be an uncomfortable prize, however, exposed as it was to German fire from three directions. Its possession was not enough to prevent the Germans from moving up an awesome array of their biggest siege mortars in preparation for Falkenhayn's coming offensive and the experiment to be conducted in conjunction with it.

Second Ypres began late on the afternoon of April 22 after forty-eight hours of the kind of intense artillery bombardment that everyone now knew to be the preamble to an infantry attack. This time, however, when the guns fell silent, they were followed not by waves of charging riflemen but by the opening of six thousand metal cylinders containing 168 tons of chlorine, a lethal heavier-than-air gas that stayed close to the ground as it was carried on the evening breeze toward the French lines. Chlorine had been chosen because it was readily available—the German chemical industry produced 85 percent of the world's supply—and because of its effects: it destroys the ability of the lungs to absorb oxygen and causes its victims to drown, generally with excruciating slowness, in their own fluids. No one on the French side knew what the gas was. It first appeared in the distance as a white mist, turning yellow-green as it drew closer. Its effects were immediate and terrifying. Every man still capable of moving ran for his life. With astonishing speed a four-mile expanse of the French front line was totally cleared. Nothing stood between the Germans and the shattered ruins of the little city of Ypres, which they had spent so many lives trying to take in 1914. In minutes, and without losing a man, they had achieved a breakthrough even more complete than the one the British had won and squandered at Neuve Chapelle five weeks before.

The introduction of gas need not have come as such a surprise. A French divisional commander, a General Ferry, had learned of the German plans to use chlorine weeks before from a captured soldier. He had informed both the

French high command and the British, suggesting that the canisters of which the prisoner had spoken should be located by aerial reconnaissance and destroyed with artillery. The only action taken in response to this warning was directed at Ferry himself. First he was reprimanded for communicating directly with the British rather than going through channels. After the battle, when the importance of Ferry's warning was beyond question, he was sacked.

The success of the new weapon was as big a surprise to the Germans as the weapon itself was to the French. The only earlier use of gas, on the Eastern Front in the depths of winter, had been such a failure that the Russians hadn't bothered to report it to their allies. Though this new attempt, unlike the first, involved a deadly chemical, the Germans regarded it as a mere experiment, a peripheral element in an operation intended only to persuade the French and British that the Germans remained strong in the west. Not enough reserves were on hand to push through and occupy Ypres, in part because so many troops had been sent to the east. And though protective breathing devices had been developed years before for industrial purposes, none had been provided to the attacking troops.

The advancing Germans were shocked by what they found: five thousand enemy soldiers on their backs, struggling for breath, suffocating in agony and terror. The Germans became so afraid of catching up with the gas as it rolled on before them that they advanced only two miles and stopped. By the time their commanders understood the scope of the opportunity that had been created, a congeries of British, French, and colonial troops had been sent forward into the gap and the opportunity was gone. From now on all the armies of the Great War would expect gas and be more or less prepared for it. And though both sides would use it extensively, never again would it disable enough men to decide the outcome of a battle. Even at Ypres the British and French needed only hours to understand what they were faced with and find ways to deal with it. First it was noticed that the brass buttons on the soldiers' uniforms had turned green. Someone deduced from this phenomenon that the mysterious cloud must be chlorine and knew of a quick preventive: by breathing through a cloth on which they had urinated (a spare sock, for example), the troops could neutralize the poison before it reached their lungs. The first improvised gas masks thus emerged almost immediately after the first use of chlorine.

It was not necessary to be exposed to the gas or in direct contact with the enemy to experience the horror of Second Ypres. Canadian Sergeant S. V. Britten tasted his share when, just hours after the start of the attack, he and his unit were assigned to strengthen defensive positions not used since the fighting of late 1914. "Left at 6:30 P.M. for reserve trenches and reached our reserve dugouts via St. Julien," he recorded. "Just rat holes! One hell of accommodation! Got to the trenches as a fatigue party with stake & sandbags, and though they were reserve trenches, they were so rotten. No trenches at all in parts, just isolated mounds. Found German's feet sticking up through the ground. The Gurkhas had actually used human bodies instead of sandbags. Right beside the stream where we were working were the bodies of two dead, since November last, one face downward in full marching order, with his kit on his back. He died game! Stench something awful and dead all round. Water rats had made a home of their decomposed bodies. Visited the barbed wire with Rae—ordinary wire strung across. Quit about 1 A.M., came back to our dugouts and found them on fire. Had to march out to St. Julien, & put up in a roofless house—not a roof left on anything in the whole place. Found our sack of food had been stolen and we were famished. Certainly a most unlucky day, for I lost my cherished pipe. Bed at 4 A.M."

After the first day Second Ypres too turned into a standard Western Front slaughterhouse. The Germans, never having intended to capture anything, settled into defensive positions as usual while the French and British launched counterattacks that accomplished nothing.

On the evening of April 24 General Sir Horace Smith-Dorrien, who had been one of the BEF's senior commanders from the start of the war and had repeatedly demonstrated his steadiness and courage, visited French at his headquarters and asked him to cancel an attack planned for the following morning. French refused, the attack went ahead, and the result was as Smith-Dorrien had predicted: a loss of thousands more British, Canadian, and Indian troops, with a gain of no ground. A division of Indian troops freshly arrived in Europe was almost annihilated while crossing a mile of open ground; the

Lt. Gen. Horace Smith-Dorrien
Removed from command for trying to do the right thing.

few who reached the enemy line alive were promptly gassed. Nearby a regiment of Senegalese troops—Africans transported to Europe by their French colonial masters—panicked after being ordered to follow the Indians and encountering chlorine. They turned on their heels, shot the officers who ordered them to stop, and kept running until they reached a supply area in the rear, where they ran amok. A corps of British cavalry had to be dispatched to bring the rampage to an end. The next day Smith-Dorrien sent a message to BEF headquarters, asking Chief of Staff Robertson to explain to French the hopelessness of further attacks. He also suggested a withdrawal to a shorter, stronger line nearer the city of Ypres. Upon receiving a curt reply, he sent another message suggesting that, if his resignation was wanted, he was prepared to submit it. Smith-Dorrien soon found himself ordered home.

Day after day, assured by Foch that Joffre would soon be sending reinforcements, French continued his offensive. The casualty lists grew longer. Not until May 1 did Foch confess that no French troops were coming—that exactly the opposite was happening; Joffre was removing troops from Ypres and sending them south for an entirely separate offensive. Finally French gave up. He ordered a pullback of three miles to precisely the position that Smith-Dorrien had been dismissed for suggesting.

The battle dragged on into late May, not ending until the Germans ran low on shells. They had taken forty thousand casualties, the British sixty thousand. "The profitless slaughter pit of Ypres," as Churchill would call it, had injected two new elements into the war: mining and gas. By introducing the latter, the Germans further damaged themselves in the eyes of the world—in American eyes most importantly. Intellectually, it was perhaps not easy to draw a moral distinction between piercing men's bodies with bullets and bayonets, blowing them apart with high explosives, and killing them with gas. On some deeper level, however, people sensed that warfare had been made monstrous in a new way, that another step had been taken toward barbarism. Not for the first time and not for the last, it was the Germans who looked most barbaric.

TROGLODYTES

THERE IS NOTHING MORE BIZARRE ABOUT THE GREAT WAR than the way in which, for four years, millions of citizens of Europe's most advanced nations lived in holes in the ground. The Western Front was unlike anything the world had seen before or has seen since.

In trying to visualize the front, the easiest mistake is to imagine a pair of ditches running parallel from the North Sea to Switzerland. The whole setup was much more complicated than that. Each side had five thousand men per mile of front on average, and this manpower was used to construct elaborate defensive *systems,* usually miles deep, that were zigzagging mazes fortified in all the ways that the latest technology made possible.

Though the methods of the three armies differed in their details, the basics were similar everywhere. First came the true front line, a trench six or more feet deep and about that wide, generally heavily manned. A mile or so to the rear was a support trench with a second concentration of troops. Farther back still, beyond the range of all but the biggest enemy artillery, was a third line for the reserves. All but the lightest guns were behind this reserve line, unreachable except by the most successful offensives.

Even this description is too simple. Trenches were often impossible to dig in the waterlogged soil of Flanders, where walls of sandbags had to be erected instead, and maintaining a continuous line could be difficult in the rough hills north of Switzerland. The German front "line" often included three parallel trenches, the first for sentries, another for the main force, the third for backup troops. However many such rows there were in any particular place, they were connected by perpendicular communications trenches, shielded by fields of barbed wire as much as thirty feet deep, and, more and more as the war wore on, studded with machine-gun nests. The trenches were less often straight than broken by dogleg turns, so that any enemy troops who got into them would have a limited field of fire.

Life in this maze embodied a cliché about war: that it is tedium punctuated by eruptions of sheer terror. The food was loathsome: bread that was a week old by the time it reached the front, canned meat when meat was available, overcooked vegetables that invariably arrived cold. Alcohol was issued daily: wine for the French (half a liter at first, then a full liter), brandy for the Germans, and rum for the British first thing every morning. Latrines, six-foot-deep pits at the end of short side-trenches, were unspeakably foul, and the traffic made them a magnet for enemy artillery. With dysentery widespread, the men often preferred to use buckets, old food containers, or the nearest shell hole.

Discipline was harsh and not infrequently arbitrary. British officers made wide use of Field Punishment Number One. Men deemed guilty of minor infractions would be lashed to a post or spread-eagled on an upright wagon wheel two hours daily (one in the morning, another in the afternoon) for as long as three months, often within range of enemy guns. And the punishments inflicted by the environment were often even worse.

There was trench foot, a fungal infection caused by prolonged exposure to cold and wet. It could lead to gangrene, then to amputation. Twenty thousand British troops were afflicted with it in the first winter of the war. Until someone discovered that daily rubbings with whale oil were an effective preventive, men crawling to the rear were a common sight and were often accused of malingering.

And there was trench mouth, which diseased the gums and caused teeth to fall out.

And when the weather was warm, trench fever erupted, caused by the excretions of lice. It began with a tingling in the shins and led to something akin to a bad case of flu. It was rarely fatal but put thousands out of action.

Lice were universal, their bites leaving red marks on the skin of every soldier. The men spent hours searching out the lice in their clothing and killing them with their fingernails or a candle flame. It was hardly worth the effort; the eggs remained in the seams and would hatch in a few hours.

The rats were even worse. A single pair can produce more than eight hundred offspring in a year. The front, with its garbage and decaying human bodies, turned into rat heaven. Soldiers wrote home of rats everywhere, rats almost as big as cats, rats eating the eyes out of corpses. Rats would chew through a sleeping man's clothes to get at the food in his pockets.

To all this was added a stench that rose to heaven, the impossibility when it rained of finding a place to lie down, and artillery fire that never quite stopped even when the front was supposedly quiet. Historians note that the armies of the Great War were made up largely of industrial and farm workers who were inured to hard labor, bad treatment, and minimal creature comforts. Even the generals most inclined to regard them as cannon fodder, however, understood that no one could endure much of this life.

And so the men were rotated. After no more than a week at the front, they would be pulled back to the support line, then to the reserve line, and finally to the rear. Even there, however, conditions were primitive. Shells still came roaring in, and exhausted, nerve-shattered troops would be drilled and harassed by officers eager to demonstrate their diligence.

The men were supposed to be given regular leave—a week every four months, in the case of the French—but often it didn't happen. When it did, the congestion of the railways and the low priority given to soldiers traveling alone could make it impossible for them to get home. Men returned to duty with venereal disease, contracted by eighty of every thousand men in the BEF. (The German rate was worse, the French somewhat lower.)

A trench culture emerged, with its own hierarchy, language, and rituals. Stretcher-bearers, many of them conscientious objectors, were admired for the courage with which they went out to rescue the wounded. Runners (Adolf Hitler was one of them, and he ended the war with two Iron Crosses) were constantly exposed to fire as they delivered messages and scouted ahead when their units prepared to move.

The setting was ideal for snipers, who became a professional elite. Sniper schools were established. Their products worked in pairs, a rifleman and an observer, firing high-powered rifles equipped with telescopic sights through holes in sheets of steel. Antisniper snipers came next. They were not always welcomed by the other troops, however; when snipers' positions became known, they drew enemy artillery fire.

Out beyond the lines lay no-man's-land. (The term has been traced back to medieval England, where it applied to disputed ground between two jurisdictions.) Pocked with shell holes, littered with debris and dead bodies, no-man's-land was sometimes half a mile or more in depth, sometimes only yards. Entering it meant death in the daytime, but at night it came to life. Raiding parties went out at sunset and returned at dawn, trying to see what enemy units were opposite, trying to capture prisoners to be questioned in the rear, sometimes just hoping for a few quick kills. For the most adventurous soldiers, this became a form of sport.

Wounds that allowed a man to go home without causing permanent damage were prized and envied. For the British these were "Blighty wounds"; for the Germans they were *Heimatschüsse*—"home shots." Veterans developed respect, even something akin to affection, for the soldiers on the other side. The enemy was suffering in the same way, after all, and was doing so with courage. Temporary truces were arranged for the bringing in of dead and injured, and some sectors came to be dominated by a live-and-let-live attitude with no one trying to make things difficult. The Bavarians were known to be particularly good-natured. When they were about to be replaced at the front by Prussians, they would warn the men opposite to expect more difficult days.

The British troops were "Tommies" to the Germans. The British called the Germans "Fritz" at first, then "Jerry." Names like "Hun" belonged to the patriots back home, from whom the men on the front felt increasingly alienated.

Officers could become objects of resentment. Even the most junior of them, often teenagers just out of the best schools, had personal servants. They lived in comparative comfort with better food and luxuries brought from home, and they never had to lift anything heavier than a swagger stick. Most despised of all were the staff officers, billeted in private homes far to the rear and rarely exposed to gunfire.

All this put officers in a different universe from the Tommies, the poilus, and the German *Frontschwein.* These common soldiers, whenever they moved, even when sent off on long marches or across no-man's-land in daylight assaults, carried a ten-pound rifle, at least 150 rounds of ammunition, bottles of water, an overcoat, a blanket with ground cloth, a trenching tool, days of rations that were not to be opened without an officer's permission, a "pocket primus" miniature stove with fuel, a mess kit with mug and cutlery, and whatever else they could manage, from socks and underwear to shaving gear, toothpaste, bandages, and books.

Chapter 16

✠

Gallipoli

"I don't order you to attack. I order you to die."
—Mustafa Kemal

The Dardanelles have always been regarded as part of the line that separates Europe from what is broadly known as Asia. They are, in the most strictly literal sense, the stuff of legend. Before the dawn of history a maiden named Helle was said to have drowned there while fleeing with the Golden Fleece, and so until modern times the Dardanelles were known as the Hellespont. Leander swam the Hellespont nightly to visit his lover, the priestess Hero, and ultimately they too drowned. Jason and his Argonauts sailed through the Hellespont. Since the nineteenth century it has been accepted as fact that the city of Troy stood on the Asian side of the Hellespont, and a mound of earth there has since time immemorial been said to contain the bones of Achilles. The Persian ruler Xerxes took his great army across the strait when he set out to conquer the Greeks in 480 B.C., and Alexander the Great crossed in the other direction a century and a half later. The poet Byron swam the Hellespont for no better reason than that doing so was the most romantic act imaginable.

The importance of the Dardanelles derives from their position at the southern end of one of the most remarkable waterways on earth, one that connects the Aegean Sea and therefore the entire Mediterranean world with the Black Sea, with the Balkan states of Bulgaria and Romania, and with nations (Ukraine, Georgia) that at the time of the Great War were parts of the Russian Empire. Entering the Dardanelles at their southern or Aegean end (the end attacked in 1915), a ship must pass through a deepwater strait forty-five miles in length before reaching the great open expanse of the Sea of Marmara, 170 miles long and fifty wide. At the northeastern end of this sea is Istanbul—Byzantium to the ancient Greeks, Constantinople from the early Christian era. It was a great city from ancient times because of its position at the entrance to a second navigable channel, the Bosporus, which is twenty miles long and leads to the immensity of the Black Sea. Even today, standing on the heights overlooking the point where the Bosporus opens onto the Black Sea, one sees an unending stream of freighters moving between the heart of easternmost Europe and the world beyond, carrying oil and grain and other riches. Nothing could be more understandable than Russia's centuries-old hunger to possess this passage, or the British belief that by wresting it from the Turks in 1915 they could win the war.

The Dardanelles owe their existence to an arid, ruggedly hilly peninsula that reaches some fifty miles southward from the Balkan mainland into the Aegean. The eastern coast of this Gallipoli Peninsula parallels the coast of Asian Turkey and is separated from it by only a few miles; it is within this gap that the Dardanelles channel lies, with steep ridges looming over it on both sides. From the peninsula's highest peaks everything is visible: the Aegean to the west and south, the entire length of the Dardanelles to the east, and the hills of Asian Turkey beyond, all of it controllable, in the years before bomber aircraft, by anyone who could get artillery onto those peaks. Once it was decided that the British and French ships would not be able to break through the narrows and that troops must be landed, the next step became obvious: to seize the heights of Gallipoli and take control of everything below. Once that was accomplished, everything else—the fall of Constantinople, the opening of the sea-lane to Russia, the winning of Greece and Bulgaria and Romania to the Entente cause—could be expected to follow.

As of March 18, the day De Robeck's battleships tried to force their way through the strait and ran into mines, the Turks had only a single ill-equipped, unprepared, and badly deployed division of infantry on the entire peninsula. Luckily for the Turks, however, the newly arrived British army commander in the Aegean, General Ian Hamilton, found his troops completely unprepared for anything as demanding as a landing on hostile shores. Everything was in disarray; the gun crews were not even on the same ships with their cannon or ammunition. Everything was going to have to be taken across the Mediterranean, unloaded, and reorganized. Accordingly, on March 22 Hamilton led his task force off to the Egyptian port of Alexandria. On that same day, in another stroke of good fortune for the Turks, Enver Pasha, who dominated the Constantinople government, had the good sense to put aside his faith in his own military brilliance. Instead of taking personal command (as he had done earlier, with disastrous results, in Turkey's winter offensive in the Caucasus), Enver created a new army for the defense of the Dardanelles and appointed as its commander General Otto Liman von Sanders, head of the German military mission in Constantinople. Sanders understood that the British, not having renewed their naval assault, must be preparing an infantry invasion. "If the English will leave me alone for eight days!" he implored the heavens when he saw the sorry state of the Turkish defenses. In the event, the British left him alone for four weeks, and he made use of every hour, pouring in troops, building fortifications, even improving the peninsula's primitive roads. The urgency of the work was increased by reports of the size of the force being assembled at Alexandria. Hamilton's command was far too big, Egypt far too thick with spies, for there to be any possibility of secrecy.

Not until April 25 did the invasion force steam over the horizon from the south and approach Gallipoli. It was the most powerful force ever to have attempted an amphibious landing in the face of an armed enemy. Two hundred transport ships were accompanied by eighteen battleships, a dozen cruisers, twenty-nine destroyers, and eight submarines. On those transports were twenty-seven thousand British soldiers, including the crack Twenty-ninth Division that before leaving England had been such a bone of contention, thirty thousand "Anzac" troops from Australia and New Zealand, and sixteen thousand Frenchmen. They had all the guns of De Robeck's great flotilla to support them and an abundance of their own artillery to take ashore. The Gallipoli expedition having been made a high priority in London and Paris, it was magnificently well equipped in virtually every way that mattered except two: hand grenades and trench mortars were in short supply.

Otto Limon von Sanders
*"If the English will leave me
alone for eight days!"*

This deficiency would prove a serious handicap in the broken and hilly ground on which the troops would soon be grappling with the Turks.

Sanders by now had six Turkish divisions on the peninsula, eighty-four thousand men. But he had more than a hundred miles of shoreline to defend, much of it nearly inaccessible, and he could only guess where his enemies intended to come ashore. As it happened, his guesses were so wrong that their consequences should have been fatal. Hamilton had decided to divide his force and send it to three places. The French would be landed—only temporarily and solely as a diversion—at a place called Kum Kale, on the Asian shore south of the tip of the Gallipoli Peninsula. Correctly anticipating this deployment, Sanders had placed two divisions not far from Kum Kale, which was vulnerable because within easy reach of naval gunfire. What he couldn't know was that Hamilton had no intention of accomplishing anything substantial at Kum Kale; Kitchener had ordered him to avoid trying to establish a permanent position on the eastern side of the strait.

The British were to be put ashore on five separate beaches at Cape Helles, the toe of the peninsula. This Sanders did not expect at all. With good reason, he thought it improbable that the invaders would land at the point of maximum distance from what was presumably their destination, the Sea of Marmara. He decided that Hamilton was most likely to send most of his troops by ship to the area around the town of Bulair, at the narrow northern neck of the peninsula. There, if successful, the invaders would be almost at the Sea of Marmara and positioned to cut communications between the Turkish forces on Gallipoli and their home base to the north. He placed two divisions at Bulair and made it his headquarters.

The Anzacs, the biggest part of the Allied force, were to be taken up Gallipoli's Aegean coast but less than halfway to Bulair. Their destination was a promisingly easy-looking beach leading to flat terrain at a point called Gaba Tepe. Air reconnaissance had found few Turkish troops in the area, and no reserves were nearby. Sanders therefore had a third of his troops on the wrong side of the strait and another third much too far north. Of the remaining third, half—a single undersize division—was sent to Cape Helles, where it would find itself trying to hold off the entire British landing force. The remaining one-sixth of Sanders's force, his last division, was sent to the middle of the peninsula, to a position from which it could move wherever needed. The only substantial Turkish force within a day's march of the Anzac landing, it was under the command of a strange, eccentric young lieutenant colonel who was so disliked and distrusted by the cabal that governed the Ottoman Empire that before the outbreak of war he had been consigned to inactive status. This was Mustafa Kemal, the future Atatürk.

The invasion should have been a triumph. The British, when they came ashore at Cape Helles, outnumbered the Turks there by six to one and met resistance at only two of their five landing beaches. Those beaches were, however, defended ferociously. At one of them, 700 of the first thousand troops to land were mowed down by machine-gun fire; at the end of the day only four hundred British were both on dry land and alive. At the other beach the Twenty-ninth Division, in action at last, fought its way through barbed wire and heavy fire, took control of the immediate area, and hunkered down to await instructions. None came, and so they did nothing. With a terrible absurdity, the same thing happened at the three undefended beaches. The British could have moved inland effortlessly and taken the crucial high ground that lay before them. They also, after advancing, could have swung around and taken from behind the Turks at the defended beaches. But no one had told their commanders what to do after getting ashore, and they stayed, uselessly, where they were.

At one of the undefended beaches, after standing by idly all day, the British spent a long hard night fighting off an enemy force that had at last come forward to meet them. In the morning, thinking their position hopeless, they returned to their landing craft and were taken away. At exactly the same time their Turkish adversaries, also having had enough, were themselves withdrawing. By then half the Turks at Cape Helles had become casualties, with barely a thousand still alive and unwounded. If the British had attacked, the sheer weight of their numbers would have been enough to sweep all resistance aside. But no orders came, and so again there was no move inland. Instead the British braced for a counterattack that the Turks were utterly incapable of attempting. Hamilton, on the battleship *Queen Elizabeth* well out to sea, had almost no idea of what was happening ashore and was able to issue no orders. By the end of the second day the French had disembarked from Kum Kale and were on their way to Cape Helles. It was too late. Sanders, having seen that there would be no landing in the north, was hurrying the Bulair divisions southward.

The landing of the Anzac force was also a disaster but of a markedly different kind. The Australians and New Zealanders, when they went ashore, encountered relatively light resistance but found themselves in a landscape far different from what they had been told to expect. Instead of the flat and easy ground that supposedly lay beyond Gaba Tepe, they found themselves having to clamber up into steep craggy hills and rock-lined ravines in the face of gunfire from Turkish riflemen concealed in the nearby hills. "A galling fire rained on us from the left where there were high cliffs," an Australian corporal would recall. "One man dropped down alongside me laughing. I broke the news to him gently: 'You've got yourself into the hottest corner you'll ever strike.' I had shown him where the enemy were, he fired a few shots.

And again I heard the sickening thud of a bullet. I looked at him in horror. The bullet had fearfully mashed his face and gone down his throat, rendering him dumb. But his eyes were dreadful to behold. How he squirmed in agony. There was nothing I could do for him, but pray that he might die swiftly. It took him about twenty minutes to accomplish this and by that time he had tangled his legs in pain and stiffened. I saw the waxy color creep over his cheek and breathed easier."

Eventually it would become clear that the Anzacs had been landed not at Gaba Tepe but, probably because of a misreading of the tidal currents, a full mile north of their destination. They were on a piece of coast so harsh and inaccessible that not even the Turks knew their way through it. Twelve thousand Anzacs got ashore in less than twelve hours, however, and almost immediately their advance units began pushing on into the hills. Soon they stood unchallenged on the ultimate prize: peaks from which they could look back to the Aegean and eastward to the Dardanelles. From here, once artillery was in place, they would command everything that mattered on land and sea.

But just then, before enough Anzac troops could be brought up to consolidate what had been gained, Mustafa Kemal arrived with a single ragged battalion at his heels. Compass in one hand and map in the other, he had been leading a forced march to the shore since getting word of the landing. As soon as he saw the enemy troops, he led his men in an attack that cleared the crest. He then ordered his men to lie down, rifles at the ready, and sent back word for the rest of the battalion to hurry forward. An epic fight for the high points called Chunuk Bair and Sari Bair was on, and what followed was a day of desperate close-quarters fighting, much of it hand to hand, with both sides constantly bringing forward more troops and launching one assault after another. Kemal, ordering his men to make yet another charge in which no one seemed likely to survive, uttered the words that would forever form the core of his legend. "I don't order you to attack," he said. "I order you to die. In the time which passes until we die, other troops and commanders can take our place."

Slowly, at terrible cost, the Turks forced the Anzacs backward down the hill toward their landing place. That night, unaware that the Turks too had reached the end of their strength, the general commanding the landing force sent a message reporting failure and asking to have his men taken off. Hamilton, after much agonizing, replied that the Anzacs must stay where they were and "dig, dig, dig."

Three days later nineteen thousand British troops attacked at Cape Helles, briefly taking the high ground overlooking the end of the peninsula. Then they were driven back, suffering three thousand casualties in the process. On May 26 twenty-five thousand British and French attacked again, made no

Mustafa Kemal
*Saved Gallipoli
for the Turks.*

progress, and gave up after nearly a third of them had been killed or wounded. The Australians and New Zealanders remained crowded into, and unable to break out of, the wretched toehold that they had named Anzac Cove. Gallipoli was turning into something almost worse than outright defeat: a stalemate as tightly locked as the one on the Western Front.

As in Europe, both sides were soon mounting sterile attacks followed by equally sterile counterattacks. As in Europe, the soldiers on both sides developed the familiar mixture of fear and respect, of hatred and admiration, for the men they were fighting. The Turks "came over in two great waves from their trenches, in great hulking mass," an Australian private observed of one attack. "They were rather big men, the Turks, fine body of men. As they came over, they were shouting 'Allah!' and blowing their trumpets and whistling and shouting like schoolboys. As they got closer, within nice rifle range, we had the order to fire and opened up with rapid fire and brought them down in hundreds, hundreds of them fell, and in front of our trenches." A corporal at Anzac Cove took a less admiring view: "The Turks suffer severely in their half-hearted bayonet attacks, usually delivered at night. They approach calling on Allah. We hold our fire until they are within twenty paces. Then they get a couple of stunning volleys and we hop out and bayonet anyone who cannot run away quick enough. I have not been lucky enough to catch one yet."

By May 8 the British and French had taken twenty thousand casualties. They had no uncommitted reserves to throw into the fight, and their supplies of shells were low. Desperation was deepening not only at Gallipoli but in London. With two more divisions, Hamilton wired Kitchener, "I could push on with great hope of success. Otherwise I am afraid we shall degenerate into trench warfare." Not everyone was even that hopeful. "Damn the Dardanelles" was Fisher's judgment—"they will be our grave."

AN INFINITE APPETITE FOR SHELLS

THE GREAT WAR IS REMEMBERED AS THE WAR OF THE machine gun. Its defining image is of doomed foot soldiers, bayonets fixed, climbing doggedly out of their trenches and being mowed down like so many stalks of corn by gun crews dispensing instant death at the industrially admirable rate of ten rounds per second. And of course that image is no mere phantasm. It happened again and again from the summer of 1914 until the autumn of 1918. The machine gun was one of the war's essential elements, a prime reason why so many offensives failed so miserably, a puzzle that the generals had to solve before they could begin to succeed.

But in fact it was artillery that dominated the battlefields. World War I was the first major war, and it would also be the last, in which more men were killed by artillery than by small arms or aerial bombardment or any other method of destruction. Until late in the war artillery was the only weapon that, when used to maximum advantage, could neutralize the machine gun. It was the one weapon without which infantry, both when attacking and when defending, had almost no chance. Armies could and did misunderstand and misuse the machine gun and survive. There was less room for error where the big guns were concerned. Huge numbers of such guns proved to be indispensable from the start, as did astronomical numbers of shells. Where this need was not met, empires tottered.

The Boer, Russo-Japanese, and Baltic Wars had all given warning of what would happen if the armies of the great powers of Europe met in battle armed with thousands of the latest rifled, breech-loading, rapid-firing cannon. No one came close to imagining, however, how great the hunger for shells was going to be when such a war came. In the years leading up to 1914 all the powers had spent heavily on artillery (in addition to its heavy artillery, Germany began the war with more than five thousand smaller field guns and twelve hundred field howitzers), and all entered the conflict with what they thought were immense quantities of ammunition. All were stunned by the speed with which their supplies were exhausted. When 1915 arrived with both fronts deadlocked, all the belligerents found themselves desperately short not just of shells but of production capacity. No amount ever seemed to be enough.

The French, who thought they had a three-month supply on hand at the end of July 1914, were rationing the number of shells given to each battery within six weeks; the Battle of the Marne nearly cleaned them out. The British, believing that they were going to war with a six-month supply, were running short before the end of October. The Russians, proud of having stockpiled a thousand rounds for every gun in their army, were likewise soon baffled by a conflict in which a single artillery piece might be called upon to fire a thousand times every couple of days.

When Grand Duke Nicholas told the Petrograd government that he needed two and a half, then three and a half *million* shells per *month,* these were numbers that Russian industry could not begin to provide. And so the Russians began placing huge orders overseas, first with British suppliers (who cheerfully accepted them and the advance payments that came with them in spite of being unable to meet their own army's needs), then with the United States. Being essentially bankrupt by early 1915, Russia was able to pay only by drawing on a line of credit of £25 million per month grudgingly extended by a British government fearful of collapse in the east. The systemic corruption and profiteering of the Russian procurement system assured that much of the money simply disappeared. Much of what was ordered was never delivered, and much of what was delivered piled up uselessly at Russia's only functioning (and woefully inadequate) ports of entry, Vladivostok at the eastern end of Siberia and Archangel in the Arctic.

Though the shortage was severe for all the belligerents, its nature varied from country to country. Austria was plagued by the need to produce

A British munitions plant, pouring out shells for the armies of the Entente

ammunition for a ridiculously large number of different *kinds* of guns, many of them antiques long since discarded by armies that had done a better job of modernizing and standardizing. But even the most modern armies encountered problems not only of quantity but of shell type. All of them, before the war, had given priority to the production and accumulation of shrapnel, an antipersonnel projectile that, upon exploding in midair, showers lethal lead pellets over a wide area. The early months of the war showed that, though shrapnel was effective in cutting away barbed wire, it was useless for destroying fortifications and killing the men inside. Only high explosives such as dynamite and nitroglycerin did the job. The consumption of high-explosive shells—much more complicated and costly than shrapnel—increased exponentially.

France and Germany adapted best. In Paris an able and energetic young socialist politician named Albert Thomas was named undersecretary for armaments in the ministry of war and hurried to make changes. He got three hundred and fifty thousand skilled industrial workers—eventually half a million—released from military service and assigned to munitions factories and coal mines. He brought tens of thousands of women onto the payrolls of private and government plants. He thereby started a gender revolution that would change European society; by the end of the war women would fill more than a third of all industrial jobs in Britain and France, and more than half of such jobs in Germany. Prisoners of war were put to work as well, and refugees. With remarkable speed France was soon coming close to meeting the needs of its army.

Germany's situation was especially perilous in the first year of the war. Moltke, uniquely among Europe's prewar military planners, had insisted on the development of industrial facilities capable of achieving and sustaining high rates of munitions production. These facilities provided a basis for rapid expansion, but they were not nearly enough. The Germans had used more ammunition in the Battle of the Marne than in the Franco-Prussian War; First Ypres and the war in the east further drained supplies; and the naval blockade put in place by Britain cut Germany off from sources of essential commodities.

To attack the problem Falkenhayn, in his capacity as minister of war, recruited a dynamic young Jewish industrialist named Walter Rathenau. Rathenau got almost miraculous results out of Germany's chemical and engineering industries. Soon camphor, essential in the production of gunpowder, was being extracted from turpentine rather than imported from Japan. Nitrogen was being drawn from the atmosphere rather than from the guano deposits of Chile, and wood products were replacing American cotton and also providing the acetone needed for making nitroglycerin. In

Germany as in France, skilled workers were exempted from military duty and women went into the factories. By the summer of 1915 Germany was manufacturing upward of four million shells per month. That was sufficient, though barely.

Historians who have examined the question argue persuasively that the shell crises of 1914 and 1915 need not have been as serious as they were and in fact were sometimes not as serious as the generals claimed. In many battles, especially when bad weather turned roads to muck, the problem was not so much a lack of ammunition as an inability to get the necessary tons of it to the waiting guns. In Serbia in 1914 horse-drawn Austrian wagons laden with shells were able to move only twelve miles in four days of hard labor. Gunners were often profligate, opening fire, for example, upon seeing just one or two distant soldiers. The Russians made especially bad use of their supplies, stockpiling mountains of shells in fortresses that usually had little military value and eventually fell to the Germans.

Generals on both sides became adept at blaming a shortage of shells for their failure to produce the results they had promised. In Russia, Minister of War Sukhomlinov was so convinced that his rivals were using such complaints to undercut him politically that he withheld urgently needed ammunition. At the end of First Ypres, Sir Douglas Haig complained to a journalist that his troops could simply have walked through the German lines unopposed "as soon as we were supplied with ample artillery ammunition of high explosives."

Haig's failures in later offensives, when his supplies of ammunition were practically infinite, make this complaint dubious at best. But it was not the last such complaint to be made—and made publicly—by a senior commander of the BEF. The result, before 1915 was half finished, would be a crisis that brought down Asquith's Liberal government and led to a radical redistribution of power among Britain's political leaders.

Chapter 17

The Ground Shifts

*"Success will come in the final analysis to
the side which has the last man."*
—HENRI-PHILIPPE PÉTAIN

By the end of April the Germans had scraped together enough troops to
form yet another new eastern army, the Eleventh. They accomplished
this through a general reorganization in which the number of battalions per
division was reduced from twelve to nine, compensating for the reduction
in manpower by giving every division more machine guns. Command of
the Eleventh was given to August von Mackensen, a ferocious-looking general who had figured importantly in the Tannenberg victory and offered
Falkenhayn the advantage of being no friend of Hindenburg and Ludendorff.

The question facing Falkenhayn would have seemed familiar in London:
how should the new army be used? Giving it to Hindenburg was out of the
question. Transferring it to the Western Front was impossible because contrary to the wishes of Kaiser Wilhelm, who though declining in influence
remained hereditary All-High Warlord with the power to set strategy. The
fact that not a single offensive on the Western Front had achieved its intended
results reinforced the kaiser's belief that victory could be achieved only in the
east.

Falkenhayn had to do *something,* he was going to have to do it in the east,
and he strongly preferred that it not happen in the northern sectors where
Hindenburg was in command. A simple process of elimination pointed him
toward the southeast—toward the Austrians and their endless problems. And
though he still had powerful political enemies, Falkenhayn also had a new
ally: Crown Prince Wilhelm, the kaiser's heir. This far-from-incapable young
officer, now developing into a seasoned army commander, suggested how
Falkenhayn might satisfy the skeptics and at the same time prepare the way

for the Western Front offensive that he wanted. The prince's idea was simple and sensible. Germany's prime objective should be not to defeat the Russians conclusively—an unrealistic goal, in light of the enemy's manpower and the vast distances of the eastern theater—but to damage them so badly that in 1916 the Germans would be free to turn their attention to the west.

Falkenhayn was thus disposed to pay heed when Conrad reported from Vienna that he saw an opportunity to break through the momentarily static Russian line between the Galician towns of Gorlice and Tarnow, and thereby preempt the inevitable resumption of Russia's Carpathian offensive. Conrad, however, remained desperately short of troops and shells, and so he added that he would be incapable of executing his plan without the assistance of at least four German divisions. Falkenhayn's answer was surprising from a man who had so long been incapable of enthusiasm where the east was concerned. He told Conrad that he was sending not just the four requested divisions but twice that many: all four of the corps that made up Mackensen's new army. Conrad, formally in charge of the campaign, was required to promise that he would do nothing without the approval of Falkenhayn or, in Falkenhayn's absence, of Mackensen. Mackensen, along with the Army of the South that was already operating with Conrad under the command of General von Linsingen, would be reporting not to the two giants of the north but to Falkenhayn himself.

Over a ten-day period Mackensen's army was moved into place, surreptitiously so as not to alert the Russians, behind a thirty-mile expanse of front facing Gorlice and Tarnow. Falkenhayn himself went east to oversee the deployment, while Hindenburg and Ludendorff remained on the sidelines. Pointedly declining to give them any direct role in the impending offensive, Falkenhayn asked them to undertake a diversionary action to draw as many Russians as possible away from Galicia. Ludendorff, interested not in diversions but in conquest, took Falkenhayn's request as justification for sending a large cavalry force into Russian-controlled territory on the far northern Baltic coast, a remote and desolate region called Courland that the war had not yet reached. At first this probe did not produce the result that Falkenhayn, at least, was hoping for: the Russians didn't regard it as important enough to require a strong response.

The southern offensive, with Conrad and his troops in a distinctly subordinate role, began on May 2 with a brief but fantastically intense artillery barrage and almost immediately turned into a success unlike anything seen in the west. In four hours fifteen hundred German and Austrian gun crews dropped seven hundred thousand rounds of high explosives, shrapnel, and poison gas onto a twenty-eight-mile front occupied by the Russian Third Army, which had not troubled to construct strong defenses and was short not only of artillery but even of rifles. Worse, the Russians' five and a half divisions—sixty thousand men—had been worn down by the winter fighting in the Carpathians and had been left in an isolated position that no other Russian force would be able to reach quickly. When the bombardment ended and Mackensen's ten divisions and Conrad's eight moved forward, the Third Army collapsed. The attackers pushed it back beyond Gorlice in less than twenty-four hours. They advanced eight miles in forty-eight hours, Tarnow fell on the fifth day, and within a week a hundred and forty thousand Russians and two hundred guns had been captured. Two other Russian armies came forward to rescue the Third, but their movements were poorly coordinated and accomplished little beyond feeding more bodies to the German gunners. General Radko Dimitriev, commander of the Third Army, was begging for approval to begin—so far as his troops were still capable of such a thing—a retreat across Galicia to the River San. This would have required abandoning the great prize of Przemysl. Grand Duke Nicholas, unable to accept the surrender of everything he had won, refused. He ordered Dimitriev to do what the German artillery made an impossibility: to stand his ground.

With winter finished, the war was heating up everywhere. A week after the start of the Gorlice-Tarnow offensive, Joffre and French launched in the Artois region directly south of Ypres (where the fighting had never entirely died down) a massive attack that both men expected to produce great results—that Joffre said could "finish the war in three months." The thinning of the German line had gone too far to remain secret. Knowledge of it helped make Joffre and French as confident as ever that the eternally hoped-for great breakthrough was at hand.

The bloody mess called the Second Battle of Artois began on May 9. After only forty-six minutes of shelling (the brevity of this bombardment was made necessary by a scarcity of high-explosive shells), three corps of Haig's recently formed British First Army hit two sectors of line defended by only two German regiments. The Germans had constructed parallel lines of defense, including dugouts reinforced with timbers that, when topped with layers of dirt-filled sandbags, could not be penetrated even by high explosives. Only eight percent of the British shells had contained high explosives, and their shrapnel hadn't been sufficient even to cut away the barbed wire in front of the trenches.

The defenders emerged from the barrage almost untouched, their machine guns so positioned as to be able to direct a heavy fire into the flanks of the two formations of British attackers. The target of the offensive was Aubers Ridge, which rose up abruptly behind the Germans' first line. Once there, the attackers were to move southeast along a line of ridges until they linked up with French troops who, according to the plan, would by then be on the march toward the town of Lens. Beyond Lens lay a flatland called the Douai plain, the wrecked Belgian fortress of Namur, and (so Joffre hoped) victory.

On that first day British casualties totaled 11,600, more than four hundred and fifty officers included, with so little result that the offensive was brought to a halt. The stop was temporary; three more divisions were thrown at the Germans May 16 through 18, suffering seventeen thousand additional casualties while gaining no ground.

The French had much greater initial success, in part because their attack was preceded by six *days* of bombardment during which twelve hundred guns poured seven hundred thousand shells onto the Bavarians of Crown Prince Rupprecht's Sixth Army. In the four hours before the infantry's advance, the gunners fired enough rounds to put eighteen high-explosive shells on every yard of front; most of their guns were 75mm field pieces with low trajectories ill suited to the shelling of trenches, but the cumulative effect was devastating. Though both flanks of the attack force were butchered by machine-gun fire, the center quickly penetrated three miles into enemy territory. For three days the center continued its advance, taking possession of three German lines.

Then heavy rain began to fall, turning the ground to a gluey mud that made further progress impossible. In the end the early success of this assault led to losses so severe that it would have been better for the French if they had been checked at the beginning as completely as the British. The attackers made no breakthrough, finally, just an impressive but temporary bending-back of the German line. Ultimately they found themselves blocked by a last-ditch line of machine-gun nests that alone stood between them and the German artillery. As usual, the fight went on long after any chance of success had evaporated, with repeated French and British attacks neutralized by German counterattacks, casualties piling up, and nothing of importance accomplished. When the battle came to its end on June 18, the French had lost more more than a hundred thousand men, the Germans just under fifty thousand.

Joffre remained undaunted. He was already making plans not only to restart the Artois offensive in the fall but to combine it with a simultaneous, even bigger attack in Champagne, thereby swamping the ability of the Germans to respond. If only in numerical terms, Joffre's optimism had a rational basis: by early summer the British and French outnumbered the Germans on the Western Front by fully half a million men. Sir John French was as confident of success as Joffre and as eager for more offensives.

But the costs of Artois did affect people whose minds were not impervious to reality. Across France this latest torrent of death produced shock, though complaint was muted by Joffre's assurances that German losses had been immensely greater. The government in Paris was deeply troubled, all the more so as some of Joffre's subordinate generals grew restive, and the humble poilus, the "hairy ones," were beginning to display an unwillingness to participate in the most suicidally hopeless assaults. Joffre was still the savior of France, but the ground under his feet was no longer quite so solid.

At the same time the prestige of Henri-Philippe Pétain, who less than a year earlier had been an obscure colonel preparing a country home for retirement, was rising rapidly. It was a corps under Pétain's command that had made all the early gains in the Artois offensive, its advance units getting to the top of Vimy Ridge before being driven off by arriving German reserves. Pétain's painstaking preparations and efficient execution had been essential to this success, limited and temporary as it was. He was a hard disciplinarian but nearly unique among the high-ranking generals of the time in the concern he showed for the living conditions of his troops and his willingness to share their risks. (He would move forward into the combat zone when his men were under bombardment.) The disdain for the cult of the offensive that had crippled his peacetime career was beginning to look like wisdom. In the crucible of combat he was emerging as a model of professional competence and common sense. Above all he was a commander who got results, and so in the immediate aftermath of the Artois campaign he was promoted to command of the French Second Army.

Plainspoken as always, he produced a report on Second Artois in which he declared that this war was not going to be won by some breakthrough, some great and brilliantly executed conclusive battle. This, he said, was a war of attrition, and it required keeping casualties at tolerable levels. "Success will come in the final analysis," he said, "to the side which has the last man." In this regard he was much closer in his thinking to Falkenhayn than to Joffre, French, and Haig. He was also ahead of his fellow French generals, and almost abreast of the best German thinking, in his understanding of how to use artillery and infantry together. It was the big guns that took enemy ground, he said. The infantry's job was to occupy what the artillery had conquered.

In London too the ground was shifting. Kitchener, as potent a national symbol in Britain as Joffre was south of the Channel, was as baffled as his French counterpart by this terrible new kind of warfare and far more prepared to admit that no solutions were at hand. Behind the scenes he was losing the iron-hard self-assurance that had for so long been an essential element of his public persona. He had lost faith in the Gallipoli campaign, where the British and French were bogged down on their landing beaches and were beginning to be ravaged by dysentery and the fly-plagued miseries of the Turkish summer. But he could see no way of extracting Hamilton's force without losing tens of thousands of men in the process. He could see no alternative to pushing ahead to victory (one of his fears was that defeat in Turkey would provoke a revolt by Britain's Muslim subjects in Egypt) and seemed prepared to pay almost any price in doing so. Early in May there had been talk of trying again to use the Entente's Mediterranean fleet to force the Dardanelles, but all such planning came to an end with the sinking at Gallipoli of the British battleship *Goliath.* The mighty *Queen Elizabeth,* crown jewel of the Dardanelles task force, was withdrawn to safer waters. Three days later, on learning that Churchill was sending still more warships to the Dardanelles, Admiral John Fisher resigned as first sea lord and sent a wildly emotional letter to the leader of the Tory opposition. Calling Churchill "a real danger," he warned that "a very great national disaster is very near us in the Dardanelles!" On May 25 the first U-boat to reach the Aegean torpedoed and sank the battleship *Triumph.* A day later it sank the *Majestic,* at which point the six British battleships remaining near the Dardanelles were sent away. With that, even the possibility of a naval attempt on the strait disappeared.

Kitchener remained skeptical about the prospects of success on the Western Front but was finding it increasingly difficult to act in accordance with his doubts. The enormous prestige that had prompted his appointment as secretary of state for war had by now shriveled considerably, at least in the eyes of his fellow cabinet members, and his hold on power was slipping. Kitchener had always been better suited to the role of satrap, to ruling distant parts of the empire, than to the compromises and collaboration of party politics, and his political skills had not improved since the start of the war. He remained secretive, autocratic, and unwilling to cooperate or delegate. "It is repugnant to me," he had said after getting a taste of cabinet government, "to have to reveal military secrets to twenty-three gentlemen with whom I am hardly acquainted." By the spring of 1915 he was sorely disliked and resented by many ministers and by the Tories as well.

In mid-May, with the bloodletting of Second Artois at its height and Haig's attack on Aubers Ridge having come to its disastrous conclusion, Kitchener canceled an order that would have sent the first of Britain's new divisions to the Western Front. Sir John French, driven half mad with frustration by news that three of the divisions were going to Gallipoli, fired off a wire to Kitchener announcing that he was so low on shells that he would not be able to resume his offensive unless immediately resupplied. When Kitchener's reply arrived—it was, to French's shock, an order to release 20,000 artillery rounds for shipment to Gallipoli—something inside the commander of the BEF snapped. Possibly too angry to notice that the message also said that the diverted shells would be replaced within twenty-four hours (a promise that was kept), French decided to make war on Kitchener. He called in an old friend and former army colleague, the London *Times* military correspondent

Charles à Court Repington, and told him, not for attribution, that the British offensives were failing because of a lack of artillery ammunition and that the fault lay with Kitchener. A few days later a series of articles based on French's accusation began appearing, with sensational impact, in London. Coupled with Fisher's resignation, these articles created the impression of a government in chaos. The situation was worsened by two staff officers dispatched to London to explain French's complaints. They found receptive listeners in Andrew Bonar Law, the leader of the Conservative Party, and David Lloyd George, who was becoming increasingly outspoken in criticizing Kitchener's dominance over military policy.

Lloyd George, long one of the most brilliant stars in Britain's political firmament, was emerging as a dominant figure. Paying a visit to Asquith, he warned the prime minister that he himself would make further public disclosures about mismanagement of armaments production unless drastic action was taken without delay. Asquith, being if nothing else skilled at self-preservation, reacted quickly. The government was dissolved and replaced with a coalition cabinet—the first wartime coalition in British history. Asquith held on to his job, but Conservative members became a major element in the cabinet and Lloyd George was the leader of the surviving Liberals. Parliament passed a Munitions War Act that established a new ministry of munitions, thereby taking responsibility for armaments out of Kitchener's hands. The prime minister ordered him to start submitting frequent and detailed reports on his actions and plans, ending his freedom to operate in as much secrecy as he wished. Eventually, as a final humiliation, responsibility for strategy would be shifted from Kitchener to the chief of the imperial general staff.

Lloyd George moved into the new munitions ministry and took drastic action. He outlawed strikes in the weapons industry and sharply increased the production of heavy artillery and high-explosive shells. Trying to come to grips with a problem plaguing all the belligerent nations, he took steps aimed at controlling profiteering by arms manufacturers.

French, in launching his press campaign, had hoped to destroy Kitchener. But Kitchener survived, albeit with his authority diminished. The only politician destroyed was one whom French liked and admired: Winston Churchill. The Conservatives had old scores to settle with Churchill, who a decade earlier had deserted them to join the Liberals. One of their conditions in joining the coalition was that Churchill could not continue as First Lord of the Admiralty. Asquith was not a man to endanger his own position in order to defend anyone else, and so Churchill was out. He departed the Admiralty in tears, certain that his career was at an end.

Kitchener retained, along with his job title, the power to decide where to send the volunteer armies that were now fully trained and ready for active service. Weakened as he was, he finally consented to send most of these units where he did not think them likely to accomplish much—to the Western Front. He also continued to feed troops to Gallipoli, where victory seemed at once imperative and unachievable. With one of these deployments went a request that Hamilton tell him how many troops he thought he would need to take control of the peninsula.

Falkenhayn too was affected by the French and British spring offensives, if not so conspicuously as Asquith, Lloyd George, and Churchill. He understood that Second Artois had been a near thing—Pétain would have held Vimy Ridge if the reserves he needed had not been too far to the rear—and had no doubt that the Entente would be attacking again within a few months. This prospect worsened his uneasiness about German weakness in the west, increased his anxiety about moving troops back from the east, and made him more unwilling than ever to commit to the kinds of grand Napoleonic schemes that Ludendorff never tired of putting forward. He was haunted by the ruin that had come to Napoleon in 1812 as a result of his movement deep into Russia. His fears ensured that there could be no resolution of his rivalry with the Hindenburg-Ludendorff team.

The Western Front remained quiet through the rest of the summer— "quiet" being a relative term indicating a state of affairs in which only scores or hundreds of men were killed daily in obscure forays, skirmishes, limited attacks, and routinely murderous sniper and artillery fire. A letter that Private Jack Mackenzie sent to his wife in Scotland on July 3 illuminates life on the line at a time of little action. "We relieved our fourth battalion in here, these are the trenches which they lost so many men in capturing, & is just one vast deadhouse, the stench in some places is something awful, the first thing we had to do was dig the trenches deeper & otherwise repair them & we came across bodies all over the place, you know the Germans occupied these trenches nearly the whole winter and have been losing heavily & has had to bury their killed in the trenches, there were legs and arms sticking out all over the place when we arrived but we have buried the most of them properly now. The ground behind us us [sic] is covered yet by dead Camerons and Germans who fell on the seventeenth of May & we go out at night & bury them, it is a very rotten job as they are very decomposed, but it has to be done." Mackenzie (who would be killed in action in 1916) goes on to thank his "own darling wife" for sending food and clothing by mail, regretting only that a recently received pair of pants was not some color other than white. "But many thanks dearest for sending them," he added, "they will do fine."

In the east, by contrast, the summer was a prolonged crisis. On May 10 the Russian Third Army, bleeding to death under the pressure of the Gorlice-Tarnow offensive, was at last given permission to fall back to the River San, where it was to make a stand. The Germans were hard on its heels and by May 16 were breaking through its new line (which was badly equipped, the Russians having sold to local entrepreneurs the mountains of supplies that had fallen into their hands with the capture of Przemysl earlier in the year). Soon the Germans were across the San, but then their offensive began to run down, encumbered by supply and transport problems in a region where good roads and railways were scarce. A Russian counterattack against the Austro-Hungarian part of the attacking force was initially successful, taking another huge batch of Conrad's troops as prisoners. But it was not successful enough to balance the German gains, and within a week it too came to a stop. The Russian government, which earlier had been indicating a willingness to send troops to Gallipoli, announced that doing so was no longer possible. Its armies, in disorderly retreat in the southeast and threatened in Poland as well, had taken more than four hundred thousand casualties in May alone (bringing their total for ten months of war to almost four million). In the south they were barely able to pull back fast enough to keep the Germans from cutting off their escape.

Fearing catastrophe, the government in St. Petersburg developed new interest in getting Italy into the war. Prime Minister Salandra, sensing that this was the moment to extract maximum concessions from the Entente and willing to gamble on the eventual defeat of the Central Powers, made Italy a party to the Treaty of London. In return for a promise to enter the war within thirty days, he was given almost everything he wanted. The matter was not settled, however. Powerful groups in Italy were opposed to war, among them the Catholic Church and the socialists, who agreed on little else. When they learned what Salandra had done, these groups protested and the government fell. Salandra's deal appeared to have died with it. But there followed a kind of protofascist coup d'état that foreshadowed the Mussolini era and led on May 23 to Italy's declaration of war on Austria-Hungary. The government did not declare war on Germany, fatuously thinking that with this omission it could avoid unnecessary trouble.

The Gorlice-Tarnow offensive, though a triumph for the German high command, set the stage for further bitter disputes. Falkenhayn had wanted to stop when Mackensen's army reached the San, but Conrad persuaded him to continue. As soon as he learned of Italy's declaration of war, Conrad urged an attack into the north Italian plain. Falkenhayn wanted to subdue Serbia—a land route through the Balkans to Turkey was badly needed. On June 3 all the major players including the kaiser met at German headquarters. Falkenhayn, warning that fresh British troops were arriving on the continent in alarming numbers, said it was time to move at least four divisions to the West. Conrad pressed his case for an invasion of Italy and was taken seriously by no one. Ludendorff laid out his latest grand plan: a move from the north (where he and Hindenburg were in command) aimed at encircling whole Russian armies. Falkenhayn argued that not enough troops were available for such an operation. Ludendorff replied that nothing less could produce lasting results—that it was futile to keep pushing the Russians back without destroying their ability to make war.

Once again the kaiser ordered a compromise that left the heart of the conflict unresolved. Mackensen's army would be reinforced with troops provided by Hindenburg and Ludendorff. (How the two must have seethed at that.) It and the Austro-Hungarian troops on its flanks would resume the Gorlice-Tarnow offensive as soon as possible. The rest of the Austrian army would move south, not to attack Italy but to prepare for a possible Italian attack.

Two weeks later, when Mackensen went into action, he was again startlingly successful. The Germans took possession of Lemberg on June 22 and crossed yet another river, the Dniester, as the Russians stumbled back to the River Bug. The Russians had been pushed completely out of Galicia, giving up everything they had gained since the start of the war, and their ability to fend off further attacks was questionable. In Courland in the far north, at the same time, Ludendorff's supposedly diversionary action was posing an increasing threat to the cities of Russia's Baltic coast. The dangers of the Courland campaign—if it continued, it could even threaten St. Petersburg—were becoming apparent to the Russians. Grand Duke Nicholas, visited at his

August von Mackensen
*His offensives drove the
Russians out of Galicia.*

headquarters by the tsar and trying to report on all the disasters coming down on his armies, collapsed in grief. "Poor Nikolasha, while telling me this, wept in my private room and even asked whether I thought of replacing him by a more capable man," Tsar Nicholas wrote his wife, perhaps hoping to make her less hostile to the grand duke. "He kept thanking me for staying here, because my presence here supported him personally." Riots broke out in Moscow. Houses and businesses owned by people with German names were looted and destroyed, but the rage was not directed at Germany only. At a huge demonstration in Red Square, people called for the tsar to be deposed, for the German-born tsarina to be confined to a convent, and for Rasputin to be hanged. The unraveling of the Romanov regime was beginning.

But even now the German generals were unable to agree on strategy. The leaders of Berlin's eastern forces met again at the end of June. Ludendorff arrived with a new plan even more ambitious than the one rejected at the start of the month. It was Hoffmann's work, and Ludendorff had accepted it only when, after an all-night debate, all four of the army commanders who would be responsible for its execution gave it their endorsement. It called for the armies in the north to move east to cut key rail lines, then swing south to trap the Russians in Poland. Encircled, the Russians would have to surrender or perish. Having been won over, Ludendorff was enthusiastic. He instructed Hoffmann to stand by at northern headquarters for a phone call announcing the kaiser's approval. When Hoffmann's phone finally rang hours later than expected, a furious Ludendorff told him that Falkenhayn had again rejected their proposal and had received the support of the kaiser for an alternative, less ambitious offensive.

What Falkenhayn had first proposed was not an alternative offensive but an end to the attacks coupled with an attempt to open negotiations with the Russians. The kaiser was taken aback by this idea and would not discuss it. But he was inclined to agree when Falkenhayn said "The Russians can retreat into the vastness of their country; we cannot go chasing them forever and ever." Another compromise emerged, a plan for a three-pronged offensive that, if not as grandiose as what Ludendorff wanted, nonetheless had a lofty objective: to force the Russians out of Poland.

Russian Poland, wedged between East Prussia and the Hapsburg domains to the south, was thus exposed on three sides. The new campaign began on July 12 with one German army group driving southward to east of Warsaw, another attacking west of the city, and Mackensen moving north toward Lublin and Brest-Litovsk. When the Russian commander in Poland sensibly suggested withdrawal, Grand Duke Nicholas refused, much as he had at first refused to permit his Third Army to pull out of Galicia. His reasons were more political than military. Some in St. Petersburg—called Petrograd now, to erase the taint of Germanism—feared that if Russia abandoned Poland while the British and French achieved a great victory at Gallipoli, Russia's claim to Constantinople might be compromised. They feared too that if Russian reverses continued while Italy was inflicting defeat on Austria-Hungary (that too was still widely expected), Italy would move into the Balkans. The Russians had strong fortresses in Poland, recently updated at tremendous expense and generously supplied with guns and ammunition that were badly needed elsewhere; the grand duke, in believing that they could hold out, ignored the lessons of Liège and Namur.

At first the German advance on Poland was slow. The emphasis was not on infantry attacks but on colossal artillery bombardments—hundreds of thousands of shells day after day—that had a ruinous effect on Russian numbers and morale. Gradually the pace accelerated. Town after town was abandoned to the Germans, and soon Warsaw, which had been in Russian hands for exactly one hundred years, was in grave danger. Townsfolk and peasants fled in all directions, leaving behind almost all their possessions and finding safety nowhere. "They are in despair, and protest bitterly," a Russian soldier wrote. "At eight in the evening we are on the march again. We come out onto the road. It is dark. But what's that noise? Oh my God, what's happening on the road ahead? It is blocked by carts, full of kids and household stuff. The cows are bellowing, the dogs are barking and yelping. The poor people are going God knows where, anywhere to get away from the fighting. But the old nags don't have the strength to pull the loads; the air is filled with the sound of horses being whipped and the Polish 'tso,' and still the carts won't move. We don't have the heart just to drive through them. It's such a heartbreaking scene, we drag one cart after another out of the mud, get them onto the main road and then onto the bridge over the river Narew. I pity them all, particularly the little children, sitting in the carts or in their mothers' arms. They don't understand what is happening around them. My thoughts turn to my own family, I feel depressed and before I know it tears run down my cheeks."

By any measure, the German achievement in the east had been tremendous. Russian resistance was crumbling everywhere. But Hindenburg, Ludendorff, and Hoffmann were contemptuous. The Germans were merely forcing the Russians to move. They were not annihilating them.

The French and British were troubled. Something big had to be done to turn the tide—to ease the danger of Russia making a separate peace. For Joffre and French, only one thing could suffice: a fall offensive big enough and successful enough to neutralize everything that had happened in the east. For others, it meant that Gallipoli had to be carried to a victorious conclusion. For still others, Kitchener among them, *both* aims now seemed imperative.

GENOCIDE

THE HOPE WITH WHICH MANY OF CONSTANTINOPLE'S Young Turks had begun the war—a hope of regaining lost territories, of taking revenge on old enemies (on Russia above all), and of restoring their empire's faded glory—soon turned to fear. A December 1914 invasion of the Caucasus, led personally by War Minister Enver Pasha, had aimed at driving the Russians out of a region whose population was overwhelmingly Muslim, but it ended in failure and the death of more than a hundred thousand Turkish troops. Then came the Entente assaults on the Dardanelles and Gallipoli—and a panicky realization that Constantinople itself was threatened. By the time the war was six months old, everything that remained of what Suleiman the Magnificent and his forebears had built was in danger of falling into ruin.

These disasters, coming hard on the heels of the Turkish expulsion from the Balkans in 1912 and a century of other humiliating concessions to the Europeans, inflamed the worst tendencies of the Turkish leadership. For more than a generation before the war, nationalist Turks and Islamic extremists had been saying that the Ottoman Empire, in order to be saved, must first be purified—must above all be purged of non-Muslim elements. By the spring of 1915 this idea was policy. The government of Turkey embarked upon the first true genocide of the twentieth century, the modern era's first effort to eliminate a whole people. The target was Armenia, which the loss of Bosnia, Bulgaria, Greece, Montenegro, Romania, and Serbia had left as the last large Christian population still inside the Turkish empire.

History had long been unkind to Armenia, which in ancient times was the most powerful independent kingdom on the eastern border of the Roman Empire and in the fourth century became the first nation to make Christianity its official religion. In the fourteenth and fifteenth centuries the northward advance of the Turks and the collapse of the Byzantine Empire reduced the Armenians, like the Christian kingdoms of the Balkans, to a persecuted subject people. In the centuries that followed they became entangled in the conflict between the Turks and the Russians, who were by then advancing southward. By the late nineteenth century Armenia was divided, upward of a million and a half of its people still subject to the Turks but another million living in areas annexed by Russia.

This division—the Armenian homeland occupying a contested borderland between two bitterly hostile empires—eventually brought disaster. Russia justified its expansion by claiming to be the champion, and where possible the liberator, of the Turks' Christian subjects. The Turks, brutish in their management of non-Islamic populations, responded by electing to deal with the Armenians as hostile aliens. They raised taxes to ruinous levels and encouraged the Kurds to enrich themselves, by force, at the expense of their Armenian neighbors. Inevitably such actions gave rise to Armenian radical groups demanding autonomy and to further Turkish suppression.

In the last two decades of the nineteenth century Constantinople's treatment of Turkish Armenia was so atrocious that it became an international cause célèbre and an early focus of the American Red Cross. Constantinople saw the attention it was receiving as interference in its internal affairs. When Armenians living in Constantinople raised a disturbance, the Turks responded with a savagery that was remarkable even by Ottoman standards. Tens of thousands of Armenians were slaughtered, many others were driven from their homes, and whole towns were leveled.

Among the Young Turks who took power in 1908 were men who wanted the Ottoman Empire to become a multicultural enterprise in which the rights of religious and ethnic minorities were respected. Such men were eventually pushed aside, however, and the government came to be dominated by fanatical nationalists who found in the Armenians a convenient object for their hatred. When a counterrevolution against the Young Turks failed in 1909, the Armenians again became scapegoats. At least fifteen thousand were butchered at the city of Adana amid grotesque scenes of rape, mutilation, and destruction of property.

When the Balkan wars sent a flood of displaced Muslims into Turkey, many were sent to Armenia (where Christians had no legal rights and were under the heel of Kurdish tribal chieftains) with license to take what they wanted and kill anyone who tried to interfere. Against this background it is remarkable that a hundred thousand Armenian men joined the Ottoman army when Constantinople entered the Great War. Rather naturally, however, loyalties were divided, and the situation became hopelessly confused. Armenians on the Russian side of the border were joining the tsar's army, and they encouraged their cousins on the other side to join in the fight against a regime that had done nothing to earn their loyalty. In December 1914 an Armenian division organized by the Russians crossed the border and killed one hundred and twenty thousand non-Armenians (most of them Turks and Kurds).

The Young Turks found here all the justification they needed for actions that in peacetime probably would have been unimaginable. They began in comparatively innocuous fashion, disarming their Armenian soldiers and assigning them to labor battalions. Then they proceeded to work, and starve, those battalions to death. Next, having eliminated the part of the population most capable of defending itself, they sent an army onto the plateau that had long been home to most of Turkey's Armenians. In town after town and city after city, all males over the age of twelve were gathered up and shot or hacked to death en masse. Women were raped and mutilated, and those who were not killed were sold into slavery. Hundreds of thousands of civilians were marched off to the deserts of Syria and Mesopotamia. Many died of exposure, starvation, or exhaustion along the way, and others were murdered by their Kurdish escorts. The pogrom spread across all of Turkey. In Constantinople thousands of convicted criminals were organized into death squads whose only assignment was to kill every Armenian they could find, giving first priority to those intellectuals, professionals, and religious and political leaders who might have the potential to serve as leaders. The families of Turkish officials took the choicest booty; the death squads and rabble took the rest.

It is estimated that more than half a million Armenians were killed in 1915, and that was far from the end of it. The massacre would continue through 1916, with further death marches in Syria. Still later, when the Russian armies withdrew from the Caucasus, the Armenians whose shield they had been fell prey to the Turks in their turn. The final convulsion would not come until 1922, when a new Turkish government took possession of Smyrna, set the city afire, and systematically slaughtered its tens of thousands of Armenian and Greek inhabitants.

No one would ever be punished. In the years after the war the United States found it more advantageous to come to terms with the Muslims of the Middle East with their oil riches than to redress the wrongs done to an Armenian nation described by the American high commissioner in Istanbul as "a race like the Jews; they have little or no national spirit and have poor moral character."

Successive Turkish governments continued into the twenty-first century not only to deny that an Armenian genocide ever occurred but to prosecute any Turk who dared to write of it.

Chapter 18

✠

Gallipoli Again, and Poland, and . . .

"Perhaps a scapegoat is needed to save Russia.
I mean to be the victim."

—Tsar Nicholas II

As the first faint hint of dawn began to glow in the eastern sky beyond Gallipoli on August 9, the men of the British Thirty-second Brigade were crouched in readiness just below the crest of Tekke Tepe Ridge, a high point dominating the center of the peninsula. These were untested but well-trained troops, some of the hundreds of thousands who had volunteered in the first days of the war, and they had landed at Gallipoli scarcely more than fifty hours before. They were also very tired troops, having spent the night clawing their way through the dark up the steep and rugged hillside. But the great prize, the heights that men from Britain, France, Australia, and New Zealand had for more than three months been trying and failing to reach, was now just yards away. And it was undefended: just the previous afternoon air reconnaissance had found no sign of Turkish forces anywhere in the neighborhood. Best of all, at the backs of the battalion, down on the beach at Suvla Bay less than three miles to the rear, were another twenty thousand newly arrived and well-equipped Tommies. They would be more than enough, once the ridge was in hand, to free the Anzacs from the nearby beachhead where they had been bottled up since July, cut off the Turkish units defending the lower peninsula, and crush them against the British and French at Cape Helles.

With the darkness fading to a predawn gray and the details of the landscape becoming visible, the order came to move. Silently, rifles in hand, the men started for the top. As they climbed, there suddenly appeared on the skyline above them, as if out of nowhere, the backlighted outlines of human beings. In another instant the silhouettes turned into a mass of shouting, shooting, bayonet-waving Turks, and the mass became a downrushing wave. Defense was impossible; those British who didn't flee were overrun and killed. The survivors were chased all the way down to the coastal flats. What they could not know was that their pursuers too had just arrived at Tekke Tepe. They had reached the crest at the end of a thirty-six-hour forced march and had been immediately sent into their attack by Mustafa Kemal, who himself had just spent three sleepless days and nights in desperate combat at Anzac Cove. Thus it had all come down to a question of minutes.

The August 6 landing at Suvla Bay had delivered to Gallipoli the four divisions that Ian Hamilton, in response to inquiries from Kitchener, had said back in May that he would need to break the stalemate. In London there had been much disagreement over whether to send those divisions—disagreement heightened by the collapse of the Liberal government and its replacement with a coalition. But when Kitchener threatened to resign if they were not sent, the opposition relented. From that point forward, events both in Europe and at Gallipoli made victory seem more imperative than ever. Repeated attempts to break out at Cape Helles and Anzac Cove had ended in bloody failure, the Turks had begun mounting attacks of their own, and the beachheads had turned into stinking pits of disease.

Back in Europe, Italy had shown itself to be unprepared for war. Its army was ill-equipped, untrained, ineptly led, and incapable of the kind of impact the Entente had hoped for and the Central Powers had feared. The Italian commander in chief, Luigi Cadorna, had marched more than six hundred thousand troops north to the Isonzo River between Vienna and Trieste, where they greatly outnumbered the Austrian defenders. They had attacked in June, losing fifteen thousand men, and again in late July, when their casualties totaled forty-two thousand. These attacks had accomplished nothing. There would be two more before the end of the year, gaining no ground of significance and producing another one hundred and sixteen thousand casualties.

The Italian failures and Russian setbacks up and down the Eastern Front had been carefully watched in the Balkans. Bulgaria now seemed closer to joining the Central Powers; Romania and Greece were less inclined to throw in with the Entente. On August 4 the Russians were pulling out of Warsaw, and British and French fears that they were giving up rose almost to the level of panic. Joffre was well along with his planning of a new offensive, but it could not be ready until autumn and British cooperation was not assured. On all the many fronts of this increasingly immense war, there remained only one place where the Entente could act immediately to end the sequence of calamities. That place was Gallipoli.

The August 6 assault had been given the highest priority and all the support that any commander could have wished in terms of manpower, weaponry, and naval and air support. Its centerpiece, the nighttime landing at Suvla Bay, was well planned and took the defenders by surprise. Sanders, the German commander, knew in advance that another invasion was coming but had no idea where. Hamilton opened the operation with attacks by the thirty-five thousand men already ashore at Cape Helles and the fifty-seven thousand at Anzac Cove, tying up the Turks in both places. To avoid drawing attention to Suvla, he had ordered no naval bombardment there before the landing.

Everything went as well as anyone could have expected when putting masses of inexperienced troops ashore on a wild and unfamiliar coast on a moonless night. By the morning of August 7 more than twenty thousand men had been landed, meeting almost no resistance and suffering practically no losses. The troops moved two miles inland and stopped to secure a perimeter. A wealth of munitions and supplies was quickly piled up on the beach. Fewer than fifteen hundred Turkish troops, armed with little more than rifles, stood between Suvla and Tekke Tepe Ridge—the key to everything beyond, the whole point of the landing. When attacked, they fled, many of them throwing down their weapons. The nearest reinforcements were at least a day and a half away. The only thing remaining to be done was for some substantial part of the invading force to move the few miles uphill to Tekke Tepe and establish a defensible position there. Rugged as those few miles were, rocky and overgrown and broken by Gallipoli's maze of ravines, they could have been traversed by noon on the first day.

British troops and supplies on the beach at Suvla Bay

Lt. Gen. Sir Frederick Stopford
in his prewar finery
*Remained far from the action
while the opportunity was lost.*

All through that first day the troops ashore were marched back and forth in confusion, their officers having been given no clear instructions as to what they were supposed to do. Hamilton himself remained miles away at his headquarters on the island of Lemnos. The commander of the landing force—a sixty-one-year-old lieutenant general named Sir Frederick Stopford, who been given the assignment by Kitchener because Hamilton's choices supposedly were needed on the Western Front—had never in his career commanded troops in combat. Satisfied that all was going well, believing that nothing more needed to be done until his artillery was put ashore, he remained aboard the ship that he had made his headquarters.

Late on the morning of August 8, half mad with frustration because of the absence of any indication that Stopford was trying to take the heights, Hamilton decided to go to Suvla himself. For a long time he was unable to find a ship to take him. It was late afternoon when he finally arrived, and when he did the senior officer ashore told him, absurdly, that no troops would be available to advance into the interior until morning. Hamilton's air spotters had reported that, although Tekke Tepe remained empty, a Turkish force was marching toward it from the north. When he insisted that morning would be too late, the Thirty-second Brigade suddenly became available. But the climb to the ridge now had to be made in darkness. The brigade repeatedly lost its way in the confusing terrain and so took seven hours to finally reach the point from which, as the night ended, it began its final ascent and was met just short of its goal by the troops of Mustafa Kemal.

The fight for Tekke Tepe Ridge had followed two days of terrible combat at Anzac Cove (where Kemal had yet again saved the day for the Turks and been vaulted by Sanders to command of all the troops in the area) and at Cape Helles. A day afterward, still without sleep, able to stay on his feet only with the aid of stimulants administered by a doctor who followed him everywhere, Kemal was shot through the wrist while driving the Anzacs from the high point of Chunuk Bair. This was the final crisis; if the Anzacs had been able to hold Chunuk Bair, it might have compensated for the failure at Tekke Tepe. When they were driven off, the second invasion of Gallipoli was essentially finished. The hapless Stopford launched additional attacks on August 12, 15, and 21, the last being the biggest battle of the Gallipoli campaign. It all but wrecked the Twenty-ninth Division that had arrived on the peninsula amid such high hopes in April. These anticlimactic offensives managed to connect the beachheads at Suvla and Anzac Cove but not to take any of the high ground on which the Turks were now positioned in strength. Both sides settled down to more stalemate. Hamilton sent a telegram to London reporting that Suvla Bay was a failure and stating that to regain the initiative he was going to need another ninety-five thousand troops. His August casualties totaled forty-five thousand, eight thousand of them at Suvla.

When Hamilton's grim news reached its destination, Kitchener was in France attending the last of a series of meetings called for the purpose of deciding what should be done next on the Western Front. The first of these conferences, at Calais on July 6, had been attended not only by the army leadership but by Prime Minister Asquith and French War Minister Millerand. It had exposed continued disagreement as to priorities and had made plain that the lines of division extended in many directions. Joffre had outlined his plan for a fall offensive. Kitchener had reacted with something close to scorn, as had Arthur Balfour, a former prime minister who had recently replaced Churchill as First Lord of the Admiralty. The next day, Kitchener and the civilians having departed, Joffre and French met at Chantilly and quietly agreed that the preparations for their offensive should proceed regardless of what the politicians thought. At a larger meeting of French and British generals on July 17, it was Haig who raised objections. He had examined the area where Joffre, Foch, and French wanted his army to attack. He declared it to be unsuitable and himself to be unwilling. The ground was too open, he said; his troops would be too exposed. And he did not have nearly enough artillery. Joffre was unmoved.

Kitchener was back in France in mid-August not only because details of the offensive needed to be settled but because of mounting trouble in the east. The fall of Warsaw—and so of all Poland—had been followed by continued German advances and increasing evidence that the Russian armies were on the verge of disintegration. The Russian retreat was turning into not just an alarming mess but a wave of crimes against humanity.

For generations most of Russia's Jews had been forcibly confined to eastern Poland, where they were required to live in ghettos and shtetls and almost entirely barred both from farming and from the learned professions. In late 1914, claiming to be addressing security concerns, the Russians had driven more than half a million of these people out of their homes and left them to the tender mercies of the long central European winter. In the first months of 1915 another eight hundred thousand of them were put out onto the roads of Poland, Lithuania, and Courland by the tsar's Cossacks, who often did not even permit them to take whatever possessions they might have been able to carry or cart away.

The Russians' final withdrawal from Poland was directed by General Nikolai Yanushkevich, a protégé of one of the tsar's favorites, the corrupt War Minister Vladimir Sukhomlinov. Yanushkevich, whom the tsar had forced a reluctant Grand Duke Nicholas to accept as his chief of staff early in the war, adopted a scorched-earth policy in which all the region's inhabitants, Jews and Gentiles alike, were put to flight. Stores of grain and other foodstuffs were destroyed; machinery was loaded onto wagons and railcars and moved east. Four million head of cattle were gratuitously slaughtered, ushering in a meat shortage that would persist in Russia beyond the end of the war. The refugees were ravaged by starvation, cholera, typhus, and typhoid. The number of lives lost will never be known.

The scale of the war in the east was breathtaking. Not long after taking Warsaw, the Germans captured the fortress city of Novo Georgievsk, taking ninety thousand soldiers, thirty generals, and seven hundred guns with it. Days later they took the equally important city of Kovno and another thirteen hundred guns. By now the Germans had taken more than seven hundred thousand Russian prisoners, the Austrians nearly that many, and their armies were still marching eastward. The Russian general staff was so alarmed by the rate at which its men were surrendering that it issued draconian decrees. Families of soldiers taken prisoner would receive no government assistance. Soldiers who surrendered would be sent to Siberia after the war.

As reports of what was happening arrived in the west, General Sir Henry Wilson, the British officer closest to the French high command and a masterful if sometimes too obvious manipulator, found ways to use them to the advantage of his friends. He began warning London that failure to give full support to France's next offensive could lead to the fall of Joffre and Millerand—and to *France* making a separate peace. Not surprisingly, Kitchener informed

Hamilton that he should expect no more troops at Gallipoli and gave the BEF unambiguous new orders for the autumn. Britain must support Joffre's offensive to the utmost, he said, "even though, by doing so, we suffer very heavy losses indeed." What is striking is that Kitchener at no point, privately or otherwise, expressed the smallest hope that the coming offensive might be a success. Its purpose, for him, was not to achieve victory but to hold the Entente together. His fears were eased though not ended when, in the closing days of August, Tsar Nicholas removed Grand Duke Nicholas as head of the Russian armies and, to the entirely appropriate horror of his ministers, appointed himself to the position. Nicholas was the soul of gentleness in dismissing his cousin, explaining in a letter that he believed it to be his "duty to the country which God has committed to my keeping" to "share the burdens and toils of war with my army and help it protect Russian soil against the onslaught of the foe." The grand duke, when he got the news, was more succinct. "God be praised," he said. "The Emperor releases me from a task which was wearing me out."

The decision to take command was characteristic of the tsar: it was courageous, even selfless, and deeply foolish. It was the last and by far the worst in a series of command changes that Nicholas made that summer. Late in June the tsar at last faced up to the incompetence of War Minister Sukhomlinov, who had rendered himself indefensible with his cavalier disregard of the most urgent problems. (When the army's chief of artillery came begging for shells, claiming that without them Russia would have to make peace, Sukhomlinov told him to "go to the devil and shut up.") The war ministry was given to Alexei Polivanov, an able and energetic general who immediately undertook a program of reforms. He made radical improvements in the supply system; created committees to take responsibility for munitions, food, fuel, transport, and refugees; and showed himself willing to work constructively with the Duma, the national assembly. Other such appointments had been similarly productive and were welcomed by almost everyone except Tsarina Alexandra, who believed that the only answer to Russia's problems was for Nicholas to become more the autocrat, less willing to tolerate reformers and liberals. "You are about to write a glorious page in the history of your reign and Russia," she wrote to her husband after persuading him to ignore the many ministers who had begged him not to become commander in chief. In her warped view, those ministers had questioned not just the wisdom of the tsar's decision but his authority as autocrat. All of them were, she decided, enemies of the crown; all should be dismissed.

It was not hard to win Alexandra's enmity, and she had a long memory. She had never forgiven Grand Duke Nicholas for refusing, during the failed revolution of 1905, to accept the leadership of a military dictatorship. In the wake of this refusal, the tsar had been left with no choice but to agree to a constitution and the creation of a national assembly. Both concessions compromised the autocracy. By making them necessary, the grand duke had shown himself too to be an enemy of the crown. Or so Alexandra thought. The possibility that the grand duke's refusal and the tsar's acquiescence had saved the regime is unlikely to have occurred to her.

Tsar Nicholas understood that from now on, as commander in chief, he would be blamed directly and personally for whatever happened to the army. "Perhaps a scapegoat is needed to save Russia," he said in explaining himself to French Ambassador Paléologue. "I mean to be the victim. May the will of God be done." Nicholas does not appear to have understood that, by keeping him far from the capital, his new responsibilities would encourage the increasingly widespread (and not mistaken) belief that the government was under the control of the tsarina and her beloved Rasputin. In any case, the British and French welcomed the change of command as evidence of Nicholas's commitment to the war. They were pleased by the tsar's choice of General Mikhail Alexeyev, a seasoned commander and a strategist of proven competence, as his chief of staff. The Germans too welcomed the change. They had learned to respect—though it is not always easy to understand why—Grand Duke Nicholas's abilities.

As before, success in the east was not giving the Germans as much comfort as might have been expected. By early September, having abandoned the cities of Brest-Litovsk and Bialystok, the Russians had withdrawn to a remote, treacherous, and largely uncharted region called the Pripet Marshes. Falkenhayn, refusing to follow them into such a morass, ordered all the commanders in the east to cease offensive operations. He began making arrangements to transfer several army corps back to the west and, at the same time, to get Bulgaria into the war by helping it to conquer Serbia. His instructions were disregarded by Conrad and Ludendorff alike; both would later claim to have misunderstood.

On August 31, apparently swept up in one of his periodic fantasies about duplicating the triumphs of the Germans, Conrad had launched his tattered forces on a sweeping offensive aimed at encircling twenty-five Russian divisions and, after defeating them, driving eastward into Ukraine. This effort started out well enough but ended badly. One of the Austrian armies, after capturing the city of Lutsk, was taken in the flank by a Russian force that had concealed itself in marshland grasses. Disaster followed upon disaster. Ultimately Falkenhayn had to detach two of the divisions preparing to invade Serbia and send them to the rescue. Conrad lost three hundred thousand men in September. Ludendorff meanwhile, continuing his Courland campaign, had taken the Lithuanian capital of Vilna. In doing so he provoked a panic in Petrograd, which though hundreds of miles from the Courland front became the scene of hasty preparations for flight. The capture of Vilna had come at such a cost, however—fifty thousand German casualties—that Ludendorff soon abandoned his hopes of taking the Russian city of Riga. He settled down to a busy winter of organizing and administering his conquests.

Max Hoffmann, unquestionably one of the most brilliant generals on either side, was by now also one of the most frustrated. He continued to blame Falkenhayn for failing to pursue a decision in the east, but now he blamed Ludendorff too, for attacking too directly at Vilna and thereby making that victory such a painful one. As for Hindenburg, Hoffmann regarded him as so passive, so utterly a figurehead, as to be little short of contemptible. "On the whole Hindenburg no longer bothers himself with military matters," Hoffmann wrote at this time. "He hunts a good deal and otherwise comes for five minutes in the morning and evening to see how things are going. He no longer has the slightest interest in military matters." Another general on Ludendorff's staff confided at about this time that "Hindenburg himself is becoming increasingly a mere stooge." The aged hero spent many hours having numerous portraits of himself painted and writing to his wife.

As for Ludendorff and Falkenhayn, all the successes of 1915 had done nothing to cool their mutual hatred. When they met at Kovno late in the year to join in the kaiser's ceremonial celebration of their conquests, Falkenhayn used the occasion to throw down the gauntlet.

"Now are you convinced," he demanded of Ludendorff, "that my operation was correct?"

"On the contrary!" Ludendorff replied. Russia had not surrendered. Russia had not sued for peace. How could anyone be satisfied? Falkenhayn was heard to say that when the war ended it was going to be necessary to court-martial Ludendorff.

The next bloodstorm broke in the west on September 25 with the opening of Joffre's fall offensive. And a very great storm it was: three distinct offensives in three places. In the Second Battle of Champagne, west of Verdun where the front ran east-west, twenty-seven French divisions backed by nine hundred heavy and sixteen hundred light guns that Joffre had stripped from his border fortresses attacked seven German divisions stretched thin across thirty-six miles of front. The Third Battle of Artois saw seventeen divisions commanded by Ferdinand Foch set out against a north-south line defended by only two German divisions. A little farther north, at Loos, the British had a comparably overwhelming advantage: six British divisions against one German. It was the spring offensive repeated on an even larger scale. The objective was to cut off the Noyon salient, break the rail line that connected the two ends of the German front, and force a general withdrawal.

Even in the spring, however, the Germans had demonstrated prodigious defensive capabilities in the face of superior numbers, and throughout the summer they had been installing new lines far to the rear beyond the reach of enemy artillery and connecting them with perpendicular trenches and tunnels. They were well equipped with heavy artillery and adept at its use, and they were learning to place their machine guns so as to neutralize any attackers who survived their artillery. All this helps to explain the lack of optimism on the British side. Kitchener, in insisting on full British participation despite not believing it could succeed, may have been motivated in part by talk of putting all Entente forces under a single commander, and by fear that a refusal to cooperate might cost him the appointment. Sir John French, though usually eager to attack, warned that in this case he had less than a third of the divisions needed for success, and that the ground over which his men were asked to advance was dangerously devoid of cover. But he too had political reasons for not complaining too vehemently: he believed that only the support of Joffre and Foch was preventing his own government from removing him from command, and that his future depended on keeping that support. General Sir Henry Rawlinson, commander of the corps that would lead the British attack, predicted before starting out that "it will cost us dearly, and we will not get very far." French General Pétain, who would be in direct charge of the Champagne offensive, was similarly skeptical.

The only optimist, oddly, was Haig, who in the beginning had been opposed to Joffre's scheme. His early gloom had been rooted in the fact that the BEF would have only 117 heavy guns to prepare its advance on a five-mile-wide front—fewer than half the number of guns per mile that Joffre was putting in place in Champagne—and in the same lack of protective cover that troubled French. His spirits had begun to lift when it was decided to precede the attack with a release of chlorine. He was so encouraged by this idea that he had a tower constructed from which to observe his troops as they rolled over the German defenses.

Haig's high spirits were briefly dampened when King George V visited BEF headquarters and borrowed one of the general's horses for a review of the troops. A corporal in the Sherwood Foresters regiment left a record of what happened when the men lined up to be inspected: "The King rode along the first three or four ranks, then crossed the road to the other three or four ranks on the other side, speaking to an officer here and there. Our instructions had been that at the conclusion of the parade we were to put our caps on the points of our fixed bayonets and wave and cheer. So that's what we did—'Hip, hip, hooray.' Well, the King's horse reared and he fell off. He just seemed to slide off and so of course the second 'Hip, hip' fizzled out. It was quite a fiasco and you should have seen the confusion as these other high-ranking officers rushed to dismount and go to the King's assistance. They got him up and the last we saw of him he was being hurriedly driven away."

The attack was preceded in the French sectors by four days and nights of shelling. This had the advantage of obliterating the German first line and many of the men in it, the disadvantage of making it obvious to the Germans that something big was coming. When the morning of the attack arrived, operations began smoothly everywhere except in the British sector, where uncertain winds made it difficult for Haig to decide whether to allow the release of the gas. His men meanwhile were huddled in the frontline trenches— "some chaps were crying, some praying," one of them would recall—and being given all the rum they could drink while waiting for the order to advance. At five-fifteen A.M., when the wind seemed favorable at last, Haig gave his approval and climbed his tower. Soon afterward, however, the wind shifted. The gas began drifting back into the faces of the British troops. When it had dissipated, the Tommies who had not been disabled began to advance. Like the French to their north and east, they were soon making rapid progress.

And then, in place after place and in an absurdly wide variety of ways, everything started to go wrong. In Champagne the French ran through the wreckage of the first German line and reached the second much sooner than anyone had expected—so much sooner that they entered the trenches just as a French artillery barrage timed to prepare the way for them came down on their heads. The survivors of this terrifying stroke of bad luck had to retreat to escape being destroyed. By the time a resumption of the attack became possible, the opportunity was gone. German reserves had come forward and, being rich in machine guns, quickly took possession of what the French had had to give up. Among these reserves were two of the corps that Falkenhayn had recently rushed to the west. Falkenhayn himself was on the scene—such was his worry about the Germans' lack of manpower—and took a hand in keeping the defenses intact. Early on, when the French were moving forward strongly, he arrived at the headquarters of the German Third Army only to discover that its chief of staff was preparing to order a retreat. Falkenhayn relieved the man on the spot and ordered that the army hold its ground at all costs while waiting for the reinforcements that he knew would soon arrive.

At Artois too, after making excellent progress and for the second time that year briefly occupying the crest of Vimy Ridge, the French were stopped by an intact German second line and ultimately driven back. Joffre, who from the start had regarded Champagne as the key to the offensive and Artois as relatively unimportant, at this point began to play what can only be regarded as an underhanded game. He wanted the British, whose attack at Loos was supposedly intended merely to support the bigger French force at Artois, to remain on the offensive. But he also now wanted to end the Artois attack, having concluded that it had no chance of accomplishing anything. Therefore he suspended operations at Artois while pretending, for the benefit of the British, that he was doing nothing of the kind. Even alone, however, the British did well at first. Like the French, they passed easily through the pulverized German first line. Unlike the French, they also broke through the second line, though with heavy losses. The ground ahead was clear, and if reserves had been available, the long-yearned-for push into open country might have been possible. French, however, had positioned the BEF's general reserves as many as ten miles to the rear, and Haig had departed from sound military practice by failing to hold part of his own army back in reserve. Getting the general reserve to the front line ended up taking many hours; by the time it arrived, the Germans had filled the hole and were hammering away with their machine guns. When the British tried to resume their advance, the result was the most one-sided slaughter of the war: 7,861 troops and 385 officers were killed or wounded in a few hours, while German casualties totaled exactly zero. As the British finally began to withdraw, the Germans stopped firing and let them go. The machine-gunners were "nauseated by the sight," a German history of the fight would state, "of the massacre of the field of corpses."

"Coming back over the ground that had been captured that day," one Tommy wrote, "the sight that met our eyes was quite unbelievable. If you can imagine a flock of sheep lying down sleeping in a field, the bodies were as thick as that. Some of them were still alive, and they were crying out, begging for water and plucking at our legs as we went by. One hefty chap grabbed me around both knees and held me. 'Water, water,' he cried. I was just going to take the cork out of my water-bottle—I had a little left—but I was immediately hustled on by the man behind me. 'Get on, get on, we are going to get lost in no man's land, come on.' So it was a case where compassion had to give way to discipline and I had to break away."

Joffre continued to batter away in Champagne into November, not giving up until Pétain began ignoring orders to continue. In the end the casualties of Second Champagne totaled a hundred and forty-three thousand for the French, eighty-five thousand (including twenty thousand men taken prisoner) for the Germans. The Loos and Third Artois offensives cost the British sixty-one thousand casualties (two generals and twenty-eight battalion commanders among them), the Germans fifty-six thousand, and the French forty-eight thousand. Again France was stunned. On the whole, however, Joffre was believed when he told the Paris newspapers that his losses had been dwarfed by the enemy's and that the campaign had been a great success. The truth was that the Germans, though almost overwhelmingly outnumbered, had inflicted huge losses on the Entente armies while preventing them from accomplishing anything. In the process they had done more than Joffre or French to demonstrate that the Entente truly did have no troops to spare for Gallipoli or other distant theaters. Joffre's credibility was freshly damaged, if only among those insiders who knew what was actually happening at the front, but Joffre himself survived.

Sir John French did not survive. Even as the Loos offensive was still in progress, Haig began to complain to his many well-placed friends that only French's incompetence had prevented it from being a success. "If there had been even one division in reserve close up," he later declared, "we could have walked right through." Haig's own position was far from unassailable—his failure to provide a reserve from his own forces was just one of his mistakes at Loos. But French, frightened and almost desperate to defend himself, made a fatal error. Foolishly, he falsified the official record of orders issued during the battle. When Haig learned of this, he made sure it was brought to the attention of King George, who intervened with the prime minister. When Asquith gave French the opportunity to resign, he yielded to what had become inevitable and agreed. Haig, to no one's surprise, was appointed to the position for which he had been angling since before the start of the war. French returned to England and was made Viscount Ypres.

As the fighting wound down in the west and the exhausted armies of the east settled in for another winter, attention swung back to the Balkans and the Aegean, where intertwined events were once again unfolding rapidly. During the summer Bulgaria had become the centerpiece of an auction much like the one that had earlier brought Italy into the war. The Bulgarian government, like Italy's, was motivated solely by considerations of which side could help it to grab the most territory from its neighbors, and early in September it opted to join the Central Powers. Even before the start of the fall campaign on the Western Front, it became clear that Germany and Bulgaria were preparing to invade Serbia. It was equally clear that, in the wake of the failures at Gallipoli, the fall of Serbia would endanger what little toehold the Entente still had in Europe's southeastern corner. Sir Edward Grey had tried desperately to win the Bulgarians over, offering them many concessions. Because Serbia was Britain's ally, however, Grey was unable to offer what Germany could: territory that Serbia had taken from Bulgaria in the Second Balkan War. Now Serbia had to be saved or Russia would be further demoralized and Greece and Romania might follow Bulgaria in joining the Central Powers. Saving Serbia meant getting Entente troops to Serbia. With the Russians gone from Galicia, there was only one possible way to accomplish that: through Salonika, the Greek port that early in the year had been an alternative to the Dardanelles as the focus of an Aegean offensive.

Before the end of September the French had several divisions, including one removed from Gallipoli, en route to Salonika. They were led by General Maurice Sarrail, who despite having been removed from command on the Western Front retained such potent political connections that the government had been obliged to find an assignment for him somewhere. Britain, unwilling to leave the Balkans to the French, ordered its Tenth Division from Suvla Bay to Salonika. For a time there were hopes of persuading the Russians to send troops as well, but on October 3 Foreign Minister Sazonov declared that this was impossible. His explanation was stark and indisputable: Russia was losing men at a rate of two hundred and thirty-five thousand a month. Its prewar professional armies had been essentially wiped out. Many of the armies that remained were wrecks.

Sarrail and the French and British divisions were ashore at Salonika on October 5. Two days later German and Austro-Hungarian troops under Mackensen entered Serbia from the north. After another two days two Bulgarian armies arrived from the east, one trying to push the Serbs toward Mackensen, the other cutting the rail lines connecting Salonika to Serbia. Sarrail, when he tried to advance, found himself blocked. The Serb army, trapped between overwhelming enemy forces approaching from two directions, decided to run for the sea. Masses of civilians fled with it; the entire nation seemed to be in flight. Exhausted, without food or other supplies, a mass of humanity tried to cross the snowbound mountains of Albania and was set upon by tribal enemies eager to settle old scores. "I remember things scattered all around," a Serb officer named Milorad Markovic would recall. "Horses and men stumbling into the abyss; Albanian attacks; hosts of women and children. A doctor would not dress an officer's wound; soldiers would not bother to pull out a wounded comrade or officer. Belongings abandoned; starvation; wading across rivers clutching onto horses' tails; old men, women and children climbing up the rocks; dying people on the road; a smashed human skull by the road; a corpse all skin and bones, robbed, stripped naked, mangled; soldiers, police officers, civilians, women, captives. Vlasta's cousin, naked under his overcoat with a collar and cuffs, shattered, gone mad. Soldiers like ghosts, skinny, pale, worn out, sunken eyes, their hair and beards long, their clothes in rags, almost naked, barefoot. Ghosts of people begging for bread, walking with sticks, their feet covered in wounds, staggering. Chaos; women in soldiers' clothes; the desperate mothers of those who are too exhausted to go on." Markovic would survive and become the father of a daughter named Mirjana. She would marry Slobodan Milošević, the Serbian strongman, who, nine decades later, was put on trial for war crimes after a later round of Balkan atrocities.

Serbia lost some two hundred thousand troops in this disaster. Of the hundred and fifty thousand who reached the Adriatic coast, only half were found to be fit for further service and transported on British ships to dismal camps on the island of Corfu.

Sarrail's failure to prevent the conquest of Serbia, coming on the heels of so many other calamities, caused the French government to fall. Premier Viviani was succeeded by Aristide Briand. Minister of War Millerand was succeeded by—of all people—General Joseph Gallieni, Joffre's unheralded partner in the saving of France a year before. Joffre found himself reporting to the man who had been responsible for his elevation to the commander in chief's post years before, and whom he had tried so jealously to keep in the shadows before and after the Battle of the Marne. Joffre's critics, increasingly numerous, hoped that Gallieni would dismiss him. Instead he once again defended and shielded him.

On October 11 Kitchener cabled Hamilton to ask his opinion of how many troops would be lost in a withdrawal from the Gallipoli beachheads. After replying that such a move would cost the British and French at least half the men they still had on the peninsula, Hamilton was relieved of command, his part in the war finished. Grey promised to give the island of Cyprus to Greece if it would join the Entente. The Greek government, intimidated by events at Gallipoli and in Serbia, declined.

In mid-November Kitchener traveled to Gallipoli, took a quick look, and said that the peninsula should be evacuated. When he returned to London, he discovered that Asquith had used his absence as an opportunity to further reduce his authority. The prime minister had reconstituted the committee responsible for war strategy, reducing it to five members with Kitchener, shockingly, no longer included. General Sir William Robertson, the onetime sergeant, was brought from France to become chief of the imperial general staff, the new War Committee's chief adviser on military operations, and the channel through whom the government's instructions were to be issued to the BEF. When Kitchener learned of this development, he went to Asquith and offered his resignation, which was refused. He still had much value as a figurehead, a symbol in the propaganda wars.

Also excluded from the new committee was Winston Churchill, who since losing his post as First Lord of the Admiralty had been left with no office except the essentially meaningless one of Chancellor of the Duchy of Lancaster (where his only duty was to appoint county magistrates). Angry and hurt, Churchill resigned from the government and entered the army as a major (he had hoped to become a brigadier general) on the Western Front. Far from an ordinary field-grade officer, he arrived in France with a servant, a black stallion with groom, mountains of luggage, and a bathtub equipped with its own boiler. He was met by a limousine and sped off to elegant accommodations at a château. By January, however, he would be serving on the front and proving to be a competent battalion commander.

One drama remained to be played out in the closing days of the year: getting the troops away from Gallipoli without incurring serious—and politically insupportable—casualties. On November 23 the War Committee approved a detailed withdrawal plan prepared by Hamilton's successor. Over the next month, though an ignominious retreat, the escape from the peninsula proved to be the closest thing to a genuine military achievement by the Entente since the Marne. Working together night after night, the soldiers on the beaches and the Royal Navy steadily and stealthily got more and more men away under cover of darkness without letting the Turks and Germans know that anything of the kind was happening. The longer the evacuation continued, the more outnumbered the remaining men were—and the more vulnerable to being overrun and wiped out. The force at Cape Helles was down to nineteen thousand men when, on January 7, 1916, General Liman von Sanders launched an assault.

Here the entire Gallipoli fiasco came to the strangest possible end. Faced with British rifle and machine-gun fire, the Turkish troops for the first time since the start of the campaign simply and absolutely refused to attack. Even when threatened by their officers, even when shoved and slapped, they would not advance. Perhaps the problem was the absence of Mustafa Kemal; his health broken, he had been sent away in December. Perhaps the Turks had just had enough. "I'm twenty-one years old," one of their lieutenants had written in November. "My hair and beard are already gray. My mustache is white. My face is wrinkled and my body is rotting. I can't bear these hardships and privations any more."

Thirty-six hours after this mutiny, the last Australian troops on Gallipoli were carried safely off to sea and it was all over. The campaign had taken the lives of at least eighty-seven thousand Turks. (That is the official number, but it is widely regarded as too low.) Forty-six thousand British, French, Australians, and New Zealanders had either been killed or died of wounds or disease. Total casualties on both sides were in the neighborhood of half a million.

Nineteen-fifteen was finished at last.

PART FOUR

1916

✠

Bleeding to Death

With hot food and room to move about, these British troops are clearly on a break from the trenches.

Chapter 19

Verdun: Preparation

"The forces of France will bleed to death."
—Erich von Falkenhayn

Shortly after seven A.M. on February 21, 1916, the third consecutive clear morning after a week of snow and muddy cold, an eight-mile sector of the German lines a hundred and fifty miles east of Paris erupted in a blaze of artillery the likes of which the world had never seen. More than twelve hundred guns, among them thirty of the gigantic mortars that had destroyed the Belgian forts at the start of the war and naval cannon capable of firing two-thousand-pound projectiles twenty miles, suddenly began blasting away at French positions on the eastern bank of the River Meuse. All through the morning and most of the afternoon they sent up a hundred thousand rounds of high explosive, shrapnel, and gas per hour—12,500 shells hourly on each mile of front. French reconnaissance aircraft reported that it was impossible to identify specific enemy gun emplacements: a solid wall of flame was rising into the sky from the woods behind the German lines. The woods on the French side were being reduced to stumps and craters amid leaping fountains of earth. Observers on both sides found it difficult to believe that any of the troops huddled in those woods could possibly survive. "Thousands of projectiles are flying in all directions, some whistling, others howling, others moaning low, and all uniting in one infernal roar," a French officer wrote after sending one of his men to repair a severed cable. "From time to time an aerial torpedo passes, making a noise like a gigantic motor car. With a tremendous thud a giant shell bursts quite close to our observation post, breaking the telephone wire and interrupting all communication with our batteries. It seems quite impossible that he should escape in the rain of shell, which exceeds anything imaginable; there has never been such a bombardment in war. Our man seems to be enveloped in explosions, and shelters himself in the shell craters which honeycomb the ground; finally he reaches a less stormy spot, mends his wires, and then, as it would be madness to try to return, settles down in a crater and waits for the storm to pass."

After noon, just as abruptly as it had started, the "rain of shell" came to a stop. The fire from the Germans' long-range guns began probing deeper, while the short-range pieces fell silent. Thinking that the worst was over, expecting that as usual the barrage would be followed by an infantry assault, the French did exactly what the Germans wanted them to do. They came up out of their hiding places, showing their heads aboveground in order to survey the damage and watch for the coming attack. German spotters observed them and directed fire onto every point where the French had revealed themselves. The bombardment went on for hours more.

At four-forty-five P.M., with the sun already slipping below the horizon, the barrage again ended. This time German troops did appear, clambering out of holes in the ground and starting toward the French. Their advance was both surprisingly timed—infantry almost always opened new offensives in the morning—and surprisingly limited in comparison with the mayhem that had preceded it. Nine divisions came forward but did so tentatively, not in a mass but in clusters scattered across four and a half miles, making use of all the protection afforded by rough hill country. Their assignment was not to overrun the French but to feel them out, to see where and to what extent the first line of defenders had survived. Wherever they encountered resistance, they stopped. In places they pulled back. The mortar fire resumed, again lobbing explosives onto whatever French soldiers had shown themselves.

All along the cutting edge of the attack, German officers were reporting that the suspension of their advance was unnecessary, that the defenses, where not annihilated, were in serious disarray. The mortars fell silent yet again. An order went out from the headquarters of the German Fifth Army for the attackers to move forward in force and take possession of as much ground as possible. But the order came too late: the sun was down, the last of the light gone. When the Germans went to ground for the night, they did so, in most cases, along what had been the first and most thinly defended French line. Their long-range guns continued to pound away as here and there snow flurries blew across the ravaged terrain. The French had been given a reprieve: one long winter night in which to reassemble their stunned troops, shore up what remained of their entrenchments, and start bringing their own artillery forward.

And so began the Battle of Verdun, the longest battle of the Great War and one of the most terrible ever fought. It had its roots in the state of the

Western Front as 1915 ended. Both sides, as they settled in for the war's second winter, had found reason to be satisfied but also many reasons for concern. The leaders of the Entente, especially, looked back on a year-long series of disappointments punctuated by disaster. Serbia had collapsed, and most of its army had been destroyed. Russia had lost Poland and Galicia. In the Gorlice-Tarnow campaign alone, a hundred and fifty thousand Russians had been killed, six hundred and eighty thousand wounded, and nearly nine hundred thousand taken prisoner. Erich von Falkenhayn told Kaiser Wilhelm that the tsar's army was "so weakened by the blows it has suffered that Russia need not be seriously considered a danger in the foreseeable future."

Though the French had been on the attack repeatedly during the year, they had accomplished essentially nothing and had done so at almost incredible cost. In the Champagne and Artois regions alone, three hundred and thirty-five thousand of their soldiers had been killed (though many were listed as missing rather than dead, their bodies lost in the chaos). This had brought to two million the number of French casualties since the start of the war. Some two hundred thousand British were dead—nearly twice the number with which the BEF had begun the war—out of total casualties of more than half a million.

Italy's entry into the war, an event that at first promised to be decisive, had simply produced another stalemate. Far off to the East, in the Caucasus region between the Black and Caspian Seas, the Russians and Turks were colliding on yet another front where heavy loss of life was producing no results that mattered.

Still, there was optimism in Paris, in London, and even in Petrograd. The Entente's manpower advantage on the Western Front was greater than ever and growing. If the Italians had not achieved the hoped-for southern breakthrough, they had nonetheless brought many hundreds of thousands of troops into the struggle. Even if they could win no battles, those troops were tying up Austro-Hungarian divisions that otherwise would have been free to go elsewhere. Russia's military administration had been put under honest and competent leadership—a phenomenon that would prove to be short-lived—and its battered armies were being refitted and rebuilt. The little army with which Britain had begun the war was growing beyond recognition in spite of its heavy losses.

By the start of 1916 the British had nearly a million troops on the continent, and that number was increasing by almost one hundred thousand monthly. Every newly arrived battalion increased the price that the Germans were having to pay for their failed bet that by invading Belgium they could take France out of the war before Britain could get fully in. Britain's and

France's armies were being steadily augmented by the arrival of troops from the colonies that both nations had around the world. The Germans and Austrians had no such resources to draw on and no possibility of moving troops by sea. The extent of London's commitment to the war was demonstrated in January 1916 with Parliament's passage of the Military Service Act. This measure, far from entirely popular even within the government (Prime Minister Asquith declined to take a position on it), was driven through the House of Commons by the steely will of David Lloyd George. It introduced conscription to Britain for the first time, ensuring that millions more men would be sent to the BEF despite a precipitous decline in enlistments. In all the nations of the Entente, the shell crisis was coming under control.

The British and French general staffs believed that their advantage was greater than it really was. Their intelligence analysts continued to assure them that the Germans were squandering troops at an unsustainable rate and soon would be exhausted. Actually, the opposite was true. The Germans had generally been far more careful than the British and French in husbanding their manpower, and their casualties through 1915 were only about half those of their enemies. Joffre and Haig, happy to accept the wishful thinking of their staffs, believed that the challenge for 1916 was simply to find the best way to overwhelm an enemy who lacked the means to respond. The answer seemed obvious: to stay on the offensive and go on killing Germans until Berlin could no longer keep its lines intact. Less obvious was where to do this, and when, but such questions do not appear to have troubled either commander very much. They concluded that their 1916 offensive, when it came, should take place *everywhere*. Determining exactly when mattered less than ensuring that all the armies attacked at the same time, making it impossible for the Germans to shift troops from one place to another to meet a sequence of threats. It was hard to imagine how, under such conditions, the Germans could avoid collapse.

The certainty that the Entente's numerical advantage could only increase with time was obvious in Berlin. Thus the Germans could find scant comfort in their successes on the Eastern Front and in fending off Joffre's offensives. They understood that the time available for bringing the war to a satisfactory conclusion was finite on their side—that regardless of how effectively they might fight a defensive war, remaining on the defensive would mean gradual exhaustion and defeat. They also understood, however, that as 1916 began they had enough troops in the west to compete effectively: ninety-four divisions on the line plus another twenty-six in reserve, versus ninety-one and fifty-nine respectively for the Entente. They understood that they needed to defeat someone somewhere while they were still capable of doing so. They had no way to decide on a specific course of action, however, without igniting the antagonism between Falkenhayn on one side and Hindenburg and Ludendorff on the other: the wearying argument about west versus east. Among the many questions for which there were no clear answers, two things seemed certain: Russia was crippled and likely to remain so for months; and the French could be depended on to continue their attacks no matter what the cost and how limited the potential gains.

The biggest strategic questions facing both sides were answered before the end of 1915. On December 6, at the great riverside château that was his headquarters in Chantilly, Joffre played host to a meeting of all the Entente's top army leaders. Britain, Russia, Belgium, Italy, and even Japan were represented. The assembled generals had no difficulty in agreeing that the Germans, fatally weakened, could be finished off with one great symphonic offensive involving all the major combatants on every major front. They agreed also that this tremendous climax should not take place until late summer. There seemed no need for hurry, and a half-year delay would give all the allies time to assemble overwhelming quantities of artillery and ammunition. It would provide time for Britain to continue the seasoning of its green new armies, and for the Russians to recover.

Later in the month Joffre and Haig met again to settle on the outlines of their part of the overall plan, the Western Front offensive. Joffre wanted it to take place in France, north of Paris, where the front was bisected by the River Somme. Haig preferred Belgium, farther north, where success could lead to the recapture of the lost Channel ports, a prime strategic prize. Joffre's Somme plan offered little chance of achieving any strategic objectives at all—nothing beyond a general pushing-back of the German line and the killing of more Germans. He prevailed nevertheless, in large part by virtue of owning a majority interest in the enterprise. Forty French divisions were to participate, while the British would contribute only twenty-five. An attack by sixty-five divisions promised to be unstoppable, especially with the Russians simultaneously launching a comparably massive offensive in the east and the Italians striking at the Austrians.

While the Entente commanders refined their plans, their German counterpart was putting together a scheme of his own. Working in his customary solitude, the secretive and deeply introverted Falkenhayn spent the first half of December ordering his thoughts. No option beyond the Western Front, he decided, could possibly produce results sufficient to Germany's need. Confident that "the Russian armies have not been completely overthrown but their offensive powers have been shattered," and believing that Russia was approaching revolution and collapse (in this he showed himself to be a man of sharp if premature insight), he thought it unwise to focus his limited resources on such an enfeebled foe. Ludendorff would have disagreed vigorously. But he was far off at the northern end of the Eastern Front, organizing the administration of conquered territories almost equal to France in size, and he was neither told anything nor asked for his opinion.

The war would never end, Falkenhayn had come to believe, until Britain was induced to give up on it. Playing artfully on Kaiser Wilhelm's resentment of his mother's homeland, he had been declaring as early as the autumn of 1915 that Britain had to be considered not just one of Germany's enemies but the archenemy, committed absolutely to the destruction of Germany. "She is staking everything on a war of exhaustion," he wrote. "We have not been able to shatter her belief that it will bring Germany to her knees. What we have to do is dispel that illusion."

But Britain herself, beyond the reach of the German army, was invulnerable. The only way to bring her to the peace table was to demonstrate that a continuation of hostilities would be pointless. Falkenhayn saw two ways of making this happen. One was a campaign of submarine warfare aimed at commercial shipping, at starving the British Isles. This was a momentous decision, as important as anything Falkenhayn did or decided to do during his tenure as chief of the general staff. He was an exception among German generals in his political sophistication—vastly more sophisticated than Ludendorff, for example—and in the aftermath of the sinking of the *Lusitania* he had sided with Chancellor Bethmann Hollweg in demanding an end to the first submarine campaign. Since then, however, his pessimism had deepened, and when their disaster at Gorlice-Tarnow failed to weaken the Russians' resolve, he had stopped hoping that anything could. When Admiral von Tirpitz assured him that the growing U-boat fleet could destroy Britain's ability to wage war within two months (other naval leaders said it would take four months—or six), he found the prospect irresistible. "There can be no justification or military grounds for refusing any further to employ what promises to be our most effective weapon," he declared. "We should ruthlessly employ every weapon that is suitable for striking against England on her home ground." His response to Bethmann's fears of American anger was that the United States "cannot intervene decisively in the war in time." This view echoed the dismissal of British intervention by the generals who had decided to invade Belgium.

The other thing Germany had to do, as Falkenhayn saw the situation, was to remove Britain's nearest and most important ally, France, from the war. Like France's Pétain, he had been convinced by the bitter disappointments of 1914 that victory in the west was not going to be achieved through a classic breakthrough and envelopment of the enemy. He understood, as Joffre and

Haig did not, that such a thing was simply not possible in this new industrial kind of war, a kind of gigantic siege in which networks of railways made it possible to seal any break in the line by moving masses of troops quickly. The sole available alternative, he concluded, was to break France's *will* to fight. In reaching this conclusion he was influenced by what he knew—and his data were better than those available to the Entente's generals—of the disparity between French and German casualties. "France has arrived almost at the end of her military effort," he told the kaiser. "If her people can be made to understand clearly that in a military sense they have nothing more to hope for, the breaking point will be reached and England's best weapon knocked out of her hand." Falkenhayn entertained no dreams of defeating France outright on the field of battle, of sweeping her armies aside and entering Paris in triumph. His thoughts were focused on driving the French to despair and, once they came to terms, making Britain despair as well. These hopes underlay his strategy at Verdun.

Powerfully influenced by Joffre's evident willingness to pay almost any price in the pursuit of limited objectives, Falkenhayn devised a plan for luring the French into a German-built killing machine. His idea was to threaten some piece of ground that the French would do almost anything to hold, some piece of ground dominated by German artillery. Under such circumstances, he said, "the forces of France will bleed to death."

Deciding where to install his machine was not difficult. Verdun, the little city nestled at the center of a bristling network of fortresses, had held out against the German advance at the start of the war and had been left as a kind of spear point jutting into the German line. Strategically its importance had diminished considerably since 1914; the French no longer needed the kind of anchor it had provided during the Great Retreat, and withdrawing from it would have put nothing in jeopardy. But it had been a bone of contention between the Germans and the French for many years, and aside from Paris itself there was no place on the map to which the French people would be likely to attach more importance. That made it perfect for Falkenhayn's purposes.

Verdun had a further advantage too, at least where persuading the kaiser was concerned. It lay opposite the German Fifth Army, which was commanded by Crown Prince Wilhelm. Responsibility for executing Falkenhayn's plan would fall to the prince, and success would give the Hohenzollern family a particularly personal kind of triumph.

Falkenhayn spent several days in December in discussions with the crown prince and the Fifth Army's chief of staff, General Konstantin Schmidt von Knobelsdorf. He won their support but was less than forthright in doing so. By not being clear about what his objective actually was (to capture Verdun,

or to draw the French army into destroying itself in a defense of Verdun?),
he planted seeds of misunderstanding that would later bear bitter fruit. He
then met with the kaiser at Potsdam, and Wilhelm approved everything.
Preparations for the campaign began immediately and in the strictest secrecy.
It was essential to take the French by surprise, and to do so before Joffre upset
everything by launching an offensive of his own.

The French of course knew nothing of the plan. But neither did Falkenhayn
know that, throughout the weeks when he was developing his ideas and getting them approved, Verdun was the centerpiece of a controversy involving
not only the French military but the most senior levels of the government in
Paris. The origins of the controversy reached back to the first days of the
war, when Joffre, seeing the speed with which the Germans had destroyed
the fortress networks at Liège and Namur, lost whatever faith he had once
had in the value of such fortifications. Before the end of 1914, with the
Germans trying to push westward out of Alsace and Lorraine, he had
ordered the abandonment of Verdun. The senior French general in the region,
the same Maurice Sarrail who now commanded the multinational force bottled up at Salonika, had disregarded this order and managed to hold on even
as the Germans almost succeeded in encircling him. Unimpressed, Joffre in
1915 began stripping the Verdun salient of guns and men in order to add
muscle to his offensives. The aged General Herr, upon becoming governor of
the Fortified Region of Verdun in August, warned that its defenses were deficient and asked for reinforcements. But his predecessor had been sacked for
making exactly the same complaint. Though Herr was not dismissed, he got
little of the help he requested.

Herr was not alone. Other generals both in Paris and in the field shared
his fears, as did a more junior officer, Émile Driant, who though sixty years
old and a mere lieutenant colonel had more influence and, apparently, more
political courage than most of the others. Thirty years before the war, early
in his career, Driant had been an aide to (and married the daughter of) a
bizarre character named General Georges Boulanger. A blustering, hapless,
ultimately ludicrous figure, Boulanger rose to become minister of war and
seemed in a moment of national hysteria in the 1880s to be on the verge of
establishing a kind of Bonapartist dictatorship, but he failed to seize his opportunity at the moment of crisis and ended by committing suicide on his mistress's grave. Driant's association with Boulanger, and afterward with a
militant right-wing faction called the Boulangists, had made him an object of
suspicion among the antiroyalist, anticlerical republicans who dominated the
army at the turn of the century. When he found himself at age fifty still a
major and without hope of promotion, Driant resigned his commission and

turned to politics and writing. He was elected to the National Assembly (a position he retained even after returning to active duty at the start of the war) and wrote a number of popular books calling for a revival of national élan in preparation for the war with Germany that he regarded as inevitable. He wrote urgently of the need to strengthen France's defenses along the eastern border, and among his works was a treatise on fortress warfare.

Perhaps because of his age, perhaps also because the cloud that had driven him out of the army still hung over his head, Driant was assigned to an obscure staff position. This position happened to be inside Verdun's central citadel. Throughout most of 1915 Verdun was practically out of the war, never seriously threatened. In time Driant managed to get himself transferred out of the citadel and placed in command of two infantry battalions posted at a hilly piece of woodland called the Bois des Caures, directly opposite the German lines.

Driant was certain that Verdun would be attacked sooner or later, and his trained eye saw how grossly unprepared it was. Unlike his superiors, he was not content to send his complaints up the chain of command and accept the lack of response. By August he was communicating with colleagues in the Assembly. "Should our front line be overrun in a massive attack," he wrote the Chamber's president, "our second line is inadequate and we're not managing to build it up: *not enough men to do the job,* and I add: *not enough barbed wire.*" Driant asked that his concerns be brought to the attention of General Gallieni, the unacknowledged hero of the Battle of the Marne who was now minister of war, and this was done. Gallieni, a strong-minded man though in precarious health, was himself by this time stewing with impatience at the conduct of the war and increasingly skeptical about Joffre's strategy. His frustration is apparent in what he wrote in his diary on December 16: "In the morning, Council of Ministers, discussion about Joffre and the trenches. Worry about the next German attack. At certain points, the defensive fortifications are not prepared. The matter is grave. Must do what is necessary towards Verdun."

Gallieni reacted quickly upon learning of Driant's warnings, dispatching an inspection team to Verdun. When the team issued a report that supported all of Driant's warnings, Gallieni passed it on to Joffre, requesting a response. Joffre, who was notoriously quick to see inquiries from the government as intolerable interference and skillful at giving no answers, responded in a kind of haughty and dismissive rage. "I consider that nothing justifies the fears you have expressed in the name of the government," he told Gallieni, claiming that the construction of "three or four successive defensive positions" was either "finished or on the road to completion." This was an outright lie, and in time it would contribute to Joffre's fall. At the end of 1915, however, he was still strong enough politically to feel free not only to lie to the government but to take the offensive against anyone who dared to challenge him. He demanded to know where Gallieni had been getting his information. In adding that "I cannot permit soldiers under my command to make their complaint or discontent about my orders known to the government through channels other than those which the military has established," and in referring to "officers serving at the front" and "politicians in uniform," he made it plain that he already knew. His failure to have Driant dismissed, transferred, or court-martialed may be explained by a reluctance to break with Gallieni, who had strong political allies and was not a man to be crossed.

Matters might have rested there except for mounting evidence of German activity opposite Verdun and rumors, reported by Entente agents in Berlin, that an offensive was coming. Rail traffic behind the German lines increased sharply, as did the use of aircraft to keep French scouts at a distance. Finally the pressure became too great for Joffre to ignore. On January 24 he sent General Noël-Edouard de Castelnau, who had recently returned to his staff after a year as an army commander, to Verdun to conduct an inspection. A Franco-Prussian War veteran who by this point had lost three sons in combat, Castelnau was alarmed by what he found. He ordered immediate steps to strengthen the defenses on the east bank of the Meuse—Herr had been concentrating his troops on the west bank—and ordered reinforcements to be brought in from other places. The first two divisions would not arrive until February 12—the day Falkenhayn had chosen for the start of his attack.

A kind of blind race now began in which both sides hurried with their preparations and neither knew what the other was doing. That the French now regarded the situation as an emergency was signaled when not only President Poincaré but even Joffre himself, perhaps eager to cover up his long neglect, paid brief visits to Verdun and some of its outlying forts. Everything possible was done to make the best of available resources, which included far too little artillery, and to bring in more men and guns. On the east bank of the Meuse, where the Germans were massing a hundred and fifty thousand men and more than eight hundred guns, Herr was able to place only about thirty-five thousand troops. Though he had more than nine hundred pieces of artillery, more than half were light field guns and many were semiobsolete models without rapid-fire recoil mechanisms. At the center of the preparations, exactly where any German attack was likely to strike first, were Driant and the thirteen hundred men under his command. They were hastily constructing concrete strongpoints in the Bois des Caures.

The Germans meanwhile were accomplishing prodigious feats in getting everything in place. Helped by the hilly, wooded countryside and the cloudy winter weather of the Verdun region, they were doing an astonishingly good job of keeping the French from learning what they intended to do, or when, or even exactly where. No fewer than five new railway lines were constructed across the German-held portion of the Woëvre plateau immediately to the east of the Verdun hills. In a seven-week period between late December and early February, thirteen hundred trains—not railcars but entire *trains*—hauled in 2.5 million shells. Earth-moving equipment, construction machinery, and everything required to prepare the offensive and support three hundred thousand troops in winter came rolling up to Verdun. The guns were positioned in the woods and covered with camouflage—a new development in warfare, made necessary by air reconnaissance. Underground chambers capable of holding as many as five hundred men each were excavated opposite the French lines and lined with steel and concrete. In the sky above all this was the greatest concentration of aircraft yet seen on any front, one hundred and fifty aircraft, a German umbrella so impenetrable that, even on the rare days when visibility was good, the French pilots were unable to get a close look at what was happening.

By the second week of February everything was in place for an offensive with the potential to change the course of the war. One thing, however, was missing: a clear and shared understanding of how to take full advantage of all the force the Germans had assembled. The worst of the tactical problems began with the strange ambiguities of Falkenhayn's plan—a plan aimed not at capturing Verdun but at bringing the French army within range of the German artillery and, in the general's words, bleeding it white. His goal at the start of the campaign was simply to mass his artillery in the hills north of the city, force the French to try to drive those guns away, and blow them to pieces as they did. The core idea was to maximize French casualties while keeping the German infantry out of the fight to the fullest possible extent. In itself this objective was entirely commendable. But it led to Falkenhayn's decision to limit the first day's attack to only four and a half miles of front, to wait until the end of the day to send the infantry in, and to advance on the east bank of the Meuse only.

There were many problems with this decision, but the most serious was also the most obvious: it would leave the French artillery on the west bank unthreatened and free to blast away across the river. The crown prince and his chief of staff, Schmidt von Knobelsdorf, battled Falkenhayn on this point, insisting that ample manpower was available for an offensive on both banks and demanding a broadening of the campaign. They were joined by the best-informed of the Fifth Army's corps commanders, General Hans von Zwehl, who before the war had participated in three war-game simulations of an attack on Verdun. Every one of those exercises had demonstrated that a move on the east bank only would be doomed to failure. The crown prince, Knobelsdorf, and Zwehl even had the implicit support of the famous French general De Rivière, who in the 1880s had directed an expansion of the Verdun defensive system. Upon completing his task, De Rivière had ruefully concluded that Verdun continued to be vulnerable at one point: the *west* bank. Falkenhayn was unpersuaded. He continued to insist that the initial infantry attack be severely limited, that the reserves necessary for exploiting success be kept well to the rear, and that those reserves be not under the crown prince's control but his own.

Falkenhayn said he simply did not have enough troops to attack on both sides of the river. His subordinates, with three hundred thousand men at their disposal, could not understand what he meant. Falkenhayn explained that troops had to be held back for use in responding to whatever counteroffensives the French or British might launch at other points along the front. His subordinates, rightly convinced that neither the French nor the British were ready to attack in force anywhere, once again were baffled. What they didn't know, because Falkenhayn didn't tell them, was that he didn't really care whether Verdun was captured or not. In all likelihood, he secretly preferred that Verdun *not* be captured—at least not quickly. He appears to have feared that a quick capture of Verdun might cause the French to withdraw and disengage, thereby spoiling his plan. One wonders if it ever occurred to him that, had he seized the city at the start of the campaign, the French would be practically certain to attack him and his massed artillery. *Not* taking Verdun, on the other hand, would leave the French in their defenses and require the Germans—assuming that Falkenhayn wanted the battle to continue—to attack again and again and again. He was relinquishing the opportunity to make one lightning strike and then fight on the defensive.

What Falkenhayn ordered, in the end, was "an offensive in the direction of Verdun." These were words of art, intended to deceive. The crown prince and Knobelsdorf, understandably, interpreted them as an order to *capture* Verdun. Literally interpreted, however, they merely meant that the German forces were to move in that direction.

All was in readiness for the attack to begin on February 12. The night before, it began to snow, and snow was still falling heavily when morning came. Visibility was zero, which meant the artillery was blind and everything had to be suspended. Conditions remained terrible for a week, but on February 19 the skies finally cleared. The next day was even better—not only sunny but warm, with the mud beginning to dry. By then the element of surprise was lost: the French knew that an attack was imminent, and they had a good idea of where it would come. That night Driant slept as usual in a house some distance from where his battalions were dug in at the Bois des Caures. He rose before dawn on February 21, gave his wedding ring and a letter addressed to his wife to his manservant, and departed for the front. He was already there when the German artillery opened fire. All that day he and his men were under bombardment, their strongpoints blasted apart one by one. Late in the day the survivors, Driant among them, were attacked by German infantry, but the attackers came in less than overwhelming numbers and the poilus held their ground. When night fell, nothing was left of Driant's battalions but Driant himself, seven lieutenants—every one of whom was wounded—and about a hundred troops still capable of fighting. But they were still in possession of the Bois des Caures.

OLD WOUNDS UNHEALED

JULIUS CAESAR WOULD NOT BE SURPRISED TO LEARN
that a great battle took place at Verdun two millennia after his conquest of
Gaul. The place was well known to the Romans, who recognized its inherent military importance. They named it, in fact—called it Verodunum,
"strong fort." As the name suggests, the Romans made it a military center
as their empire grew. It was a base from which they could move against
still-unconquered tribes, and a refuge to which they could withdraw when
barbarian hordes came plundering.

Verdun had almost certainly been a stronghold long before Roman
times. Its importance grew out of its position on the River Meuse, which
snakes northward from headwaters in the French Alps into Belgium and
Holland on its way to the North Sea. Any geographer could have predicted
that a town would emerge where Verdun did in fact appear: it was the only
point on a long stretch of the Meuse where even Bronze Age travelers
could cross the river with comparative ease. From earliest times it was a
gateway connecting the Rhineland with central France and the two little
river islands where Paris would be born. Any mass of warriors on the rampage in western Europe was likely to find itself drawn to Verdun.

Thus Verdun's whole history has been written in blood. Even Attila the
Hun sacked and burned the place. When the quarreling grandsons of
Charlemagne met in 843 to divide the Frankish empire, they did so at
Verdun. Their agreement, the Treaty of Verdun, created three new realms.
In the west was the Kingdom of the West Franks, which would evolve over
the centuries into France. The Kingdom of the East Franks became
Germany (and gradually broke into hundreds of fragments). Between the
two was a long and vulnerable strip-kingdom, called Lotharingia (the root
of the name Lorraine) for the unfortunate grandson, Lothair, who received
it as his share. It ran from what is now Holland south through the old kingdom of Alsatia (thus Alsace) all the way to Rome. It became a battleground
between its neighbors and soon disappeared from history.

It is not much of an exaggeration, in light of this history, to say that not
only France and Germany but also their twelve hundred years of struggle

over the territories between the Meuse and the Rhine all were born at Verdun.

For a while Verdun belonged to the western kingdom. In 923, at a time when France was feeble and the Holy Roman Empire strong, the Germans took it. Verdun and the territories around it, Alsace and Lorraine included, remained German for more than six hundred years, which might have been expected to settle the question of its cultural identity. But by the sixteenth century the balance of power had shifted. France was centralizing under the king at Paris and growing stronger, while the Holy Roman Empire was almost too fractured to defend itself. Verdun was plucked away by Henry II of France. In the seventeenth century Cardinal Richelieu, chief minister to Louis XIV, seized Alsace and Lorraine as well, shifting the border between France and Germany eastward to the Rhine.

Louis XIV, the Sun King, had in his service possibly the greatest military engineer in history, Sébastien Le Prestre de Vauban. When Vauban installed a great chain of frontier fortresses west of the Rhine, he made Verdun its northern anchor. He transformed it from a fort into a network of forts spread across the rugged, wooded hills at the center of which the town sits like a plum in the bottom of a bowl. Until advances in artillery and siege warfare overtook Vauban's work, Verdun remained impregnable.

Every war drew armies to Verdun. It withstood a siege during the Thirty Years War and fell to the Prussians in 1792, when the monarchies of eastern Europe were making war on Revolutionary France. The French soon got it back, but the idea of retaking and keeping Alsace and Lorraine became a key element in the German nationalism that Napoleon's wars had ignited.

Verdun held out longer than all of France's other eastern fortresses in the Franco-Prussian War of 1870. The Germans returned it to France as part of the settlement of that war, but they kept Alsace and a substantial part of Lorraine—five thousand square miles in all. Now the recovery of the two provinces became a *French* dream, their loss a wound so painful as to destroy any possibility of reconciliation with Germany. In Paris's Place de la Concorde, a statue representing Strasbourg, principal city of the lost territories, was permanently draped in black.

The latest, westward shift of the border had left the French with no major defenses between Verdun and Germany. Verdun became, therefore, part of France's first line of defense. In the final years of the nineteenth century, it and a line of fortress cities to its south (Toul, Épinal, and Belfort) were further expanded and strengthened. Observing this work, Alfred von Schlieffen concluded that the only feasible way to take the offensive against France was to go through Belgium.

Just a few years before the Great War, the largest of the Verdun strong-points, Forts Douaumont and Vaux, were covered with protective shells that not even the biggest guns could destroy. By the outbreak of the war, the word *Verdun* signified a ten-mile-wide military region bisected by the Meuse and including a dozen major fortresses, eight smaller strong-points, and forty additional redoubts that, though smaller still, also bristled with guns.

Verdun proved crucial to France's survival in the opening weeks of the war. It remained the anchor that Vauban had intended it to be, allowing the French armies to maintain an unbroken line as they fell back toward the Marne. Almost but never quite cut off, by October 1914 it was the hard nucleus of a salient protruding into the German line. Early in 1915, the Germans tried to pinch it off but failed. Thereafter that sector of the front became quiet, and Joffre began stripping Verdun of its firepower. Ulti-mately 80 percent of its artillery was sent off for use in offensives else-where. Its manpower was reduced to levels that every commander on the scene found to be cause for alarm.

Alsace and Lorraine by this time had been invaded by the French and retaken by the Germans, but their status remained unsettled. The popula-tion of the two provinces was largely German-speaking and German in culture—even today their architecture and place names are more German than French. But loyalties were mixed. The region had been French at the time of the Revolution and had remained French long enough to become republican in its sympathies and unaffected by the rise of nationalist sen-timent inside Germany proper. After the Franco-Prussian War it had been put directly under the governance of Berlin, rather than being given the kind of semiautonomy enjoyed by other German states. Its people had lit-tle liking for the Prussians, who moved in like an occupying force. On the other hand, most of the Alsace-Lorrainers were Catholic, and the militant anticlericalism of the French government in the decade before the war (a prejudice so potent that it put even senior French army officers under a cloud of suspicion) made many of them wary of Paris.

The behavior of the Prussians seemed almost calculated to push Alsace and Lorraine into the arms of France. In 1913 a young Prussian lieutenant insulted the people of the town of Zabern and injured a protesting civilian with his sword, but Berlin took no disciplinary action and offered no apol-ogy. Anti-Berlin feeling became inflamed, and the overreaction of the authorities quickly made things worse. In August 1914, when mobilization was not greeted with universal enthusiasm, the German military authori-ties felt confirmed in their disdain.

Mobilization went smoothly enough, though in all of Alsace and

Lorraine only eight thousand men volunteered and a fourth of the sixteen thousand conscripted men living abroad reported for duty as ordered. Many of those who did report were deemed to be of questionable loyalty, and when it became clear that disproportionate numbers of them were being sent to the Eastern Front, they naturally grew resentful. More than seventeen thousand Alsace-Lorrainers, meanwhile, were slipping across the border to volunteer in France.

Ultimately, three hundred and eighty thousand men from Alsace and Lorraine served in the German army during the war. Their desertion rate was eighty out of every ten thousand, compared with one in ten thousand for other German troops. The high command responded with increased distrust and even harsher treatment both of the provinces themselves and of the soldiers who had come from them, and the sense of alienation deepened. It widened beyond possibility of repair when the government's postwar plans for the provinces became public knowledge. Rather than being granted autonomy as one of the German states, they were to be punished: Alsace was to be given to Bavaria, Lorraine to Prussia.

Thus did Germany, through its own actions, lose Alsace and Lorraine long before France took them back.

Chapter 20

✠

Verdun: Execution

"It wouldn't take anything, just a slightly harder blow,
for everything to collapse."

—ANONYMOUS FRENCH SOLDIER

Anyone inclined to believe that some dark force beyond human compre-
hension intervened again and again to make the Great War long and
ruinous would have no difficulty in finding evidence to support such a thesis.
There is no better example than the Battle of Verdun, which in its length and
cost and brutality and finally in its sheer pointlessness has always and rightly
been seen as a perfect microcosm of the war itself.

Nothing at all was inevitable about the battle. Though Falkenhayn may
have been right in thinking that Germany had to take the offensive somewhere early in 1916, he had other targets to choose from, even on the Western
Front. Ludendorff, if given the chance, could have argued persuasively for
action in the east.

And if Verdun was in fact the right choice, Falkenhayn's tactics were questionable at best. They stripped his troops of the opportunity that his artillery
had created to capture the heart of Verdun's defenses. They gave the French,
who by midday on February 21 were in no condition to withstand an attack
in force, time to pull themselves together.

The French for their part had little real need to hold Verdun. Their front
was firm at all points at the start of 1916, and historians have argued that they
would have been wiser to abandon Verdun, fall back on the hill country to
the southwest, and oblige the Germans to settle for a symbolic victory of
minor strategic value. But the fates decreed otherwise. The defense of Verdun
fell to men who were not willing to consider even an advantageous retreat.
And so it continued.

The second day began with a German bombardment as shattering as that

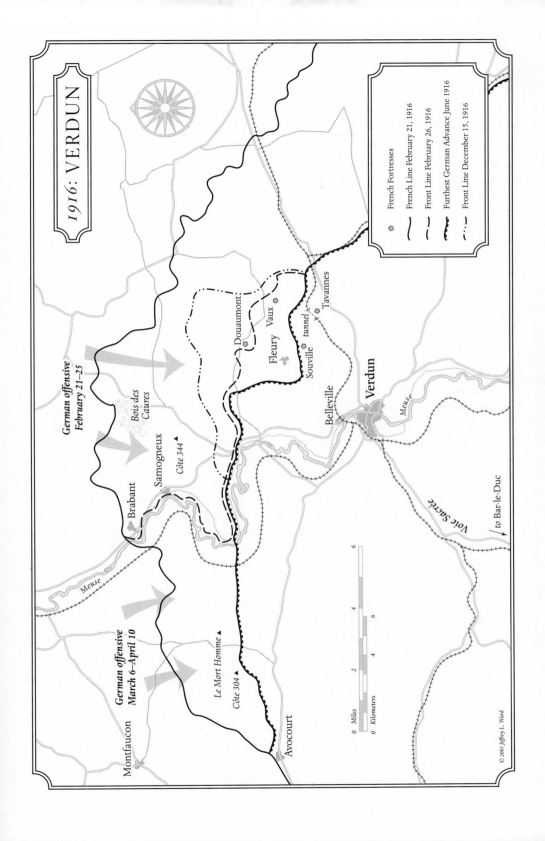

1916: VERDUN

French Fortresses ●
French Line February 21, 1916
Front Line February 26, 1916
Furthest German Advance June 1916
Front Line December 15, 1916

German offensive February 21–25

Brabant

Bois des Caures

Samogneux
Côte 344 ▲

Montfaucon

German offensive March 6–April 10

Le Mort Homme ▲
Côte 304 ▲

Avocourt

Meuse

Douaumont
Fleury
Vaux
Souville
tunnel
Tavannes

Belleville

Verdun

Meuse

Vôie Sacrée

to Bar-le-Duc

0 Miles 2 4 6
0 Kilometers 4 6

© 2005 Jeffrey L. Ward

of February 21. The French could do nothing but curl up at the bottom of whatever bunkers or holes they could still find amid the rubble and pray not to be vaporized or buried alive. This time the Germans began their advance at the end of morning, and they came forward in far greater numbers. They found the French forward positions even more obliterated than on the previous afternoon, and they had hours of daylight in which to keep moving.

The courage of the French troops in the face of all this defies belief. On the first day they had held their ground first with rifle and machine-gun fire, then with grenades, and finally, even in the face of that horrific new weapon the flamethrower, with gun-butts and stones. Now they somehow managed, even before the lifting of the barrage, to launch small, scattered, and uncoordinated counterattacks. It was, once again, the French doctrine of attacking whenever possible and trying immediately to recapture any lost ground. It confused and slowed the Germans, but it also led the French into exactly the kind of slaughter upon which Falkenhayn had built his hopes.

An entire German division was sent to the Bois des Caures, still held by the surviving members of Émile Driant's battalions, with orders to take it at all costs. During the first day's bombardment an estimated eighty thousand shells had fallen on the Bois des Caures, an area measuring five hundred by one thousand yards. Now, on the second morning, thousands more had come screaming down. Driant lost still more of his men, most of his bunkers were unrecognizable, and his position was nearly surrounded. Coolly, he burned his papers and ordered a withdrawal during which he was killed—shot in the forehead, according to men who were with him.

When the day ended, the Germans had again pushed the French back, but their gains were again less than spectacular. Casualties on the German side were as light as Falkenhayn could have hoped: the two infantry divisions on the cutting edge of the attack would report fewer than two thousand men killed or missing in the first *month* of the battle. By contrast, French deaths exceeded twenty-three thousand in the first five days. Of this total, nearly twenty thousand were listed as "missing," which meant they had been taken prisoner or, more commonly, that their bodies had been destroyed or buried by the shelling. It was a rare case—extremely rare for the Western Front—of defenders suffering substantially heavier losses than their attackers. Three-fifths of the troops with which the French began the battle became casualties within two weeks.

On the third day, after a night of intense cold that deepened the misery of the troops on both sides and ended the lives of hundreds of the wounded scattered across the landscape, the situation appeared to stabilize. The French troops continued to display an astonishing willingness to die rather than surrender or retreat, and they were inspired by the arrival of reinforcements from the rear and by increasing artillery support. The Germans again advanced, but their gains again were modest. The situation appeared to be moving toward a restoration of the old and familiar stalemate.

But suddenly on the fourth day, February 24, the French line began to fall apart. The day was a series of disasters for the defenders, and the first occurred hours before dawn. The Germans had been threatening the town of Samogneux on the right bank of the Meuse some four miles southeast of the Bois des Caures. On the night of February 23 a unit of French troops outside Samogneux broke in the face of an attack. After fleeing through the town, these soldiers told everyone they encountered, wrongly if understandably, that Samogneux had been lost. In fact it was still in French hands, but the commanders in the rear were sent reports of its fall. One general ordered a counterattack. Another directed artillery fire onto the town. At fifteen minutes after midnight French shells began falling both on the French in Samogneux and on those hurrying to retake it. By four A.M. the Germans were in possession.

The German artillery continued to blast away, and when dawn came and the infantry returned to the offensive, it quickly broke through a new line of defense that Castelnau had ordered to be put in place during his visit to Verdun late in January. With the breaching of this line, which had proved to be a powerful obstacle until it was overrun, French resistance seemed to dissolve. When the Germans attacked the next line in their path, the French ran. The Germans gained more ground on this day than on the first three days of the battle. They advanced three and a half miles, stopping only when the great bastions of Fort Douaumont and Fort Vaux, the two strongest points on the east side of the Meuse, blocked their way. French reinforcements continued to arrive, but as they did so they were sent off to whatever points appeared to be in greatest trouble without being concentrated or coordinated. They were quickly shot up without achieving anything. "It wouldn't take anything, just a slightly harder blow," said a French ambulance driver observing the situation, "for everything to collapse."

The French general with overall responsibility for the Verdun region, Fernand de Langle de Cary, telephoned Joffre to say that he wanted to withdraw from the Woëvre plain, the expanse of gently sloping farmland several miles east of the city. This was an astonishing proposal: the Germans had not even attacked on the Woëvre. Withdrawal there would gravely compromise the French army's ability to threaten the Germans' great salient at St. Mihiel, south of Verdun. It would imply eventual abandonment of the entire east bank. Joffre, however, responded with the preternatural calm for which he was by now famous. Telling Langle de Cary to do as he thought best, he returned to his supper. Langle de Cary went ahead with the withdrawal. Almost as soon as he did so, German troops moved in from the north to fill the vacuum. It was another part of the spreading French collapse.

Shortly after Joffre finished his meal, Castelnau arrived to tell him of the deteriorating situation. He recommended that the French Second Army, commanded by General Henri-Philippe Pétain and currently being rested at the town of Noailles in Normandy, be sent to the west bank at Verdun. Joffre agreed and retired for the night. At eleven P.M., having received alarming reports of fresh reverses, Castelnau was again at Joffre's door. When a frightened aide reminded him that the commander in chief's rest was not to be disturbed, Castelnau swept past him. Joffre, roused from his sleep, listened impassively to the latest news. He remained confident that the attack at Verdun was not a serious threat—his intelligence staff had assured him that it was a diversion in advance of a bigger German offensive planned for Champagne. When Castelnau asked permission to proceed to Verdun with authority to do there whatever he found to be necessary, Joffre again assented. He returned to bed and Castelanau departed by automobile.

At Noailles, meanwhile, another little drama was being played out. Castelnau's telegram ordering the Second Army to Verdun had been delivered to Pétain's headquarters, but Pétain himself was not there. He had left earlier in the day without telling anyone his destination. His aide, Bernard de Serrigny, knew his chief well. He summoned a car and set out through the dark countryside for Paris. It was almost three A.M. when he entered the sleeping city and directed his driver to the hotel at the Gare du Nord. There he roused the night manager. When she insisted that no General Pétain was

General Noël de Castelnau
Rushed to Verdun at start of battle.

on the premises, he refused to believe her. A search of the upper floors proved him right. Outside the door to one of the guest rooms stood a pair of army boots of yellowish leather—Pétain's boots. Next to them—all suspicions confirmed—was a dainty pair of ladies' slippers.

When he answered the knock on his door and saw who was there, Pétain stepped into the hall in his nightclothes. Serrigny briefed him, displaying the message instructing him to meet with Joffre at Chantilly at eight that morning. From inside the dark room came the sound of a woman weeping. Pétain, as calm as Joffre had been, told Serrigny to take a room, get some sleep, and meet him in the lobby at seven. Four hours later the two were speeding northward out of the city toward Chantilly.

At about the same time, miles to the east, Castelnau was arriving at Verdun, where the sun was rising over an icy landscape and the German Fifth Army was beginning the fifth day of its offensive. The French were in such disarray, and so demoralized, that they almost certainly would have been routed if hit with sufficient force. The crown prince and Knobelsdorf saw the opportunity and were eager to exploit it, but their meager reserves had already been committed. The main German reserve force was still under the control of Falkenhayn, who refused to release it. He thereby wasted his second chance to take Verdun. He was sticking with his plan and in so doing was fatally outsmarting himself.

All that day Castelnau traveled from place to place, bringing order out of confusion and quietly taking stock. As he did so, stunning news reached him. Mighty Fort Douaumont, the centerpiece of the Verdun defensive system, a stronghold built to be impregnable, and impregnable in fact when properly defended, had been captured by the Germans. This was not supposed to happen.

The story of how it happened is like something out of Kafka. The Germans had brought to bear upon Douaumont the same monster howitzers with which they had destroyed the Belgian forts a year and a half earlier, but this time their bombardment failed. The latest improvements had covered Douaumont's interior with alternating layers of reinforced concrete and loose rock and earth, a shock-absorbing dome that no shell could penetrate. The fort remained intact through explosion after explosion, the men inside badly rattled but unhurt.

Those men, however, numbered only sixty. Most of the fort's garrison, along with every piece of artillery that could be moved, had been sent away months before. On February 25 the troops who remained were huddled deep in the interior, as far as possible from the mayhem above. Three little parties of Germans—one of them consisting of a solitary sergeant—crept up on the fort at different points and met no resistance. Each party, unaware of the others, found an undefended entrance. Once inside they wandered unchallenged through empty chambers and passageways. After much confused exploring during which the solitary sergeant discovered a commissary and paused to gorge on hard-boiled eggs, they eventually and half-accidentally took the French by surprise, capturing them and the fort itself. German reinforcements were quicker than the French to rush forward, so that one of the anchors of Verdun fell into German hands without a shot being fired by either side.

In spite of the disasters occurring all around him, Castelnau decided that Verdun could be held. Being a firm adherent of the doctrine that when unable to attack the French should never give ground, he did exactly what Falkenhayn would have wanted him to do: he resolved that Verdun *must* be held.

Meanwhile not everything was going well for the Germans. For reasons that will never be known because every witness was instantly reduced to his constituent molecules, an enormous German ammunition dump at the village of Spincourt suddenly blew up. Four hundred and fifty thousand shells disappeared in an explosion that seemed to rend the heavens, leaving the Germans instantly and gravely short of ammunition. And from the west bank of the Meuse, a haven for French artillery because of Falkenhayn's refusal to include it in his offensive, long-range guns were methodically putting the big German howitzers out of action one by one.

At three-thirty in the afternoon Castelnau telephoned Joffre and told him of his decision to stand and fight. He announced another decision as well: all the other senior generals in the area having been found wanting, Pétain should be given command not just of the west bank but of the entire theater. When Pétain arrived near midnight, at the end of a day that had included a pro forma meeting with the sphinxlike Joffre and long hours on crowded wintry roads, he was coming down with what appeared to be a bad cold. Castelnau briefed him, gave him handwritten orders to take command and to hold the east bank at all costs, and departed. Pétain slept for a few hours in an armchair in an unheated room, and when he awoke he was burning with fever. A doctor was called in, and after a hurried examination he declared that the general had double pneumonia. This condition was debilitating and potentially lethal in the days before antibiotics, especially for a man of sixty. Pétain would have been amply justified in declaring himself unable to continue. Instead, issuing strict orders that his illness be kept secret, he organized a system in which members of his staff would serve as his eyes, ears, and voice, and he himself would rarely have to leave his room. For most of the next week he reorganized the defense of Verdun from a sickbed. During part of that week his life hung in the balance.

The appointment of Pétain put Verdun in the hands of a man who, probably more than any other in the French army, was capable of organizing an effective defense while at the same time protecting his troops from unnecessary destruction. Pétain was an infantryman who had taken the trouble, in the course of his long career, to make himself expert in the science of artillery. At a time and in a place that put nearly unendurable pressure on France's common soldiers, he was unique in his ability to understand the troops under his command: in his unwillingness to throw their lives away, and in his willingness to share their dangers. He was a leader, and the poilus responded to him. His was a remarkable case of the right man being in the right place at the right time.

From his first day in command, too weak to stay on his feet, Pétain began

Generals Ferdinand Foch (*left*) and Henri-Philippe Pétain

moving men and guns back into the strongholds that Joffre had all but abandoned. He ordered an end to hopeless attacks on lost positions, Fort Douaumont included. He installed a so-called "line of panic" where the French could gather for a last stand if the Germans broke through. He took charge both of the artillery and of the system by which Verdun was supplied. The guns were positioned, and their fire coordinated, to inflict maximum damage on the German assault troops as they came forward through the gullies between the hills. This turned the tables on Falkenhayn. Now the Germans were advancing not just against battered infantry but into a concentrated barrage. The French soldiers were soon aware of the change, and their morale rose swiftly.

Though still concealed behind his wall of secrecy, Pétain saw that Verdun's greatest vulnerability was its tenuous line of supply. Because it was a salient, a bulge in the line left exposed by the Germans' 1914 advances to the east and south, the city had only one connection to the rear: a road that ran northward from the ancient hill town of Bar-le-Duc, forty miles to the south. Everything needed to sustain the fight—men, guns, ammunition, food—had to travel along this road. It had been widened in 1915, providing barely enough room for two trucks side by side. Never in history had an embattled army the size of Pétain's been supported for an extended period through such a thin line.

Pétain's staff could find only seven hundred trucks. All of France was searched for more, so that ultimately thirty-five hundred would be streaming north and south day and night. At the peak of the conflict, trucks arrived in Verdun at a rate of one every fourteen seconds. Any vehicle that broke down was rolled into the ditches that lined the road, and at any given time as many as fifteen thousand men were at work keeping the roadbed in usable condition. Upon unloading, the trucks would be filled with men—not with the wounded only, but with soldiers being sent away for recuperation from the horror of an unending artillery barrage—and returned to Bar-le-Duc. This too was part of Pétain's plan: he ordered a constant rotation of units into and out of the combat zone, so that relatively fresh troops were always arriving and the men under fire had something more to look forward to than remaining under fire until they were dead. In time three-fourths of the entire French army—125 divisions—would be rotated through Verdun, so that it more than any other battle of the war became a shared national experience. The French writer and politician Maurice Barrès would call the Bar-le-Duc road the Voie Sacrée, the Sacred Way, and it has been remembered by that name ever since.

The actions taken by Pétain, coupled with the Germans' lack of reserves, changed the character of the fight. On February 27, barely forty-eight hours after standing on the brink of taking the city, the Germans for the first time captured no new ground at all during a full day of combat. Kaiser Wilhelm, after days of waiting at his son's headquarters to enter Verdun in triumph, gave up and left the area.

February 28 brought a thaw, melting the ice and snow and turning frozen earth to mud—and threatening to make the Bar-le-Duc road impassable. Thousands more men were assigned to shoveling gravel and scrap metal and whatever else was available onto and into the mud, and the trucks kept moving. Between February 24 and March 6 twenty-five thousand tons of supplies and a hundred and ninety thousand men were carried into Verdun.

For the Germans, the thaw was a disaster. Their roads had been severely damaged by French artillery fire, and as they softened into a quagmire, the movement of guns and shells became nearly impossible. Howitzers in forward positions remained short of ammunition and under fire. Forward units of German infantry found themselves under a barrage little less deadly than the one that had descended on the French a week earlier. Much of this fire was coming from a long ridge west of the Meuse that for centuries had borne the ominous and suddenly prophetic name of Le Mort Homme, the Dead Man. With every new day the Germans were paying a higher price for Falkenhayn's refusal to include the west bank in his offensive.

Even at this juncture, one way remained open for the Germans to deliver a mortal blow without expending infantry. They could have directed artillery fire onto the Bar-le-Duc road, the Verdun lifeline, which was jammed to capacity around the clock and in constantly deteriorating condition. In preparation for his offensive, Falkenhayn had sent batteries of long-range naval

German troops struggling to move a piece of light field artillery

guns to Verdun; the road was within their range. The Germans also had almost total control of the air over Verdun at this early stage; with bombing and strafing their aircraft could have reduced the road to chaos. Somehow— another of the war's many mysteries—the Germans failed to make use of these opportunities. They continued to allow men and equipment to pour into Verdun even as movement of their own forces became all but impossible.

On the last day of the month, February 29, the crown prince and Knobelsdorf met with Falkenhayn to decide the biggest possible question: whether the offensive, which had obviously come to nothing, should be continued. There was much to be said for stopping, with German losses not yet at all painful by Great War standards. The capture of Douaumont alone was sufficient for propaganda purposes. The assembled generals surely were mindful of the reasons for stopping: among military strategists it has long been a truism that prolonging an unsuccessful offensive invariably proves futile.

The crown prince, however, appears to have been seduced by visions of what might have been achieved if his ideas rather than Falkenhayn's had been allowed to shape the attack of February 21. He and Knobelsdorf declared themselves in favor of continuing if three conditions were met. The offensive must be widened to include the hills west of the Meuse, the French artillery positions around Le Mort Homme especially. The reserves held back by Falkenhayn must be brought forward and used. Finally, this widening of the fight and raising of the stakes must not be open-ended. The entire operation had to be called off, the crown prince said, as soon as it became clear that the Germans were losing as many men as the French. Falkenhayn agreed. His goal remained what it had been all along: "not to defeat but to annihilate France."

And so the Germans, having in the space of a week thrown away two opportunities to capture Verdun, cast aside the chance to get out cheaply.

THE LIVING DEAD

BY 1916 THE ARMIES OF BRITAIN, FRANCE, AND GERMANY were being diminished not just by the numbers of men killed and wounded but by something so new to human experience that the English had to coin a name for it: *shell shock.* By the thousands and then the tens of thousands, soldiers on the Western Front were being turned into zombies and freaks without suffering physical injuries of any kind.

The phenomenon appeared in 1914, and at first no one knew what to make of it. The medical services on both sides found themselves confronted with bizarre symptoms: men in a trancelike state, men shaking uncontrollably, men frozen in weird postures, or partly paralyzed, or (though unwounded) unable to see or hear or speak. By December British doctors were reporting that between three and four percent of the BEF's enlisted men and up to ten percent of its officers were displaying symptoms of this kind. Their German counterparts would record almost twelve thousand such cases in the first year of the war.

The victims got little sympathy. Career officers were accustomed to separating soldiers into four groups: the healthy, the sick, the wounded, and the cowards. They were predisposed to put men with nervous and mental disorders into the last category, to order them back to duty, and to mete out harsh punishment to any who failed to obey. But the number of men unable to obey became too big to be ignored or to be put in front of firing squads; it has been estimated that twenty-four thousand had been sent home to Britain by 1916.

The army's career physicians agreed with their generals: this was not illness but malingering, and the solution was punishment. Any who failed to agree were met with contempt. But doctors who had been brought out of private practice with mobilization looked for medical explanations. Theories were offered. An early favorite was that the soldiers' nervous systems were being damaged in some mysterious way by shock waves from high explosives. Thus the term *shell shock* came into general, even diagnostic, use.

Gradually it became clear that the words did not fit the facts. Many of the victims had not been shelled—at least had not been exposed to

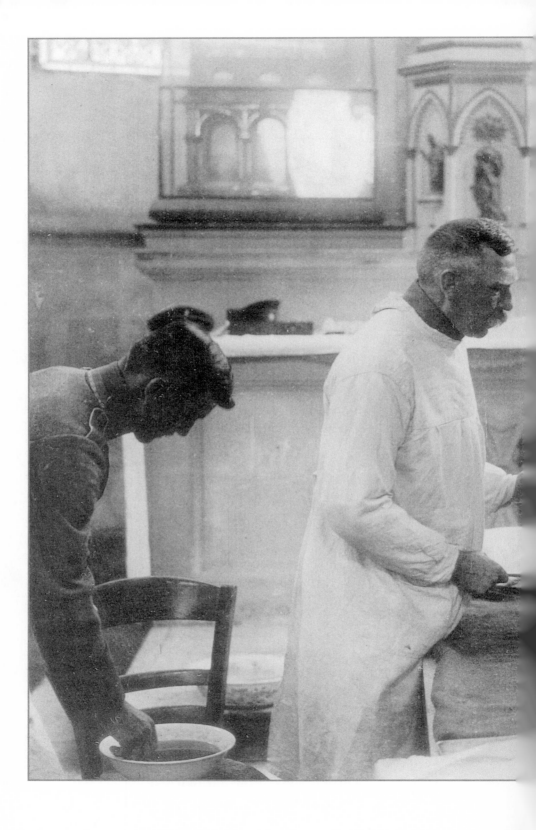

shellfire shortly before breaking down. More oddly, *none* of the victims had been physically injured. By 1916 a more sophisticated understanding was emerging. Charles Myers, a young English psychiatrist, decided after making a close study of the subject that *shell shock* was "a singularly ill-chosen term." The condition, he said, had nothing to do with the physics of shellfire or with physical damage to nerves. It rose out of the peculiar conditions of trench warfare, an experience beyond anything the human psyche was built to endure. The troops were cracking because they could not absorb what was happening to them, because they knew themselves to be utterly powerless (bravery had little survival value when one was on the receiving end of a bombardment), and because they had no confidence that the generals who had put them in danger knew what they were doing. Men whose courage was beyond challenge could and did break down if subjected to enough strain of this kind. Conversely, many shell shock victims recovered sufficiently to be returned to action, and some performed heroically after doing so.

Myers's analysis of the relationship between trench warfare and breakdown—which came to be called *hysteria* when the victims behaved manically, *neurasthenia* when they sank into depression—was confirmed as the war continued. Observers noticed that breakdowns had been least frequent in the opening months of the war, before the Western Front became rigid (and later that their frequency declined when the deadlock was broken and the armies again began to move). Further confirmation came in the fact that one in six victims was an officer, although the BEF had only one officer for every thirty men. Junior officers on the front lines not only bore heavier responsibilities than the men they commanded but were more often exposed to enemy fire.

By trial and error, it was discovered that soldiers who broke down were most likely to recover when treated almost immediately, at casualty clearing stations behind the lines, rather than being sent to hospitals. Various treatments were tried—hypnosis, electric shock, simple and often bullying forms of talk therapy—and several proved to be at least somewhat effective. Treatment was often indistinguishable from punishment. Men unable to talk were given electric shocks until they screamed in pain, at which point they were declared to have recovered. Always the objective was not to "cure" the victim, to identify and deal with the underlying causes of his symptoms, but to get him back into action. The British created two categories of cases: men who had broken when actually under fire, and those who had not been under fire. Only those in the first category were entitled

Previous pages: Surgery in a French church

to wear on their sleeves the stripe awarded to men wounded in action, and only they, if they did not recover, were entitled to disability compensation. It remained inadmissible for physicians to suggest that a loss of the will to fight could ever be justified. The few who dared to suggest that it might be rational for a man to disobey an order that could not possibly lead to anything except sudden death—an order to climb out of a hole into blanketing gunfire, for example—were likely to be dismissed. Any nonmedical officer who seriously challenged such orders was dismissed or worse.

The problem remained immense. This is an area in which data are scarce—little is known about the incidence or treatment of shell shock among the Austrians and Russians, though the continued fluidity of the Eastern Front may have limited the problem there. But by the end of the war, two hundred thousand shell shock cases entered the medical records in Germany, eighty thousand in Britain. Sixteen thousand cases were reported by the British just in the second half of 1916, and this total included only those men in the first category, the ones whose problems were judged to be less dishonorable. Fifteen percent of all the British soldiers who received disability pensions—one hundred and twenty thousand men in all—would do so for psychiatric reasons. In 1922, four years after the war's end, some six thousand British veterans would remain in insane asylums.

Chapter 21

✠

Verdun Metastasizes

*"Verdun was the mill on the Meuse that ground to
powder the hearts as well as the bodies of our soldiers."*
—CROWN PRINCE WILHELM

On March 6, after a week when the artillery on both sides continued to
pound away but infantry operations were limited to attacks and counterattacks of little consequence, the Germans attempted to restart their
stalled offensive. In keeping with the conditions that the crown prince had set
in agreeing to continue, they did so with many more troops this time
(Falkenhayn had released a corps of reserves) and on a much broader front.
They again attacked in the craggy wooded hills east of the Meuse, but now
they also made a complementary move on the west or left bank. There the
main objective was Le Mort Homme, the ridge from which French gunners
had been sending fire across the river. The battle remained above all an
artillery contest. As on February 21, the Germans began by trying to use
their firepower to obliterate the defenders. Once again men died by the hundreds without seeing or being seen by the men who killed them.

The balance had shifted, however. The French had hurried two hundred
thousand troops up the Voie Sacrée from Bar-le-Duc, and the long-range
guns that they had positioned all through the region were wrecking the
Germans' howitzers. Pétain, anticipating a German advance on the west bank,
had positioned four divisions of infantry there—something on the order of
sixty thousand troops—with a fifth in reserve. Though not fully recovered
from pneumonia, he was back on his feet and directing everything.

Conceivably, if he had been free to make his own decisions, Pétain might
have elected to withdraw from Verdun. He understood that he would have
sacrificed nothing of strategic importance in doing so, and he would have left
the Germans in a difficult position from which to proceed. But he knew too

that President Poincaré, for reasons of national morale, had demanded that the city be held, and that if he proposed anything different he would likely be dismissed. Fortunately for him, the Falkenhayn plan had by this point lost all coherence. The dynamics of the situation were drawing the Germans into a nearly obsessive willingness to attack and attack again regardless of cost, and to attack not only with guns but with troops. Blindness, loss of perspective, had become a more serious affliction on the German side than on the French.

On the ravaged ground of the east bank, after again throwing masses of infantry against reinforced French defenses and murderous artillery fire, the Germans found themselves reeling under the magnitude of their losses and unable to advance. On the new battleground west of the river too, the center of the attack was quickly stopped. Only on the left flank of the west bank offensive, the flank directly adjacent to the Meuse, was the story different. There the attackers made rapid and substantial progress, managing to blast the French out of village after village, capturing the first and then the second lines of defense along four miles of front, taking thousands of prisoners. The situation became so desperate, the danger of a general collapse so great, that the sector's French commander issued a warning to his troops. If they tried to withdraw, he would order his own artillery and machine guns to fire on them.

The Battle of Verdun began to settle down into stalemate. On March 7 the Germans' drive on the west bank brought them up against a woodland called the Bois des Corbeaux, one of several points protecting the approaches to Le Mort Homme. Artillery wiped out many of the defenders, put the survivors to flight, and allowed the Germans to take possession of the woods. Early the next morning the French returned in a wildly courageous counterattack that should have been a disaster but through sheer audacity panicked the Germans and sent them running. But the next day, when a blast of artillery blew off both legs of the dashing colonel who had led the counterattack carrying only a walking stick, the Germans yet again captured the Bois. This time they held it. But the victory was little more than pyrrhic. It left the Germans exhausted and pinned down. Not only Le Mort Homme but the high points nearest it remained in French hands, bristling with artillery and machine guns, guarded by entrenched riflemen. Further movement was out of the question.

The crown prince's attack on two sides of the river had miscarried as badly as Falkenhayn's on one. If the French were being bled white, so were the Germans. The two sides were draining each other in a fight so huge and costly, so rich in drama, that it had captured the imagination of the world. Verdun had been elevated to such colossal symbolic importance that France needed only to hold on in order to claim a momentous victory. Falkenhayn, originally indifferent to whether Verdun fell or not, now desperately needed to take it. The trap that he had wanted to construct for the French now held him firmly in its grip.

As a direct result of Verdun, the war in the east flared back into life. Late in 1915, when the Entente's senior commanders met to make plans, the Russians had complained about what they saw as their allies' failure to help when the Germans were hammering them out of Poland. General Mikhail Alexeyev, sent to Chantilly as the tsar's new chief of staff, demanded an agreement that whenever one front was threatened, an offensive would be launched on the other to relieve the pressure. The Battle of Verdun was only days old when the French reminded Petrograd of this commitment. The Russians responded with yet another expression of their almost touching readiness to try to come to the rescue whenever asked—an eagerness that contrasted sharply with the cynicism and contempt that so often tainted relations between the British and the French. It is difficult to imagine Joffre or Haig responding as the Russians did if the situation had been reversed.

Only the tsar was really eager. When the Russian general staff gathered at his headquarters on the third day of fighting at Verdun, the army group commanders argued that they were not ready for an offensive and attacking now could only spoil their chances of doing so successfully later. They pointed out that the spring thaw was approaching and that the resulting floods would usher in the annual "roadless period," during which movement of men and guns became all but impossible. Tsar Nicholas decided otherwise. He ordered not only that an attack be launched but that it take place in advance of the thaw. The only remaining question was where to hit the Germans.

The Russians appeared to have good options from which to choose. The loss of Poland had enormously shortened their lines, increasing the number of troops available for each mile of front. In the north, in the sector commanded by Hindenburg and Ludendorff on the German side, the Russians had three hundred thousand troops to the Germans' one hundred and eighty thousand. In the center the Russian advantage was even greater: seven hundred thousand men facing three hundred and sixty thousand Germans. In the south, where the front slanted eastward toward the Balkans, things were more evenly balanced, with half a million men on each side. Here, however, the enemy troops were mainly Austro-Hungarian rather than German and therefore considerably less intimidating. That the Russian troops were largely half-trained recruits and deplorably ill equipped (tens of thousands remained without rifles) seems to have caused little more concern than the questionable quality of their leadership. Though the whole vast Russian army was a sorry mess by the standards of the Germans, French, and British, War Minister Alexei Polivanov was improving training and supply. Recent events gave cause for encouragement. Grand Duke Nicholas had launched an offensive in the Caucasus in January and within a week had won a major victory over the Turks at Koprukov. On February 16 his forces had captured Erzerum, the Ottoman Empire's most important northern stronghold. Obviously Russian armies were capable of winning.

It was decided that the new offensive should take place in the northwest, at Lake Naroch near the Lithuanian capital of Vilna, and should include the northern and central army groups. Together they could provide ten corps, more than twenty divisions, enough to outnumber the Germans by what promised to be a decisive margin. They were commanded by two of the most senior Russian generals, Alexei Evert and Alexei Kuropatkin.

After a series of delays that gave the Germans ample foreknowledge of what was coming, the Russians kicked off their attack on March 18. The dreaded thaw had begun the day before, covering the terrain with knee-deep slush, but success seemed certain nevertheless. Of all the Russian armies, those commanded by Evert and Kuropatkin were richest in guns and ammunition. They began Verdun-style, in eight hours firing thirty thousand three-inch shells and nine thousand heavier projectiles at the entrenchments of the German Tenth Army. When the Russian infantry moved forward—four corps on a front of twelve miles—it did so against a defending force that was barely one-fifth its size, and in short order it overran the Germans' first two lines. In less than a week, however, the attack broke down completely, with the Russians trying and failing to take the high ground beyond the positions they had captured.

There are several explanations for this failure. Bad weather and inadequate air reconnaissance had left the Russian artillery almost blind, so that much of the barrage fell harmlessly on unoccupied ground. Even when the gunners had the opportunity to support their infantry, they often failed to do so. The end of winter, with the snow cover melting and then freezing hard and melting again, made conditions terrible for the infantry. The quality of the troops was low on the Russian side, high on the German, and the sixty-eight-year-old Kuropatkin was a deplorable product of the Russian autocracy's tendency to keep mediocrities in important positions long after their unfitness had been demonstrated beyond doubt. A favorite at court, he had served as minister of war from 1898 to 1904 and then was given command of all Russian ground forces in the Russo-Japanese War. Though he had been replaced after causing a disastrous defeat at Mukden, his connections got him returned to senior command. He again performed clumsily early in the Great War but had nevertheless been made commander of the Northern Army Group in 1915. Now, at Lake Naroch, he failed to support the cautious Evert in much the same way that Rennenkampf had failed Samsonov at Tannenberg, and with equally painful results. Evert's men, trying to advance in deep ice-melt against an enemy firing down on them from defenses that Ludendorff had been strengthening all winter, were massacred. Twelve thousand unwounded Russians, still flimsily dressed after a year and a half of war, froze to death when temperatures plunged overnight. The offensive ended so quickly, at so little cost to the Germans, that it had no impact on Verdun. Outnumbered as they were, the Germans had required no reinforcements.

At this same time there departed from the stage possibly the best leader, almost certainly the best man, in the French military establishment. Joseph Gallieni, whose interventions as a sidelined general had led to the victory at the Marne in 1914 and as minister of war had helped to save Verdun in February 1916, resigned in March in preparation for surgery needed to save his life. Worn down by the demands of office, told that he should wait six months to recover his strength before undergoing the operation, he refused. He hoped to be able to return to duty quickly (although, disgusted by politics, he vowed that upon recovering he would serve wherever he was wanted *except* as a member of the cabinet). But the doctors' warnings proved accurate: he did not survive the surgery, dying on March 27. He was still a comparatively obscure figure at his death, his greatest contributions to the war effort unknown to the public. In 1921, posthumously, he would be made a Marshal of France.

Gallieni was not the only major figure to depart the stage in 1916. The year became a kind of parade of personalities, with high generals, admirals, and government leaders falling from power in all the combatant countries and being succeeded by new faces. Great changes in the French command structure began early in April with the arrival at Verdun of General Robert Nivelle, the dashing figure who in 1914, as a colonel in command of field artillery, had won fame by breaking up one of the last attacks by German forces advancing on Paris. A passionate adherent to the cult of the offensive, Nivelle in the year and a half following the Marne had become a favorite of Joffre's, rising almost as rapidly as Pétain. Upon reporting at Verdun, he became commander of a corps on the east bank of the Meuse. That part of the battleground was, at the time, almost inactive. The Germans were focused on the west bank, pouring steel and flesh into their increasingly desperate, increasingly bloody efforts to drive the French from Le Mort Homme. "One must have lived through these hours in order to get an idea of it," a French chaplain said of life in one of the fortresses blocking approaches to the hill. "It seems as though we are living under a steam hammer...You receive something like a blow in the hollow of the stomach. But what a blow!... Each explosion knocks us to the ground. After a few hours one becomes somewhat dumbfounded." He wrote of badly wounded men left unattended for eight days, "lying down, dying of hunger, suffering thirst to the extent that they were compelled to drink their urine."

Pétain's artillery too was taking a fearsome toll, but literally foot by foot the attackers were clawing their way forward in what was by now a war of attrition of the rawest and most savage kind. Though the French defenses were once again firm—the Pétain system of rotating troops into and out of the battle was making the nightmare less intolerable for the French than for the Germans—the pressure on them remained intense.

And the losses were mounting: eighty-nine thousand French and eighty-one thousand Germans dead or wounded by the end of March. Nivelle, however, was intent on attacking. He began to do so repeatedly in spite of Pétain's disapproval, blithely and with unshakable confidence shrugging off one costly failure after another. He had the enthusiastic support of a man who had come with him to Verdun: General Charles Mangin, now commander of the crack Fifth Division, known to his own men as "the Butcher" for his indifference to casualties. The aggressiveness of this pair won them Joffre's admiration. Pétain, by contrast, was sinking into disfavor. Joffre was impatient with his stubborn unwillingness to go on the offensive and stay there, his repeated efforts to keep Nivelle and Mangin in check. Pétain regarded himself as fortunate to be able to stand his ground in the face of the onslaught on the west bank, and he was content to hold back and make the Germans pay the price of their persistence. But Joffre was always quick to remove officers who failed to do as he wished.

On April 8, blind or indifferent to the fact that only one day before the east bank had erupted in a German assault that pushed back the French front line, Joffre sent a telegram urging Pétain to launch "a vigorous and powerful offensive to be executed with only the briefest delay." This was nonsense under the circumstances, and it was rendered moot by what followed the next day: an enormous, convulsive renewal of the German offensive on both banks simultaneously. The intensity of this new attack rivaled that of February 21; before sending their infantry into action, the Germans fired off seven trainloads of artillery shells. Only the guns that Pétain had concentrated on the west bank prevented a breakthrough. Then it began to rain, and the rain continued for twelve days, bogging everyone down and saving the French from being overrun.

For the Germans this newest failure was crushing. It led Crown Prince Wilhelm to conclude that the entire campaign was a failure, that continuing could no longer possibly produce results commensurate with the costs. (After the war, in his memoirs, he would write that "Verdun was the mill on the Meuse that ground to powder the hearts as well as the bodies of our soldiers.") It would deepen the divisions within the German general staff and lead to a change of command. In the near term, however, only Pétain's fate was sealed. Joffre could see nothing except that Pétain was still on the defensive, still not attacking. But Pétain was now a national hero in his own right, known to the public as the savior of Verdun and therefore safe from being sacked. Joffre's solution was to kick Pétain upstairs. He dismissed Langle de Cary, hero to no one and savior of nothing, as commander of Army Group Center, which included Pétain's Second Army. Pétain became Langle de Cary's successor. The French Second Army, and with it responsibility for conducting the Battle of Verdun, were given to Nivelle, who soon discontinued Pétain's system for allowing no division to remain under fire for more than a week at a time. This system had contributed immeasurably to French morale. But its end pleased Joffre, who had always regarded it as an unnecessary complication as he tried to prepare for an offensive on the Somme.

German and French gunners continued to blast away at each other on the west bank, and slowly the Germans inched forward. By April 21 there was hand-to-hand fighting for control of the Mort Homme crest.

It can only be mentioned here that intense but fruitless fighting was in process all around Ypres:

That on Monday, April 23, the city of Dublin exploded in an Easter Rebellion that British troops needed a week to suppress;

That the Russians and Turks were continuing their war in the Caucasus and around the Black Sea;

And that in Berlin the German government was once again engaged in a bitter struggle over whether to restrict the operations of its growing fleet of U-boats.

In the far South Atlantic the explorer Sir Ernest Shackleton arrived at a whaling station on South Georgia Island at the end of a horrendous year and a half stranded with his men amid the ice floes fringing the Antarctic continent. It had been 1914, the fighting in its earliest stages, when Shackleton lost contact with the outside world.

"Tell me," he asked the first man he encountered. "When was the war over?"

"The war is not over," he was told. "Millions are being killed. Europe is mad. The world is mad."

The Eastern Front had fallen quiet in the aftermath of Lake Naroch, but there too important changes were taking place. On the day Nivelle arrived at Verdun, Tsar Nicholas peremptorily discharged Alexei Polivanov as minister of war, thereby removing a man who, in the months since his appointment, had been achieving near-miracles. Polivanov had been fearless in flushing corruption and incompetence out of the administration of the Russian war effort and in repairing the damage done to the tsar's armies in 1915. He was dismissed not because of the defeat at Lake Naroch, in which he had no role, but because Tsarina Alexandra hated him and had long wanted him put out of the way. As a reformer, Polivanov was despised by the court's inner circle; he was willing to work cooperatively with the national legislature that the tsar had been forced to create in the bloody turbulence following the Russo-Japanese War; and he had tried to dissuade Nicholas from assuming command of the army in 1915. All these things, in Alexandra's small and rigid mind, made him an enemy of the autocracy that she was pathologically committed to preserving for her son. His final offense, the one that finished him, was to intervene when he learned that four of the war ministry's fastest automobiles had been handed over to Rasputin to enable him to escape police agents. Polivanov departed in official disgrace and without a word of thanks. With Nicholas II away at army headquarters, the government was essentially under the control of the tsarina. And she was essentially under the control of the mysterious Rasputin. "I shall sleep in peace," she told her husband upon learning that Polivanov was gone.

There followed the appointment, as commander on Russia's southwestern front, of a still-obscure general named Alexei Brusilov. It happened—perhaps for no better reason than that even a blind hog finds an acorn once in a while—that this appointment put into a crucial position at a crucial time the most talented Russian field commander of the Great War. A member of a military family of noble origins (his own father had been a general), Brusilov had performed brilliantly at the start of the war, leading the forces that drove

General Alexei Brusilov
*Turned the war around
on the Eastern Front.*

the Austro-Hungarians out of Galicia and back into the passes of the Carpathians. Later his army absorbed the German Carpathian offensive of May 1915, preventing a calamity bigger than Tannenberg. Brusilov had directed a two-hundred-mile fighting retreat, striking out at the advancing Germans night after night, disrupting their movements, and saving the Russian forces from being encircled. His appointment gave him the opportunity to transform the war in the east, and he would not be slow to seize it.

Just days after Brusilov took up his new command, with Joffre demanding that the Russians do something more helpful than the Lake Naroch debacle, the tsar's staff and front commanders met to decide what to do next. New as he was to such august assemblies, Brusilov showed himself to be the only general willing to commit to a new offensive. Thus he dominated the proceedings, proposing a joint attack by his four armies and the larger forces commanded by Evert and Kuropatkin to his north. In this way, he said, the Germans could be pinned down at every point on the front. They would be unable to shift their forces to wherever the danger was greatest. Evert and Kuropatkin, careful men under the best of circumstances and stunned by the failure at Lake Naroch, were unwilling to agree. They were overruled by the tsar's chief of staff, General Alexeyev, an able strategist who had been Brusilov's superior in 1914 and had personal experience of his capacities. Alexeyev decreed that all the front commanders should prepare for a joint offensive to take place in July. Brusilov was warned (perhaps because his group was the only one that did not greatly outnumber the enemies facing it) that he must expect no reinforcements. He returned to his headquarters and got to work. Evert and Kuropatkin did essentially nothing.

On April 28, after waiting more than a month for the ground to firm up, Hindenburg and Ludendorff launched a counterattack at Lake Naroch. It was as spectacular a success as the original Russian attack had been a failure, recapturing in a day everything that the Russians had managed to take in a week in March. The ease with which the Germans swept back over their lost ground was in part the result of an innovation introduced by the commander of their artillery, a lieutenant colonel of retirement age named Georg Bruchmüller. This was the *Feuerwalz*, or dance of fire. (The British would give it the more prosaic name "creeping barrage" when they adopted it later in the year.) It replaced days of shelling with a shorter, shockingly intense bombardment that, when the infantry advanced, moved ahead of it into enemy territory like a protective wall. Its effectiveness lay in the way it gave defenders no time to adapt, and attackers the sense that they were being literally shielded from the enemy as they advanced. It was, implicitly, a rejection of the artillery tactics being used by both sides on the Western Front. Ultimately it would prove to be one of the war's most important tactical innovations. Ludendorff's strategist Max Hoffmann recognized its brilliance in bestowing on its inventor the nickname Durchbruchmüller— Breakthroughmüller.

In the two fights at Lake Naroch the Russians had suffered at least one hundred thousand battlefield casualties, a total that excludes the twelve thousand troops who froze to death. German losses totaled twenty thousand. But it was not the direct results of the battle (neither side gained any ground) that made it important. Lake Naroch changed the course of the war in the east by persuading Evert and Kuropatkin that further offensives could not succeed regardless of how many men, guns, and shells the Russians used.

AIRSHIPS AND LANDSHIPS

THE GREAT WAR DID NOT GIVE BIRTH TO AVIATION; THE Wright brothers made their first flight at Kitty Hawk eleven years before the war began. It did not even give birth to *combat* aviation; the Italians had used nine primitive airplanes in snatching Libya away from the Ottoman Empire in 1911 and 1912.

But the war transformed aviation with dazzling speed. In a matter of months it changed the airplane from a novelty of uncertain value—"a useless and expensive fad," Britain's top general said as late as 1911—to an essential element in the arsenal of every nation.

The Great War *did* give birth to the tank, which would not have been invented nearly as early as it was if not for the stalemate on the Western Front.

Both phenomena, air *forces* as opposed to mere airplanes and tanks as an antidote to trenches and machine guns and barbed wire, made their first appearance in 1916.

It is sometimes claimed, falsely, that Europe's military leaders remained almost entirely blind to the potential of the airplane during the decade before the war. Skepticism was indeed widespread, and sometimes it was absurd: Ferdinand Foch, when he was commandant of the French War College, had declared the new flying machines "good for sport but not for war." But in 1909, when Louis Blériot crossed the English Channel in a plane he had designed and built himself, more than a few British leaders understood that their island nation was suddenly no longer as safe as it always had been. When the French began using aircraft effectively in their annual military exercises, the Germans understood that their fledgling aviation industry and its inferior products had better catch up—and fast.

France (not America, despite the Wright brothers) was the leader in heavier-than-air flight throughout the prewar years. Though both France and Germany began the war with more than two hundred airplanes in military service, those of the French were distinctly superior. The British lagged behind with fewer than a hundred aircraft, only forty-four of which were sent to the continent with the BEF. The Russians, though they had acquired substantial numbers, were entirely dependent on foreign sources for their planes. Few and simple as they were, however, airplanes quickly proved their value. Weeks after French fliers confirmed the shift of the German First Army away from Paris, setting the stage for the Battle of the Marne, the British began using their aircraft as artillery spotters. When the Western Front became static and cavalry were rendered useless, aircraft became essential in reconnaissance. Aerial photography reached a high level of sophistication as early as 1915.

Air combat followed as the fliers on both sides began trying to knock each other out of the sky. French and German pilots (often enlisted men at first—mere chauffeurs) went aloft carrying passengers who fired at each other with rifles and shotguns. Somebody got the idea of mounting a Hotchkiss light machine gun at the front of France's Morane Saulnier monoplane, which with a top speed of a hundred miles per hour was the best of the war's first aircraft. Another innovation soon followed: steel plating on the back side of the propeller blades, to spare pilots the indignity of shooting themselves down. So armed, the French began destroying their adversaries in numbers that mattered. The Germans, who until then had been spending most of their aviation budget on massive lighter-than-air Zeppelin dirigibles, again had to scramble to catch up. There began a game of technological leapfrog that continued through the war, with first one side and then the other gaining temporary advantage. The rudimentary technology of the time made the game a fast one. As the British aviation pioneer T.O.M. Sopwith said, "We literally thought of and designed and flew the airplanes in a space of about six or eight weeks."

A major advance came in the form of a new German biplane (a term indicating that it had two main wings, one above the other) designed by the Dutch engineer Anthony Fokker. In most respects this Fokker Eindecker, introduced in 1915, was little more than a copy of a captured Morane Saulnier. But in one respect it was revolutionary: Fokker equipped it with an interrupter gear (an idea he got from a Swiss engineer) that permitted its two machine guns to fire through the propeller without hitting the blades. This innovation completed the integration of piloting and killing. It turned airplanes into true weapons—flying gun platforms built for attack. With it the Germans dominated the air by late 1915. They were able to establish a virtually impenetrable umbrella over Verdun, keeping their preparations for the attack there a secret from the French. Even so, the Eindeckers needed half an hour to climb to ten thousand feet and had a top speed of only eighty-seven miles per hour.

The French and British regained the lead with three new and distinctly superior models: the Nieuport and Spad biplanes, and a Sopwith triplane that was a marvel of climbing power and maneuverability. The Entente armies assembled hundreds of these aircraft in preparation for their offensive on the Somme. The Germans, inevitably, responded with even more potent new aircraft that were ready for service by the fall of 1916. The race would go on from there.

The war's great fighter aces have since become romantic legends—the Red Baron and his kind, knights on flying horses—but there was more to air combat than chivalry. Before the war was a month old, the Germans were dropping bombs on Antwerp from their Zeppelins. In 1915 Zeppelin raids over southern England became almost commonplace, killing and wounding hundreds. As airplanes became more capable, they also became specialized: scout planes, fighters, and aircraft equipped for strafing troops on the ground. The vulnerable Zeppelins were replaced with increasingly heavy bombers, making the war terrible in a wider variety of ways. February 1916 brought the first sinking of a ship, a British merchantman, by bombardment from the air. In July a French raid on the city of Karlsruhe inadvertently bombed a circus, killing 154 children.

The tank, unlike the airplane, came out of nowhere. In fact there was no such thing as a tank when the war began; only a few obscure visionaries had even imagined such a weapon, and none might have been built by the war's end if not for Winston Churchill. As early as 1914, impressed by the effectiveness of armed and armored cars in the early weeks of fighting (they would become useless as soon as the war of mobility ended), Churchill was asking the naval designers at the Admiralty to see if they could turn such vehicles into some kind of "trench-spanning" machine. Such a machine proved impracticable, there being no way to drive wheeled vehicles across trenches, but by January 1915 Churchill had found a different approach. Convinced that human flesh and bone were never going to be a match for artillery and machine guns, and encouraged by military engineers, Churchill sent a memorandum to Prime Minister Asquith proposing the development of "steam tractors with small armored shelters, in which men and machine guns could be placed, which would be bulletproof" and would "enable trenches to be crossed quite easily." Asquith passed the suggestion along to Kitchener, who was not enthusiastic but ordered that design work should begin. After another month, dissatisfied with the pace at which the war ministry was proceeding, Churchill assembled his own design team and funded it out of the Royal Navy's budget. By the time he was replaced as First Lord of the Admiralty, contracts had been let for the construction of eighteen prototype "landships."

The project slowed down drastically after Churchill was dismissed, and it probably would have died if he had not intervened to persuade his successor of its potential. In January 1916 a first working prototype—it would be nicknamed "Mother"—was ready for testing. It was a mother indeed, thirty-three feet long and eight feet wide and high. It carried a crew of eight with two machine guns and two cannon firing six-pound shells. It weighed twenty-eight tons and under optimum conditions could achieve a top speed of four miles per hour. It moved not on wheels but on caterpillar-type steel tracks capable of crossing trenches and crushing any barbed-wire barricades in its path.

As the first of the new vehicles came off the production line, the project was shrouded in deepest secrecy. Anticipating the questions that would be provoked by huge, strangely shaped objects concealed under tarpaulins, officials at the war office decided to say that they were special water carriers—mobile *tanks*—bound for Russia. That was the name that stuck. Among the names rejected were *landship* (too descriptive), *reservoir,* and *cistern.*

In the summer of 1916, when Churchill learned that Britain's (and the world's) first forty-nine tanks were being sent to France for use on the Somme, he was horrified. He thought it essential that the new weapon be kept out of action and unknown to the Germans until sufficient numbers could be assembled to produce a decisive breakthrough. He appealed first to Lloyd George and then to the prime minister. Asquith agreed that delay seemed advisable, but when he suggested it to Haig, he was politely ignored.

Chapter 22

Maelstrom

*"These were the happiest days of my life,
and my joy was shared by all of Russia."*
—General Alexei Brusilov

By the end of April casualties at Verdun totaled one hundred and thirty-three thousand for the French, one hundred and twenty thousand for the Germans. And the slaughter continued. The Germans were still doing most of the attacking, forcing their way onto the slopes of Le Mort Homme, taking part of the crest at one point but unable to hold on. General Max von Gallwitz, a skillful artillery commander and a veteran of the conquest of Serbia, arrived to take command on the west bank. Upon getting a look at the situation he declared that Le Mort Homme must indeed be taken, but that it never would be until the guns protecting it were cleared from an adjacent ridge called Côte 304. To that purpose he assembled more than five hundred heavy guns along a single mile of front, an even greater concentration of firepower than the Germans had mustered for their earlier attacks, and on May 3 he opened fire. The idea was the usual one—to blow the French away, so that the infantry could then move forward almost unopposed. As usual it didn't quite work.

Gallwitz's barrage continued through all the first day and all of the night that followed and another entire day beyond that. But though it reduced thousands of the defenders to body parts and buried many others alive, and though neither food nor water could be got through to the French troops cowering in the depths of their ruined bunkers and trenches, those troops were not annihilated and the ones who survived did not run. (The mystery of how men could hold their ground under such circumstances is explained in part by what awaited them in the rear: their own sergeants and junior officers, ready to shoot them on the spot if they tried to escape.)

The Germans captured Côte 304 in the end, taking possession of ten thousand rotting French corpses with it (the victors got double rations of tobacco as an escape from the smell), but they had needed three terrible days of fighting at close quarters to do so. They had broken off another important piece of the Verdun defensive system, taking another step toward gaining control of the west bank, but they had paid dearly for their success. What was worse, Le Mort Homme still stood unconquered in front of them, its guns still in action. But again the attackers were ordered to push on.

The Germans' nightmare deepened on May 8, before anyone had an opportunity to celebrate the conquest of Côte 304, when Fort Douaumont suddenly blew up. No one lived to explain what had happened, but there had been complaints that ammunition was not being handled properly as it was moved into and out of the fort. The prevailing theory, based on evidence collected after the disaster, is that it began when a group of Bavarian soldiers sheltering inside Douaumont opened a hand grenade to get a few thimblefuls of explosive for use in heating coffee. The resulting fire is believed to have ignited a cache of grenades, which in turn set off some flamethrower fuel tanks, which in turn started a chain reaction among stacked artillery shells. Whatever the cause, some six hundred and fifty German soldiers were killed. The few survivors, emerging from the depths of the fort with faces blackened by the blast, were immediately shot by German troops who had no idea what had happened inside and assumed that the fort had been overrun by French colonial units from Africa.

Spirits were not high, understandably, when the staff of the German Fifth Army met at the crown prince's headquarters on May 13 to discuss an east bank offensive that had been repeatedly delayed because of weather, the disruptive though otherwise unsuccessful attacks being launched repeatedly by Nivelle and Mangin, and ongoing artillery fire from Le Mort Homme. The crown prince, having given up on Verdun, was urging both Falkenhayn and the kaiser to call off not only the new offensive but the entire campaign. In doing so he was putting himself at odds with Knobelsdorf, who before the war had been his tutor in tactics, since August 1914 had been his chief of staff and mentor, and remained convinced that Verdun could be taken. He and Falkenhayn were encouraged by the false belief (mirrored by equally wrong French estimates of German casualties) that their enemies had by now lost well over two hundred thousand men.

A surprising unanimity emerged. Even Knobelsdorf conceded that enough was enough. He promised, in fact, to visit Falkenhayn that same day and try to persuade him to bring Verdun to an end. What happened next has never been explained. When he reached Falkenhayn's headquarters, Knobelsdorf did the opposite of what he had promised. He told Falkenhayn that the French guns at Le Mort Homme would soon be silenced and that the east bank offensive could then be safely resumed. Getting agreement from Falkenhayn, who by now had staked his place in history on Verdun, is not likely to have been difficult. No doubt Falkenhayn was mindful of the fact that the leading pessimists—the crown prince, Gallwitz, and others—all had opposed his elevation to commander in chief after the fall of Moltke. The crown prince, when he learned of Knobelsdorf's betrayal, could do nothing. Though heir to the imperial throne, he had been treated with disdain by the kaiser all his life. Even now, after a year and a half as an increasingly competent and serious-minded army commander, during which time he had gradually acquired the confidence to stand up to the iron-willed Knobelsdorf, he was kept at a distance from his father.

And so the carnage would continue. It would be accelerated, in fact, as Knobelsdorf hurried with Falkenhayn's encouragement to complete the capture of Verdun before Joffre and the British were ready with the offensive that they were obviously preparing along the Somme. The crown prince could only complain that "if Main Headquarters order it, I must not disobey, but I will not do it on my own responsibility."

The hopes of the optimists were about to be upended by the man who supposedly was their one great military ally, the Austrian Conrad. In the course of his career Conrad had been obliged to watch the new Kingdom of Italy encroach on the Austro-Hungarian territories to its north, and he had developed a nearly pathological hatred and contempt for the Italians. ("Dago dogs," he called them.) Since late 1915 he had been badgering Falkenhayn for help in mounting an offensive southward out of the Alps, a campaign that would destroy Italy's ability to wage war and restore Vienna to possession of the north Italian plain. Falkenhayn, his armies outnumbered on every front and his attention focused on Verdun, had brushed these appeals aside. He pointed out that while conquests in Italy might bring pleasure to Vienna, they could contribute little to the winning of the war. He had done so with unnecessary brusqueness. An outwardly cold figure, Falkenhayn had no close friends even among his fellow Junkers, and he disliked and distrusted Conrad. He demolished whatever possibility remained of a constructive working relationship with Conrad by keeping him in the dark. The Verdun offensive had come as more of a surprise to the Austrians than to the French. And though Falkenhayn's secretiveness had not been directed exclusively at Conrad (for valid reasons he had drawn such a curtain of security over his preparations that not even the commanders of the German armies west and south of Verdun knew exactly what was coming), the Austrian was deeply offended. He decided not only to proceed with an Italian campaign but to tell the Germans nothing of what he was doing.

His plan was to attack not at the Isonzo, already the scene of four battles and still the place where the Italians were concentrating most of their forces, but farther west, in the mountainous Trentino region northeast of Lake Garda. He began by sending more than a dozen of his best remaining divisions to an assembly point just north of the passes leading into Italy. From there they would be able to descend upon the farmlands and cities of Lombardy, lands and cities that in Conrad's view rightfully belonged to Vienna. Once in open country, the Austrians could wheel around and take the Italians on the Isonzo in the rear. Not for the first time and not for the last, Conrad smelled triumph. Six of the divisions committed to the Trentino were taken from Galicia, where he saw no possibility of trouble. The Russians had been thoroughly thrashed in Galicia in late 1915 (though mainly by German troops that Falkenhayn had since sent to Verdun), and their numerical advantage was smaller there than at any other point on the Eastern Front. If Conrad was even aware of the appointment of Alexei Brusilov as commander of Russia's southwestern front, he could not have regarded it as significant. He secured pro forma approval of his plan from the Hapsburg archduke who was his official commander in chief and assumed personal command of operations in Italy.

Conrad consistently asked his troops to do things that were beyond their capacity. If he was the strategic genius that some historians have called him, he was also less than a realist. He would venture forth not just to meet and fight his enemies but to crush them, to destroy them even when he was terribly outnumbered. And there was a pattern to his campaigns. They would begin thrillingly, with spectacular gains, and they never failed to end in disaster except when the Germans came to his rescue. Their cumulative result, by early 1916, was the loss of so many troops (more than two million casualties in 1915 alone, including seven hundred and seventy thousand men taken prisoner) that the Austro-Hungarian military was at the end of its ability to mount independent operations. Perhaps this accounts for Conrad's eagerness to invade Italy. Perhaps even he had lost confidence in his ability to accomplish anything on the more challenging Russian front.

In taking charge of the Trentino campaign, Conrad did not move his headquarters to or even near the places where the invasion force was being assembled. He did not even pay them a visit. He remained in Silesia, six hundred miles to the north, where he had happily settled with a new wife and all the comforts of prewar aristocratic life. He perfected his isolation by keeping all communications on a one-way basis, and by sending out detailed instructions as to exactly what the Austrian divisions in the Trentino were to do, and when and where, while ignoring questions and suggestions. He drew marks on maps showing which objectives each division was supposed to reach each day, and as far as he was concerned that was that. If following his instructions required the troops to climb through deep snow over a mountain crest when they could have reached the same objective by moving downhill through a valley, that too was that. No discussion was wanted or tolerated. When the chief of staff of the army group being formed in the Trentino requested permission to travel to Silesia and confer with Conrad, he was refused.

Conrad had wanted his offensive to begin almost immediately, in April, but on this point he had to bend to reality. Neither his troops nor their supply trains could get into position that quickly at that time of year, though hundreds froze to death or were buried in avalanches in the attempt. When the Austrians finally attacked on May 15, they were one hundred and fifty-seven thousand strong. The one hundred and seventeen thousand Italians standing in their path were rather easily pushed back. True to the Conrad pattern, the Austrians made progress for three weeks, sweeping southward on a broad front. By the end of May they had captured four thousand prisoners and 380 guns. The tsar, accustomed by now to urgent appeals from Joffre, found himself being begged for assistance by the King of Italy as well.

There were good reasons for Nicholas to pay heed, and they went beyond Verdun and the Austrian invasion of Italy. Everything seemed to be working in favor of the Central Powers. North of Paris, a German attack intended mainly to disrupt French and British preparations for their summer offensive had shocked Joffre by driving the British out of positions from which they had been preparing to take Vimy Ridge, an immense strongpoint dominating the plain of Artois to the west. The French had sacrificed mightily in establishing those positions, and had regarded them as secure when, in March, they handed them over to the British. Haig, though humiliated by the loss, was unable to organize a counterattack because so many of his resources were now being concentrated at the Somme.

At Verdun on May 22, "Butcher" Mangin, dreaming his dreams of glory and confident of success, opened an attack aimed at retaking Fort Douaumont. The bitterness of the struggle was becoming unnatural, almost psychotic. "Even the wounded refuse to abandon the struggle," a French staff officer would recall. "As though possessed by devils, they fight on until they fall senseless from loss of blood. A surgeon in a front-line post told me that, in a redoubt at the south part of the fort, of 200 French dead, fully half had more than two wounds. Those he was able to treat seemed utterly insane. They kept shouting war cries and their eyes blazed, and, strangest of all, they appeared indifferent to pain. At one moment anesthetics ran out owing to the impossibility of bringing forward fresh supplies through the bombardment. Arms, even legs, were amputated without a groan, and even afterward the men seemed not to have felt the shock. They asked for a cigarette or inquired how the battle was going."

In the five days preceding the start of his attack, Mangin's three hundred heavy guns had fired a thousand tons of explosives onto the quarter of a square mile centered on the fort, and the assault that followed broke into the fort's inner chambers. The Germans regrouped, however, and after days of hellish close-quarters underground combat drove the attackers out. The failure had been so complete and the costs so high—more than fifty-five hundred troops and 130 officers killed or wounded out of twelve thousand French attackers, another thousand taken prisoner—that Mangin was relieved of command. "You did your duty and I cannot blame you," Pétain told him resignedly. "You would not be the man you are if you had not acted in the way you did." Meanwhile, in almost equally intense fighting nearby, the Germans were forcing their way closer to Le Mort Homme.

By this time General Mikhail Alexeyev, still in place as the tsar's chief of staff in spite of having been the fallen Polivanov's partner in reform (he had survived, probably, by virtue of being at army headquarters and therefore remote from the intrigues of Petrograd), was asking his sector commanders when they could attack. Evert said predictably that he was able to do nothing. Brusilov surprised even Alexeyev by answering that his preparations were essentially complete, his four armies ready to go. It was decided that Brusilov would attack at the beginning of June. Evert, directly to his north, was coaxed into agreeing that he would send his immensely larger forces into action on June 13. He was reluctant in spite of having a million men under his command and two-thirds of Russia's heavy artillery.

On May 26 Joffre met with Haig, at the insistence of Pétain, and asked him to move up the date of the Somme offensive from mid-August. Haig disliked the idea, but when Joffre told him that if he waited another two and a half months "the French army could cease to exist," he yielded.

On May 31, for the first and last time in the war, the dreadnoughts of the British Grand Fleet and Germany's High Seas Fleet met in battle. The German commander, having concocted a plan to lure Britain's battle cruiser force southward away from the protection of dreadnoughts, had steamed into the North Sea the previous day with a mighty array of ships: sixteen dreadnoughts, six older battleships, five battle cruisers, eleven light cruisers, and sixty-one destroyers. Unknown to him, the British, having intercepted and decoded his radio messages, were coming at him with a hundred and fifty ships that outnumbered him in every category.

They met near Jutland, a peninsula on the Danish coast, and what followed was the greatest sea battle in history until the Second World War. It was a complex and confused affair, unfolding in five distinct stages as the fleets separated and converged and changed directions again and again, and it was marked by serious mistakes and much ingenuity on both sides.

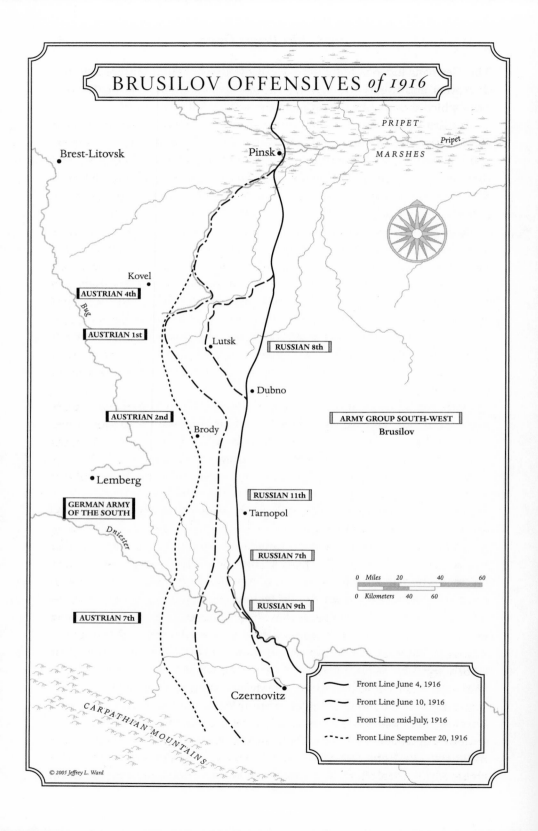

BRUSILOV OFFENSIVES *of 1916*

PRIPET

Pripet

Brest-Litovsk

Pinsk

MARSHES

Kovel

AUSTRIAN 4th

AUSTRIAN 1st

Lutsk

RUSSIAN 8th

Dubno

AUSTRIAN 2nd

Brody

ARMY GROUP SOUTH-WEST
Brusilov

•Lemberg

GERMAN ARMY
OF THE SOUTH

Dniester

RUSSIAN 11th

Tarnopol

RUSSIAN 7th

| 0 | Miles | 20 | | 40 | | 60 |

| 0 | Kilometers | 40 | | 60 |

RUSSIAN 9th

AUSTRIAN 7th

Czernovitz

———— Front Line June 4, 1916

– – – – Front Line June 10, 1916

–·–·– Front Line mid-July, 1916

········· Front Line September 20, 1916

CARPATHIAN MOUNTAINS

© 2005 Jeffrey L. Ward

The Germans lost one battleship, one battle cruiser, four light cruisers, five destroyers, and twenty-five hundred men before withdrawing to home ports from which they would never again venture.

The British losses were heavier: three battle cruisers, three cruisers, and eight destroyers, sixty-two hundred men. Technically the battle was a draw, and strategically it changed nothing. The British had been outgunned and outmaneuvered. Though the public was told of a glorious victory, and British fleet commander John Jellicoe was celebrated as a hero, the Admiralty knew better.

At about the same time the Germans took possession of Le Mort Homme at last, eliminating the artillery threat from that quarter. Now they were free to shift over to the defensive on the west bank and start the climactic east bank offensive that was going, according to Knobelsdorf, to carry them into Verdun. By June 1, with the main force for the new offensive still being put in place, German units making an exploratory attack fought their way up to the final approaches to Fort Vaux. This fortress, smaller than Douaumont but formidable nevertheless, was now the last major strongpoint standing between the Germans and the city. Everything needed for the capture of Verdun appeared to be falling into place.

One blow after another was falling on the Entente. The Austrians were out of the Alps and on open ground. They appeared to be positioned to encircle the Italians retreating before them. In Flanders the Germans captured a piece of high ground called Mont Sorel two and a half miles south of the heaps of broken stone that once had been the beautiful city of Ypres.

But then it was June 4, and Brusilov ordered his guns to open fire. Brusilov's preparations had been imaginative and aggressive, with everything focused on taking the Austrians by surprise across such a broad front that they would find it impossible to react effectively. His use of air and ground reconnaissance to identify enemy weak points was without precedent in Russian military operations, and his efforts to deceive the Austrians had gone so far as to include the painting of phantom trenches on the ground behind his lines. His barrage lasted only one day, its purpose not to obliterate the Austrians' defenses but to neutralize their artillery and clear away their barbed wire. It did both things. His infantry, when it attacked on June 5, found the Austrians in confusion. Its advance stunned them with its scope, extending as it did along a line of more than two hundred and fifty miles. Brusilov's idea was that by attacking everywhere, he was sure to find holes somewhere, and he had moved his reserves (scant though they were) close enough to the front that they could exploit opportunities as soon as any appeared. On point after point—the brevity of his bombardment, his refusal even in the face of appeals from Alexeyev to mass his troops on a narrow piece of the front, his willingness to attack forces equal to his own in numbers—he ignored what had become by now the tactical orthodoxy of the Great War. And the result was, from the first hour, a success of almost incredible magnitude. The Austro-Hungarian Fourth Army disintegrated when hit; seventy-one thousand of its men, more than half of the army were killed, wounded, or captured. The Seventh was wrecked even more completely, losing one hundred and thirty-three thousand men. It was the same almost everywhere; after three days Brusilov found himself in possession of three hundred thousand prisoners. Before the end of the first week, more than half of the Austrian defenders had become casualties.

The remnants (most of them Slavs, the more trusted Austrian units having been sent off to Italy) fled back toward the Carpathians. They were incapable of restoring their lines both because they had no reserves—what could have been their reserve force was south of the Alps—and because their senior commanders were absent. They were at a Hapsburg castle in the faraway town of Teschen, partying with Conrad.

June 4 was, by what turned out to be a singular stroke of bad luck for the Austrians, the birthday of the nonentity who was titular commander in chief of all the Austro-Hungarian armies. This was Archduke Frederick, a nephew of Emperor Franz Joseph and one of the several Hapsburg grandees holding ceremonial posts in the upper reaches of the army. A great celebration had been arranged in honor of the occasion, and Conrad, confident that the impending conquest of Italy would give the empire and its dynasty much to celebrate, had attended not only with senior members of his own staff but also with generals from Galicia. The festivities were still in progress when word arrived that the Russians had suddenly become active on their southern front. Conrad serenely assured all present that there was no reason for concern.

It did not take long for him to learn otherwise. Two days after the party the Italian commander in chief, General Cadorna, used troops taken from his fifth (and brief and unsuccessful) Isonzo offensive to counterattack the Austrians who had descended out of the Trentino. He was successful this time and Conrad's Italian campaign came to its end. In Galicia, Brusilov had shattered the Austro-Hungarian forces on his flanks and was positioned to encircle the center. Only one thing was stopping him: he lacked the necessary manpower. Many times the number of troops needed to do the job were with Evert in the northwest, but Evert remained unwilling either to attack or to let go of any of his divisions. June 13, the day on which Evert had pledged himself to an attack, came and went without action. This was a mortal failure. Max Hoffmann wrote afterward that if Evert had attacked, "the crisis

General Luigi Cadorna (right)
Launched attack after attack at River Isonzo.

would probably have developed into the complete defeat of the Austro-Hungarian Army." Instead, the Germans opposite Evert's army group remained unengaged and free to shift southward against Brusilov.

Even without Evert's assistance, a conclusive defeat of Austria-Hungary seemed inevitable. Conrad, thoroughly alarmed, hurried by train not to the front but to Berlin, where he reported the end of his Italian adventure and begged Falkenhayn for help. Falkenhayn responded even more coldly than usual, promising nothing. But the German Army of the South was still in Galicia, and now it hit the Russian Eighth Army at exactly the point where the Brusilov offensive was achieving its deepest penetration. Brusilov, his troops exhausted and the Russian supply system failing him in its usual fashion, had to halt to regroup.

He had achieved tremendous things. He had destroyed two Austro-Hungarian armies and all but wrecked others, delivering a deeply damaging blow to the shaky morale of Vienna's armies. His hordes of prisoners included thousands of officers, and he had captured hundreds of machine guns and pieces of artillery. The ground taken by his troops was not crucially important when measured against the vastness of the eastern theater, but with his enemies in such disarray he faced rich opportunities for further conquest. He had redeemed every pledge that Russia had ever made to its allies. If he had not stopped the Austro-Hungarian descent upon Italy—Cadorna had seen to that—he had made certain that the Austrians could not reinforce the Trentino campaign.

No less important was the sense of confidence that he had restored to the armies of the tsar. "This town today is a veritable maelstrom of war," a British correspondent wrote of the entry of Brusilov's troops into newly conquered Lutsk. "From not many miles away, by night and day, comes an almost uninterrupted roar of heavy gunfire, and all day long the main street is filled with the rumble and clatter of caissons, guns, and transports going forward on one side, while on the other side is an unending line of empty caissons returning, mingled with wounded coming back in every conceivable form of vehicle, and in among these at breakneck speed dart motorcycles carrying dispatches from the front. The weather is dry and hot, and the lines of the road are visible for miles by the clouds of dust from the plodding feet of the soldiery and the transport. As the retreat from Warsaw was a review of the Russian armies in reverse, so is Lutsk today a similar spectacle of the Muscovite armies advancing; but now all filled with high hopes and their morale is at the highest pitch."

Perhaps most important of all, Brusilov had suddenly and terribly complicated Falkenhayn's manpower problems at a point when the Germans seemed once again on the brink of forcing their way into Verdun. Knowing that an Entente offensive on the Somme was drawing near, Falkenhayn had been planning a preemptive attack. Now, thanks to Brusilov, that plan had to be abandoned. As scornful as he was of Conrad, as reluctant as he was to use scarce resources to pull Conrad's chestnuts out of a fire that Conrad himself had made possible, Falkenhayn had no choice but to start transferring troops—eighteen divisions, ultimately—away from the Western Front.

But Brusilov too was in a difficult position. He had paid a great price for his victory: three hundred thousand men lost, huge stores of ammunition expended, and other supplies depleted to the point of exhaustion. And Brusilov, more than any of his enemies, more even than the Austro-Hungarians, lacked any hope of making good his losses. With the war ministry in the hands of an inoffensive but superannuated general whose only qualification was his unquestioning loyalty to the Romanov family, the Russian military administration was barely functioning except for the benefit of profiteers. In a real sense Russia's collapse and the revolution that followed stemmed directly from Petrograd's inability to resupply Brusilov and from Evert's failure to give him support. Balancing the Russian calamity was Ludendorff's refusal to send troops from his base in the north to help either Falkenhayn at Verdun or Conrad in Galicia. It can be said in Ludendorff's defense that he continued to be faced with Russian armies that outnumbered his and had to be expected to attack.

As events on four fronts—Verdun, the Somme, Galicia, and Italy—began to interlock, the strain was intense everywhere. The Italian government fell as controversy erupted over Cadorna's handling of the Trentino offensive. For the first time in the war the French National Assembly was forced to meet in secret session, the opposition demanding answers about Joffre's strategy.

The whole month of June was a time of terrible and sometimes weird events. The British were shocked to learn that a cruiser bound for Russia had struck a mine near the coast of Scotland, and that among those lost was Earl Kitchener of Khartoum. The ever-amazing Conrad, many of his armies barely functional, proposed to an incredulous Falkenhayn a giant offensive aimed at surrounding and destroying Brusilov's army group. He was not just ignored but laughed at; even his Austrian colleagues were learning to despise him. And as if there were not enough active fronts already, an Arab revolt was breaking out with British support in the desert wastes at the southern end of the Ottoman Empire, while at Salonika French General Sarrail was nearly ready to take his force northward into the Balkans.

Fort Vaux, the all-but-final obstacle on the Germans' long and bloody road down the east bank of the Meuse to Verdun, surrendered after days of bitter and brutal combat. Its defense had been so heroic that the French commander, who had given up at last only because his men were literally dying of thirst, was honored personally by the crown prince, who gave him a sword to replace one lost in the fight. The captive Major Raynal returned the favor by noting that young Wilhelm Hohenzollern was "not the monkey that our caricaturists have made him out to be." The fall of Fort Vaux left only one final small strongpoint, Fort Souville, between the Germans and the city. It cleared the way for the climactic offensive that Knobelsdorf had been hungering for since April.

The last of Falkenhayn's reserves went into this attack: thirty thousand men on a front of just three miles against an objective that, if taken, would leave them only two and a half miles from the central citadel at Verdun. Knobelsdorf was so confident of success that he invited the kaiser to join him. June 22 was reserved for the artillery barrage, which was as savage as

ever and ended with the firing of shells containing a new kind of gas, phosgene, that killed every living thing, even plants and insects. "Our heads are
buzzing, we have had enough," a French lieutenant somehow was able to
write in his journal while this attack was in process. "Myself, Agnel, and my
orderly are squashed in a hole, protecting ourselves from splinters with our
packs. Numb and dazed, without saying a word, and with our hearts pounding, we await the shell that will destroy us. The wounded are increasing in
numbers around us. These poor devils not knowing where to go come to us,
believing that they will be helped. What can we do? There are clouds of
smoke, the air is unbreathable. There's death everywhere. At our feet, the
wounded groan in a pool of blood; two of them, more seriously hit are
breathing their last. One, a machine-gunner, has been blinded, with one eye
hanging out of its socket and the other torn out: in addition he has lost a leg.
The second has no face, an arm blown off, and a horrible wound in the stomach. Moaning and suffering atrociously one begs me, 'Lieutenant, don't let
me die. Lieutenant, I'm suffering, help me.' The other, perhaps more gravely
wounded and nearer death, implores me to kill him with these words,
'Lieutenant, if you don't want to, give me your revolver!' Frightful, terrible
moments, while the cannons harry us and we are splattered with mud and
earth by the shells. For hours, these groans and supplications continue until,
at 6 P.M., they die before our eyes without anyone being able to help them."

The infantry attacked at five A.M. on June 23, breaking through the center
of the French lines. Pétain, learning of this, decided that in order to save hundreds of artillery pieces from capture he was going to have to abandon the
east bank. Trenches were being dug, and barricades erected, in the streets of
Verdun.

But the Germans were paying the price of advancing on a narrow front:
they were exposed to murderous fire on both flanks while aircraft strafed
them from above. The forward edge of the advance got to within twelve
hundred yards of the crest of the last ridge before Verdun, but that was as far
as it could go. At the end of two days of horror for the men on both sides,
the Germans had to give up. This failure too came down to a shortage of
troops. Just days before, faced with telegram after telegram detailing the
emergency in the southeast, Falkenhayn had decided that he had no choice
but to begin pulling divisions out of Verdun and getting them onto trains
bound for Galicia. Just one of those divisions, if thrown into the final lunge
at Souville, might have swung the balance. That no division was available has
to be considered part of Brusilov's achievement.

The French, at the climax, had appeared to have no chance of holding on.
Joffre's view of the situation is clear in his decision to dispatch to Verdun four
of the divisions he had been saving for the Somme. Everywhere there was

panic and an almost frenzied shuttling of troops. Conrad ordered the transfer of eight divisions from Italy to Galicia, and a desperate Aristide Briand, Premier of France, traveled to Haig's headquarters to beg him to begin his offensive on the Somme. He must have been powerfully persuasive: Haig began his bombardment that afternoon. Pétain, when he telephoned Joffre to report that he was removing his artillery from the east bank, was told of the start of action on the Somme and ordered to stand fast. He did so, and with what must have seemed miraculous speed the pressure lifted.

The fight for Verdun—a prize that would have cost the French little if they had lost it and done the Germans little good if they had won it—was at an end. Falkenhayn diverted still more troops and guns to the east.

For the French, at least where Verdun was concerned, the worst was over. But a nightmare of a different kind, the Battle of the Somme, had just begun.

THE JEWS OF GERMANY

THE MIDPOINT OF THE WAR BROUGHT A GREAT TURNING point in the long history of Jews in Germany. Until 1916 that history had been largely a striving for acceptance, for integration, for official and popular recognition that a Jew could be as good a citizen as any Christian and deserved to be treated accordingly. After 1916 many Jews abandoned such hopes.

What precipitated the change was less the war itself, during which more than a hundred thousand German Jews became soldiers (German cemeteries along the Western Front are studded with markers bearing the Star of David), than the government's attitude toward its Jewish troops. Specifically, it was the Prussian minister of war's October order of a census to determine how many Jews were in every army unit, how many had not yet been called up, and how many had been released from service or found to be unfit.

News of this census came as a shock to the Jewish community. It gave rise everywhere to a painful question: *Why?* Jewish volunteers had rallied to the colors at the start of the war. Jews were putting millions of marks into war bonds, and Jewish industrialists and scientists were making important contributions to Germany's ability to fight. Why were *they* being singled out for investigation? The answer, for many, was that their loyalty counted for nothing, and that it was folly to expect anything else.

To say that Germany at the start of the war was a culture steeped in anti-Semitism is to say nothing that sets it apart from the other countries of Europe. The whole Western world was so anti-Semitic that its prejudice was taken for granted: it was simply assumed, at every level of society, that Jews were not only different but different in ways that made them a problem. Germany was not the worst in this regard. That distinction belongs to Russia, which barred almost all Jews from citizenship, regarded its Jewish population as a threat to security, and continued to single the Jews out for atrocious mistreatment after the start of the war. France was not nearly that bad, Britain was a paragon of tolerance by comparison, but in every country to be a Jew was to be an alien to a greater or lesser extent. In all of them there were outbreaks of violence against Jews during the course of the war.

The German situation had always been particularly complicated and particularly marked with hypocrisy. As early as 1812, at the climax of the Napoleonic wars, the Kingdom of Prussia had issued an Emancipation Edict granting citizenship to Jews. In its way and for its time this edict was modestly progressive, but only within narrow limits. It excluded Jews from serving as military officers—that was the preserve of the Junkers—and from the government bureaucracy, including the judicial system. The rationale was that the Christian citizens of a Christian nation should not have to take orders from Jews.

In 1869, with Germany midway through its wars of unification, another new law guaranteed that all government appointments would be made without regard to religion. Formally, this meant that every career, including the army, was open to every qualified candidate. In reality, it meant almost nothing. Whenever a Jew applied for a position, reasons were found for selecting someone else. It meant even less after the creation of the German Empire, when exclusion became unofficial policy.

The intensity of the problem is explained by the peculiar nature of the Prussian state, and by the Junkers' belief that the state belonged to *them.* Anyone who was not a Junker was an outsider, and in the last decades of the nineteenth century Berlin launched campaigns of persecution against the Catholics who made up a third of the Reich's population, against Social Democrats with their demands for democracy, and against ethnic Poles. And of course, against the Jews. All these groups were systematically excluded. Even to have a Social Democratic relative was enough to close the doors of advancement to an able and ambitious young man.

Jews, meanwhile, were distinguishing themselves in every field that was open to them: the professions, industry, banking, science, journalism, and the arts. With every generation their prosperity improved. In Prussia more than five hundred out of every ten thousand Jewish boys became university students; the corresponding numbers were fifty-eight for Protestants and thirty-three for Catholics. Some Jews became rich, others prominent. But their very success bred trouble. When the economy declined or things went badly for Berlin on the international stage, "the Jews" were commonly blamed.

From 1885 to 1914 not one Jew was given a commission in the Prussian army. (The same was not true in Catholic Bavaria, which maintained a separate army.) Again the problem was the Junker mentality. The expansion of the military establishment during the prewar arms race made it impossible to fill the officer corps with sons of the landed aristocracy—there weren't enough of them. Others had to be admitted. Increasingly if grudgingly, the offspring of the new urban middle class were deemed to be acceptable—

assuming that their families were sufficiently respectable and unimpeach-
ably Lutheran. Jews continued to be unacceptable. They applied for commissions, they were often superlatively well qualified in terms of education
and other criteria, the law said that religion was not to be taken into
account—and without exception, decade after decade, every candidate
was turned away.

This exclusion became a major symbolic issue for Germany's Jews,
especially for those most determined to win acceptance by the community
at large. Abandoning the hope that the regular army might ever accept
Jews, they focused on the reserves. And with good reason. Reserve commissions carried extraordinarily high prestige in Prussia. They provided
access to the best society and could be essential for advancement in civilian careers. They, more than anything else, represented inclusion.

Jewish leaders complained, petitioned, and tried to use their influence.
They found support in liberal non-Jewish groups, and the question was
debated repeatedly in the Reichstag. But one war minister after another
refused to acknowledge that a problem existed. Whenever a particular
case was offered as proof of flagrant discrimination, whoever was war minister at the time would order an investigation (which meant nothing more
than asking local military officials to decide if they themselves had broken
the law) and report that, regrettably, the candidate in question had proved
to be unfit.

August 1914 seemed to change everything. Kaiser Wilhelm, who before
the war had called the Jews "the curse of my country," proclaimed the
dawn of *Burgfrieden,* a new era in which all Germans were accepted fully
and all would join together to save Germany from her foes. There were six
hundred thousand Jews in Germany at the time, about one percent of the
population, and with no important exceptions they embraced the war.
Even the small Zionist minority accepted it as a means of liberating the
Jews of Poland and giving the Russians a lesson. This, Jewish leaders said,
was the hour they had been waiting for. And there seemed to be reason for
hope. Jews were made officers—though they were not to be promoted to
any rank higher than captain.

From the start, the conservatives were not happy with *Burgfrieden.* They
had always sought national unity through the exclusion of anyone not
regarded as a real German, and they warned that the changes brought by
the war would lead to the end of Germany as a truly German state. But
early in the war the people holding such views were often prevented from
publishing or speaking in public—the first suppression of anti-Semitic
propaganda in German history. Again the Jews were encouraged, but the
new era proved to be a short one. As the war dragged on and life became

difficult and the hope of victory faded, the inevitable search for scapegoats began. Capitalism was to blame for Germany's predicament, and the capitalists were Jews. Or socialism was to blame, and the socialists were Jews. Jewish profiteers were draining the nation's lifeblood, Jewish liberals were contaminating the young with democratic ideas, Jews who cared more about Jews than about Germany were trying to turn the Fatherland into a refuge for undesirables from Poland.

Disillusionment set in, affecting Jews at the front no less than those at home. They had gone to war filled with expectations that by sharing in the national sacrifice, they would dissolve the barriers that had so long kept them apart from other Germans. What they found, more often than not, was an unbridgeable cultural gulf between themselves and the Gentile soldiers. What they did not find, usually, was acceptance as *German* troops.

This was the climate in which War Minister Adolf Wild von Hohenborn ordered his census. It was supposed to be secret, but it soon became known everywhere and aroused an angry Jewish reaction. Within the army it was widely misinterpreted; officers who received it sometimes reacted by sending all their Jewish soldiers immediately to the front. Hohenborn's motives, ironically, appear not to have been malign. He was responding to a rising chorus of complaints that the Jews were shirking, using their notorious wiles to avoid doing their share. He could simply have joined the chorus—plenty of other officials, the kaiser included, were doing exactly that. Instead he decided to establish, in coldly objective terms, what the facts were. And the facts turned out to be very different from the complaints: the Jews were doing their share and more. By the time these findings were disclosed, Hohenborn was no longer war minister. His successor, trying to quiet the furor, stated rather obscurely that "the behavior of Jewish soldiers and fellow citizens during the war gave no cause for the order by my predecessor, and thus cannot be connected with it."

But there was no apology, nobody in a position of authority said anything about the Jews who were fighting and dying, and much damage had been done. The Jewish troops continued to do their duty—twelve thousand would be killed—but the dream of 1914 was dead. In its place was fear of what Germany would be like after the war was over.

"A war after the war stands before us," said the newspaper of the Central Association of German Citizens of Jewish Faith, long an optimistic voice for full Jewish integration into German life. "When the weapons are laid to rest, the war's storm will not have ended for us."

Chapter 23

✠

The Somme

*"When we started to fire we just had to load
and reload. They went down in their hundreds.
We didn't have to aim, we just fired into them."*

—German machine-gunner

If it had been possible to win the war in the west by sheer force, by overpowering the enemy with manpower and firepower, the Battle of the
Somme would have done the job. The British and French attacked a German
army that they outnumbered by an enormous margin. They had an equal
advantage in artillery and total control of the air. They were backed by all the
resources that modern industrial economies could put at the disposal of their
soldiers.

First conceived in the closing days of 1915 as one part of a great combination of attacks by Britain and France and Russia and Italy on every one of
Europe's many fronts, the battle was long in the making. The whole first half
of 1916 was devoted to building up great masses of armaments, to bringing
forward the green new armies that Kitchener had recruited in 1914, to literally laying the groundwork (in the form of new roads and railways and lines
of communication) for a success so complete that the enemy would be
crushed and stalemate would be transformed into sudden, final, total victory.

As originally planned, the offensive was to be a French show primarily,
with forty of Joffre's divisions providing most of its weight and the British in
a secondary role. But the unexpected upheavals of the first half of 1916—
Verdun first, then Lake Naroch, and finally Conrad's offensive in Italy and
Brusilov's in Galicia—disrupted everything on all sides. As Verdun went on
and on, most of the French army was run through Falkenhayn's killing
machine. As unit after unit was chewed up, Joffre gradually (and resentfully)
found himself unable to assemble even half the number of troops he had orig-

inally wanted for the Somme. Lake Naroch meanwhile paralyzed the will of the men commanding Russia's central and northern fronts; Conrad's Trentino campaign rendered Italy incapable of a summer offensive; and the Brusilov offensive (undertaken, it should be remembered, in response to French appeals for help) had a similar impact on the Russians in the south.

The British alone were untouched. Of all the Entente commanders, only Haig remained free to proceed almost as if no battles were happening anywhere. And Haig cannot be accused of failing to make use of his great gift of time. He devoted the first half of 1916 to two things: to preparing for a fresh offensive in Flanders, where he hoped to join with the Royal Navy in retaking Belgium's Channel ports, and to getting ready (reluctantly at first) for the offensive that Joffre was determined to launch on the Somme. As the so-called "Kitchener's armies" arrived on the continent, they were alternated between routine line duty on quiet sectors of the front and training that included mock assaults on simulated enemy trenches. By June Haig had half a million men on and behind the Somme front. New guns were arriving as well, along with mountains of the shells being bought from America and produced by Lloyd George's ministry of munitions. Along with them came all the bewildering panoply of equipment and supplies required by a modern army readying itself for action. Seven thousand miles of telephone lines were buried to keep them from being cut by German artillery, and 120 miles of pipe were laid to get water to the assembling troops. Ten squadrons of aircraft—185 planes—were brought in to drive off the suddenly outclassed German Fokkers and serve as spotters for the gun crews as they registered on their assigned targets. Tunnelers were digging out cavities under the German lines and packing them with explosives. It was a massive undertaking, all done as efficiently as anyone could have expected, and ultimately Haig was responsible for every bit of it.

The planning of the attack was his responsibility too, and there lay the rub. Haig had eighteen divisions on the Somme by early summer, and two-thirds of them were used to form a new Fourth Army under General Sir Henry Rawlinson, who had been with the BEF from the start of the war. Rawlinson was a career infantryman—the only British army commander on the Somme not, like Haig, from the cavalry—and his ideas about how to conduct the coming offensive differed sharply from those of his chief. Haig wanted a breakthrough. He was confident that his artillery could not merely weaken but annihilate the German front line, that the infantry would be able to push through almost unopposed, and that this would clear the way for tens of thousands of cavalry to reach open country, turn northward, and throw the whole German defensive system into terminal disorder.

Rawlinson, by contrast, had drawn the same lessons as Falkenhayn from a year and a half of stalemate. He thought breakthrough impossible, and that trying to achieve it could only result in painful and unnecessary losses. He opted for a battle of attrition, one intended less to conquer territory (there being no important strategic targets anywhere near the Somme front, actually) than to kill as many Germans as possible. To this end he favored "bite and hold" tactics similar to those with which Falkenhayn had begun at Verdun. Such tactics involved settling for a limited objective with each attack, capturing just enough ground to spark a counterattack, and then using artillery to obliterate the enemy's troops as they advanced. Rawlinson and Haig never resolved their differences; rather, they opened the battle without coming to an understanding on what they were trying to do or how it should be done.

The men of the Fourth Army were as new to war as they were eager for it after eighteen months of training. Haig was untroubled by their lack of experience. In this regard it was he who was like Falkenhayn at the start of Verdun. He had fifteen hundred pieces of artillery, one for every seventeen yards of the eighteen miles of curving front along which the BEF would be attacking. Between them the British and French had 1,655 light, 933 medium, and 393 heavy guns. The corresponding numbers on the German side were 454, 372, and eighteen. Haig's confidence that his batteries could paralyze the German defenses before his infantry climbed out of its trenches was communicated down the chain of command. "You will be able to go over the top with a walking stick, you will not need rifles," one officer told his troops. "When you get to Thiepval [a village that was one of the first day's objectives] you will find the Germans all dead. Not even a rat will have survived."

Every part of the attack was planned to the minute. Every unit was told what points it would reach in the first hour and exactly where it would be at the end of the day. And though in the end Haig did not have quite as many weeks to prepare as he wanted—the emergency at Verdun made that impossible—the tightening of the schedule still left him with time to do everything needed. It had no effect on the conduct of the campaign, or on his serene confidence that the machine gun, "a much-overrated weapon," could be overcome by men on horseback. He was ready enough by June 24, when French Premier Briand came to implore him for help, to begin his artillery barrage.

The French had one corps of Ferdinand Foch's Army of the North positioned on the north bank of the Somme, immediately south of Rawlinson, and five others arrayed along an eight-mile line extending southward from the river. They were even better equipped than the British with artillery, especially heavy artillery, a weapon in which France had been deficient at the start of the war. Their assignment was a holding attack intended to make it impos-

Field Marshal Sir Douglas Haig
Commander of the British
Expeditionary Force
*Attacked often—and continued
his attacks too long.*

sible for the Germans opposite to shift their reserves (of which they had virtually none) northward to stop Rawlinson's advance.

Facing them all, bracing for the attack that was all too obviously coming, was a stripped-down German Second Army under General Fritz von Below. Below had only seven divisions along the entire front, five north of the river and two to the south. Because they were so few, all of them were up on the front line—a dangerous arrangement, but an unavoidable one in light of how badly the Germans were outnumbered. The particular thinness of the German line opposite the French was Falkenhayn's doing: confident that Verdun had left the French incapable of attacking anywhere else, he had instructed Below to deploy his troops accordingly. But the German preparations had been superb, and Falkenhayn was responsible for that too. Under his instructions the Germans had been doing much more than merely digging trenches. The infrastructure they had put in place was a marvel of engineering, designed so that all the strongpoints protected each other and any enemy penetration could be quickly isolated. Beneath and behind the trenches, thirty feet and more deep in the chalk that underlay the rich topsoil of Picardy, the Germans had created what was almost an underground city, a long chain of chambers and passageways reinforced with concrete and steel. This human beehive was equipped with electric lighting, running water, and ventilation and was

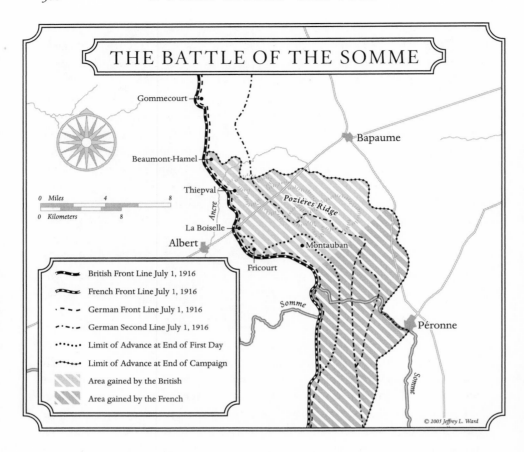

THE BATTLE OF THE SOMME

Gommecourt

Bapaume

Beaumont-Hamel

Thiepval

Pozières Ridge

0 Miles   4   8

0 Kilometers   8

Ancre

La Boiselle

Albert

Montauban

Fricourt

Somme

British Front Line July 1, 1916

French Front Line July 1, 1916

German Front Line July 1, 1916

German Second Line July 1, 1916

Limit of Advance at End of First Day

Limit of Advance at End of Campaign

Area gained by the British

Area gained by the French

Péronne

Somme

© 2005 Jeffrey L. Ward

impervious to all but the most powerful artillery. Above it, slowly crumbling under Haig's barrage but still largely ready for use when the time came, were three (and in some places more) lines of trenches that together formed a defensive zone up to five miles deep.

Haig's plan called for five days of bombardment, but when rain began to fall on June 26 and continued into June 28 a two-day postponement had to be ordered to allow the ground to dry. The intensity of the barrage was reduced so that the supply of shells would not run too low. Still, it remained a staggering display of power. By the time the troops went over the top on July 1, more than 1.5 million shells had descended upon the German lines—a quarter of a million on the morning of the attack alone. A ton of munitions had been dropped on every square yard of German front line with the same spirit-crushing results that both sides had been experiencing at Verdun for more than four months. "Shall I live till morning?" one of Below's soldiers wrote in his diary. "Haven't we had enough of this frightful horror? Five days and five nights now this hell concert has lasted. One's head is like a madman's; the tongue sticks to the roof of the mouth. Almost nothing to eat and nothing to drink. No sleep. All contact with the outer world cut off. No sign of life from home nor can we send any news to our loved ones. What anxiety they must feel about us. How long is this going to last?"

The Tommies and poilus looked on happily, rejoicing in the thought that nothing could survive such an inferno. And indeed the Germans were hurt, and badly. Nearly seven thousand of them died under the shellfire, and many of their guns were destroyed. Even for the survivors, the underground city became a chamber of horrors in which they could only cower in the dark, unable to bury the dead bodies around them, waiting for death. But tens of thousands survived, especially opposite the British lines. Somehow they remained sane, watching through periscopes for signs of movement on the other side. Their artillery was likewise invisible. Weeks before, the German gunners had taken the range of the British and French trenches and likely lines of advance. Then they too had gone underground, their weapons concealed in woods and covered with camouflage. Their unbroken silence made it seem certain that they too had been destroyed.

The attack, when it came, could scarcely have been less of a surprise. The area through which the front snaked is open, rolling farmland. Though the landscape was studded with woods, there were none in no-man's-land, which was clear at almost every point, open to view. Late on the afternoon of June 30 the British units chosen to lead the assault were mustered out of the villages where they had been waiting and started toward the front. As they filled the roads, they became obvious to German observers on high points behind the front. Great columns of cavalry came forward as well. It took no Napoleon to perceive the meaning of it all. As the Germans settled in for another night of agony, they did so knowing that the hour of truth was at hand.

Midsummer nights are short in the north of Europe, and in July in Picardy the sky is dimly alight by five A.M. This is also a region of predawn mists and low-lying fog. Haig could have kicked off his offensive in the early light; had he done so, his troops might have crossed no-man's-land almost unseen. But the French had insisted on a later start, and Haig found it necessary to comply. At exactly 6:25 A.M., as on all the days preceding, the British ended their usual early-morning cease-fire and started blasting away as usual. They had established this routine as a way of lulling the Germans into thinking that July 1 was going to be just another day. But this was an unlikely conclusion for them to reach, considering what they had seen the evening before.

Ten minutes before the start of the attack, at 7:20 A.M., the British detonated a huge mine that they had excavated under a German redoubt at Hawthorne Ridge, near the village of Beaumont-Hamel. "The ground where

I stood gave a mighty convulsion," a distant British observer reported. "It rocked and swayed . . . Then, for all the world like a gigantic sponge, the earth rose in the air to a height of hundreds of feet. Higher and higher it rose, and with a horrible grinding roar the earth fell back on itself, leaving in its place a mountain of smoke." Terrifying and deadly as the explosion was, it was too limited in its effects to justify the final alert that it sent to the Germans up and down the line. And now it was the turn of the British to receive a signal—a chilling one. The supposedly extinct German artillery suddenly opened up, its fire falling with stunning accuracy on the trenches in which the British soldiers waited. Obviously the Germans were still out there. Obviously they still had guns, and obviously those guns were registered for maximum effect. Ten remaining British mines, none of them as big as the one at Hawthorne Ridge, went off at 7:28. Two minutes later whistles blew and scores of thousands of British troops hauled themselves up onto exposed ground and started toward what every one of them must have hoped was nothing more than the dirt tombs of their enemies.

At this same moment the British artillery, which on every previous morning had continued until 7:45, was lifted off the German front line and shifted to more distant targets. There was supposed to be a creeping barrage for the infantry to advance behind, but it was badly managed and moved too quickly. In short order most of the British shells were falling in the German rear. The shift provided the defenders with yet another alert. As soon as they saw—felt, heard—that the barrage had moved beyond them, they scrambled up out of their hidden chambers, took their positions, and unlimbered their machine guns.

Even up on the surface, the extent of artillery damage turned out to be astonishingly limited. What seemed most inexplicable, the German barbed wire and the wooden posts from which it was strung remained in place almost everywhere. It provided the defenders, as wire always did where it was left uncut, with a nearly impenetrable protective barrier.

For the attackers, who were forced to converge wherever they could find openings, it was a death trap. At this point certain hard truths about the fantastic British bombardment became apparent. Huge numbers of shells—as many as a third by some estimates, almost certainly hundreds of thousands—had been duds that failed to detonate. Too many of the shells that did explode contained shrapnel rather than high explosives, and more than half of the others were too small to penetrate the German dugouts. Even the fuses had turned out to be defective. Part of the problem was a collapse of quality control as Lloyd George rushed the British factories, many of them

Previous pages: British troops amid the mined landscape of the Western Front employing unskilled workers, to increase shell production. Another was Haig's decision to keep many of his heaviest guns in Flanders, where he continued to hope for a coastal offensive. What turned these misfortunes into a scandal was the refusal of senior British commanders, in spite of repeated warnings from observers up on the front lines, to believe that the wire had not been destroyed.

The Tommies knew nothing of this as they set out. Their inexperience and ignorance of what lay ahead helped to keep their enthusiasm high. They had also been fortified—steadied, dulled—by extra rations of rum. (In some units the men were given as much as they would drink.) To the extent that further motivation was required, it was provided by warnings that any man who failed to advance would be shot by his sergeants. Such practices were common and often backed up with action, though the orders were never put into writing. Nor were any officers foolish enough to put into writing the orders they issued with respect to the taking of prisoners. For a number of the units attacking at the Somme, these orders were simple beyond possibility of misunderstanding: no quarter was to be given. Any Germans attempting to surrender were to be dispatched forthwith.

The Germans were astonished by what they saw. Instead of coming forward in a rush, instead of ducking and dodging and making use of whatever cover the terrain offered, the British were lined up shoulder to shoulder in plain view. Instead of running, they were walking almost slowly, as if to demonstrate their skill at close-order drill. Rifles and bayonets at the ready, they were like a vision out of the era of flintlock musketry. If this was little short of insane, it was also exactly what had been ordered: a high-precision advance by soldiers in tidy rows. This was Rawlinson's idea. He thought that his troops, inexperienced as they were, would be incapable of advancing in any other way. "The attack must be made in waves," he said, "with men at fairly close interval in order to give them confidence." This would have made perfect sense if the Germans had in fact been wiped out. Each row was to proceed at a pace of exactly one hundred yards every two minutes, with everything timed to the second and all of it made tolerable by a creeping barrage that turned out not to be there.

According to the immensely detailed British plan of the day, the advancing soldiers were not to break into a run until within twenty yards of the enemy. Running would in any case have been nearly impossible: every man in the first wave carried some seventy pounds of weaponry, ammunition, and gear, so that even getting out of the trenches had been a challenge. The men in the later waves were more heavily burdened still. Their assignment was to consolidate the ground taken by the men ahead of them, and they had been equipped accordingly. They carried all the same things as the first wave plus everything needed to construct a new defensive line: boards, rolls of barbed wire, bundles of stakes, machine guns. If ordered to run, they would have been unable to do so, especially over ground that the bombardment had turned into an obstacle course. "Fancy advancing against heavy fire," one survivor would recall, "carrying a heavy roll of barbed wire on your shoulder!"

No-man's-land was a mile across at some points, a few hundred yards at others. The ground sloped downward toward the Germans in some places, more commonly upward, but everywhere it left the advancing troops as exposed as tin figures in a shooting gallery. Wherever they found themselves approaching uncut wire, as happened to unit after unit, they had no choice but to search out gaps and try to crowd through. Thus their slow-moving lines, or the parts of them that reached the wire, had to jam together in clusters barely able to move at all.

The Germans simply pointed their machine guns at these knots of flesh and cut them down in swaths. "We were surprised to see them walking," said a German machine-gunner. "We had never seen that before...When we started to fire we just had to load and reload. They went down in their hundreds. We didn't have to aim, we just fired into them."

"The infantry rushed forward with fixed bayonets," another of the German defenders remembered. "The noise of battle became indescribable. The shouting of orders and the shrill British cheers as they charged forward, could be heard above the violent and intense fusillade of machine guns and rifles and the bursting bombs, and above the deep thunderings of the artillery and the shell explosions. With all this were mingled the moans and groans of the wounded, the cries for help and the last screams of death. Again and again the extended lines of British infantry broke against the German defense like waves against a cliff, only to be beaten back. It was an amazing spectacle of unexampled gallantry, courage and bulldog determination on both sides."

Of the sixty-six thousand men in the first wave, few got close to the German line. More than half were killed or wounded, including three-quarters of the officers. Some did make progress: the Thirty-fourth Division captured all of twenty acres, losing three of four men in the process. At Beaumont Hamel nine out of every ten members of a Newfoundland battalion advancing toward the Hawthorne Ridge crater were shot down in forty minutes. Injured men streamed back to their own lines, throwing the later waves into deeper disorder, but as the day went on still more long rows of troops were sent forward one after another.

At day's end perhaps a third of all the units involved in the attack had reached what were supposed to be their objectives for the first hour. Few had gone farther. Not one of the five villages that were supposed to be taken in an hour had fallen. The units at the British center and left had accomplished nearly nothing. Three divisions of cavalry, having stood poised for action throughout the day, were still blocked and idle when the light failed. The number of casualties had reached sixty thousand, and almost twenty thousand of them were dead. It was the worst day in the history of British warfare. (England's casualties at Waterloo a century earlier had totaled eighty-four hundred. A generation later, at the Normandy invasion, the British and Americans together would be in combat for twenty days before their dead, wounded, and missing totaled twenty thousand.) German losses for the first day on the Somme totaled approximately eight thousand, including two thousand men taken prisoner—not by Rawlinson's army.

Before it was over the German gunners, at points in the center where the carnage had been most terrible, found themselves unwilling to continue firing. Shutting down their guns, they watched in silence as the British departed with whatever wounded they were able to take with them. Later, though, when some of the wounded left behind began to shoot from where they lay, the Germans too resumed firing.

There had been two successes, neither of them expected. South of the river, what was supposed to have been a holding action by units of Foch's battle-hardened "Iron Corps" turned into exactly the kind of breakthrough that Haig had planned for his own line. It had torn open the defenses, capturing several villages and losing only two thousand men. This happened in part because German troops were so sparse in the area, in part as a result of an effective creeping barrage. It happened mainly, however, because of what Great War historian Cyril Falls would call the "speed, dash, and tactical brains" of the French infantry. Foch and his generals made none of the British mistakes. Their poilus, when they advanced, were allowed to leave behind everything not required for the day's fighting. They were able to run and were encouraged to do so. They advanced not in marching lines but helter-skelter, platoon by platoon, darting from one shell hole to another, encircling the German machine guns rather than hurling themselves frontally against them. Foch was unable to use his gains to swing around and help out farther north, however. He was blocked by the Somme and its marshy banks.

The French corps north of the river, using the same tactics, made almost equal gains. Its advance shielded the flank of the southernmost British unit, a corps commanded by General Sir Walter Congreve, enabling it to drive northward two thousand yards and reach its objective, the village of Montauban. This was a startling achievement in comparison with what was happening elsewhere on the British line. It led, however, only to more frustration. Beyond Montauban, the countryside was open and undefended—ripe for the taking. But Rawlinson, in keeping with his bite-and-hold approach, had told his commanders that "no serious advance is to be made until preparations have been completed for entering the next phase of the opera-tions." Congreve reported his success, requesting permission to resume his advance, but he received no answer. The French on his right were then like-wise unable to advance farther, because doing so alone would have exposed their flank. Congreve had opened a path through which Haig's cavalry could, that very afternoon, have charged unobstructed into the German rear. But Haig and Rawlinson were fighting different wars, and the opportunity was lost.

When darkness finally descended, the Battle of the Somme was already deadlocked. Verdun remained deadlocked too. So did the Italian front, and the east.

FAREWELLS, AND AN ARRIVAL AT THE TOP

THE EMPEROR OF AUSTRIA AND APOSTOLIC KING OF Hungary developed a cough. Soon he had a fever that went up and down and up again. Franz Joseph was eighty-six years old in November 1916, and the sixty-ninth anniversary of his coronation lay just weeks ahead. Among all the monarchs in European history, only Louis XIV of France had had a longer reign.

Narrow and backward-looking and rigid though he was (he refused to use the telephone or ride in automobiles), Franz Joseph was in many ways a good and simple man. All his life he had done his best to be faithful to the code in which his strong-willed mother had raised him. Every night he got down on his knees to pray before retiring, and every morning he knelt down again as soon as he was out of bed. His dedication to what he saw as his duty almost surpasses understanding, especially in light of how little benefit he had derived from being so faithful. Even now, aged and coughing and fevered, he had himself awakened at three-thirty in the morning and was at his desk long before sunrise. With brief interruptions he would stay at that desk until after nightfall, struggling to manage the empire that his ancestors had built up over a thousand years and that was falling in around him.

A cloud of doom hung over once-gay Vienna. Franz Joseph's great palace of Schönbrunn, so long the scene of so much Hapsburg splendor, had grown dark and somber. His prime minister had recently been shot to death by a socialist.

As his illness worsened, the old man refused to rest. He would put his head down on his desk and let his pen fall to the floor but then recover himself and return to his papers or his next official visitor. When he was put to bed for the last time, he had to be carried there against his will. "I still have work to do," he complained. "Wake me tomorrow at half past three." That night he was given the last rites, lost consciousness, and quietly died.

His was one of the good deaths of 1916; it is impossible not to feel grateful that Franz Joseph did not live to see what the rest of the war would bring. Something similar can be said of the passing of Kitchener in June.

He too was getting on, and by the time of his drowning he was clearly a failure as minister of war. His autocratic ways had been totally unsuited to cabinet government, and only his stature as a public hero kept him in his job. He had been free to accept the tsar's invitation to visit Russia because nobody really wanted him in London. The sinking of his ship gave him a kind of warrior's death that he might have welcomed. His future, like the Austrian emperor's, would likely have been laden with disappointment.

December 29 would bring a different kind of death. Late that night the monk Rasputin made a visit to the palace of Prince Felix Youssopov, husband of the tsar's niece Irina and heir to a fortune bigger than that of the Romanovs. This young nobleman was a degenerate who had spent his life in the pursuit of every kind of sensual excess. As early as 1915 he had become obsessively committed to the notion that Rasputin was a threat to the survival of the regime of which he and his family were such spectacularly conspicuous beneficiaries. Rasputin, he decided, must die. Slowly, hesitantly, he assembled a little circle of conspirators, among whom was the young Grand Duke Dmitri Romanov, cousin to the tsar.

It is alleged, though some say otherwise, that what drew Rasputin to the palace that night was Youssopov's hint that the beautiful Irina would be

Grigori Rasputin with some of his many female admirers

made available to him there. This might explain why the customarily foul monk arrived in a new silk blouse, his boots polished and his person heavily perfumed. It is also said that after his arrival he was given wine and candies heavily laced with potassium cyanide, but other accounts say that whoever was responsible for providing the poison lost his nerve and used cooking powder instead. The poison story is particularly questionable: nothing Rasputin ate or drank that night appeared to have any effect beyond helping to keep him drunk. After a long period of music and dancing, with Rasputin not only failing to expire but suggesting a visit to Petrograd's brothels, Youssopov directed his attention to a silver and crystal crucifix displayed in a nearby cabinet. When the monk went to look, Youssopov pulled out a revolver and shot him in the back. Rasputin fell to the floor, apparently dead.

Youssopov's accomplices, who had been waiting in concealment upstairs, joined him in nervous celebration. Sometime later Rasputin opened his eyes. Then he was on his feet, lunging at Youssopov. The prince broke free and ran up the stairs, Rasputin close behind. When Youssopov escaped through a door and locked it behind him, Rasputin left the palace. He was on his way to the gate when one of Youssopov's accomplices began firing at him with a pistol. The first two shots missed, but the third brought Rasputin down. The gunman drew nearer and fired yet again, believing that this time he had shot his prey in the head. Youssopov came running out of the palace with a club in his hand. After several hard blows Rasputin sank into the snow, again apparently dead. His body was wrapped in a curtain, bound with rope, and dumped into the icy waters of the canal outside the gate. Later, when the corpse was fished out of the ice, police investigators found that before dying Rasputin had worked free of his bindings. An autopsy determined that the cause of his death was drowning. He had still been alive when thrown into the water and was not yet out of fight.

The mystery of Rasputin is impenetrable. That he was a singularly low character is beyond question, but if he did not also have strange powers he was singularly successful at seeming to do so. Among his effects was a letter written days before his death. It was addressed to "the Russian people, to Papa [his name for the tsar], to the Russian Mother and to the Children, to the land of Russia." In it he predicted that he would not live to see the new year, which was only days away when he wrote, and offered a warning. "Tsar of the land of Russia," he wrote, "if you hear the sound of the bell which will tell you that Grigori has been killed, you must know this: if it was your relations who have wrought my death then no one of your family, that is to say none of your children or relations, will remain alive for more than two years. They will all be killed by the Russian people."

The news of Rasputin's murder caused public jubilation. Youssopov and his accomplices, though they denied involvement, were acclaimed as heroes. Rasputin was buried in Romanov parkland, his funeral secret and attended by scarcely a handful of people. Among that handful, however, were the tsar and tsarina and their children. Whether anything would have turned out differently if Rasputin had died a year or two earlier, there is no way of knowing. By the time it came, his death was too late to change anything.

At almost exactly the same time, at the end of an almost indescribably complex struggle that split Britain's major parties into a jumble of disconnected fragments, Herbert Henry Asquith was displaced as prime minister. What broke Asquith in the end was not any failure on his part (through more than two years of war he had been a skillful if cautious leader, first of the Liberal government, then of the coalition that replaced it) but the demands of David Lloyd George for an ever-larger role in the management of the war. Finally those demands grew to a point where Asquith felt he could not accede to them without becoming a mere figurehead. A showdown was inevitable, and it came at a time when Asquith, absorbing the shock of his son's death in the Battle of the Somme, was unable to keep himself focused. ("Whatever pride I had in the past and whatever hope I had for the future—by far the largest part was invested in him," Asquith wrote after learning of this death. "Now all that is gone.") When Asquith misplayed his hand, Lloyd George unseated and replaced him.

The new prime minister had had the kind of career that causes people on the western side of the Atlantic to say "Only in America!" Born into exceedingly humble circumstances, orphaned at an early age and raised in Wales by a shoemaker uncle, he began as a law clerk, struggled to gain admission to the bar, married a farmer's daughter, and won election to Parliament at the age of twenty-seven. A firebrand reformer, a champion of progressive legislation and of industrial and agricultural workers, he rose fast in the Liberal party and by 1908, at forty-five, was chancellor of the exchequer. Along the way he built a record of opposing military spending and overseas adventures, favoring domestic programs instead. He paid a political price for doing so and learned to be careful not to alienate the Conservatives too much.

In July 1914 Lloyd George was a leading figure among the Liberal ministers resisting the slide into war. When the German invasion of Belgium radically changed public opinion, he quickly and adroitly moved with it. From then on he was not only a supporter of the war but a tireless agitator for total British commitment, controversial at times for his absolute rejection of any possible settlement short of victory. He more than anyone else was the force behind Britain's conscription laws, and it was he who created and then took charge of the ministry of munitions in response to the shell crisis of 1915, giving up his post at the treasury to do so.

In the summer of 1916, when Kitchener drowned, Lloyd George bullied where necessary and maneuvered where possible to get himself named secretary of state for war. In that position he soon became more powerful and effective than Kitchener ever had been. His rise to prime minister at the end of the year ensured that, however long the war lasted, Britain would have strong and capable and unwaveringly determined political leadership. It also ensured that that leadership would often be bitterly at odds with the leading British generals—with Robertson, the chief of the imperial general staff, and with Haig at the BEF.

Chapter 24

Exhaustion

*"It is not surprising if the effect on some
intelligent men was a bitter conviction that
they were being uselessly sacrificed."*

—OFFICIAL AUSTRALIAN HISTORY OF
THE BATTLE OF THE SOMME

Throughout the second half of 1916, great irruptions of violence followed one after another as the forces set in motion earlier in the year
overflowed into places previously untouched and finally played themselves
out in failure and despair. The Battle of the Somme, after its terrible first day,
contracted immediately though not permanently into a more limited conflict. On July 2 Haig, aware by now of the extent of his losses, sent only three
divisions into attacks—barely more than a fifth of the number that had gone
into action the preceding day. Not one of those divisions, strangely, was sent
to exploit Congreve's breakthrough at Montauban, and Congreve himself
was again not allowed to move. Along much of the front, action was limited
to gruesome nighttime forays into no-man's-land for the purpose of finding
those still alive among the heaps of corpses. At Beaumont-Hamel, where the
number of dead and wounded was unmanageably large, German soldiers
slipped out of their trenches after dark and, without a word being exchanged,
helped the British rescue parties with the work of retrieval.

Also on July 2, at Baranovitchi in the northern reaches of the Eastern
Front, Russian General Evert at last launched the offensive that he had promised weeks earlier in support of Brusilov. Evert had a thousand guns, each of
which fired a thousand rounds in advance of the assault, and he had more
than twenty-six divisions to send against two Austrian divisions backed by six
German divisions in reserve. The result was a disaster almost equal to Lake
Naroch in its magnitude. Though one of the Austrian divisions collapsed, the

other held its ground, and when the Germans came forward, they inflicted eighty thousand casualties on the attackers, losing only sixteen thousand men themselves. This ended any possibility of further Russian initiatives in the north.

For the first time the Brusilov offensive was given first priority by the tsar's headquarters. All available troops found themselves headed toward his theater of operations. Brusilov resumed his campaign even before the Barano-vitchi fight was over, and in short order he was again producing stunning victories. In four days he took forty thousand prisoners and captured three hundred and thirty guns. He began moving his armies, which now outnumbered those facing him by two to one, northward toward the Austro-Hungarian stronghold at Kovel.

On July 10, in a final lunge at glory, Knobelsdorf sent off a cobbled-together force roughly equivalent to three divisions in another attempt to take Verdun. A handful of these troops reached Fort Souville and stood briefly atop its protective shell waving flags. But Knobelsdorf had no reserves with which to follow up, and they were soon blown away by French artillery. The attack was suspended with a speed that was merciful to the troops on both sides. It was the Germans' last spasm at Verdun, though by no means the end of the killing. It was also the end of Knobelsdorf's part in the drama; on the orders of the kaiser, who had been driven by mounting disappointment to begin listening to his son, he was sent off to command a corps on the Eastern Front. Falkenhayn, harried by the crises on the Somme and in the southeast, increased the number of troops being transferred to both places.

At the Somme, meanwhile, the British continued to pound away with their artillery at the German defenses. One German soldier, after being taken prisoner, described for an English journalist the experience of having to take turns huddling in overcrowded bunkers under a barrage so intense that supplies could not get through. "Those who went outside were killed or wounded," he said. "Some of them had their heads blown off, and some of them had both their legs torn off, and some of them their arms. But we went on taking turns in the hole, although those who went outside knew that it was their turn to die, most likely. At last some of those who came into the hole were wounded, some of them badly, so that we lay in blood."

Sir Henry Rawlinson was slowly and with difficulty winning Haig's approval for another attack on the Somme. His plan this time was to send four divisions (with others guarding their flanks) across no-man's-land in the middle of the night, pause while the artillery pounded the Germans for only five minutes, and attack in the earliest predawn light. The French, judging the dangers of being caught on open ground after sunrise to be unacceptably great, refused to join in. But when the attack went off on July 14, it was a complete success—at first. There were only four battalions of defenders, and the British quickly overran their first line and broke through parts of the second. This time (and for the first time since 1914) the British cavalry did get into action, but it had been positioned so far behind the lines that it needed nine hours to reach the point of breakthrough. By the time it arrived, the Germans had been able to rush forward reserves to block the hole. Men and horses were mowed down by machine guns, and by the end of the day the Germans were once again in control of their second line. It had been a near thing, however. Although Haig by now had given up on achieving and exploiting a breakthrough, this latest attack persuaded him that the Germans really were at the end of their manpower. He decided that the Somme was worth continuing as an attrition battle. Encouraged by his staff's exaggerations of German losses, he approved Rawlinson's plan for yet another assault later in the month.

Across Europe it went on and on, new offensives coming one after another like waves on a sea of blood. At Verdun, a day after Rawlinson's July 14 offensive, Mangin the Butcher, lifted out of disfavor by Nivelle and promoted to command of a corps, sent a division to capture the village of Fleury. This was such a total failure, costing the French so many men, that Pétain intervened. He ordered that there were to be no more attacks without his specific approval, and he made it clear that he would approve no actions that had not been properly prepared. Mangin and his chief, Nivelle, began laying plans for an even bigger assault of a kind that Pétain would have to approve.

On July 23 Rawlinson launched his next attack. The troops of the Anzac Corps, many of them veterans of Gallipoli, took possession of part of Pozières Ridge, their assigned objective. But that was the only thing gained in another round of heavy losses, and the fight dragged on fruitlessly for another two months. "Although most Australian soldiers were optimists, and many were opposed on principle to voicing—or even harboring—grievances, it is not surprising if the effect on some intelligent men was a bitter conviction that they were being uselessly sacrificed," the official Australian history of the battle later observed.

On July 25 a Russian general nearly as talented as Brusilov, Nikolai Yudenich, commander of an army that had been winning victory after victory in the Caucasus, found that masses of Turks were converging on him from two directions. He struck at the Turkish Third Army and shattered it, killing or wounding seventeen thousand of its men and capturing another seventeen thousand while causing thousands of others to desert. He then turned to meet the Turkish Second Army, which continued to bear down on him and included among its corps commanders Mustafa Kemal, the hero of Gallipoli.

As the month ended, Brusilov continued his drive on the transportation center at Kovel, doing further damage to what remained of the Austro-Hungarian army. But he was being slowed down by an all-too-familiar problem: inadequate transport, supplies, and reinforcements. What was new and worse, German divisions were arriving in significant numbers from the west. This was a potentially mortal danger, but Brusilov could take pride in the fact that it was happening. Three months earlier the Germans had 125 divisions in the west, forty-seven in the east. But the ratio had been changing steadily ever since in response to the crisis that Brusilov had created, and by August it was 119 west, sixty-four east. Hundreds of thousands of German troops who could have made a critical difference at Verdun were in Galicia instead, or on their way there.

Though the year was unfolding in nothing like the way envisioned at Chantilly in December, by August it was beginning to appear possible that Joffre's objectives would still be achieved. The Germans were outnumbered and on the defensive at Verdun and on the Somme, and the same was true of the combined German-Austrian force in the southeast. The Austrians were on the defensive in Italy (where the Sixth Battle of the Isonzo began on August 6, generating more than a hundred thousand casualties before petering out after twelve days), and Turkey too was an empire in extremis, tormented by Yudenich's Caucasus campaign and the revolt in the Arabian desert. To complete the picture, French General Sarrail was preparing to move his quarter of a million men—twenty-three British, French, Italian, and Serbian divisions—northward out of Salonika. There seemed good reason to expect that, if all this pressure could be maintained, Germany would crack as Austria-Hungary had already done. This belief—that the Germans couldn't possibly still have enough men and guns to keep their defensive wall intact—persuaded Haig to keep hammering away at the Somme.

At this juncture, however, two things happened to turn everything upside down again. The Brusilov crisis forced Vienna to consent to putting almost all its armies under unified German command. Conrad howled in protest, but no one now cared what Conrad thought; undoubtedly he would have been dismissed if his many critics had been able to agree on a successor. Almost the whole Eastern Front was placed under the command of Hindenburg, which meant under Ludendorff, who could emerge at last from his isolation in the Baltic wastes. As soon as he had authority over the southeast, Ludendorff stopped insisting that none of the divisions he had been hoarding in the northeast could be spared for duty elsewhere. Hundreds of trainloads of his troops, guns, and supplies began pouring toward Galicia. As they took up positions, Brusilov's chances of restarting his campaign rapidly grew smaller.

Romania chose this moment, after months of hesitation, to throw in with the Entente. This decision was taken in spite of the fact that Romania's royal family was a junior, Catholic branch of the Hohenzollerns. It was precipitated by Brusilov's successes, especially his occupation of the Bukovina, a Hapsburg province on the northern border of Transylvania. This little conquest, of modest importance by every other measure, mattered because the Romanians hungered to annex Transylvania, which not only included many Romanians in its mixed population but had been part of Romania until seized by the Austrians in 1868. The Romanians feared that if they failed to act now, Transylvania would fall permanently to the Russians.

On August 17 Romania signed a secret agreement under which it joined the Entente and was promised Transylvania in return. It was assured of protection from its neighbor Bulgaria (now on the side of the Central Powers and eager to recoup what it had lost in the Second Balkan War) by the army that Sarrail was bringing up from Salonika. On that same day, ironically, a mainly Bulgarian force under German General Mackenson hit Sarrail's army at the village of Florina in Greece. Sarrail was forced into a retreat that would continue for more than three weeks. The die was cast, however.

On August 27 Romania issued a declaration of war, and that night it sent four hundred thousand troops, twenty-three divisions, through the mountain passes separating it from Transylvania. On the other side of those passes were only thirty-one thousand Austro-Hungarian soldiers. A quick and almost painless conquest seemed certain.

The addition to the Entente of Romania with its army of more than half a million men was one of those Great War triumphs that turned out to be less than met the eye—infinitely less, in this case. It was controversial before it happened, with Britain's David Lloyd George and Russia's General Alexeyev among those opposed. Alexeyev warned that the Romanian army was useless in spite of its size, and that Russia would find itself forced to protect hundreds of miles that had until now required no protection because of Romania's neutrality. He argued, in short, that Russia would be worse off with Romania as an ally than if Romania stayed out of the war. The tsar ignored Alexeyev. He listened instead to Boris Stürmer, the craven, conniving, and inept courtier who (to the shock of everyone, including Petrograd's conservative old guard) had been appointed prime minister in February and in July, after Sazonov was dismissed, had taken on the additional duties of foreign minister. Stürmer, who had absolutely no experience in such matters and was despised by nearly everyone who knew him, told Tsar Nicholas that the Romanians would sweep across Transylvania and into Hungary. He effortlessly carried the day.

Romania's declaration of war seemed a disaster to the Germans, and for Falkenhayn it was. He had been assuring Kaiser Wilhelm that if Romania entered the war at all, it couldn't possibly do so before late September, after the harvest was brought in. Chancellor Bethmann Hollweg, who had wanted Falkenhayn's dismissal since the two split over unrestricted submarine warfare, seemed suddenly justified. The coup de grâce was delivered when Hindenburg, prodded by Ludendorff and Hoffmann, threatened to resign if he was not made commander in chief. Kaiser Wilhelm, deeply discouraged about the state of the war and too weak politically to face down Hindenburg, gave up. On August 29 he sent a message inviting Hindenburg and Ludendorff to meet with him in Potsdam. When Falkenhayn, reading the signs, offered his resignation, it was accepted without discussion. Falkenhayn then made a final effort to save himself, warning Wilhelm that Hindenburg's appointment would mean the end of his, the kaiser's, ability to command the army or the nation. His power would be usurped not by Hindenburg, who scarcely mattered except as a symbol adored by the public, but by Ludendorff. Much as he resented Hindenburg and despised Ludendorff as a ruffian upstart, Wilhelm could see no alternative. The next day Hindenburg accepted Falkenhayn's job. Falkenhayn, offered appointment as ambassador to Constantinople, asked for a military position instead. Soon—perhaps it was Ludendorff's idea of a joke, or of ironic revenge—he was given the job of subduing Romania.

Ludendorff, explicitly given joint authority with Hindenburg over the German armies, was no longer satisfied with being chief of staff. He had the title of Quartermaster General of the German Army conferred on himself instead. He then departed by train for Verdun, taking Hindenburg with him. After getting a brief and appalling look at the situation there (the entire region was a blasted waste, its landscape described by a French aviator as like "the humid skin of a monstrous toad"), he made the inevitable official, decreeing that there would be no more German attacks.

The Romanian army, meanwhile, was showing itself to be even more hopeless than Alexeyev had warned. It was untrained and disorganized, so ill equipped that most of its divisions didn't possess a single machine gun, with an officer corps so bizarre that its senior commanders had issued an order permitting only those above major in rank to wear makeup. The divisions entering Transylvania should, by sheer force of numbers, have been able to push the Austrians out. Instead they proceeded with excruciating slowness, waiting for Russian help that wasn't coming. Alexeyev was disgusted by the entire enterprise, certain that Romania could not be defended, and unwilling to add to the small number of Russian troops already there.

The timidity of the Romanians in Transylvania, coupled with a period of quiet at Verdun and the Somme (where the French and British were not yet ready for their next attacks), gave the Germans precious time. Whole armies were being hurried across Hungary—fifteen hundred trainloads of men and equipment during September alone—while Mackensen, having stopped

Sarrail, began shifting the bulk of his Bulgarian force northward out of Greece. Only now did the full extent of Romania's unreadiness begin to make itself felt, turning war into low farce. Planning nothing more than a feint, Mackensen sent a smallish force to threaten the Romanian fortress of Turtukai on the Danube. The commander of this fortress, whose garrison greatly outnumbered the troops sent by Mackensen, declared boldly that "this will be our Verdun." One day later, upon being attacked, 80 percent of the Romanians at Turtukai surrendered almost without a fight. Those who did not surrender ran away, so that three Romanian divisions essentially evaporated. Mackensen then crossed the Danube into the province of Dobruja on the edge of the Black Sea. His arrival sparked celebrations: Dobruja had been taken by Romania in the Second Balkan War, and most of its population was Bulgarian.

At almost every point where they encountered enemies, the Romanian units simply collapsed. In their haste and confusion some of them attempted to surrender to one of the few Russian units in Dobruja—their own allies, who were distinctly unamused. The local Russian commander, ordered by Alexeyev to try to organize a joint defense, replied that trying to turn the Romanians into a disciplined force was like trying to get a donkey to dance a minuet. Greece too had by this time been drawn into the Entente (temporarily, as it would turn out, and as the result of indescribably complicated political machinations), and it too was putting troops in the field. But those troops saw no more reason to fight than the Romanians did. An entire corps surrendered to Mackensen without a shot being fired and was happily sent off by train to Silesia, where it would pass the rest of the war in the safety of internment camps. When Romania's commanders responded to the Dobruja crisis by shifting troops from the west, the only result was to thin their inert force in Transylvania.

In mid-September Falkenhayn arrived in Transylvania and took command of a new German Ninth Army, which was being assembled out of the many troops now arriving in the region. He was a man with something to prove—giving him an army to command rather than an army group had been an insult—and one day after taking up his new duties he started his forces toward the mountain passes leading to Romania. Meanwhile new convulsions erupted from France to the Caucasus. A September 15 assault by eight British divisions on the Somme included the battlefield debut of the tank. Only sixty of the new machines were in France at the time; of them only thirty-two were able to go into action, and only nine got far enough to help in temporarily pushing back the German line. (Ultimately the attack was another failure.) Churchill, who had wanted to keep the new weapon secret until enough could be assembled for a major surprise, was in anguish. "My poor 'land battleships' have been let off prematurely and on a petty scale," he wrote. "In that idea rested one real victory." Haig, who had insisted on not waiting, was not discouraged. He told the war office that he wanted a thousand more tanks as soon as possible. The French and the Germans got to work on tank programs of their own.

In the Caucasus Yudenich and Kemal, determined and able and well matched, struck at each other again and again, capturing towns and then having to give them up. In Greece Sarrail stopped his retreat with a counterattack against the Bulgarians and again began trying to push toward the north.

Three of the disasters of this period were particularly pointless. The Italians started the Seventh Battle of the Isonzo, which like its predecessors lasted only a few days, generated thousands of casualties, and accomplished nothing. On Brusilov's front, Tsar Nicholas sent an elite army of Imperial Guard units that were nominally under his personal command (he didn't go with them, however) to join in the advance on Kovel, now largely defended by Germans. The Guards, a hundred and thirty-four thousand of the best infantry and cavalry remaining to Russia, outnumbered the defenders and were better supplied with guns and shells. But their commander, a Romanov grand duke handpicked for the job by the tsar, ignored the lessons of the Brusilov offensive. Regarding flank attacks as unworthy of a force as superb as his, he sent the Guards in frontal assaults straight at the guns of the Germans. He sent them seventeen times—they found themselves trying to advance through waist-deep water while being strafed by aircraft—and every attempt ended in slaughter. Brusilov, who was not even consulted, could only read the reports and grieve. When the enterprise was called off at last, fifty-five thousand Guardsmen were casualties. As news of this disaster spread among the troops and into the civilian population, anger and resentment boiled to the surface. The heads of generals rolled, but the damage had been irretrievable.

At Verdun, which otherwise remained quiet by Verdun standards, the French on September 4 experienced a disaster that uncannily mirrored the earlier German explosion inside Fort Douaumont. In a fourteen-hundred-foot railroad tunnel that was being used by Nivelle's troops as a barracks, communications channel, storage depot, medical treatment center, and refuge, a fire somehow broke out where rockets were being moved by mule. It spread to a chamber where grenades had been stockpiled, then to the fuel for the tunnel's generators. It burned out of control for three days, trapping and killing more than five hundred men. The poilus too were finding reason to grumble.

September 25 brought another British thrust on the Somme. Again Haig used his tanks—only 30 percent got as far as no-man's-land before breaking down—and as usual the Tommies paid a high price in lives for gains that included the village of Thiepval, which had been a prime objective back on

July 1 and now fell at last after two days of hard fighting. Thereafter the weather failed, the onset of autumn rains making further movement impossible.

Falkenhayn, at the same time, was clearing Transylvania. Late in September he delivered a thrashing to a Romanian force at Hermannstadt. (As the name of this town indicates, Transylvania had a substantial German population, one eager to help Falkenhayn's army with intelligence and in all other possible ways.) The Romanians fell back to the so-called Transylvanian Alps and prepared to make a stand in the passes. They were reinforced by two hundred thousand of their countrymen sent from the Danube. Their numbers, and the fact that they were on high ground protected on both sides by mountains, appeared to make them secure. Falkenhayn desperately needed to get past them and link up with Mackensen. His whole plan depended on that. But with winter approaching in the high country, time was running out. If this thrust were not to degenerate into another stalemate, he had to force the Romanians out of the passes before the snows came.

Early October brought a three-day Eighth Battle of the Isonzo, which cost many lives but otherwise had no results, and preparations for a new French attack at Verdun. On October 19, satisfied that this was not going to be another squandering of lives, Pétain allowed Nivelle to begin bombarding the Germans with six hundred and fifty pieces of artillery (among them new siege guns bigger than the German Big Berthas) and fifteen thousand tons of shells assembled for the purpose. It was February in reverse: for four days the French blasted away at demoralized German troops who, huddled under an intermittent freezing rain, saw their defenses blown apart around them. On October 22 Nivelle played a trick. Suddenly all his guns fell silent, after which, by prearrangement, the thousands of French troops positioned along the front line sent up a great cheer—always until now a sure sign of an attack. Thoroughly fooled, the Germans uncovered the artillery that they had kept concealed until now and opened fire, thereby disclosing their positions. This was what Nivelle had wanted. There followed not an infantry attack but another day and a half of French shelling, during which sixty-eight of the Germans' 158 batteries were destroyed. Many of those that remained were so worn out by almost a year of heavy use as to be no longer accurate. The new French guns slowly began to break Fort Douaumont apart, setting its interior afire. The German garrison was pulled out, leaving the fort undefended.

The assault force was commanded by Mangin. When it attacked on the morning of October 24, its soldiers were concealed in mist, shielded by a creeping barrage, and thoroughly prepared. (At least partly to satisfy Pétain, a full-scale model of Douaumont had been constructed behind the French lines, and one French unit after another had captured it in mock assaults.) The attack was a total success. In one day the French retook positions on the east bank of the Meuse that the Germans had spent four and a half months and tens of thousands of men capturing. The retaking of Douaumont sparked national jubilation. When Fort Vaux fell nine days later (it too was abandoned by the Germans and captured almost without a fight), France was prepared to believe that at Verdun its army had won one of history's great victories. Nivelle, almost overnight, became the nation's new hero, the man who had "the formula" (so he himself declared) for turning the tide. Few wanted to notice that the Germans still held all their gains on the west bank, so that their artillery could block further advances on the other side of the river. Nor did it seem to matter that though the Germans were giving ground, they were doing so slowly and in good order. The hills retaken by the French were without strategic value, and nothing remotely like a breakthrough had been achieved. But Nivelle and Mangin were eager to strike again.

Nor was Haig quite finished (or the Italians, who on November 1 began a three-day Ninth Battle of the Isonzo that brought to almost one hundred and forty thousand the number of casualties suffered by both sides on that little front during 1916). On November 13 the British detonated a mine that their tunnelers had dug under a German redoubt on the blood-soaked ground of Beaumont-Hamel, and the subsequent attack by seven divisions captured both the redoubt and twelve hundred German soldiers. This fight went on for six days. Then on November 18 a blizzard brought it to an end. The Battle of the Somme was at an end as well. Absurdly, in their final forward plunge the British commanders had pushed their line downhill from a freshly captured ridge to the low ground beyond. The only result was that thousands of troops would, for no good reason, spend a miserable winter entrenched in cold, deep mud dominated by enemy guns.

Casualties on the Somme totaled half a million British and more than two hundred thousand French. Though the British and French originally estimated German casualties at above six hundred and fifty thousand and this number was long accepted by historians, it cannot be accurate. Official German sources place their Somme casualties at two hundred and thirty-seven thousand, a total that corresponds approximately to the calculations of Australia's official historian. The extent to which the British and French exaggerated is clear in the various governments' official (and credible) tabulations of total deaths on all sectors of the Western Front in all of 1916: one hundred and fifty thousand British, two hundred sixty-eight thousand French, and one hundred forty-three thousand German.

Whatever the numbers, many of Kitchener's armies were now not only battle-seasoned but seriously reduced. German losses, though far from outlandish in comparison with those of their enemies, had been higher than necessary. The reason was that Fritz von Below, commander of the Second Army at the Somme, had threatened to court-martial any officer who allowed his men to withdraw and later launched hundreds of useless counterattacks. Ultimately Falkenhayn was responsible. "The first principle in position warfare," he had decreed, "must be to yield not one foot of ground; and if it be lost to retake it by immediate counterattack, even to the use of the last man." Ludendorff, upon making his first visit to Verdun, ordered an end to such practices and began the introduction of more flexible, less costly tactics.

Just ahead of heavy snows that might have kept them blocked all winter, Falkenhayn's divisions now forced their way through four mountain passes. The Romanians, virtually out of ammunition, were unable to resist. Mackensen began moving toward Falkenhayn from Dobruja, which he had thoroughly subdued. The Romanian commander divided his force to strike simultaneously at Falkenhayn and Mackensen, trying to keep them apart. It was a bold move but completely beyond the capabilities of the army that attempted it. It might have had a chance of success with Russian support, and by now Alexeyev had relented. In response to the threat that Romania's collapse was beginning to pose for Russia itself, he did what he had feared from the start that Romania's entry into the war would force him to do. He told Brusilov to extend his line more than two hundred miles to the east and south. This ended the danger of a German move into Russia, but it so dispersed Brusilov's troops as to render him incapable of continuing his offensive. Alexeyev was trying to send troops into Dobruja from the east, but he had acted too late in a theater that was without adequate railroads. Sarrail, meanwhile, was again trying to come to the rescue from the south. He raised hopes by capturing the city of Monastir in southern Serbia, but thereafter his advance stalled.

At the start of December Falkenhayn and Mackensen came together and finished the destruction of the Romanian army in the Battle of Arges. Since their government's declaration of war, two hundred thousand Romanians had been killed or wounded (half the dead were victims of disease, actually) and one hundred and fifty thousand had been taken prisoner. Those able to flee went northward into Russia. The Germans, Bulgarians, and Austrians (plus some Arab units contributed by the Turks) had lost about sixty thousand men. On December 6 they crowned their victory by taking possession of the capital city of Bucharest. The forces that Alexeyev had been trying to send against them were able to do nothing more than block Mackensen from advancing northward out of Dobruja along the shore of the Black Sea.

The consequences of the Romanian campaign transcended the numbers of men lost and the propaganda benefits reaped by the victors. Over the next year and a half the Central Powers would remove from Romania more than two million tons of grain, one million tons of oil, two hundred thousand

tons of timber, and three hundred thousand head of livestock. To a considerable extent, Romania fueled Germany's ability to stay in the war.

All the battles were now over except the oldest, the one at Verdun. On
December 13 the political ice under Joseph Joffre broke at last. Questions
about his leadership, above all about his failure to prepare at Verdun, had
finally generated more pressure than his defenders were able to withstand.
The hero of the Marne, the revered savior of France, was moved into an
empty position as adviser to the war cabinet. To satisfy his supporters, to
keep them and Joffre himself from resisting or protesting, he was made a
Marshal of France. His successor as commander in chief was not his able
deputy Castelnau (too aristocratic and Catholic to be acceptable to the republicans who dominated the government), not the demonstrably effective Foch
(also too Catholic—he was a member of a lay religious order, and one of his
brothers was a Jesuit priest), and not the supremely competent and sensible
Pétain (too chronically contemptuous of politicians and his fellow generals
to be digestible by either the government or the army). The new chief was
France's new darling, Robert Nivelle, the self-styled genius credited with
changing Verdun from a tragedy into a national triumph.

Two days after Nivelle's promotion, his man Mangin attacked for the last
time at Verdun. This was another success, at least from Mangin's perspective.
It resulted in the capture of eleven thousand Germans and 115 of their guns.
But it lacked any real importance—by the third day the Germans were successfully counterattacking—and by the time it was brought to a halt the
number of French casualties since the end of the German offensive had risen
to forty-seven thousand.

Verdun was over at last. For months the battle had been little more than a
struggle over a symbol. No one seemed capable of asking why the French
were attacking or the Germans were bothering to defend. The crown prince,
in his postwar memoir, offered the German rationale. To have walked away
from ground over which so much blood had been spilled, he wrote, would
have been politically impossible—would have caused explosions at home.
The French in the end were fighting for nothing more substantial than
glory—not France's so much as Mangin's glory.

Meaningless as it was, the last assault of 1916 brought an ominous if
largely unnoticed foreshadowing of the year that lay ahead. As they moved
forward to the trenches from which they would once again have to throw
their flesh against machine guns, the French troops began to bleat like sheep.
The sound echoed all around. *Baaaa, baaaa*—the one pathetic form of protest
available to men condemned to die. More than the fighting, more than any
piece of ground won or lost, this was the sign of what was coming next.

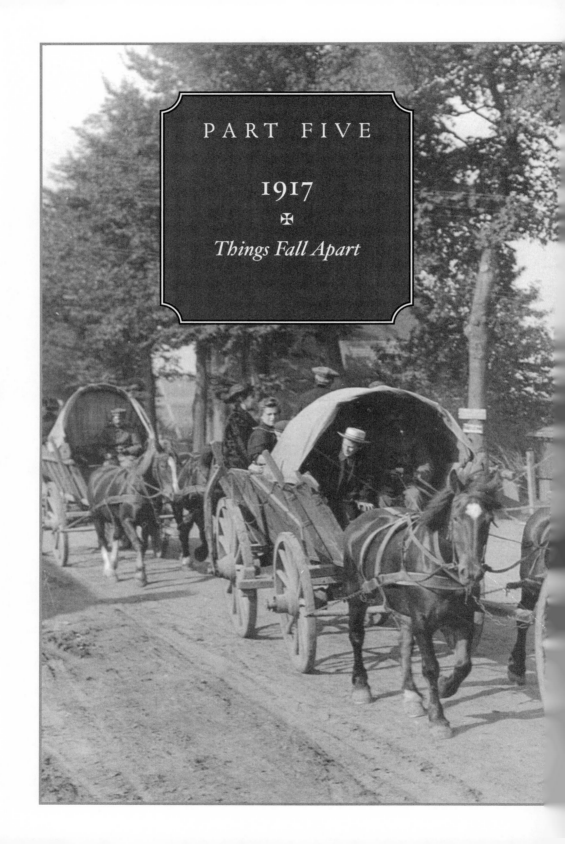

PART FIVE

1917
✠

Things Fall Apart

*Innocent, but not bystanders: these French refugees join
the countless millions of civilians whose lives were turned
upside down by the world's first total war.*

Chapter 25

✠

Turnips and Submarines

*"I could not advise His Majesty to do otherwise than
accept the opinion of his military advisors."*
—THEOBALD VON BETHMANN HOLLWEG

By the winter of 1916–17 the Central Powers had more reason than ever
to want the war brought to a swift conclusion. Their military situation
was far grimmer than it had been a year earlier: the Austro-Hungarian armies
broken beyond hope of repair, the Germans exhausted by Verdun and the
Somme and the scramble to cope with the Brusilov offensive, and the Ottoman
Empire unraveling north and south. On the home front things were even
worse. Germany and Austria alike were beginning to die from within, their
cities sinking into want and despair, their children literally starving.

As early as October 1916 Germany's Chancellor Bethmann Hollweg was
seeking to get the American president to interject himself as a mediator
between the warring sides. This proved infeasible, Woodrow Wilson being
embroiled in an election that he was by no means certain of winning. So
Bethmann sent a diplomatic note to Europe's neutral nations, declaring that
Germany was prepared to enter into negotiations. He offered no concessions
but also set no conditions, rather grandly making note of recent German successes including the conquest of Romania. In spite of support from the pope,
within days this initiative was rejected by all the members of the Entente.
The Russian Duma passed a resolution stating that peace would be possible
only after "victory over the military powers of Germany." The tsar, in a message to his troops, scornfully characterized Bethmann's offer as evidence of
German desperation. In London, David Lloyd George said the British would
"put our trust rather in an unbroken army than in broken faith." The Entente's
leaders pointed to Bethmann's failure to say anything about Belgium—a

particularly serious issue for the British, for whom permanent German domination of Belgium would be an intolerable security threat. Bethmann himself had recognized that in not addressing this question he was reducing his chances of accomplishing anything, but divisions within the German leadership had forced him to keep silent. Generals and admirals too powerful to be ignored were insisting that Belgium must at the war's end remain a German dependency or even be absorbed into the Reich. Ludendorff was typical in this regard: Belgium's postwar dependence on Germany, he said, must be "economic, military and political."

President Wilson, once he was safely reelected on a campaign slogan of "He kept us out of war," set out eagerly to become the world's peacemaker. He issued a diplomatic note in which he proposed an international peace conference. To establish a basis for discussion, he asked all the belligerents to state their war aims—to explain what they hoped to accomplish in continuing the struggle. Germany reacted first, endorsing the idea of negotiations and making lofty affirmations of its innocence and its willingness not only to talk but to participate in the creation of a new international system to prevent wars. It said nothing specific, however, about what Berlin would regard as an acceptable settlement concerning Belgium or any other question. This was the best Bethmann could do; putting the Ludendorff position in writing would have ended any possibility of negotiations.

Bethmann's reticence did not help. The Entente dismissed the German

President Woodrow Wilson
"He kept us out of war."

position as empty posturing and repeated its demand for a withdrawal from Belgium and France. On January 10 the Entente's leaders amplified their reply, complaining that Wilson had implied "a likeness between the two belligerent groups" when, in their view, Germany and its allies were solely responsible for the war. They outlined an array of demands that began with the "restoration" of Belgium, Serbia, and Montenegro and the payment of reparations by the Central Powers. Most ominously from the perspective of the Central Powers, they called for "the reorganization of Europe." They wanted not only the return of Alsace and Lorraine to France but the dismemberment of the Austro-Hungarian and Ottoman Empires.

This was followed by recriminations from both sides, and all hope of substantive discussion evaporated. We have no certain way of knowing whether the Entente really was unwilling to consider anything short of victory or was simply attempting to begin discussions on the strongest possible footing. What is certain is that both sides were afraid to say anything that might be interpreted as weakness either by their enemies or by their own people, and that powerful factions in both camps were determined to win the war. Lloyd George, for one, was mindful that his position as prime minister was dependent on the support of the Conservatives, who would have rebelled if he had displayed any willingness to compromise with the Germans. On the other side, the contempt with which the Entente had responded not only to Bethmann's but to Wilson's notes made Germany's conservatives feel justified in opposing further attempts to make peace.

It had become easier than ever to argue that Berlin had no option but the military one. But its military prospects seemed bleak. Ludendorff, in the weeks since taking charge of the high command, had been reviewing the situation on the Western Front. After two years in the east, he brought a fresh eye to the deadlock—and he did not like what he saw. "Our position was extremely difficult, and it seemed impossible to find a way out," he would write later. "We ourselves were not in a position to attack, and we dared not hope that any one of our enemies would collapse. If the war continued for any length of time, defeat seemed inevitable." What was definitely inevitable was that the Entente would be launching new offensives on both fronts in 1917, and Ludendorff believed that Falkenhayn's defensive system was sacrificing too many troops by holding doggedly to ground of little value. In any case, Germany clearly could not survive indefinitely, much less win the war, by standing on the defensive. The challenge, as Ludendorff saw it, was twofold: to find a less costly defensive doctrine and to arrive at some way of seizing the initiative, of carrying the war to the enemy. The search for a new defense brought out the best in the German general staff. The search for a way to widen the war, for a kind of new front where Germany could have the advantage, led to a reopening of the long-festering dispute over submarine warfare.

By 1917 the war was affecting civilian populations throughout Europe, but the naval blockade had raised suffering in Germany and Austria-Hungary to a uniquely high level. The French, from the beginning of the war to the end, had to sacrifice less than any of their enemies or allies. The Paris government never imposed effective controls on food production or distribution for the simple reason that it never had to: consumption actually increased throughout the war. This fact—astonishing in light of what was happening elsewhere—was made possible by shippers' nearly unimpeded access to France's Atlantic and Mediterranean ports, and by the high priority that the Paris government gave to food imports, at least partly as a way of limiting popular discontent with the war. Almost the only general inconvenience was a shortage of coal resulting from German occupation of France's prime coal-producing region, but even this was eventually made good. Problems had arisen, inevitably, from the 1914 induction of fully one-fourth of France's farmers and agricultural workers, from the military's requisitioning of thousands of horses, and from the diversion of rail facilities to military use. But these problems too proved to be manageable. By 1917 butter was still almost as plenti-

Planting time in France
Across Europe, with men and animals gone to war,
women took on new labors.

ful and inexpensive as it had been at the start of the war—this at a time when, in Germany and Austria, butter was virtually unobtainable at any price and only expectant mothers and the smallest children were allowed even a meager ration of milk.

The situation was worse in Britain, which in the years before the war had been importing 60 percent of the calories consumed by its population, but there too things were short of desperate. With its centralized administration and strong executive—all the stronger after Lloyd George became prime minister—Britain was able to impose controls on all aspects of the system by which its people were fed. Nevertheless there had been food shortages in 1916 (as much because of the year's bad harvest as because of the U-boats), and early in 1917 Lloyd George took measures to increase agricultural production. Voluntary rationing was tried, and when it proved ineffective, it was followed by mandatory controls on the distribution of the staples that were in shortest supply. A decline in nutrition manifested itself in a 25 percent increase in deaths from tuberculosis in England and Wales, and in rising infant mortality. Civilian health care deteriorated: hundreds of doctors were with the BEF on the continent, and hospitals throughout the British Isles were flooded with sick and wounded soldiers.

American agriculture boomed as exports to Britain and France increased; more and more land was put into production. Skyrocketing demand, however, caused prices to rise on the U.S. domestic market. Paradoxically, in the midst of abundance and the prosperity that came with it, there were food riots in several eastern U.S. cities during the winter of 1916–17.

In the management of food as in so many other areas, Tsarist Russia was a dismal failure. It had ample capacity to feed its population, and throughout the war it produced more than enough food to do so. Millions of tons of surplus grain were on ships in Black Sea ports, ready for export but unable to get through the Dardanelles. Russia was increasingly unsuccessful, meanwhile, in getting food and fuel to its cities, which were crowded with refugees, including the millions of Jews whom the Russians themselves had driven out of Poland in 1915. Much of the nation's railway system had been given over to the military, and much of what remained was in disarray. In the large cities, the price of food increased much faster than wages. The infant mortality rate doubled in Petrograd from 1914 to 1916, and by 1917 women working ten-hour days in factories were also spending forty hours weekly standing in line to get food and fuel for their children. Riots and strikes began to break out—six hundred seventy-six thousand workers struck in Petrograd in January and February 1917—and even in 1916 troops sent to suppress disturbances had refused to do so. By early 1917 the capital had only a few days' supply of grain in reserve and was a tinderbox ready to ignite.

On the other side of the Eastern Front, inside Germany and Austria-Hungary, the situation was equally grim if not quite so explosive. Here it was not only the urban centers that were in trouble. The problem was not just bad management—though there was enough of that—but a true, protracted, and by 1917 pervasive absence of the necessities of life. Neither empire had done anything to prepare for a long war, let alone for what amounted to a years-long siege, and both had begun experiencing shortages of food when the war was only a few months old. As early as October 1914 ten thousand horses were slaughtered in Vienna. The following spring, when German farmers defied a ban on feeding grain and potatoes to livestock, the Berlin bureaucracy ordered the mass butchering of all hogs. Nine million animals perished in this *Schweinemord,* and the consequences were uniformly unfortunate. After a brief collapse, pork prices rose sharply and permanently, and there was no longer enough breeding stock to replenish the supply.

A number of factors contributed to making the naval blockade as devastating as it was. The jerry-built political structures of the German and Austro-Hungarian Empires made consistent central control and even coordination practically impossible; Bavaria blocked the removal of its produce to other parts of Germany, while Hungary began selling its agricultural surplus to Germany rather than sharing it with Austria. Before the war Germany had been importing two million tons of nitrate and phosphate fertilizers per year, plus six million tons of grain for fodder and a million seasonal agricultural workers. As this input dwindled, agricultural productivity fell; grain production declined by half between 1914 and 1917. Inevitably, the needs of the armies were given first priority, and these were colossal and inexorable: seventeen million pounds of meat, sixty million pounds of bread, and one hundred thirty million pounds of potatoes every week. The first food riots erupted in Vienna in May 1915, in Berlin five months later. Food prices rose 130 percent in Berlin during the first year of war, 600 percent in two years. Even for industrial workers wages did not come close to keeping pace, climbing only 78 percent for men employed in German war plants from 1914 to 1917 (women were paid substantially less) and 52 percent for men in nonmilitary factories. Profiteering was widespread, creating new millionaires whose conspicuous prosperity made them objects of popular hatred.

Heavy rains, early frost, and shortages of fertilizer and labor made the 1916 harvest a disastrous failure, and outright famine became widespread. The potato crop, increasingly essential as meat and dairy products became nearly unobtainable, fell by half in Germany and more than that in Austria-Hungary. Scores of thousands of people were lining up at soup kitchens every day. Textiles were being manufactured from paper and plant fiber, shoes from paper and wood, coffee from tree bark. Destitute war widows—

Germany already had tens of thousands—spent their days waiting in long lines with their children for pathetically tiny rations. The diet of adult Germans consisted of a grotesque black "war bread" containing little real grain, fatless sausage, and a weekly allowance of three pounds of potatoes and one egg. Germans increasingly relied, for sheer survival, on one of the least appealing vegetables known to man, the humble turnip.

The bad harvest was followed by the long, cold winter of 1916–17, remembered ever after as "the turnip winter." The chief physician at one of Berlin's principal hospitals reported that eighty thousand children had died of starvation in 1916. In Austria families were allowed to heat only one room of their houses, which led to an epidemic of frozen and burst pipes. People were using dogs to pull their carts through the streets of Vienna—until it became necessary to eat the dogs. Even in Hungary, once rich in agricultural output, people were eating horses and dogs. German schools were closed for want of heating fuel. The average daily adult intake of calories, estimated at thirty-four hundred before the war, fell to twelve hundred. Deaths from lung disease increased from fourteen to nearly twenty-three per 100,000 women. Rickets, a deformation of bones and joints caused by malnutrition, became widespread among children.

"One of the most terrible of our sufferings was having to sit in the dark," a German woman wrote of life during the blockade. "It became dark at four in winter. It was not light until eight. Even the children could not sleep all that time. One had to amuse them as best one could, fretful and pining as they were from under-feeding. And when they had gone to bed we were left shivering with the chill which comes from semi-starvation and which no additional clothing seems to alleviate, to sit thinking, thinking." A German who was a schoolboy during the war would recall that "everybody seemed to be keeping rabbits because of the shortage of meat. They took us out in whole classes and sent us into the country to help the farmers. We liked that, but it meant we didn't get much teaching. All the teachers were out as soldiers anyway, and generally the whole life of the country was becoming grimmer. There was a strong sense of people saying, 'This war is lasting too long.' Some became quite outspoken. The feeling was that the war was lasting too long and that Germany didn't have much chance of winning it, because the conditions within the country were getting so very difficult."

Even the expected bounty from the conquest of Romania made little difference, increasing the amount of grain available in Germany and Austria by barely six percent. In both countries once-prosperous city-dwellers were venturing out into the countryside to trade jewelry and prewar clothing made of authentic wool and cotton for whatever food they could find. In Vienna tens of thousands of women were trying to survive through prostitution. As governments repeatedly expanded the work week to increase factory output, strikes by workers not earning enough to feed their families grew in frequency, size, and violence. Mobs of women looted stores and government food depots.

This is the dark background against which, on the ninth day of 1917, Germany's leaders met for a showdown over the question of submarine warfare. The kaiser was there, of course, still his empire's All-High Warlord though increasingly passive and incapable of asserting himself. Hindenburg and Ludendorff were there as well, recently back from their inspection of the Western Front and freshly convinced that continued stalemate was the best Germany could hope for there in the coming year. Also present were the navy's leaders, most notably Henning von Holtzendorff, chief of the navy's general staff and a passionate advocate of the submarine as the only way of bringing Britain to its knees. Finally—last to arrive, because not invited until almost too late—was Chancellor Bethmann Hollweg.

In response to pressure from the United States, Germany had been keeping its submarine fleet in check since September 1915, when unrestricted operations were brought to an end. Bethmann had insisted on this measure, and though the kaiser supported him, most of the generals and admirals were furious at him for refusing to lift restrictions. Their estimates of what a renewed campaign could accomplish, however, had changed with the passage of time. At the beginning of 1915, in urging the removal of all restrictions, the admirals had said that such a step would put Britain in serious trouble within six weeks. Now, with the submarine fleet considerably expanded, Holtzendorff was saying that the job could be done in six months. Bethmann was horrified. He remained certain that what Holtzendorff was proposing would bring the United States into the war, and he dreaded the consequences. The kaiser asked Holtzendorff for his view. "I will give Your Majesty my word as an officer," the admiral replied, "that not one American will land on the Continent."

Ludendorff's views on the subject were no secret to anyone. Two weeks earlier he had sent Bethmann a telegram stating that a U-boat campaign was "the only means of carrying the war to a rapid conclusion," and that "the military position does not allow us to postpone." Though Kaiser Wilhelm shared Bethmann's fears, a far stronger ruler than he would have found it difficult to resist the demands of his officers. Virtually the entire German nation was clamoring for an end to restrictions on U-boat operations. Industry, the armed forces, the population at large—all were experiencing the ruinous effects of the blockade, and all had come to see submarine warfare not only as justified morally and legally but as absolutely necessary in practical terms.

The Reichstag passed a series of resolutions opposing the limits that Bethmann was now nearly alone in trying to maintain.

The issue was quickly settled. Bethmann dutifully restated his reasons for opposing any change. But then, having done so, he withdrew his opposition. "I declared myself incompetent to criticize the judgment of the military experts who insisted that the war could not be won on land alone," he wrote later. "In view of these facts and of the declared readiness of Headquarters to risk war with the United States, I could not advise His Majesty to do other than to accept the opinion of his military advisers." In yielding as he did, Bethmann removed whatever basis the kaiser might still have had for resisting. He surrendered the last barrier to an unrestricted submarine campaign—very nearly the last barrier to America's entry into the war. More than one fateful page was turned. Control of German policy passed conclusively out of the hands of the kaiser, out of the hands of the kaiser's government, and into those of Erich Ludendorff.

The ultimate tragedy, from the German perspective, is that the decision taken on January 9 arose out of profoundly mistaken assumptions. Holtzendorff was wrong in his appraisal of the submarines' effects, and of America's military potential; this would become clear soon enough. Ludendorff was equally wrong in believing that Russia remained capable of offensive operations on the Eastern Front. If the U-boat decision had been deferred by just a few months, the truth about Russia's collapse would have made it unnecessary. Washington's principal grievance against Germany would have been removed.

The decision having been made, the Germans had no time to waste. It seemed essential, in order to demonstrate that if the war continued the British would starve as Germany was starving, to cut off British imports before the 1917 harvest was brought in. This meant before August 1, which in turn meant—Holtzendorff having predicted that the U-boats would need six months—starting by February 1. These calculations were as sound as they were simple, but the conclusions drawn from them were pure wishful thinking. Holtzendorff estimated that the submarines could sink six hundred thousand tons of shipping monthly from February through May, four hundred thousand monthly thereafter. He believed that losses of this magnitude would discourage many neutral shippers from trying to reach Britain, whose ability to continue the war would thereby come to an end.

These forecasts were accurate enough in the near term. Even in January, while still allowing American merchantmen to pass by unharmed, the U-boats would sink one hundred and eighty thousand ships totaling more than three hundred thousand tons. The lifting of restrictions became effective on February 1, and in that month five hundred and forty thousand tons would

Homeward bound
U-boats returning to port at the end of a North Atlantic hunting expedition.

be sunk—well over half of them British. This total was followed by five hundred and ninety-three thousand tons in March, eight hundred and eighty-one thousand in April, five hundred and ninety-six thousand in May, and six hundred and eighty-seven thousand in June.

The German public rejoiced over the start of the campaign and the deliverance that it seemed to offer. But there was no deliverance. Life became more difficult in Britain but never nearly as difficult as in Germany and Austria. The flow of imports slowed for a time but never came close to stopping. The British and Americans put into service many of the German freighters that they had impounded in ports around the world at the outbreak of the war. As they became more adept both at sinking German submarines and at eluding them, it became obvious that the U-boats were going to deliver none of the things that Holtzendorff had promised, and that American entry into the war was going to be anything but unimportant.

Holtzendorff, who had been so terribly wrong, would nevertheless keep his job. Ludendorff, who had supported Holtzendorff with every political weapon at his disposal, not only kept his job but became de facto autocrat of Germany. Only Bethmann Hollweg would be purged.

CONSUMING THE FUTURE

UNDER PRODDING FROM ERICH LUDENDORFF, THE REICHS-
tag late in 1916 approved an Auxiliary Service Law that carried the concept of total war to a level previously unimagined. It put every German
male between the ages of seventeen and sixty at the government's disposal. Anyone not sent to the war could be assigned to a munitions factory, to agricultural labor, to a desk in the bureaucracy—to whatever the
war ministry decided. Once in an assignment, no one could quit without
permission. Those who disobeyed could be jailed for a year and fined.

At the same time, presumably because the law had made cheap labor
plentiful, the government ordered massive increases in the manufacture of
war matériel. Gunpowder and light artillery production quotas were doubled to twelve thousand tons and three thousand barrels per month respectively. The target for machine guns was tripled to seven thousand per
month, and rifle production was boosted to one hundred and twenty-five
thousand monthly.

The service law did not go as far as Ludendorff had wanted. He had proposed applying it to women, particularly to all the childless war widows
who were, or so he complained, idling away their days. He had wanted to
close the schools and universities. He had proposed these things in spite
of the fact that unemployed women far outnumbered the available jobs,
and every youth of sufficient age and fitness was already in uniform. But
even in the limited form accepted by the Reichstag, the measure proved to
be unenforceable, a bureaucratic nightmare that angered the workers and
their unions while accomplishing little. It was soon abandoned.

The new production quotas likewise were often not met. But they were
typical of what all the belligerent countries were trying to do as the war
entered its third year. They were throwing everything they had—their people, their production capabilities, all the wealth accumulated over generations of industrial development—into the effort to destroy one another.
The longer the war continued, the deeper they were willing to dig. Even as
they weakened physically, with able-bodied men growing scarce and
essential commodities even scarcer, their commitment to fighting on grew
stronger. Almost no plausible measure was regarded as too extreme.

Which gives rise to a rather elemental question: where did the money come from? How did Germany and Austria-Hungary and Turkey and Bulgaria on one hand, Britain and France and Russia and Italy on the other, pay for such an immense and protracted struggle?

The answer, in a nutshell, is that they didn't. None of them even tried. In addition to being the greatest bloodbath in the history of western Europe and the greatest in eastern Europe until the Second World War, the Great War was a process by which all the great powers, victors and vanquished alike, transformed themselves from bastions of prosperity into sinkholes of poverty and debt. Financially as in so many other ways, the war was a road to ruin.

This development was not unforeseen. As technological progress accelerated in the nineteenth century and fueled tremendous military expansion, the question of how much a general war would cost became one of the great imponderables facing the governments of Europe. In 1898 a Russian named Ivan Bloch produced a six-volume study, *Future War,* in which he postulated that armed conflict between the great powers would mean "not fighting, but famine, not the slaying of men but the bankruptcy of nations and the break-up of the whole social organization." He predicted that any such war would be short because financially insupportable. Twelve years later a book titled *The Great Illusion,* by the Englishman Norman Angell, became an international best-seller by predicting that not even the winners could possibly benefit from a major war. Military power, Angell said, had become "socially and economically futile, and can have no relationship to the prosperity of the people exercising it." Such a warning seemed credible: when Angell's book appeared, all the great powers were spending scores and even hundreds of millions of dollars annually on their armies and navies. Such spending continued to increase through the last four years of peace, and much of the increase was made possible by borrowing. Only Britain, wealthiest of the European powers and the one with the smallest army, was balancing its budget.

What was not foreseen was the ability of the industrialized nations to go on fighting year after year even while devouring themselves financially. As astute an economist as John Maynard Keynes was a year into the Great War before he understood that total war would not cause total financial collapse. "As long as there are goods and labor in the country the government can buy them with banknotes," he wrote in September 1915, "and if the people try to spend the notes, an increase in their real consumption is immediately checked by a corresponding rise of prices." The truth, he concluded, was that bankruptcy would never force the great powers to stop fighting. They could be stopped only by the exhaustion of their manpower, their physical resources, or their will to continue. The next few years showed him to be entirely right.

With the start of the war, every one of the nations involved cast aside any semblance of financial restraint. As early as October 1914 Chancellor of the Exchequer David Lloyd George was admonishing the British war office not to come to him for approval before ordering whatever it thought it needed. It was the same in every capital: governments worried not about how much they were spending but about whether their military leaders were doing everything possible (which often meant *buying* everything possible) to outmatch the enemy. Budgets ceased to matter.

Great nations found themselves unable not only to pay their bills but even, in some cases, to pay the interest on what they were borrowing. By 1917 the German government's expenditures amounted to 76 percent of net national product; they had been 18 percent just before the war. Tax revenues were covering only 8 percent of the spending. That same year Britain's military spending was 70 percent of national output, and revenues were about a fourth of expenses. France's military budget, thanks to heavy borrowing, was equal to or even more than total output.

On the home front
A French couple with what remains of their home.

The strategies adopted by the various countries for maintaining sources of credit varied greatly and were almost indescribably complicated. The problems were greatest for the least developed nations, Russia and Austria-Hungary in particular. The solution in both cases was reliance on stronger senior partners. Russia began borrowing from its allies as early as October 1914. Eventually it borrowed £568 million from London and three and a half billion francs from Paris—colossal sums for the time, equivalent to billions of dollars. Germany found it necessary to be similarly generous to Austria-Hungary, and later to Turkey and Bulgaria as well. The Russians had compounded their difficulties by shutting down the state monopoly on alcohol early in the war as a gesture of austerity, patriotism, and willingness to sacrifice. This accomplished nothing except cutting off a fourth of Petrograd's revenues, creating a huge black market in vodka, and worsening inflation.

Not one country attempted to meet its expenses or even reduce its deficits through increased taxes. Where taxes were increased, the purpose was either to inhibit inflation by soaking up some of the wages flowing to workers or to maintain a flow of revenue sufficient to satisfy the credit markets. New taxes were sometimes imposed on profiteers, but more to maintain public morale (damaged everywhere by the spectacle of tycoons reaping fortunes while everyone else suffered) than to increase revenue. Tax systems became less rather than more progressive. Governments tried to limit the amounts of money available to working people for the pursuit of increasingly scarce goods while simultaneously helping the wealthy to retain their assets for investment in postwar rebuilding.

The situation first became serious for the Central Powers, which virtually from the first day of the war had lost their merchant fleets and access both to their own overseas investments and to global sources of credit. They had to do nearly all their borrowing internally, through loans from domestic financial institutions and the sale of bonds. They were surprisingly successful. Germany issued war bonds twice annually. The many marks raised in this way covered two-thirds of its war costs.

The British and French were far more able than the Germans to repatriate money they had invested overseas, and because of the naval blockade only the Entente was able to buy and borrow from the United States. But gradually, inexorably, their treasuries were depleted. Questions arose in New York and Washington about their ability to make good on their debt. In November 1916 the U.S. Federal Reserve Board warned its member banks against continuing to buy foreign—which meant British and French—treasury bills. The result was a near-panic in which London retaliated by briefly ceasing to place orders in the United States and urged

France to do likewise. By April 1917 the British were spending $75 million a week in the United States, were overdrawn on their American accounts by $358 million, and had only $490 million in securities and $87 million in gold to draw on to make good their debt. In short, they were only weeks away from insolvency.

But this was a crisis for the United States too. American manufacturers and farmers had become dependent on sales to the Entente, and American banks were owed immense amounts. A British and French financial collapse—never mind the outright defeat of the two nations—would have been a disaster for the U.S. economy. Thus the German submarines were not Washington's only reason for wanting to save the Entente. In purely practical business terms, it became dangerous for the United States *not* to enter the war.

It is estimated that the war ultimately cost $208 billion—this at a time when skilled workers were paid a few dollars a day. The final bill was $43.8 billion for Britain, $28.2 billion for France, and $47 billion for Germany. In each case, the result was the same. The wealth of all the belligerent countries was drastically reduced.

The ultimate result is expressed in the word *disinvestment.* All the European powers stopped making the kinds of investments required for real economic growth. Everything, even the future, went into the flaming cauldron of the war. Britain, that paragon of affluence and commercial success in 1914, ended the war sunk in debt, its civil infrastructure a shambles. The Europeans had begun the war at the pinnacle of the world's economic and financial hierarchy, and they ended it as wrecks. Ivan Bloch had been wrong about the feasibility of keeping such a war going. About the consequences, however, he had turned out to be dead right.

Chapter 26

✠

A New Defense, and a New Offensive

"This is a plan for the army of
the Duchess of Gerolstein."

—Louis Lyautey

O n February 24 British troops near the French city of Arras reported
something exceedingly strange. The German lines opposite them were
being shelled—by *German* artillery. Scouting parties sent out to investigate
discovered something even stranger: the enemy's trenches had been abandoned. The men who had occupied them were nowhere to be seen. The purpose of the shelling, clearly, was to destroy what the departing soldiers had
left behind.

One of the most remarkable tactical moves of the Great War, in its
improbable way one of the boldest, was in process. After two and a half years
of Western Front combat in which both sides had clung desperately to every
yard of barren turf, the Germans were pulling back. Though the extent of
the withdrawal remained for a time not at all apparent—at Arras the line
shifted just a short distance, so that the British thought they were witnessing
nothing more than a minor adjustment—over a period of several weeks the
Germans would withdraw twenty miles along seventy miles of front
between Arras and St. Quentin. Quietly, voluntarily, they would give up a
thousand square miles of conquered French territory. They would turn their
backs on ground soaked with their own blood, on positions that Erich von
Falkenhayn, when he was head of the high command, had ordered held at all
costs.

The withdrawal was Ludendorff's doing, and it was fraught with risk. If
the British and French had attacked while the Germans were abandoning
their old line and before they were settled into new positions, the results

could have been disastrous. It was also a task of almost unbelievable magnitude; Ludendorff's plan was not only to shift to a new line but to make that line immeasurably stronger than the one being given up. Three hundred and seventy thousand men (German reserves and civilians, Russian prisoners of war) worked for four months on the construction of the new defenses, digging trenches and subterranean chambers for the concealment of men and equipment, building fortifications of concrete reinforced with steel, and erecting huge barricades of razor-edged concertina wire. Farther east another hundred and seventy thousand workers assembled the necessary materials and sent them forward to the construction crews. More than twelve hundred trains were assigned to the project, hauling steel and concrete and everything else that was needed. And aside from that mystifying bombardment at Arras, most of it was accomplished in secret.

The withdrawal was code-named Alberich, after a maliciously tricky dwarf king in German (and Wagnerian) mythology. The new wall of defense that it created was named the Siegfried-Stellung Line by the Germans, but the Entente would call it the Hindenburg Line. The decision to construct it was among those taken by Ludendorff after he and Hindenburg replaced Falkenhayn as joint commanders in chief, and it showed once again Ludendorff's ability to think and to act on a grand scale. It grew out of the conclusions he had drawn after an inspection of the Western Front in the aftermath of Verdun and the Somme: that his armies were no longer capable of taking the offensive, that too many of Germany's diminishing manpower resources had been squandered, and that the defensive doctrine currently in use had to be scrapped.

"The decision to retreat was not reached without a painful struggle," Ludendorff would write later. "It implied a confession of weakness bound to raise the morale of the enemy and lower our own. But as it was necessary for military reasons, we had no choice." The decision was made possible by the enormous power that Hindenburg and Ludendorff together exercised in Berlin. They were the conquerors of the east, the people looked to them as saviors, and no one in the civil government, not even the kaiser, was prepared to stand against them. Again and again, in crisis after crisis, they almost always got their way—by threatening to resign if not by other means. Late in 1916, when Ludendorff demanded the mobilization of Germany's entire civilian population for the war effort, he did not get everything he wanted, but he got a great deal. Sectors of German industry that had not already converted to the production of war matériel now did so. The army itself was restructured: Ludendorff created thirty-one new divisions in the fall of 1916 and thirteen more in January 1917, mainly by making each existing division smaller while giving it more machine guns and artillery. Boys born in 1899 were drafted ahead of schedule—though they proved, upon reporting for training, to be alarmingly malnourished.

The benefits of the withdrawal, if it could be pulled off, promised to be substantial. The front as it ran southward from Arras to Soissons and the area of the Chemin des Dames ("the Ladies' Road," so named because it had been a favorite bridle path of the daughters of King Louis XV) was a great ninety-mile bulge curving westward to include the city of Noyon, only a few days' march from Paris. The Hindenburg Line would be twenty-five miles shorter, freeing thirteen divisions and fifty batteries of heavy artillery (roughly the equivalent of an entire army) for use elsewhere. This was a crucial consideration, because the German manpower situation had been difficult since mid-1916. At the start of 1917 the Germans had two and a half million men, 134 divisions, on the Western Front. Facing them were nearly four million Entente troops organized into 175 divisions (a total expected to rise substantially by year end as the BEF continued to expand). The danger that Germany would be numerically overwhelmed seemed to be increasing with every new month.

The creation of the new line would also enable Ludendorff to install, from scratch, the kind of physical infrastructure needed for a new kind of defense. Under his new approach, there was no longer to be a German front line in the traditional sense. The now-customary continuous line was replaced by small, mutually supportive steel-and-concrete camouflaged blockhouses laid out in a checkerboard pattern and manned by machine-gun crews. Wherever possible, these blockhouses were positioned on the forward slopes of hills, from which they would look down on attacking troops. They would be shielded by high rows of razor wire configured so as to channel attackers into narrow, lethal passages as had happened more or less inadvertently at the Somme. The men in the blockhouses, rather than standing their ground and fighting to the death, were to fall back when they had done what they reasonably could to slow the enemy's advance. The old, brutal system, in which troops were packed together in the forward trenches in an effort to create an immovable mass and were expected to die at their posts, became obsolete. In its place was something intended to be significantly more flexible and much less costly in terms of lives.

The first true defensive line, in the new system, would be far to the rear—as much as a mile behind the blockhouses, beyond the reach of enemy mortars and light artillery. Another line would be another mile back, and the reserves would be positioned even farther in the rear than that, safe from most artillery but ready to counterattack as soon as an opportunity appeared. The result would be an elastic defensive network designed to draw the enemy into a miles-deep killing zone, one in which the reserves were no longer reserves at all in the traditional sense but a strike force poised to throw the enemy back at that point of maximum vulnerability where his initial thrust had exhausted its energy.

This was Ludendorff's vision for the Western Front in 1917. It had everything to recommend it except for the short-term risk—the possibility that an Entente offensive (and one was sure to come before long, possibly early in the year) might catch the Germans midway through their withdrawal and between their old and new lines. This risk seemed so great that even Ludendorff hesitated—until fate intervened.

At the beginning of February the Germans intercepted and decoded a message sent from the Italian foreign office in Rome to Petrograd. It contained bad but not surprising news: the British and French were preparing an attack on the Western Front. It was to be yet another massive offensive, bigger even than the Somme, involving some one hundred divisions. But there was good news too, and it was very good indeed. The attack would not be coming until April—two months or more in the future. The Germans would have time enough to complete and man their new line. They would have time to school the troops in the execution of the new system. On February 4 Ludendorff ordered work to proceed, and it was fully under way five days later.

The Hindenburg Line, as it took shape, proved far too formidable for the humble term *trench warfare* to remain appropriate. It began with a trench, but one that was to remain unoccupied. This trench was almost ten feet deep and twelve feet across—a trap for tanks, and an equally forbidding obstacle for men advancing on foot. Behind it, one after another, were five or more rows of barbed and razor wire, each row twelve feet deep and twice a man's height, each twenty yards distant from the next. Then came the blockhouses, with two machine guns in each. Beyond them—dangerously far beyond, for enemy infantry trying to advance under fire—lay the first true line, a largely underground beehive of chambers and passageways covered with up to eight yards of earth and impregnable to artillery and bombs. Farther back still, also down below the surface and positioned wherever possible on a reverse slope so as to be almost unreachable by artillery, were two lines of guns. This was defensive warfare raised to a new plane. It appeared to be invulnerable. It was the work of a commander of immense vision, energy, and ambition—a man prepared to bend the entire German Empire to his purposes.

And it was made possible by the fact that the British and French would not be attacking until April.

Entente planning for 1917 had begun in much the same way as the preparations for 1916: with a gathering of the high commanders at Joffre's château in Chantilly, and with all the assembled generals eager to get back onto the offensive and finish off the Germans. This meeting took place on November 15, and the British, French, Italians, and Russians had no difficulty in agreeing once again that they would all attack simultaneously. They agreed also that they would wait until May, so that snow would not be a problem on the Eastern Front or for Italians pushing into the Alps. French General Robert Nivelle, now popular in Paris as the supposed hero of the final stages of the Battle of Verdun, presented a plan for a February attack on the Chemin des Dames, but it was set aside.

The assembled commanders even repeated themselves in failing once again to agree on where, exactly, the British should attack. As usual, Haig wanted to strike in Flanders, on the old Ypres battleground, with the old objective (dear to the Royal Navy, and of unquestionable strategic value) of capturing the Belgian ports. Once again Joffre wanted the British to be concentrated farther south, near if not actually on the old Somme line, and once again he was able to argue that his wishes should prevail because the French would be providing most of the troops. This point of disagreement was a mere detail, however. The generals more or less cheerfully left it to be decided later. Even Haig was optimistic. David Lloyd George, then still minister of war, arrived at Chantilly late in the discussions, after the decisions had been made. Though he had long since evolved into one of Britain's most determined advocates of victory at whatever cost, he was also appalled by the Western Front's casualties and not at all satisfied that they had been necessary or worthwhile. He was infuriated when he discovered that the military men had once again shown themselves to be incapable of coming up with anything better than a continuation of what was, in his view, their "legacy of inevitable disaster." But there was nothing he could do—at the time.

During the six weeks remaining until the end of the year, the earth shifted under all their feet. Lloyd George became Prime Minister of England. Joffre fell from power and was replaced by Robert Nivelle. Suddenly the agreements reached at Chantilly mattered hardly at all.

The new year began with a January 5 conference of Entente leaders at Rome. Neither Haig nor Nivelle attended. They were separately engaged in developing their plans for the next offensive, the former still focusing his hopes on Flanders, the latter on a Chemin des Dames attack that would leave little room for action in Flanders. Lloyd George used the occasion to try to reduce the bloodletting on the Western Front. To the surprise and annoyance of General Robertson, who had accompanied him to Rome as chief of the imperial general staff, he proposed giving first priority in 1917 to a reinforced strike out of Italy aimed at destroying the remains of the Austro-Hungarian armies and taking Vienna out of the war. This idea had been conceived originally by Luigi Cadorna, the Italian commander in chief, and it had strategic merit. For Lloyd George it had the attraction of making another Somme or Ypres almost impossible in the near term. It would also take precedence over Nivelle's Chemin des Dames campaign and a supporting British attack that Nivelle wanted at Arras. It would involve Italian infantry, mainly; the principal British and French contribution would be enormous quantities of artillery.

Cadorna, when he saw how hostile the British generals were to his idea, began to backpedal. The French premier, Aristide Briand, also was unenthusiastic, perhaps because he knew that Nivelle would never agree. Having so recently participated in the displacement of Joffre, Briand would be in an awkward position if he disregarded the wishes of the man to whom he had entrusted the armies of France. Lloyd George, despite his recent elevation, had no leverage with which to impose his will on the others. He had become prime minister in spite of having few real friends in positions of power anywhere. Many members of his own Liberal Party resented him for having colluded in the fall of Asquith, the Conservatives had long and with good reason regarded him as a foe, and it was widely expected that his government could not last more than a few months. His hopes for an Italian offensive having died for want of support, he departed Rome a thwarted and disgruntled man.

Lloyd George stopped in Paris on his way home, and upon arrival he was met by Nivelle, who greeted him with a smart, flatteringly respectful salute. By all accounts Nivelle was a man of extraordinary charm. His ability to

David Lloyd George
Weary of the generals'
"legacy of inevitable disaster."

make political friends had contributed at least as much as his aggressiveness and dash to his startlingly rapid rise. He now worked his wiles on Lloyd George, who, accustomed to the disdain of his own country's generals (Haig had called him a "cur," though not to his face), must have been delighted. Nivelle brought unique advantages to his meeting with the Welsh Lloyd George. He was not only not Catholic but Protestant, and not only a Protestant but one who did not hesitate to display contempt for the faith of his Catholic countrymen. This had made him attractive to the French republicans, and now it made him attractive to the British. He spoke perfect English without an accent (his mother was English-born), which again made him exceptional among France's senior commanders. And—no small matter, as it turned out—he had a pleasing skull. Lloyd George was a believer in phrenology, the then-popular pseudoscientific discipline based on the idea that character and destiny are revealed in the shape of one's head. He considered the contours of Nivelle's head and saw victory there.

Nivelle explained his plan for the Chemin des Dames. It would involve a multipronged attack on the German line west of Reims, and he proclaimed with invincible confidence that it would decide the war in twenty-four to forty-eight hours. It would be a French attack primarily (Lloyd George had to be pleased to hear that), supported by a complementary British offensive. It would use the same tactics that had produced such supposedly glorious results in the final weeks at Verdun. (Lloyd George was unaware that those results were achieved only after the Germans had given up on Verdun, and that the operation that produced them was on a comparatively tiny scale.) The death blow would be delivered by a strike force (Nivelle called it his Mass of Maneuver) made up of twenty-seven divisions of French infantry and cavalry. Best of all, Nivelle offered assurances that the offensive not only would not but *could* not turn into another Verdun or Somme. He promised that if somehow the impossible happened and it did not succeed within two days, he would bring it to a stop.

Lloyd George was won over. He invited Nivelle to travel to London and meet with the British war cabinet on January 15. There again Nivelle proved irresistible, winning over British politicians who had been steeped in skepticism by the failures of 1915 and 1916. The only difficulty was the question of timing. Nivelle wanted to start quickly—as early as February. Haig, not happy about what amounted to a rejection of his Flanders offensive, was suggesting May. The result was compromise: what would go down in history as the Nivelle offensive was approved for April 1. It was only two weeks later that Ludendorff learned of it and ordered completion of the Hindenburg Line to proceed.

When the Entente leaders met again at Calais on February 26, they made it clear to Haig that he was expected to be ready at the beginning of April, and that he was to cooperate fully with Nivelle. In letters written after the conference, Haig referred to a proposal that Lloyd George had rejected out of hand. "The French put forward a terrible scheme for putting the British under a French commander in chief," he wrote in a letter to a friend. "Thank God even Lloyd George thought it went too far." This incident requires note because of Haig's later claim, made after the war and long widely believed, that Lloyd George had himself suggested putting the BEF under Nivelle and had been stopped only by the threat of Haig, Robertson, and other British generals to resign or face courts-martial rather than agree. Though required to attack at Arras rather than in Flanders, in all matters tactical Haig retained control of the BEF. He was explicitly given the right, if in disagreement with Nivelle, to appeal directly to London. He left Calais with the further assurance that Nivelle's campaign would be ended if it did not lead quickly to a breakthrough, and that the BEF would then be free to resume preparations for an offensive in Flanders.

Nivelle remained supremely confident. He moved his headquarters to a magnificent château that had once been the property of Marie Antoinette. He took his wine cellar with him—took all the appointments appropriate to a generalissimo, along with the favorites ("Butcher" Mangin prominent among them) who had been with him at Verdun. Those he did not favor found themselves sidelined. Foch was banished to the dormant front near Switzerland. Pétain, Castelnau, and others found that they too no longer mattered. No one mattered but Nivelle. In his lofty and splendid isolation, he proceeded with arrangements for a Napoleonic stroke that was now just weeks in the future.

But a problem emerged: several of France's most proven commanders were convinced that the Nivelle plan had no chance of success. The reluctance of Haig and his generals might be written off as sour grapes, but Pétain, Foch, Franchet d'Esperey, and even General Alfred Micheler (who had been given command of Nivelle's Mass of Maneuver) all were soon arguing that Nivelle was preparing to do the wrong thing in the wrong place and was headed for disaster. No one wanted to listen: not Lloyd George, not the president or premier of France.

Late in 1916 France's most brilliant colonial soldier, a onetime protégé of Gallieni's named Louis Lyautey, had been brought back from Morocco for what would prove to be a short tour of duty as minister of war. When he learned what Nivelle was planning, this future Marshal of France was incredulous. "This is a plan for the army of the Duchess of Gerolstein," he exclaimed, making reference to a popular operetta. But still no one would listen. When in March Paul Painlevé became minister of war (the Briand government had fallen because Lyautey refused to share military secrets with other members of the government), he tried strenuously to persuade Nivelle to make his attack more limited, less ambitious, less risky. No one in a position to make a difference would listen.

HEARTS AND MINDS

BY 1917 MORALE HAD BECOME A CRITICAL PROBLEM BOTH in the armies of the great powers and among their home-front populations. As the level of sacrifice being demanded of people in and out of uniform came to seem almost insupportable, and as the death and deprivation seemed to be achieving practically nothing, the enthusiasm that had marked the beginning of the war fell ever closer to the vanishing point. Soldiers wanted to go home and wanted to know why they couldn't. Their families wanted them home and wondered what their sons were dying for. All of them wanted a return to what had been lost.

Governments responded in a variety of ways. They became harsher in suppressing dissent. They increased their emphasis on propaganda, on bolstering the loyalty of people whose suffering had not yet turned them into dissenters. The control and manipulation of information that all the warring nations had been practicing since August 1914 became more systematic, more sophisticated, and farther-reaching. It came to be an essential function of government.

Inevitably, to the extent that the propaganda was effective, it made an end to the fighting more difficult to achieve. "However the world pretends to divide itself," the English writer Rudyard Kipling declared in a London newspaper, "there are only two divisions in the world today—human beings and Germans." Similar things were being said about the British by writers in Berlin. People everywhere were being told that this war was no continuation of politics by other means, no traditional struggle for limited objectives. It was a fight to the death with the forces of evil, and the stakes were survival and civilization itself. It is no simple thing to make people believe such things and later persuade them to accept a settlement based on compromise.

Control of public opinion was made possible by the same economic and technological developments that had made Europe capable of fighting such a war. In all the belligerent countries, the most developed of them especially, industrialization had drawn millions of people from traditional, predominantly rural ways of life into fast-growing urban centers. It created a need for the education of these people—for a literate workforce—while

slashing the cost of producing newspapers. Both an enormous new reading public and new means of reaching that public came into existence.
London alone had sixteen daily papers by 1914, and the largest were
selling nearly a million copies a day. Germany had four thousand newspapers—half of them dailies—with a huge total circulation.

If the readers of these newspapers were not necessarily well informed,
they were certainly receiving information of a kind that their ancestors had
rarely seen. The strains and pressures and opportunities of modern life
were politicizing them as never before. People understood that they had a
stake in the issues of the day, they formed opinions on those issues, and
increasingly they felt entitled to express themselves and be heard. As the
war made their lives darker and harder, governments found it increasingly
necessary to persuade them to endure.

The war's first propaganda fell into place almost effortlessly. As invariably happens at the start of a war, people everywhere were swept up into
ecstasies of patriotism. Almost everything they heard and read assured
them that their glorious armies would soon be victorious, that their cause
was a noble one, and that the enemy was wicked in ways rarely seen
in history. Formal censorship of the press was scarcely necessary; many
newspaper owners were themselves caught up in the general frenzy, and
few of those who had doubts found it convenient to express them. There
were exceptions in all countries—the *Manchester Guardian* said Britain
was entering "a war in which we risk everything of which we are proud,
and in which we stand to gain nothing"—but they rapidly grew rare.

British public opinion had been particularly well prepared for the conflict. Throughout the two decades leading up to the war, Germany's growing economic strength and emergence as a naval power provoked cries of
alarm in many of the most influential newspapers. The Rupert Murdoch of
the day, Alfred Harmsworth (more famous as Lord Northcliffe after he was
elevated to the peerage), owned a number of important papers aimed at
different segments of the public. He used all of them to alert his readers to
what he saw as the German menace, fostering, one of his competitors
complained, "an anti-German frame of mind that takes no account of the
facts." When war came and no correspondents were allowed near the
front, neither Northcliffe nor his competitors complained about having to
depend on official sources for information about what was happening
there. Nor did they see reason for complaint. Many saw it as their mission
not to inform the public (which long remained ignorant of the realities of
the war) but to do their bit to keep morale high.

A Press Bureau was established in August 1914 (by Winston Churchill,
ready as always to take the broadest possible view of his responsibilities)

to determine what should and should not be published. Soon thereafter a Defense of the Realm Act made it unlawful to print anything "of such a nature as is calculated to be or might be directly or indirectly useful to the enemy." At about the same time a new Secret War Propaganda Bureau was given responsibility for assisting the foreign office in wooing neutral nations. Where the home front was concerned, the propaganda machinery remained fairly primitive. It placed less emphasis on actively manipulating public opinion than on preventing the publication of anything that might limit confidence in the success or heroism of the BEF. The task was simplified by a general absence of people prepared to publicly question the cause.

The French government began by leaving the management of war news in the hands of General Joffre and his staff. Throughout the first half of the war this simple system worked about as well as Britain's, and for similar reasons: the newspapers tended to be content to get their information from the military, and few people with a voice in public life wished to question or complain. The Germans entered the war with probably the world's most fully developed information-and-propaganda system, but it was directed not at the home front but at other countries—the United States especially—and was crippled when the British navy cut the only cable connecting Germany with the Western Hemisphere. From the beginning, the Berlin government was even less sophisticated than the British and the French in trying to shape the opinions of its own people. Like so many other problems that would grow worse for the Germans as the war dragged on, this one arose at least in part from the peculiarities of German society. The Junker elite loathed and feared the urban masses, wanted nothing from them but acquiescence and obedience, and was loath to do anything to indicate that public opinion mattered.

For two years all three countries relied primarily on a strict but easily maintained press censorship (often banning publications that refused to cooperate), on assuring their populations that the war was being won, and on depicting the enemy as evil incarnate. Their methods were predictable and in retrospect sometimes seem ridiculous. The German story line was that the Reich was fighting a defensive war against a cabal of unscrupulous enemies determined to destroy it. The British and French followed an exactly opposite script, one in which they were defending civilization against Huns who wanted to rule the world. Even the atrocity stories that were staples in the newspapers of the Entente were mirrored in those of the Central Powers. The Germans were reported to be cutting off the hands of French boys so they could never become soldiers, to be raping children and bayoneting infants. The German public was told that the Russians were poisoning the lakes of East Prussia and cutting off the limbs of captured German soldiers, and that the French and Belgians made a specialty of gouging out prisoners' eyes. Lying was epidemic—newspapers ran old photographs of Russian pogroms against Jews as evidence of Germany's "rape of Belgium"—and officials with access to the facts were not immune. David Lloyd George, long before he became prime minister, was declaring in public that "the new philosophy of Germany is to destroy Christianity."

This state of affairs began to change, and to change in ominous ways, as the war entered its third year. The British government, alarmed by spreading strikes and protests, singled out pacifists and conscientious objectors for blame. Pacifist leaders (many of them socialists who had remained silent earlier) were arrested if they attempted to address assemblies of workers. As labor unrest became commonplace everywhere (British munitions production was briefly brought almost to a stop in May 1917), the governments of Britain, France, and Germany all tried to ignore the real causes: rising living costs, long hours working under harsh conditions, and shortages of food. In all three countries strikers were accused of treason, and governments increased their efforts to make the public agree.

Nineteen-seventeen was the turning point. In February of that year Lloyd George established a Department of Information to tighten control over what the public was told. Four months later he created a National War Aims Committee, with former prime minister Asquith as its president. Despite its name, the committee's purpose was not to articulate the nation's war aims (which were intentionally kept vague so as not to bring political divisions to the surface), not to respond to German propaganda, but to neutralize domestic dissent. The unprecedented sum of £240,000 was appropriated to finance its activities, which were focused on blanketing areas of labor unrest with gruesome (and generally fabricated) tales of German atrocities. The committee's aim was to persuade workers that there could be no negotiated peace with such a barbaric foe.

France created a new propaganda agency, a Maison de la Presse that was part of the ministry of foreign affairs but aimed at the home front. It too focused on atrocity stories, on the war as a crusade to save justice and liberty, and on what it depicted as the essentially spiritual character of the struggle. Ludendorff followed suit by starting a program of "patriotic instruction." Its purpose, inevitably, was to remind an increasingly disheartened German public that it was involved in a struggle to save civilization. "Good propaganda must keep well ahead of actual political events," said Ludendorff. "It must act as pacemaker to policy and mold public opinion without appearing to do so. Before political aims are translated into action, the world has to be convinced of their necessity and moral justification." He was becoming a thoroughly modern general, an innovator not just in battlefield tactics but in the uses of PR.

The results of all the propaganda would be tragic. By raising the stakes of the war beyond the limits of reason, the propagandists ensured that whichever side lost would feel terribly, irredeemably wronged. And that whichever side won would find it difficult to deal rationally with the populations it had defeated.

Chapter 27

✠

Revolution and Intervention

"All this is really no business of mine but something must be done. And if I don't do it nothing will be done."

—Erich Ludendorff

The six weeks leading up to the Nivelle offensive brought two of the most world-changing events since the French Revolution. The Romanov dynasty that had ruled Russia for three centuries came to an end, and the United States entered the Great War.

Like many of history's great upheavals, the end of the Romanovs was both a long time coming and shockingly sudden. In military terms, Russia's situation had seemed mildly promising as 1917 began. The Brusilov offensive, in spite of its costs, had been one of the war's most brilliantly successful campaigns and had given the Russian commanders new confidence. The winter had provided the army with months in which to regroup, Austria-Hungary was obviously no longer dangerous, and France and Britain were sending huge amounts of equipment—artillery and shells in particular, but other weapons and essential matériel as well—to the Eastern Front. Even Germany, its forces stretched thin, no longer seemed as intimidating as before. As Churchill would write after the war, to emerge victorious Russia had only, from 1917 on, to maintain an intact front. Its generals thought they could do more than that. When Joffre originally proposed a multifront offensive for 1917, they showed no reluctance to join in. When Joffre fell and was succeeded by Nivelle, and when Nivelle's plan for the Chemin des Dames became the Entente's Western Front plan for 1917, the Russians said they would have seventy divisions ready for action when Nivelle attacked. Those divisions would be equipped with tens of thousands of machine guns and pieces of artillery. Such numbers made even generals as cautious as Evert, whose timidity in 1916 had saved the Germans from ruin, willing to attack.

These promising developments would mean nothing in the end, however, because the Russian home front was slipping into chaos. The winter of 1916–17 was exceptionally hard, with extraordinarily deep snows and temperatures so low that more than a thousand steam locomotives froze up and exploded. The railway system, never more than satisfactory, became barely capable of functioning. Throughout most of Russia the situation remained manageable, but the flow of food and fuel into the largest cities slowed to a trickle. The problem was especially serious in Petrograd—which in addition to being the capital was Russia's most important industrial center—because of its remoteness from the interior. By early in the new year factories were shutting down for lack of fuel. The workers were left with nothing to do but roam the streets, cold and hungry, frightened and angry. The bakeries that had flour could not make bread because they could not heat their ovens; the women of the city, unable to get their usual scant rations even by waiting in line for hours, began to loot. The tens of thousands of troops stationed in Petrograd, many of them untrained and bewildered recruits, were harangued by wandering agitators calling for revolution and an end to the war.

Almost everyone by now was demanding change, especially the appointment of a "responsible" Council of Ministers—one willing and able to carry out the duties for which the tsar's cabinet was supposed to be responsible. But nothing changed, and the expectation of a final crisis came to be almost universal. That any such crisis would almost certainly topple the regime

Russian women reading the latest list of deaths on the front

seemed obvious, and outbursts of hostility toward the tsar and tsarina became commonplace even in privileged circles. General Sir Henry Wilson, a senior member of the British general staff, visited Russia and reported that "everyone—officers, merchants, ladies—talks openly of the absolute necessity of doing away with them." When the young democratic socialist Alexander Kerensky told the Duma that Nicholas and Alexandra must be deposed "by terrorist methods if there is no other way," he was cheered and promised protection. Though his words were suppressed by the newspapers, they spread through the capital and were everywhere applauded. On February 23 the Duma's president, ending a meeting with the tsar, said he thought they would not meet again because revolution was imminent. Nicholas, who had retreated deep within himself by now, did not respond. Among the civil authorities, however, an uprising was regarded as so nearly inevitable that the police were issued machine guns.

Nicholas was weary, isolated, impervious to advice, incapable of action, possibly aware of what lay ahead and internally preparing himself for it. He had spent much of the winter secluded with his wife and children in their palace at Tsarskoe Selo near the capital. Almost everyone who had access to him—Alexandra excepted—was begging him to appoint a new cabinet, but he did nothing. The tsarina, a majority of one, was urging him to rule autonomously and ruthlessly. "Lovy, be firm, because the Russians need you to be," she wrote him after he left home for army headquarters. "At every turn you show love & kindness—now let them feel your fist, as they themselves ask. So many of late have told, that we need the knout. It's strange, but that is the Slav nature." But even to her appeals Nicholas made almost no response.

Alexander Kerensky
His fatal error: trying to keep
Russia in the war.

People who met with him would remember how distant and detached he had become, seemingly untouched by what was happening. He would listen patiently to repeated appeals for action, smile vacantly, and say and do nothing. The only official in whom either Nicholas or Alexandra placed any confidence was the ludicrously incapable Alexander Protopopov, who gave less attention to his duties as minister of the interior (which duties were supposed to include getting essential supplies into the cities) than to the séances at which he assisted the tsarina in trying to establish contact with the late Rasputin. Protopopov was a singularly manipulative fool: in the presence of the tsarina he would fall to his knees and declare in tones of wonder that he had seen the figure of Jesus standing behind her.

On Wednesday, March 7, Nicholas raised the hopes of every reasonable member of the government by abruptly announcing that on the following day he would go to the Duma and declare his intention to appoint a new cabinet. That same evening, however, he made a second announcement—that he was leaving immediately for army headquarters, that there would be no visit to the Duma, that he was, in short, breaking his promise. Within hours he was gone from the capital. It is likely that he departed both at the insistence of his wife, who thought Nicholas was being intolerably weak if he so much as acknowledged the existence of the Duma, and to escape from her constant instructions and appeals. He had no particular need to be at army headquarters, with the Eastern Front still locked in winter. That may be precisely why he went—to escape from everything. He was perhaps in a depression, perhaps simply resigned. As soon as he was gone, events began to unfold rapidly.

On Thursday street demonstrations in Petrograd turned as before into riots and looting. Cossack troops, the cavalry traditionally used by the tsars to control unruly or merely disfavored civilian populations, were sent into the streets to restore order. These Cossacks, however, were mainly young, inexperienced, and half-trained; those of their elder brothers who had not by now died in the war were off at the front. Significantly, they did not carry with them the whips with which Cossacks customarily subdued crowds. Instead of attacking the rioters, most of whom were women, they mingled with them and assured them that they were in no danger.

On Friday the crowds were even larger than before, the rioting more violent. The leaders of the capital's most radical leftist groups, suddenly bold after years of ferocious repression, called for a general strike.

On Saturday the crowds and the Cossack horsemen were once again out in force. The latter, ordered to fire on the demonstrators, turned their guns on the police instead. This almost unimaginably shocking turn of events, the end of generations of Cossack loyalty to the regime, sent the cabinet into a panic. Members sent a telegram to the tsar offering their resignations and asking him to return to Petrograd and form a new government. The reply that he sent was magnificently absurd in its irrelevance to the situation: "I order that the disorders in the capital, intolerable during these difficult times of war with Germany and Austria, be ended tomorrow."

That tomorrow, Sunday, March 11, was in fact comparatively quiet, the streets almost empty. Before leaving the capital Nicholas had given his newest prime minister, an aged and well-intentioned but ineffectual veteran of the Petrograd bureaucracy, a signed order for the dismissal of the Duma. His instructions had been to hold this document in reserve and use it if necessary. Now it was delivered to the assembly, whose members promptly voted to disregard it. In doing so they effectively joined the revolution.

On Monday tens of thousands of soldiers joined it as well. Many simply deserted. Others joined the civilians in a fresh outbreak of rioting. The capital's huge armory was attacked, taken, and pillaged. Thousands of rifles were carried off into every corner of the city and into the hands of every would-be revolutionary. Courthouses and the offices of the secret police were set ablaze. Prisons were broken into, their inmates freed to flee or join the mob.

On Tuesday, March 13, Tsar Nicholas finally left army headquarters and began the five-hundred-mile rail journey back to Petrograd. His progress was slow. In yet another of his endless acts of well-intentioned foolishness, Nicholas had ordered that his train should follow an indirect route so as not to interfere with the flow of troops and matériel to the front. As he drew closer to the capital, he encountered increasing signs of disorder. Finally, with the imperial train still far from its destination, reports of violence along the line ahead made it clear that further progress would be impossible. The locomotive pulling Nicholas and his entourage was shunted into the railyard of the obscure provincial town of Pskov, where it came to a halt.

Telegrams arrived from senior military commanders—one came from Grand Duke Nicholas in the Caucasus—telling the tsar that it had become imperative that he surrender the crown. Nicholas seemed unsurprised. He showed concern only for his wife and children, virtually prisoners since the forty-thousand-man garrison at Tsarskoe Selo had joined the rebellion. All five of the royal children were sick with the measles—no trivial disease in 1917. The tsarina, unable to communicate with her husband, at first found it difficult to believe that any of these things were happening. Soon, however, she recovered. She threw herself into the care of her daughters and twelve-year-old son, and into arranging meals and warm quarters on the ground floor of the palace for the two companies of Cossacks that alone remained loyal. After years of almost insanely self-destructive behavior, she began to display the strength and calm acceptance that would support her family through the months of life that remained to them.

On March 15 two new Russian governments came into existence. One was proclaimed by the Duma, now dominated by the thirty-six-year-old Kerensky, who became minister of justice. Its rival was the Soviet of Soldiers' and Workers' Deputies, made up, as its name indicated, of representatives of army units and industrial laborers. The two set up operations in the same building and agreed that the tsar must abdicate. Members of the cabinet, instead of resisting, presented themselves to the Duma and, pathetically, asked to be arrested for their own protection. A delegation set out from Petrograd to get Nicholas's signature on an act of abdication. By the time its train reached the tsar, he had made up his mind to sign. On one point, however, he refused to cooperate. Asked to pass the crown to his son, he insisted not only on abdicating himself but on doing so on behalf of the boy as well. He understood that the delicate Alexis, his life in almost constant jeopardy because of his hemophilia, would if made tsar be handed over to the care of strangers. This, Nicholas declared, was out of the question.

And so the crown passed to Nicholas's younger brother Michael, a feckless individual who years before had made himself the black sheep of the Romanovs by secretly marrying a twice-divorced commoner with whom he had already had a son. But the new Tsar Michael II, fearing for his life as revolution and chaos spread, abdicated almost immediately. He declared his willingness to resume the crown later, but only if it were offered to him by an assembly of the people's elected representatives. With that, the Romanov dynasty ended. The Duma's provisional government declared its determination to continue the war until victory was achieved. The former Tsar Nicholas, displaying no bitterness, supported the government in this respect without reservation. In a farewell message to the troops, he said that "whoever now dreams of peace, whoever desires it...betrays...the land of his fathers."

The end of the tsarist regime was soon known to the world. Paris and London, and also those members of the U.S. government who were eager to join the war, received it with something like jubilation. Alliance with the Russian autocracy had from the start been an embarrassment for the French and the British, one that complicated their efforts to depict the war as a conflict between democracy and dictatorship. Now, apparently, Russia too was becoming a democracy—and one no less eager to continue the war than the tsar had been. The Entente was being purified.

In Russia itself the news was tragic for many, a cause of celebration for many more. "God in heaven, it's like a miracle of miracles, it all happened so quickly," a soldier serving as a clerk in a field hospital recorded in his diary.

"Such joy, such anxiety that I can't get on with the work. I want to convince all the doubters that these developments are good news and that things will get better for us now. Good Lord, it's so great that Tsar Nicholas and the autocracy no longer exist! Down with all that rubbish, down with all that is old, wicked and loathsome. This is the dawn of a great new Russia, happy and joyful. We soldiers are free men, we are all equal, we are all citizens of Great Russia now!... The police are being arrested, their weapons are taken away from them. Please God let it be like this forever."

The tsar's abdication came six weeks after Germany's announcement that it was resuming unrestricted submarine warfare. It immediately made clear just how great a mistake that announcement had been, and that Germany's political system had broken down almost as completely as Russia's. That system, by putting virtually all authority in the hands of a tiny elite with little connection to the nation as a whole, had been creaking badly even before the war. In the best of times it was superficially tidier than Britain's parliamentary monarchy and the French republic with its innumerable changes of government. But even under strong and brilliant leadership (a rare commodity in a political culture as stunted as imperial Germany's), the German system operated in a kind of splendid isolation, with no mechanism for adapting and renewing itself in response to trouble. When its leadership fell as far short of strength and brilliance as it did after Bismarck, it had few outside resources to draw on. Under pressure of war its isolation became pitiable rather than splendid. Thus the Germany of 1917: a civil government unable to control or even compete with the army's high command, and a military inept in politics and diplomacy and blind to its own ineptness. And thus the emergence, more by default than by anyone's design, of a dictatorship led by a man, Erich Ludendorff, who though one of the outstanding generals of German history was devoid of political gifts, experience, or skills.

This dictatorship was quick to produce political disasters equal in magnitude to Ludendorff's military achievements. The first came in October. Like those that followed, it had its roots in Ludendorff's fixation on strengthening the German war machine by every possible means, and in his consequent embrace of what would come to be called "war socialism"—the subordination of every available human being and every particle of the economy to the imperatives of the war. Manpower was in short supply not only in the army but on the home front, and even before Ludendorff's rise to supreme power some thousands of Belgian industrial workers had been forcibly transferred to the factories of Germany. The factory owners wanted more, and almost as soon as he arrived in the west, Ludendorff decided to satisfy them. He set a quota of two hundred thousand transfers. Bethmann, other members of the government, and even the general in command in Belgium all dissented, saying that the program could have little impact on industrial output but would be a propaganda fiasco, a boon for the Entente in its tireless campaign to portray Germany as nothing better than an outlaw nation.

These arguments were swept aside. Late in October Belgian industries that were not contributing directly to the war effort were shut down and mass deportations began. In three months more than sixty thousand Belgians, many of them in bad health, were herded onto cattle cars and transported to Germany under brutal conditions. Ultimately the entire program proved to be as useless as its opponents had warned and had to be brought to an end. By that time, however, it had done terminal damage to Germany's international reputation, ending any possibility that the American public might respond other than with revulsion to the resumption of unrestricted submarine warfare.

A second great blunder came soon afterward. Early in November Germany announced that it intended to create a new Kingdom of Poland out of an unspecified portion of the territories from which the Russians had been expelled in 1915. Like the Belgian deportations, this idea had not originated with Ludendorff, but he had seized upon it and forced it on the government in spite of the reservations of Bethmann Hollweg and others. The underlying hope was that the Poles would be so grateful for the gift of a nation of their own after generations of partition and occupation that they would eagerly fight on the side of the Central Powers. The originators of the plan, in selling it to Ludendorff, held out the vision of quickly recruiting five divisions of Polish soldiers—a million men eventually—to fight against the Russians. Desperate for manpower, incapable of listening to those who knew far more than he about the psychology of the Polish people, Ludendorff lunged at this mirage.

The idea was doomed from the start. Long experience of tsarist rule had taught Poland's rural peasantry to hate the very idea of military service. And the promised "kingdom" was far too vague, too obviously false, to tempt anyone to die in the service of Germany. It was not to be created until after the war's end, and its hereditary ruler would be a German rather than a Slavic prince. It was to include only part of the former Russian Poland, other parts of which were to be annexed by Austria or Germany. Some of it was to be not Polish at all but territory stripped from Russia proper. Its army was to be under German command, and the kingdom was to be barred from entering into treaties without German approval.

It was an absurdity, and it produced predictable results. In all of Poland only a few thousand men answered the call to arms, barely enough to make up a few battalions which would be disbanded before the war's end without ever seeing active service. What mattered far more—what turned the episode into a disaster—was the impact on Russia. Throughout the summer and autumn of 1916 Bethmann Hollweg had been sending out feelers to Petrograd, exploring the possibility of a separate peace. The response had been ambiguous—Tsar Nicholas had no interest—but not hopelessly negative. This was the period of Boris Stürmer's tenure as prime minister and foreign minister in Petrograd. (Significantly, he was able to hold on to both offices despite being so anti-British and pro-German as to be frequently accused of treason. The Russian court had always included a pro-German faction, and that faction was still in place after two years of war.) But the loss of Poland had been a grievous blow to Russian pride and a profoundly disturbing threat to what the Petrograd government saw as its security needs in Europe. The announcement of a make-believe Polish state amounted to a declaration that Poland could never again belong to Russia. It ended any possibility of a separate peace between Germany and the government of the tsar—a peace that Germany urgently needed. By provoking resentment in every part of Russian society, it ensured that when revolution came and the provisional government succeeded to power, it too would be determined to continue the war. In the longer term, by weakening the provisional government and opening a path to power for the Bolsheviks, it would have even more disastrous consequences for Russia than for Germany. But Ludendorff would misplay that card too.

It has to be said, in fairness to Ludendorff, that his intrusions into diplomacy and politics and even industrial management appear to have been motivated less by a desire to aggrandize himself than by a determination to win the war and by frustration with the inertia and incompetence of the German governing system. "All this is really no business of mine but something must be done," he lamented to Crown Prince Wilhelm. "And if I don't do it nothing will be done."

The greatest blunder was Germany's handling of its relations with the United States during the first three months of 1917. It began with the decision to resume unrestricted submarine warfare, but that set in motion a whole series of subsequent mistakes that proved to have terrible consequences. Those mistakes culminated in an American declaration of war that more competent German leadership might very well have averted.

At the center of the story stands Arthur Zimmermann, who had become head of the German foreign ministry at the end of 1916 after Hindenburg and Ludendorff purged Gottlieb von Jagow for being too inclined to side with Bethmann. Zimmermann was neither inexperienced nor inordinately self-serving; before the war he had declined the foreign ministry because he didn't want to have to deal with the Reichstag and the other chronic headaches that went with the job. A man of considerable charm, he was enjoyed

Arthur Zimmermann
Author of history's most costly telegram.

by everyone who knew him, including the American ambassador in Berlin, who was otherwise no admirer of Germany or the Germans. But he was also one of those men capable of believing that they know everything about subjects of which they actually have no useful experience. Years before the war, upon returning to Germany from the Far East, Zimmermann had crossed the United States by train, spending a few days in San Francisco and New York along the way. Ever afterward he had postured as an authority on all things American, and too many Germans who had never been across the Atlantic accepted his pronouncements. Such Germans were all too willing to ignore the cabled warnings of their own ambassador to the United States, the intelligent and capable Count Johann von Bernstorff, who had been in Washington for eight years and understood that the nation that had fought the American Civil War was not to be trifled with.

In the weeks between the decision to lift restrictions on U-boat operations and the public disclosure of that decision, Zimmermann cast about for ways to exploit it to Germany's advantage. He devised a plan, a scheme for winning new allies—Mexico and Japan, of all the improbable candidates—while at the same time entangling the United States in a war on the North American continent. He began the execution of this scheme by addressing a message to the German ambassador in Mexico City:

WE INTEND TO BEGIN UNRESTRICTED SUBMARINE WARFARE ON THE FIRST OF FEBRUARY. WE SHALL ENDEAVOR IN SPITE OF THIS TO KEEP THE UNITED STATES NEUTRAL. IN THE EVENT OF THIS NOT SUCCEEDING, WE MAKE MEXICO A PROPOSAL OF ALLIANCE ON THE FOLLOWING BASIS: MAKE WAR TOGETHER, MAKE PEACE TOGETHER, GENEROUS

FINANCIAL SUPPORT, AND AN UNDERSTANDING ON OUR PART
THAT MEXICO IS TO RECONQUER THE LOST TERRITORY IN
TEXAS, NEW MEXICO AND ARIZONA. THE SETTLEMENT IN
DETAIL IS LEFT TO YOU.

WE WILL INFORM THE PRESIDENT OF THE ABOVE MOST
SECRETLY AS SOON AS THE OUTBREAK OF WAR WITH THE
UNITED STATES IS CERTAIN AND ADD THE SUGGESTION THAT
HE SHOULD, ON HIS OWN INITIATIVE, INVITE JAPAN TO
IMMEDIATE ADHERENCE AND AT THE SAME TIME MEDIATE
BETWEEN JAPAN AND OURSELVES.

PLEASE CALL THE PRESIDENT'S ATTENTION TO THE FACT
THAT THE UNRESTRICTED EMPLOYMENT OF OUR SUBMARINES
NOW OFFERS THE PROSPECT OF COMPELLING ENGLAND TO
MAKE PEACE WITHIN A FEW MONTHS.

ZIMMERMANN.

Zimmermann originally intended to have his proposal delivered by hand
via a submarine being prepared for a voyage across the Atlantic. When
that venture was canceled, he sent the message by telegram, and in code,
to Bernstorff in Washington, with instructions to relay it to Mexico City.
Germany's transatlantic cable having been cut by the British navy early in the
war, he used a British-owned telegraph line that President Wilson had made
available to Germany for communications having to do with possible peace
negotiations. Like everyone else in the German government, Zimmermann
was unaware that British naval intelligence had long since broken the German
encryption system and was intercepting virtually every transatlantic message
sent by Berlin. Thus the Royal Navy knew the contents of Zimmermann's
telegram almost as soon as Bernstorff did. Its intelligence chief, as soon as
he saw an incompletely decoded version, understood that the Germans had
bestowed upon the Entente a propaganda weapon of incalculable power. He
also understood, however, that he had a problem: how to make Zimmermann's
proposal known to the Americans without also revealing to the Germans that
their code had been compromised. He locked the message in a safe and kept
it secret even from his own government. There it would remain for more
than five weeks, a bomb waiting to be detonated.

On January 22, still ignorant not only of the telegram but of Germany's
impending resumption of submarine warfare, President Wilson gave a speech
to Congress in which he spoke of the sacredness of freedom of the seas, his
vision of a League of Nations that would make future wars impossible, and
his hope that the war could end in "peace without victory." The British and

French were scornful, furious at Wilson for refusing to say that peace was impossible until Germany had been crushed. Ambassador Bernstorff was barraging Berlin with messages, begging his government to respond to Wilson's request for peace terms and delay its submarine warfare declaration long enough to give Wilson an opportunity to get a conference scheduled. Even if Wilson failed, Bernstorff observed, a display of German willingness to cooperate would have a favorable impact on American opinion. His pleas were ignored. Soon the German admirals were able to say that it was too late for a change of plans—the first of the U-boats had put to sea and could not be recalled.

On January 31, pursuant to his instructions, a disconsolate Bernstorff announced the resumption of unrestricted submarine warfare to U.S. secretary of state Robert Lansing, expressed his regret at having to do so, and withdrew. Foreseeing the outcome, he began preparations for a return to Germany.

On February 2 Wilson met with his cabinet, found that its members were almost unanimously in favor of going to war, and replied that he still had hopes of staying out, of acting as a peacemaker. An American liner, the *Housatonic*, was sunk by a U-boat that day without loss of life.

On February 3 the United States severed diplomatic relations with Germany, giving Bernstorff his passport and inviting him to depart. Cornered by reporters, the ambassador said simply that "I am finished with politics for the rest of my life."

The situation remained static for nearly three weeks, with Republican leaders of the Senate and former president Theodore Roosevelt calling for war and Wilson remaining silent. The ports of the East Coast became gridlocked with loaded merchant ships, their owners afraid to order them to sea. The rail lines leading into those ports began to back up as well, unable to unload the huge quantities of freight bound for Europe. Farmers and manufacturers, workers and shippers, labor unions and corporations all began to scream as costs rose, perishable goods began to rot, and sales and jobs were jeopardized. Everyone looked to the White House and waited. It began to seem possible, to the astonishment of many and the delight of some, that not even the U-boat campaign was going to persuade Wilson to make war. The public remained unsettled where the question of war was concerned. There was much support in the east, much opposition in other regions, and millions remained undecided.

But then on February 23, British intelligence having found a way to disguise the means by which it had learned the contents of the Zimmermann telegram (this involved pretending that a copy had been found on an intercepted ship), Foreign Secretary Arthur Balfour shared its contents with the American ambassador in London. It was forwarded to Secretary of State

Lansing, who had long been an advocate of war and so was pleased to present it to Wilson. The president was furious. Lansing persuaded him to keep the telegram secret until its disclosure could have maximum impact.

On February 26 Wilson again addressed Congress, this time requesting approval for the arming of American commercial ships with navy guns and gun crews. The House of Representatives approved his request almost immediately and by an overwhelming majority. There was no vote in the Senate because of a filibuster organized by the antiwar progressive Robert LaFollette of Wisconsin. Prowar factions in the Senate and elsewhere were seething, calling LaFollette and his allies traitors and Wilson a coward.

Late on February 28, with Wilson's approval, Lansing released the Zimmermann telegram to the press. It made banner headlines from coast to coast the next morning, stunning the nation. The story had only one flaw: it was almost too astonishing to be believed. Opponents of war denounced it as a fraud, a British concoction. Many Americans found this denunciation easier to believe than that the German government's foreign minister could have done such a thing.

Then, after days of dispute, Zimmermann again came to the rescue of the Entente. Questioned by reporters—he was unique among German officials in his willingness to talk with the press—he blithely declared that of course the telegram was authentic. *Of course* he had sent it. Why not? he asked innocently. Obviously he had not intended it to be used unless and until the United States declared war.

On March 7 the president went into deep seclusion, refusing to see or confer with anyone. On March 12 he emerged to issue an executive order for the arming of American merchant ships, thereby bypassing the LaFollette filibuster. Then he again withdrew, and the days crept past with the world holding its breath. On March 18 three American ships were sunk by U-boats. Two days later Wilson called his cabinet together and again asked its members for their opinion. To a man, they favored war.

On April 2 Wilson delivered the speech, never to be forgotten, in which he told Congress that war was unavoidable because "the world must be made safe for democracy."

The House approved a War Resolution with 373 members in favor, fifty opposed.

On April 4 the Senate approved the same resolution eighty-two to six.

And on April 6 the United States declared war on Germany.

THE COSSACKS

FOR MANY AMERICANS, GETTING INTO THE EUROPEAN war was a thrilling prospect. It was an opportunity not only to have an adventure, not only to make the world safe for democracy, but to demonstrate to the Old World the superiority of the New.

The Old World, after all, was *old:* tired, benighted, corrupt. The New, by contrast, was the natural habitat of the free and the brave. The inability of the Entente to defeat the forces of evil in more than two years of war was itself an expression of Old World decadence, and it was time for the Yanks to show the British and French how to get it done.

If the Americans had looked for a European people akin to their image of themselves, for a population of rugged, even cowboylike individualists with a history of fighting for their independence, they might have found one in an extremely improbable place. The closest counterparts to the legendary heroes of the Wild West were, ironically, the Cossacks of the Russian steppe—the ultimate symbols of tsarist repression.

No one had been surprised, when Petrograd began to dissolve into chaos, that it was Cossack horsemen who were sent into the streets to restore order. Russians had learned to expect to see Cossacks wherever there was trouble. As often as not, it was Cossacks who *made* the trouble. They were the tsar's enforcers, the scourge of peasants and Jews, a bludgeon used by the Romanov regime to smash whoever seemed to need smashing.

Their very name had become synonymous with despotism. Even today it conjures up images for people who know little of Russian history: rifles and sabers, boots and saddles, mustachioed killers in big shaggy hats. Cossacks had put the first Romanov on the throne in 1613, conquered and settled Siberia, and broken the back of Napoleon's invading army in 1812. They formed the core of Russia's enormous cavalry throughout the Great War.

"Age-old subduers and punishers," Trotsky called them. But that was only part of the story. Tolstoy, who had lived among them in his youth, said that what made them Cossacks was their "love of freedom."

They were unlike any other people in Europe—not exactly Russian but

Cossack fighters
*"Age-old subduers
and punishers."*

not an entirely distinct tribe, certainly not a military caste like the Junkers
of Germany. For centuries their homelands were a kind of melting pot
open to anyone brave or desperate enough to enter. There is no better
analogy than the gun-toting freebooters of the American West.

Until the fifteenth or even sixteenth century there was no such thing as
a Cossack. The Cossacks emerged in the period when the Mongols of
Genghis Khan, having forced their way deep into central Europe, controlled an enormous expanse of the fertile open plain, the steppe, that rolls
almost without interruption from Hungary to northern China. As the
Mongols' expansion ceased and the Great Khan's empire was divided into
pieces, what is now southern Russia and Ukraine was left in possession of
a subgroup called the Tatars. These warlike nomads lived by plunder, constantly raiding the Russian domains centered on Moscow to the north.
They carried away not only treasure but thousands of captives to be sold
in the slave markets of the Ottoman Empire. To the Russians, the Tatars
were a terror, the lands they controlled a dark pit of barbarism.

By the sixteenth century the tsars were consolidating their control of

Muscovy and, in the process, reducing the Russian peasants to serfdom—to mere property, a condition not far removed from outright slavery. Not surprisingly, the peasants were less than pleased. Their only choices, however, were to submit, to die, or to flee. There was no place to go except southward into the lands of the Tatars, and those who went were, almost by definition, the boldest and most defiantly self-reliant members of the Russian peasantry. Once beyond the reach of Moscow, they clashed with, learned from, gradually dominated, and finally merged with the Tatars. A new phenomenon among the peoples of the world arose: a community of untamed Orthodox Christian warrior horsemen, of mixed Slavic and East Asian blood, living by the sword and ruled by no one.

The early Cossacks (the origins of the name are shrouded in mystery but apparently have roots meaning both "wanderers" and "free people") created an extraordinary society. Unlike any of the surrounding peoples, they were radically democratic. Even their women were remarkably free. Every member of the community voted, and a leader called the *ataman* was elected for a term of only one year so that power could not be gathered permanently into any single pair of hands. Anyone wishing to join the community—runaway serf, Tatar nomad in search of home and fellowship—had only to declare a wish to do so and accept at least nominally the Orthodox faith. Ethnic or racial origin meant nothing, property was held in common, and there was no such thing as a hereditary elite.

As their numbers and power increased, the Cossacks became both worrisome as a potential threat and attractive as potential allies. For a time the tsars were pleased to have them as a buffer between Russia and its traditional enemies to the south and east. Eventually, however, Moscow attempted to change them from allies into subjects, and that gave rise to conflict. The Cossacks refused to take an oath of loyalty to the tsar, causing much trouble, but Moscow allowed them to keep any territories they conquered (Siberia being one example) so long as those territories became officially part of Russia. In this way the Cossacks came to occupy vast domains. The ambivalence of their relationship with the tsars was never plainer or more painful than during the lifetime of Michael Romanov, the first member of Russia's last dynasty. It was Cossack support, after years of chaos, that allowed Michael to assume the throne. Later, however, when he sent a representative into the Cossack lands to demand submission, the unfortunate emissary was put into a sack and thrown into the River Don.

The seventeenth and eighteenth centuries brought Russian wars on the Cossacks and repeated Cossack rebellions. They ended in defeat for the Cossacks, their absorption into the Russian nation, and the gradual dilution of some of their most distinctive traditions. The *ataman* came to be an appointee of the tsar. Some of the strongest Cossack families seized large estates and established themselves as a landowning aristocracy on the traditional Russian model. Even serfdom was introduced into the Cossack lands. The old traditions were not entirely extinguished, however, and the tradition of every Cossack male being a proudly independent warrior proved to be least extinguishable of all. The price, however, was high. Cossack youths owed the tsar first twenty, then eventually thirty years of military service. Each was required to provide his own horses and equipment, a heavy burden for ordinary families. Sadly, the Cossacks' contempt for outsiders made it easy for the tsars to convert them into instruments of repression, even of genocide. In 1648–49, in just one of the crimes that steep their history in blood, they massacred three hundred thousand Jews. The reward, for a Cossack soldier, was a grant of land at the end of decades of service.

They were never mere murderous robots, however. During the 1905–6 revolution, their arrangement with the Romanovs threatened to break down when Cossack regiments mutinied rather than allow themselves to be used to stamp out rebellion by peasants and workers. A crisis was averted only by the dissolution of the disloyal units. When the Great War came almost a decade later, the Cossacks were once again ready for duty. They were mobilized en masse, boys and middle-aged men alike, creating severe hardships for the families left behind. They made up at least half of the Russian cavalry, and the willingness of the Russian general staff to send them and their horses against German machine guns made the war even more disastrous for them than for most Russians. By 1917, when they were called upon once again to put down popular uprisings, many of them had had enough. They stood aside and allowed the revolution to proceed.

Of all the signs that Nicholas II and his whole system were finished, this was the clearest.

Chapter 28

✠

The Nivelle Offensive

*"Do you know what such an action is called?
It is called cowardice."*

—GENERAL ALFRED MICHELER

Amazingly, the first three months of 1917 had passed without huge effusions of blood on any of Europe's fronts. Men were still being killed by the hundreds, but not in great offensives. They were dying in what had become merely the routine way. They died every day in the almost absent-minded exchanges of artillery and sniper fire that punctuated life in the trenches. They died every night in the dark bloody excursions into no-man's-land that had become so common that almost no one noticed.

On April 6 France's political and military leadership gathered in President Poincaré's railroad car in the forest of Compiègne near Paris. The subject was the impending offensive that would, General Robert Nivelle promised, bring the war to an end. The purpose of the meeting, however, was not to complete the planning of that offensive. It was to settle the question of whether the offensive was going to happen at all. Among those opposed were General Alfred Micheler, a Somme veteran chosen by Nivelle to command the army group that would attack at the Chemin des Dames, and Paul Painlevé, the recently appointed minister of war. The latter had not abandoned his efforts, which began almost the day he took office, to persuade Nivelle to reconsider. By the start of April he was practically begging, promising Nivelle that in light of the German pullback to the Hindenburg Line no one would think less of him if he changed his mind. Painlevé lacked the authority to decide the issue, however. Only Poincaré could do that.

The arguments for not proceeding were almost overwhelming. It was certain that the United States was coming in—its declaration of war became effective, in fact, on the day of the Compiègne meeting. This meant that the

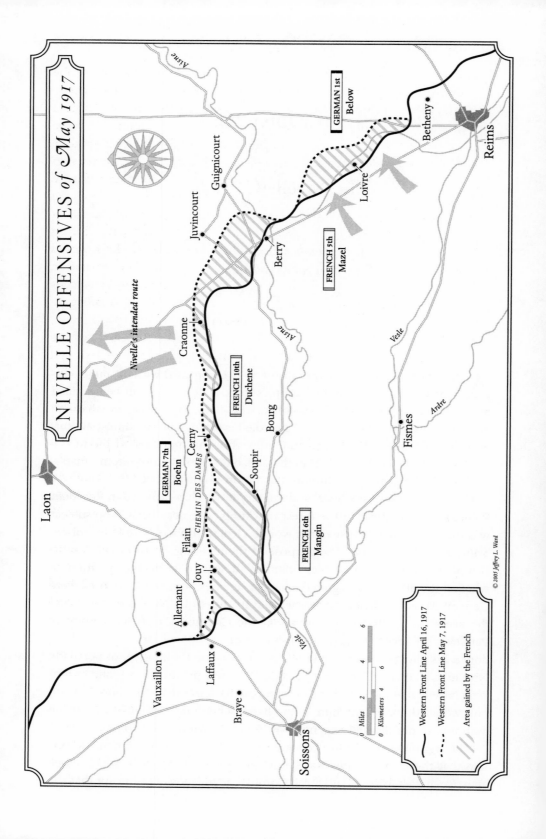

NIVELLE OFFENSIVES of May 1917

Aisne

GERMAN 1st
Below

Betheny

Reims

Guignicourt

Loivre

Juvincourt

FRENCH 5th
Mazel

Berry

Nivelle's intended route

Aisne

Craonne

Vesle

FRENCH 10th
Duchene

Ardre

Bourg

Fismes

GERMAN 7th
Boehn

Cerny

Soupir

CHEMIN DES DAMES

Filain

Laon

FRENCH 6th
Mangin

Jouy

Allemant

Vauxaillon

Vesle

Laffaux

Braye

Soissons

Miles   2   4   6
0

Kilometers   4   6
0   2

Western Front Line April 16, 1917

Western Front Line May 7, 1917

Area gained by the French

© 2005 Jeffrey L. Ward

French could afford to rest their worn-down armies while waiting for the Americans to arrive. The fall of Nicholas II, which promised democracy in Russia and a restoration of Russian morale, also suggested that 1917 would be a good year for France to husband her strength. What mattered even more was the German withdrawal to the Hindenburg Line; this move, as Painlevé and others pointed out repeatedly, had destroyed many of the premises on which Nivelle's plan had been based from the start. The German defensive line was miles shorter and much stronger than it had been at the turn of the year. Many of the positions that Nivelle had intended to attack were now abandoned. The territory beyond those positions had been left a barren wasteland; Ludendorff, in pulling his forces back, had imitated the scorched earth policy used effectively by the Russians in retreating from Poland in 1915. Every building, every tree, every bit of railway, and every crossroads had been destroyed in the thousand square miles that the Germans gave up, and the Entente was slow to take possession of the resulting desolation. The British and French would have to attack at the two extremities of the Hindenburg Line, with a mixed command under Haig at the western end near Arras and most of the French miles to the east. Neither would be able to support the other directly.

The focal point of the French attack, the Chemin des Dames, could hardly have been a more formidable objective. The German defenses lay atop a high wooded ridge along the base of which the River Aisne followed its east-west course. The roads and railways behind the French lines almost all ran the wrong way, laterally instead of toward the front. Despite the difficulties, Nivelle proposed to overwhelm the Germans with a single crushing blow. When Joffre had first proposed a 1917 offensive, his plan had been to attack on a front of about sixty miles. Nivelle, convinced that the tactics that had worked in the final days of Verdun could be equally effective on a larger scale, had expanded that to a hundred miles. The Germans meanwhile, aware of what was coming, had increased the number of their divisions on and behind the Chemin des Dames ridge from nine to thirty-eight. Nivelle was undeterred. The more enemy divisions were on the scene, he said, the more he would be able to destroy.

Haig was skeptical, but his doubts were neutralized by Lloyd George's disdain for him and enthusiasm for Nivelle and for his plan. Several of France's most senior generals remained skeptical as well, but because some of them had been passed over when Nivelle was promoted to commander in chief, it was easy to attribute their objections to petty jealousy. Painlevé was so certain that disaster lay ahead that he had tried to resign from the cabinet and been refused. Now, at Compiègne, he explained his fears one final time. Again Nivelle shrugged him off. He said that if he were not allowed to proceed, he would resign. Poincaré, aware that Nivelle's resignation would mean the fall of yet another government, hoping that the offensive would save the Russians and Italians from attack and impressed anew with his new commander's absolute certainty, ended the discussion by telling him to proceed.

The offensive began on April 9 with an attack by four armies, three British and one French, on the northern edge of the old Somme battleground. It was intended partly to draw German reserves away from Chemin des Dames, but it was more than just a diversion. One of the hopes for it was that, if Haig's troops broke through, they could advance to the east and link up with Nivelle's advance. Once combined, the two forces would have enough mass to uproot Crown Prince Wilhelm's army group and drive it out of France. As at the Somme, the British preparations had been on a colossal scale. Their dimensions are apparent in the details: 206 trainloads of crushed rock brought forward to build firm roadways behind the British front, and days of preparatory bombardment by more than twenty-eight hundred cannons and heavy mortars—one for every twelve yards of line.

Haig's Canadians were particularly well prepared and rehearsed. Early on the morning of the attack they moved undetected to within a hundred and fifty yards of the German defenses through a maze of sewers and tunnels that honeycombed the earth under Arras. Upon emerging they were able to advance under the protection of a perfectly timed creeping barrage. The Germans, their attention fixed on the French buildup at the Chemin des Dames, had not expected anything on this scale. Taken by surprise, within a few hours they were driven off most of Vimy Ridge, which dominates the countryside east of Arras. Thereafter, the advance was slowed by wintry storms and a stiffening of resistance as German reserves came into play.

"We moved forward, but the conditions were terrible," a British artilleryman reported. "The ammunition that had been prepared by our leaders for this great spring offensive had to be brought up with the supplies, over roads which were sometimes up to one's knees in slimy, yellowish-brown mud. The horses were up to their bellies in mud. We'd put them on a picket line between the wagon wheels at night and they'd be sunk in over their fetlocks the next day. We had to shoot quite a number. Rations were so poor that we ate turnips, and I went into the French dugouts, which had been there since 1914, and took biscuits that had been left by troops two years previously. They were all mouldy but I ate them and it didn't do me any harm. We also had crusts of bread that had been flung out of the more fortunate NCOs' mess at a previous date, we scraped black mud from them and ate them. One could make two biscuits last for about three quarters of the day."

Haig continued to attack for weeks, partly to give continued support to Nivelle, partly because the success of the first day had caused him to believe (as he was inclined to do in the middle of all his offensives) that he was on the verge of a breakthrough. But little more was gained. Entente casualties had been fairly light in the early going—almost trivial by the standard of the Somme—but as Haig persisted into mid-May, the total mounted at a rate of four thousand every day. Haig tried as usual to get the cavalry into action, but by the time this was possible the Germans were ready. Machine guns and artillery massacred horses and riders alike.

One of many
Arras Cathedral, destroyed by shelling

From a strategic perspective, the results of Arras were ambiguous. Haig had grounds for claiming success: Vimy Ridge was a valuable trophy, the Germans had had to rush in tens of thousands of reinforcements from other points along the front, and in the exhilarating first three days the British had captured fourteen thousand prisoners and one hundred eighty guns. They had also advanced between three and six miles at various points—major gains on the Western Front. On the other hand, they had achieved no break-through and had no hope of linking up with Nivelle. By the time it all ended, the Germans had taken one hundred and eighty thousand casualties, Haig's armies a hundred and fifty-eight thousand. Back in London, Lloyd George was freshly disgusted by the expenditure of so many men for such limited results.

Ludendorff was alarmed. April 9 was his fifty-second birthday, and his staff had prepared a party to observe the occasion, but he withdrew into isolation soon after getting the first reports from Arras. The early British gains, the loss of Vimy Ridge especially, seemed at first to indicate that his new system of defense did not work. "I had looked forward to the expected offensive with confidence, and was now deeply depressed," he would recall. "Was this to be the result of all our care and trouble during the past half-year?" Closer exam-ination, however, revealed that the fault lay in the failure of the German Sixth Army's commander to *use* the system. General Ludwig von Falkenhausen had not followed instructions. Instead he had continued to do the things that he, like all the Western Front veterans on both sides, had been learning to do in two and a half years of trench warfare. He had tried to block the Canadian advance with a heavily manned and continuous front line; instead of falling back when pressed, that line had been ordered to stand its ground and so had been overwhelmed. He had kept his second and third lines close together and near the front, so that like the first they were shattered by the British artillery and overrun. He had positioned his reserves fifteen miles to the rear, too far away to make a difference at the crisis of the attack.

Where the system had been tried, however, it proved its effectiveness. The attackers had been allowed to advance into a killing zone where they were raked with artillery and machine-gun fire and then driven back with counter-attacks. German losses had been kept at tolerable levels. As soon as this became clear, Falkenhausen was dismissed. Efforts were redoubled to ensure that the new system would be fully in place at the Chemin des Dames by the time the French attacked there.

Nivelle's attack came at six A.M. on April 16. From start to finish it was a contest between an offensive of the most conventional kind—more than a week of intense artillery preparation, massed formations of infantry slog-ging in plain view toward their objectives—and the Germans' new defense. Almost immediately it turned into something very like the debacle that

Painlevé and so many others had feared. The idea that had governed all of Nivelle's planning—that the tactics he and Mangin had used to retake Forts Douaumont and Vaux at Verdun would work in this different and much larger theater—proved to be totally inadequate to the occasion. (Nor had Nivelle considered that, by the time of his attacks at Verdun, the Germans were quite prepared to abandon ruined fortresses for stronger positions in the rear.) In many places French troops had to cross the Aisne at the start of their advance, then climb a steep hillside obstructed with trees, a ragged network of ravines, and the inevitable German wire. The entire hillside was studded with German machine-gun nests so well dug in and protected with steel and concrete that they had survived the bombardment; they poured fire on the French as they came forward. The German first line was on the reverse slope, beyond the crest of the ridge. Thus most of the French shells had passed harmlessly over it, and those attackers who reached the crest were exposed against the sky. The German reserves were far enough back to be beyond reach of most of Nivelle's batteries (he was undersupplied with long-range guns), but not too far back to enter the battle quickly.

In raw manpower terms, the advantage lay entirely with the French. Nivelle had three armies that among them included fifty-three divisions—at least 1.2 million men—and all three were used in the initial assault. But twenty-seven divisions were held back as the Mass of Maneuver, which was to exploit the breakthrough when it came. To absorb this attack the Germans had twenty-one divisions in position on or near the Chemin des Dames, and another twenty-seven as their counterattack force. They had been in possession of the ridge since September 1914, so that they knew every inch of it and had had more than two and a half years to shape it to their needs. And they were commanded by Crown Prince Wilhelm; he and his staff had become well acquainted with the Nivelle offensive formula at Verdun, and they had had the winter to adapt to it. And of course they held the heights.

One hundred and twenty-eight of France's new tanks participated in the assault but accomplished nothing. As part of the new German tactics, every artillery battery was ordered to direct the fire of one of its guns at any tank that came into view. This tactic proved devastating: fifty-two tanks were blown to bits on the first day, and another twenty-eight broke down. Those that remained either fell into ditches excavated by the Germans or bogged down in mud.

The weather was on the side of the Germans. It had started to rain the night before the attack, and the rain turned to sleet followed by snow—an improbable development at this time of year. At many points the French never got close to their objectives. At others they were able, heroically and at great cost, to advance as much as two and a half miles. "A snow squall swept our position," a French tank officer wrote after observing the opening of the attack. "Our first wounded soldiers were coming in, men from the Eighty-Third Infantry Regiment. We gathered round them, and learned from them that the enemy positions were very strong, the resistance desperate. One battalion did reach the top of the Cornillet—probably the one whose gallant advance we had watched—but it was decimated by fire from intact machine gun positions, and was unable to withstand the enemy's counterattack. One of the wounded men, his arm in a sling and patches of blood on his forehead, shouted while driving by:

"'The Boches are still holding out in the Grille Wood, but we are attacking them with grenades.'

"A helmetless lieutenant, his clothes disarrayed and with a wound in his chest, walked slowly toward our group:

"'Ah! If only you [the tanks] had been with us! We found nothing but intact barbed wire! If it hadn't been for that, we'd be far ahead now, instead of killing each other on the spot.'

"'We just couldn't keep moving,' an alert corporal shouted, while using his rifle as a crutch. 'Too many blasted machine guns, against which there was nothing doing!'

"'The Boche certainly knew we were going to attack there,' the lieutenant went on, 'their trenches were jammed.'"

Even the French gains were in accord with the German defensive system. By midday the Germans were moving both their reserves and their masses of light artillery forward from the rear. They hit the French after they had been wearied and battered, sending them reeling back toward their starting point. As the day ended, the French had succeeded in moving their line forward approximately six hundred yards on average. (Nivelle had forecast gains of six miles on the first day.) The Mass of Maneuver had had no opportunity to go into action. It was another Somme.

Nivelle attacked again on the second day, this time sending his forces off in two directions in a forking maneuver. One army was to move toward the northeast and try to link up with a French force that was at the same time launching a separate, supporting assault in Champagne. This was a complete failure, first absorbed by the German defenses and then forced back. The other tine of the fork, commanded by Mangin, had some success in pushing to the north and west. It captured three towns of no great importance, but finally even Mangin's relentless aggressiveness could not keep it from bogging down. In the end his men too were driven back. The French were everywhere stymied. Nivelle kept scheduling and canceling and rescheduling attacks by his Mass of Maneuver. The strain of having to prepare again and again to die unnerved the waiting troops.

On April 19 War Minister Painlevé again intervened, trying to get Nivelle to stop. The general, who in demanding approval of his grand plan had promised to call it off if a breakthrough were not achieved within forty-eight hours, refused. The very next day he found to his chagrin, however, that he had no choice but to pause: the divisions at the front were breaking down, both their morale and their supplies of ammunition dangerously low. Late on the day after that, April 21, a new phenomenon appeared. African troops—members of elite units that had often led the assaults of Mangin's army—shocked and embarrassed their officers by shouting *Vive la paix*. "Peace! Down with war! Death to those who are responsible!" Other units were getting drunk en masse and refusing to march to the front.

On April 25, with Paris awash in rumors that put the casualty figures even higher than they actually were, President Poincaré humiliated the commander in chief by ordering an end to the attacks on the Chemin des Dames. Nivelle reacted ignobly. He blamed Mangin for the failure of the offensive and dismissed him from command of the Sixth Army. He then tried to blame Micheler as well. Micheler, who had regarded the offensive as hopeless from the start and had become almost insubordinate in saying so, responded with witheringly wrathful contempt. "What, you try to make me responsible for the mistake, when I never ceased to warn you?" he demanded. "Do you know what such an action is called? It is called cowardice."

By the time the offensive was shut down, it had cost the French two hundred and seventy thousand casualties, including tens of thousands killed. Total German casualties have been estimated at one hundred and sixty-three thousand. These were losses that neither side could afford. Nivelle was destroyed, not so much because of his failure but because he had promised so much. On April 28 Painlevé elevated Pétain to chief of staff of the French army and asked Nivelle to resign as commander in chief (a post distinct from chief of staff). Nivelle, astonishingly, refused. Instead he became increasingly reckless in assigning blame. He completed his self-humiliation by refusing to resign even after Pétain was named commander in chief in his stead. By that time Pétain was faced with an entirely new kind of crisis—an army mutiny so widespread that for a while it appeared possible that France might be unable to stay in the war.

The war had reached a point at which several of the belligerent nations were not only in trouble but in danger of breaking down. The disintegration of the Ottoman Empire was by now well advanced. The Turks, their hard-fighting but weary soldiers chronically low on supplies and reinforcements, had lost the Caucasus to the Russians in 1916. In March 1917 British forces operating out of Egypt had captured the Mesopotamian capital of Baghdad, one of the greatest jewels in the Ottoman crown. The only thing keeping Turkey in the war was the certainty that its empire was doomed if Germany went down to defeat.

Russia's provisional government too was faced with monstrous problems. It was being financed and generously supplied by the British and French but was increasingly unable to keep either its armies intact or its home front under control. On April 11 an All-Russian Conference of Soviets voted to support a continuation of the war, but it also called for negotiations aimed at achieving peace without annexations or indemnities on either side. On April 15 tens of thousands of Russian troops came out of their trenches to join with their German and Austrian adversaries in impromptu and nearly mutinous Easter celebrations. On the following day Lenin arrived in Petrograd from his long exile in Switzerland; Ludendorff, hoping to foment further disruption inside Russia, had approved his travel by rail from Switzerland via Frankfurt, Berlin, Stockholm, and Helsinki. Upon his arrival the Bolshevik leader began maneuvering his followers into an antiwar stance calculated to take advantage of public discontent. The Russians had promised a May 1 attack in support of the Nivelle offensive and had assembled a massive force for the purpose. The offensive proved impossible, however, to carry out. The troops had become ungovernable, and not enough coal could be found to operate the necessary trains. On May 2 Kerensky became leader of the provisional government. He tried to address the army's problems, but everything he did ended up making them worse. When he released all men over age forty-three from military service, a transportation system that was already on the verge of collapse found itself mobbed by middle-aged veterans desperate to get to their homes. When he abolished the death penalty for desertion, a million soldiers threw down their weapons. Many were drawn homeward by the hope of getting a piece of land when the great estates of the aristocracy were distributed to the people. Many were simply sick of war.

Austria-Hungary was a broken and empty shell barely held together by the resentful support of Berlin. Its new emperor, Karl I, not yet thirty, was a pious, earnest, and cultivated idealist who had succeeded to his family's dual thrones after having received no training in politics and no experience in the administration of anything. He desired sincerely not only to hold his empire together but to deliver its people from further carnage. In March he embarked upon one of the most quixotic undertakings of the Great War. He recruited his wife's two young brothers, the Princes Sixtus and Xavier of Bourbon-Parma, both of whom had served as stretcher-bearers in the Belgian army earlier in the war, to be his emissaries in a secret effort to initiate peace discussions with the Entente. This effort was as naïve as it was well intentioned, its naïveté most apparent in Karl's failure to tell the Germans what he was doing. When the inevitable happened and Berlin found out, Karl stood convicted in the eyes of his allies of having attempted to save himself while cutting Germany adrift (something that he does not appear to have intended). When the details of his proposal appeared in the Paris newspapers (the Germans were freshly appalled to learn that Karl was offering Alsace and Lorraine to France), he panicked and denounced the story as a malicious fabrication. This persuaded the French that he was not only a fool but a liar.

His effort had been doomed from the start. At first it generated small sparks of interest, especially in London, but by this point a negotiated peace that did not involve the dismantling of Austria-Hungary was hardly possible. Russia, Italy, and Romania had all been promised great pieces of Karl's patrimony. It was difficult to see how Britain and France could agree to a settlement that did not redeem these pledges. Karl's initiative had been little more than a last gasp of an impotent and dying regime.

If Germany was a tower of strength when contrasted with Turkey, Russia, or Austria-Hungary, serious cracks were appearing in the tower's foundations. The German nation was continuing slowly to starve, and when the flour ration was further reduced in mid-April, workers went on strike in hundreds of factories. As prices continued to rise, workers in steel and munitions plants along with miners by the tens of thousands struck for higher wages and more and better food. Behind this unrest was a deepening weariness with an endless war and with all the tragedy the war had brought. Germany's political parties, which were a barometer of public opinion even if they lacked any role in making policy, began to break apart over how to end the war and how the experience of the war should be translated into reforms. In March the Reichstag created a special committee to study a reform of the German constitution. In April the socialists, echoing their counterparts in Russia, called for peace without annexations or indemnities.

Such ideas were anathema not only to Ludendorff and the rest of the high command but to all the most powerful elements of German society. The Junkers of Prussia, the owners of German industry, and the conservative and center-right parties all were opposed to reforms that might require them to surrender any part of the power that had long belonged to them alone. Nor were they without popular support: ordinary citizens were easily persuaded that any settlement of the war must both repay the nation for its suffering and increase its security through strategic annexations of, for example, Belgium's Liège. In Germany as in all the belligerent countries, propaganda was contributing to making peace impossible. The German public had been taught that the war had been started by an Entente committed to the destruction of their nation, that in prosecuting the war the Entente had flouted international law, and that the armies of the Entente were guilty of unspeakable atrocities. To people who believed these things, it was inconceivable that

Germany could accept a peace in which the aggressors were not held to account or were left with the ability to attack again.

Bethmann Hollweg saw things more clearly. Though he exasperated friends and enemies alike with his shifting opinions and pursuit of compromise, the chancellor was consistent in believing that a negotiated peace was Germany's only hope. He also saw constitutional reform—democratization—as necessary to maintain the morale of the nation. By April he was publicly advocating the elimination of Prussia's three-tiered electoral system, which reserved almost all political power to the property-owning classes. Bethmann understood that the war had made such arrangements no longer sustainable: the people were unwilling to tolerate them. In proposing reform, however, he accomplished nothing except a multiplication of his influential enemies. Hindenburg and Ludendorff felt confirmed in their certainty that he was a radical in bureaucrat's clothing and must be removed. The kaiser, himself a waffler and increasingly unable to assert himself, was generally inclined to agree with Bethmann. By repeatedly refusing to replace the chancellor, he made himself an object of contempt among the conservatives and accelerated the process by which he was becoming a marginal figure.

In the near term Germany's problems were almost trivial when compared with those facing the French in the aftermath of the Nivelle offensive. The French army, or a dangerously big part of it, was in open rebellion, refusing to obey orders, assaulting and even killing officers, deserting. Troops were crowding into Paris in a state of extreme disorder. French archives on the mutiny have been sealed since the war and will remain so until 2017, but enough is known to make clear that at its peak it was a threat to the survival of the republic. Within six weeks of its start half of the French divisions on the Western Front were rendered nonfunctional as a result of what one officer called "a sort of moral nihilism, an army without faith." The government, more euphemistically, described the problem as "collective indiscipline."

With minor exceptions, the mutiny was never genuinely revolutionary in impulse—it was not aimed at overthrowing the government or even at ending the war. Rather, it was a kind of spontaneous strike through which the soldiers declared their refusal to continue living in intolerable conditions and dying to no purpose. Thus it was susceptible to being defused with practical remedies aimed at legitimate and manageable grievances. And France, unlike Russia, possessed the means to make the necessary reforms. It had ample food and matériel and money and a reasonably competent government.

For a variety of reasons the Germans remained ignorant of the mutiny and unable to take advantage of it. Had they done so when the rebellion was at its height, they might have met with little resistance in moving on Paris.

Before that could happen, however, Henri-Philippe Pétain took up his new responsibilities as commander in chief. His appointment was a stroke of good fortune for the Entente.

Pétain acted as quickly and firmly as he had upon arriving at Verdun in 1916. And he displayed great delicacy of judgment, neither cracking down so hard on the troops as to provoke worse resistance nor allowing the army to drift into deeper confusion. His first moves were aimed at reestablishing discipline. Thousands of soldiers accused of being the mutiny's ringleaders were arrested and brought to trial. Approximately five hundred of them were condemned to death, though fewer than a hundred were actually executed. (The exact numbers will remain uncertain until the records are made public.) Many went to prison, many were exiled to France's colonies, and those returned to active service found themselves subjected to the traditional forms of discipline in undiluted form.

Almost as quickly, however, Pétain also began addressing the abuses that had sparked the mutiny, "not forgetting the fact," he said, "that the mutineers were men who have been with us in the trenches for three years, our soldiers." He promised to provide many of the things that the men demanded— better food, decent shelter when not on the front lines, fairness in such matters as the granting of leave, an end to the pointless offensives that had squandered so many lives. And he saw to it that his promises were kept. Pétain himself visited ninety divisions during the crisis, standing atop his automobile to talk with the troops, listening to questions and complaints, giving straight answers. He had the great advantage of his reputation as a general who had always showed genuine concern for the well-being of the poilus.

It worked. At the height of the crisis, in late May and early June, new outbreaks were occurring at a rate of more than half a dozen every day. There began to be talk of political revolution, of forcing an end to the war. But by mid-July the mutiny was essentially at an end. Pétain had been as good as his word: not only were hundreds of thousands of soldiers given leave, but they received preferential treatment from the railroads in order to get home without delay. Not only were new facilities constructed for units being rested after service at the front, but these facilities were for the first time situated far enough behind the lines to be safe from enemy guns. It was too soon for Pétain to keep his promise that there would be no more insanely wasteful offensives, but the troops had been given reason to trust him and seemed prepared to do so.

Still, even with the crisis behind it, the army was in a badly shaken state. Major new campaigns were out of the question. The Germans too were in fragile condition after Arras and the Chemin des Dames; much of the

Russian army had disintegrated; and the Austrians, Turks, and Italians could do little more than flail feebly away on their various fronts. In every case outright collapse appeared to be somewhere between possible and imminent.

Britain seemed in a universe of its own, somewhere above the general calamity. The U-boat campaign was at its height and creating serious problems, sinking more than eight hundred and forty tons of shipping in April, a third more than the campaign's planners had said would be needed monthly to bring the British to their knees. But the solution had emerged. Early in May a first convoy of merchantmen guarded by destroyers set out from Gibraltar and reached England without loss. The British admirals had been reluctant to try the convoy system because it was in a sense counterintuitive, requiring every ship in a formation to proceed at the speed of the slowest. But Lloyd George insisted, and as soon as the idea was tried, any possibility that the U-boats would achieve their objectives disappeared forever. Britain experienced industrial and to a lesser extent political turbulence, with workers striking for better pay and conditions and the socialists demanding peace. But this was nothing compared to what was happening in Russia, Austria-Hungary, and Germany. The BEF had taken substantial losses at Arras, but that problem too was small compared with those of the French.

Britain and its army seemed blessed.

That would be the next thing to change.

THE WAR AND POETRY

HISTORIC EVENTS ARE OFTEN SAID TO HAVE "CHANGED
everything." In the case of the Great War this is, for once, true. The war
really did change *everything*: not just borders, not just governments and
the fate of nations, but the way people have seen the world and themselves
ever since. It became a kind of hole in time, leaving the postwar world permanently disconnected from everything that had come before.

As Samuel Hynes details in his brilliant study *War Imagined,* the events
of 1914–18 produced "the most important and wide-ranging cultural
change in modern English history." To grasp the truth of this—and it does
not apply to England only—it is necessary only to look at the literature
of the war years, and at the strange way that literature came to a stop,
appeared to be dead for a while, and then started up again on an entirely
new plane.

The start of the war brought an explosion of writing everywhere. It was
the age before radio and television, when poetry still mattered to millions
of people, and in August 1914 newspapers were being sent hundreds of
poems every day. Almost all of them were amateurish at best, but the subject matter was uniformly lofty: the greatness of this new crusade, the glory
of the cause, the heroism of those who had "fallen" on "the field of honor."
If poems expressing a less exalted view of the conflict were submitted, few
editors in Austria, Britain, France, Germany, or Russia showed any interest
in printing them.

Many leading men of letters enlisted their pens in the war effort. In
England James Barrie, Arnold Bennett, Robert Bridges, G. K. Chesterton,
Arthur Conan Doyle, John Galsworthy, H. Rider Haggard, Thomas Hardy,
John Masefield, Arthur Pinero, H. G. Wells—they and many others
accepted the Asquith government's invitation to help the nation understand what it was fighting for and why the sacrifices that lay ahead could
be embraced with pride. German writers, artists, and intellectuals, stung by
stories in Entente newspapers about atrocities committed by Berlin's troops
in Belgium and elsewhere, signed and published declarations of the justice of their homeland's cause. The most conspicuous, bearing the sig-
natures of nearly a hundred prominent figures, was addressed "To the

Cultured World." Thomas Mann, a future Nobel Prize winner, was among those swept up in the euphoria. The war, he said, was "a purification, a liberation, an enormous hope. The German soul is opposed to the pacifist ideal of civilization, for is not peace an element of civil corruption?"

There were side currents in the flood of patriotic words. The novelist Henry James, an American who had made England his home and would take up British citizenship before his death during the war, was in despair from the beginning. He called the war "this abyss of blood and darkness" and saw the fact that such a thing could happen as a nullification of everything he had believed about Europe, its civilization, and his own work. At the other end of the spectrum were men who, like Mann, wrote of the war as a kind of gift, a purifying fire that would burn away the rotten parts of a sick and effete culture.

The young Rupert Brooke saw it as heroic, beautiful, *and* purifying. He contemplated death in battle and found it pleasing.

> If I should die, think only this of me:
> That there's some corner of a foreign field
> That is forever England. There shall be
> In that rich dust a richer dust concealed;
> A dust whom England bore, shaped, made aware,
> Gave, once, her flowers to love, her ways to roam,
> A body of England's, breathing English air,
> Washed by the rivers, blest by suns of home.
>
> And think, this heart, all evil shed away,
> A pulse in this eternal mind, no less
> Gives somewhere back the thoughts of England given;
> Her sights and sounds; dreams happy as her day;
> And laughter, learnt of friends; and gentleness,
> In hearts at peace, under an English heaven.

As art this is High Treacle, but to English readers in 1914 it was Shakespearean. Brooke was dead several months after he wrote it. Of blood poisoning from an infected mosquito bite on a troop ship off Gallipoli. His "corner of a foreign field" is on the Aegean island of Skyros.

As the war wore on without result, the flow of noble feelings set to verse continued unabated. Increasingly, though, it was mere empty verbiage, an unloading of exhausted and irrelevant clichés, poetry done by the numbers. Almost nothing authentic, nothing that expressed the experiences of the men in the trenches or even their families at home, was showing up in print. More and more of the great men of letters were falling silent, as if acknowledging that there was nothing they could say. Those who continued in the old vein began to meet with resentment from men who had been to the front. When a young infantry officer named Roland Leighton received a volume of Brooke's poems from his fiancée, he wrote back in a tone the young lady could not have expected.

"Let him who thinks that War is a glorious golden thing, who loves to roll forth stirring words of exhortation, invoking Honor and Praise and Valour and Love of Country with as thoughtless and fervid a faith as inspired the priests of Baal to call on their own slumbering deity," he wrote, "let him look at a little pile of sodden grey rags that cover half a skull and a shin bone and what might have been its ribs, or at this skeleton lying on its side, resting half-crouching as it fell, supported on one arm, perfect but that it is headless, and with the tattered clothing still draped around it; and let him realize how grand & glorious a thing it is to have distilled all Youth and Joy and Life into a foetid heap of hideous putrescence. Who is there who has known and seen who can say that Victory is worth the death of even one of these?"

Leighton too was soon dead. Killed hours before he was to go home on leave and be married. (His fiancée, Vera Brittain, went on to write a book, *Testament of Youth*, which has remained in print ever since and is among the Great War's classics.)

Literary and artistic life came to be paralyzed by a sense that the established and accepted ways of representing reality—pictures of romantic warriors performing wondrous feats, words about honor and duty and glory—didn't fit with what was happening on the Western Front, and that every effort to make them fit could produce only rubbish. The words died and became hollow, unusable. Something similar was happening in the visual arts, and in fiction and theater; painters and novelists and playwrights, if they were at all serious, seemed not to know what to do. The less serious continued to treat the war as a medieval jousting match, but everything they did was stillborn, irrelevant, even vile. Virginia Woolf attended a concert where "the patriotic sentiment was so revolting that I was nearly sick."

But slowly, finally, in ways that could anger minds that wanted not to be disturbed, new voices began to emerge. A poetry and a kind of painting were born that did not deny reality—new and "ugly" expressions of an ugly thing. The new work came from the only possible source: men who had been there. One such man was the German artist Otto Dix, who had volunteered in 1914 in the expectation that war would bring him "tremendous experiences." Four years of service including fighting in Champagne, the Somme, and Russia changed him and his art profoundly and permanently. "Lice, rats, barbed wire, fleas, shells, bombs, underground caves, corpses, blood, liquor, mice, cats, artillery, filth, bullets, mortars, fire, steel: that is what war is," he wrote. "It is the work of the devil." He survived and spent the rest of his life putting his horror and disillusionment on canvas. Others—poets first, then writers of fiction—did the same in print. Some of them are still famous today. The Englishmen Robert Graves and Siegfried Sassoon. The German Erich Maria Remarque. Henri Barbusse and Guillaume Apollinaire of France.

And Wilfred Owen, a young teacher who had never attended a university, enlisted in 1915 and was wounded three times before being diagnosed with shell shock and sent to a hospital in Scotland. There he met Sassoon, a captain from the landed gentry who had been decorated for heroism and later sent for treatment rather than being court-martialed for declaring his intention never to fight again. Owen showed his early efforts to write verse to Sassoon, who found them conventional and urged him to deal with what he had actually experienced and what he really felt. This is the most famous result:

> *Bent double, like old beggars under sacks,*
> *Knock-kneed, coughing like hags, we cursed through sludge,*
> *Till on the haunting flares we turned our backs,*
> *And towards our distant rest began to trudge.*
> *Men marched asleep. Many had lost their boots*
> *But limped on, blood-shod. All went lame; all blind;*
> *Drunk with fatigue; deaf even to the hoots*
> *Of tired, outstripped Five-Nines that dropped behind.*
>
> *Gas! Gas! Quick, boys!—An ecstasy of fumbling,*
> *Fitting the clumsy helmets just in time,*
> *But someone still was yelling out and stumbling*
> *And flound'ring like a man in fire or lime . . .*
> *Dim through the misty panes and thick green light,*
> *As under a green sea, I saw him drowning.*
>
> *In all my dreams before my helpless sight,*
> *He plunges at me, guttering, choking, drowning.*
>
> *If in some smothering dreams you too could pace*
> *Behind the wagon that we flung him in,*
> *And watch the white eyes writhing in his face,*
> *His hanging face, like a devil's sick of sin,*

If you could hear, at every jolt, the blood
Come gargling from the froth-corrupted lungs
Obscene as cancer, bitter as the cud
Of vile, incurable sores on innocent tongues,—
My friend, you would not tell with such high zest
To children ardent for some desperate glory,
The old lie: Dulce et decorum est
Pro patria mori.

Sweet and fitting it is, to die for one's country. The poems of Lieutenant Wilfred Owen got almost no notice before the war ended. Afterward critics found in them a major voice. Owen never knew. He was killed exactly one week before the war ended, shot while leading his platoon across a canal in Belgium. The telegram reporting his death was delivered to his parents' door as church bells rang in celebration of the armistice.

Chapter 29

✠

Wars Without Guns

"It would be laughable to depart over fantasies."
THEOBALD VON BETHMANN HOLLWEG

I n the aftermath of Russia's March Revolution and the failed offensives at Arras and the Chemin des Dames, struggles for power erupted in Petrograd and London. And although for Germany these events had not been the disasters that they were for the Entente, a struggle of the same kind occurred in Berlin too at exactly the same time. Paris, meanwhile, slipped into a deepening gloom, its leadership demoralized and adrift.

The stakes were perhaps highest in Russia. With the tsar deposed, with the tsar's ministers under arrest and hateful factions battling for control of the provisional government, the Russian nation was faced with the most elemental of political questions. It had to decide not only *who* would govern but *how*. It had to settle on a *form* of government, and on some way of organizing its disintegrating economy. It had to do so in the middle of a war that it was losing, and with few established mechanisms in place. Through the first half of 1917 support for continuing the war remained substantial. Kerensky was saying that the revolution had been in part an angry reaction to rumors that the Romanov government might enter into a separate peace. He and the general staff, though their efforts to mount the offensive promised at Chantilly late in 1916 had ended in chaos, were preparing a more modest campaign for the summer. Resistance, however, was growing, and it was strongest where loyalty was needed most: in the army and the industrial workforce. By late spring more than thirty-five thousand troops were deserting monthly. The home front too remained dangerously turbulent, almost, at times, to the point of anarchy. The recently formed soviets, representing soldiers and sailors and workers, were deeply skeptical of what Kerensky was doing. The Communist

Party's Bolshevik faction, with Lenin now in charge, was increasingly bold in stirring up opposition.

The question for Germany was simpler: who was going to be in control? The contest was singularly unequal. On one side were virtually all the dominant elements of German society, united in opposition to reform of any meaningful kind. Their only real opposition was a single man, Chancellor Bethmann Hollweg, with the kaiser floating uncertainly between the two camps. Though his own thinking often coincided with Bethmann's (in 1917 he issued an Easter message endorsing the chancellor's proposals for electoral reform), he knew himself to be disappearing into the shadows cast by Hindenburg and Ludendorff. The two generals blamed Bethmann for everything. His failure to maintain control of domestic politics, they complained, was eroding the loyalty of the Reichstag. His pursuit of peace negotiations was making Germany look weak and encouraging the Entente to fight on. When strikes broke out in Berlin, they too were Bethmann's fault.

The result was a standoff that lasted for months. At an April 23 conference, when Hindenburg and Ludendorff demanded approval of a war aims memorandum that declared Germany's intent to annex large portions of the Balkans as well as parts of Belgium and France, Bethmann did not resist. A week later, however, he placed in the files a note stating that he regarded the memorandum as meaningless because it implied Germany's ability to dictate terms to the Entente—an outcome that seemed worse than improbable at the time. "I have co-signed the protocol," he wrote, "because it would be laughable to depart over fantasies." The ambiguity of his position became public when, in a May 15 speech to the Reichstag, he declared himself to be "in complete accord" with the generals on war aims but also willing to offer Russia a settlement "founded on mutually honorable understanding." This statement was self-defeating. It deepened Ludendorff's hostility while at the same time confusing and alienating the increasing number of Reichstag members who understood that the U-boat campaign was failing, wanted a negotiated settlement, and could have provided the chancellor with a base of public support.

Hindenburg and Ludendorff drew their strength from two sources. One was their record of success in the field—a record that reached back to Tannenberg and had raised them to the stature of demigods. The other was the support they received from the richest, most powerful, most conservative elements of German society—groups convinced that only victory could deflect the general population from demanding reform of the entire system at war's end. This coalition was potent if not entirely stable. But when it pressed for Bethmann's removal, Kaiser Wilhelm showed surprising strength in resisting. He foresaw that any new chancellor was likely to be Ludendorff's tool, and that this would be the end of the Bismarckian system. But the pressure was tremendous. Even the kaiser's wife and Crown Prince Wilhelm were badgering him for the appointment of a new chancellor. And the generals had not played their last card. In contrast to Bethmann and the kaiser, they had the advantage of knowing what they wanted and being willing to do practically anything to get it.

In Britain too the struggle was between the head of the government and the general staff, but beyond that there were few similarities to the situation in Germany. The British political system, being so much more mature than Germany's, made a military challenge to the government's control of policy virtually inconceivable—nothing of the kind arose in the course of the war. The struggle was over control of the BEF only, but was no less intense for being limited. The adversaries were Lloyd George, who had always had strong opinions about how the war should be conducted and now as prime minister was subordinate to no one, and Haig and General Sir William Robertson, based in London as chief of the imperial general staff. At issue, as the summer of 1917 began, was the question of what to do with the BEF, which in two and a half years had grown to be among the most powerful armies in history. Lloyd George, his government now enjoying solid public support after a shaky start, remained scornfully skeptical of the generals' tactics and strategies. Arras and the Chemin des Dames had destroyed whatever inclination he once might have had to leave such matters in the hands of the professionals. He could see no reason to attempt further offensives before American troops were present in large numbers. He continued to push for an Italian offensive while the French and the Russians recovered their strength and the United States translated its potential into an army ready to fight. The generals, inevitably, disagreed.

The importance that Lloyd George attached to the arrival of an American army required, that May, a considerable act of faith. It had not been certain, in the immediate aftermath of Washington's declaration of war, that the United States would be doing more than sending money, equipment, and ships to its new allies. When the chairman of the Senate Appropriations Committee declared that "Congress will not permit American soldiers to be sent to Europe," Wilson quickly proved him wrong, but the president had stunningly little to work with. Until a gradual buildup was authorized in 1916, the U.S. regular army included one hundred and thirty thousand men, which barely put it among the twenty largest armies in the world. It had no tanks, almost no aircraft, and few machine guns in spite of the fact that the machine gun was an American invention. The nation's distrust of military establishments was reflected in a law limiting the general staff to fifty-five officers, no more than twenty-nine of whom could be based in Washington.

The American army also had no divisions; its largest unit was the regiment. A First Division was hurriedly put together and dispatched to France as a demonstration of the seriousness of Washington's intentions. Led by General John J. Pershing, a stern West Pointer who had started his career in the Indian wars, it would march through the streets of Paris on July 4 to an ecstatic reception. It was far too small to make a difference and was not trained for combat, however, and no other divisions were ready to follow it.

The difficulties of creating an army capable of making a difference on the Great War's Western Front are almost impossible to exaggerate. The first draft since the Civil War was put in place, and by mid-1917 every American male between the ages of twenty-one and thirty-one (later this would be raised to forty-five) was registered. Thirty-two training camps, each occupying eight to twelve thousand acres and containing fifteen hundred buildings capable of accommodating forty thousand men, were constructed in sixty days. Nearly every noncom in the old regular army was commissioned, and new schools in every specialty from gunnery to baking were brought into existence up and down the East Coast. The Entente was sending combat

Veteran and newcomer
Ferdinand Foch, left, and John J. Pershing.

veterans across the Atlantic to show green American instructors how to teach even greener inductees the arts of modern war. The French tutors specialized in artillery, liaison, tactics, and fortifications, the British in machine guns, bayonets, mortars, sniping, and gas. Managing all this required expanding and restructuring the War Department and general staff even more rapidly than the new camps were thrown together.

Ambitious as the expansion was, it did not prepare Washington for Pershing's estimate, sent shortly after his arrival in France, of how many troops he was going to require within a year. "It is evident that a force of about one million is the smallest unit which in modern war will be a complete, well-balanced and independent fighting organization," he reported. "Plans for the future should be based ... on three times this force—i.e., at least three million men."

None of which was of the smallest interest to Douglas Haig, whose attention was focused not a year ahead but on Flanders in 1917 and whose faith centered not on the United States but on his own ability to produce a breakthrough at Ypres. He was supported by the Royal Navy, the leaders of which saw the Belgian coast as a place where their seaborne guns could support infantry operations and as a strategic prize urgently needing to be recovered. The Admiralty had been developing plans for an amphibious invasion since 1915. By the spring of 1917, in cooperation with the army, it had begun the construction of huge floating docks capable of putting ashore infantry and tanks. Haig seized at the opportunity that this appeared to present. He and his staff developed a plan of their own, one that would combine a new offensive out of the Ypres salient with an amphibious landing and unhinge the German position in Belgium. Pressed from two directions, Haig believed, the Germans would have to give up the coast. Without room for maneuver, they might be driven out of Belgium entirely. Then, their flank exposed, they might even be forced back from the Hindenburg Line. At a minimum, the British would capture the ports of Ostend, Zeebrugge, and Blankenberge, thereby depriving the Germans of the ports from which some of their smaller submarines were venturing into the Channel. Such gains would greatly strengthen Britain's position in any peace negotiations.

The amphibious operation was the only novel aspect of the plan. The attack out of Ypres was to be a traditional Western Front offensive: a supposedly overwhelming artillery bombardment followed by a supposedly irresistible infantry attack resulting in a breakthrough that the cavalry could then exploit. The whole thing could not have been better calculated to provoke Lloyd George, who fumed from the moment he learned of it. To him it seemed nothing more than another foredoomed recipe for throwing away thousands of lives and wrecking what remained of the new armies that Britain had been nurturing since 1914. The landing of troops from the sea, genuinely innovative though the idea was, could not be safely attempted until after the main breakthrough was achieved. To quiet Lloyd George, Haig set down a criterion for the landing. The breakthrough would be counted as real, and the amphibious force sent into action, when the British took possession of the town of Roulers, seven miles inside German territory. Lloyd George was unimpressed. He was certain that Roulers was out of reach. Haig and Robertson thought it presumptuous of the prime minister to have an opinion on such matters.

Weather, always a factor in war, had to be a particular concern for anyone planning operations in western Belgium. Flanders is an exceedingly flat geography, one almost devoid of anything more notable than scattered farmhouses, sleepy villages, and occasional patches of trees. Today, when visitors search out the battlegrounds around Ypres, they have difficulty identifying the so-called ridges and hills that the Great War made immortal; these features are rarely more conspicuous than wrinkles in a tablecloth. Flanders is also an exceptionally low part of northern Europe's great coastal plain, so near to being an extension of the sea that its inhabitants spent centuries installing drains, canals, and dikes to bring it to the point where it could be farmed. Even today it is about as wet as terrain can be without becoming an estuary. Even in what passes for dry weather in Flanders, one has to turn over only a few spadesful of earth before striking water. When it rains—as it almost always does in late summer, and heavily—the whole area turns to mud. The composition of its soil is such that, when saturated, it becomes a bottomless, unmanageable, uniquely gluey mess.

Haig was warned. The summers of 1915 and 1916 had been unusually dry by Flanders standards, but his staff examined records back to the 1830s and reported that normally "in Flanders the weather broke early each August with the regularity of the Indian monsoon." The retired lieutenant colonel who was military correspondent of the *Times* of London cautioned Robertson against trying to mount a major operation in the low country in late summer. "You can fight in mountains and deserts, but no one can fight in mud and when the water is let out against you," he said. "At the best, you are restricted to the narrow fronts on the higher ground, which are very unfavorable with modern weapons."

"When the water is let out against you": this must have been a reference to what the Belgians had done in the depths of their desperation in 1914, opening the dikes and inundating the countryside east of the River Yser to stop the Germans from breaking through. It was a warning that the Germans might do something similar if in similar jeopardy. It should have brought to mind yet another danger: that heavy bombardment might so wreck the whole region's fragile drainage system as to make flooding inevitable whatever the

Germans did. Haig did not brush these warnings aside, but neither did he allow them to deflect him. They made him impatient to get started while Flanders remained dry. As soon as the Arras operation was behind him, he shifted to building up an attack force at Ypres. He proceeded without Lloyd George's approval and even though Pétain had advised him (a warning never communicated to Lloyd George) that his plan had no chance of success.

Haig hoped to prepare by establishing a new strongpoint on the edge of the salient, some piece of relatively high ground that, once reinforced, could serve as an anchor for troops moving forward to pry the Germans out of their defenses. In this connection he was given a magnificent gift by one of his army commanders. General Sir Herbert Plumer, a pear-shaped little man with the bristling white mustache of a cartoon Colonel Blimp, had been commander of the Second Army on the southern edge of the salient for two years—two terrible years during which the fighting at Ypres had accounted for fully one-fourth of all British casualties. In 1915 Plumer had begun a tunneling program aimed at the German positions opposite his line, and in 1916 he expanded it into the most ambitious mining operation of the war. Twenty shafts, some almost half a mile long and many of them more than a hundred feet deep to escape detection and drained by generator-driven pumps, were extended until finally the diggers were beneath the Messines Ridge, from which the German artillery spotters had long enjoyed an unequaled view of the area. One of the mines was discovered and destroyed by the Germans, but by May the other nineteen were finished, packed with explosives, and still unknown to the enemy.

At 3:10 A.M. on June 7, after a week of bombardment by the heaviest concentration of artillery seen on any front up to that time (Plumer had a gun

Sir Herbert Plumer
*Found the key to Ludendorff's
new system.*

for every seven yards of front), the mines were detonated. All nineteen went off nearly simultaneously, sending the entire ridge into the air. Tremors were felt in London—Lloyd George himself heard a faint boom while working through the night at 10 Downing Street. "When I heard the first deep rumble I turned to the men and shouted, 'Come on, let's go,'" a lieutenant with a British machine gun corps recalled. "A fraction of a second later a terrific roar and the whole earth seemed to rock and sway. The concussion was terrible, several of the men and myself being thrown down violently. It seemed to be several minutes before the earth stood still again though it may not really have been more than a few seconds. Flames rose to a great height—silhouetted against the flames I saw huge blocks of earth that seemed to be as big as houses falling back to the ground. Small chunks and dirt fell all around. I saw a man flung out from behind a huge block of debris silhouetted against the sheet of flame. Presumably some poor devil of a Boche. It was awful, a sort of inferno." A private, a member of a tank crew, got a closer look at the devastation. "We got out of the tank and walked over to this huge crater. You'd never seen anything like the size of it, you'd never believe that explosives could do it. I saw about a hundred and fifty Germans lying there dead, all in different positions, some as if throwing a bomb, some still with a gun on their shoulder. The mine had killed them all. The crew stood there for about five minutes and looked. It made us think. That mine had won the battle before it started. We looked at each other as we came away and the sight of it remained with you always. To see them all lying there with their eyes open."

Plumer's infantry took possession of the long chain of seventy-foot-deep craters that now gaped where the ridge had been. It had been a spectacular success, one that achieved its objectives in minutes at almost no cost in British lives, but it was also distinctly limited. The British penetration was about two miles at its farthest point, and no effort was made to push deeper. Haig, interested in the operation only insofar as it contributed to his preparations for a main assault that was still more than a month in the future, had ordered it stopped as soon as the ridge was taken. His reasons were not trivial: he did not want the Second Army so far forward that his artillery could no longer protect it, and he did want it to dig in before the Germans could counterattack. Still, for a few hours there had been an opportunity to cut deeply into and possibly even through the broken German defenses, and that opportunity was not put to use. Perhaps the most important consequence of Messines Ridge was the taste it gave Plumer, a capable commander, of the advantages of a limited attack.

Haig still did not have London's approval for his main offensive, and the success at Messines Ridge (which had, in the end, left the British still confined inside the old Ypres salient) had done nothing to ease the prime minister's doubts. Lloyd George summoned Haig to a June 19 meeting with his recently created Cabinet Committee on War Policy to explain his plans in detail. Robertson also attended. Like Lloyd George one of those "only in America," up-from-nowhere figures who appear in almost every nation in almost every generation, "Wully" Robertson was a genuinely remarkable individual, especially for the class-bound society that Britain was a century ago. Born in humble circumstances in 1860, he had joined the army at seventeen. ("I shall name it to no one for I am ashamed to think of it," his mother wrote him when she learned of his enlistment. "I would rather bury you than see you in a red coat.") He did well during ten years in the ranks, was changed by a commission from the army's youngest sergeant major to its oldest lieutenant, and during long service in India mastered an array of languages, including Gurkhali, Hindi, Pashto, Persian, and Urdu. He served with distinction in the Boer War and returned to England to become both a reform-minded authority on military training and an expert on the German army. To this day he remains the only Englishman ever to rise from private soldier to field marshal (a rank he was given at his retirement, along with a baronetcy), but throughout his career he never attempted to shed the rough Lincolnshire accent that made his origins clear to all. From early in the war he had been committed to victory on the Western Front (opposing, among other alternatives, the Dardanelles campaign), and since his elevation to the lofty position of chief of the imperial general staff in December 1915 he had been Haig's most important supporter. This made him deeply suspect in the eyes of Lloyd George.

The London conference went on for three days and was a contest from start to end. Haig laid out his plan and the great things he expected it to accomplish. Lloyd George peppered him with questions. He wanted to know why the generals believed a Flanders offensive could succeed this time, what their estimate of casualties was, how the enemy's forces were disposed, and what the consequences of failure might be. He made it plain that he was not satisfied with the answers. The Royal Navy was called in and, to no one's surprise, sided with the soldiers. Admiral Jellicoe, the semidiscredited semihero of the Battle of Jutland, raised Lloyd George's furry eyebrows by asserting that Britain would be unable to continue the war for much more than another year unless the Belgian coast was taken. This warning was far-fetched (only a small number of Germany's smaller submarines was based in Flemish ports) but so purely speculative that neither Lloyd George nor anyone else could prove that it was wrong. All the representatives of the army and navy were impatient with Lloyd George and offended by what they saw as his meddling. The cheek of this craggy Welshman, a man utterly lacking in military training or experience, seemed to them ludicrous and offensive.

In the end the prime minister yielded without having been won over. He gave in to political rather than military realities. After everything had been hashed out and hashed over, he had only one other member of the committee firmly on his side. A third member, the Conservative leader Andrew Bonar Law, also expressed doubt that Haig and Robertson had made their case. But, unknowingly echoing what Bethmann Hollweg had said in Berlin under almost identical circumstances five months earlier, he added that he did not think the committee could "overrule the military and naval authorities on a question of strategy." Lloyd George understood that to countermand Haig and Robertson without broad bipartisan support would leave him exposed and vulnerable in the House of Commons. Also, one of Haig's promises had to be taken into account. In a way reminiscent of what Nivelle had proclaimed when his plans for the Chemin des Dames were challenged, Haig said that if his scheme did not succeed it could quickly be called off. The losses could be ended while still at tolerable levels. Reluctantly and resentfully, certain that he was witnessing Great War stupidity at its worst, Lloyd George told Haig to proceed with his preparations while awaiting final approval.

Thus the meeting ended in a conditional victory for the generals. Viewed in a broader context, however, it had demonstrated the strength of the British system. When Haig and Robertson departed, they took with them not control of strategy but only permission to get ready for one more attack. That permission had been granted by the civil government, the power of which had in no way been diminished. The discussion had happened at the insistence of the prime minister, and the prime minister had the last word. Everyone knew and accepted, if unhappily in some cases, that ultimate authority lay with Lloyd George and his committee. The constitution was intact.

Imperial Germany's constitution was supposed to work in somewhat the same way. Its chancellor was supposed to be in control and in fact had been in control when Bismarck held the office (though even he could have been dismissed by the kaiser at any time and ultimately was). But because the government's leaders had no power base of their own (were not, as in Britain, chosen by the legislature), the strains and uncertainties of a protracted and total war caused control to slip out of the chancellor's hands. The system broke down, finally, and a new one had to be improvised. The improvising could have been done by the one man whom almost the whole German nation trusted, but Hindenburg had no interest. Thus it fell to the one man who both wanted it and seemed able to get Hindenburg to do whatever he wished—Ludendorff, a man elected by no one, a man the kaiser disliked intensely. Thus the war turned Germany into a true military dictatorship, something that it had in fact never before been.

The Russian authorities, meanwhile, were struggling to hold together their forces on the Eastern Front and having distinctly limited success. Among the German troops opposite those forces was a young newly commissioned officer, recently returned to duty after being wounded in action, named Rudolf Hess—the same Hess who in later years would be one of Hitler's top henchmen. "Yesterday we saw heavy fighting," he observed sardonically in a letter to his parents, "but only among the Russians themselves. A Russian officer came over and gave himself up. He spoke perfect German. He was born in Baden but is a Russian citizen. He told us that whole battles are going on behind their lines. Their officers are shooting each other and the soldiers are doing the same. He found it all too ridiculous. They can all get lost as far as he's concerned. We invited him to eat with us and he thanked us. He ate well and drank plenty of tea before going off. There was a lot of noise coming from the Russian side yesterday. They were fighting each other in the trenches. We also heard shots coming from their infantry but they were firing at each other. Charming!"

On July 1, in spite of such disorders and to the delight of Paris and London, Kerensky somehow launched his offensive. Though not nearly as large as what had been promised before the fall of the tsar—not enough troops could be assembled for that—it still involved two hundred thousand men and more than thirteen hundred guns on a thirty-mile front. The mere fact that the Russians were able to take the initiative was cause for happiness, and there seemed to be grounds for optimism. The offensive was under the overall command of General Brusilov, father of the great offensive of 1916 and now commander in chief. It took place in Galicia, where Brusilov had achieved his earlier successes and the Russian forces were in better order, their morale higher, than in the north. They had been superbly equipped by their allies with artillery and aircraft, and nearly half of the defenders were Austrian rather than German troops.

The offensive appeared to go brilliantly at first, with a bombardment that destroyed much of the enemy's forward defenses. The infantry attack that followed swept forward into enemy-held ground. It was all an illusion, however. The Russians were unaware of the new defensive system that Ludendorff had put in place on both fronts and that even the Austrians were using under German direction. The counterattack, when it came, was more than the Russian soldiers were able or willing to endure. They didn't simply retreat, they quit the war on the spot, refusing to obey further orders. Officers who attempted to restore order were shot dead. On July 8 the Russian Eighth

Army essentially went out of existence. Ten days after that Brusilov, who had had misgivings from the start but had been ordered to proceed by Kerensky, found himself relieved of command. By July 19 it was the Germans who were on the offensive, driving a disorderly mob of Russians before them. Their commander was the same Max Hoffmann who had been Ludendorff's strategist at Tannenberg and was now chief of staff on the Eastern Front. Wherever the Germans advanced, the Russians fled. When the Austrians joined in, the Russians fled even from them.

It was, for all practical purposes, the end of the war in the east. Russian casualties had been almost trivial by the standards of the preceding three years—only seventeen thousand killed, wounded, or missing—but such numbers were meaningless in the context of a general collapse. The Germans would attack again later, in the north, but by then success would come so easily as to be almost a formality. Russia really was finished this time. It was the end of the provisional government as well. The future belonged to the Bolsheviks.

Hindenburg and Ludendorff, fortified by this success, now settled the question of who was in charge in Berlin. On July 6 the leader of Germany's Catholic Center Party, a moderate and monarchist named Matthias Erzberger, had delivered a speech that shocked the nation. Using information obtained through international contacts made available by the Vatican, Erzberger not only argued but persuasively demonstrated that the submarine campaign had failed. He demanded reform, including a stronger governing role for the Reichstag, and German renunciation of territorial gains in order to secure a "peace of reconciliation." This speech came at a point when the struggle for control over policy was particularly intense (many factions were involved, and their positions were too varied to be dealt with here), and it outraged the conservatives. The Reichstag's annexationists bitterly attacked Bethmann. But in the face of renewed demands for his dismissal, the kaiser continued to support him.

On July 12, with the crisis at its height, there came a new and even greater shock. A telegram from the headquarters of the army high command announced the resignations of both Hindenburg and Ludendorff. It said the resignations of other members of the general staff would soon follow and that the reason was the impossibility of working with Bethmann Hollweg. It was blackmail plain and simple. In Britain or France, the resignation of any general behaving so high-handedly would have been accepted without comment. Kaiser Wilhelm was indignant, but he was also impotent and knew it. He responded by asking Hindenburg and Ludendorff to come to Berlin to see him. Bethmann resigned.

The timing was deeply unfortunate. Monsignor Eugenio Pacelli, the future

Pope Pius XII, had called on the chancellor shortly before his resignation and presented an offer by Pope Benedict XV to attempt to mediate an end to the war. The first essential step, Pacelli explained, had to be a declaration of Berlin's intentions with respect to Belgium. It was as clear to the Vatican as to everyone that no peace talks were possible unless Germany demonstrated a willingness to restore Belgium to its prewar status. Even the kaiser, who had long and pompously insisted that Germany's security interests required it to maintain control of at least part of Belgium, had come to understand that such a goal was not realistic. Bethmann had responded encouragingly, telling Pacelli (without seeking the army's agreement, of course) that Germany would agree to Belgium's autonomy if Britain and France would do so as well. He even spoke of resolving the question of Alsace and Lorraine to mutual satisfaction. The Reichstag's increasingly liberal majority almost certainly would have supported Bethmann if given the opportunity. But with Bethmann gone there could be no such opportunity. The papal initiative came to nothing.

After some difficulty in finding a new chancellor (various factions put forth their candidates, who one by one were rejected), the job was given to an obscure bureaucrat named Georg Michaelis. It is a measure of the depths to which Germany had fallen politically that Kaiser Wilhelm had not only never met Michaelis, he had never even heard of him. Michaelis would prove so lacking in experience, judgment, and strength of character that even Ludendorff—whom he was eager to please—was soon disappointed. Ludendorff, a complex and paradoxical character who despite always wanting his way did not really want to become dictator (he scoffed at suggestions that he himself should become chancellor), found himself responsible for everything, with no one of consequence to help on the political and diplomatic side. It hardly needs saying that neither he nor his agents (nor the hapless Michaelis) had any success in bringing the Reichstag under control. On July 19 a substantial majority of its members approved a resolution that offended the conservatives anew. "The Reichstag strives for a peace of understanding and the permanent reconciliation of peoples," the resolution declared. "Forced territorial acquisitions and political, economic or financial oppressions are irreconcilable with such a peace." The German government remained at war with itself.

France was a different case. The Third Republic was, in a sense, *always* at war with itself. It had been so in the days just before the war, when Caillaux with his pacific inclinations would have become prime minister if not for his wife. In the years since then one government after another had fallen, in one case after only days in power. But behind the turmoil France retained the machinery needed to produce coherent political, military, and diplomatic decisions, and that machinery had continued to function. The government, after Joffre's period of total control, had reestablished its authority over military strategy. It had done so in part because the army's high command, divided between republicans and never-quite-trusted Catholics such as Ferdinand Foch, was never a coherent enough force to become a political threat.

In the summer of 1917 France needed only one final ingredient in order to operate effectively. It needed a prime minister as strong and determined and politically savvy as Lloyd George, one capable of making himself master of the nation.

That prime minister had been waiting in the wings all along, and he was about to emerge.

ENTER THE TIGER

BY 1917 GEORGES CLEMENCEAU HAD BEEN A PROMINENT figure in French politics and journalism—a magnetic, troubling, disruptive figure, hated and feared and adored—for half a century. All four of the governments that had come and gone in Paris since 1914 had kept him on the outside (that was where Clemenceau had always been happiest, making the insiders squirm), but he remained a force in public life.

And now his hour had come round at last. The nation, exhausted and confused, desperately needed new leadership. So many men had tried and failed that only one possibility remained. It was the man they called, by no means always affectionately, *Le Tigre*. With many misgivings, seeing no choice but to ignore the savagery with which the Tiger had been striking at him since the war began, President Poincaré asked him to form a government. Clemenceau, who throughout most of his career had been refusing invitations to come inside, accepted immediately. And immediately everything began to change. France had found its war leader, its Lloyd George.

Clemenceau was seventy-six years old in 1917, which meant he had been thirty at the end of the Franco-Prussian War, but he was still a volcano of energy. He rose at five every morning, wrote and read for two and a half hours, and then spent half an hour with a calisthenics coach before going to his office. All through the war he had been a member of the French Senate. His position on its army and foreign affairs committees enabled him to know more than most about how the war was being managed and what was happening behind the scenes, and he used his newspaper to complain about what he knew. When the war began, the paper was called *L'Homme Libre,* The Free Man. Before the war was two months old, the government, offended by its biting criticism, ordered it shut down. One day later Clemenceau launched a replacement, *L'Homme Enchaîné,* The Man in Chains. It too was briefly suppressed. When publication resumed, Clemenceau became somewhat less indiscreet but no less critical. He regarded it as his mission to raise difficult questions. "The danger of speaking out and the danger of remaining silent," he observed, "balance agonizingly in our minds." His articles were the scourge of the Viviani gov-

Premier Georges Clemenceau
"Home policy? I wage war!
Foreign policy? I wage war!"

ernment, then of the Briand government, then of the governments of Ribot and Painlevé. They also heaped scorn on generals. Clemenceau showed no more deference than Lloyd George to the expertise of military professionals. He admired only two, Foch and Pétain, and deferred not even to them. The poilus loved his paper and bought a hundred thousand copies of every edition.

Not surprisingly, French officialdom regarded him as an impossible man. "So long as victory is possible he is capable of upsetting everything!" Poincaré said early in the war. "A day will perhaps come when I shall add: 'Now that everything seems to be lost, he alone is capable of saving everything.'" It was perhaps the most prophetic statement of the war. It reflected the fact that, regardless of how many enemies Clemenceau had made and how much his enemies resented him, it was impossible to question his patriotism, his ability, his hatred of Germany, or his commitment to victory at any cost.

He had been a singular character from youth, and life had made him more so. The son of a provincial physician who served time in jail for his outspoken criticism of the Second Empire, Clemenceau shaped himself in his father's image: radically republican, antimonarchist, anticlerical, cynical and scornful of the whole French establishment. He completed medical studies but afterward went to the United States, arriving while the Civil War was in progress and remaining for four years. He supported himself as a teacher and correspondent for French newspapers and married a nineteen-year-old American girl named Mary Plummer, who had been his student in Stamford, Connecticut. (The marriage, the only one of

Clemenceau's long life, produced three children but ended unhappily after seven years.)

Back in France and living in Paris in 1870, when Napoleon III was captured by the Germans in the Franco-Prussian War, he was already prominent enough in leftist politics to be appointed mayor of the eighteenth arrondissement, working-class Montmartre, after radicals seized control of the city. From there he went on to serve in the Chamber of Deputies, to write for and found radical publications, and to champion such causes as separation of church and state and the rights of miners and industrial workers. Among his passions was one that alienated him from the Jaurès socialists who might otherwise have been his best allies: military preparedness. He regarded the loss of Alsace-Lorraine as an intolerable humiliation and renewed war as not only inevitable but desirable, the only way of putting things right. "One would have to be deliberately blind not to see," he wrote, "that the [German] lust for power, the impact of which makes Europe tremble each day, has fixed as its policy the extermination of France."

Clemenceau gloried in opposition, and for many years he led one of the Chamber's many factions. He regarded the middle classes that dominated French politics, the most respectable people in the country, as enemies of progress and justice. During the years of conflict surrounding the Dreyfus case, in which the leadership of the French army was exposed as having knowingly sentenced an innocent Jewish army captain to a life of penal servitude for allegedly selling state secrets to Germany, Clemenceau led the coalition that broke the power of the conservatives and brought the government and the military under republican control. He had repeatedly refused ministerial appointments, but in 1906, with antagonism between the multitudinous factions causing one government after another to fall in quick succession, Clemenceau consented to become minister of the interior. In this position he surprised and delighted the conservatives by using the army and police to subdue striking miners. Though he continued to advocate the eight-hour day, the right to unionize, accident and old-age insurance for workers, and a progressive income tax, the socialists from that point on regarded him as untouchable. But his unexpected firmness won so much support from the center that later the same year he became premier. His government lasted almost three years—itself an achievement. It affected the course of the war to come by strengthening France's Entente with Russia (which Clemenceau saw as vital to survival, though he professed to despise the tsarist regime) while laying the foundations of her secret alliance with Britain.

As the Great War became years old and the costs mounted and victory seemed more and more distant, the legislature separated into two irreconcilable camps. On one side were those who believed in the possibility of negotiating an acceptable peace. This group was led by the same Joseph Caillaux who would have become premier in the summer of 1914 if his wife had not chosen that moment to buy and use a pistol. The other, convinced that no peace could be tolerable that was not preceded by the defeat of Germany, lined up behind the Tiger.

The Chamber was so polarized that it became impossible to put together the kind of coalition with which France had been muddling through. War Minister Paul Painlevé became premier in September 1917 when the six-month-old Ribot government fell, but within weeks he too was tottering. The socialists were indignant about sudden food shortages, the conservatives bewailed the state of the army and the war, and in November the Bolshevik takeover in Petrograd shocked everyone. Painlevé, neither experienced nor skillful enough to manage it all, had to go. Poincaré as president had to find someone to form a government. At this point only two men could have done so: Caillaux or Clemenceau. Selection of the former would have meant a search for compromise with the Germans. Clemenceau, by contrast, represented *la guerre à l'outrance,* total war to the end. For Poincaré, the choice was obvious.

The new premier brought many advantages to the job. He knew America, spoke English, and was almost the patron saint of the alliance with Britain. Best of all, from the perspective of the conservatives who were now his strongest supporters, his first term as premier had proved beyond doubt that he was no socialist, that under his administration France need not fear Bolshevik contamination, that he would use any means necessary to maintain order. He had become the establishment's Tiger, and from the day he took office he behaved more tigerishly than he ever had in his life. He took charge completely, filling his cabinet with capable but minor figures who lacked a political base from which to challenge his authority. Instead of naming a war minister, he took that position himself and made it plain to the generals that he, not they, would have the final word. Ironically in light of his own history, he suppressed publications that questioned government policy. Dissenters were sent to prison. Stunningly—years later Clemenceau would express some remorse about this—even Caillaux was charged with disloyalty and put behind bars. Clemenceau embraced the elites—the bankers, the manufacturers, the leaders of the *haute bourgeoisie*—that he had reviled all his life. Talk of limiting or confiscating excess war profits was extinguished as completely as talk of a compromise peace. The moneyed classes could help to win the war, and therefore they were Clemenceau's friends. Anyone expressing doubt was his enemy.

Making decisions was easy in the Clemenceau government. Whatever could contribute to victory was done. Whatever might make victory more difficult was, whenever possible, stamped out. Anything irrelevant to the war no longer mattered.

"Home policy?" Clemenceau declared when questioned about his plans. "I wage war! Foreign policy? I wage war!"

Chapter 30

Passchendaele

*"Blood and mud, blood and mud,
they can think of nothing better."*
—David Lloyd George

July was exactly half finished when the British began their bombardment in advance of the great offensive that Haig had been waiting so long to undertake at Ypres. In intensity and duration the barrage dwarfed what the Germans had done in opening the Battle of Verdun, dwarfed what the British themselves had done at the Somme almost exactly a year before. Along fifteen miles of front, more than three thousand guns, more than double the density at the Somme, began pouring a day-and-night deluge of high explosives, shrapnel, and gas onto the Germans opposite. During the two weeks ending on July 31 they would fire four million rounds, a hundred thousand of them gas, compared with a mere million during the Somme preparation. These shells had a total weight of sixty-five thousand tons and would inflict thirty thousand casualties on the German Fourth Army even before the British infantry was engaged.

The landscape, already a barren expanse of shell holes and rubble, was rearranged again and again and again, burying the living while excavating the dead. Not incidentally, the rearrangement process destroyed what remained of the area's intricate drainage system. If rain came—and rain was almost certain to come to Flanders at this time of year—there would be no place for the water to go.

Douglas Haig was now in much the same position that Nivelle had put himself in earlier in the year: proceeding in the face of alarmed skepticism (Foch had called Haig's plan "futile, fantastic and dangerous") and refusing to be dissuaded. His goal, once the infantry and the tanks that had been assembled for the offensive went into action, was to drive the Germans back at least three miles on the first day, fifteen miles in eight days. As soon as the railway junction at Roulers had been captured, a meticulously trained division with its own tank force was to be landed on the coast behind the German lines. The Fourth British Army, positioned near where the River Yser enters the sea, was then to move eastward under the protection of the Royal Navy's shipboard guns and link up with the landing force. The Germans, at the end of their strength, would not have enough troops to form a new defensive line once they were forced to withdraw from the coast.

That was the plan. One of its problems—by no means the only problem, but one of the most serious—was that the Germans knew what was coming. Haig appears to have resigned himself to the impossibility of concealing anything except the amphibious landing, which was put under such tight security that the men training for it in the Thames estuary on the north side of the Channel were not allowed to write home. The Germans, from the air and from their observation points on the low ridges circling Ypres, had a clear view of the gathering of the greatest concentration of soldiers and weapons in the history of the British army. And of course they reacted. Fourteen German divisions were transferred to Ypres, four of them from the Eastern Front, while the British were making ready. A week after the Germans were blown off Messines Ridge, Ludendorff sent Fritz von Lossberg, the originator of the new system of flexible defense in depth, to Ypres as chief of staff of the German Fourth Army. This gave Lossberg more than fifty days to prepare. As he did so, the confidence of the German commanders grew. "My mind is quite at rest about the attack, as we have never possessed such strong reserves, so well trained for their part, as on [this] front," Crown Prince Rupprecht of Bavaria, head of the army group in Flanders, observed in his diary.

On July 10 the Germans had launched a preemptive raid on the Yser bridgehead from which the British Fourth Army was to move eastward to join the landing force. This raid, in addition to driving most of the British back to the west side of the river, led to the discovery of a tunnel they had planned to use to blow up key German positions at the start of their advance. The discovery confirmed that something big was being planned for the coast, and the Germans' capture of the high ground (high as such things are measured in Flanders) just east of the Yser left the British in a far less advantageous position.

On both sides the preparations were on the vast scale that industrialized total war was making commonplace. Just the construction of the concrete pillboxes that were Lossberg's first line of defense and the underground bunkers being installed behind the lines to shelter his counterattack troops required a seemingly endless supply of gravel. It was purchased in Holland and carried across Belgium on a stream of trains.

Hanging over everything was the question of whether, his enthusiasm notwithstanding, Haig was preparing anything really different from what the generals of the Entente had been trying without success since the end of the Battle of the Marne. Lloyd George thought not. Winston Churchill thought not as well and said so. Lloyd George had appointed him minister of munitions in July, and though at the insistence of the Conservatives he was not allowed to join any of the government's key war committees, he never hesitated to express himself on policy matters. Pétain, no less than Foch, also thought not. If the immensity of Haig's resources justified his confidence, if his barely concealed contempt for the French made him feel certain that he could succeed where Nivelle had failed, the bloody futility of all previous Western Front offensives provided equal justification for the doubts of the skeptics.

Then there was the weather. It continued to be unusually dry, but this was unlikely to continue, and Haig was determined not to waste time. Tensions rose as one rainless day followed another and the pieces of the plan failed to fall into place. Haig had decided, to the disappointment of older and more senior generals, to assign responsibility for the main part of his offensive to the youngest of his army commanders, the forty-seven-year-old Hubert Gough. Gough was chosen for his boldness, for his eagerness for action, and probably in part for his being, like Haig, a cavalryman by origin. He was also an indifferent executive who had gathered around himself a staff better known for its arrogance than for its ability to perform. At Ypres the ability to manage enormous numbers of men and matériel mattered a good deal more than dash, and difficulties were not slow to appear. On July 7 Gough reported that his preparations were not on schedule and that he was concerned about the readiness of the French forces on his left. He said he needed more time. Haig (who would have been justified in remembering what Napoleon had said to his generals—"ask me for *anything* but time") replied with a flat no. Six days later the two generals met, and again Gough asked for a postponement. He said he needed five days. Haig granted him three, moving the start of the attack from July 25 to July 28. On July 17, with the bombardment under way but fog now impeding preparations, yet another delay of three days was found to be unavoidable. The danger of rain made every one of those days a painful loss, and Haig, increasingly anxious, knew it.

Lloyd George and his War Policy Committee, caught between their fears of what this offensive could turn into and the political risks of forbidding it, seemed paralyzed. Five days into the barrage, they still had not approved the offensive. Finally on July 20, having through their own inaction left themselves with almost no choice, they informed Haig that he was free to proceed. They did so grudgingly at first, warning him that he would have to stop if his attack were not quickly successful and asking him to specify his objectives. Haig was offended, and when he said so he received another message assuring him that he had the committee's "wholehearted support." From that point everything began to move rapidly. On July 22 the barrage was raised to a higher level of intensity. On July 26 seven hundred British and French aircraft took to the air and cleared it of Germans. Two days later came the final stage of the bombardment, a counterbattery barrage intended to knock out the German artillery, which had been inflicting heavy damage on British positions. It came to a premature end as fog returned and made it impossible for the gunners on either side to find their targets. The weather continued to hold. The British would be advancing over terrain that artillery had made a mad jumble of shell holes, but at least the surface was dry. The last two weeks had been punctuated with showers but not to a troublesome extent.

The offensive went off at 3:50 A.M. on July 31, with seventeen Entente divisions advancing and seventeen waiting in the rear. At the northern end were two French divisions whose mission was to protect Gough's flank. At the other end were five divisions of Plumer's Second Army. Their objectives too were modest: to capture a few strongpoints but mainly to stand in place and hold the Messines Ridge as a pivot point for Gough's advance. Ten divisions of Gough's Fifth Army were the battering ram, their assignment to force the Germans back and set the stage for the reserves to come forward. Gough had almost twenty-three hundred guns on his seven-mile section of front, one for every six yards. Together he and Plumer and the French had nearly half a million men.

Waiting for the attack was a hornets' nest of German machine-gun nests arranged in a rough checkerboard pattern. Behind them the Fourth Army's twenty divisions were arranged in four clusters: nine nearest the front, six behind them, two more to their rear, and the last three even farther back. Almost anywhere the British or French succeeded in making a hole, German reserves would be in position to move forward and seal it.

Some things went exactly according to Haig's plan. The troops on Gough's flanks made good progress, advancing to their objectives with comparatively little difficulty. Even in the center, the forward units managed to fight their way through the first German zone (which was, after all, supposed to yield when pressed) and into the second. They penetrated nearly two miles at a few points, no more than half a mile at others. Six thousand German soldiers, shattered by the frenzied final hours of the bombardment, were taken prisoner in a few hours. But by early afternoon, with a light rain sprinkling the field and the leading British units no longer in contact with their artillery, the Germans opened fire with field guns positioned on elevated ground to the north and south of the salient created by the advance. This was artillery that might have been destroyed if not for the fog of the preceding days. The British, taking heavy losses, were forced to pull back. Of the fifty-two tanks that had advanced with Gough's troops, twenty-two broke down and another nineteen were put out of action by German fire. By late afternoon the attack was at a standstill and the drizzle had turned to hard rain. Haig, not aware that twenty-three thousand of his men had been killed or wounded, perhaps drawing a comparison with the first day on the Somme, reported to London that the day's events had been "highly satisfactory and the losses light for so great a battle."

On this same day Pope Benedict XV sent a letter to the governments of the Entente and the Central Powers, offering to mediate a peace of no territorial conquests. As before, a clear response from Berlin, an agreement to give up Belgium, would have been the essential next step. Once again the Germans were unable to respond. A young new foreign minister, Richard von Kühlmann, decided to ignore this latest Vatican initiative and approach London directly instead. He hoped to separate the British from their allies with a private promise to withdraw from Belgium in return for a cessation of hostilities. But the new chancellor, Michaelis, destroyed whatever tiny potential this idea may have had. He yielded to Ludendorff's insistence that Germany must retain effective control not only of most of Belgium but of the coal and iron mines of France's Longwy-Briey district and must be promised extensive portions of Africa as well. There were other clumsy efforts at arranging talks at about this time—Austria and France became involved in various ways at various points—but nothing could come of them because on both sides the people with the power to decide were determined to dictate any final settlement. The performance of Michaelis was so unimpressive through all of it, and like Bethmann Hollweg he came to be so hated in the Reichstag, that he had to resign after only three months in office.

Rain was falling in torrents when Haig resumed his attack on August 2. With the Flanders drainage system in ruins, every hole filled with water and the ground became a soupy morass to a depth that no man's foot could reach. The tanks could not move, the airplanes could not fly, and the German artillery was taking an increasing toll. Still Haig tried to push on. But after two more days, with the rain continuing and the number of French and British casualties up to sixty-eight thousand, he finally ordered a halt until the rain stopped and the ground could dry out.

For the troops, the break in the fighting was something less than deliverance. One British officer would record the experience of waiting day after day in a bunker taken from the Germans. "Inside it was only about five foot high and at the bottom there was about two foot of water. This water was simply horrid, full of refuse, old tins, and even excreta. Whenever shells burst near it the smell was perfectly overpowering. Luckily, there was a sort of concrete shelf the Boche had made about two foot above ground level. It was on this shelf that four officers and six other ranks spent the night. There wasn't room to lie down, there was hardly room to sit upright, and we more or less crouched there. Outside the pillbox was an enormous shell-hole full of water, and the only way out was over a ten-inch plank. Inside the shell-hole was the dead body of a Boche who had been there a very long time and who floated or sank on alternate days according to the atmosphere. The shell-holes were crowded with dead and dying men, the latter crying out for help as they slowly expired."

Haig had to wait until August 10, when at last it became possible to mount a fresh assault aimed mainly at capturing or driving away the German light artillery. This was another limited and costly success. As soon as it ended, Haig began planning for a resumption on August 14. But the rain started again, causing one and then a second postponement of twenty-four hours. When it came, the next attack was more of the same: much death, little to show for it. Haig decided not to give up, which he would have been amply justified in doing and was probably obligated to do under the promises he had made to London. Instead he prepared to change directions.

Thus ended the first phase of the Third Battle of Ypres. In three and a half weeks Haig's troops had advanced two miles—not much more than half of his objective for the first day. The amphibious force remained idle, waiting for the capture of Roulers. As it became clear that Roulers was never going to be captured, that force would be quietly disbanded. On both sides divisions too battered to continue had to be replaced. There were twenty-three such divisions on the German side, fourteen on the British. "Blood and mud, blood and mud," Lloyd George complained back in London, "they can think of nothing better."

The weight of the campaign was now shifted away from Gough to Plumer's Second Army. In two years at Ypres, Plumer had won the loyalty of his troops with a Pétain-like concern for their welfare and a marked unwillingness to waste their lives. The morale of his army was high, the soldiers eager for action. And unlike Gough or Haig, Plumer had paid attention to the Germans' new defensive methods. He devised a countertactic, one possibly inspired by his experience at Messines Ridge, and was given Haig's approval and three weeks to get ready. While he was doing so, Haig was called to London for another meeting with Lloyd George and the War Policy Committee. It was an arid repeat of the earlier discussions. Haig, again supported by Robertson, argued the necessity of continuing to pound away at the Germans until they broke, which he was sure they were about to do. He returned to France with his authority unimpaired, leaving behind a most unhappy prime minister.

At this point Haig had more reason for confidence than he knew. Plumer had in fact found the key to the German defense, one that neutralized its strengths and exploited its inherent weaknesses. Like most truly brilliant military plans, Plumer's approach was elegant in its simplicity and straightforward in its recognition of the facts on the ground. It began with the premise that relatively short gains—gains of a mile or less—had become available almost for the asking as a result of the thinness and elasticity of the Germans' forward positions. Premise number two was that gains of several miles—never mind breakthroughs of the kind that Entente commanders had been seeking since 1914—were now more out of the question than ever because of the Germans' increased ability to counterattack in force. The conclusion was so blindingly obvious that only Plumer and his staff had seen it: the German system could be outsmarted with attacks that stopped upon capturing the easy ground and never went far enough to trigger a counterattack. Cumulatively, a series of such attacks might drive the Germans backward out of their defenses and into a war of maneuver that they lacked the manpower to survive.

Plumer was too good a general to rely on cleverness alone. He used the first three weeks of September—weeks suddenly, blissfully free of rain—to pull together a mass of artillery even more awesome than those of July and August. At the end of his preparations he had one artillery piece for every five yards of front. The Germans would be subjected to five waves of fire, each a zone of destruction two hundred yards deep. The first zone was shrapnel exclusively, the second high explosives, and the third indirect machine-gun fire ("indirect" meaning that the gunners, unable to see their targets, aimed into the air so as to bring the bullets arcing down on the defenders from above). The last two were more high explosives. Every German position would find itself in one zone after another as the entire pattern, half a mile deep from front to back, swept over it in a storm that changed its character every few minutes. Plumer's artillery would fire three and a half million rounds in this way before and on the day of his attack.

Plumer was able to conceal his preparations behind the slightly elevated ground that he had captured first at Messines Ridge and later in moving forward on Gough's flank. When he attacked on September 20, his troops advancing behind a creeping barrage, those Germans who had not been killed by the artillery or pulled back from it were subdued almost with ease.

Upon reaching their assigned objectives, the attackers stopped and hurriedly began constructing defenses. The main body of German troops, meanwhile, remained in the rear, waiting for the British to come at them. By the time they realized that the British were finished for the day, it was too late for a counterattack to be effective. The whole operation had been quick and clean, and within the limits of its objectives it had been a complete success. Though it did not come cheaply in the end—British casualties ultimately totaled more than twenty thousand, mainly as a result of German artillery fire after the advance—it was clear to both sides that the game had entered a new phase. The Germans were as alarmed by the results of this Battle of the Menin Road as the British commanders were elated.

The attack had captured not just German ground but part of the German infrastructure—pillboxes and bunkers essential to the new system. This increased the defenders' vulnerability to further attack. Seeing this, Plumer hurried his artillery forward and on September 26 attacked again in what has gone into the chronicles as the Battle of Polygon Wood. The weather remained clear, so that scores of British and French pilots were able to fly low over the German defenders, strafing them and dropping bombs. After another horrendous barrage the infantry advanced on a front of four miles, dug in after advancing the assigned half-mile, and again left the main German forces looking on helplessly. The Germans had lost another set of strongpoints. If this happened several times, they might be left with no infrastructure at all.

Desperate, the Germans gave up on their new system. They reverted to older tactics, positioning large numbers of troops in a strong forward line to block the attackers from making easy early gains. Plumer again had his guns on the move, preparing for another strike. The fates seemed to have turned entirely in his favor: the meteorological record contained no evidence of a Flanders September as dry as the last month had been.

But a light drizzle began on October 3, and it was still falling the next morning when a fresh British assault began the Battle of Brookseinde. Even more than September 20 and 26, this was a day of disaster for the Germans. The men in the new forward line, having had a mere handful of days in which to improvise their defenses, were slaughtered wholesale by Plumer's barrage. The reserves, positioned too far forward by generals too eager to get at the attackers, were caught in the same inferno. The British troops advanced only seven hundred yards before, maddeningly for the Germans, stopping as before. In the process they killed or wounded thirty thousand of the defenders, taking twenty-five thousand casualties themselves. This rate of loss, painful for the British, was unsustainable on the German side. And conventional tactics plainly were incapable of keeping it from happening again.

Man and beast, together in war
A German rider and his mounts, prepared to encounter gas.

At his headquarters, alarmed by the dispatches arriving from Flanders, Ludendorff cast about for some way to launch an offensive that would draw British troops away from Ypres. No such thing was possible. The necessary troops were not available, in part because Pétain was now launching holding attacks at Verdun and elsewhere with French divisions sufficiently recovered to be trusted in action. Ludendorff ordered the Sixth Army to shift back to the new system. At least this would keep most of the troops out of reach of the British artillery. Beyond that there was nothing for the Germans to do but hope for deliverance. "The fighting on the Western Front became more severe and costly than any the German Army had yet experienced," Ludendorff would recall of this period. "I myself was put to a terrible strain.

The state of affairs in the West appeared to prevent the execution of our plans elsewhere. Our wastage had been so high as to cause grave misgivings, and had exceeded all expectations."

Deliverance came literally from the heavens. The drizzle that had started on October 3 turned to a steady rain, and after a few days more it became a downpour that went on and on. Flanders was turning into an enormous shallow lake, every shell hole and piece of low ground filled to the brim. It would have been a sensible time to wrap up Third Ypres, and when the British commanders met on October 7, Plumer and Gough both were in favor of doing so. Haig would not hear of it. Plumer's advance had left his troops deployed along a line that would be difficult to hold without exceptional hardship through the coming winter. One remedy would have been to pull back to slightly higher and dryer ground—a horrifying prospect for Haig in light of the price paid for his gains and what was sure to be Lloyd George's reaction. The only acceptable course, Haig declared, was to push forward to the capture of Passchendaele Ridge, the northern extension of the same snakelike strip of high ground of which Messines Ridge was also a part. Virtually every British division in the Ypres salient having been reduced to tatters, the lead role was to be played by divisions from the Commonwealth—from Australia, New Zealand, and Canada.

The first attack at Passchendaele, the Valley of the Passion, went off in the rain on October 9 under conditions that were not merely difficult but impossible. Standing water covered almost everything, and what was not under water (the men included) was covered with mud that seemed to go down and down forever. It was impossible to find a foothold, impossible to move the artillery or set it firmly in place where it was, nearly impossible even for men on foot to move. Big guns sank out of sight. So did an entire light railway. The only way to bring shells forward was by pack mule, but many of the mules sank and drowned. When fired, the shells disappeared without exploding because the surface, even the mud beneath the water, had become too soft to activate their fuses. Somehow the Australians and New Zealanders at the center of the attack managed to fight their way forward, but their progress served only to expose them to machine-gun fire from three directions instead of one. Finally they had no choice but to struggle back to where they had begun. The wounded, unavoidably left behind, disappeared into the muck.

"The slope," said an Australian officer of a scene he came upon while on reconnaissance, "was littered with dead, both theirs and ours. I got to one pillbox to find it just a mass of dead, and so I passed on carefully to the one ahead. Here I found about fifty men alive, of the Manchesters. Never have I seen men so broken or demoralized. They were huddled up close behind the box in the last stages of exhaustion and fear. Fritz had been sniping them off all day, and had accounted for fifty-seven that day—the dead and dying lay in piles. The wounded were numerous—unattended and weak, they groaned and moaned all over the place...Some had been there four days already." Moving on again, he came upon another bunker with "twenty-four wounded men inside, two dead Huns and six outside, in various stages of decomposition. The stench was dreadful...When day broke I looked over the position. Over forty dead lay within twenty yards of where I stood and the whole valley was full of them."

When the Canadians were selected to lead the next assault, their commander, Sir Arthur Currie, expressed his reservations. He predicted that taking Passchendaele would cost him sixteen thousand men. He did not, however, refuse. When his men attacked on October 26, they took heavy casualties, inflicted equally severe losses on the Germans, and were brought to a halt well short of Passchendaele Ridge and the sorry assortment of low rubble that had once been Passchendaele village. The Canadians tried again four days later, and the results were no different. A shortage of drinking water, ironically, added to the torment of the men. Bringing water forward was as difficult as hauling shells, and the swamp that extended in all directions had been poisoned by human waste and the rotting cadavers of animals and men.

Another of Europe's battlegrounds was now fully ablaze—the Italian front this time, where the bloodletting that had marked Italy's entry into the war in the summer of 1915 suddenly soared to new heights. The Italian commander in chief, Luigi Cadorna, had launched two more Battles of the

General Sir Arthur Currie
*Foretold the cost of
taking Passchendaele.*

Isonzo earlier in the year, in May and August, and these two fights had cost his armies more than two hundred and eighty thousand casualties. The Austrians too had suffered hideously, and when the two battles were over, both sides were begging their allies for help. The monstrous Cadorna, a kind of savage in uniform who seriously advocated the shooting of every tenth man in units that failed to perform to his satisfaction, feared that the collapse of Russia was going to free Austria-Hungary to send all of its armies against Italy. He turned to the British and French for reinforcements, but found them willing to do no more than continue to send artillery. Austria-Hungary's young Emperor Karl, warned by his general staff (no longer headed by Conrad, who had been demoted) that the Austrians were unlikely to survive another of Cadorna's assaults, asked Ludendorff for help. Rebuffed, he appealed directly to Kaiser Wilhelm, who intervened. When a general sent to evaluate the Italian front reported that the Austrians were indeed at the end of their strength, Ludendorff reluctantly created a new German Fourteenth Army out of infantry, artillery, and aircraft taken from the Baltic, Romania, and Alsace-Lorraine. He sent this army southward under the veteran Otto von Below with orders to stabilize the Italian front with the shortest, most limited campaign possible.

The resulting Battle of Caporetto—also known, inevitably, as the Twelfth Battle of the Isonzo—began on October 24 with a joint German-Austrian attack that quickly developed into an unexpectedly far-reaching success. The Germans and Austrians, whose thirty-three divisions faced forty-one divisions of Italians, advanced more than ten miles on the first day, and the retreat that Cadorna attempted to organize soon degenerated into headlong flight and the surrender of hundreds of thousands of his troops. Below's orders were to proceed no farther than the River Tagliamento, which flows southward into the Adriatic west of the Isonzo, but his forces reached that objective so quickly that they pushed on in hot pursuit. The government in Rome fell, Cadorna was sacked, and the Italian forces continued to run until they were on the banks of the River Piave twenty miles beyond the Tagliamento. There they were able to make a stand. They were helped in doing so by the exhaustion of the pursuing Germans and the onset of winter rains. Below had advanced eighty miles in seventy days, shortening the southern front by a crucial two hundred miles. Italian casualties totaled three hundred and twenty thousand during the retreat to the Piave, including two hundred and sixty-five thousand men taken prisoner, and the stand on the Piave had claimed another one hundred and forty thousand. Tactically, Caporetto had been one of the war's most spectacularly successful campaigns, and when it ended the war on the southern front seemed almost over. But it was not conclusive. The upheavals that it generated brought the government in Rome and its army under more capable leadership. The gross mistreatment that had destroyed the morale of the Italian troops ended. All this would work to the detriment of the Central Powers.

Not until November 6, under nightmarish conditions, did fresh Canadian troops finally drive the Germans off a large enough portion of Passchendaele Ridge for Haig to claim victory. The price had been almost exactly what Currie had predicted: nearly sixteen thousand men. A final attack four days later allowed the Canadians to consolidate their new positions and brought the Third Battle of Ypres to an end. In three months and one week the forces of the Entente had advanced all of four and a half miles, taking ground that Haig described as a splendid starting point for further fighting in 1918 but that less ecstatic generals dismissed as worthless. The British, Canadians, Anzacs, and French between them had taken a quarter of a million casualties, the Germans nearly as many. The Germans had used—and in many cases used up—118 divisions. The British, whose divisions were considerably larger than their German counterparts at this point, had used forty-three, the French six. Both sides were exhausted, the BEF nearly as broken as the French army had been after the Chemin des Dames.

Haig, however, was not satisfied. On November 20, near Cambrai east of the old Arras battlefield, he sent nineteen divisions and the largest force of tanks yet assembled into an attack on a thinly defended section of the

Not invincible
Burnt skeleton of a British tank, in German hands.

Hindenburg Line. Like Caporetto, this was a tremendous success for the attackers from the start, but unlike Caporetto the success was short-lived and soon reversed. Of the 216 new Mark IV tanks used in the initial assault, seventy-one broke down mechanically, sixty-five were destroyed by enemy fire, and forty-three bogged down. Some of them, however, bulled their way through the forward defenses, terrifying the Germans and putting them to flight. But Haig had intended Cambrai as a mere demonstration, a year-ending morale-booster. No follow-through had been planned, and none was attempted. The British found themselves with enemies on three sides—always the curse that followed success on a narrow front—and on November 30 a counterattack by twenty German divisions recovered almost all the lost ground.

A German lieutenant at Cambrai left a record of how he and his comrades learned to cope with Haig's tanks. "When the first tanks passed the first line, we thought we would be compelled to retreat towards Berlin," he wrote. "I remember one tank, by the name of Hyena, which advanced very far and suddenly stopped about 1,000 yards from my little dugout. Some of the boys soon discovered they could stop the tanks by throwing a hand grenade into the manhole on the top. Once this was known, the boys realized that there was a blind spot—that the machine guns couldn't reach every point around the tank, and these points were very important in the defense.

"I was shocked and felt very sorry for those fellows in the tanks, because there was no escape for them. Once a man was on top of the tank it was doomed to failure, and the poor fellows were not able to escape. The fuel would start to burn and after an hour and a half or two hours we saw only burning tanks in front and behind us. Then the approaching troops behind the tanks still had to overcome the machine guns of our infantry. These were still effective because the British artillery had to stop shooting as the tanks were advancing, and naturally some of our machine gun nests were still in full action.

"Anyhow, the attack came to a standstill and we waited for several regiments of cavalry to sweep up and drive us towards Berlin. But this didn't happen, much to our surprise. When new troops were pulled together near this break-in of the British tanks, the situation settled down, we were formed anew, and afterwards we could clearly see the spot where the British tanks had driven into the German lines. Then after a few days we made a counterattack. It didn't succeed on the first or the second day, but on the third day we were finally successful."

Yet another British offensive had been for nothing. It had not, however, been without meaning. Generals on both sides saw that the new tanks, if properly used, could have produced very different results—that Cambrai was a sign of things to come.

And so ended 1917. On the Western Front, the year had taken the lives of two hundred and twenty-six thousand British, one hundred and thirty-six thousand French, and one hundred and twenty-one thousand German soldiers. And still the stalemate continued.

Between them, Arras, the Nivelle offensive, Third Ypres, and Cambrai had rendered the French and the British incapable of mounting a major offensive at the end of the approaching winter.

At the same time they had destroyed the Germans' confidence in their defensive system.

These two facts would shape the year ahead. They would put the conflict on the road to its end at last.

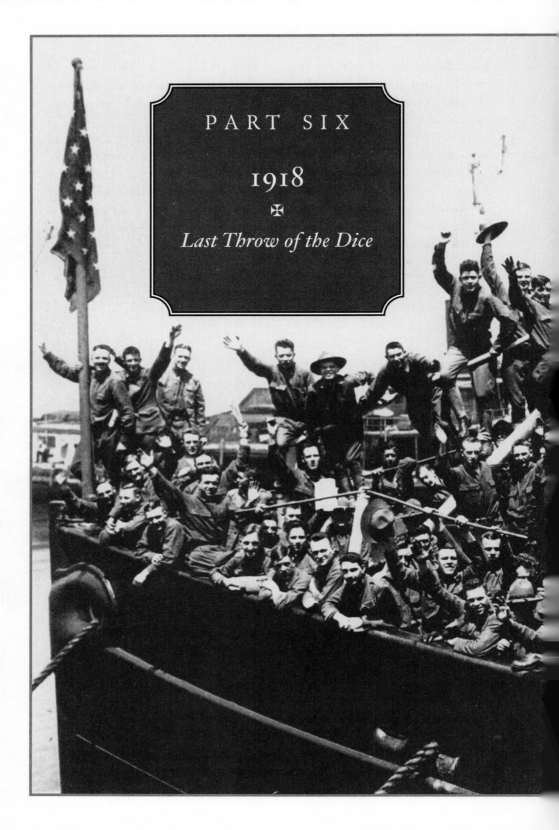

PART SIX

1918

✠

Last Throw of the Dice

Doughboys: American soldiers embark for France.

Chapter 31

✠

Going for Broke

"We make a hole, and the rest will take care of itself."
—Erich Ludendorff

The Europe that settled in for the war's fourth winter was beginning to give evidence of being a dying civilization. Russia, often hailed before the war as the European nation with the most brilliant future, was in ruins. Tsar Nicholas and his wife and children were prisoners, Kerensky's potentially democratic government was gone, and Lenin and his Bolsheviks were taking control of the wreckage. The people were sunk in destitution, without security or stability, millions of them so sick of the war as to be unwilling to participate in it. Lenin, accordingly, was almost desperately eager to give them peace.

Conditions were less terrible elsewhere, but not always a great deal less. Even in France and Great Britain, where access to the riches of the New World had prevented discomfort from deepening into general deprivation, there was weariness with the war and the heartbreak it had brought. There was also weariness, unmeasurable because harshly suppressed, with governments committed to fighting on no matter what the cost. Everyday life had become dark. The "democracies" allowed little in the way of liberty to citizens not fully in favor of the war, information not bent to the purposes of propaganda was difficult to find, and there seemed no reason to expect anything except more of the same, conceivably for years to come.

For Germany and even more for Austria-Hungary, strangled by a blockade that there was now no hope of breaking, the fate of Russia was a warning of what could lie ahead. Here there was no mere discomfort but widespread malnutrition and the prospect of another winter without heat or light or enough food to sustain health or even life. Here was the despair of watching one's children starve. Life had become tragic—unlivable, even—in the most elemental terms. The possibility of rebellion against the war and the people responsible for continuing it was becoming real.

As winter brought with it the usual suspension of major military operations, the general staffs began once again to make their plans for the year ahead. On both sides, this annual ritual was becoming more difficult. The failure of one campaign after another to deliver what the generals promised— the failure of *every* offensive on the Western Front, from the initial German drive on Paris to Passchendaele—made it hard to believe that the next great scheme could have any chance of success. The armies on both sides were in deplorable condition.

Although Russia had not surrendered or made peace, the two-front war was at an end. Until American troops could be mustered in sufficient numbers and adequately trained—no such thing was expected for another half-year at best—Britain and France would have to fight the Germans alone. There were the Italians, of course, but in the aftermath of Caporetto little could be expected of them.

And Italy's losses seemed almost unimportant compared with those of Britain and France. The latter's casualties totaled three million by late 1917; they had occurred at an average of forty thousand per month throughout that murderous year, and replacements were hard to find. General Pétain, the commander in chief, forecast that he would need 1.02 million troops on the Western Front in 1918 but would have only 85 percent of that number. (As things worked out, he never had 75 percent.) Under Pétain's ministrations the army had largely recovered from the mutiny of 1917. It had fought off more than a hundred German attacks from June through August and had attacked successfully at Verdun and the Chemin des Dames, capturing ground and taking prisoners. However, Prime Minister Clemenceau and his principal military adviser, Ferdinand Foch, had limited regard for Pétain's achievement. In their opinion his caution was excessive, and his determination to carry the fight to the enemy much too qualified.

With its larger population, its global empire from which to draw manpower, and "only" two million casualties since the start of the war, Britain should have been in a better position than France. But in fact it was not, at least in the view of its commanders. The problem was not, strictly speaking, a shortage of soldiers. Rather it was Prime Minister David Lloyd George's refusal to let the commander of the BEF, Douglas Haig, have enough divisions for a repetition of the Somme or Passchendaele. Some four hundred and fifty thousand fit and ready combat troops were being held at home at Lloyd George's insistence, and only labor units that were neither trained nor armed for battle were allowed to cross the Channel. Haig was so short of replacements that he reduced the number of battalions per brigade from four to three to avoid having to dissolve whole divisions. This gave rise to organizational confusion that would be far from resolved when the British found themselves once again in heavy fighting.

In terms of the matériel needed to support their populations and troops, however, Britain and France were entirely out of danger. The American cornucopia was disgorging itself across the Atlantic, overwhelming the German U-boats as they tried to stem the flow. Virtually everything needed by the Entente, money included, was being generously provided. British production of ammunition had been increased by nearly 3,000 percent during the two years beginning in March 1915, when Lloyd George became minister of munitions. It underwent a further quadrupling in the nine months after Winston Churchill, exonerated by a commission investigating the Gallipoli disaster, took charge of production. By late 1917 a quarter of a million tons of shells was being shipped across the Channel monthly, and this was less than a third of the tonnage of supplies arriving at BEF bases on the north coast of France. The problem, for the Entente, was management. After three years of war there was still no effective mechanism for coordinating British and French operations.

In November 1917, shortly after the Battle of Caporetto, the Entente's leaders had met at Rapallo in Italy and agreed on the creation of a grandly titled Inter-Allied Supreme War Council. This body included the heads of the governments and representatives of their general staffs. The United States, though not involved at first, soon joined. Lloyd George welcomed the council as a counterweight to his own general staff—to Haig and "Wully" Robertson. Lloyd George had regarded Haig as an unfit commander of the BEF since before he became prime minister. He had never stopped wanting to remove Haig, but doing so had remained impossible.

The Supreme War Council proved to have value, but principally in improving administration. It was effective in coordinating the various national transportation systems, and in allocating matériel and, to a limited extent, manpower. It even, before the end of 1917, satisfied Lloyd George's highest aspirations for it by rejecting Haig's proposal of another offensive in Flanders. At its second meeting, in December at Versailles, the council decided that there should be no great offensives anywhere in 1918. Where the active direction of military operations was concerned, however, the council was useless. Neither Haig nor Pétain wanted to surrender control to an international authority, and neither cooperated with efforts to get them to do so. Early in 1918 King George V underscored Haig's untouchability—the strength of his support in high places—by promoting him to field marshal. At almost the same time, ironically, South African General Jan Smuts was on the continent on Lloyd George's behalf, secretly trying to identify a replacement for Haig. Both Herbert Plumer and Henry Rawlinson were regarded as possibilities.

The Central Powers had no comparable problems of coordination; Germany no longer had allies substantial enough to require much coordination with. Turkey, in her northern theaters, had been saved by Russia's collapse. But she was exhausted and overextended. To the south she was in increasing peril from British forces pushing eastward out of Egypt and a British-supported Arab revolt. Falkenhayn was in the Middle East now, as was Otto Liman von Sanders, the onetime commander at Gallipoli. Their assignment was to help the Turks, but they had neither the troops nor the matériel to make a decisive difference. Bulgaria was safe enough, for the time being, but unable to do more than help in the Balkans. It was unsettled by domestic opposition to the regime that had taken it to war on the side of the Central Powers.

That left Austria-Hungary, now little more than an empty shell. In 1917 Vienna conscripted into its tattered armies the hundred and sixty thousand eligible men—boys, really—born in 1900. That left it with no remaining sources of manpower except for whatever wounded veterans and repatriated prisoners of war (four hundred thousand of these would be recovered from Russia early in 1918) could be returned to combat duty. The Austrians were dangerously short of coal, iron, oil, guns, ammunition, and food for men and animals. The horses needed to move artillery were dying by the tens of thousands because there was no fodder. The 1917 potato harvest, one of the few substantial sources of new food, would be exhausted by spring. Monthly rifle production was plummeting from one hundred and thirteen thousand in March 1917 to nine thousand the following February. Production of heavy shells, which exceeded four hundred thousand per month in the autumn of 1917, would be down to a third of that less than a year later. Bandages were being made of paper because there was no cotton. Paper underwear was being issued to the troops. For soldiers and civilians alike, life had become a degrading struggle for survival.

In November the Austro-Hungarian general staff, in reviewing its options, was forced to the conclusion that its armies would be incapable of mounting offensive operations in 1918. It still had forty-four divisions on the now-quiet Russian front and thirty-seven in Italy, but these were so depleted of men and equipment, typically including between five and eight thousand troops each, as to be barely worthy of being called divisions. Desertion was epidemic, those troops who did not desert were displaying an increasing inclination to revolt (this was especially true of returning prisoners of war), and in rural areas life was reverting to a kind of Dark Ages barbarism. Deserters formed themselves into bandit gangs and preyed on local populations.

Conrad had been displaced as chief of staff but commanded an army on the Italian front. And evidently he had learned nothing in three years of mounting grand campaigns beyond the capabilities of his forces. He began hatching plans for an offensive southward out of the Tyrolean Alps onto the plains northwest of Venice—yet another scheme for punishing the despised Italians, made more attractive this time by the hope of capturing as much territory as possible before the hoped-for German victory. Soon Conrad was peddling his ideas in Vienna. His superiors did their best to ignore him.

All of which left Germany on her own. Even so, the situation seemed far from hopeless. In spite of another year of heavy casualties, in spite too of shortages of many essentials, the end of the war in the east was making it possible to bring Berlin's military might fully to bear on the Western Front. And if the German armies were no longer what they had been two or three years earlier, they were no more badly damaged than those of Britain and France. If they were wretchedly ill equipped in comparison with their enemies—even Germany's front-line troops could be given small rations of meat only three or four times weekly, and their trucks and wagons had no rubber tires—in other ways they enjoyed significant advantages.

High on the list of such advantages was the strength of the German defenses in Belgium and France. At all points except where the difficulties of the terrain made enemy attack improbable, these defenses had been improved beyond recognition since 1914. They were massive, sophisticated, ten-mile-deep systems of interconnected and mutually supportive machine-gun pillboxes, moatlike traps for infantry and tanks, and artillery-proof bunkers, all of it guarded by shoals of barbed and razor wire. Hundreds of thousands of laborers, many of them prisoners of war and civilians from captured territory, had been engaged in building this system since the start of the stalemate. The result was a barricade that, once reinforced with troops from the east, promised to be all but impregnable.

In the second half of 1917, first on the northeastern front and then at Caporetto and Cambrai, the Germans had introduced a new offensive system to complement their defenses. Called the "Hutier method" because it was first used by a cousin of Ludendorff's named General Oskar von Hutier, this system promised to be a way of breaking the deadlock in the West. It involved a new kind of assault unit made up of detachments of only six or eight men, so-called storm troops trained not to try to overwhelm the enemy's defenses with sheer mass but to make use of whatever cover the terrain afforded, slip around and past the strongest positions (instead of stopping to destroy them), and so move deep into enemy territory with

General Oskar von Hutier, at left
First to employ the new offensive doctrine.

unprecedented speed. The bypassed strongpoints would later be reduced by larger, more heavily armed units following in a second wave. Though such tactics had been tried on only a modest scale on the Western Front, there seemed no reason why they should not prove effective in much larger operations—*if* the Germans took the offensive.

That was the question facing the high command: whether to attack or stand on the defensive as in 1915 and 1917. The decision was Ludendorff's, and from the start he favored the offensive. He was influenced in that direction by what Plumer had achieved with his limited attacks at Ypres late in 1917, but what decided him was the U.S. army. American troops were arriving in France by the scores of thousands every month (the number would grow to a quarter of a million monthly by mid-1918). Though almost all were still in training, they would soon be a force of overwhelming size. Green though they were, the Yanks were well fed, enthusiastic, and equipped with the best of everything. Still unbloodied, they displayed a kind of innocent eagerness that was no longer possible for the British, French, or Germans.

Ludendorff calculated that the Americans could not be a problem until the middle of 1918, but that thereafter they would tip the scales conclusively. If Germany was to win the war in the west, it had only the first half of the year in which to do so. It was with this in mind that a new booklet, "The Attack in Trench Warfare," a treatise explaining the Hutier method and how to use it, was distributed to the armies of Germany. Selected officers were pulled out of the line for an eight-day retraining course that was soon expanded to four weeks. The best German divisions in the east, along with soldiers under age thirty-five culled from less capable units, were loaded onto trains and moved back to Germany for rest, refitting, and instruction. The goal was to create forty-two elite mobile divisions made up of the best soldiers Germany still had—fit young fighters skilled in the use of grenades, light machine guns, flamethrowers, and trench mortars and schooled in the new system. After years of standing in a defensive posture that offered no chance of victory, after ordeals like Passchendaele, these men wanted to attack. They "pined for the offensive," Ludendorff said, "and after Russia's collapse expected it with relief." Something similar was true of the home front. People not only wanted an end to the war but expected—had been taught to expect by German propaganda—that the end would come soon and in the form of an unambiguous victory.

The remaining question was where to attack. That came down to a question of *whom* to attack—the British or the French? To explore it, on November 11 Ludendorff met with Generals Friedrich von der Schulenburg, chief of staff of Crown Prince Wilhelm's army group, and Hermann von Kuhl, chief of staff of the army group commanded by Crown Prince Rupprecht of Bavaria. Both were seasoned commanders (Kuhl had been Kluck's chief of staff during the 1914 drive on Paris), and both had strong opinions. Schulenburg urged an attack on both sides of the Verdun salient—not as ridiculous an idea as it might at first seem, the French having drastically reduced their defenses in that sector. He saw a possibility of shattering the line around Verdun and driving the French back toward Paris. Kuhl pushed for Flanders, arguing that it was the only place where strategic objectives could be achieved. If the BEF's line could be pierced, the British would have their backs against the sea and might be destroyed or forced to escape to England. Ludendorff himself laid out a number of other possibilities, giving particular attention to the point near St. Quentin where the British and French lines met. He declared that no offensive could go forward unless three conditions were met. The Russians and Italians must continue to pose no threat. The attack must come at the earliest possible time—in March at the latest, in February if possible. Wherever it came, even if against the French, the objective must be the defeat of the British. The BEF, so tiny at the start of the war, was now the dominant element in the Entente's strength. If it could be eliminated, the French would be unable to continue. If it could be eliminated by midyear, the Americans would not matter.

Fifteen days later any lingering worries about a possible revival of the war on the Eastern Front were put to rest when three Russian soldiers waving a white flag approached the German line in Courland in the far north. They said they had been sent by General Kirilenko, a new chief of staff appointed by the Bolsheviks. Their mission was to communicate their government's wish for a negotiated peace. Within days German and Russian delegates, among them Max Hoffmann and German foreign minister Richard von Kühlmann (who had succeeded Arthur Zimmermann), were gathering in the city of Brest-Litovsk.

Many peace feelers were being put forward at about this time, usually secretly and with tangled motives, and the leaders on both sides were speaking publicly about their willingness to make peace on reasonable terms. The Entente was trying to arrange a separate peace with Vienna, which would have been fatal to Germany in the east. The Germans were using intermediaries to see if one member of the Entente or another—now London, now Paris, now Petrograd—might be ready to talk. And the pope, who had regarded the war as madness from the start, continued to rouse the ire of Italian nationalists by looking for some common ground upon which an armistice might be arranged. The story of these pronouncements and initiatives, some of them sincere and others cynical, is complicated, interesting, and at points amusing or sad. But there was never much chance of working out a general peace.

The only conceivable peace, as long as the deadlock continued, was a return to the status quo ante. But at this stage only Russia and Austria-Hungary would have embraced such an idea, and they were willing to do so only because they had failed. Berlin and London and Paris and Rome still saw victory as possible or even likely in the long run, and none would settle for less. In a sense, all were *unable* to settle for less. Having told their peoples that this was a fight of good against evil, they would have found a decision to reconcile with the enemy (not to mention everything sacrificed in fighting that enemy) awkward to explain.

Germany's leaders were more divided than those of the Entente on the question of war aims. Hindenburg and Ludendorff still expected to win, and therefore they had no interest in peace terms not dictated by Berlin. By contrast, Count Georg von Hertling, the aged Bavarian Catholic and former professor of philosophy who had become chancellor on November 1 after Michaelis resigned, said he wanted a place in history as the "reconciliation chancellor." But even for him reconciliation meant a peace that brought gains to Germany—Luxembourg and Liège, perhaps, as well as France's Longwy-Briey basin with its rich deposits of coal and iron. In this he was supported by Richard von Kühlmann, who pursued negotiations in many directions so energetically and ingeniously that Hindenburg and Ludendorff came to regard him as another of their problems. But he never did so with the intention of ending the fighting; his objective was to get any one member of the Entente to drop out of the war, freeing the generals to finish off the others.

If Kühlmann's activities were less disastrous than Zimmermann's had been, they were sterile nevertheless. With Lloyd George secure as prime minister in Britain and Clemenceau totally dominant in Paris, separating their two countries was impossible. Both men understood that Europe could not possibly be returned to what it had been at the start of the war. The Russia that had been France's most important ally in 1914 no longer existed. Postwar Russia, broken and reduced, would be little better than a satellite of Germany—unless Germany too were broken. More than at the beginning, this was now an all-or-nothing war.

It was all or nothing for Ludendorff too. On December 27 he met again with Schulenburg and Kuhl. (It is revealing of Ludendorff's power that he was free to settle momentous questions without involving the two crown princes to whom Schulenburg and Kuhl formally reported, or Hindenburg or the kaiser, or any member of the government.) Schulenburg continued

Georg von Hertling
Aspired to be
"the reconciliation chancellor."

to want an offensive at Verdun, and Kuhl still favored Flanders. Undecided, Ludendorff instructed army and army group staffs all along the front to develop plans for possible offensives: not only at Verdun and in Flanders but at St. Quentin, Arras, Champagne, and even the all-but-impenetrable Vosges Mountains west of Strasbourg. He feared that an attack at Verdun could be answered and undone by a British response in Flanders. Though he agreed with Kuhl that Flanders was ideal strategically, he feared that the ground there would be dangerously muddy so early in the year. He continued to show particular interest in the St. Quentin option, but his colleagues were not enthusiastic. Kuhl had already sent him a memorandum arguing that although a breakthrough might be fairly easy at St. Quentin, exploiting it would require defeating the British while simultaneously blocking the French from coming to their aid. This, he said, was likely to be asking too much of the troops. Ludendorff's own operations chief, Major Georg Wetzell, expressed his own fears that the St. Quentin option was too ambitious and that either Flanders or Verdun would be preferable. There was of course nothing unhealthy in open disagreement over such questions; the debate reflected Ludendorff's ingrained willingness to consider the opinions of those military (as opposed to his civilian) associates whom he trusted. But the fact that he remained undecided about the location of an attack that he wanted to take place within ten or twelve weeks is suggestive of a lack of strategic clarity.

Fresh good news came from the Eastern Front: by Christmas the Germans and Russians had agreed to a thirty-day armistice during which negotiations would proceed, and Bolshevik leader Leon Trotsky arrived at Brest-Litovsk to take charge of the Russian delegation. But this development was balanced by trouble behind the lines. On January 14 cuts in bread and flour rations ignited strikes across Austria. Seven hundred and fifty thousand workers went out, including hundreds of thousands in Vienna, and they demanded not just food but peace. The disorder spread to warships in Austria-Hungary's Adriatic ports and to Germany's Kiel naval base, where authorities apprehended the protest leaders and inducted them into the army. The intensity of the discontent, and the extent to which the dissidents were organized, became clear when the executive committee of a Workers Council issued a January 27 call for a general strike and as many as a million German workers (exact numbers, in these matters, remain impossible to establish) went out the next day. Many of the strikers were munitions workers, which made the walkout intolerable to the military authorities. Equally intolerable—and deeply troubling—was the political content of the strikers' rhetoric. The Workers Council, echoing its allies in the Reichstag, called for "the speedy conclusion of peace without annexations and indemnities, on the basis of self-determination of peoples." After a week of street violence in which a

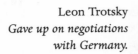

Leon Trotsky
*Gave up on negotiations
with Germany.*

number of people were killed, the strike was not settled but crushed by the army. Forty thousand strikers, supporters, and family members were arrested. Between thirty-five hundred and six thousand of the leaders were inducted into military service and told they were bound for the front. In the eyes of conservatives and even moderate elements of the German public, Ludendorff and the army had preserved law and order. The episode heightened Ludendorff's sense that the home front was dangerously unstable, that the war had to be won before the urban rabble became absolutely unmanageable and the nation's resolve was destroyed.

He found additional reason for concern when, on February 11, liberal members of the Reichstag issued a statement calling for a *political* offensive against Great Britain—emphatically not a *military* offensive—"including an unequivocal declaration of the sovereignty and integrity of Belgium." This statement served as a highly unofficial (and officially repudiated) response to a January speech in which Lloyd George had suggested a willingness to accept a negotiated settlement. Lloyd George had not been looking for a response—the purpose of his speech was not to get negotiations started but to persuade the British labor unions that responsibility for the continuation of the war lay with Berlin—and Ludendorff was not wrong in regarding the whole affair as meaningless. He remained confident that Germany could come out of the war as master of Belgium and more *if* his domestic adversaries were not permitted to deflect him from the victories that lay ahead.

On January 21, after a tour of the Western Front, Ludendorff announced his decision. The attack would be at St. Quentin, in Picardy east of the old Somme battleground at the juncture of the British and French lines. This was not the attack he really wanted—that would have been farther north. But

Flanders would have to wait until it was sure to be dry enough not to suck the Germans into another Passchendaele. St. Quentin presented no such danger. It would be code-named "St. Michael" after the sword-bearing archangel who was patron saint of the German Reich. By forcing Haig to shift his reserves southward it would, according to Ludendorff's plan, set the British up for a later pair of Flanders offensives, St. George One and Two.

Crown Prince Rupprecht of Bavaria was puzzled by the Michael plan (the "St." prefix was soon abandoned). An intelligent and skillful army group commander, a descendant through his mother of the Stuart kings of England, he asked what its strategic objective was supposed to be. "We make a hole and the rest will take care of itself," Ludendorff replied. "That's how we did it in Russia." It was not an answer that many strategists, thinking calmly, would have found satisfactory.

Wetzell had offered a word of caution before the question was closed. If Michael went ahead, he suggested, it should be kept within strict limits. If the troops succeeded in breaking through, the generals should be content to allow the resulting threat to draw the British reserves down from Flanders. The advance should *not* continue into the tangled wasteland that the Battle of the Somme had created and that the Germans had made worse with their scorched-earth withdrawal to the Hindenburg Line.

Ludendorff disregarded this advice.

KAISER WILHELM II

ALTHOUGH WILHELM II HAD ACTUALLY *DONE* VERY LITTLE to ignite the war (his biggest contribution was a careless failure to restrain the Austrians at the outset, and he tried to reverse course as soon as he understood the danger), the war might never have happened if not for what he *was.*

That was the story of his life. In the quarter of a century between his becoming emperor and the outbreak of hostilities, he had accomplished almost nothing. If Germany flourished in almost every sphere from economics to the arts, its success was not his doing. But his personality had cast an unsettling shadow across Europe all the same, alienating powerful neighbors, increasing Germany's isolation, and worsening the tangle of ambition and fear that finally drew all the Great Powers into the abyss.

To take a word from *Wilhelm II and the Germans,* a penetrating psychoanalytic study by Professor Thomas A. Kohut of Williams College, the kaiser's personality was "fractured." It made him an immensely complicated, dangerously unstable, deeply damaged public figure, sometimes appealing but more often offensive, full of bluster and swagger but terribly insecure, intelligent but only in superficial and unreflective ways, made up of parts that never formed a coherent whole. He was "one of those strange figures in history whose personalities have had more effect on the course of affairs than their deeds."

The kaiser's complexities rose partly out of his ancestry. The grandson on the paternal side of modern Germany's first emperor, on the maternal side of the majestic Victoria who was Queen of Great Britain and Ireland and Empress of India, he was heir to two awesome and radically different traditions. Britain at the time of his birth was not quite a democracy by today's standards, but it was a distinctly liberal society in which most political power resided in Parliament and the monarch was well along the path to becoming a revered figurehead. Hohenzollern Prussia on the other hand, and the empire that Prussia created when Wilhelm was still a boy, were autocracies that concentrated nearly all power in the crown. England had long been the richest country on the planet and the center of the world's greatest empire, and it possessed all the assurance that came from generations of dominance. Germany by contrast, after centuries of frag-mentation and weakness, was a newcomer to the world stage. Like an overgrown adolescent it was both surprised by and overly proud of its new strength, unsure of itself, often unsure of how to behave. It had an inferi-ority complex that made it quick to respond resentfully to trivial, even imaginary, slights.

All this was made personal for the boy Wilhelm by his parents, the character of their marriage, and their unhappy destinies. Princess Victoria of Britain (Queen Victoria's eldest child) and Crown Prince Friedrich of Prussia and Germany were an attractive, intelligent, and well-intentioned couple who unquestionably loved each other and their many children. Despite the immense advantages with which they began, however, their lives and careers were tragic. Vicky, as she was known in the family, was a strong-willed and opinionated young woman who had been raised by her parents—especially by her adored father Prince Albert, who had begun life as a member of provincial German royalty—to regard English culture and England's liberal political traditions as pinnacles of human achieve-ment. When she went to Berlin as Fritz's teenage bride, she did so with a self-imposed mission: to transform the backward Germans and their feudal politics into a mirror image of enlightened Britain. She made little effort to conceal her disdain for her new home, making herself an object of distrust not only to the Junker establishment but to her in-laws.

It was part of Fritz's tragedy that, though he played a distinguished part in Prussia's victories over Austria and France, he not only accepted his wife's attitudes and aspirations but allowed himself to be so completely dominated by her as to become an object of contempt in official Berlin, a male-chauvinist society if ever there has been such a thing. He lost the confidence of his father, the king-emperor, and of Chancellor Bismarck, who came to see him as the mere instrument of his wife's dangerous notions. The couple's first son, Willy, was therefore from earliest childhood pulled in two directions. His mother wanted desperately for him to become another Prince Albert, an English gentleman of German origin, a progressive and reformist liberal. But the world in which he was raised—his grandfather the emperor most definitely included—was equally deter-mined to ensure that he grew up to become a worthy heir to the long line of Prussian warrior-kings. The court looked to him to display a proper Hohenzollern hatred for anything tainted with such decadent abomina-tions as liberalism or, even worse, an even quasi-democratic sharing of power.

The difficulties of the child's situation were made worse by serious physical disabilities. He nearly died during a horrendously difficult breech birth from which he emerged with the muscles, tendons, and nerves of his left shoulder nearly destroyed. His arm and hand were paralyzed, and his upper torso and neck were affected to such an extent that in early childhood he could neither walk normally nor hold his head consistently upright. Throughout his life he would be incapable of dressing himself or cutting his food. It is possible though not provable that he suffered minor brain damage as a result of oxygen deprivation during the birth ordeal.

Little Willy's deformities made him an object of concern for the Hohenzollern family and court. For his mother, they were a nightmare. The princess was laden with guilt over having produced so defective an heir. Still a teenager when her son was born, she was unable to conceal her horror from the child. "He would really be so pretty," she wrote mournfully to her mother in England, "if not for [the birth damage]." Inevitably if unintentionally, she implanted in him the conviction that he was not what he should be. This message was reinforced by the Hohenzollern inner circle. A great-uncle declared sternly that "a one-armed man should never be king of Prussia."

His mother hoped desperately to make the boy whole. He underwent years of treatment that, however well intentioned, was not far from torture. His limp left arm was regularly wrapped in the body of a freshly killed hare to warm it. Electric current was applied in an effort to stimulate muscle growth. For an hour each day he was locked into a brace that forced his head upright against the resistance of stiffening muscles and tendons. Ultimately, tendons on one side of his neck had to be severed to correct his distorted posture and facial expressions.

The child was unable to stay atop a horse—an inconceivable failing in a Hohenzollern heir. And so, weeping, he was forced to mount and fall and remount and fall again until finally, after weeks of agony and humiliation, he became the skilled and confident horseman that he would be throughout his reign. It was a splendid achievement for a small boy, but he does not appear to have received praise for it. The same iron discipline was applied in all his early training: his education had been entrusted to a taskmaster, the cold and distant Herr Hinzpeter, who not only demanded a round-the-clock Spartan regimen but believed that praise corrupted the soul. Thus Willy's hunger for approval, for assurance that he was not a misfit, remained totally unsatisfied. Out of that hunger there grew a habit of covering his self-doubts with bravado and responding with wrath to even the appearance of rejection.

Freudians will argue that young Willy, in order to have a chance of establishing his own identity, was bound to rebel against his mother, against her anxieties and her frustrated efforts to mold him into a replica of her father. (She was always disappointed in his academic performance.) Be that as it may, rebel he did. As he approached manhood, he broke with his parents, moving in the one direction certain to appall them: toward his grandfather the emperor, toward Bismarck, toward the whole reactionary Junker ethos including what his grandmother in England called "that terrible Prussian pride and ambition." As he took up a commission in one of the elite regiments, he said that he found there his first real home. He married a girl who could scarcely have been less like his mother—a dull, unquestioning German girl who in short order bestowed on him six sons in whom he took little interest and a daughter on whom he doted. His approving grandfather began to send him on diplomatic missions that should rightfully have been given to his father, humiliating poor Fritz and dividing the family into two openly warring camps.

All this history went into the making of the man who in 1888—the year his grandfather and his cancer-stricken father both died—became at twenty-seven the master and All-High Warlord of the most powerful nation on the European continent. Wilhelm II's youthful impetuousness, compulsive self-aggrandizement, and painstakingly concealed insecurity so perfectly mirrored the nation he led that throughout the early years of his reign he and his brilliant uniforms and his theatrical displays of self met with public adulation. He was a precociously modern figure in his obsession with how he was covered in the press, an early and for a time successful practitioner of the dubious art of public relations. But it could not last. Wilhelm himself was psychologically too fragile to hold together the image, the facade, that he had worked long and hard to create. In his need to prove himself master of everything, he dismissed the mighty Bismarck two years after taking the throne. He intruded constantly into domestic and international affairs that he had neither the knowledge nor the skill to manage. "The emperor is like a balloon," Bismarck had said. "If one did not hold him fast on a string, he would go no one knows whither." With Bismarck no longer holding the string—Wilhelm could tolerate no underlings except those who made obsequious displays of submission—he soon went out of control. The last ten years of peace were punctuated with scandals and sometimes outlandish political and diplomatic blunders. He suffered a series of nervous breakdowns, the first of which, interestingly, occurred when his one close friend was revealed to be homosexual. He emerged from each setback and collapse more depressed than ever, more obviously a hollow man swollen with pretense, less able to function as a real—as opposed to a make-believe—ruler.

And through it all like a dark thread there ran his immensely complicated relationship with his mother's homeland. He admired and even loved, craved the approval of but also envied and resented, the grand-mother, uncle, and cousin who successively reigned in Britain. He built a fabulously expensive navy in the improbable hope that somehow this would cause Britain to want Germany's friendship. "Nothing will change," he said, "until we are so strong on the seas that we become valuable allies." When the result was exactly the opposite of what he had hoped—when Britain felt so threatened that she was driven to friendship with Russia and even her ancient enemy France—Wilhelm reacted with angry, bitterly uncomprehending complaints of betrayal.

What he was, finally, was a weak and often foolish man who neverthe-less managed to persuade much of the world that he was a monster and a danger. By 1914 he was only marginally capable of heading his gov-ernment and even less prepared to direct Germany's massive military machine. By 1918 he was little more than a figurehead in whom the real leaders of Germany had no confidence. By autumn his story would be very nearly finished.

Chapter 32

✠

Entangling Misalliances

"I am sick of this d—d life."
—General Sir William Robertson

The British and the French, once they agreed that no large-scale offensives should be attempted in the new year, were left with much to guess at where German intentions were concerned. They had to try to figure out where (if anywhere) the Germans were likely to attack, and to settle on tactics and how to deploy their troops.

It was not easy to agree on any of these matters. The possibilities were too numerous for comfort. At the end of 1917 the Western Front still ran in the old zigs and zags from the Belgian coast down to Picardy in France, from there westward to Verdun, and then southward again to Switzerland. The eighteen miles nearest the English Channel were defended by thirteen Belgian divisions and, more decisively, by the broad shallow lakes created when the coastal dikes were opened in 1914. This flooding made the northern end of the front impregnable—essentially took it out of the war. Nearly as impregnable were the 150 miles at the southern end, where the steep pine forests of the Vosges Mountains, the heights looming over the River Meuse, and France's mighty chain of fortresses formed a formidable wall.

That left hundreds of miles of potential battleground. German initiatives were feasible everywhere from the start of the British line at a Belgian stream called the Coverbeeck to south of Verdun. Flanders, Picardy, Champagne, the Argonne, the big German salient at St. Mihiel—all remained in play. The known fact that the Germans were now transferring large numbers of troops to the west made it probable not only that an attack was coming but that it would be on a bigger scale than what had been seen thus far.

Lloyd George's miserliness with replacements notwithstanding, Douglas

Haig had an immense army under his command. Fifty-seven British, Indian, Australia–New Zealand, and Canadian divisions, along with two unhappy Portuguese divisions that their government had tossed into the war as a gesture of friendship with England, held a hundred and twenty-five miles of front on a line running north-south from Flanders to the Somme. The BEF had held much of this ground exactly as long as the Germans opposite, but they had been far less conscientious about improving their defenses. Like his French allies, Haig had always been focused on the offensive, and so he had always regarded his position less as a fortress to be secured than as a series of launching points for attacks. He had encouraged his subordinates to think likewise, with the result that his front line was not what it could have been and his rear defenses were in many places rudimentary. These weaknesses could not be blamed on Lloyd George. While withholding infantry, the prime minister had dispatched more than a hundred thousand laborers to the continent. But as 1917 ended, only seventeen hundred of these men were at work on the British defenses. Even the following March, with Ludendorff's blow known to be coming, only twenty-seven hundred would be so employed.

There was also a problem with how Haig's forces were deployed. Passchendaele had been a drive out of the Ypres salient toward the north and west. The success of that drive, meager though it was, had drawn the British forward into a tight pocket between Ypres and the sea. Haig had kept his heaviest troop concentrations in and near this pocket, where there was little room for maneuver. He did so in part to protect the ports through which the BEF's lifeline ran from England. His doing so was also a function of his belief, which revolted Lloyd George, that the ground taken at such cost at the end of 1917 could be an ideal starting point for a resumed offensive in the new year.

Another problem was the approach to defensive warfare taken by most of Haig's army commanders. All but the savvy Plumer adhered to the old practice of packing large numbers of infantry into the line nearest to the Germans. They also left their second line within reach of enemy guns.

Lloyd George and the generals continued to be at loggerheads. At the turn of the year the prime minister forced Haig to replace his chief of staff, deputy chief of staff, and heads of intelligence, engineering, and medical services. Haig was not pleased. The new men were not drawn from the cavalry fraternity he favored, and having them imposed upon him was an embarrassment— the closest Lloyd George could come to replacing Haig himself. But they proved markedly more competent than their predecessors (Haig's original chief of intelligence had been reviled and ridiculed for an optimism untroubled by facts), and so ultimately the changes would work to Haig's advantage. As a further affront, Lloyd George appointed one of Haig's rivals and critics, the venomously charming Henry Wilson, to be Britain's military representative on the Supreme War Council.

Little more harmony was evident in the French camp, or in relations between the British and the French. Pétain, who commanded the army groups that would have to deal with any German attacks between Picardy and Verdun, was becoming an isolated figure. Only he among the French appeared to see the implications of what the Germans had achieved with their new assault tactics, and to understand that these innovations required a new kind of response. When on January 8 he promulgated his Directive No. 4, which offered such a response, his army commanders received it with indifference or poorly concealed scorn. Clemenceau, who understood what Pétain had achieved at Verdun and in dealing with the mutiny, saw also that the general no longer showed much confidence that the war could be won. This troubled him and contributed to his rejection of Pétain's idea for a 1918 offensive in Alsace. Its purpose was to have been limited: a capture of coveted ground that would improve France's bargaining position if peace talks began. That was not nearly enough for Clemenceau. For inspiration—for a professional's assurances that victory could be achieved—the prime minister looked not to Pétain but to Foch. But instead of putting Foch in Pétain's place, he held him in reserve. He was convinced that the Entente needed a supreme military commander. He was determined to put a French general in that post, and to see that Foch got the job.

And so Pétain remained the commander in chief, if not a greatly appreciated one. His Directive No. 4 offered badly needed changes. It drew on the lessons of the chess game that Plumer and the Germans had played in Flanders, and of the German counteroffensive at Cambrai, in calling for a thinly manned and flexible front line. This amounted to a revolution in French tactical thinking, an abandonment of the old idea, long since abandoned by the Germans, of holding every foot of ground at all costs. It was heresy to most of the army group, army, corps, and divisional commanders. Some of them protested. When Pétain did not withdraw his directive, they united in ignoring it. For support they had to look no farther than to Foch, who had never stopped worshiping at the altar of *offensive à l'outrance* and was known to have Clemenceau's ear.

But it was Pétain who, with little support from above or below, had to get on with the job of preparing for a German offensive. He had ninety-nine divisions with which to do so, sixty of them spread along the front and the others in reserve. (There were also more than a hundred thousand American troops in France by this time—four oversize U.S. divisions—but Pershing did not regard them as ready to play an active role at the front. Nor was he willing to put them at the service of British or French commanders.)

They seemed immense, the forces at Pétain's disposal, until one took into account the amount of territory they had to defend and the number of German divisions being brought from the east. He had only four divisions in reserve at the northern end of his line, not nearly enough for safety. In the hope of freeing more troops, late in 1917 he asked Haig to extend the British line fifty-five miles to the south, so that it would reach to and even beyond St. Quentin. Haig had no interest in doing anything of the kind.

Both Pétain's request and the broader question of how to create an adequate reserve force in Picardy—precisely the place, as it happened, that Ludendorff chose for his attack—were still unresolved when, on January 24, the senior British, French, and American generals gathered at Compiègne. When the idea of creating a general reserve out of divisions contributed by Haig and Pétain was proposed, both men backed away from it with all possible haste. United only in their determination to continue operating independently of each other, they insisted that they had no troops to spare for such experiments. The conference ended without result.

Six days later the third meeting of the Supreme War Council brought the generals together with Lloyd George and Clemenceau. This meeting went on for four days and was contentious. Lloyd George made the last of his many efforts to shift the focus of the war away from the Western Front, trying to persuade the others to make Turkey the primary target in 1918. The idea was not without potential—the Turkish army was little better than a wreck, and taking it out of the war could have exposed Austria-Hungary's eastern flank, and created tremendous problems for Germany in the Balkans and beyond. But the others were not interested. Clemenceau was absolutely opposed; nothing mattered to him so much as driving the Germans out of France. When Robertson supported Clemenceau instead of his own prime minister, his name went to the top of Lloyd George's unwritten list of nuisances to be eliminated.

Inevitably, the reserve issue came up again. Lloyd George, by prior arrangement with Clemenceau, nominated Foch to be chairman of an executive committee responsible for establishing a general reserve. For him it was another way of keeping Haig in shackles, for Clemenceau a first step toward giving Foch authority over Pétain and Haig. As before, these two generals wanted nothing to do with any such proposal. Though unable to block the creation of the new committee or Foch's appointment as its head, they regarded the whole exercise as unnecessary and unimportant. They had already agreed that, if either was seriously threatened, the other would send as many as six divisions to the rescue. This agreement seemed sufficient to them.

Haig, abandoning his hopes for an offensive in Flanders, agreed to extend his right wing far enough to the south to take over twenty-five miles of

French line. This was less than half of what Pétain had requested, but it would allow him to shift two corps, at least four and possibly six divisions, to his reserve. It did not, however, prevent Foch from requesting that Britain, France, and Italy between them contribute thirty divisions to the new general reserve, which otherwise would exist only on paper. Haig, who had been obliged to send five divisions to Italy in November and now had only eight in reserve, declared that he would resign rather than comply.

A dispute broke out within the British camp over the role of Henry Wilson and, by implication, of Robertson. Wilson, a French-speaking Francophile, had long been the French general staff's favorite Englishman. (He was a passionate Ulsterman, actually, and would be assassinated in Ireland after the war.) As London's principal agent in the secret prewar sessions that had first brought the staffs of the two armies together for joint planning, he had developed such an admiration for Foch that some who did not share his enthusiasm referred to him as Foch's lapdog. He made little effort to conceal his disdain for Haig and Robertson, which won him favor in the eyes of Lloyd George. The new trouble erupted over the question of whether Wilson, in his new position as Britain's military representative on the Supreme War Council, should report to Robertson as chief of the imperial general staff or to the government—to Lloyd George. Wilson wanted to report to the prime minister. Robertson's position was that Wilson, being a general representing the army, must report to him directly and only through the chain of com-

"Wully" Robertson
Targeted by Lloyd George.

mand to the government. Lloyd George, weary of Robertson's insistence that the war had to be won on the Western Front and his unwavering support of Haig, no doubt saw in the situation an opportunity to rid himself of a problem. He therefore supported Wilson. Robertson, demonstrating that he was standing on principle rather than trying to aggrandize himself, offered to serve in either position, as chief of the imperial general staff or as council member, so long as the latter reported to the former. When Lloyd George refused, Robertson resigned.

Lloyd George added insult to injury, and made the entire disagreement seem contrived from the start, by appointing Wilson to replace Robertson as chief of the imperial general staff. (The job was first offered to Herbert Plumer, whose refusal may have stemmed from indignation at how Robertson had been treated.) Wilson completed the farce by replacing himself on the council with a junior general whom he was easily able to control. Robertson was consigned to the British home forces. Thus was neutralized one of the most capable and respected generals to serve in the British army during the Great War. Robertson himself appeared to have few regrets. As he had written to Haig, "I am sick of this d—d life."

Haig extended his line to the south in the simplest possible way: by ordering the commander of the army that formed his right wing, Hubert Gough, to spread out his troops to cover the additional twenty-five miles. The advantage of this approach was that it required no thinning of Haig's left, where he continued to expect the enemy to attack. Such an expectation was not foolish. Haig knew at least as well as Ludendorff that the proximity of the sea put his left in an awkward position, and that the loss of the port towns of northeastern France would be a disaster from which recovery might not be possible. What he failed to anticipate was Ludendorff's decision to strike elsewhere first because of the weather factor. The problem for Gough—one that he recognized and quickly reported—was that the thinning of his line made him alarmingly vulnerable. The front-line defenses that he had inherited from the French were in a poor state of preparedness, and in some places rear defenses barely existed.

Gough, whose Fifth Army was the smallest in the BEF, was being asked to cover forty-two miles of front with fourteen divisions. The two armies immediately to his north had sixteen divisions each and together had to defend only sixty-one miles. Gough complained, asking for more troops and for labor units with which to improve his position. He got no response. Haig believed, evidently, that in the unlikely event of an attack on his right, Gough would have ample room to pull back to the east and north while Pétain moved French troops from the south to fill any gaps. He is not known to have been aware that Pétain was under instructions, in case of an emergency, not to support the British but to fall back to a position from which he could protect Paris.

The Germans too remained tangled in disagreement and uncertainty. The preparations for the Michael offensive were moving forward efficiently enough—Ludendorff decided that the attack would begin on March 21, the earliest practicable date—but the generals and politicians were divided over how, and on what terms, to shut down the war in the east. This led to a breach between Ludendorff and certainly the cleverest, possibly the most brilliant general officer in the German army, the recently promoted Major General Max Hoffmann. On New Year's Day, when Hoffmann returned from the peace talks in Brest-Litovsk for a meeting of the kaiser's Crown Council, Foreign Minister Kühlmann invited him to lunch. Kaiser Wilhelm invited himself to join them. He asked Hoffmann for his views on what Germany should claim as the spoils due to it as the victor in the east. Hoffmann, mindful that Ludendorff had forbidden all officers to talk with the kaiser without first consulting him, tried to avoid answering. When Wilhelm insisted—he was, after all, the monarch to whom every German officer swore obedience— Hoffmann had little choice except to comply. He explained, knowing that everything he said was in direct opposition to Ludendorff's thinking, that in

General Max Hoffmann
*Master tactitian of
the Eastern Front.*

his opinion it would make no sense to take permanent control of large expanses of territory in the east. Adjustments along the frontier with Poland could have military value, he said, but absorbing substantial non-German populations would bring only trouble.

After lunch Hoffmann attempted to telephone Ludendorff and explain what had happened. He was unable to reach him: Ludendorff was in transit, en route to the next day's council session. When that meeting began, the kaiser launched into a lecture about the inadvisability of demanding too much from the Russians. Then, with the astounding lack of judgment of which he was capable, Wilhelm proudly declared that he was supported in this matter by a general of unquestioned ability: Max Hoffmann. Ludendorff was almost apoplectic. Soon he was demanding Hoffmann's dismissal.

Ludendorff was blind where the settlement with Russia was concerned. He could see only that Russia was no longer capable of defending herself, and he took this as Germany's opportunity to become master of everything east of Berlin. What he did not see, or more likely did not care about, was that stripping Russia bare would persuade the surviving members of the Entente that there was no possibility of negotiating an acceptable end to the war. It would convince them that Germany wanted nothing less than the destruction of her enemies and dominance of all Europe. Such worries had no meaning for Ludendorff. He *did* want the destruction of Germany's enemies—the European ones, at any rate—and he intended to achieve exactly that. He was opposed not only by Hoffmann but by Kühlmann and Chancellor Hertling, both of whom urged restraint. Kühlmann in particular understood that if Ludendorff's demands were satisfied, Germany and Russia could never be other than enemies. He wanted to lay the groundwork for postwar friendship—albeit with a Russia that had been seriously weakened. He hoped that at least a gesture in the direction of generosity would encourage Britain to enter into negotiations.

A week after the Crown Council meeting, Woodrow Wilson delivered an address to Congress in which he unveiled his famous Fourteen Points. These were a loftily idealistic expression of what America sought to achieve in the war: self-determination for all peoples, open covenants openly arrived at, and other fine notions that would prove to be entirely unachievable when put to the test. Characteristically, the president had not deigned to consult with his allies in preparing his speech. Though they were pleased with some of his words (a call for the restoration of Belgium, a suggestion that Alsace-Lorraine should be returned to France and that Austria-Hungary's Italian possessions should be surrendered), they were surprised and confused by others and not much inclined to take them seriously. When news of the speech reached Berlin, it strengthened Ludendorff. Wilson the would-be peacemaker, by indicating that such fraught questions as Belgium and perhaps even Alsace-Lorraine might not even be open to discussion, had given Ludendorff new ammunition to use in insisting that the war had to be fought to a conclusion.

The mercurial Kaiser Wilhelm had altered his thinking on an eastern settlement by the time the Crown Council next met on February 13. Ludendorff was aggressive as always, urging not only that Estonia, Livonia, Finland, and Ukraine should be taken from Russia but that the German army should continue driving eastward until they had overthrown the Bolsheviks. The kaiser went even further. He proposed breaking what had been the Romanov empire into four separate entities: a truncated Russia proper, Ukraine, Siberia, and a Union of the South East. Such skeptics as Hoffmann, Kühlmann, and Hertling were not only powerless but by now essentially voiceless.

The Russians were shocked by what was demanded of them in the aftermath of this meeting. Trotsky threw up his hands, telling the Germans that he would never agree to what they wanted and urging Lenin to adopt a "no war, no peace" policy in which Russia would neither continue to fight nor agree to Germany's terms. When the negotiations broke down completely, the Germans swiftly put fifty divisions back into motion along the Eastern Front. The Russians were so helpless that the Germans, though their best men and equipment were now in France, advanced a hundred and fifty miles in five days. The Turks, also unimpeded, advanced through the Caucasus to oil-rich Baku in Azerbaijan. The Ukrainian capital of Kiev fell to the Germans on March 1. Trotsky, furious, said that Russia should rejoin the Entente and resume the war. Lenin, fearing the capture of Petrograd and the destruction of his fledgling regime, moved his government to Moscow and said no.

On March 3 the Russian delegation, with Trotsky no longer participating, signed at Brest-Litovsk one of the most punitive peace treaties in history. Russia relinquished (not to Germany but to puppet regimes to be put in place by Germany) Courland, Estonia, Finland, Latvia, Lithuania, Livonia, Poland, Ukraine, and White Russia (or Belarus). With these territories went something on the order of fifty million people, a third of the old empire's population, and hundreds of thousands of square miles. Russia also lost a third of its rail system and agricultural land, more than half of its industry, three-fourths of its iron ore, and nine-tenths of its coal mines. The Russians agreed to demobilize what remained of their armies.

The Russian delegation treated the settlement as a bad joke. The delegation's chief refused even to read the document that he signed, dismissing its contents as meaningless. There was no possibility that the Russian nation, regardless of who governed it, ever would accept such a settlement as anything other than an act of coercion without a trace of legitimacy. The settlement was precisely the opposite of what Bismarck had done after Prussia's nineteenth-century victory over Austria-Hungary, taking no territory at all to avoid embittering a humiliated foe. Brest-Litovsk guaranteed that there could be no reconciliation—no true peace—between Russia and Germany.

Even in the short term, the treaty was a greater misfortune for Germany than for Russia. The Bolsheviks gave away little—what they surrendered was beyond their power to hold. The Germans got a liability of enormous dimensions. At a time when they needed every available man and gun and locomotive in the west, they took on a new, ramshackle, unmanageable, and doomed eastern empire, the occupation of which would require one and a half million troops. They had to send soldiers to subdue Finland, Romania, Odessa, Georgia, Azerbaijan—an almost endless list of distant places with little relevance to the outcome of the war. Ukraine alone soaked up four hundred thousand German and a quarter of a million Austro-Hungarian troops. And for what? The payoff never came. Ukraine was supposed to become a bread basket for the starving populations of the Central Powers. But the troops sent there consumed thirty rail cars of food daily. The grain that eventually reached the German and Austrian home fronts was never more than ten percent of what had been hoped for. The situation would continue to deteriorate, compounding the problems of the Germans, as civil war erupted in Russia and its former possessions.

Even this outcome was overshadowed by the impact that Brest-Litovsk had on Germany's principal enemies. The draconian treatment of Russia was taken as a stern lesson in what had to be expected if imperial Germany was not broken. Those leaders most determined to fight on—Lloyd George for one, Clemenceau for another—could claim to have been vindicated. On both sides of the Western Front, potential peacemakers were left without influence.

Ludendorff could scarcely have cared less. He basked in the satisfaction of having achieved a triumph as complete and world-changing as any in history. In the west he was assembling an astoundingly powerful force—191 divisions, three and a half million men—trained in new tactics and eager to put them to work.

He was within days of bringing down on his enemies the greatest series of hammer blows in the annals of war. If he could succeed this one last time, Germany would be master of east and west.

LAWRENCE OF ARABIA

BY THIS TIME A WHOLE OTHER WAR, ONE BETWEEN THE British and the Turks (but with Arabs doing much of the fighting and dying), was growing up from small beginnings on the fringes of the Sinai Desert east of Suez and west of Palestine. Even at its height it would be a tiny war compared to what was happening in Europe, and viewed from a sufficient distance it could seem a wonderfully exotic affair.

It was also more fertile ground than the battlefields of Europe for the emergence of heroes. Trenches and massed artillery and machine guns had a way of putting would-be heroes underground before they properly got started. But in the desert, men wearing burnooses rode camels into battle. Even an *Englishman* could do so. Out of that possibility grew the greatest romantic story of the Great War, the legend of Lawrence of Arabia, the man the Bedouins called El Aurens.

The story began in the Egyptian capital of Cairo in September 1916, with the preparations of a British diplomat named Ronald Storrs to travel into the Hejaz region east of the Red Sea. Storrs wanted to make contact with the followers of Sherif Hussein, Arab emir of the sacred city of Mecca. The British had earlier duped and bribed Hussein, making promises they had no intention of keeping, to get him to raise a rebellion against the Ottoman Empire. He had done so, and the Turks had responded. In February and again in August, Turkish troops led by German officers had unsuccessfully attacked the Suez Canal, which ran north and south along the western edge of the Sinai and was the jugular through which Britain maintained contact with India and the Far East. Though thrown back, the Turks were threatening to take Mecca from the Arab rebels and crush Hussein's small force of warrior-tribesmen.

A young and very junior lieutenant, Thomas Edward Lawrence, requested permission to accompany Storrs. Still in his twenties, a deskbound intelligence officer with no military experience or training, Lawrence was on the staff of a recently created entity called the Arab Bureau, which was to develop policies to guide British relations with the Arabs. Lawrence said he wanted to gather information about how the Arab troops were organized, and to identify competent, dependable Arab leaders. His superiors granted his request; evidently he was not popular among the Cairo officer corps, so that "no one was anxious to detain him."

It was a perfect meeting of man and situation. One of five sons of a baronet named Chapman and the governess with whom he had run away from his first family—creating such a scandal that they had adopted a new family name—he already had extraordinary knowledge of the Arabs and their world. As a student at Oxford he had become fascinated with medieval military fortifications, and while still an undergraduate he traveled through Ottoman Syria and Palestine studying castles constructed by the crusaders. The resulting thesis, later published in book form, led to a degree with highest honors and a traveling fellowship. From 1911 to early 1914 Lawrence worked on archaeological digs and broadened his knowledge of Arabia, its people, and their language and culture.

In England when the Great War began, he joined the war office in London and was put to work making maps. Before the end of the year he was given a commission and sent to Cairo. Though he looked utterly unlike the Peter O'Toole who would one day play him on the screen (Lawrence was short and lantern-jawed), he had exceptional intellectual gifts and made himself valuable during a year spent questioning prisoners, analyzing information procured from secret agents, and continuing to make maps. His appreciation of the magnitude of the war on the far-off Western Front was no doubt strengthened by the death of two of his brothers there in 1915.

Though his background and peculiarities (which included a powerful masochistic bent) meant that Lawrence had a limited future at best in the regular army, from the start of the Storrs mission his liabilities became assets. Instead of returning to Cairo with the rest of the mission, Lawrence went deeper into the Arabian desert, traveling by camel and adopting Arab garb (the only sensible way to dress in that uniquely inhospitable environment). South of the city of Medina he met one of Hussein's sons, Prince Feisal. The two quickly formed a bond. When Lawrence returned to Cairo, he told his superiors that the Arab revolt had the potential to seriously weaken the Turks everywhere from Syria southward, that Feisal was the man to lead it, and that he should be given money and equipment. Lawrence was sent back into the desert to become Britain's liaison and to deliver promises of support.

This eccentric academic intellectual turned out to be a guerrilla fighter of almost incredible courage, a shrewd military strategist, an absolutely brilliant tactician, and an inspiring leader of Arabs. Having won the confidence of Feisal, he was able to open a new, miniature, but important, front. It became a war of his own creation, it kept the Turks constantly off balance, and ultimately it would protect the flank of a conventional British force moving out of Cairo to the conquest of a Sinai, Palestine, and Syria. Coming at the same time as the collapse of Bulgaria, which opened Constantinople to attack out of the Balkans, the advance into Syria would help make it impossible for Turkey to continue the war. By then young Lawrence was a lieutenant colonel and holder of one of Britain's highest military decorations, the Distinguished Service Order or DSO.

Lawrence's approach was to probe into enemy territory with the smallest, most mobile force possible, hitting hard and escaping quickly. He led the raids that he planned, taking the Turks by surprise by approaching across murderously hot and waterless wastes, blowing up bridges and railways, then disappearing back into the desert. He was engaged in countless gun battles, was wounded several times, and was once captured while on a spying mission by Turks who didn't know who he was but beat him severely before letting him go. Probably he was sexually assaulted during this episode, though in later years he was evasive on the few occasions he made reference to it. The war in the desert was a savage affair in which terrible atrocities were committed by both sides. At the same time that Lawrence's activities made him an international hero (an American journalist named Lowell Thomas brought his exploits to the world's attention), they left him physically and emotionally exhausted and psychologically damaged.

The traumatic effects of the war were worsened, for Lawrence, by the knowledge that Britain was deceiving Hussein, Feisal, and the Arabs generally. Britain and France had signed but kept secret the Sykes-Picot Agreement, according to which, after the war, the southern parts of the Ottoman Empire were to be divided between the two. Britain was to get southern Mesopotamia (Iraq to us) and ports on the Mediterranean. Lebanon and Syria were promised to France. The Arabian Peninsula was to be divided into spheres of influence that, if nominally autonomous, would be dominated by the Europeans.

Sykes-Picot could not be reconciled with what the Arabs had been promised: autonomy across their homeland, from the southern tip of the peninsula up through Lebanon and Syria. Lawrence revealed much of the true situation to Feisal, urging him to strengthen the Arabs' bargaining position by capturing as much territory as possible before the war ended. Though his credibility with the Arabs was enhanced when the Bolsheviks published the details of the Sykes-Picot deal in 1917, his position remained difficult all the same. When it became certain, after Damascus fell to the Allies, that the pledges made to the Arabs were not going to be redeemed, Lawrence departed for London without waiting for the war to end.

His postwar life would be as improbable as his wartime career, though in a radically different way. He refused a knighthood and promotion to brigadier general, resigning his commission instead. He went to the Versailles Peace Conference, where he appeared in Arab headdress and robes and lobbied in vain on behalf of the Arabs. Thereafter, offered lofty academic positions and high office by Colonial Secretary Winston Churchill, he joined the Royal Air Force as a private under the name Ross. When this was discovered and became a sensation in the press, he was discharged. With the help of influential friends, he became a private in the Royal Tank Corps, this time using the name Shaw. In the years that followed he kept this identity but simultaneously produced books that are today minor classics, maintaining friendships with some of the important literary and political figures of the day. He retired from the RAF in 1935, moved to a cottage in the countryside, and died, forever mysterious, in a motorcycle accident.

Chapter 33

✠

Michael

"There must be no rigid adherence
to plans made beforehand."
—GERMAN INFANTRY MANUAL

Ludendorff's hammer came down on the British through an impenetrable fog early on the morning of Thursday, March 21, shattering everything it struck. For a long breathless moment, the fate of Europe hung in the balance.

The force of the blow was magnified by surprise. In spite of the immensity of their preparations—building up huge ammunition dumps, concentrating sixty-nine divisions and more than sixty-four hundred guns between Arras to the north and St. Quentin to the south—the Germans had managed to keep their intentions secret. By early March Haig and Pétain knew that an offensive was coming: troop movements on such a scale could not be concealed and could not be without purpose. But the Germans had been in motion all along the front that winter as Ludendorff, unable to decide where to attack, ordered his generals to be ready everywhere. It was impossible to know which movements actually mattered. The final placement of the guns did not begin until March 11. The assault divisions did not start for the front until five days after that, and even then they marched only by night, staying under camouflage by day. Between February 15 and March 20 ten thousand trains hauled supplies forward, but they too moved by night. Early in March Ludendorff moved his headquarters to Spa, in southeastern Belgium. On March 19 he moved again, to Avesnes in France.

Ludendorff had had 150 divisions in the west in November. By mid-March the total was 190—three million men, with more on the way. And to the extent that after years of slaughter there was still cream at the top of the German army, Ludendorff had drawn it together for this operation. He had

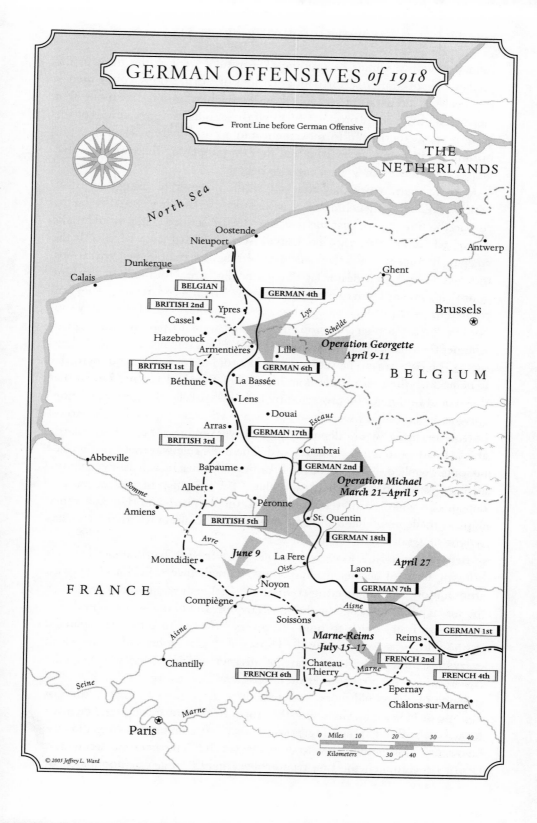

refined it with a winter of training. The results were at the front in the predawn fog of March 21: forty-four divisions of storm troops, young men at the peak of preparation, equipped with the best mobile weapons that German industry could produce. Many of these soldiers were veterans of the eastern war, experienced in movement and accustomed to winning. They brimmed with confidence. Told that they were opening the campaign that would end the war, they were eager to believe.

Many of them, when they attacked, would not even be using their rifles, which would be slung behind them across their backs. They would be on the run, in the tiny groups that the new doctrine prescribed. They would make use of whatever cover they could find, scrambling to keep pace with the creeping barrage that was their shield. When they encountered enemy troops, they would hurl grenades or lay down a field of fire with the light machine guns that some of them carried—whatever it took to keep moving. They had colored flares with which to signal success or trouble, a need for artillery support or for the artillery to stop firing. They were to pay no attention to whether their flanks were exposed or enemy troops remained in place behind them. The pace was to be set by whoever could move fastest, and there was to be no such thing as a continuous line. When they had advanced so far that they could no longer be protected by friendly artillery, the junior and non-commissioned officers were to make their own decisions about what to do next. Everything would depend on initiative, boldness, flexibility, and the ability to adapt to whatever developed. The main rule was that the old rules no longer applied. "The objective of the first day must be at least the enemy's artillery," said a newly issued pamphlet. "The objective of the second day depends on what is achieved on the front; there must be no rigid adherence to plans made beforehand... The reserves must be put in where the attack is progressing, not where it is held up."

Behind this assault force would follow a wave of "battle unit" divisions bringing forward heavier machine guns, flamethrowers, field artillery with ammunition, and engineering equipment. Their job was twofold: to reduce the strongpoints bypassed by the storm troops, and to throw together defensive works from which to hold off counterattacks. To their rear, manned by the third-best divisions, lay the Hindenburg Line, a home base to which everyone could withdraw in case of disaster. Farther back still were the reserves, ready to go wherever they were sent.

None of this could work, could produce more than another Verdun or Somme or Passchendaele, unless the storm troops got through the enemy's front line with their fighting power intact. To ensure that they did, the Germans had something new to show the British. That something was a man: Georg Bruchmüller, the one true artillery genius of a war dominated by artillery, the same retirement-age lieutenant colonel (throughout the war he was never promoted) whom Hoffmann had nicknamed "Breakthroughmüller" for his dazzling accomplishments in the east. The Germans had never indulged in the weeks-long bombardments with which the British had so often tried and failed to annihilate their enemies before attacks, but Bruchmüller was the first on either side to fully grasp the futility of such tactics. Heavy barrages told defenders that an attack was coming and where. When they went on for days, they created opportunities for defenders to adapt either by digging in deeper or, as happened more and more commonly, by pulling back out of range. The damage they caused rarely proved to be enough to make a decisive difference.

The Bruchmüller answer was as complex and sophisticated as a twenty-first-century Fourth of July fireworks display. It lasted for hours instead of days, preserving the element of surprise, and involved a constant back-and-forth shifting between front-line and rear targets, high explosives and shrapnel and gas. When it was properly executed, the surprise was total, because there had been no preliminary registration of the guns on their targets. Instead, every gun was registered on firing ranges before being brought to the front. Then it was locked onto its targets silently, by mathematical calculations including adjustments for atmospheric conditions. Bruchmüller barrages concluded with an overwhelming concentration of high explosives on front-line positions, throwing any survivors into shock before the appearance of the storm troops. Beyond the first line, heavy reliance on gas avoided the cratering of the ground over which the infantry would have to advance. Bruchmüller had been with Hutier in the northeast, where his methods had made possible the rapid conquest of strong Russian defenses. A month later those same methods produced similar results at Caporetto. Ludendorff had brought Bruchmüller to the west. He was, in all likelihood, the most valuable individual in the entire German army during the great climax of 1918.

There was a way for the enemy to deal with a Bruchmüller bombardment, as the Germans themselves had demonstrated at Ypres in 1917. It required giving up the idea of a strong, solid front line, leaving only a screen of machine-gunners in forward positions and moving most of the troops far enough back to be out of reach of the guns. Pétain understood this, but he was not Ludendorff's target. The British commanders who would be hit by Michael showed no understanding at all.

Those commanders were Henry Horne, whose First Army defended Arras at the northern end of the attack zone, Julian Byng and his Third Army immediately to Horne's south, and Gough with the Fifth Army on the right, centered on St. Quentin. Among them the three had almost fifty divisions, with the strongest concentration in the north and Gough's line the longest and thinnest, much of it recently inherited from the French. Byng and Gough had fully a third of their troops in forward positions, and most of the remainder were no more than two or three miles in the rear. Haig's main reserve was fifteen miles behind the front, too far back to be able to go into action quickly.

As March unfolded, Haig remained certain that the BEF would be the target. But he thought the attack would come in Flanders, where he was strongest—which gave him confidence. "I was only afraid," he wrote in his diary after an inspection of his northern line, "that the enemy would find our front so very strong that he will hesitate to commit his Army to the attack with the almost certainty of losing very heavily." In fairness to Haig, the reports he received from his intelligence staff were sometimes woefully wrong and cumulatively confusing. "There are strong indications," one such report stated on March 2, "that the enemy intends to attack on the Third and Fifth Army fronts, with the object of cutting off the Cambrai salient [also known, in its abbreviated 1918 form, as the Flesquières salient] and drawing in our reserves." This was a virtually letter-perfect account not only of what Ludendorff was planning but why, and it was confirmed by another report a week later. Nothing was done in response, perhaps because other intelligence pointed in other directions. On March 16 Haig was assured that there was no evidence of a German buildup south of the line running from Cambrai to Bapaume, the sector that included the Flesquières salient. This report, though correct in its facts, was dangerously wrong in its conclusion that there was no reason to fear an attack south of Cambrai-Bapaume. The German attack force had indeed not yet arrived in the area by March 16, but forty-seven of its divisions were moving in that direction and were only a few nights' march from the front.

Every new day brought fresh indications that *something* big was coming—and soon. On March 11 the Germans changed their codes, always a sure sign of impending action.

By March 20 the fourteen divisions and twenty-two hundred guns of the German Seventeenth Army were in position on nine and a half miles of front opposite Horne and Byng. This army was to be the cutting edge of the offensive. Commanded by Otto von Below, the victor of Caporetto, it was to break through Horne's line, push westward past Arras, and then swing to the right. By threatening to circle around behind the British, it was supposed to force Haig to shift his reserves to block Below's path, weaken his forces in Flanders, and so accomplish Michael's primary objective.

On Below's left was the German Second Army under Georg von der Marwitz, who had directed the 1917 counteroffensive at Cambrai and earlier was chief of staff of the army that cleared the Russians out of Galicia. He was to advance in step with Below, broadening the penetration of the British line. Immediately to the south of Marwitz, on his left, was the Eighteenth Army, commanded by Hutier himself, freshly arrived from the east. Little was expected of Hutier in this campaign. His army was to provide an anchor for Below and Marwitz as they swept forward. It included twenty-one divisions and more than twenty-six hundred guns; that was expected to be enough to block any French forces coming up from the south. Hutier's artillery was directed personally by Bruchmüller. Together, Below, Marwitz, and Hutier had a million men—an avalanche of infantry.

At about two A.M. on March 21 the kind of thick fog that is common in Picardy at that time of day and year came up out of the ground and reduced visibility to a few yards. Shortly before five, after some hesitation about whether the wind would blow the gas in the right direction, the bombardment began. Along a line of more than forty miles between the Sensée and Oise Rivers, 6,473 pieces of artillery began pouring out fire and steel and gas. Heavy and light cannon and howitzers alternated ammunition and angles of fire according to Bruchmüller's symphonically intricate schedule. At eight-fifteen all the guns came together in a final convulsion of maximum-rate fire concentrated on the defenders' front line. This went on and on, the explosions coming too rapidly to be distinguished, until after eighty minutes it climaxed in a five-minute crescendo surpassing everything that had come before. Then, with shocking abruptness, there came five minutes of silence during which the guns were adjusted for their next task: a creeping barrage that drew the storm troops out of their trenches and led them toward the west. The fog had not lifted. This was a problem for the Germans, who could barely see where they were going and easily lost their sense of direction. But it created far worse problems for the British who had survived the barrage. They were able to see and fire only at whichever attackers happened to stumble directly onto them as they advanced through the murk.

The fog, the soul-shattering power of the artillery, and the speed with which the storm troops followed the creeping barrage—all of it combined to produce a rout. The first lines of defense were quickly overrun, the troops in them killed or captured or put to flight. In the center, units of Byng's army hung on stubbornly in the Flesquières salient, the little bulge that was all that remained to the British of the ground they had won in the Battle of Cambrai the previous fall. But with Gough's troops falling back on their right, the men in the salient were in danger of being cut off. Gough's army, driven not only out of its first line but out of its second as well, could find no place to make a stand. "It was flamethrowers forward," a young storm trooper later wrote home. "The English dugouts were smoked out and we took our first prisoners. They were trembling all over. Now we went forward without resistance.

The next dugouts were passed, and we came to the railway. There the English had dug a field post in a declivity, and before it were corrugated iron huts. Here they had their kitchen, canteen, etc. The kitchen was naturally stormed immediately. I was astonished at what the English still had. The stove was still lit, bacon was sizzling, a side of beef lay on the table ... We stuffed our knapsacks. Each man took an English iron ration. In the next hut, a canteen, we found English cigarettes in great supply. Each man lit up ... On the entrance to the village we found a machine gun nest. We made an effort to take it, but there was much barbed wire in front, and it would have cost many lives. It was very hazy still, and our artillery could not help us. We let it go and went on."

To the extent that Gough's army could maintain the semblance of a continuous line, the retreat was making that line longer by the hour; by day's end it would be stretched a harrowing five miles. By then Hutier's troops had taken possession of Gough's entire battle zone, including its artillery line. After dark, to save his army, Gough ordered a ten-mile withdrawal to the only natural defense available to him, the River Somme at a point where its meandering course runs north-south and connects to the Crozat Canal.

The Germans had captured hundreds of Gough's guns and achieved something almost never before seen on the Western Front: a breakthrough into open territory beyond the enemy's lines. But that breakthrough had been achieved only in the south—the one place where Ludendorff neither expected nor particularly wanted any such thing. That night, in considering his next steps, Ludendorff found himself confronted with something more complicated than clear-cut success or failure. Though some things had gone brilliantly, nothing had gone according to plan. On the German right, where the deepest penetration had been expected and Below's army was supposed to punch through toward Arras, nothing of the kind had happened. The fog had been lightest on the right and had burned off more quickly than elsewhere, the bombardment had been less effective there than where Bruchmüller was in charge, and the advance had been fought to a standstill at the British second line. Marwitz in the center had done better but not dramatically so. All the drama was on the left, where Hutier and Bruchmüller had been on the scene to implement the tactics bearing their names and had done so with impressive efficiency.

Ludendorff had limited numbers of storm troops in reserve. One of the questions facing him was how to use them to best effect. Staying with his original plan would have required reinforcing Below and trying again to break through on the right. That would have been a Haig-like or Falkenhayn-like decision, another in the long series of attempts to turn failure into success by increasing the amount of force being applied. Ludendorff decided to do otherwise. He sent six of his best divisions to Hutier and none to Below. This was consistent with the Germans' new doctrine, a reinforcement of success rather than of failure, but it also reflected Ludendorff's worsening lack of focus. If Hutier continued to advance, his troops would be moving into territory that had been turned into a barren obstacle course by the Battle of the Somme and by the Germans' own scorched-earth withdrawal to the Hindenburg Line. It would be a difficult advance at best, exhausting the men who undertook it. It was precisely what Ludendorff's operations chief had urged him to avoid.

No one including Ludendorff himself could have said at that point what the purpose of a continued Hutier advance was supposed to be. Below and Marwitz had had a clear mission from the start, but there had never been a comparable goal for Hutier. His astonishing progress gave rise to a question: progress toward *what?* What actually was the *value* of the ground he had taken and the great expanses of territory that lay open in front of him? The absence of an answer exposed the emptiness of the Michael operation after the first day's failure on the right. "We tear a hole in the enemy line," Ludendorff had said when challenged, "and everything else follows." Now he had his hole—though not the hole he had wanted—and his next step was going to be to jump into it. Whatever his decision should be called, it was not strategy. It was more like an act of faith—of Micawberish blind hope that something, somehow, would turn up.

On Friday morning all three German armies returned to the attack. There could be no surprise this time, and because the troops on both sides were in new positions and the fog had returned to blind the gunners, there could be no Bruchmüller barrage. Below's troops, running head-on into reserves sent forward by Byng, got nowhere. Marwitz managed to inch forward on both sides of the Flesquières salient, but the salient itself, which Ludendorff had expected to crush on the first day, again refused to fall. Again almost all progress was on the German left, where Hutier's men continued to advance almost as fast as their legs could carry them. They got across the Somme and the Crozat Canal—the British had failed to blow the bridges—and forced Gough to resume his retreat.

Gough's efforts to find a foothold became increasingly desperate. Military police stopped fleeing troops at gunpoint and forced them into whatever defenses could be found or thrown together. Officers stood in the rear, pistols in hand, to keep the men at their posts. None of it was enough, and the retreat always resumed. Haig sent an appeal to Pétain, asking him to send help. By the time this message arrived, Pétain already had seven divisions on the way—one more than he and Haig had promised to send if either came under attack.

By nightfall on March 22 the Germans had again accomplished something new to the Western Front: they had kept a major offensive moving forward through a second day. Also again, their success had been limited to the left wing. Ludendorff's plan had been completely overtaken by events. As he tried to adapt, his difficulties mounted. His supply system, positioned for an advance in the north, was not prepared to follow Hutier's army. That army, weary after two days of rapid pursuit over difficult ground, was running out of essentials as basic as water. French and British reserves, meanwhile, were racing to intercept it.

Dawn on Saturday, March 23, found the British on the verge of ruin. Not only Hutier's army but even Marwitz's advance units were now fifteen miles beyond their starting points. Gough's army was ceasing to be a coherent fighting force. Eight of the divisions with which Gough had begun the battle were in shambles. Hutier's troops were west of the Somme, gobbling up mile after mile. As it disintegrated, Gough's left wing had lost contact with Byng's right. Byng's flank was exposed, and the line he had to defend grew longer. Haig asked Pétain for an additional twenty divisions. Pétain replied that this was impossible—he was expecting an attack in Champagne. He did, however, send another six divisions. This was in addition to the seven sent earlier—divisions that were now reaching the battlefield but finding it impossible to get around behind Gough's fast-fleeing troops and into the path of the Germans. Pétain had done far more than he had ever promised. His doing so has to be considered a magnanimous act, especially in light of the fact that he was right about Champagne: the Germans *were* preparing an attack there. Haig, however, was not satisfied. To the contrary, he was resentful of Pétain.

On the third day the Germans' advance put them within reach of a bona fide strategic prize. Directly ahead, due west of St. Quentin, was the city of Amiens, the importance of which can be made clear even today by a glance at an ordinary road map. Almost all the highways in the region run into Amiens, which sits at their center like the hub of a great wheel. In 1918 all the railways ran through Amiens too, creating a transport center very near to where the British sector ended and the French began. The town was vital to the British, to the French, and to their ability to maintain contact. On March 23 it was thinly defended. If Ludendorff had ordered it taken, he could have separated the two allies so completely that it might then have become possible to destroy their armies one by one.

Instead, turning away from a vital target that the enemy was unprepared to defend, Ludendorff sent his armies in three directions, each of which had comparatively minor potential. Below, once again bogged down, was given reserves and told to turn farther toward the north. Marwitz was to push westward on a trajectory that would carry him not to Arras, not to Amiens, but to a point between the two. Hutier was directed southward toward the town of Noyon in the direction of Paris.

Perhaps Ludendorff thought he could finish both of his enemies with one master stroke, a great combination of separating and enveloping movements that would simultaneously destroy the British on his right and the French on his left. If that was the idea—no alternative explanation seems equally plausible—it was beyond the capabilities of the German forces. It brings to mind the campaigns of Conrad von Hötzendorf, who had wrecked the Austro-Hungarian armies with theoretically brilliant but unrealistic lunges at instant glory. The March 24 orders issued by Ludendorff—a Ludendorff alienated from the Max Hoffmann whose brains had so often been so useful, and increasingly remote from his own staff and the commanders of his armies—provide early evidence that he was breaking down under the strain with which he had been living for nearly four years.

On this same day an explosion mysteriously occurred in the heart of Paris. People searched the sky for enemy aircraft but found nothing. Then came another explosion, and another. Finally the mystery was solved: this was the work of artillery. An enormous new cannon called the Kaiser Wilhelm gun was firing eight-inch shells from freshly conquered territory more than seventy-five miles from the capital. Between its March debut and August, it would fire 283 rounds into Paris, killing civilians and destroying property at random, accomplishing absolutely nothing.

Kaiser Wilhelm himself was exceptionally active on this day. Rocketing about in his private train, declaring victory to everyone within earshot, he ordered the schools of Germany closed in celebration. He had champagne served at dinner. "If an English delegation came to sue for peace," he pronounced, exposing the childishness of his daydreams, "it must kneel before the German standard."

Also on March 23 a young German pilot was shot down behind the British lines—the second of Ludendorff's beloved stepsons to die in this way.

Early on the morning of Sunday, March 24, the commanders of the six British battalions clinging to the Flesquières salient agreed that, with their position rapidly deteriorating, their choice was to withdraw or to be destroyed. They ordered a retreat that left the British center without its anchor. The entire British line was now pulling back, the Germans advancing everywhere. Even Below was making slow progress. Hutier continued to encounter almost no resistance, though his army was running down badly. Looting and drunkenness were breaking out wherever tired, hungry German troops came upon some of the enormous stores abandoned by the British. Not as malnourished as their families back home but chronically ill-fed nonetheless, they were astonished to find the enemy so abundantly provided with food, liquor, and good wool and cotton clothing—things almost unavailable in Germany. They had been told that the Entente was suffering as severely as they were. They saw that this was untrue.

The greatest weakness of Ludendorff's attack force had come fully into play: he had no pursuit capability with which to run down and destroy the defeated British divisions. What remained of the German cavalry was in the east, where vast open spaces afforded scope for operations of a kind not possible in the west. Ludendorff had neither tanks nor enough armored cars to make a difference. Germany being without access to rubber, its few motor vehicles were fitted with steel tires that destroyed whatever roads they used. Hutier could advance no faster than his men could walk, and those men had been walking and fighting for four days. They ended Sunday's march eight miles short of their assigned objective. Farther north the Germans took possession of Bapaume but also did not reach their goal.

This was no consolation to Haig and Pétain. The Germans were not only continuing to advance but positioned to drive a wedge between them. Relations between the two commanders were badly strained, Haig unimpressed with the two hundred thousand troops that Pétain had sent to his aid. Haig understood the importance of maintaining the connection between his line and that of the French—"our Army's existence in France depends on keep-

Without access to rubber, the Germans equipped their vehicles with steel tires

ing the British and French armies united," he declared—but somehow he regarded this as Pétain's responsibility. When the two generals met on Sunday night, Haig learned that if the German advance continued, the French intended to fall back toward the south. His reaction appears to have been a mixture of rage and panic. He blamed Pétain, who had no choice in the matter: his orders, direct from the French cabinet, were to defend Paris at all costs and to the exclusion of other priorities. Pétain sent a telegram asking his government to get the British to stay far enough to the south that he would not be required to overextend himself in order to maintain contact.

The crisis produced in Haig an abrupt change of mind on the subject of a supreme commander for the Entente armies. Knowing that such an assignment was sure to go to Foch, judging that Foch was likely to be far more willing than Pétain to advance to the north rather than withdraw, Haig that night sent a telegram to Lloyd George asking him to reopen the question. It happened that just hours earlier Clemenceau, prodded by Foch, had sent a wire of his own to London suggesting the same thing. Lloyd George dispatched Lord Alfred Milner, the war minister, to France to make it happen.

On Monday Ludendorff awoke at last to the importance of Amiens. With French and British reserves now pouring into the front lines, Below was once again blocked, his objectives hopelessly out of reach. But Amiens, if captured, could justify the entire campaign. Ludendorff ordered Marwitz to link his left wing with Hutier and move to take the city. The head of the French rail system, meanwhile, was begging Foch to "save Amiens or everything's lost—it's the center of all our communications." Foch, Pétain, and Clemenceau met at Compiègne, trying to figure out how to balance Haig's appeals for more help with the defense of Paris. Haig was meeting with his army commanders—all but Gough, who had more pressing concerns—at Doullens, not a great distance away from Compiègne. When Clemenceau offered to join them the next day, the British readily agreed.

On March 26, with the Germans sixteen miles from Amiens and still advancing, the French leaders arrived at Doullens. They were a formidable group: President Poincaré, Clemenceau, Pétain, and Foch, who was delighting the premier with talk of shifting over to the offensive. On hand to greet them were Haig and his generals plus, from London, Wilson, the new chief of the imperial general staff, and Lord Milner. Haig was, for once, eager to cooperate. In response to a question from Clemenceau, he declared his determination to stand and fight at Amiens rather than pull back to the north. It was Milner who brought up the matter that had brought all of them together. He proposed that Foch be named "coordinator" of the Entente forces "around Amiens." The French, of course, assented, all but Pétain enthusiastically. Haig, of all people, objected that Foch must be given more authority than Milner's words implied. His motives were obvious. Foch's new role would permit a more thorough and systematic sharing of reserves, and under current circumstances that could only benefit the British. The wording was changed, accordingly, to extend Foch's responsibilities to the entire Western Front. Haig's diary entry of this date reveals his thinking. "In my opinion," he wrote, "it was essential that Foch should control Pétain."

To the extent that Foch's elevation was an implicit criticism of Pétain's response to the German offensive, it was undeserved and unnecessary. By March 26 the offensive was essentially at an end, in large measure because Pétain had stripped so many troops from his own line and reserves that twenty-four French divisions were now assembling in the path of Hutier's and Marwitz's armies. As more arrived and the tide began to turn, Foch would win much credit—less because of anything he had done than because of the timing of his appointment. Still, the appointment was important. A step had been taken toward unified command.

Foch, immediately after his promotion, complained of having been given the task of winning a battle that was already lost. Something closer to the opposite was true. The Michael offensive was losing its force and coherence, deteriorating at times into a kind of blind and almost random lashing out at the defenders. Hutier's worn-down troops continued, where they were confronted only by the remains of Gough's army, to move forward at a pace that would have seemed incredible except that the British were not even trying to resist.

Hutier moved forward nine miles on March 26, ten on the day following. The character of the campaign was becoming almost farcical, with the British retreating at an easy walk and Germans following at the same pace. When the British stopped to rest, the Germans would stop as well, keeping a safe distance. They had left behind most of their artillery and were short of almost everything. Their officers were unable to prevent them from looting whenever an opportunity arose. "Today the advance of our infantry stopped near Albert," a German captain observed. "Nobody could understand why. Our airmen had reported no enemy between Albert and Amiens. The enemy's guns were only firing now and again on the very edge of affairs. Our way seemed entirely clear. I jumped into a car with orders to find out what was causing the stoppage in front... As soon as I got near the town I began to see curious sights. Strange figures, who looked very little like soldiers, and certainly showed no signs of advancing, were making their way back... There were men driving cows before them on a line; others who carried a hen under one arm and a box of notepaper under the other. Men carrying a bottle of wine under their arm and another one open in their hand. Men who had torn a silk drawing-room curtain off its rod and were dragging it to the rear as a useful piece of loot. Men with writing paper and colored notebooks. Evidently they had found it desirable to sack a stationer's shop. Men dressed up in comic disguise. Men with top hats on their heads. Men staggering. Men who could hardly walk... When I got into the town the streets were running with wine. Out of a cellar came a lieutenant of the Second Marine Division, helpless and in despair. I asked him, 'What is going to happen?' It was essential for them to get forward immediately. He replied, solemnly and emphatically, 'I cannot get my men out of this cellar without bloodshed.'"

The retreat continued everywhere except at Amiens, where the British straggled onto the high ground east of the city and found themselves welcomed by French and British reserve divisions already in place there. They prepared to make a stand. The Germans stopped opposite them and waited for their guns to catch up.

Although the meaning of Michael had come down to the fate of Amiens, on March 28 Below's army was launched on another attack on Arras. It lacked enough troops to do the job, there was no fog that morning, and because Byng had pulled back most of his troops, the opening bombardment fell on empty trenches. The result was a slaughter of the attackers and a decision by Ludendorff not to try again. No possibility remained except Amiens.

Recently so vulnerable, the city was now heavily defended and growing stronger by the day. Ludendorff sent nine of Below's divisions to reinforce Marwitz's army for an assault, but the shift came too late. The French Fifth Army, detached from Champagne by Pétain, arrived on the scene. This was the third army that Pétain had moved into the British sector, and it settled the issue. Soon, with the Germans no longer able to advance anywhere, both sides were digging in for a resumption of trench warfare. By April 5, sixteen days after it began, Michael was at an end. Gough, the scapegoat, was sent home and never granted the official review of his actions that he demanded. Haig would have been sacked as well, but Lloyd George remained unable to find a politically acceptable replacement.

The Germans had captured twelve hundred square miles, ninety thousand prisoners, more than a thousand guns, and mountains of supplies. They had inflicted more than one hundred and sixty thousand casualties on the British (the men taken prisoner included) and seventy thousand on the French. But one hundred sixty thousand of their own best troops had been killed or wounded as well, and seventy thousand had been taken prisoner. And all the ground they had won was worthless or less than worthless. It included not a single place of true strategic value. The German line had been lengthened by fifty miles at the same time that the number of troops available to defend that line had been significantly reduced. In moving forward into a huge and worthless new salient, the Germans had left behind the best defensive infrastructure on the Western Front. They had to start from scratch on ground where they had no finished defenses, no support system, no anything.

Ludendorff had driven his enemies to make changes that would have momentous consequences in the months ahead. Not only were the rudiments of a system of unified command now in Foch's energetic hands, but the Americans were involved as never before. Until Michael, Pershing had been jealously husbanding his growing force, concentrating on getting it ready to make war in 1919. But Michael changed his thinking. "The Allies are very weak and we must come to their relief this year," he told Washington in asking for an acceleration in the shipment of troops to France. "The year after may be too late. It is very doubtful if they can hold on until 1919 unless we give a lot of support this year." On March 28, having no way of knowing that the emergency was coming under control, he had gone to see Foch and invited him to use the American troops in any way he wished. From that day the Americans were in the fight.

LUDENDORFF

THINGS HAD NEVER GONE SO BADLY FOR ERICH LUDENDORFF, or gone badly in so many ways over such a long period, as they did in 1918. As his problems mounted, he grew visibly fragile.

All his life he had displayed an insatiable appetite for work, but now his staff noticed him slipping away from headquarters without explanation. A member of the medical staff, writing of Ludendorff, would recall that at this juncture "there were reports of occasional crying episodes."

Officers who served him became concerned for him personally and about his ability to function. Quietly, with considerable trepidation, they arranged for a psychiatrist who knew Ludendorff, a Dr. Hocheimer, to visit and see what might be done.

Everyone was on pins and needles the day Hocheimer arrived, wondering how he was going to approach Ludendorff and how the general was going to react. Ludendorff was a stiff, distant man with no visible sense of humor and firm control over all emotion except the rage that could break out in moments of intense stress. An ugly explosion was by no means out of the question. What happened was more unexpected than that. It revealed the depth of Ludendorff's neediness.

He was predictably impatient at being interrupted but consented to see the doctor. "I talked earnestly, urgently and warmly, and said that I had noticed with great sadness that for years he had given no consideration to one matter—his own spirit," Hocheimer recalled afterward. "Always only work, worry, straining his body and mind. No recreation, no joy, rushing his food, not breathing, not laughing, not seeing anything of nature and art, not hearing the rustle of the forest, nor the splashing of the brook."

Ludendorff sat for a long time without answering. "You're right in everything," he said at last. "I've felt it for a long time. But what shall I do?"

Hocheimer urged a move from Ludendorff's cramped quarters at Avesnes back to the more pleasant accommodations at Spa in Belgium. He recommended walks, breathing exercises, and a change in routine calculated to induce relaxation and the ability to sleep. Ludendorff followed these instructions conscientiously, even eagerly. As long as he continued to do so, his torments eased.

The High Command, posing for the camera
From left: Hindenburg, Kaiser Wilhelm, and Ludendorff.

He and Hocheimer continued to confer. The doctor's ultimate diagnosis: "The man is utterly lonely."

Utterly lonely: the theme of Ludendorff's life. He had spent his first four and a half decades in a terrible solitude. Then, suddenly and unexpectedly, he had found an escape. And now the solitude was closing in on him again. That is almost certainly part of what he meant when, upon receiving heartbreaking news not long before Hocheimer's visit, he said that "the war has spared me nothing."

The third of six children in a respectable family of very limited means (his mother's family was of aristocratic origin but impoverished), Ludendorff in childhood was notable for three things. He was so obsessed with cleanliness that he spurned games that might dirty his shoes. He was a diligent and talented student, especially in mathematics. And he had no capacity for making friends. He was drawn to a military career—his father had been a cavalry captain—and when he took the entrance examination for cadet school he did so well that he was not only admitted but advanced to a class of boys two years older than himself. His performance remained exceptional in everything except gymnastics—he was without physical grace, another thing that separated him from his classmates. The age dif-

ference and his extreme fastidiousness (he never showed the slightest interest in the adventures and misadventures to which schoolboys and junior
officers are naturally drawn) kept him always on the outside. He was a
drudge and a grind, if an able one.

After receiving his commission, he went through the usual rotation of
assignments, distinguishing himself at every step. In his late twenties he
was selected for study at the War Academy, an honor reserved for only the
most promising young officers. The commandant there, observing his intelligence and performance, singled him out for the ultimate recognition:
eventual assignment to general staff headquarters. By age forty he was in
Berlin, a major working closely with the chief of the general staff, the
fabled Field Marshal Alfred von Schlieffen, whom he came to regard as
"one of the greatest generals who ever lived." After Schlieffen's retirement,
Ludendorff was promoted to lieutenant colonel and became a protégé of
the new chief, Moltke the younger. He assisted Moltke in translating
Schlieffen's secret scheme for an overwhelming envelopment of the French
army into settled German policy.

But he was still alone.

Then one evening when he was forty-four and apparently consigned to
permanent bachelorhood, he noticed a woman stranded in the rain as he
was walking home after one of his long days of work. He offered to share
his umbrella, and the woman gratefully accepted. She was Margarethe
Pernet, beautiful, lively, the mother of three young sons and a daughter,
unhappily married. Somehow—it seems miraculous for a man as sealed up
inside himself as Ludendorff—the two connected. They were married as
soon as Margarethe could divorce her husband.

A new life, a new world, opened for Ludendorff. He delighted in his
new family, and the children worshiped him. He remained addicted to
a rigid routine, always departing for work no later than seven A.M. and
expecting meals to be served not a minute early or a minute late. But now
a new dimension was added, a connection, thanks to his ready-made family, to a wider and cheerier range of experience. All the evidence indicates
that the marriage was genuinely intimate and happy, and Ludendorff's
career flourished. He became an influential member of Moltke's planning
staff, winning important admirers and powerful enemies as he pushed
hard (much too hard, his enemies said) for an expansion of the army in
anticipation of war. He was promoted to colonel in 1911, to command
of a Düsseldorf regiment in 1913, and to one-star general in charge of a
brigade less than a year after that. The outbreak of the war brought an
immediate second star and assignment as chief of staff of the Second Army
as it prepared to join the invasion of France. Before he could take up this

new position, he was detached for temporary duty with the special force created to capture Liège; the plans for attacking the Belgian fortifications were largely his work. This led to his first taste of glory, to his receiving Germany's highest military honor, and to his reassignment with Hindenburg to the East Prussian front.

His stepsons, all of whom emulated Ludendorff and had been preparing for military careers, went eagerly to war. The eldest, Franz, a promising youngster almost as gifted academically as his stepfather and far more popular with his peers, suffered such serious grenade wounds in 1914 that, after being awarded the Iron Cross, he was declared unfit for further duty. He began to apply for the Flying Corps and finally was accepted, possibly with Ludendorff's help. His brothers followed his example, and soon all three were pilots flying combat missions on the Eastern Front. Franz suffered a concussion and broken hip in a crash landing, but as soon as he recovered he went back into action. In September 1917 he was shot down over the English Channel and killed. When Ludendorff learned of this, he hurried to Berlin to break the news to his wife. He was stricken, and perhaps guilty at having made the boy's flying career possible. Margarethe was shattered.

Ludendorff was especially close to the youngest of his stepsons, who happened to share his first name. In March 1918 he received word that young Erich, still a teenager, had been shot down behind British lines, his fate uncertain. Not long afterward, with German troops advancing across France in the Michael offensive, Ludendorff was told of the discovery of a fresh grave. Its marker said, in English, "Here rest two German pilots." He went to the grave and had the bodies dug up. One was Erich's. It was temporarily reburied at Avesnes while arrangements were made for its transfer to Berlin.

That was where Ludendorff was going when he began to disappear from headquarters: to brood at Erich's grave. That was also when an army doctor heard "reports of occasional crying."

Nothing could ever be the same. Margarethe was broken, permanently in the grip of depression, grief, and fear. Ludendorff, in his own words, felt that the war had taken everything.

Chapter 34

✠

An Impossibly Complex Game

*"With our backs to the wall and believing in the
justice of our cause, each man must fight to the end."*
—SIR DOUGLAS HAIG

In departing from his plan for Michael, in pursuing Hutier's breakthrough all the way to Amiens, Ludendorff had used up the resources needed for the next stage of his campaign. Ninety German divisions had been thrown into the fight, and many emerged with only a few thousand of their men alive and unwounded. The scale of the losses, and the fact that he now had a huge new salient to defend, left Ludendorff with only eleven intact assault divisions to commit to Flanders—barely a third of the number originally planned. Nothing that he had originally intended was now feasible in the near term. The dream of winning the war by midyear was losing whatever grounding in reality it might have had at the start.

Probably what should have come next was a diplomatic initiative. The Germans were not in a weak position from which to offer to open negotiations. Brest-Litovsk had sealed their success in the east, and Michael had been if nothing else a persuasive demonstration of their power in the west. Germany could have offered to relinquish vast amounts of what it had won and still, possibly, have emerged from the war with gains. Even if it gave up all of its conquests, the war would still have demonstrated that Germany was at least as powerful as all its European enemies combined. No one could have denied its claim to world power status.

France, meanwhile, had reached a point where it could no longer replace its battlefield losses; it had almost no eligible recruits except those reaching the age for induction. Britain was not notably better off. In the spring of 1918 the Lloyd George government abandoned a pledge never to send boys under eighteen to the front, and it was considering conscription in Ireland. Neither

Lloyd George nor Clemenceau had any interest in a peace that would leave Germany undefeated, but if Berlin had addressed the most abrasive issues— agreeing to give up Belgium and to reverse the draconian provisions of Brest-Litovsk—the Entente's hawks might have been forced to compromise. Certainly they would have been pressured to do so by a public hungry for peace. If improbable, such an outcome was not impossible.

There continued to be Germans in high places, even influential members of the military, who wanted to make peace. Early in 1918 Max Hoffmann had agreed with the idea of trying for a military decision in the west, but when Michael produced nothing but gains of useless territory, he decided that a change of course was necessary. He would write later that the high command, faced with the hard fact "that it could not take Amiens, in other words, that the breakthrough had not succeeded...should also have realized that decisive victory on the Western Front was no longer within reach...It was its bounden duty to tell the government that the time had come to begin negotiations."

Ludendorff saw no such duty. He was a man for whom, in the words of a longtime member of his staff, "all political questions were military questions." He had settled the political questions of eastern Europe with his victories, and Michael's disappointing conclusion did nothing to deflect him from wanting to do the same in the west. It is by no means clear that in the aftermath of Michael he remained an entirely rational man. He became not only bent on but obsessed with victory, impervious to the promptings of reason and reality alike.

Speed—haste—continued to be essential to Ludendorff's plans. The number of American troops in France was growing explosively. If they or the British and French were given an opportunity to take the offensive, the Germans might never regain the initiative. If the St. George One operation that Ludendorff had planned for Flanders was no longer feasible and St. George Two could go forward only on a reduced scale, Ludendorff would settle for that. The British, after all, had also been weakened by Michael. They had been forced to reduce their reserves in the north to stop the German advance. By late March, even before the end of Michael, Ludendorff was shifting troops and artillery to Flanders. Arrangements were hurriedly made for a scaled-down operation to which Ludendorff's staff gave the almost derisory name Georgette. It was a feeble substitute for the showdown toward which all of Ludendorff's changing plans continued to be aimed, but he embraced it as a step in that direction.

While Michael was limping to its close and preparations for Georgette were just getting started, Lloyd George traveled to France for an April 3 meeting at which, with the Americans participating, the Allies agreed to strengthen the authority earlier conferred on Foch. He was given "all powers necessary" for "the strategic direction of military operations" on the Western Front. Haig had by now lost interest in this idea. With the French taking over part of his line and fresh British troops arriving from Egypt and Mesopotamia (Iraq), he no longer saw any need to be strategically directed by anyone. His reluctance fueled Lloyd George's enthusiasm. His chagrin would reach its peak, as would Lloyd George's satisfaction, when on April 14 Foch was given the title of General in Chief of the Allied Armies. In terms impossible to mistake, this made the Frenchman Haig's commanding officer.

Georgette (sometimes called the Battle of Lys, or Fourth Ypres) opened modestly on April 9 with an attack by nine German divisions on an eleven-mile front. As at the start of Michael, there was heavy predawn fog. Again Bruchmüller preceded the advance of the storm troops with a five-hour barrage of crushing intensity, and again the Germans made startling early gains. The British were taken by surprise; Haig's intelligence specialists, having observed German artillery moving to the north, guessed wrongly that the attack would come at Vimy Ridge. The worst of the barrage fell on the pair of Portuguese divisions that had been more or less donated to the Entente by a Lisbon government, since fallen, friendly to England. The morale of the Portuguese troops was low—they had been left in the trenches far too long and had never understood what they were doing in this war in the first place—and they were to have been rotated out of the line and sent home later that very morning. When Bruchmüller's fire came down on them, they broke and ran. The storm troops advanced three and a half miles, running into resistance toward the end of the day and beginning to take heavy losses. It happened to be Ludendorff's fifty-third birthday, and the kaiser was at German headquarters. He gave a little speech celebrating this latest triumph—so he saw it—and extolling Ludendorff's brilliance. He honored the general by presenting him with a little metal statuette of—Kaiser Wilhelm II!

Georgette's main objective was Hazebrouck, a railway junction from which, if they captured it, the Germans would be able to disrupt the BEF's supply lines and shell the Channel ports. The defenders, through the first two days of fighting, were Horne and his British First Army. But by the second night, the Germans having torn a thirty-mile hole in his line, Haig was asking for French assistance and sending in the Second Army under Herbert Plumer, who had just returned from helping to stop the Germans' Caporetto campaign in Italy. The fighting was ferocious and costly to both sides, and as day followed day it continued to be inconclusive. On April 11 Haig issued an order of the day that would be derided in the trenches and celebrated at home: "Every position must be held to the last man. There must be no retirement. With our backs to the wall and believing in the justice of our cause, each man must fight to the end." These words were marvelous theater, grist for the propaganda mills of London, but otherwise empty. Many of the troops greeted them with sarcasm. The part about holding every position was tactically deplorable, as Plumer would soon demonstrate. As for the BEF having its back to the wall, Haig knew very well that there were doors in that wall, and he was not unwilling to use them. At the time he issued his order, he was discussing with General Wilson a possible removal of his armies from France via the Channel ports.

On April 12 Ludendorff attacked again with an increased number of divisions. This new effort got to within five miles of Hazebrouck but then petered out. On the following day, probing for weak spots, the Germans attacked on the northern edge of the Ypres salient, where Plumer's defenses were thin. To avoid having his line shattered and his troops overrun, Plumer

Shock troops
German soldiers advance over ground pocked with shellholes.

disregarded Haig's order of April 11 and began to pull back, abandoning all the ground for which Haig had paid a quarter of a million casualties in 1917. Lloyd George, when he learned of this, sourly rejoiced. He felt vindicated in his criticism of the assault on Passchendaele. "The conquest was a nightmare," he said. "The relinquishment of it was a relief and inspiration." He was right on both counts. By shortening his line, Plumer strengthened it enough to make a German breakthrough impossible. Once again he demonstrated to his men that he would not sacrifice their lives in pointlessly heroic gestures.

Through two long weeks Plumer slowly fell back and back, giving up ground but inflicting heavy casualties on the attackers and relieving the pressure that otherwise would have broken his line. French help was beginning to arrive—infantry and dismounted cavalry that Foch had taken from Pétain,

whose own lines were left even weaker than they had been at the end of Michael. The Germans noted these movements. Ludendorff ordered Crown Prince Wilhelm, whose army group faced Pétain's forces in Champagne, to complete his preparations for an offensive there. The game was becoming almost impossibly complex.

Meanwhile Ludendorff had no more to show for Georgette than he did for Michael—nothing but more casualties and another salient that increased his vulnerability without providing anything of value in return. He had told the kaiser that he could end the war in 1918, cautioning that it would be "a gigantic struggle beginning in one place, continuing in another, and demanding much time" but promising victory all the same. After so much futile action he needed to capture something, some specific *thing*, that actually mattered. His troops stood just short of Amiens, just short of Hazebrouck, and not far from a pair of high points called Mont Kemmel and Mont des Cats that, if taken, could allow him to dominate Ypres and everything around it. Any one of these would have been a great prize. Instead of making a choice, Ludendorff decided, as at the Michael crisis, to do everything at once.

On April 24 nine divisions of Marwitz's Second Army attacked on a narrow front in the direction of Amiens. It was a rare instance of the Germans using tanks; Marwitz had thirteen of Germany's monstrous and cumbersome new A.7.V tanks, each carrying a crew of eighteen. They routed the British until the BEF's smaller, more agile Whippet tanks met and routed them. The Germans made progress that day, though at high cost, but after nightfall a fierce counterattack by Australian and French troops drove them back to their starting point. Ludendorff gave up on Amiens. The forward edge of the Michael salient became static once again, this time permanently.

The next day, at the edge of the Georgette salient, French troops who had just relieved the British on Mont Kemmel (being in Flanders, this was less a real "mount" than part of a long, low ridge) were beginning a Foch-ordered attack when they were hit by a Bruchmüller barrage followed as always by an infantry advance. Many of the French survivors were put to flight, and those who tried to resist were soon overwhelmed. "Gray-blue figures out of the half-buried entrances of the dugouts spring up and try to pull machine guns after them," one of the attackers observed. "Once they bring one into position, but the hand grenades of our first wave destroy weapon and crew before it can be used. Most of the defenders think no more about resistance; then the firestorm has passed over them, the German shock troops are already before them, and it is better to raise one's hands. Ever more frequently come the blue figures creeping out of the ground, smeared with mud, with fixed, bewildered eyes."

By ten A.M. the Germans had possession of the high ground. They had not only captured Mont Kemmel but swept the defenders away, creating a wide hole in the line. Mont des Cats, a more valuable objective, lay directly ahead and completely open. But Ludendorff, having grown wary of unexpected successes that drew his troops too far into worthless terrain, had ordered the attack force to stop upon reaching Mont Kemmel and wait there for instructions. All that day the Germans remained in place, doing nothing to exploit one of the best opportunities to fall within their grasp during all of 1918. Toward the end of the day a British reserve division arrived from the rear and began filling the gap. It was followed by others, until a resumption of the German advance became impossible. It was a repeat of the earlier failure to make a timely move against Amiens. General von Kuhl, chief of staff of the army group in that sector, said afterward that if the Germans had taken Mont des Cats, the British would have found themselves threatened from their rear and forced to abandon not only Ypres but their positions along the River Yser nearby. Much of what Ludendorff hoped to accomplish in Flanders could have been achieved with that one move. Instead, his troops were once again short of their goal and blocked.

He made one more try. On April 29, again in the Lys valley, he sent his Fourth Army with all available reserves into an attack aimed at taking Cassel, a town overlooking the port of Dunkirk. It was another bloody fight, it gained nothing, and the Germans' failure brought Georgette to an end.

Ludendorff's situation was now worse than it had been at the start of Michael. He still regarded the destruction of the BEF in Flanders as both possible and the key to everything, but because Georgette had brought French and British reserves streaming back northward, he again needed to draw those reserves away before delivering the conclusive blow. To accomplish this, he decided to attack the French where the movement of their reserves had left them weakest, along Pétain's thinned-out line in the Champagne country around Reims. Bruchmüller's artillery and all available infantry divisions were loaded onto trains and sent to join in an offensive that Crown Prince Wilhelm's army group had long been preparing east of the Michael battleground.

But Ludendorff no longer had the army with which he had begun the year. His casualties since the start of Michael now totaled nearly three hundred and fifty thousand, one of every ten German soldiers in the western theater. More than fifty thousand of his best troops had been killed, and replacements of comparable quality did not exist. More than a hundred of his divisions, nearly all of the elite assault units among them, had seen action, often suffering mightily. "The absence of our old peace-trained corps of officers was most severely felt," Ludendorff would observe in his *War Memoirs*.

Taken prisoner
French troops being marched to the rear by their German captors.

"They had been the repository of the moral strength of the country." He was writing euphemistically. In using the word "absence," he was speaking of annihilation.

Many of the surviving troops were demoralized by the failure of their ordeal to produce the promised victory. Though French and British losses had been comparably horrendous, Americans were now arriving in France in army-size numbers: eighty thousand in March, one hundred and eighteen

thousand in April, two hundred and forty-five thousand in May. Though they had seen no action of consequence, their best-trained divisions were now part of Foch's reserve and available for use.

Making them available had been a stupendous challenge. In 1916 the U.S. army was smaller than the number of British casualties in the Battle of the Somme, smaller than the French or German losses at Verdun. It had so few senior officers that, after the American declaration of war, the volunteers and

draftees were organized into divisions of twenty-seven thousand men each—
nearly twice the size of European divisions, so that only half as many commanders and staffs were required.

After hurrying the First Division to France, the War Department kept the
rest of its army at home for months of training. As troops began to cross the
Atlantic in serious numbers, arguments arose over how to deploy them. The
Entente commanders, the British especially, wanted to absorb them into their
own armies piecemeal, as they arrived. "Black Jack" Pershing, whose taciturn
dignity was at variance with the Europeans' image of Americans, refused
absolutely. The American Expeditionary Force, he made clear, would go into
action only when it was ready. It would do so as an autonomous entity, operating separately from the British and the French. First, however, he was going
to put it through considerably more training behind the front.

The next question was where to put the AEF. The northern part of the
front was British home ground and out of the question. The Champagne
region, blocking the way to Paris, belonged to Pétain and the French. That
left the east, the region just south of Verdun. This was agreeable to Pershing:
a breakthrough there, if it captured the rail center at Metz, could hurt the
Germans badly. He established his headquarters at the town of Chaumont in
Lorraine. The First Division went into training nearby, and as more troops
arrived a Second Division was assembled. The men were quartered in barns,
the officers wherever French families had bedrooms to spare. At the midlevel
of Pershing's officer corps were men who would be giants of another, later
war: Douglas MacArthur, George Marshall, and George Patton.

Pershing himself had much to learn about combat on the Western Front,
and though a capable executive, he was not a military genius. He refused to
follow the advice of his allies and give first priority to the disciplines of trench
warfare. With the confidence of a newcomer, he insisted that what lay ahead
was a war of movement, of breakthrough and advance. Blind to the impact
of the machine gun on infantry operations (his troops would pay a high price
for this blindness), he saw skill with the rifle as the key to success.

There was no greater challenge than supplying the AEF as it took shape
not only far from home but far from France's coasts. Three Atlantic ports
were given over to the use of the Americans and were expanded to permit the
unloading of a swelling stream of ships. The French were reluctant to give up
control of rail lines connecting the ports with the American theater of operations, but they were won over with a kind of bribe. France was given three
hundred American locomotives, and the Americans got hundreds of miles of
track.

Millions of tons of matériel had to be moved from the coast, along with hundreds of thousands of men. An office was established in Paris under a friend of Pershing's, the Chicago banker and newly minted Brigadier General Charles G. Dawes (a future vice president of the United States), to manage the purchase of still more matériel—12 million tons by the end of the war, more than was shipped from America. The management of all these supplies had to be improvised on a day-by-day basis, and for a time the whole system teetered on the brink of chaos. Its magnitude is apparent in the details—in what was required, for example, just to provide the AEF with telephone communications. The Americans would install twenty-two thousand miles of phone lines and lease an additional twelve thousand from the French. The War Department, in response to a request from Pershing, found, recruited, and sent several hundred American telephone operators who were fluent in French.

As May began, however, little of the American presence was visible to the people of Britain or even France. In London, Lloyd George's government was under pressure to send more men to the continent and, at the same time, to demonstrate to a restive public that it was not ignoring opportunities for bringing the war to an end. It responded in two ways. It broadened conscription, drafting fifty thousand coal miners and men in other occupations that were previously off-limits. On May 15 Foreign Secretary Arthur Balfour declared in the House of Commons that Britain was prepared to enter into negotiations. There was one condition, and it was no surprise to anyone: Germany must declare her willingness to restore Belgium to her prewar autonomy and neutrality. This was an opportunity for the Germans. But the men who might have responded positively—Chancellor Hertling, Foreign Minister Kühlmann—continued to be overshadowed by Ludendorff and his unbending rejection of compromise. Just a week earlier, on May 7, Ludendorff's domination of German policy had manifested itself in a settlement with Romania. Nearly as shortsightedly greedy as Brest-Litovsk, the Treaty of Bucharest made Romania permanently subject to Berlin. It gave Germany a majority interest in the Romanian oil fields (Vienna was given 24 percent) under a lease of ninety-nine years.

What Ludendorff planned now was a pair of offensives in rapid sequence: first at the Chemin des Dames line and then, farther west, across the little River Matz between the towns of Montdidier and Noyon less than sixty miles from Paris. The defenders, in both cases, would be Pétain's troops. The immediate objective was a familiar one: to so threaten the French line (and also Paris) that Foch would be forced to shift his (and Haig's) northern reserves to the south. The ultimate objective was equally familiar: to set the stage for a death blow in Flanders.

Preparing for the new attacks would require a month. The artillery needed for Bruchmüller's fireworks show, and all the necessary ammunition, had to be moved yet again. Many divisions of infantry—tired, disheartened troops— had to be moved as well. The French would have plenty of time to prepare.

The French had 103 divisions on their home soil. (Others were in other places, such as Italy, Salonika, and the Middle East.) But of this total, forty-five were north of the River Oise. Even if some of these divisions were moved quickly to the southeast, Pétain could have no more than sixty with which to defend everything from the Oise to beyond Verdun. This at a time when Ludendorff had more than two hundred divisions—albeit badly battered divisions—in the west. Verdun, supposedly France's most sacred citadel after Paris itself, was now almost undefended. Preparations for German initiatives all along Pétain's line had been obvious for months, but determining where an attack might come had remained impossible. The challenge of responding to these difficulties was one of the greatest faced by Pétain during the war. His difficulties were magnified by the recurrent need to share whole armies with Haig.

Pétain's problems were further deepened by opposition, at almost every step, from Foch and other generals. These men continued to believe that the only way to wage war was to attack and attack again almost regardless of the circumstances, and that when the enemy attacked the only acceptable response was to stand in place and die rather than retreat. They saw Pétain's openness to other tactics, his willingness to learn the lessons of the past year, as weakness bordering on cowardice. When Pétain repeated his order for the implementation of Directive No. 4, which called for an elastic defense-in-depth, he was again ignored. Foch, in his new capacity as supreme commander, explicitly undercut him by issuing, on May 4, an order of his own to the effect that when attacked the French commanders were not to consider even temporary withdrawal.

The line along the Chemin des Dames was commanded by General Denis Duchesne, a former chief of staff to Foch and one of the new generalissimo's most ardent disciples. His force, though mainly French, included three British divisions that after being severely mauled in the Michael fighting had been sent to this long-quiet area to recover. Contemptuous of Pétain and his directive, encouraged in his insubordination by Foch's example, Duchesne crowded his troops into poorly prepared entrenchments up on the front line. His entire array of defensive positions, artillery included, was five miles deep at most. And all of it was north of the River Aisne, so that the defenders would have to fight with water at their backs. The whole arrangement was magnificently bold and ripe for disaster.

General Hamilton Gordon, commander of Duchesne's British corps,

Corporal Hitler, seated at left: Winner of two Iron Crosses

questioned the French general about his arrangements. *"J'ai dit,"* Duchesne haughtily replied. *I have spoken.* The troops were to stay where they were. If attacked, they were to yield nothing.

As before Michael, and despite the fact that their preparations filled four weeks with the movement of men and guns, the Germans were almost miraculously successful in maintaining secrecy. More than twenty divisions were assembled opposite Duchesne, and more than three hundred thousand shells were stockpiled for each corps of two or three divisions. And yet as late as May 26, when the British reported signs of imminent trouble, Duchesne was unconcerned. "There is no indication," he said, "that the enemy has made preparations which would enable him to attack the Chemin des Dames tomorrow." He then departed for Paris and an assignation with his mistress.

Hours later, at one A.M. on May 27, four thousand German guns and four thousand mortars began their work of devastation. The barrage fell mainly on the unfortunate British, whose worst fears suddenly became real. At four A.M. fourteen divisions of storm troops with seven more in close support attacked behind a wall-solid creeping barrage. They found the defenders either dead or in shocked disarray. Discovering a gap between the French and the British, they pushed through. By midday they had advanced five miles and (the British and French having failed to destroy the bridges) were across the Aisne. Corporal Adolf Hitler, armed only with a pistol and operating alone, captured twelve French soldiers during the advance. For this action he was given an Iron Cross First Class, complementing the Iron Cross Second Class he had received almost four years earlier.

By nightfall the Germans were across a second river, the Vesle, and still moving. Once again, however, their lack of cavalry or armored motor vehicles deprived them of the means to overtake the fleeing French and British. In an effort to compensate, the commander of the German Seventh Army ordered that the advance continue all night—a thing that proved to be physically impossible. By the time exhaustion made a halt imperative, the lead German units had moved forward twelve miles across twenty-five miles of front. It was a spectacular achievement, comparable to what Hutier had done at the start of Michael.

All was not well, though. On the German left, near the city of Reims where the French defenses were stronger and had been more intelligently arranged, the offensive had failed. This compromised all the gains at the center and on the right, leaving the advancing units with an exposed flank. To support his offensive as it moved south, Ludendorff needed the rail centers of Soissons and Reims, the former at the western end of the entry to the new salient, the latter to the east. German troops would enter Soissons on the second day of the battle but, bizarrely, be ordered out again, apparently because their looting went out of control and their commander feared a collapse of discipline. Ludendorff, upon learning of this, would order them to go back in and stay. Soissons was not enough, however. Until Reims fell, the Germans would be advancing into a kind of sack that, while growing bigger at the bottom, had a dangerously narrow mouth and only one vulnerable lifeline.

Pétain and Foch were surprised that Ludendorff had attacked in such force at the Chemin des Dames. As the attack resumed on May 28 and continued to progress, they puzzled over how he was sustaining his momentum, not knowing how many troops he had taken from the north. For once they were in agreement: Reims must be held, along with a wooded plateau just beyond Soissons. This would keep the mouth of the new salient from opening wider. Neither general thought Paris was in danger. To threaten the capital, the Germans would have to shift their attack toward the west. If they did so, the French Tenth Army that was part of Foch's reserve was in position to fall on their flank. Pétain ordered one of the armies north of the Oise to come south. He also asked Foch to send reserves but was refused. Clemenceau, never one to leave military operations in the hands of the generals, traveled to Foch's headquarters and was surprised to learn of this refusal. When Foch explained that he believed the new offensive to be intended not to capture Paris but to drain the Flanders reserve, Clemenceau declined to interfere.

By the end of the second day, the Germans were in possession of high, easily defended ground south of the Vesle. They had reached nearly all the objectives that Ludendorff had set for their offensive, and in doing so they had captured huge quantities of desperately needed supplies. The familiar pattern was once again emerging. At one end of their line, around Soissons, the Germans had succeeded more easily and completely than they had expected. But at the other end, in the attempt to take Reims, they had failed. As before, the question was what to do next—whether to push on where the troops had been so successful, or try again where they had failed, or simply call the whole thing off. German intelligence was watching keenly for evidence that Entente reserves were moving out of Flanders. Thanks to Foch, no such evidence existed: the reserves were staying put. The entire effort had to be judged a failure. At an evening meeting at Crown Prince Wilhelm's headquarters, all the generals in attendance, Ludendorff among them, agreed that the offensive had to continue. Once again losing sight of what he had originally intended, Ludendorff ordered seven of the divisions being saved for Flanders to be brought south to join in the attack. He was like a roulette player trying to recoup his losses by putting chips on more and more numbers.

THE WOMEN

ONE OF THE STAPLES OF GREAT WAR PROPAGANDA WAS
the poster showing a nurse (always beautiful and composed, always
immaculate) bending over a handsome young soldier (calm and alert, seriously but not mortally wounded, never injured in ways unpleasant to the
eye) who gazes up at her in gratitude and admiration.

Such art had always been a fantasy, and by the war's climax it was an
affront to truth. Many thousands of female nurses were doing heroic service near the front lines in the summer and autumn of 1918, but there was
nothing romantic about their experience. The avalanche of casualties on
both sides had turned field hospitals into places of horror.

"Hundreds upon hundreds of wounded poured in like a rushing torrent," an American nurse remembered. "The crowded, twisted bodies, the
screams and groans, made one think of Dante's *Inferno*." Men came in
with parts of their faces missing, with their sexual organs gone, with limbs
reduced to dripping shreds.

Things were even more terrible on the other side. "We are supposed to
care for up to three hundred wounded here, but there are absolutely no
supplies!" a German nurse recorded in her diary. "In the morning helpful
soldiers found us some mattress ticking. We began by tearing it up for bandages, since there was no material for dressings. Later we took down the
curtains and made bandages of them. Our charges are starving, and all we
can give them is dry army bread."

There was the stink of gangrene, and the pathetic shell-shock cases.
Dying boys cried out for their mothers, and, in the second half of 1918,
more and more fevered men were dying of influenza.

More than fifteen thousand women were with the American Expeditionary Force and auxiliary organizations such as the Red Cross by that
time. (Ten thousand American nurses had volunteered to serve with the
Entente forces before the end of 1914.) The BEF had twenty-three thousand
nurses and fifteen thousand nurses' aides, the armies of France sixty-three
thousand, the Germans ninety-one thousand. They performed magnificently—a hundred and twenty American nurses died in Europe, and two

hundred were decorated for bravery under fire—but they were only a tiny percentage of the women whose lives were affected by four years of war.

The start of the conflict, and the outburst of patriotism to which it gave rise, had brought out masses of women volunteers in all the belligerent nations. At first their governments scarcely knew what to do with them. Women had few rights in those days. (New Zealand had granted them the vote in 1893, but two decades later it remained almost alone.) Women of "good" family had little access to careers and almost none to the world of public affairs. Nurses were obviously essential and quickly put to work, but in other respects things continued—for a time—in the old familiar ways. The volunteer associations of women that sprang into existence in Britain, France, and Germany were not only dominated but monopolized by the upper and middle classes. If working-class women had been accepted, many would not have been able to afford the required uniforms.

But soon, with so many millions of men at the front, women were needed badly. The volunteers were put to work as clerks, cooks, drivers, canteen workers, telephone operators—in nearly any job, as time passed, where they could free a man for combat. The British would ultimately have a hundred thousand women in service in this way—all carefully screened to ensure that they came from the right kind of background. For young women who had expected the future to be limited to marriage and child-bearing, it all could be wonderfully thrilling. "For the first time I was going to be someone," said a French girl. "I would count in the world."

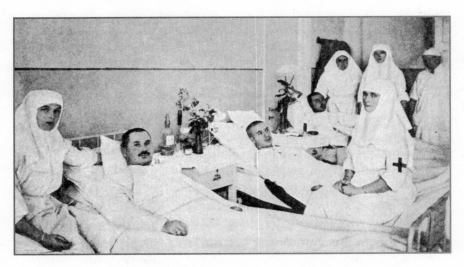

Russia's Tsarina Alexandra, seated at right, in a hospital far from the front

Members of Britain's Auxiliary Ambulance Corps
making a morning milk delivery

For the women of the lower classes, millions of whom were employed before the war began, more than adventure was involved. The pay of common soldiers was minuscule, allowances for dependents not sufficient to sustain life. (The allowance for a wife was one and a quarter francs per day in France, nothing for a dependent mother or sister.) And ironically, the war destroyed many women's jobs. In France 85 percent of women in industry when the war began were employed in textile manufacturing. As many of the factories were shut down, 60 percent of those women were thrown out of work. Sixty-seven percent of garment industry jobs disappeared. In France and elsewhere many of the women who went into the munitions factories were no doubt motivated by patriotism. But for many it was also a matter of survival.

The resulting changes were dramatic. In Germany more than five million women entered the labor force, rising from 35 to 55 percent of the total employed. In Britain the comparable total was more than one and a half million, with seven hundred and fifty thousand women taking jobs previously held by men, three hundred and fifty thousand moving into new war-related positions, and almost a quarter of a million becoming agricultural laborers. In France, whose population was more heavily rural than Britain's or Germany's, food production became increasingly the work of women. Female employment in French munitions factories rose from fifteen thousand early in 1915 to six hundred and eighty-four thousand in 1917. The French railways, which had employed six thousand women before the war, had fifty-seven thousand on their payrolls by the end. Female employment in the Paris subways rose from 124 to more than three thousand.

Neither France nor Germany integrated women into its armed forces, though the Germans were preparing to do so late in 1918. The British were pioneers, creating women's branches of their army, navy, and air force in 1917. Female officers were called "administrators" rather than given military rank. Noncommissioned officers were "forewomen," the privates "workers." In what was a bold innovation by British standards, the army began to accept women from the working class. Traditionalists were shocked. A letter to an English newspaper complained of women "making themselves and, what is more important, the King's uniform, ridiculous."

The Americans followed Britain's example and soon went further. As early as March 1917 the U.S. Navy was enlisting female clerks as "yeomanettes," who were barred from sea duty but given formal naval rank. In the summer of 1918 the Marine Corps advertised for female volunteers, got two thousand responses just in New York City, and eventually accepted three hundred.

All this took place against a background of vast suffering for the women of Europe. In Germany alone more than a million and a half soldiers were dead by late 1918, and nearly a third of them had been married. Widows, many of them living in severe deprivation and struggling to support children, had become a significant element of every country's population. Little better off were the families of prisoners of war. Hundreds of thousands of unmarried young women would never find husbands.

In western Europe the new roles assumed by women proved to be surprisingly short-lived. Women's suffrage movements had been gaining strength up to 1914—had appeared to be on the verge of success in places—but the war brought them to an end. In January 1918 Britain granted the vote to women, but only to women who owned property. Later in the year, in an odd twist, it allowed women to hold elective office while continuing to deny them the vote. Women who had expected to be given the vote and other rights in return for their service and sacrifice learned that they were mistaken.

The changes wrought by the war proved to be most permanent in the most improbable places. In Turkey, before the war, women had been virtually excluded not only from employment but from education and even social life beyond the walls of their homes. The lynching of women deemed to be of bad moral character was accepted practice. The war turned Turkey's women into office workers, organizers of charities, teachers, nurses, and even transporters of ammunition. The veil was abolished, and schools for girls appeared in surprising numbers. Things later reverted to the traditional pattern in rural areas, but in Constantinople the changes stuck.

Change was most dramatic in revolutionary Russia. Huge numbers of women had gone to work in war factories where conditions were even more abominable than in the west. This and the severe deprivations of the long conflict—never enough food or fuel, vast numbers of men killed—radicalized the women of Russia's cities. They figured importantly in the uprisings that brought down the tsar. When the Bolsheviks took power late in 1917, equal pay and rights for women became the law of the land. The final irony is that civil rights in Russia soon became once again meaningless for women as well as for men.

Chapter 35

✠

The Black Day of the German Army

*"The scale and nature of operations required
a 'big business' type of commander, a great
constructing and organizing brain."*
—Basil H. Liddell Hart

On a morning at the end of May, for the first time in more than three and a half years, German soldiers stood on the banks of the River Marne barely fifty miles from Paris. They were bone-weary and threadbare, and in days of moving south some had made themselves sick gorging on captured enemy stores. Still, the return to this place must have felt like triumph. Since the start of the Chemin des Dames offensive, they had rolled over or swept aside every enemy unit in their path. They had wrecked seven French and British divisions, taken fifty thousand prisoners, and advanced thirty miles. And the way ahead looked clear: the troops retreating before them were thin on the ground, almost without artillery, and unable to find a place to stop and turn and fight. The Germans must have felt that, if they found the strength, they could keeping on walking to the Eiffel Tower.

It is unlikely that many of them understood how empty their triumph was. Their advance was creating an enormous salient, the biggest yet, a kind of sack with a narrow mouth. They were inside the sack, and every step they took made it deeper or wider. But the mouth was not growing at all. It was in danger of becoming smaller. If it were closed altogether—if the French held on to Reims and retook Soissons—the German assault troops would be trapped.

The Allied side too (with the Americans in the fight, the term *Allies* becomes appropriate as a substitute for *Entente*) had little appreciation of how vulnerable the Germans were. They had taken Soissons, they appeared to be on the brink of taking Reims, they had advanced so far between the two cities that they were starting to cross the Marne, and they appeared to be unstoppable. The crisis bore all the earmarks of a disaster, and a contagion of panic set in. At the eastern end of the front, south of St. Mihiel, French General Castelnau began laying out a plan for a withdrawal to the west—for abandoning the fortresses that had long made his sector all but impregnable. To the north Haig's staff was dusting off its plans for an evacuation back to England. Even the irrepressible Foch was infected. He suggested that Clemenceau prepare the government to leave Paris, whose citizens were fleeing by the hundreds of thousands, and talked of fighting all the way to the Pyrenees. Franchet d'Esperey, the "Desperate Frankie" of 1914 fame, ordered the French Fifth Army to give up Reims. Lloyd George, having returned to Versailles, yielded at last to Foch's appeals for more troops from England. (They were desperately needed; Haig was disbanding 145 battalions to replenish those that remained.) Only Pétain, the supposedly overcautious pessimist, remained untroubled. He felt certain that the Germans had fatally overextended themselves and that their ruin was inevitable if the Allies just held on.

But then, just as everything seemed to be unraveling for the Allies, the situation began to turn around. Two of Pershing's big divisions, ordered to converge where the Germans were crossing the Marne, linked up with French units and met the enemy at Château-Thierry. It was the Americans' first major engagement, and it brought the German advance to a stop. The commander at Reims disobeyed Franchet d'Esperey, stayed in place, and stopped the Germans there as well. When the Germans pulled themselves together for another assault on Reims, they had to do so without storm troops or Bruchmüller's artillery and failed miserably.

Ludendorff, thwarted again, turned to the next phase of his plan: the attack at the River Matz west of Soissons. The goal here—it had become an urgent need—was to broaden the mouth of the salient at its western end, pushing the Allies far enough back that they could no longer threaten the one rail line carrying German supplies and troops southward toward the Marne. The attack was to begin on June 9, with Hutier's army taking the lead. Everything had to be done so hurriedly that secrecy was impossible. As the preparations proceeded, American Marines launched an attack at Belleau Wood to block one of the Germans' approaches to Paris. They did so artlessly, advancing shoulder to shoulder in a way rarely seen since the slaughter of the British at the Somme in 1916, but their high morale and the sheer weight of their numbers kept them inching forward. It would take them almost three weeks and many casualties to secure the wood, but the process consumed German troops that Ludendorff could ill afford to lose.

Hutier's preparations at the Matz were so rushed and unconcealed that the French began to suspect a German ruse designed to draw their attention away from some other, more secret operation elsewhere. German deserters even told the French the exact times when the bombardment and the infantry's advance would come. Nevertheless, when the attack began—another Bruchmüller barrage, a forward rush by experienced troops who had been allowed to rest since Michael—it was a complete success, and for the least excusable of reasons. Once again the defenders were commanded by a Foch disciple who had scorned Pétain's instructions and put his main force on or near the forward line, where the German artillery devoured it. Hutier's troops advanced six miles that day, demolishing three French divisions and taking eight thousand prisoners.

But then on June 11, as if from out of nowhere, the French counterattacked west of Soissons. Their advance was directed by Charles Mangin, "the Butcher," the almost maniacally aggressive French general who throughout the war had alternately been glorified for his ferocious offensives and censured, even removed from command, for carrying things too far. Thanks to Foch, he was back in command of a corps, and he was unquestionably the right man for the job at hand. This time it was the French who were concealed by fog. Rushing eastward, they caught Hutier's troops on open ground without prepared defenses. The Germans were thrown back with such shocking force that Ludendorff immediately called off the Matz operation.

There followed a month of comparative quiet that the armies on both sides used to catch their breath and pull themselves together. Not only the Germans but now the French as well were preparing fresh attacks. Something new made its appearance on the Western Front during this period: the first cases of the Spanish influenza that would spread around the world and in eleven months kill more people than the war itself. All the armies were affected, but chronic malnutrition made the problem worse on the German side. Thousands of men all along the front became too sick for duty—as many as two thousand per German division. By the end one hundred and eighty-six thousand German soldiers would die of the disease along with four hundred thousand German civilians.

The quiet was interrupted on July 4 by the Battle of Hamel, one of the most remarkable (if largely forgotten, perhaps because comparatively bloodless) operations of the war. It took place near Amiens, its aim was to clear away the German threat to that city, and it was planned and executed by John Monash, who in April had been knighted by King George, promoted to lieutenant general, and made the first non-English commander of the BEF's Australia–New Zealand Corps.

Monash himself was one of the war's most fascinating figures and arguably the most effective commander on either side. Raised on the Australian outback by Jewish shopkeeper parents who had emigrated from Prussia (the Monasch family home—that was the original spelling of the name—had been not far from Ludendorff's birthplace), he had risen from humble beginnings to take degrees in engineering, liberal arts, and law, to become an accomplished musician and linguist, and to found a consulting firm that directed the construction of bridges and railways all across Australia. Along with all these accomplishments, almost as a kind of avocation, Monash distinguished himself as a reserve officer in Australia's tiny army, designed a breech-loading cannon, and became popular as a lecturer on tactics and military technology. He was given command of one of Australia's first brigades at the start of the war and spent 1915 at Gallipoli, where his brigade went ashore with the first invasion and stayed until the end. He contributed significantly to Plumer's success at Messines Ridge in 1917 and, as a major general, commanded a division at Third Ypres and Passchendaele.

Powerful people in Australia had tried to keep Monash out of the war, and powerful people in Europe later tried to obstruct his advancement. Eyebrows went up, in 1918, at the thought of giving a third star and command of two hundred thousand Anzac troops to a man who was not only an amateur soldier, not only a colonial, but a Jew whose parents had come from Germany. He survived only because every general who served with him became his admirer and defender, and because the king came to respect him.

It was at Hamel that Monash showed what he could do. He used his organizational genius and experience in the management of huge projects to integrate as never before all the terrible new machinery of war: machine guns, artillery, aircraft, and tanks. Executing Monash's plan of attack, his troops needed only ninety-three minutes to reach all their objectives, capturing thousands of enemy soldiers and suffering only light casualties, making Amiens secure and opening a way for further Allied offensives. Their success explains why Captain Basil Liddell Hart, a veteran of the Great War who spent the rest of his life writing its history, said that Monash "had probably the greatest capacity for command in modern war among all who held command." It was a kind of capacity, Liddell Hart continued, that abandoned the old-school dash and flair of the British and French professionals and "fulfilled the idea that gradually developed in the war—that the scale and nature of operations required a 'big business' type of commander, a great constructing and organizing brain."

Hamel has been called the first truly modern battle. It became the model for later British operations; a brochure describing Monash's tactics was distributed to every officer in the BEF. It set the stage for the Anzacs, often operating jointly with the Canadians, to serve as Britain's shock troops for much of the rest of the war.

Eleven days after Hamel—one wonders how such things continued to be possible—forty-nine divisions of Crown Prince Wilhelm's army group made yet another attack on Reims. It was intended as the climax of Ludendorff's Chemin des Dames operation. It was to open a second rail line into the Marne salient and prepare the way for the long-awaited push in Flanders, which was to follow in just five days. But again things did not go according to plan. Pétain, with patient argument, had won the commander of the French Fourth Army over to his way of thinking, so that an effective system of defense in depth was put in place east of Reims. The result validated Pétain's ideas: the German attack on that side of the city got nowhere. On the west side, where the Foch school still prevailed, the Germans achieved a quick and deep penetration in spite of a total lack of surprise. By the second day, it was clear that the German failure east of the city had left the advancing troops to the west dangerously exposed. Ludendorff called the attack off. He left to meet with Crown Prince Rupprecht at Tournai in the north. It was time to finalize preparations for Flanders. Bruchmüller's guns were already heading there on trains.

After four months of struggle and sacrifice, the German situation in Flanders was not remotely as good as Ludendorff had hoped to make it. Haig had greatly improved his defenses—his hundred thousand laborers were fully employed at last, building new fortifications and laying out miles of wire— and powerful reserves remained nearby, thanks to Foch's refusal to release them for the Marne. But Flanders was the last card left to Ludendorff, and he was determined to play it. He and the Bavarian crown prince were deep into their discussion when shocking news arrived. The Germans south and west of Soissons had been hit by a massive French offensive and were in retreat.

This was another of Mangin's surprises, and again it had come out of the forest west of the Chemin des Dames. Twenty-three divisions, four of them American, had followed five hundred tanks in an eastward attack aimed at recapturing Soissons and sealing off the salient. By nine-thirty A.M., with Ludendorff speeding south by train, the Americans and French had overrun three German lines. The American First and Second Divisions were at the center of the attacking force, and the fighting was ferocious. "Machine guns raved everywhere; there was a crackling din of rifles, and the coughing roar of hand grenades," one soldier would recall. "Company and platoon commanders lost control—their men were committed to the fight—and so thick was the going that anything like formation was impossible. It was every man for himself, an irregular, broken line, clawing through the tangles, climbing over fallen trees, plunging heavily into Boche rifle pits. Here and there a well-fought Maxim gun held its front until somebody—officer, non-com, or private— got a few men together and, crawling to left or right, gained a flank and silenced it. And some guns were silenced by blind, furious rushes that left a trail of writhing khaki figures, but always carried two or three frenzied Marines with bayonets into the emplacement; from whence would come shooting and screaming and other clotted unpleasant sounds, and then silence."

Eventually arriving German reserves stopped the advance, and field artillery firing at point-blank range destroyed most of Mangin's tanks. By day's end the Germans had managed to cobble together a defensive line some five miles back from where they had started, but fifteen thousand of them had been taken prisoner, and they had lost four hundred guns. They had stopped Mangin short of Soissons, but he continued to pose a mortal threat. With all hope of taking Reims gone and Soissons in increasing danger, the Marne salient had become untenable. Ludendorff was left with no choice but to postpone Flanders indefinitely.

He dispatched an army to the defense of Soissons. Late in the day he met with Kaiser Wilhelm and told him that, as in 1914, it was necessary to withdraw from the Marne. Preparations began for getting the troops and as many guns and supplies as possible—much would have to be left behind—out of the salient and up through Soissons to safety.

The balance of power had shifted. In March the Germans had had three hundred thousand more troops than the Allies, but between the start of Michael and the end of July more than a million of those troops, a large proportion of them the prime young men trained as storm troops, had been killed, wounded, or captured. The British and French lost half a million men each, and the French, like the Germans, had almost no replacements. But the Americans were continuing to arrive in France at a rate of more than a quarter of a million a month, and they were going into action. Now the Allies had two hundred thousand more troops than the Germans, and the difference was widening daily. Though the Allies still had fewer divisions, that statistic has little meaning. The German divisions were ravaged. More than a hundred were classified as unfit for use on the offensive.

All the force that Ludendorff had expended in driving his troops south to the Marne had gone for nothing. The men who had fought their way across the Marne were being destroyed at a horrendous rate by the Allied armies now opposing them, and the only remaining question was whether they could be got back out of the salient before their escape was cut off. "Midnight," a German soldier remembered of the start of the withdrawal. "Time to leave, to escape the annihilating fire at daybreak. The Sixth Company remains behind to cover the retreat. The first group starts off, ten minutes later the second, and then after a few rifle salvoes the rest. We leave the ruined glade, climbing over the numerous shell holes in the underbrush. Here and there rises a sandy mound in which a rifle is stuck, a steel helmet over its butt. There they lie buried, those who would never come back from the battle of the Marne... Along the road back to Romigny the column passes rattling artillery, the riders in the blowing rain bent over in their saddles, the cannoneers hanging on the limbers of the guns. Between slouch the dispersed fragments of infantry, the remnants of companies, guns slung round necks, tarpaulins over heads against the rain, the knapsacks underneath bulging with the effect of a line of comic hunchbacks... The long lines of infantry file in the gray morning out of the woods, over the open field, without haste... Behind us thunder the engineers' demolitions. The engineers soon come running down the slope, followed by the infantry rearguard... Only our dead remain behind."

The great Flanders offensive that was supposed to be the point of everything the Germans had done was overdue and unlikely ever to take place. Ludendorff himself was in obvious torment—self-isolated, distracted, easily enraged, on the edge of collapse. To all the weight of his military problems was added the fear of what would happen when the German public, still assured daily that its armies were victorious in the field, awoke to the magnitude of his failure.

The fighting was not only bloody and continuous but extended over huge sections of front. Allied troops, at Foch's prodding, were attacking all around the edges of the Marne salient, which shrank rapidly as the Germans hurried to extricate themselves from it. On July 24 Foch, Haig, Pershing, and Pétain met and agreed, with some difficulty, on a coordinated series of major offensives. Haig was to attack eastward out of Amiens (Monash's success at Hamel had made this possible), Pétain northward across the Marne. Pershing, who was demanding the return to his sector of the divisions that had been scattered to help deal with the German offensives, would advance on the old St. Mihiel salient south of Verdun. The objective in each case was to capture rail lines that were essential to the Germans and that, if taken, would tremendously improve the Allies' ability to move their troops and supplies. The fact that the Allies were able to make plans on such a tremendous scale demonstrates the extent to which they now had the initiative, while Ludendorff could only react.

Nevertheless, the next day Ludendorff made a final, desperate effort to encircle Reims. It was another complete failure; his armies no longer had real offensive punch. The retreat back toward Soissons proceeded in orderly fashion in spite of continuous attacks from three directions; it was punctuated with counterattacks that kept the Allies from getting too close. When Pétain attacked along the Marne, his troops made little headway against a thin but tenacious rear guard. His attack drew in additional German troops, however, thereby preparing the way for the next French blow. It came on August 1, when Mangin advanced from the west in a renewed attempt to take Soissons. It was a near-triumph. Mangin's combined French-American force pushed the Germans back five miles in a day and captured the high ground south of the Vesle, from which they could train their guns on Soissons. By the tiniest of margins, however, the attack had come too late. The Germans slipped safely out of the salient and took up new positions north of its mouth. They gave up Soissons, and the French moved in behind them, with scarcely a shot being fired.

It had all been weirdly like 1914. Once again the Germans had reached and crossed the Marne, had been unable to sustain their advance, and had recovered their footing along the Aisne after a hurried withdrawal. But the German army of August 1918 was not what it had been in September 1914. It faced bigger and stronger enemies, and it had fewer resources with which to establish a defensive line. Ludendorff, strangely, could not accept or perhaps even see this. As late as August 2, in a communication to his army commanders, he spoke of an imminent return to the offensive. Nothing of the kind was even remotely possible.

Reality came crashing in on August 8, remembered ever since by the name Ludendorff conferred upon it: the Black Day of the German Army. It arrived in the form of the British attack east of Amiens. This too was planned, organized, and executed by Monash, whose corps had become part of a new army created to replace Gough's broken Fifth. The attack had been put together hurriedly in order to deny the Germans any opportunity to regroup after their race back from the Marne, but it proceeded flawlessly. With six hundred tanks and Monash's Anzac troops in the lead, it took the Germans by surprise and scattered them in all directions. Their organization collapsed as completely as their morale. The Anzacs advanced six miles by ten-thirty A.M., nine miles by noon. What was new and shocking was the refusal of the German troops to respond to orders, even to attempt to stop and fight. Reinforcements coming up from the rear were taunted as "scabs" and "strikebreakers." The Germans lost more than six hundred and fifty officers and twenty-six thousand troops that day. Two-thirds of them surrendered. They did so willingly, eagerly, often in large and well-armed groups.

Almost as surprising as the Germans' initial disintegration was Marwitz's success in bringing the situation under control. He sealed the hole in his line with reserves and organized a counterattack that shrank the British gain to a few miles. Not all his troops were out of fight, obviously, and those willing to continue were learning that the Allied tanks were not invincible. Many tanks would break down after an hour or two in action. Others overturned or became stuck in muddy, shell-pocked terrain, and the rest could be perforated by heavy machine guns or blown apart with field artillery. The Germans were also helped by the British and French infantry's lack of experience on the offensive. As black as August 8 may have been for the Germans, as clearly as it showed the extent of their decline, it showed too that finishing them was likely to be a slow and costly process.

August was a hard and bitter month across Europe. On the Western Front the initiative lay entirely with the Allies. With Foch in command, the British, French, and Americans were constantly either attacking or preparing to do so. The Germans recovered their cohesion and defended effectively under conditions that Ludendorff was making unnecessarily difficult. Though his own staff and the army group commanders begged him to order a pullback to the Hindenburg Line and other redoubts left behind by his offensives, he refused to do so, perhaps finding it impossible to acknowledge that his gains were worth nothing and in fact were barely defensible. The weakness of the positions he was requiring his divisions to hold was increasing their losses and making things easier for the enemy.

At meetings of the German leadership, it came to be generally acknowledged, even by Ludendorff, that military victory was now out of the question. Somehow, however, no one did anything to try to get negotiations started. At one point Kaiser Wilhelm instructed Foreign Minister Kühlmann to approach the Queen of the Netherlands about acting as an intermediary, but Kühlmann did nothing to follow up. He and the others clung to the hope that, by restabilizing the front and returning it to stalemate, Germany would be able to initiate peace talks from a position of strength. It was a vacuous hope. The troops were in such a sorry state, many of them rebellious and undependable, that Ludendorff had ordered deserters to be summarily executed and whatever property they possessed confiscated by the state. This was another sign of desperation: throughout the war, up to this point, the German army had been far more restrained than either the British or the French in its use of the death penalty for cowardice and desertion.

The Western Front was far from Germany's only problem. If any embers of life and force had continued to glow inside Austria-Hungary, they were extinguished in mid-June in an offensive out of the Tyrolean Alps. The architect of this final disaster was, inevitably, Conrad von Hötzendorf, long since replaced as Vienna's chief of staff but now in a field command. In May he had bullied the young and thoroughly demoralized Emperor Karl into approving his scheme. Actually, the emperor did worse than simply allow Conrad to proceed—he suggested expanding the offensive into a two-pronged affair, making it doubly certain that at no point would the Austrians have enough strength to succeed. Originally planned for May 28, the operation was delayed by problems with Austria's barely functional transport and supply systems. When they finally attacked on June 15, the Austrians managed to push the Italians back and cross the River Piave. This gave Ludendorff a moment of hope that, with continued progress, they might cause a diversion of American troops to Italy. But then the Austrians ran into a British-French rear guard and were abruptly brought to a stop. On the second day they were driven back to their starting line with a loss of forty-six thousand men. By June 25 their losses were ruinous: one hundred and forty-two thousand men, of whom eleven thousand had been killed and tens of thousands had surrendered. Those not yet dead, wounded, captured, or absent without leave found themselves without food or ammunition.

This campaign left the armies of Austria-Hungary incapable of maintaining a credible defense. On July 25 Conrad was relieved of command and elevated from baron to count, presumably for some reason other than his contributions to the destruction of the Hapsburg empire. Desertions were accelerating, the armies melting with the Alpine snows. Soon Vienna was informing Berlin that it could not continue. If Germany would not join it in seeking peace, Austria would do so alone. When it attempted to approach the Allies, however, it was rebuffed. It had acted too late to save itself.

Farther to the east, the folly that had been Brest-Litovsk was continuing to draw German troops into a military, political, and economic quagmire. They had to occupy the city of Kharkov deep inside Ukraine to maintain some vestige of control and any hope of extracting grain from that distant and unmanageable corner of their new eastern domains. They had to move into the Donets Basin, which since the start of the war had been Petrograd's primary source of coal, in search of fuel for the decrepit railways taken from the Russians. They had to stretch their lines of communication into the Crimea to discourage an Allied advance from the Middle East. The Turks, meanwhile, had overextended themselves in the Caucasus by advancing in the aftermath of Russia's collapse, and elsewhere they were entering a state of disintegration almost as advanced as that which had overcome the Austrians. They were being outmaneuvered and outfought by British and Arab forces in the crumbling southern reaches of their dying empire.

All was not hope and glory on the Allied side, either. The end of the German threat to Paris had ended also any possibility that the Clemenceau government would fall, a development that might have brought to power a government willing to negotiate with the Germans. But Britain and France alike were staggering under the weight of 1918's cascade of casualties; the British were drafting fifty-year-old men, while the French were organizing combat units made up almost entirely of men over forty. Economic dislocations also were taking a toll. Workers at ammunition factories in Birmingham and Coventry went out on strike, returning only when Lloyd George threatened to draft them into the army. In August Britain's police declared a one-day strike in protest of inflation's ruinous impact on their wages. This was followed by a railway strike in several regions. Strikes were even more widespread in France, and the strikers were often at least as intent on pressuring the government to make peace as on winning financial concessions.

Such unrest reflected the fact that, to the uninformed eye, 1918 could still have the appearance of a year of German gains. The map continued to show Germany in possession both of eastern Europe and of more of France and Flanders than it had held at the beginning of March. The breakdown of the German army was not readily apparent behind the front lines as its remnants continued to put up a stubborn defense, hold the Allied advance to a glacial pace, and kill British, French, and Americans.

The German forces too were paying heavily, of course, and the relentlessness of the Allied attacks gave them no chance to rest, reorganize, or throw together adequate defenses. Their casualties in August alone totaled two hundred and twenty-eight thousand. Of this total, a hundred and ten thousand men were listed as missing, a gentle way of saying that many had deserted. German soldiers were celebrating when they managed to surrender without being killed. When newly captured troops arrived at the holding pens created by the Allies for their growing hordes of prisoners, those already inside welcomed them with cheers. By September the number of German divisions on the Western Front would be down to 125, and only forty-seven of those were considered capable of combat. The Allies by then were up to more than two hundred divisions, increasing numbers of them fresh and double-sized American units.

The impossibility of a German victory had become clear to all the senior commanders on the Allied side and to most of their German counterparts. Germany's only hope, if any hope remained, was to take action on the diplomatic front before it, like Austria-Hungary, had nothing left to offer.

THE GARDENERS OF SALONIKA

THERE IS A NICE SYMMETRY TO THE FACT THAT, AS AUGUST 1918 arrived and the war became four years old, a huge multinational army lay bottled up in the Greek port city of Salonika under the command of French General Louis-Félix-Marie-François Franchet d'Esperey.

The idea of establishing an Entente base in Salonika had originated with Franchet d'Esperey as early as October 1914, when he was commanding the French Fifth Army on the Western Front and had already been nick-named "Desperate Frankie" by his British allies. He suggested it to President Poincaré, who was interested enough to ask him to draw up a detailed proposal. Franchet d'Esperey did so, explaining that by opening a front in the southern Balkans, France could protect Serbia and drain off German and Austrian troops from other places. But by the time the pro-posal was ready for consideration, the attention of the French and British was focused on the Dardanelles.

The possibility remained dormant for almost a year. Then, with the Gallipoli campaign in ruins and the Russians driven out of Galicia by the Gorlice-Tarnow offensive, Erich von Falkenhayn decided that the time had come to take possession of Serbia and secure an overland route to Constantinople. In October 1915, facing an invasion, the Serbs appealed for help. Paris was eager to respond. It wanted not only to keep Serbia intact but to win over Greece and Romania through a show of force. It also saw an opportunity to give France a strong presence in the Balkans—one that could be valuable after the war. Britain's leaders, with the exception of David Lloyd George, were skeptical. But they agreed to send one bat-tered division from Gallipoli as junior partner to a much larger French con-tingent.

The expedition was put under the command not of Franchet d'Esperey, who by then commanded an army group in the west, but of Maurice Sarrail, an able but notoriously political officer who had recently been relieved by Joffre after a German offensive in the Ardennes caught his Third Army off guard. Uniquely among senior French generals, Sarrail was closely affiliated with the socialists in the National Assembly. He had become popular with critics of Joffre's management of the war. His dismissal created an outcry, the leftists accusing Joffre of trying to eliminate a potential successor. The Salonika assignment was a convenient way of restoring him to command while getting him as far away from Paris as possible.

The first troops arrived at Salonika on October 5, and in short order Sarrail had them on the march toward Belgrade. They had only one single-track railroad to make use of, and the troops had to advance over some of the roughest, most barren hill country in Europe. They were met by Bulgarian troops who had recently been drawn into the war by German promises of rich territorial concessions—everything Bulgaria had lost in the Second Balkan War and more. They were still a hundred miles from Serbia when word arrived that the Serbs had been defeated and were fleeing for the coast through Albania. Sarrail could do nothing to help them. By late November he was pulling his troops back to their starting point.

He began building defenses that turned Salonika into a minature Western Front, practically impregnable. The British wanted out. Even Lloyd George had changed his mind, and Prime Minister Asquith was describing Salonika as "dangerous and likely to lead to a great disaster." But France, Russia, and Italy all demanded that they not only remain but send more divisions. London complied for the sake of harmony.

Sarrail's Army of the Orient grew rapidly. It included one hundred and sixty thousand men by January 1916, three hundred thousand by May. French, British, Italian, and Russian troops were gradually absorbed into it, along with Serbs who had been refitted on the island of Corfu. Sarrail involved himself so deeply in Greek politics (which were indescribably confused, with King Constantine leaning toward his brother-in-law the kaiser while leading politicians favored the Entente) that Britain and Russia became suspicious of French ambitions in the Balkans. Rumors circulated to the effect that Sarrail wanted to establish a kind of crusader kingdom in the region with himself as potentate.

The next complication was Romania, which both sides had been courting since the start of the war. When the Romanians agreed to join the Entente on condition that Sarrail attack the Bulgarians, the French government ordered him to proceed. It wanted to expand its reach in the Balkans and to draw German troops away from Verdun. Sarrail was preparing his offensive when the Bulgarians, as part of their role in Germany's campaign against Romania, seized the initiative and attacked him first. Sarrail counterattacked in September (allowing the Serbs to take the lead and sacrifice a fifth of their army in the process) and took the Serbian city of Monastir before being stopped. Stalemate was restored, and civil war broke out in Greece. Sarrail was actively supporting the king's political rivals.

The deadlock continued through 1917. The Entente had more than half a million men in Salonika by early that year, and in Europe the enterprise came to be regarded as a bad joke. German generals called Salonika their largest internment camp. Clemenceau, in his newspaper, called Sarrail's troops "the gardeners of Salonika," a waste of manpower needed on the Western Front. The place was far from a rural idyll, however. It was humid, swampy, and filled with pestilence. Hundreds of thousands of soldiers were stricken with a virulent strain of malaria. The city of Salonika, which had belonged to the Ottoman Empire until four years earlier, was a hell-hole. Refugees from the Balkan wars were crowded together in makeshift slums, and unsavory entrepreneurs grew rich by providing amusement for restless Entente troops. Venereal disease was epidemic, and a French division that had not had leave in more than a year briefly mutinied.

Sarrail tried an offensive in the spring of 1917, but it quickly failed. The Serbian army became embroiled in rumors of a plot to replace Serbia's king with a military dictatorship. Colonel Dragutin Dmitrijevic, the same "Apis" whose Black Hand had plotted the assassination of Franz Ferdinand three years earlier, was arrested, convicted of conspiracy, and executed on June 26. That same day King Constantine of Greece was forced to abdicate and move to Switzerland. A provisional government that Sarrail had been fostering in exile took power in Athens, and Greece declared war on the Central Powers. Everything was in confusion, and Sarrail was widely despised.

When Clemenceau became premier, he sent Sarrail into retirement. The new commander was General Adolphe Marie Guillaumat, a veteran of France's colonial wars and a Western Front army commander who offered the advantage of being determinedly apolitical. Guillaumat began making preparations for a 1918 attack on the Bulgarians; it was to be a limited operation with modest objectives. The Germans, meanwhile, were pulling their troops out of the Balkans for use in Ludendorff's coming offensive in the west. Even the British generals in Salonika grew optimistic. The Bulgarians, left on their own, seemed unlikely to stand their ground if seriously threatened.

In June 1918, with the Western Front in crisis, Guillaumat was called home to become military governor of Paris. (There was more to this appointment than met the eye. Clemenceau and Foch, their minds made up to sack Pétain if conditions in France continued to deteriorate, had selected Guillaumat as his replacement.) It happened that Franchet d'Esperey was out of work at the time. In May, after the German breakthrough at the Chemin des Dames, Clemenceau had half-apologetically offered him up as a scapegoat to politicians demanding change. ("I bear you no ill-will," he had told the general in dismissing him.) Franchet d'Esperey had been offered the Salonika command late in 1917, before Guillaumat. He had turned it down out of fear that, because he was known to be one of the army's Catholic, even quasi-royalist conservatives, his appointment would outrage the leftists. Invited to succeed Guillaumat rather than Sarrail, however, he felt free to accept.

Almost as soon as he arrived in Greece, he began expanding Guillaumat's plans. "I expect from you savage vigor," he told the generals who greeted him when he landed. Two hundred and fifty thousand Greek troops had become available as a supplement to his army, and soon he was cabling Paris, demanding permission for a major campaign. Clemenceau was in favor. With the Germans on the defensive in Belgium and France and masses of Americans in action, there was no longer a need for more troops in the west, and with Austria nearly defenseless southeastern Europe seemed to offer rich opportunities. He got London and Rome to agree.

In September the Army of the Orient began moving north. This was its last chance to show that the whole thing had not been a tragic waste.

Chapter 36

✠

The Sign of the Defeated

"No no no!... You do not finish a war like this!...
It is a fatal error, and France will pay for it!"

—GENERAL CHARLES MANGIN

Forced to accept the impossibility of victory in the west, Ludendorff clung to the hope that he could deny victory to the Allies. He persisted in believing that Germany could emerge from the war in possession of part of Belgium and of France's Longwy-Briey basin. "The man could escape even now," Foch said of him on August 28, marveling at his stubbornness, "if he would make up his mind to leave behind his baggage."

That Ludendorff was living in a fantasy was soon made plain. The British were readying an offensive out of Arras, and Foch was demanding that the Americans contribute divisions to it. Pershing, variously described by frustrated French commanders as "tactless" and even "obtuse," would not agree. He wanted to concentrate his troops on his own sector of the front, where he could use them to pursue his own objectives. Foch was indignant. Pétain brokered a resolution of the dispute that provided French support for the attack that Pershing was preparing at St. Mihiel. This attack would have three objectives: to drive the Germans out of their salient; to cut the rail line running laterally behind the salient; and to threaten Longwy-Briey. It was to take place in just five days. The Allies were doing everything in a rush now, thinking for the first time that it might be possible to finish the war before the onset of winter.

The push at Arras, with Canadian troops in the lead, was another success for the Allies; they broke through everywhere they attacked. The defense proved so porous that Ludendorff agreed at last to a pullback to the Hindenburg Line—to the surrender, finally, of everything taken in the year's offensives. His decision came too late, however, for an orderly retreat to be possible. On the British part of the front alone, during the two weeks of the withdrawal, the Germans lost one hundred and fifteen thousand men, four hundred and seventy guns, and stores that they had no means of replacing.

The war had come down to a rapid succession of hard Allied blows that the Germans could only do their diminishing best to contain. A disproportionately large number of these blows were being delivered by the Anzac and Canadian corps, which after four years of hard fighting remained so potent that Haig turned to them repeatedly as a battering ram with which to smash the German line. A strong case can be made that these were the best fighters of the war, their divisions the most effective on either side. This was made possible partly by John Monash, partly by his Canadian counterpart, Lieutenant General Sir Arthur Currie.

Currie, like Monash, came from a background that set him apart from almost all the other BEF generals. He had grown up a farm boy in British Columbia, wanting to become a lawyer but obliged after his father's death to settle for schoolteaching instead. From there he went into insurance, then into real estate speculation. At twenty-one he joined the Canadian Garrison Artillery, a weekend-warrior operation, as a lowly gunner. A combination of competence and amiability opened the doors to advancement: he was commissioned at twenty-five, promoted to captain a year later, and at thirty-three became a lieutenant colonel commanding a regiment.

He had been keenly disappointed when medical problems kept him out of the Boer War, and when the Great War came he was eager to go. He was as well qualified as it was possible for a Canadian soldier to be at that time and was put in command of one of Canada's first four brigades. Trouble, however, pursued him. A real estate bubble had burst early in 1914, leaving him deep in debt. He borrowed regimental funds to stave off bankruptcy and might have been charged with embezzlement if not for the intervention of friends. To the end of the war he would be haunted by the obligations he had left behind. In sending $10,000 to a creditor in 1917, he wrote that "for nearly three years the last thing I thought of at night and the first thing in the morning was this"—the money he owed.

By then, however, he was one of the BEF's most respected commanders. In April 1915 the courage and tenacity of his brigade in holding off a German attack on the village of St. Julien had kept Second Ypres from turning into a disaster for the British. A year later the brilliance with which his Canadian First Division captured Vimy Ridge provoked General Henry Horne to declare it "the pride and wonder of the British Army." But in June 1917, when the British selected Currie to become the first Canadian commander of the Canadian Corps, politicians back home complained of not having been consulted and proposed other candidates. They urged Currie's creditors to demand payment in full. His promotion was changed to "temporary" and seemed likely to be rescinded. He had always been a kind of alien among the BEF's generals; even the Australian Monash was a model of gentlemanly refinement by comparison. "He had a tremendous command of profanity," his own son would recall. "He didn't swear without a cause. But boy, when he cut loose he could go for about a minute without repetition."

Currie was saved—and knighted—when two of his officers advanced him $6,000, and when the veneration in which he was held by Canada's troops made it clear that his removal would spark protests. At the end of the summer of 1918 those troops were keeping intact a record that is nothing less than astonishing in the context of the Great War. They never once failed to capture an objective, never were driven out of a position they had an opportunity to consolidate, and never lost a gun.

At the beginning of September, Ludendorff's worst headache was not the Canadians or the Anzacs but the huge numbers of Americans assembling near Verdun. Anticipating an attack, temporarily free of his obsessive determination to hold his ground everywhere, he ordered the abandonment of the two-hundred-square-mile, thirteen-miles-deep St. Mihiel salient. This timely move would disappoint Pershing, who had originally planned to attack at St. Mihiel on September 7 but was forced to delay by difficulties in getting French artillery into position. He wanted not only to capture the salient but to destroy its defenders, and he had the resources to do so: a million U.S. and a hundred and ten thousand French troops, three thousand artillery pieces, absolute air superiority, and unlimited ammunition.

The attack began on September 12 with a four-hour barrage, but when the infantry went in, it encountered not dug-in resistance but merely a rear guard shielding the escape of eight shabby, undermanned German divisions. The entire salient fell in a single day. Fifteen thousand German troops succeeded in getting themselves captured, handing over four hundred and fifty guns in doing so. Pershing and his staff immediately began preparations for another attack in an area bordered by the heights of the River Meuse and the Argonne Forest. Here the Germans would be waiting with a twelve-miles-deep defensive system nearly as formidable as the Hindenburg Line. But Pershing had eight hundred and twenty thousand men to throw against them, six hundred thousand of them Americans, plus four thousand guns and enough shells for those guns to fire at their maximum rate until their barrels burned out. The staff was given fourteen days to get everything ready.

The rest of the world was falling apart for the Germans. The Serbian, British, French, Greek and Italian troops of Franchet d'Esperey's Army of the Orient, though weakened by malaria and influenza, unleashed their attack on strong Bulgarian and German entrenchments outside Salonika. For several days the defenders held their ground so successfully that yet another effort to break out of Salonika seemed doomed to end in failure. But then, their confidence flagging because of shortages of ammunition and supplies, the Bulgarians attempted a limited retreat aimed at drawing the attackers into an ambush. It proved a fatal mistake: Franchet d'Esperey's aircraft began to attack almost as soon as the Bulgarians were out of their defenses. The withdrawal turned into a rout. The Bulgarian troops, weary of a long war that had accomplished nothing and disaffected from the king who had consigned them to the Central Powers, abandoned the fight. Franchet d'Esperey's advance units reached a position from which the Hungarian interior lay open to them. German troops were dispatched to salvage the situation, but they had no real hope of doing so. "We could not answer every single cry for help," Ludendorff would lament later. "We had to insist that Bulgaria must do something for herself, for otherwise we, too, were lost." On September 25 the Bulgarians asked for an armistice; it was granted five days later. The Turks, having been defeated by an Allied force under British General Edmund Allenby in Palestine, were in retreat toward Damascus and could do nothing about Bulgaria without leaving Constantinople unprotected. The war in the Balkans was over.

On September 28, meeting at their headquarters at Spa, Ludendorff and Hindenburg abandoned their illusions. They admitted to each other that not only the Balkans but the war itself was lost. A few days later Hindenburg would write that this admission had been made unavoidable in large part "as a result of the collapse of our Macedonian front" and Germany's consequent exposure to attack from the east. In the long story of the war, there are few greater ironies than the fact that this was accomplished, after years of disease-ridden idleness, by the gardeners of Salonika.

Ludendorff, all options exhausted, sent his army group commanders a message of desperation. He told them (it is unlikely that they were comforted by his words) that there would be no more withdrawals in the west. Once again he was demanding that every position be held, even against impossible odds. He told his staff that something called pneumonic plague had broken out in the French army—he had heard a rumor of such a development and, he would recall, "clung to that news like a drowning man to a straw." It was nonsense.

The BEF and the French were attacking the Hindenburg Line, capturing soldiers by the thousands and guns by the hundreds, and the Americans and French were attacking on a forty-mile front in the Meuse-Argonne. The war had rarely been bloodier—the British took a hundred and eighty thousand casualties between August 28 and September 26, and the Americans would have twenty-six thousand killed and ninety-five thousand wounded in approximately the same period. But for the Allies such losses were made bearable by the hope that a satisfactory end was coming within sight. Obviously the Germans could not possibly stand up against all the blows being directed at them without collapsing eventually. "I have seen prisoners coming from the Battle of the Somme, Mons and Messines and along the road to Menin," a British sergeant wrote home. "Then they had an expression of hard defiance on their faces; their eyes were saying: 'You've had the better of me; but there are many others like me still to carry on the fight, and in the end we shall crush you.' Now their soldiers are no more than a pitiful crowd. Exhaustion of the spirit which always accompanies exhaustion of the body. They are marked with the sign of the defeated."

The end of the story is as much a tale of politics as of combat. The fighting continued on its immense scale, with the dominance of the Allies increasingly undeniable. Though the best of the surviving German units continued to resist with a determination that at times almost defies belief, they were obviously sacrificing themselves in a lost cause. The Allies now had six million men in the west, but as their artillery and tank advantage became overwhelming and the tactics pioneered by Monash were widely adopted, not all those men were needed. Guns, tanks, and aircraft rather than the bodies of the troops became the hammers with which the Germans were destroyed and driven back. The French now had nearly 40 percent of their army—more than a million men—assigned to the artillery. They had nearly six thousand medium and heavy guns, compared with three hundred in 1914. When the Canadians finally broke through the Hindenburg Line on September 28 and 29, they were able to do so in large part by firing almost nine hundred and forty-four thousand artillery rounds in those two days. Early in October twelve thousand *tons* of munitions were being fired every twenty-four hours. France's 75mm light field guns were firing two hundred and eighty thousand rounds daily. To be a German soldier on or near the front was to live under a round-the-clock Bruchmüller barrage.

Though the German line was being punctured with increasing regularity— on October 5 each of Haig's four armies broke through the Hindenburg Line at one or more points—none of these successes turned into a rout. Low on food and ammunition, never able to get a day's rest, the hard core of the German army continued to give up its ground grudgingly, to take a heavy toll of the advancing Allied troops, and even to counterattack at critical junctures. In some places the German line was manned only by officers with machine guns, but still it never dissolved. Amazingly, the number of British, French, and American troops being killed in combat continued to exceed German fatalities.

Almost 90 percent of the men in an American Marine battalion were killed or wounded in an ultimately successful effort to drive the Germans off a hill in Champagne—a region, as one of the attackers would recall, that years of fighting had reduced to "blackened, branchless stumps, upthrust through the churned earth...naked, leprous chalk...a wilderness of craters, large and small, wherein no yard of earth lay untouched." This same Marine left a vivid account of how horrifically difficult it could be to advance against the German defenders even at this late and, for them, hopeless stage in the war: "All along the extended line the saffron shrapnel flowered, flinging death and mutilation down. Singing balls and jagged bits of steel spattered on the hard ground like sheets of hail; the line writhed and staggered, steadied and went on, closing toward the center as the shells bit into it. High-explosive shells came with the shrapnel, and where they fell geysers of torn earth and black smoke roared up to mingle with the devilish yellow in the air. A foul murky cloud of dust and smoke formed and went with the thinning companies, a cloud lit with red flashes and full of howling death. The silent ridge to the left awoke with machine guns and rifles, and sibilant rushing flights of nickel-coated missiles from Maxim and Mauser struck down where the shells spared. An increasing trail of crumpled brown figures lay behind the battalion as it went. The raw smell of blood was in men's nostrils."

Heavy autumn rains also slowed the Allied advance. So did the difficulty of the terrain and the strength of the remaining German infrastructure, especially along the eastern sections of the front where the Americans were attacking. Still another problem was the sheer size of the Allied forces—the difficulties of keeping so many men and guns deployed, supplied, and in motion. Things became so complicated in the Argonne that Pershing suspended his offensive for most of a week to get them sorted out.

In the immediate aftermath of the Salonika disaster, Ludendorff met with Admiral Paul von Hintze, who had become foreign minister after the forced resignation of Kühlmann. Ludendorff, echoing what he had already acknowledged to Hindenburg, outlined the truth of the situation. He said an armistice was not only advisable but needed immediately. Hintze was shocked to discover that Ludendorff thought a cease-fire could be secured within a few days. More astonishingly, he wanted an agreement that would allow the German armies to pull back to their own border, rest their troops and build their defenses, and later resume the fight if they chose to do so. The conversation was not a calm exchange of views; at one point Ludendorff, in one of his rages, collapsed to the floor.

Hintze's objectives were to save Germany and the Hohenzollern dynasty. To this end, once he and Ludendorff had agreed to approach Woodrow Wilson about an armistice based on his Fourteen Points, he made a surprising proposal. He suggested something that he called "revolution from above." This was to be a transformation of the German political system that would demonstrate to the Allies that Germany was now under progressive, even democratic leadership, and that the change had been accomplished by, rather than in spite of, Kaiser Wilhelm. Actually, the plan was far from revolutionary; its most radical innovation was giving representatives of the Reichstag a place in the cabinet. This made it possible for Ludendorff, and later the kaiser, to assent. Modest as the changes were, however, in the context of Prussian and Hohenzollern history and in the eyes of the conservatives they were a shocking violation of tradition. Even Hertling, not a Prussian, resigned the chancellorship rather than accept what Hintze proposed. On September 27 the kaiser—a "broken and suddenly aged man," according to one officer, but doing everything possible to salvage something of his inheritance—signed a proclamation of parliamentary government, a thing that, as he knew, every one of his forebears except his own father would have considered an abomination. His signature was the strongest imaginable evidence of how desperate the German leaders now understood their situation to be. It was also, sadly, a way of maneuvering the liberals and socialists in the Reichstag into taking a share of the blame for the disaster that was unfolding.

Hintze insisted that, to demonstrate that the proclamation was not mere empty rhetoric, he must join Hertling in resigning. The kaiser and Ludendorff tried to dissuade him but failed. The situation was unraveling rapidly. On September 30 a member of Ludendorff's staff, a mere major, was dispatched to Berlin to inform the Reichstag of what was happening on the Western Front. The truth so totally contradicted everything that the Reichstag deputies (and the public) had been told previously that it dealt a mortal blow to the credibility of government and military alike. Three days later "the one prominent royalist liberal in the empire," Prince Max of Baden, succeeded Hertling as chancellor and was charged with arranging a peace. He was a man of ability though in poor health, and the fact that he was well known within the German establishment for reformist sympathies was supposed to show the Allies that a new kind of government, one with which the democracies could come to terms, was in place in Berlin. The Allies saw only the elevation of a man who was both a relative of the kaiser's and a member of Baden's royal house. The choice of Prince Max was ill conceived not because of who he was but because of how he appeared to Germany's enemies: as simply more of the same.

On the day he took office the prince signed a note that had been drafted by Hintze and was addressed to Woodrow Wilson. It requested an immediate armistice, accepting the peace terms that the president had been issuing through the course of 1918. Wilson replied promptly and in firm but almost friendly terms, advising the Germans to confirm their acceptance of the

Fourteen Points and their willingness to withdraw from all occupied territory. Prince Max's government, encouraged, signaled its agreement. The Allied armies, meanwhile—this was the second week of October—were briefly stymied on the Western Front. The Americans were finally clearing the Argonne (a dashing young brigadier general named Douglas MacArthur constantly exposed himself to enemy fire), but they had taken heavy casualties during a hard, protracted fight at the end of which they found themselves

Brigadier General Douglas MacArthur
A dashing—and risk-taking—young division commander.

facing still stronger defenses farther east. Ludendorff found new straws to clutch at. He began to talk of line-shortening measures that could, he insisted, enable the Germans to hold out through the approaching winter, wear down the Allies through attrition, and extract acceptable terms.

But Wilson was under pressure at home. The American public, after a year and a half of propaganda and patriotic oratory, had become so passionately anti-German as to be in a state resembling mass hysteria. Members of Congress responded in ways calculated to enhance their own popularity. The president had been severely criticized for what was seen as the gentle tenor of his response to the German request, his party had only a thin majority in both houses of Congress, and the midterm elections scheduled for November 5 threatened to give control to his Republican foes. Everything and everyone, the French and British not least, were pushing him to take a harder line.

Then on October 12 a young U-boat commander fired two torpedoes into the hull of the steamer *Leinster* as it plied its usual course between Ireland and the west coast of England. Almost four hundred and fifty people perished, a hundred and thirty-five women and children among them. Once again the war was repeating itself. It was the *Lusitania* revisited, though this time with even more devastating political consequences. All the Allies seized the opportunity to toughen the peace terms that they had proposed earlier, when the outcome of the war had been less certain. Wilson extricated himself from his domestic problems by sending a new note to Berlin. He not only demanded an end to submarine warfare but adopted an entirely new tone. He made reference to the "arbitrary" power of Germany's military elite and the threat it posed for the world. He declared that any armistice terms must be settled not with him, not even with the Allied governments acting jointly, but with the commanders in the field. With this he took himself off the hook.

Ludendorff's talk of holding the line in the west, meanwhile, was being rendered meaningless by events in the east. Hungary had separated itself from the Austro-Hungarian empire, declaring itself an autonomous nation. Emperor Karl, attempting to save something from the wreckage, issued a manifesto that transformed what remained of the empire into a federation in which all the members, even nationalities as obscure as the Ruthenians, would have their own national councils. No one paid attention. All the pieces of Karl's empire were going their own ways. The remnants of his army were breaking up as well. Various non-Austrian units—Croatian, Czech, Magyar, Romanian, and others—were marching home. The road to central Europe lay open to Franchet d'Esperey's Army of the Orient. Romania, the source of oil supplies without which the Germans could not have continued the war beyond several months, was his for the taking.

October 17 brought a gathering of the German Council of War—Kaiser

Wilhelm, Hindenburg, Ludendorff, and the new government's leading officials. Ludendorff was at his least rational, not only repeating his determination to hold out through the winter (that very night he would learn that the
British had made a new breakthrough and were again advancing) but threatening to resign if other generals were allowed even to express their opinions.
He demanded that the pointless submarine campaign be continued in defiance of Wilson. The kaiser, somehow, found it possible to agree. Prince Max
alone dissented. He adopted Ludendorff's old tactic, threatening to resign if
Wilson's terms were not accepted in every detail. He carried the day—letting
him go so soon after attaching such importance to the creation of his "liberal" government was impossible. In so doing, he broke Ludendorff's power
at a single stroke.

Crown Prince Rupprecht of Bavaria, still commanding the German army
group in the north, sent a warning (no longer to Ludendorff, significantly, but
to Prince Max) that if an armistice were not arranged soon the enemy could
not be kept from invading Germany. General Wilhelm Gröner, who had
started the war as head of the German railway system and held other important positions since, finding himself at odds with Ludendorff along the way,
reported that at least two hundred thousand troops, possibly as many as a
million and a half (it was no longer possible to keep track), were missing,
many of them having deserted.

Crown Prince
Rupprecht of Bavaria
*Descendant of English kings,
left by the war without a
home to return to.*

The blood continued to flow—one hundred and thirty-three thousand French troops were killed, wounded, or reported missing in October—but always the Allies were attacking and always the Germans were slipping deeper into disorder. The Germans were without replacements, almost without reserves, while the Allies had grown so rich in manpower that they were able to pull the Anzac Corps out of the line. Monash's troops were near the breaking point. Monash himself had adopted the habit of keeping his left hand pocketed because he could not keep it from trembling.

On October 22 Admiral Franz von Hipper, newly appointed chief of the German High Seas Fleet, tried to execute what he called Operation Plan 19, according to which his ships were to put to sea and engage the British and American fleets in a final, suicidal *Götterdämmerung*. Learning of this plan, the crews of three dreadnoughts mutinied at Kiel and ran red banners of revolution up their masts. The Kiel army garrison joined the revolt, which quickly spread, and the kaiser's prized fleet ceased to exist even as a potential fighting force.

On October 23 the Germans were shocked to receive a third note from Wilson, who was now only two weeks from the congressional elections. "If the Government of the United States must deal with the military masters and monarchical autocrats of Germany," the president declared, "... it must demand not peace negotiations but surrender." Wilson's harsh new tone provoked a message to the German troops, written by Ludendorff and signed by him and Hindenburg. "Our enemies merely pay lip service to the idea of a just peace in order to deceive us and break our resistance," it said. "For us soldiers Wilson's reply can therefore only constitute a challenge to continue resisting to the limit of our strength." Ludendorff traveled from his headquarters to Berlin, where his purpose was to terminate Prince Max's dialogue with Washington. Upon arrival he found that his message had created a furor. It had aroused the indignation of a public hungry for peace, of a large part of the Reichstag, of Prince Max, and even of the military. It had provoked so many protests from the army's field commanders that it had to be withdrawn—a fresh humiliation for Ludendorff. Members of the Reichstag were demanding his removal. Some were saying that if peace was impossible as long as Kaiser Wilhelm remained on the throne, then Wilhelm too must go.

Every day, almost every hour, brought word of new disasters. In Italy an Allied force of fifty-six divisions, three of them British and two French, was attacking northward in what would be known as the Battle of Vittorio Veneto, an effort by the Italians to seize as much territory as possible before the fighting ended. The Austrians, rather than resisting, rose up in revolt. Half a million of them surrendered. Their generals, helpless, sent a delegation to Trieste to beg for an armistice.

Ludendorff in Berlin began talking of upholding something that he termed "soldier's honor" through a mustering of the entire German nation for a final Wagnerian fight to the death. The deputy chancellor, after listening to the general's rant, replied simply and poignantly. "I am a plain ordinary citizen and civilian," he said. "All I can see is people who are starving." On October 26 Hindenburg and Ludendorff met privately with the kaiser. Ludendorff, understanding that his position had become impossible, coldly offered his resignation. When the kaiser offered him transfer to a field command, he refused and asked to be relieved. This time the kaiser accepted. Hindenburg too asked to be relieved. "You will stay," Wilhelm told him curtly. Hindenburg bowed in acquiescence. For the rest of his life Ludendorff would regard Hindenburg's obedience as an unforgivable betrayal.

When news of Ludendorff's departure was announced in Berlin movie houses, audiences cheered. Germany had become so dangerous for him that he slipped away in disguise and soon was in exile in Sweden.

On October 27 a fourth German note went to President Wilson. It was a capitulation, stating almost abjectly that Germany "looked forward to proposals for an armistice that would usher in a peace of justice as outlined by the President." In other words, the Germans were now prepared to have the president tell them what the terms of peace would be, though they assumed that those terms would correspond to the Fourteen Points. For nine long days Wilson did not deign to reply. While Berlin waited, the Americans captured the city of Sedan and severed the Germans' last north-south rail line in France. Turkey and Austria surrendered, and even Bavaria began to explore a separate peace. Revolution broke out in nearly every provincial capital. In Munich a republic was declared, the king fled, and Crown Prince Rupprecht found himself without a home to return to.

On October 28 the commanders in chief of the Allied armies met to decide on the armistice terms to be offered the Germans. The discussion was not amiable. Haig had the easiest expectations, proposing that the Germans be required to withdraw from Belgium and France and surrender Alsace-Lorraine. Pétain was tougher, demanding that the Germans withdraw east of the Rhine even north of Alsace-Lorraine and so hand over large areas of their homeland to the Allies. Pershing was even more demanding, laying out terms far more punitive than anything suggested by the others.

A new dynamic came into play: the desire of the British and French to end the war as quickly as possible out of fear that, if it continued, the Americans would become so dominant that they could dictate the peace. Such fears were not irrational; they had begun with Wilson's earlier failure even to consult with the Entente while communicating with the Germans. And serious issues divided the Allies. Lloyd George had very different ideas from Wilson's on how such questions as postwar trade, freedom of the seas, and the German colonies should be decided. When the president's Fourteen Points were introduced into the discussion, the generals had to send out for a copy. None of them could say just what it was that the president had proposed.

On November 1 Kaiser Wilhelm was asked to abdicate. He refused and talked of leading the armies back to Germany to put down the spreading revolt. General Gröner, having been appointed quartermaster general in Ludendorff's place, asked the most senior generals on the Western Front if their troops would follow the kaiser home and participate in suppressing the population. An able and decent man who in future years would twice save a fledgling German democracy from collapse, becoming an enemy of Hitler's by doing so, Gröner had little doubt about what the answer would be. He received thirty-nine replies. One said yes, fifteen said possibly, and twenty-three said no. Soon after being informed of this, told by Hindenburg that his safety could no longer be assured, Wilhelm abdicated. He crossed the border into Holland, where the queen had agreed to accept him.

On November 8 a German delegation led by Matthias Erzberger, head of the Catholic Center Party, arrived at Allied headquarters in Compiègne. The Berlin government, faced with civil war and fearful of a Communist take-over, had instructed Erzberger to accept whatever terms were offered. Foch, after making it clear that there would be no discussion of terms, pre-sented the conditions under which the Allied commanders would agree to a thirty-day armistice. These included German withdrawal to east of the Rhine within fourteen days; repudiation of the Treaty of Brest-Litovsk and with-drawal to the eastern borders of August 1, 1914; the handover of five thou-sand artillery pieces, three thousand mortars, thirty thousand machine guns, and two thousand aircraft; and the surrender of Germany's possessions in Africa. The Allied naval blockade would continue—alarming news for the representatives of a nation desperate for food. The Germans were given three days to decide—take it or leave it. Eventually a few minor adjustments were permitted: the Allies too feared a Communist revolution in Germany and so reduced the number of machine guns to be surrendered in order to give the German authorities means with which to restore order. Erzberger, who would later be assassinated for his "betrayal" of the Fatherland, led his fellow delegates in signing.

It was over. The armistice went into effect at eleven A.M. on November 11. Not everyone on the Allied side was pleased. "No no no!" Mangin exclaimed when he learned of the terms. "We must go right into the heart of Germany. The armistice should be signed there. The Germans will not admit that they are beaten. You do not finish wars like this . . . It is a fatal error and France will pay for it!"

THE FATE OF MEN AND NATIONS

WHATEVER IT WAS THAT FOLLOWED THE ARMISTICE OF November 11, 1918, it was not peace.

Something on the order of 9.5 million men were dead: four million from the Central Powers, almost a million more than that on the Allies' side. Among them were 1.8 million Russians, nearly 1.4 million French, eight hundred thousand Turks, seven hundred twenty-three thousand British, five hundred seventy-eight thousand Italians, and one hundred fourteen thousand Americans. (Romania and Serbia each lost more than twice as many men as the United States.)

The tally was two million dead for Germany, one million for Austria-Hungary. Germany had lost fifty-five men for every hour, thirteen hundred thirty for every day, of the fifty-two months of the war. One in every fifty citizens of the Hapsburg empire had been killed.

These numbers do not include the more than fifteen million men wounded, or the nearly nine million who had become prisoners of war. Nor do they include the numberless millions of civilians who had died in every imaginable way.

Whatever else it did, the armistice did not end the killing. Life in Europe had become too deranged, too many things remained unsettled, and too many young men who knew nothing but war found that there was nothing for them to go home to, for that to be possible.

Russia proceeded almost seamlessly to an enormous civil war that would go on for years, kill more of its people than the Great War, draw in troops from western Europe and the United States, and end with the Communists in firm control. Just weeks after the armistice, an uprising aimed at establishing something like a Bolshevik regime in Germany erupted in Berlin and was bloodily suppressed not by the civil authorities but by rough paramilitary "Free Corps" made up of demobilized German soldiers unwilling to lay down their arms. Communist governments briefly seized power in Budapest and Munich. Fighting over territory erupted in the newborn nations of Poland and Czechoslovakia, in Transylvania, in Ukraine, in the Caucasus, and in the disputed borderland between Turkey and Greece. "Central Europe is aflame with anarchy," American Secretary of State Lansing wrote in April 1919. "The people see no hope."

The disorder was beyond anyone's power to control, and the soldiers who had won the war had little interest in trying. They wanted to go home. When troops based near Folkestone in Britain learned of plans to send them to Russia, they mutinied. Crews of French ships in the Black Sea did the same thing for the same reason.

This was the state of affairs as the victors gathered in Paris in January 1919 to remake the world. Dozens of nations were invited to attend, but from the start it was clear that all decisions would be made by a very small number of them. At first the proceedings were dominated by a Council of Ten, the heads of government and foreign ministers of Britain, France, Italy, Japan, and the United States. Eventually even this group was found to be too large for secrecy to be maintained, and the foreign ministers were excluded. Japan interested itself only in issues related to Asia and the Pacific, Italy eventually walked out in indignation over not getting everything it wanted, and in the end the conference was dominated by three men: Georges Clemenceau, David Lloyd George, and Woodrow Wilson.

The Moscow government of V. I. Lenin was absent because its former allies not only feared and refused to recognize it but were supporting its White Russian enemies. In a radical departure from historical practice (a tradition that had given France, for example, a prominent part in the Treaty of Vienna after the final defeat of Napoleon), Germany was excluded as an outlaw nation. The Austro-Hungarian and Ottoman empires had ceased to exist, and Austria and Turkey hardly seemed to matter. Out of the ruins new countries were emerging almost overnight: Czechoslovakia, Finland, Hungary, Lithuania, Poland, and the Yugoslavia that had coalesced around Serbia. They and others that would soon emerge—Estonia and Latvia in the Baltic, Lebanon and Syria in the Middle East—could only wait on the sidelines (often fighting with their neighbors as they did so) while the great powers decided their fates.

Those powers assembled in Paris with very different agendas. By the end of the war Britain had already achieved its primary objectives. Belgium was saved, the German naval threat was eliminated, and the British army had made spectacular conquests in the Middle East, where the collapse of Russia had eliminated a longtime rival. Lloyd George, his coalition government having been resoundingly returned to office in a December election, had few major aspirations beyond protecting the British Empire's gains, restoring some kind of balance of power on the continent, and satisfying popular demand for the punishment of Germany. The public's hunger for revenge, white-hot after four years of suffering and anti-German propaganda, had somehow to be balanced against the desirability of maintaining Germany as a buffer against Communist Russia and as a future trading partner.

It was very different with Clemenceau. Germany, though defeated, remained larger and more populous than France, which no longer had a Russian ally to even the scales. Clemenceau's vision, one shared by the French nation, was of a Germany either dismantled or so permanently disabled as to be incapable of posing a threat.

And then there was Wilson, who fancied himself a disinterested mediator free of the cynical and selfish calculations of the Old World. He arrived in Paris aspiring to end not only the Great War but all war through the creation of a League of Nations, and to make the world "safe for democracy" through the implementation of his Fourteen Points (in which he would gradually lose interest). In light of the strict secrecy with which he and his allies undertook to redraw the map of the world, there is irony in his first point's demand for "open covenants of peace, openly arrived at." The irony is deepened by the contrast between Wilson's preachments about the right of national self-determination and the haste with which Britain, France, Italy, and Japan were gobbling up whole regions all around the world without pausing to consider what the peoples affected might want. Irish Americans were outraged by Wilson's refusal to support Ireland's demands for separation from Britain. Other ethnic groups felt similarly betrayed.

Eventually, probably in an effort to maintain some degree of influence with Clemenceau and Lloyd George, Wilson abandoned even the pretense of championing the Fourteen Points. He became as vengeful toward Germany as Clemenceau, accusing Americans who questioned his ideas for the League of Nations of being "pro-German."

A further irony is that Italy and Japan, neither of which had contributed greatly to the defeat of Germany (Japan had contributed essentially nothing), achieved more at Paris than any other country and yet came away not only unhappy but alienated. Italy was given even more territory than it had been promised by the 1915 Treaty of London (Wilson consented while complaining that the United States had not signed that agreement and was not bound by it), absorbing Alpine regions inhabited by hundreds of thousands of ethnically German Austrians. But when it was refused Fiume in Croatia, its delegates indignantly packed up and returned to Rome. For centuries Italy had been dominated by Vienna. Now, its empire gone, Austria was an almost negligible little country of seven million, a poor and landlocked place so alone that it petitioned to be absorbed into Germany. Italy found itself stronger than at any time since the fall of the Roman

Empire and with no neighbors dangerous enough to be feared. It saw little need to remain on friendly terms with Britain or France and chose to be aggrieved. Its young democracy had been badly compromised by wartime struggles for power in Rome, and the way was cleared for the emergence of Benito Mussolini.

Japan had prospered during the war, selling industrial products and raw materials to the West. It emerged in possession of Germany's North Pacific colonies, in control of China's Shantung Province (China protested, but to no effect), and with big ambitions on the Asian mainland. At Paris, their conquests ratified, the Japanese asked for one thing more: inclusion in the covenant of the new League of Nations of an "equality clause" that would declare discrimination on the basis of race to be unacceptable. No enforcement provisions were demanded; for the Japanese this was a symbolic issue, an assurance that they were accepted as equals by Europe and America. When Wilson offered no support (the United States excluded Asian immigrants, and the western states were determined to continue doing so) and the Australians objected vehemently for similar reasons, the Japanese washed their hands of the West. Dominant in East Asia, they like Italy saw no need to seek the approval of their onetime allies before pursuing their next objectives.

Turkey was quietly accepting the loss of its empire until, at the insistence of a French government seeking to strengthen its position in the Balkans, the Aegean port city of Smyrna was given to Greece. This sparked anger in Constantinople, the rise of a Turkish nationalist movement under Mustafa Kemal, the hero of Gallipoli, and a war that would continue until Smyrna was taken from the Greeks. To the south, Britain and France came into conflict over how to divide their Middle Eastern spoils. Britain took Palestine, opening it to emigration by European Jews under the Balfour Declaration. After suppressing a rebellion in Mesopotamia, it threw Kurdish, Sunni, and Shia populations together in a new puppet kingdom called Iraq. France was allowed to have Lebanon and, despite deep reluctance on Britain's part, Syria.

Every one of these developments planted seeds for generations of discord. All of them were peripheral, however, to the great central question of Germany. Clemenceau proposed breaking it up—separatist movements had appeared in Bavaria and the Rhineland, and he was eager to exploit them—but Lloyd George would have none of it. Clemenceau then suggested turning Germany's Rhineland regions into an independent ministate that would in practical terms be a French dependency. This too went nowhere. While such questions were being debated, the naval blockade was kept in place, needlessly causing the death from starvation and disease of perhaps a quarter of a million Germans, many of them children. Future president Herbert Hoover, in charge of European relief operations, begged for permission to send food to Germany and was rebuffed even by Wilson. Those Germans who did not die were left deeply, and justifiably bitter.

The complications were endless. The Allies refused to be bound by the terms of the November armistice, and Clemenceau and Lloyd George (neither of whom liked or respected Wilson) happily joined the American president in forgetting the Fourteen Points. The question of reparations moved to center stage. Britain and France had hoped that the loans they had received from the United States would be forgiven after the war. When Wilson refused, both men looked to German reparations as the solution to their financial problems. Colossal amounts were suggested—sums sufficient to cover not only all damage to Belgian and French property but the costs incurred by the Allies in fighting the war and the pensions due to their veterans. The question of how much to demand, and when to require payment, became impossibly tangled. Lloyd George worried that, if Germany were pushed too hard, it would fall to the Communists. Clemenceau feared that, if the wrecked German economy was not drained white, it would fuel a military resurgence. Both, as a kind of sidelight, wanted to put the former kaiser on trial for war crimes, but the Queen of Holland refused to hand him over. Wilson, once the advocate of peace without victory, now regarded Germany as undeserving of the slightest consideration. Neither he nor Lloyd George nor Clemenceau considered the possibility that, Berlin's imperial regime having been removed, welcoming the new Weimar Republic into the family of nations might have been a sensible next step.

Not until May was the Weimar government directed to send a delegation to Paris. Upon arrival, the delegates were confined behind barbed wire and allowed no contact with anyone. On June 7 they were summoned to appear before the Allies and presented with what would be called the Treaty of Versailles. The terms included:

German acknowledgment that it was solely and entirely responsible for the war.

Germany's exclusion from the League of Nations, the creation of which was embedded in the treaty.

The return of Alsace and Lorraine to France without a plebiscite in either province.

The surrender of small amounts of German territory to Belgium.

French occupation of Germany's coal-rich Saar for fifteen years, after which the region's disposition was to be determined by plebiscite.

Allied occupation of all German territory west of the Rhine for fifteen years.

No union of Austria and Germany.

The award of the Sudetenland, a region whose population was overwhelmingly German, to Czechoslovakia.

The award of German port cities on the Baltic to the new nation of Poland, creating a "Polish corridor" that would separate East Prussia from the rest of Germany.

The surrender of Upper Silesia, long part of Germany, to Poland.

The surrender of northern Schleswig to Denmark.

The limitation of the German army to one hundred thousand volunteer troops, the dissolution of the general staff and the air force, and the destruction of all U-boats and all but six of Germany's battleships.

Germany was to pay reparations, but the amount and the time over which they were to be paid remained unspecified. This was to Clemenceau's liking. He hoped that Germany would be unable or unwilling to pay, that its noncompliance would allow France to stay on the Rhine indefinitely, and that the people of the occupied territories might eventually choose to become part of France.

The head of the German delegation, when he saw what was in the treaty, summed up his interpretation of it in four words. "Germany," he said, "renounces its existence."

The terms of the treaty united the warring factions of German society. Officials in Weimar complained that Germany had been deceived and betrayed, that it had accepted an armistice under the Fourteen Points, and that the Allies were now ignoring both the terms of that armistice and the Wilson formula. But Germany was continuing to starve, and it was incapable of defending itself. When the Allies threatened to invade, the government had little choice but to sign.

It did so in much the same spirit in which the Russians had accepted Brest-Litovsk, conscious of being coerced, convinced that Germany had no moral obligation to comply. A further source of poison was the fact that the Allies had chosen to deal with the Weimar government exclusively, leaving the German army uninvolved. The ground was prepared for claims that the army, never having surrendered and still in possession of vast conquered territories at the time of the armistice, had been "stabbed in the back" by cowardly and traitorous liberal politicians. Germans were given an excuse to despise their new government.

By the time the Treaty of Versailles was signed, several of the characters in the drama of the war's beginnings were dead. Tsar Nicholas and his wife and their five children had been executed by their Bolshevik captors in

Siberia. István Tisza, the Hungarian prime minister who in July 1914 tried to slow Vienna's rush to war, was assassinated by Communists as Hungary began to disintegrate in October 1918. Gavrilo Princip, the killer of Franz Ferdinand, had died in jail of tuberculosis in April 1918, regretting nothing except the inadvertent shooting of the archduke's innocent wife.

Others didn't last long.

Theobald von Bethmann Hollweg, whose son had been killed in the war, died in retirement in 1921.

Henry Wilson, who left the British army to become a member of Parliament from Ulster, was shot to death by Irish Republican army gunmen on the doorstep of his home.

Karl I, deposed as the last Hapsburg emperor but refusing to abdicate, died of pneumonia in exile, barely thirty-five years old.

Woodrow Wilson, his League of Nations rejected by the U.S. Senate, left the White House in poor health in 1921 and died in 1924.

President Wilson's end was paralleled by that of Lenin, who was also disabled by cerebral hemorrhages and also died in 1924.

Many of the old soldiers faded slowly away.

Robert Nivelle finished his career in North Africa and was heard of no more.

William Robertson commanded the British occupation troops in the Rhineland in 1919 and 1920, was made a field marshal and baronet, and went into retirement.

Alexei Brusilov served the Bolsheviks until 1924.

Ferdinand Foch was made a Marshal of France and heaped with honors. Then, like Joseph Joffre and Erich von Falkenhayn, he withdrew from the world stage.

Luigi Cadorna, in disgrace after his calamitous failure at Caporetto, would be rehabilitated by Mussolini and made a field marshal in 1924.

Franz Conrad von Hötzendorf moved to Germany and, like many others, devoted the twilight of his life to writing self-serving memoirs of limited historical value.

Douglas Haig, though made an earl and voted a gift of £100,000 by Parliament at the end of the war, was too controversial and too hated by Lloyd George to be made chief of the imperial general staff. He devoted himself to raising money for needy veterans until his death in 1928.

John Monash, the brilliant commander of the Anzac Corps, stayed in Europe long enough to oversee the return of his troops and establish educational programs to help prepare them for civilian careers. He was an Australian national idol after the war, and a university was named for him.

The comparably brilliant Arthur Currie of the Canadian Corps had a

much different postwar career. The shadows that had pursued him to
Europe followed him home, and he was given an insultingly chilly welcome by Canada's political leaders. He filed suit when a journalist charged
him in print of squandering the lives of his troops at Passchendaele. When
his accuser was found guilty, Currie was put in a carriage and paraded
through the streets by crowds of cheering veterans. He found employment
as vice chancellor of McGill University and faded into inexplicably deep
obscurity. His name does not appear in *The Macmillan Dictionary of the
First World War*, a hefty volume that gives substantial attention to the likes
of Admiral Alexander Kolchak and Ante Trumbic of Croatia. Nor is it listed
in the 834-page *Harper Encyclopedia of Military Biography.*

The only senior Great War general who played a genuinely major role
in the postwar world was Mustafa Kemal. Taking the name Atatürk (father
of the people), he became president of the Turkish republic in 1924 and
began turning it into a secular, westernized state.

Kaiser Wilhelm lived quietly on a small estate in Holland until 1940,
putting pins in maps, at the end, to mark the progress of Germany's armies
in a new war.

His cousin George V died four years before Wilhelm, his last years troubled only by the refusal of his eldest son and heir to break off a scandalous
relationship with an American divorcée named Wallis Simpson.

Georges Clemenceau, who had already been in his late seventies when
he became Premier of France in 1917, lived on to have probably the fullest
postwar years of any of the heads of government. Resented by many
French politicians for the way he had monopolized the management of the
war in its last year and the negotiations that followed, he ran for president
in 1920, lost, and resigned as premier. He then traveled the world, hunting tigers in India, wrote books, and made a tour of the United States to
warn of the dangers of American indifference to affairs in Europe before
dying at eighty-eight. His hatred of Germany never waned.

Some of the war's great figures lived too long. David Lloyd George lost
his place as prime minister in 1922, when the Conservative Party left his
coalition and took power independently. His own Liberal Party had withered by then, and Labour had become Britain's most important opposition
party. Lloyd George remained in Parliament for more than two decades, a
sadly marginal figure without a power base. He never again held office.

Erich Ludendorff, upon returning from exile in Sweden, associated himself with the darkest elements in German politics. He became involved in
efforts to overthrow the Weimar Republic in 1920 and 1923 (the second
time in affiliation with Adolf Hitler), ran unsuccessfully for president of the
republic in 1925, and divorced his wife Margarethe. His second wife

encouraged him in a crackpot cultish campaign to rid Germany of Christians, Jews, and Freemasons—of almost the entire population, in short. Ludendorff thus isolated himself not only from everything progressive but even from the Nazis and the Junker officer corps. In the months before his death in 1937, when in a return to something like sanity he began to raise the alarm about the dangers of the Hitler dictatorship, no one was listening.

The most brilliant and dynamic of the Bolsheviks, Leon Trotsky, lost out in a power struggle with Joseph Stalin in the years after Lenin's death. He was expelled from the Russian Communist Party in 1927, exiled to Central Asia in 1928, and expelled from the Soviet Union altogether in 1929. Endlessly pursued by Stalin's agents, he moved on to Turkey, to France, to Norway, and finally in 1936 to Mexico. He was murdered four years later, killed by an ax blow delivered to the back of his skull.

Paul von Hindenburg retired from the German army after the war, already in his seventies. Despite being an avowed monarchist with no respect for the new republic, he consented to run for president in 1925 and, still a national hero, was elected. In 1932, in his eighties and an even more passive figurehead than he had been during the war, he ran for reelection because there seemed to be no alternative to Hitler. Again he was successful. A year later he was persuaded to name Hitler to the chancellorship by associates who assured him that, once in office, Hitler would be easily contained. He was still alive, if barely, as the Nazis began the reign of terror with which they seized control of the government and the country.

An even more melancholy story is that of Henri-Philippe Pétain, who at the start of the Great War had been an aging colonel near retirement and at its end was a Marshal of France and commander in chief of the armies of his nation. In his sixties in 1918, he remained on active duty and moved from one exalted position to another. Eighty-four when Germany invaded France in 1940, he was asked to form a government. When the Germans conquered two-thirds of France, Pétain arranged an armistice and was named chief of state with nearly unlimited powers by a new government based at Vichy. His performance during the German occupation was ambiguous at worst—he remained in office out of fear that his departure would lead to worse Nazi outrages, and attempted in many ways to obstruct the occupiers—but after liberation he was put on trial by the new French government and condemned to death. The sentence was reduced to life imprisonment by Pétain's onetime protégé Charles de Gaulle. He died in confinement on an island off France's Atlantic coast in 1951, aged ninety-five.

One of the war's youngest leading figures also appeared to live too long. Winston Churchill's career prospered in the decade after the Treaty of Versailles. He served as secretary of state for war from 1919 to 1921, as colonial secretary in 1921 and 1922, and as chancellor of the exchequer from 1924 to 1929. Along the way he left the Liberals to return to the Conservative Party, where he had begun a quarter century earlier, but the Conservatives despised him for his old apostasy and distrusted him deeply. From 1929 on he was consigned to what he called "the political wilderness," a has-been issuing warnings about the rearmament of Nazi Germany that few were prepared to take seriously.

But that is another story.

Notes

PART ONE
July 1914: *Into the Abyss*

The causes of the First World War, and the culpability of the nations and individuals involved, have been controversial through nine decades and appear likely to remain so forever. The relevant literature is almost infinite in quantity and in the variety of conclusions offered. The author, having attempted to consult as much of this literature as possible, found many works to be helpful but four to be particularly so: Immanuel Geiss's *July 1914, The Outbreak of the First World War, Selected Documents*, William Jannen, Jr.'s *The Lions of July, Prelude to War, 1914*, Eugenia V. Nomikos and Robert C. North's *International Crisis: The Outbreak of World War I*, and the second volume of Gerhard Ritter's *The Sword and the Scepter: The Problem of Militarism in Germany*. Geiss's book is an invaluable collection of diplomatic communications and government records during the July crisis, though the interpretation that Geiss puts on these communications is itself controversial to the point of being generally discredited. Jannen's day-by-day, hour-by-hour recounting of the crisis is unparalleled in the amount of detail provided, and Ritter offers a uniquely thorough analysis of what was happening on the German (and Austro-Hungarian) side and why.

Page

7 "For heaven's sake!" and "Sophie dear": Taylor, *Fall of the Dynasties*, 13.

7 "It's nothing": Fromkin, 136.

8 "A higher power": Remak, 160.

8 "My purpose...was to plant": Millis, 23.

9 "the imperative duty": the quotes from Bryan, the *Review of Reviews*, and Elihu Root are in Millis, 9–14.

14 "some young Serb might put": Marshall, 25.

15 "he only wanted to die": Z.A.B. Zeman, "The Balkans and the Coming of War," in Evans and Strandmann, *Coming of the First World War*, 20.

16 "In 1908–1909 we would": Ritter, 2:235.

17 In the course of 1913: Conrad's 1913 calls for war are in Strachan, *First World War*, 69.

18 "a final and fundamental": Ibid., 71.

18 "a man...the monarchy needed": Jannen, 3.

19 He had at his disposal: Austria's and Serbia's 1913 manpower figures are in Herrmann, 123.

20   People who knew Franz Ferdinand: The archduke's views on trialism are in, among other sources, Strachan, *First World War,* 68.

25   *Bella gerant alii:* Taylor, *Dynasties,* 75.

27   "Yes, yes, but one is": Remak, 162.

28   Gangs of hooligans: Details about disturbances in Sarajevo and Belgrade are in Jannen, 10; Marshall, 24; and Remak, 147.

28   "into one another's arms": Jannen, 10.

28   "behaving shamefully": Fromkin, 143.

29   "The event almost failed": Ibid.

29   Either of the Austro-Hungarian: Austria-Hungary's mobilization plans are described in Strachan, *First World War,* 291.

30   "Then he's a false rascal!": Geiss, 346.

30   "Who authorized him to act that way?": Jannen, 21.

31   "How often have I asked myself": Ibid., 18.

31   "It was his opinion": Geiss, 77.

31   "did not succeed in convincing me": Ibid., 78.

32   "I don't believe we are headed": MacDonogh, 354.

32   At the July 5–6 meetings: Berchtold's scheme for using Bulgaria to separate Romania from Russia is in Jannen, 30.

33   "put an end to Serbia's intrigues": Ibid., 41.

33   "Our exactions may be hard": An Austro-Hungarian government summary of the council's proceedings, and the quotes in this and the following paragraphs, are in Geiss, 80.

35   "would, as far as can humanly be": Berghahn, 194.

37   "You are setting fire to Europe": Lincoln, 428.

45   "The most brilliant example": Fay, 2:340.

45   "The Royal Government cannot accept": Geiss, 203.

46   The Austrian mobilization that followed: The numbers of divisions are in L.C.F. Turner, "The Russian Mobilization in 1914," in Kennedy, 262.

46   They involved the mustering: troop numbers are in Fay, 298.

48   "I would like to call your attention": Geiss, 206.

49   "a question of the balance": Ibid., 209.

50   "in the most decided way": Ibid., 236.

52   "He was always lecturing me": Jannen, 37.

52   "Nothing has helped": Ibid., 56.

52   "This was more than one could have expected": Ibid., 147.

53   "a capitulation of the most humiliating": Ibid.

53   "Orientals...therefore liars": Fay, 420.

54   "Austria has declared war on us": Jannen, 138.

54   "has left us in the dark concerning": Geiss, 259.

54   He wanted to discuss a number of ideas: The content of the conversation, and the nature of the misunderstanding to which it gave rise, are detailed in Jannen, 133.

55   "complete readiness of France to fulfill": Turner, "Russian Mobilization," in Kennedy, 252.

60   "faith in the power": Massie, *Nicholas and Alexandra,* 16.

60   "Among the falsest": Ibid., 14.

61   "What am I going to do?": Ibid., 43.

62   "ignoble war has been declared": The words of the telegrams, and the kaiser's marginal notes, are in Geiss, 260.

63   One ordered the mobilization: The numbers of army corps and divisions are in Ritter, 2:253.

64   Crowds were gathering in Vienna: The anecdotes about reactions to the impending war, including the words of Russell, Grey, and Churchill, are in Ferguson, 176ff.

65   "the leading nations of Europe": Ritter, 2:253.

65   "kindly impress upon M. Sazonov": Turner, "Russian Mobilization," in Kennedy, 265.

65   In one of his middle-of-the-night: this exchange is in ibid., 263.

66   "Think of the responsibility": Fay, 2:265.

66   Russia's general mobilization: Nomikos and North, 6.

67   "Let Papa . . . not plan war": Taylor, *Dynasties,* 243.

67   "unless Austria is willing": Geiss, 286.

68   "serious error": Jannen, 223.

68   "We are of course, ready": Geiss, 293.

68   "how difficult it would be": Ibid., 317.

69   "What a joke!": Fromkin, 229.

71   "Fear is a bad counselor": The words of Ambassador Nikolaus von Temerin Szécsen are in Jannen, 186.

71   "You must inform German Chancellor": Grey's message to Ambassador Sir Edward Goschen is in Geiss, 315.

72   "must follow in case Russia": The double ultimatum is dealt with in Jannen, 256.

72   "If France had actually": Renouvin, 224.

72   "the peace of Europe": Geiss, 324.

72   "technically impossible": Ibid., 323.

72   "the same guarantee from you": Ibid., 344.

77   "Wherever the Sultan went": Barber, 85.

82   "France will have to regard": Mayeur and Reberieux, 350.

82   An hour later the French government: Joffre's warning is in Fay, 531.

82   Their conversation turned into: An exceptionally thorough and lucid account of the dispute between Germany's military and diplomatic leaders over whether and how to mobilize and declare war is in Ritter, 2:267.

82   "if I thought I could assure": Geiss, 343.

83   "We shall simply march": Jannen, 298.

83   "I assured His Majesty": Strachan, *First World War,* 90.

84   "This pained me a good deal": Renouvin, 251.

85   "it is understandable that each increase": Röhl, 43.

86   "would make it difficult": Geiss, 346.

86   "My impression": Ibid., 347.

87   "I have no other reply": Samsonov and Pourtalès each left an account of their
      last meeting. Not surprisingly, these accounts are not identical in their
      details, but they do not conflict substantially. Elements of their accounts
      have been taken from Gilbert, *First World War,* 30, and Jannen, 311.

PART TWO
August–December 1914: *Racing to Deadlock*

Entering upon August 1914 and the opening of hostilities, the student of
the Great War encounters problems having to do with the number of
casualties suffered by the various belligerent nations in specific battles and in
specific time periods shorter than the war as a whole. Years of research that
included visits to the Imperial War Museum in London, the Library of
Congress, and a variety of archives in and near Paris brought the author to
the conclusion that there is no single, simple, or absolutely authoritative
solution to such problems. Many of such numbers must be taken as approx-
imations, especially in the case of countries whose record-keeping was never
meticulous or whose records have been lost since the war. The best approx-
imations are at a minimum useful as measures of the scale of the fighting
and of the comparative effectiveness of the various armies, and they are
used for this purpose in the present work. The number of published sources
on the Battles of the Marne, Tannenberg, and First Ypres is of course
immense. Different authors shed light on these subjects from different
angles, and many of the resulting works are valuable. The author found the
following works to be notably helpful as guides to these contests: Robert
Asprey's *The First Battle of the Marne* and *The German High Command at War,*
Georges Blond's *The Marne,* Holger H. Herwig's *The First World War:
Germany and Austria,* Henri Isselin's *The Battle of the Marne,* and the first volume of Hew Strachan's epic work-in-progress, *The First World War.*

Page

91   "If the iron dice roll:" Tuchman, *Guns of August,* 74.

91   "a long weary struggle": Barnett, 40.

92   "too reflective, too scrupulous": Ibid., 23.

92   "Art is the only thing": Blond, 30.

93   The so-called Grand Program: Strachan, *First World War,* 62.

93   By 1914, 1.4 million Russian troops: Rutherford, 20.

94 "We should exploit in the West": L.C.F. Turner, "The Significance of the Schlieffen Plan," in Kennedy, 200.

94 His commentaries, which he continued to produce: The weaknesses of the Schlieffen Plan, and Schlieffen's recognition of those weaknesses, are described briefly in Stevenson, *Cataclysm*, 38, and in vastly greater detail in Ritter, 2:193–216.

95 Bismarck had joked: Bismarck, 134: The kaiser said that this quip was Bismarck's "pet motto."

95 As late as 1913: France's alertness to British sensitivities on the subject of Belgium, and Britain's role in discouraging France from planning to violate Belgian neutrality, is described in Asprey, *Marne*, 24.

95 "for the civilian side to have": Ritter, 2:206.

95 "If we were to": Ibid., 2:195.

96 The infantry would have to do this: Herwig, 60.

96 Schlieffen calculated: Schlieffen's estimates of the number of divisions required for executing his plan are in Farrar-Hockley, 6.

96 "Before the Germans reach the Somme": Turner, "Schlieffen Plan," in Kennedy, 202.

96 "It must come to a fight": Asprey, *Marne*, 11.

96 The most challenging aspect: Herwig, 60.

97 "will hardly be possible": Turner, "Schlieffen Plan," in Kennedy, 212.

97 As the years passed: Moltke's changes in the proportions of troops assigned to the German right and left wings are in Stevenson, *Cataclysm*, 39.

97 In its 1914 iteration: Turner, "Schlieffen Plan," in Kennedy, 212.

98 In the thirty days following: The troop and division numbers given here and in the next paragraph are in Ferguson, 92.

100 This measure was a requirement: French and German conscription percentages are in Stevenson, *Cataclysm*, 161.

101 "the most hated man in France": Berenson, 71.

101 Though his enemies accused him: Caillaux's handling of the Morocco crisis is detailed in ibid., 76.

102 "bring Jaurès's pacifist dream": Ibid., 71.

102 "comic interlude": Ibid., 22.

103 "Do not touch me": Ibid., 2.

105 Joffre was demanding: Joffre's demands, and Poincaré's restraining influence, are in Herwig, 58.

106 "The danger is great": Jackson, *Jean Jaurès*, 181.

106 "We have no wish to incite" and "if on the eve of war": Ibid., 176.

107 "everything is finished": Goldberg, 471.

108 His little army: The size of King Albert's force is in Ferguson, 92.

108 Each of these forts contained: Information about the defensive forces at Liège is in Mosier, 58.

108 The Germans, as part: The Liège assault force is described in Herwig, 96.

110 His First Army: The size of Kluck's army is in Stevenson, *Cataclysm*, 43.

110 The first three of these armies: Ibid.

110 This was war on a truly new scale: The size of Wellington's Waterloo force is in Herwig, 48.

114 An advancing army's worst: Strachan, 237.

115 "In such a case": The Joffre-Lanrezac exchange is in Blond, 57.

117 The day after that: Herwig, 88.

118 On August 13, after taking: Belgian casualties at Fort Chaudfontaine are in Mosier, 60.

118 "I ask you to bear witness": Keegan, *Illustrated History,* 78.

118 More than five hundred trains: rail transport data are in Asprey, *German High Command,* 52.

118 Kluck's First Army alone: The German First Army's requirements are in Herwig, 100.

118 August 17: A collision: Russian prisoner totals are in Gilbert, *First World War,* 28.

119 "We cannot ask our Bavarian": Isselin, 33.

119 On this same day: Austrian casualties are in Gilbert, *First World War,* 50.

121 "Our advance in Belgium": Moltke's words are in Keegan, *Illustrated History,* 71.

122 "Do you already hold me": Ritter, 3:14.

122 His intelligence bureau: French estimates of German strength are in Blond, 22.

122 The fourteen French divisions: Numbers of divisions are in Bruce I. Gudmundsen, "Unexpected Encounter at Bertrix," in Cowley, 25.

122 The fight at the town of Rossignol: Casualty totals are in Mosier, 71.

123 French casualties for the war's first month: The numbers are in Stevenson, *Cataclysm,* 45.

123 Among the dead: The ten percent figure is in Asprey, *Marne,* 59.

123 "In a moment it is clear": in Lacouture, 30.

123 The Germans, except on their right: Germany's combat death figure is in Mosier, 72.

128 "Squiff" and "filthy cabinet": Jannen, 325.

131 Grey told his fellow ministers: In later years, criticized for not acting more forcefully during the July crisis, Grey would state that "the idea that one individual sitting in a room in the Foreign Office could pledge a great democracy definitely by his word, in advance, either to take part in a great war or to abstain from taking part in it, is absurd." See Hazelhurst, 51.

133 "the precipitate and peremptory": Ibid., 67.

133 "My own opinion...is that L.G.'s mind": Ibid., 68.

133 "I suppose...that a good three-fourths": Ibid., 32.

134 "The Liberals, very few of them": Ibid., 44.

134 "This is not my crowd": Ibid., 117.

134 "It is curious...how": Jenkins, 328.

135 "It will be obvious that the greatest care": Terraine, *Western Front,* 38.

137 "Bülow was a solid professional": Bülow's background is Mombauer, 68.

139 Every private in the BEF: The capabilities of British riflemen are in Pound, 46.

139 When the day ended: Mons casualties are in Keegan, *Illustrated History*, 86.

140 It was all nonsense: The origins of the Mons legends are in Hayward, 46.

140 Le Cateau turned into a bigger: Casualty figures are in Stevenson, *Cataclysm*, 47.

140 They had taken some eight thousand: Casualty figures are in Keegan, *Illustrated History*, 90.

140 A French counterattack that marked: Ibid., 86.

141 "the most terrible August": Marshall, 58.

141 "forced to take defensive action": Blond, 19.

141 The BEF marched: Strachan, *First World War*, 225.

142 "capable of taking up the offensive": Isselin, 37.

143 "complete victories": Asprey, *Marne*, 64.

143 He also decided to send: Marshall, 63.

143 Combined with Moltke's earlier adjustments: Details about Moltke's troop dispositions are in Asprey, *German High Command*, 100; and *Marne*, 65, 103; Herwig, 99; and Strachan, *First World War*, 241.

144 That commander, the fat and elderly: Prittwitz's manpower is in Stevenson, *Cataclysm*, 52.

144 Moving against this Eighth Army: The Russian manpower advantage is in Strachan, *First World War*, 316.

146 "I know of no other man": Asprey, *German High Command*, 69.

149 Nine divisions were formed into an arc: The troop dispositions are in Marshall, 61.

150 Rennenkampf's troops had been on the march: Strachan, *First World War*, 320.

151 "I will not allow General Samsonov": Marshall, 61.

151 He had lost seventeen thousand: Asprey, *German High Command*, 58.

152 In the course of the next three days: Prisoner and casualty figures are in ibid., 80.

152 "the fate of Russia will be decided": "Moltke and Conrad," in Kennedy, 224.

163 On Lanrezac's left: The hours spent retreating daily are in Strachan, *First World War*, 259.

164 "If you refuse": Blond, 62.

165 "my confidence in the ability": The French-Kitchener exchange is in Magnus, 293.

166 "I think you had better trust me": Asprey, *Marne*, 81.

166 French's account states: French's memoir of the conversation is in Magnus, 68.

167 Joffre by this point: The number of general officers removed by Joffre is in Asprey, *German High Command*, 103.

168 The number of divisions facing: The increase in the strength of Joffre's left is in Strachan, *First World War*, 243.

168   The French, in contrast to the Germans, were reaping: Information about Joffre's rail system is in ibid., 243.

168   Apparently he was discouraged: the effect of railroad damage on Moltke's thinking is in Mombauer, 243.

168   "A natural reluctance to abandon": Blond, 90.

169   "We must not deceive ourselves": Asprey, *Marne*, 94.

170   "the will to conquer is the first": Tuchman, *Guns of August*, 32.

171   "for the attack only two": Ibid., 34.

173   "Battles are beyond everything": Ibid., 32.

175   But his army was in danger: Austin, 2:232.

176   "a comedian" . . . "no British": Liddell Hart, *Reputations*, 85.

177   "One of our battalions": Austin, 2:272.

178   In pulling back to the Ourcq: The size of the gap is in Keegan, *Illustrated History*, 31.

180   "Attack, whatever happens!": Tuchman, *Guns of August*, 435.

180   "For my part I preserve": Asprey, *Marne*, 120.

180   "What a mess!" Isselin, 156.

181   "voluntary concentric retreat": Keegan, *Illustrated History*, 107.

182   "the decision will be": Ibid., 101.

183   He had sent thirty-one: Numbers of Austrian and Russian divisions are in Stevenson, *Cataclysm*, 58.

183   Conrad had lost more: Austrian losses are in ibid., 58.

183   "shackled to a corpse": Falls, 54.

183   "I have one of my sons": Herwig, 96.

184   "I cannot find words": Blond, 215.

185   "There was not a moment's hesitation": Clark, *Donkeys*, 21.

186   Late in the nineteenth century: Robertson's first opportunity to become an officer is in Bonham-Carter, 29.

188   "I have often made up my mind": Winter, *Haig's Command*, 33.

188   "the role of cavalry on the battlefield": Clark, *Donkeys*, 22.

189   "such a terrible intriguer": Ibid., 32.

189   "as much an enemy": Tuchman, *Guns of August*, 201.

189   "He means well and will succeed": Winter, *Haig's Command*, 25.

191   "After five days and nights": Isselin, 228.

191   It is one measure: French munitions production figures are in Marshall, 73.

191   "Three days ago our division": Austin, 2: 293.

192   British and French headquarters: French's prediction is in ibid.

193   To strengthen his right: Falkenhayn's troop movements are in Herwig, 114.

193   That left Antwerp, which was already: The Antwerp defenses are in Mosier, 116.

194   Members of the cabinet were said: The varying responses of Kitchener and other cabinet members are in Marshall, 74.

195   These movements set the stage: the forces engaged in the Battle of Warsaw are in ibid., 80.

195   "From Czestochowa we advanced": [*Story*], 193.

196   The Ninth Army retreated sixty miles: Ibid., 82.

196   Overall the campaign had cost: German losses are in Stevenson, *Cataclysm*, 64.

199   When Scotland's Second Highland Light Infantry: The unit's losses are in Farrar-Hockley, 180.

201   The enemy turned every house: Schwink, 65.

201   Lombartzyde was captured: A chronology of the times Lombartzyde changed hands is in Gleichen, 30–38.

202   "This . . . is not war!": Marshall, 77.

202   By the time the Flanders front: Casualty totals are in Asprey, *German High Command*, 124.

202   *Burke's Peerage*, the registry: The losses to England's titled families are in Pound, 77.

203   They had lost another ninety thousand: The numbers in this paragraph are from Herwig, 109–10.

203   "Only about half had overcoats": Austin, 2:421.

204   A counterattack organized by Serbian: The Austrian and Serbian troop numbers are in Herwig, 112.

204   Again their losses were outlandish: Casualty totals are in Stevenson, *Cataclysm*, 65.

204   With almost four years of war remaining: Vienna's losses are in Herwig, 120.

204   By March it would add another hundred thousand: This number is in Stevenson, *Cataclysm*, 75.

PART THREE
1915: *A Zero-Sum Game*

The first full calendar year of the Great War was dominated by two epic struggles: the fight for mastery on the Eastern Front, and the Dardanelles-Gallipoli campaign. In connection with the former, particularly helpful works include *The Eastern Front, 1914–1917* by Norman Stone and (a little-known gem that proved to be indispensable) *The Russian Army in World War I* by Ward Rutherford. Trumbell Higgins's *Winston Churchill and the Dardanelles*, Robert Rhodes James's *Gallipoli* of 1965, and Alan Moorehead's more recent *Gallipoli* all provide useful guidance to their subject.

Page

209   On New Year's Day: Gilbert, *First World War*, 124.

209   In the last five months of 1914: The casualty figures in this paragraph are from Stevenson, *Cataclysm*, 75.

210 In Paris the dominating fact: Data on French resources lost to Germany are from Ferguson, 250, and Marshall, 73.

211 "great incalculable": Stone, 122.

211 "a broken instrument": Asprey, *German High Command,* 152.

212 "If we succeed in bringing Russia to terms": Zeman, 83.

216 "a few months hence" and "keep hammering away": Ferguson, 292.

216 "The German armies in France": Magnus, 311.

217 "by extended operations": James, 28.

217 The Champagne operation alone: Keegan, *Illustrated History,* 159.

218 "I have grown into close union": Churchill, *The Unknown War,* 279.

219 "a dubious character": Asprey, *German High Command,* 153.

220 "theater of decision": Churchill, *Unknown War,* 280.

220 "I can only love and hate" and "the fatherland's evil angel": Herwig, 132.

220 Conrad's offensive began: Stone, 113.

221 While one Austrian army captured: Herwig, 137.

221 The Germans began their assault: Asprey, *German High Command,* 162.

222 Counterattacks by eleven Russian divisions: Stone, 112.

222 Russia, at this time, had approximately: The numbers of Russian and Central Powers divisions are in Stone, 112.

223 Ludendorff claimed that a hundred thousand soldiers: Ibid., 118.

223 "we failed strategically": Churchill, *Unknown War,* 299.

223 The winter campaign, by the time it ended: Stone, 122.

226 It was invented in 1884: Ellis, 36.

227 Rudimentary methods of underground tunneling: This matter is the sole subject of Barrie, *War Underground.*

228 A war that introduced so many: Buehr, 5.

233 The Germans calculated: Marshall, 85.

234 "I intensely disliked the thought": Rutherford, 115.

234 "in no circumstances can we": Ibid., 116.

236 "it would have been possible": Liddell Hart, *Real War,* 147.

236 "To attack Turkey . . . would be": Higgins, 104.

236 "The unavoidable losses must be accepted": Magnus, 323.

236 "having entered on the project": Ibid., 325.

239 It was defended by only: Figures on German and British troop strength are in Clark, *Donkeys,* 49.

239 Their way would be cleared: Winter, *Haig's Command,* 37.

240 "led by donkeys": Clark, *Donkeys,* frontispiece.

241 He had lost 11,600 men: Keegan, *Illustrated History,* 174.

241 "I was wounded": Arthur, 76.

243 "I am being most reluctantly driven": Higgins, 164.

243 "must be a deliberate": James, 65.

245   All along the strait: Moorehead, 67.

245   "The first ammunition dump": Arthur, 83.

245   With Przemysl the Russians had captured: Herwig, 139.

253   "Out of approximately 19,500 square miles": Asprey, *German High Command*, 180.

253   "supreme contempt for death": Tschuppik, 121.

256   The offensive began on April 5: French data are in Mosier, 145.

256   When Joffre finally allowed: Ibid., 148.

257   The explosion was followed: Casualty figures are in Groom, 97.

257   This time, however, when the guns: Data on chlorine gas are in Barrie, 62.

258   The advancing Germans were shocked: Groom, 102.

258   "Left at 6:30 P.M. for reserve": Lewis, 83.

260   They had taken forty thousand: Asprey, *German High Command*, 180.

260   "The profitless slaughter pit": Gilbert, *Churchill*, 3:516.

267   "If the English will leave me alone": Marshall, 110.

267   Two hundred transport ships: Ship and troop numbers are in Moorehead, 107.

268   Sanders by now had six Turkish divisions: Keegan, *Illustrated History*, 219.

268   The British, when they came ashore: Moorehead, 140.

269   By then half the Turks: Ibid., 141.

269   "A galling fire rained on us": Palmer and Wallis, 125.

270   Twelve thousand Anzacs got ashore: James, 111.

270   "I don't order you to attack": Moorehead, 131.

270   "dig, dig, dig": James, 130.

270   Three days later nineteen thousand: Ibid., 141.

270   On May 26 twenty-five thousand: Ibid., 150.

271   "came over in two great waves": Arthur, 114.

271   A corporal at Anzac Cove: Palmer and Wallis, 127.

272   By May 8 the British and French: Casualty figures and the quotes by Hamilton and Fisher are in Moorehead, 156.

273   In the years leading: German figures are in Strachan, *First World War*, 995.

274   The French, who thought they had: British, French, and German consumption data are in ibid., 998.

274   When Grand Duke Nicholas told: Stone, 144.

274   Being essentially bankrupt: Ibid., 153.

275   He got three hundred and fifty thousand skilled industrial workers: Stevenson, *Cataclysm*, 189.

275   He thereby started a gender revolution: Ferguson, 268.

276   Historians who have examined: Uses of shell shortages for political advantage are explored at length in Stone, 144–63, and Strachan, *First World War*, 993–1005.

276   "as soon as we were supplied": Strachan, *First World War*, 1001.

278   Conrad, however, remained desperately short: Churchill, *Unknown War*, 308.

278   In four hours fifteen hundred: details of this bombardment are in Falls, 122; Gilbert, *First World War*, 154; and Rutherford, 121.

279   Worse, the Russians' five and a half: Austro-Hungarian, German, and Russian troop and division totals are in Stone, 130.

279   They advanced eight miles: Ibid., 139.

279   "finish the war in three months": Marshall, 123.

279   After only forty-six minutes: Clark, *Donkeys*, 106.

279   Only eight percent of the British shells: Douglas Porch, "Artois 1915," in Cowley, 76.

280   On that first day: Asprey, *German High Command*, 179.

280   The French had much greater initial success: Porch, "Artois," in Cowley, 76.

280   When the battle came to its end: Evans, *Battles*, 23.

280   If only in numerical terms: Asprey, *German High Command*, 194.

281   "Success will come in the final analysis": Gilbert, *First World War*, 173.

282   "a real danger . . . a very great national disaster": Higgins, 196.

282   "It is repugnant to me": Woodward, 48.

284   "We relieved our fourth": Lewis, 112.

285   Its armies, in disorderly retreat: Casualty figures are in Herwig, 144, and Rutherford, 133.

287   "Poor Nikolasha, while telling me this": Massie, *Nicholas and Alexandra*, 313.

288   "They are in despair": Palmer and Wallis, 107.

291   It is estimated that: Death totals for Armenians in 1915 are in Balakian, 179.

291   In the years after the war: U.S. high commissioner Mark Bristol is quoted in ibid., 367.

296   Hamilton sent a telegram: Hamilton's troop request is in James, 307.

296   His August casualties totaled forty-five thousand: Casualty figures for Suvla and Gallipoli are in James, 297 and 301, and Marshall, 118.

297   In late 1914, claiming: Numbers of Polish Jews displaced in 1914 and 1915 are in Rutherford, 152.

297   Four million head of cattle: Ibid.

297   Not long after taking Warsaw: Data on what was captured at Novo Georgievsk are in Gilbert, *First World War*, 180, and Rutherford, 153.

297   By now the Germans: Prisoner of war totals are in Stone, 165.

298   "even though, by doing so, we suffer": Stevenson, *Cataclysm*, 129.

298   "duty to the country which God": Massie, *Nicholas and Alexandra*, 320.

298   "God be praised . . . The Emperor releases me": Rutherford, 155.

298   "You are about to write a glorious page": Ibid., 156.

299   "Perhaps a scapegoat is needed": Ibid., 156.

300   The capture of Vilna had come: Asprey, *German High Command*, 190.

300   "On the whole Hindenburg no longer bothers" and "Hindenburg himself is becoming": Ibid., 204.

300   "Now are you convinced" and "On the contrary!": Ibid., 188.

300   In the Second Battle of Champagne: Troop numbers are in ibid., 197, and artillery totals are in Keegan, *Illustrated History,* 185.

300   The Third Battle of Artois: The number of divisions at Artois and Loos are in Liddell Hart, *Real War,* 188.

301   "it will cost us dearly": Ibid., 187.

301   His early gloom: BEF data are in ibid., 190.

301   A corporal in the Sherwood: Arthur, 104.

302   His men meanwhile were huddled: Liddell Horta, 101.

303   When the British tried to resume: Casualty figures are in Clark, *Donkeys,* 173.

303   "nauseated by the sight": Winter, *Haig's Command,* 41.

303   "Coming back over the ground": Arthur, 421.

303   In the end the casualties: Casualty numbers for Second Champagne, Third Artois, and Loos are in Evans, *Battles,* 25.

304   "If there had been even one division": Liddell Hart, *Real War,* 195.

304   Haig's own position was far from unassailable: Haig's duplicity is examined in detail in Winter, *Haig's Command,* 38–41.

305   His explanation was stark: Rutherford, 168.

305   "I remember things scattered": Arthur, 116.

306   Serbia lost some two hundred thousand troops: James, 348.

307   "I'm twenty-one years old": Palmer and Wallis, 141.

PART FOUR

1916: *Bleeding to Death*

An enormous literature on the great battles of 1916 has grown up over nine decades. In approaching the Battle of Verdun, the author found two works to be particularly helpful as overall guides: *The Price of Glory: Verdun 1916* by Alistair Horne, and *The Road to Verdun* by Ian Ousby. A volume requiring special acknowledgment in connection with the Battle of the Somme is *The First Day on the Somme* by Martin Middlebrook. Both battles are dealt with helpfully in *Attrition: The Great War on the Western Front, 1916,* by Robin Neillands, and the year's diplomatic background is illuminated by *Divide and Conquer: German Efforts to Conclude a Separate Peace, 1914–1918,* by L. L. Farrar, Jr. In connection with 1916 as well as other years, Stone's *The Eastern Front* and Herwig's *The First World War: Germany and Austria* are rich in information about the war in the east.

Page

311   More than twelve hundred guns: The size of the German bombardment at the start of the Battle of Verdun is, like so many aspects of the Great War, a question to which there appears to be no conclusive answer. Stevenson, on page 132 of *Cataclysm,* says the Germans had 1,220 guns. Divergent numbers in other recent histories are 1,300 (Clayton, 100), "about 1,200...over half of them heavy caliber" (Ousby, 63), "1,521 heavy guns" (Herwig, 183), and "850 heavy guns" (Gilbert, *First World War*, 231).

311   All through the morning: Asprey, *German High Command*, 222.

311   "Thousands of projectiles": Austin, 4:54.

312   Nine divisions came forward: Stevenson, *Cataclysm*, 132.

313   In the Gorlice-Tarnow campaign: Casualty figures and the Falkenhayn quote are in Herwig, 179.

313   Three hundred and thirty-five thousand: Ousby, 7.

313   This had brought to 2 million: Mosier, 18, puts French casualties by the end of 1915 at 2,478,000 with 941,000 dead or missing. Neillands gives comparable totals of 1,932,051 and 1,001,271 respectively.

313   Some two hundred thousand British were dead: Neillands, 36.

313   Italy's entry into the war: Isonzo casualty figures are in Banks, 201.

313   By the start of 1916 the British: Mosier, 34, gives a total of 987,000.

314   The Germans had generally been far more careful: The success of the Germans in keeping their casualties below Entente levels is examined and discussed at length in several parts of Mosier and Ferguson.

314   They also understood, however: The German and Entente division totals are in Herwig, 178. Clayton, 196, says the Entente had ninety-five French, thirty-eight British, and six Belgian divisions versus 117 German.

315   Forty French divisions: The number of divisions that Joffre originally planned for the Somme offensive is in Clayton, 96.

315   "the Russian armies have not been completely": Neillands, 60.

316   "She is staking everything on a war": Ibid.

316   Since then, however, his pessimism: The assurances of the German naval leaders are in Asprey, *German High Command*, 219.

316   "There can be no justification": Ibid.

316   "We should ruthlessly employ every weapon": Neillands, 66.

316   "cannot intervene decisively": Herwig, 181.

317   "France has arrived almost at the end": Goodspeed, 176.

317   His thoughts were focused: An exceptionally illuminating explanation of Falkenhayn's Verdun strategy and the thinking behind it is in Farrar, *Divide and Conquer*, 49–56.

317   "the forces of France will bleed": Ousby, 52.

319   "Should our front line be overrun": Ibid., 74.

319   "In the morning, Council of Ministers": Mosier, 188.

319   "I consider that nothing justifies": Ibid., 189.

320   "I cannot permit soldiers under": Ousby, 75.

320   On the east bank of the Meuse: Manpower data are in ibid., 76.

320   Though he had more than nine hundred: Ibid. Horne, *Price*, 55, says the French had only 270 artillery pieces at Verdun at the start of the battle; this total differs greatly from other sources.

321   No fewer than five new railway lines: Marshall, 170.

321   In a seven-week period between late December: Stevenson, *Cataclysm,* 132.

321   In the sky above all this was: details of the German air umbrella are in Clayton, 100, and Mosier, 208.

322   "an offensive in the direction of Verdun": Asprey, *German High Command,* 221.

323   When night fell, nothing was left: Driant's surviving force on the night of February 21 is in ibid., 221.

326   By the outbreak of the war: Clayton, 99.

326   Ultimately 80 percent of its artillery: Neillands, 73.

326   The behavior of the Prussians seemed: Conflicts between German authorities and residents of Alsace-Lorraine are described in Alan Kramer, *"Wackes at War: Alsace-Lorraine and the Failure of German Mobilization, 1914–18"* in Horne, *State,* 110–20.

330   During the first day's bombardment: Keegan, *Illustrated History,* 257.

330   Casualties on the German side were as light: Numbers are in Mosier, 213–14.

331   They advanced three and a half miles: Falls, 189.

331   "It wouldn't take anything": Ousby, 100.

333   Those men, however, numbered only sixty: Ibid., 108.

334   Four hundred and fifty thousand shells: Herwig, 190.

336   Pétain's staff could find only seven hundred: Data about truck traffic are in Keegan, *Illustrated History,* 262; Clayton, 106; and Ousby, 146.

336   In time three-fourths of the entire French army: Ousby, 128.

337   Between February 24 and March 6: Asprey, *German High Command,* 190.

338   "not to defeat but to annihilate France": Ibid., 184.

339   By December British doctors: Shephard, 21.

339   Their German counterparts would record: Ibid., 98.

339   But the number of men unable: Ibid., 38.

342   "a singularly ill-chosen term": Ibid., 31.

342   Further confirmation came: Ibid., 75.

343   This is an area in which data: British and German totals are in Stevenson, *Cataclysm,* 170.

343   Sixteen thousand cases were reported: Shephard, 41.

343   Fifteen percent of all the British: Ibid., 144.

343   In 1922, four years after: Ibid., 158.

344   Pétain, anticipating a German advance: French west bank troop deployments are in Neillands, 175.

346   In the north, in the sector: German and Russian troop strength in the three main sectors of the Eastern Front is in Stone, 227.

347   They began Verdun-style: Information about shells expended, and the five-to-one troop margin, is in Rutherford, 188.

348   Twelve thousand unwounded Russians: Gilbert, *First World War,* 237.

348   "One must have lived through": [Story], 10:2881.

349   And the losses were mounting: Ibid.

349   "a vigorous and powerful offensive": Mosier, 218.

349   "Verdun was the mill on the Meuse": Neillands, 197.

350   "Tell me...when was the war over?" Gilbert, *First World War,* 257.

351   "I shall sleep in peace": Rutherford, 193.

353   In the two fights at Lake Naroch: Stone, 231, says Russian casualties totaled one hundred thousand. Rutherford, 191, says the total was between one hundred ten and one hundred twenty thousand.

354   "a useless and expensive fad": Neillands, 82.

354   "good for sport but not for war": Ibid.

354   Though both France and Germany: Details about prewar aircraft development and numbers of planes acquired by the Great Powers up to 1914 are in Herrmann, 140–42 and 201–06.

355   "We literally thought of": Marshall, 316.

355   Even so, the Eindeckers: Michael Spick, "The Fokker Menace," in Cowley, 261.

356   "steam tractors with small": Gilbert, *Churchill,* 3:535.

357   It was a mother indeed: The specifications of the first tank are in Cooper, 26.

358   "These were the happiest days of my life": Jamie H. Cockfield, "Brusilov's Immortal Days," in Cowley, 227.

358   By the end of April: Mosier, 108.

358   To that purpose he assembled: Horne, *Price,* 170.

359   The Germans captured Côte 304: Neillands, 211.

359   Whatever the cause: Ousby, 275.

359   He and Falkenhayn were encouraged: Horne, *Price,* 229.

360   "if Main Headquarters order it": Ibid.

360   "Dago dogs": Herwig, 204.

361   Six of the divisions committed to the Trentino: Conrad's removal of six prime divisions from Galicia is in Herwig, 205.

361   Their cumulative result: Austria-Hungary's 1915 casualty figures are in ibid., 204.

362   When the Austrians finally attacked: Initial Austrian and Italian troop strength is in ibid., 206.

362   By the end of May: Numbers of soldiers and guns captured by the Austrians are in Stone, 246.

362   "Even the wounded refuse": Austin, 4:224.

363   In the five days preceding: Bombardment details are in Horne, *Price,* 236.

363   The failure had been so complete: French casualty figures are in Ousby, 267.

363   "You did your duty": Ibid.

363   He was reluctant in spite of: Cockfield, "Brusilov's Immortal Days," in Cowley, 225.

363   "the French Army could cease": Horne, *Price,* 293.

366   The Austro-Hungarian Fourth Army: Casualty figures are in Herwig, 213.

366   It was the same almost everywhere: Prisoner-of-war totals are in ibid., 209.

366   Before the end of the first week: Stone, 254.

366   "the crisis would probably have developed": in Rutherford, 204.

368   "This town today is a veritable maelstrom": [Story], 9:2668.

369   "not the monkey our caricaturists": Horne, *Price,* 264.

369   The last of Falkenhayn's reserves: Data on the force attacking Fort Souville are in ibid., 284.

370   "Our heads are buzzing": Lewis, 209.

370   Joffre's view of the situation: Horne, *Price,* 289.

373   From 1885 to 1914 not one Jew: This history, and the associated data, are in Christhard Hoffmann, "Between Integration and Rejection: The Jewish Community in Germany, 1914–1918," in Horne, *State,* 96–104.

374   "the curse of my country": MacDonogh, 439.

375   "A war after the war stands before us": Horne, *State,* 100.

377   Seven thousand miles of telephone lines: Johnson, 60.

377   Ten squadrons of aircraft: Middlebrook, 66.

377   Haig had eighteen divisions on the Somme: Falls, 198. Different historians give divergent numbers of British, French, and German divisions at the start of the Battle of the Somme, perhaps because of the frequency with which divisions were being shifted from place to place during the multiple crises of mid-1916.

378   He had fifteen hundred pieces of artillery: Middlebrook, 68.

378   Between them the British and French: Artillery totals are in Herwig, 199.

378   "You will be able to go over the top": Middlebrook, 78.

378   The French had one corps: Johnson, 57. Here again different writers give different numbers in describing the French forces on the Somme. For example, Johnson says the French had two divisions in reserve in addition to those on the front line, while Herwig, 199, says they had six.

379   Below had only seven divisions: Mosier, 233, and Herwig, 199, give this number, while Falls, 198, says the total is six.

380   By the time the troops went over the top: Shell numbers are variously in Cowley, 321; Herwig, 199; and Johnson, 61.

380   "Shall I live till morning": Macdonald, *Somme,* 49.

381   Nearly seven thousand of them died: Tim Travers, "July 1, 1916: The Reason Why," in Cowley, 327.

381   "The ground where I stood": Johnson, 67.

385   "The attack must be made in waves": Travers, "July 1," in Cowley, 329.

386   "Fancy advancing against heavy fire": Ibid., 321.

386   "We were surprised to see them walking": Mosier, 235.

386   "The infantry rushed forward":Lewis, 215.

386   the Thirty-fourth Division: Middlebrook, 248.

386   At Beaumont-Hamel: Casualty figures are in Travers, "July 1," in Cowley, 326.

387   The number of casualties: Numbers are in Middlebrook, 244. The following casualty figures from Waterloo and Normandy are in Middlebrook, 246.

387   German losses for the first day: Travers, "July 1," in Cowley, 327.

387   It had torn open the defenses: Ibid., 324.

387   "speed, dash and tactical brains": Falls, 200.

387   "no serious advance is to be made": Johnson, 63.

391   "Tsar of the land of Russia": Massie, *Nicholas and Alexandra*, 374.

392   "Whatever pride I had": Cowley, 354.

394   On July 2 Haig: Middlebrook, 225.

394   Evert had a thousand guns: Artillery numbers and the Russian and German casualties that follow are in Stone, 260–61.

395   In four days he took: Ibid., 261.

395   On July 10, in a final lunge: Horne, *Price*, 296.

395   "Those who went outside were killed": Austin, 4:247.

395   His plan this time was to send: The size of Rawlinson's attack force and the German defense is in Liddell Hart, *Real War*, 240.

396   "Although most Australian soldiers were optimists": Ibid., 244.

396   He struck at the Turkish Third Army: Falls, 248.

397   Three months earlier the Germans: Numbers of German divisions in the East and West in May and August 1916 are in Mosier, 252.

397   The Austrians were on the defensive: Casualties for the Sixth Battle of the Isonzo are in Banks, 201.

397   To complete the picture, French General Sarrail: Mosier, 255.

398   On August 27 Romania issued a declaration: The size of the Romanian force invading Transylvania and of the Austrian forces defending is in Stone, 274, and Liddell Hart, *Real War*, 264.

398   The addition to the Entente of Romania: The size of Romania's military forces is in Mosier, 254. Stone, 264, says Romania had six hundred and twenty thousand soldiers.

399   It was untrained and disorganized: The Romanian makeup order is in Stone, 265.

399   Whole armies were being hurried: Train numbers are in ibid.

400   The commander of this fortress: The Turtukai episode is in ibid., 276.

400   "this will be our Verdun": Ibid., 277.

400   Only sixty of the new machines: Liddell Hart, *Real War*, 245.

400   "My poor 'land battleships'": Gilbert, *Churchill*, 3:810.

401   The Guards, a hundred and thirty-four thousand of the best: Details of the Kovel offensive are in Rutherford, 213–15, and Stone, 261–63.

401   It burned out of control: the Tavannes Tunnel disaster and its casualties are in Horne, *Price*, 305–7.

401   Again Haig used his tanks: Neillands, 285.

402   On October 19, satisfied: French artillery preparations are in Horne, *Price*, 308 and 314.

403   Nor was Haig quite finished: Isonzo casualties for 1917 are in Banks, 201.

403   On November 13 the British detonated: The number of British divisions is in Liddell Hart, *Real War,* 247; the number of German prisoners is in Falls, 206.

403   Casualties on the Somme totaled: The facts about British, French, and German casualties are explored at length in Mosier, 241.

404   "The first principle in position warfare": Cowley, 350.

404   Since their government's declaration: Casualties of the Romanian campaign are in Mosier, 260.

404   Over the next year and a half: Amounts of materials extracted from Romania in 1917 and 1918 are in Stone, 265.

405   Meaningless as it was: The story of the bleating French troops is in Horne, *Price,* 318.

PART FIVE

1917: *Things Fall Apart*

Three books with suggestively divergent subtitles—*Ludendorff, Genius of World War I* by D. J. Goodspeed, *Ludendorff, The Tragedy of a Military Mind* by Karl Tschuppik, and *Tormented Warrior: Ludendorff and the Supreme Command* by Roger Parkinson—become increasingly valuable as the war enters 1917 and their subject emerges as something very like a military dictator of Germany. In dealing with the Western Front in 1917, the author found much of value in *The Defeat of Imperial Germany, 1917–1918* by Rod Paschall and *In Flanders Fields: The 1917 Campaign* by Leon Wolff. *Paths of Glory: The French Army 1914–1918* by Anthony Clayton is a helpful guide to its subject at this stage in the war, *The War to End All Wars* by Edward M. Coffman and *Illusion of Victory* by Thomas Fleming to America's entry into the conflict.

Page

409   "victory over the military powers": Gleichen, 117.

409   "put our trust rather": Gilbert, *First World War,* 303.

410   "economic, military and political": Parkinson, 114.

411   "a likeness between the two": Gleichen, 278.

411   "the reorganization of Europe": Woodward, 237.

411   "Our position was extremely difficult": Ludendorff's words are in Tschuppik, 66.

412   Almost the only general inconvenience: Data on lost coal production are in Ferguson, 250.

412   Problems had arisen, inevitably: Heyman, 199.

413   The situation was worse in Britain: Ibid., 197.

413   A decline in nutrition manifested itself: Tuberculosis data are in Ferguson, 277.

413   Russia was increasingly unsuccessful: Refugee numbers are in Stevenson, *Cataclysm*, 234.

413   The infant mortality rate doubled: Hours spent by women working and standing in line, and the numbers that follow on strikes in January and February 1917, are in ibid., 249.

414   As early as October 1914 ten thousand horses: Herwig, 274.

414   Nine million animals perished: Ferguson, 276.

414   Before the war Germany had been importing: Herwig, 272.

414   As this input dwindled: The decline in German grain production is in Ferguson, 251.

414   Food prices rose 130 percent: The Berlin percentage increase is in Herwig, 286, the Vienna increase in Herwig, 276.

414   Even for industrial workers: German wage increase percentage is in Stevenson, *Cataclysm*, 305.

415   The chief physician at one of Berlin's: The doctor's estimate is in a report by an American journalist excerpted in Thoumin, 274.

415   The average daily adult intake: Asprey, *German High Command*, 314.

415   Deaths from lung disease increased: Ferguson, 277.

415   "One of the most terrible": Wolff, 22.

415   A German who was a schoolboy: Arthur, 200.

415   Even the expected bounty: Percentage increase from Romanian exports is in Wolff, 251.

416   "I will give Your Majesty my word": Gilbert, *First World War*, 306.

416   "the only means of carrying the war": Parkinson, 123.

417   "I declared myself incompetent": Tschuppik, 87.

417   Holtzendorff estimated that the submarines: Stevenson, *Cataclysm*, 213.

417   Even in January, while still allowing: Gilbert, *First World War*, 306.

417   The lifting of restrictions became effective: Tons of merchant shipping sunk February through June 1917 are in Stevenson, *Cataclysm*, 264.

419   Under prodding from Erich Ludendorff: Details of the Auxiliary Service Law are in Herwig, 263; the increases in gunpowder and weapons production are in the same work, 260.

420   "not fighting, but famine": Ferguson, 9.

420   "socially and economically futile": Angell, 72.

420   "As long as there are goods and labor": Keynes's words are in Strachan, *First World War*, 817.

421   By 1917 the German government's expenditures: British, French, and German government spending as a percent of net national product is in Stevenson, *Cataclysm*, 179. The percentages of Britain's and the German federal government's budgets covered by tax revenues are in *Cataclysm*, 180.

422   Eventually it borrowed £568 million: Strachan, *First World War,* 956.

422   This accomplished nothing: The percentage of Russia's prewar tax revenue provided by the vodka monopoly is in Stevenson, *Cataclysm,* 181.

422   Germany issued war bonds twice: Ibid., 182.

423   By April 1917 the British were spending: Strachan, *First World War,* 975.

423   It is estimated that the war ultimately cost: numbers are in Stevenson, *Cataclysm,* 183.

424   Though the extent of the withdrawal: The dimensions of the withdrawal are in Johnson, 96, and Parkinson, 126.

425   Three hundred and seventy thousand men: The numbers of men and trains used to construct the new line are in Herwig, 250.

425   "The decision to retreat": Parkinson, 127.

425   The army itself was restructured: The number of newly created divisions is in Mosier, 269.

426   The Hindenburg Line would be twenty-five miles: The number of miles the front was shortened is in Johnson, 96; the number of divisions and batteries freed is in Herwig, 250.

426   At the start of 1917 the Germans had: The number of men is in Liddell Hart, *Real War,* 298; the number of divisions in Herwig, 247.

427   It was to be yet another massive offensive: The number of divisions planned for the Entente attack is in Paschall, 29.

427   This trench was almost ten feet deep: a physical description of the new defenses is in Herwig, 251.

428   They also agreed that they would wait until May: British generals (most importantly Haig and Robertson) would later claim that the plan approved at Chantilly called for the attack to begin in February 1917, which would have made the German withdrawal to the Hindenburg Line impossible and allowed the subsequent Flanders attack to take place before the onset of seasonal rains. This version of events has been accepted by historians ever since. Denis Winter, however, using documents not available until half a century after the war, offers persuasive evidence that the Chantilly conference ended in agreement to launch the joint offensives in May. The examination of this issue is in Winter, *Haig's Command,* 70–84.

428   "legacy of inevitable disaster": Lloyd George's words are in Wolff, 37.

430   "cur": Ibid., 40.

430   The death blow would be delivered: The number of divisions planned for Nivelle's Mass of Maneuver is in Johnson, 92.

430   The only difficulty was the question of timing: The difficulties over when to start the Nivelle offensive, and the final compromise, are in Winter, *Haig's Command,* 76.

431   "The French put forward a terrible scheme": Ibid., 83. Haig's letters are important as one part of Winter's demonstration that Lloyd George did not propose the appointment of a French supreme commander as Haig would later claim.

431   "This is a plan for the army": Clayton, 125.

433 "However the world pretends": Haste, 81.

434 London alone had sixteen daily papers: Ibid., 29.

434 Germany had four thousand: Welch, 29.

434 "a war in which we risk everything": Ferguson, 216.

434 "an anti-German frame of mind": Haste, 5.

435 "of such a nature as is calculated": Ibid., 83.

436 "the new philosophy of Germany": Ibid.

436 The unprecedented sum of £240,000: Ibid., 40.

436 "Good propaganda must keep well ahead": Welch, 195.

438 When Joffre fell and was succeeded: The number of Russian divisions to be involved in the 1917 joint offensive is in Rutherford, 235.

440 General Sir Henry Wilson, a senior member: Massie, *Nicholas and Alexandra,* 388.

440 "by terrorist methods if there is": Taylor, *Dynasties,* 257.

440 "Lovy, be firm": Radzinsky, 174.

442 "I order that the disorders": Nicholas's message is in Massie, *Nicholas and Alexandra,* 400.

442 He showed concern only for his wife: The size of the rebelling garrison is in Radzinsky, 180.

443 "whoever now dreams of peace": Taylor, *Dynasties,* 290.

443 "God in heaven, it's like": Palmer and Wallis, 290.

444 He set a quota of two hundred thousand transfers: The size of the quota, and the number of Belgians deported, are in Asprey, *German High Command,* 317.

445 The originators of the plan: The numbers are in Goodspeed, 197.

446 "All this is really no business of mine": Parkinson, 119.

447 WE INTEND TO BEGIN UNRESTRICTED: Tuchman, *Zimmermann Telegram,* 146.

449 "I am finished with politics": Ibid., 149.

450 The House approved a War Resolution: The vote totals are in Ferrell, 2.

451 "Age-old subduers and punishers": Taylor, *Dynasties,* 262.

451 "love of freedom": Tolstoy, 46.

457 The Germans meanwhile, aware: The number of German divisions is in Paschall, 46.

458 The offensive began on April 9: The number of attacking armies is in Clayton, 128.

458 Their dimensions are apparent in the details: The trainloads of rock are in Paschall, 33, and the number of guns and heavy mortars in Paschall, 38.

458 "We moved forward, but the conditions": Arthur, 206.

459 Entente casualties had been fairly light: The average of four thousand per day is in Johnson, 119.

460 Haig had grounds for claiming success: Prisoner and captured gun numbers are in Wolff, 62.

460   By the time it all ended: Casualty figures are in Evans, *Battles*, 35.

460   "I had looked forward": Parkinson, 129.

461   Nivelle had three armies that among them: Division and troop totals are in Herwig, 327.

461   But twenty-seven divisions were held back: The size of the Mass of Maneuver is in Paschall, 33, and the number of German line and reserve divisions in Paschall, 46.

461   One hundred and twenty-eight: Tank numbers are in Clayton, 129.

461   "A snow squall swept our position": Lewis, 286.

463   "Peace! Down with war!": Herwig, 329.

463   "What, you try to make me responsible": Marshall, 211.

463   By the time the offensive: French and German casualty figures are in Herwig, 329.

466   Within six weeks of its start: The words of the unnamed officer are in Clayton, 130.

467   Approximately five hundred of them: Various writers give exact but widely differing numbers. For example, Clayton, 134, says 499 were condemned and twenty-seven were executed; the corresponding numbers in Herwig are "between 500 and 600" and "perhaps as many as 75."

467   "not forgetting the fact": Clayton, 134.

468   The U-boat campaign was at its height: Tons of shipping sunk in April 1917 is in Herwig, 318.

469   "the most important and wide-ranging": Hynes, 11.

470   "a purification, a liberation": Tuchman, *Guns of August,* 311.

470   "this abyss of blood and darkness": Ibid., 3.

470   "If I should die, think only this of me": Silkin, 81.

471   "Let him who thinks that War is a glorious": Hynes, 112.

471   "the patriotic sentiment was so revolting": Ibid., 36.

471   "tremendous experiences": Winter, *Sites of Memory,* 160.

472   "Bent double, like old beggars under sacks": Ward, 21.

474   By late spring: Rutherford, 248.

475   "I have co-signed the protocol": Feldman, 34.

475   "in complete accord": Farrar, *Divide and Conquer,* 80.

476   "Congress will not permit": Coffman, 8.

476   Until a gradual buildup was authorized: 1916 troop totals and the provisions of the National Defense Act are in Eisenhower, 22 and 23.

476   The nation's distrust of military establishments: Ibid., 22.

477   Thirty-two training camps: Coffman, 30.

478   "It is evident that a force": Ibid., 127.

479   "in Flanders the weather broke early": Wolff, 81.

479   "You can fight in mountains": Ibid., 79.

480   General Sir Herbert Plumer: Ypres as the scene of one-fourth of BEF casualties 1914–16 is in ibid., 83.

480 One of the mines was discovered: Paschall, 62, says five hundred tons of explosives were placed under the ridge. Herwig, 330, and Liddell Hart, *Real War*, 331, both put the total at six hundred tons. Johnson, 126, gives a total of "nearly four hundred tons," and Wolff, 90, gives a most improbable figure of one million tons.

481 "When I heard the first deep rumble": Lewis, 292.

481 "We got out of the tank": Arthur, 217.

481 Plumer's infantry took possession: The number of Germans killed is estimated at ten thousand to twenty thousand in various sources. Mosier, 281, offers evidence that the total is not likely to have been as high as ten thousand.

482 "I shall name it to no one": Bonham-Carter, 5.

483 "overrule the military and naval authorities": Wolff, 118.

484 "Yesterday we saw heavy fighting": Palmer and Wallis, 292.

484 Though not nearly as large as what: The numbers are in Rutherford, 250.

485 Russian casualties had been almost trivial: Ibid., 254.

486 "The Reichstag strives": Feldman, 42.

488 "The danger of speaking out": Bruun, 121.

489 "So long as victory is possible": Jackson, Clemenceau, 120.

490 "One would have to be deliberately blind": Bruun, 116.

492 "Home policy?": Jackson, Clemenceau, 126.

493 Along fifteen miles of front: Evans, *Battles*, 40, and Wolff, 124, give 3,091 as the number of British guns. The comparison with the Somme is in Johnson, 139.

493 During the two weeks ending: The number of shells fired is in Evans, *Battles*, 40.

493 These shells had a total weight: The weight of the shells fired is in Paschall, 66, and the German casualties are in Paschall, 69.

493 "futile, fantastic and dangerous": These words are actually General Sir Henry Wilson's, in a diary entry presumably paraphrasing what Foch had said to him, in Wolff, 79.

494 Fourteen German divisions: Paschall, 69.

494 "My mind is quite at rest": Wolff, 135.

495 "ask me for *anything* but time": Ibid., 122.

496 "wholehearted support": Ibid., 124.

496 The offensive went off: Division numbers are in Groom, 185.

496 They penetrated nearly two miles: Paschall, 67.

497 Of the fifty-two tanks: Ibid., 67.

497 Haig, not aware that twenty-three: Haig's words are in ibid., 69.

497 But after two more days, with the rain: casualty figures are in ibid., 71.

498 "Inside it was only about five foot": Arthur, 229.

498 There were twenty-three such divisions: Paschall, 71.

498 "Blood and mud": Wolff, 165.

499   At the end of his preparations: One gun for five years of front is in Paschall, 73.

499   Plumer's artillery would fire three and a half million: Wolff, 171.

500   Though it did not come cheaply: Casualty numbers are in Paschall, 73.

500   In the process they killed: Casualty figures are in ibid., 75.

501   "The fighting on the Western Front": Parkinson, 137.

502   "The slope," said an Australian: Wolff, 239.

503   The Italian commander in chief: Casualty figures for Tenth and Eleventh Isonzo are in Banks, 201.

504   The Germans and Austrians, whose thirty-three divisions: The numbers of divisions are in Mosier, 292.

504   Italian casualties totaled three hundred and twenty thousand: The numbers are in Evans, *Battles*, 43.

505   The price had been almost exactly: Paschall, 77.

505   The British, Canadians, Anzacs, and French: Casualty figures for Third Ypres are in Evans, *Battles*, 41, and Paschall, 79.

505   On November 20, near Cambrai: The numbers are in Mosier, 290.

506   Of the 216 new Mark IV tanks: The numbers are in Paschall, 126.

506   The British found themselves: The number of divisions is in Mosier, 298.

507   On the Western Front, the year had taken: Numbers of soldiers killed on the Western Front in 1917 are in ibid., 284 and 299.

PART SIX
1918: *Last Throw of the Dice*

Several books previously credited for their usefulness in earlier parts of this book were also particularly helpful in connection with 1918. Among them are L. L. Farrar's *Arrogance and Anxiety* (illuminating in connection with diplomacy), Holger H. Herwig's *The First World War*, and the fourth volume of Gerhard Ritter's *The Sword and the Sceptre*. The author is also indebted to Corelli Barnett for the final section of *The Swordbearers*, to Roger Parkinson's *Tormented Warrior: Ludendorff and the Supreme Command*, to Alan Palmer's *The Gardeners of Salonika*, and to the following works dealing with 1918 exclusively: *The Battle for Europe 1918* by H. Essame; *Crisis 1918* by Joseph Gies; *1918: The Last Act* by Barrie Pitt; and *To Win a War* by John Terraine.

Page

512   The latter's casualties totaled: King, *Generals and Politicians*, 194.

512   General Pétain, the commander in chief: Clayton, 161.

512   It had fought off more than: Details of the French operations are in Terraine, *To Win a War*, 11.

512   With its larger population: British casualty figures are in King, *Generals and Politicians*, 194.

512   Some four hundred and fifty thousand fit and ready: Essame, 32.

513   British production of ammunition: Tonnage of shells and total British shipments to the continent are in ibid., 23.

513   Lloyd George had regarded Haig: Haig's pledge to the Conservatives not to replace Haig and Robertson is in Pitt, 33.

514   In 1917 Vienna conscripted: Herwig, 353.

514   That left it with no remaining: Ibid., 366.

514   Monthly rifle production was plummeting: Weapons production figures are in Herwig, 357.

514   It still had forty-four divisions: Numbers of divisions are in Herwig, 366.

517   "The Attack in Trench Warfare": Pitt, 44.

517   The goal was to create: Herwig, 395.

517   "pined for the offensive": Barnett, 280.

518   He declared that no offensive: Ludendorff's conditions are in Pitt, 42.

519   "reconciliation chancellor": Gies, 17.

519   Kühlmann, who pursued negotiations: Kühlmann's diplomatic objectives, and the divide-and-conquer objectives of German diplomacy generally, are the subject of Farrar, *Divide and Conquer.*

520   Seven hundred and fifty thousand: Herwig, 362.

520   The intensity of the discontent: Pitt, 39.

520   "the speedy conclusion of peace": Parkinson, 159.

521   Forty thousand strikers: Pitt, 39.

521   Between thirty-five hundred and six thousand: Herwig, 381.

521   "including an unequivocal declaration": Gies, 66.

522   "We make a hole": Asprey, *German High Command,* 367.

523   "fractured": Kohut, 47.

523   "one of those strange figures": Steinberg, 26.

525   "He would really be so pretty": Kohut, 47.

525   "a one-armed man should": Ibid., 43.

526   "The emperor is like a balloon": Ponsonby, 363.

527   "Nothing will change": Kohut, 214.

529   Fifty-seven British, Indian: Essame, 26.

529   While withholding infantry: The numbers of laborers sent, and the numbers put to work, are in ibid., 15.

530   He had ninety-nine divisions: Pitt, 62.

532   This was less than half: The number of corps to be shifted is in Gies, 75.

532   Haig, who had been obliged: King, *Generals and Politicians,* 47.

533   "I am sick of this d—d life": Terraine, *To Win a War,* 37.

533   Gough, whose Fifth Army: Miles and division totals are in Gies, 76.

536   Ludendorff was aggressive as always: The positions of Ludendorff and Kaiser Wilhelm at this meeting are in Herwig, 383.

536   "no war, no peace": Terraine, *To Win a War*, 21.

536   The Russians were now so helpless: German gains are in Stevenson, *Cataclysm*, 321.

536   Russia relinquished: Details of what Russia signed over at Brest-Litovsk are in Pitt, 45; Terraine, *To Win a War*, 22; and Asprey, *German High Command*, 360.

536   The delegation's chief refused: Goodspeed, 239.

537   At a time when they needed: The number of occupation troops that Germany required is in Ritter, 4:116.

537   Ukraine alone soaked up: Herwig, 386.

537   In the west he was assembling: The number of German troops is in Stevenson, *Cataclysm*, 325; the number of divisions in *Cataclysm*, 326.

539   "no one was anxious to detain him": Bruce, 60.

542   In spite of the immensity: The numbers are in Pitt, 45.

542   Between February 15 and March 20: Herwig, 392.

542   Ludendorff had had 150 divisions: Terraine, *To Win a War*, 22.

544   The results were at the front: The number of divisions is in Herwig, 395.

544   "The objective of the first day": Barnett, 291.

545   Among them the three had almost: Division numbers are in Gies, 76.

546   Byng and Gough had fully a third: The deployment of troops is described in Barnett, 291.

546   "I was only afraid": Pitt, 57.

546   "There are strong indications": Barnett, 300.

546   The German attack force: Division and gun numbers are in Palmer, *Victory 1918*, 167.

546   By March 20 the fourteen divisions: Barnett, 293.

547   It included twenty-one divisions: Ibid., 293.

547   Along a line of more than: Pitt, 71.

547   "It was flamethrowers forward": Gies, 82.

548   To the extent that Gough's army could maintain the semblance: The extension of Gough's line is in Barnett, 307.

549   He sent six of his best divisions: Ibid., 311.

549   By the time this message arrived: Ibid., 312.

550   Eight of the divisions with which Gough: Ibid.

550   Haig asked Pétain for an additional: Haig's request, and the number of divisions sent by Pétain, are in Pitt, 95.

551   An enormous new cannon: Asprey, *German High Command*, 383.

551   "If an English delegation came": Herwig, 406.

551   Early on the morning of Sunday, March 24: Pitt, 93.

552   They ended Sunday's march: Parkinson, 157.

552   Haig understood the importance: Terraine, *To Win a War*, 46.

553 "save Amiens or everything's lost": Gies, 99.

554 "In my opinion . . . it was essential": Barnett, 326.

554 By March 26 the offensive was essentially: Pitt, 100.

554 "Today the advance of our infantry": Terraine, *To Win a War*, 48.

555 The Germans had captured twelve: Pitt, 109.

555 They had inflicted more than: Casualty and prisoner numbers are in Asprey, *German High Command*, 391.

556 "The Allies are very weak": Freidel, 85.

557 "there were reports of occasional": Parkinson, 174.

557 "I talked earnestly, urgently": Hocheimer's treatment of Ludendorff is described in ibid., 176.

558 "the war has spared me": Ibid., 157.

559 He was promoted to colonel: In their biographies Goodspeed, Parkinson, and Tschuppik all explore the meaning of Ludendorff's transfer away from the high command headquarters.

561 Ninety German divisions had been thrown: Herwig, 408.

561 The scale of the losses: Essame, 48.

561 Britain was not notably better off: Pitt, 111.

562 "that it could not take Amiens": Ritter, 4:233.

562 "all political questions were": Barnett, 278.

563 "all powers necessary": Pitt, 111.

563 Georgette . . . opened modestly: Details are in ibid., 120.

563 "Every position must be held": Essame, 48.

565 "The conquest was a nightmare": Gies, 118.

566 "a gigantic struggle beginning": Parkinson, 149.

566 On April 24 nine divisions: Keegan, *Illustrated History*, 374.

566 "Gray-blue figures out of the half-buried": Gies, 121.

567 General von Kuhl, chief of staff: Kuhl's view of the consequences of the failure are in Pitt, 130.

567 His casualties since the start of Michael: Numbers are in Barnett, 331.

567 "The absence of our old": Terraine, *To Win a War*, 53.

568 Though French and British losses: Numbers of arriving American troops are in Palmer, *Victory 1918*, 177.

571 An office was established in Paris: The 12-million–ton figure is in Freidel, 73.

571 The Americans would install: Eisenhower, 57.

571 It broadened conscription, drafting: Gies, 124.

572 The French had 103 divisions: Ibid., 143.

573 "J'ai dit": Essame, 58.

573 More than twenty divisions were assembled: The numbers and the words in quotes are in Essame, 59.

576 "Hundreds upon hundreds of wounded": Heyman, 122.

576 "We are supposed to care": Ibid., 124.

576 More than fifteen thousand women: Ibid., 120–21.

577 "For the first time I was going": Ibid., 122.

578 In France 85 percent of women: The data are in Steven C. Hause, "More Minerva than Mars: the French Women's Rights Campaign and the First World War," in Higonnet et al., 106.

578 In Germany more than five million: Ferguson, 267–68.

579 Female employment in French munitions factories: Hause, "More Minerva," in Higonnet et al., 104.

579 In Germany alone more than one and a half million: The data are in Karin Hausen: "The German Nation's Obligation to the Heroes' Widows of World War I," in Higonnet et al., 128.

583 Hutier's troops advanced: German gains are in Essame, 72.

583 By the end one hundred and eighty-six thousand German: Terraine, *To Win a War*, 150.

584 "had probably the greatest capacity": Serle, 377.

584 Eleven days after Hamel—one wonders how: Pitt, 179.

585 Twenty-three divisions, four of them American: Gies, 229.

585 "Machine guns raved everywhere": Terraine, *To Win a War*, 78.

586 In March the Germans had had three hundred thousand: The numbers in this paragraph are in Essame, 101.

586 "Midnight," a German soldier: Gies, 248.

588 The Germans lost more than six hundred and fifty officers: Ibid., 131.

589 The troops were in such a sorry state: Parkinson, 164.

590 On the second day they were driven back: Herwig, 370.

590 But Britain and France alike: Drafting of fifty-year-old Britons is in Paschall, 165.

590 Workers at ammunition factories: British labor troubles are in Terraine, *To Win a War*, 126.

591 Their casualties in August alone: German casualties, and the following sentence on the declining number of divisions, are in Herwig, 424.

593 "dangerous and likely to lead": Palmer, *Gardeners of Salonika*, 49.

593 It included one hundred and sixty thousand men: Troop numbers are in ibid.; the January 1916 total on 52, the May total on 63.

593 Rumors circulated to the effect that: Ibid., 95.

594 The Entente had more than half a million: Pope and Wheal, 418.

594 "the gardeners of Salonika": Palmer, *Gardeners of Salonika*, 71.

595 "I bear you no ill-will": Ibid., 183.

595 "I expect from you savage vigor": Ibid., 186.

595 Two hundred and fifty thousand Greek: Pope and Wheal, 418.

596 "The man could escape even now": Parkinson, 175.

597 On the British part of the front: Essame, 149.

597 "for nearly three years the last": Swettenham, *33.*

597 "the pride and wonder of the British": Ibid., 171.

598 "He had a tremendous command of profanity": Dancocks, 18.

598 They never once failed: Ibid., 174.

598 He wanted not only to capture: Essame, 155.

598 Fifteen thousand German troops: Ibid., 158.

598 But Pershing had eight hundred and twenty thousand men: Ibid., 157.

599 "We could not answer every single cry": Terraine, *To Win a War*, 131.

599 "as a result of the collapse": Palmer, *Gardeners of Salonika*, 228.

599 Ludendorff, all options exhausted: Ritter, 4:339.

599 "clung to that news like a drowning": Ibid., 4:340.

599 The war had rarely been bloodier: Terraine, *To Win a War*, 224.

600 "I have seen prisoners coming": Ibid., 129.

600 The French now had nearly 40 percent: Clayton, 163.

600 When the Canadians finally broke through: Terraine, *To Win a War*, 166.

600 Almost ninety percent of the men: Terraine, *To Win a War*, 163.

601 "revolution from above": Ritter, 4:342.

602 "broken and suddenly aged man": Terraine, *To Win a War*, 158.

602 "the one prominent royalist liberal": Palmer, *Victory 1918*, 234.

605 General Wilhelm Gröner: Gröner's report on missing troops is in Herwig, 442.

606 The blood continued to flow: French casualties are in Clayton, 162.

606 "If the Government of the United States": Parkinson, 181.

606 "Our enemies merely pay": Ritter, 4:365.

606 In Italy an Allied force of fifty-six divisions: division numbers are in Herwig, 436.

607 "soldier's honor": Ritter, 4:366.

607 "I am a plain ordinary citizen": Ibid., 367.

607 "You will stay": Ibid., 368.

607 "looking forward to proposals": Ibid., 369.

608 He received thirty-nine replies: Herwig, 445.

608 These included German withdrawal: The terms of the Treaty of Versailles are examined clearly and in detail in Sharp, 102–29.

608 "No no no!": Essame, 205.

609 Something on the order of 9.5 million men: Overall casualty figures are in Ferguson, 295.

610 "Central Europe is aflame": Sharp, 130.

Bibliography

Allen, Kenneth. *Big Guns of the Twentieth Century and Their Part in Great Battles.* Hove, England: Firefly, 1976.

Angell, Norman. *The Great Illusion.* London: William Heinemann, 1910.

Arthur, Max. *Forgotten Voices of the Great War.* Guilford, Conn.: Lyons Press, 2002.

Asprey, Robert B. *The German High Command at War.* New York: William Morrow, 1991.

———. *The First Battle of the Marne.* Philadelphia and New York: J. B. Lippincott, 1962.

Audoin-Rouzeau, Stephane, and Annette Becker. *1914–1918: Understanding the Great War.* New York: Hill and Wang, 2000.

Austin, Walter F., ed. *Source Records of the Great War.* [no city given]: National Alumni, 1923.

Bach, H. I. *The German Jew.* London: Oxford University Press, 1984.

Balakian, Peter. *The Burning Tigris.* New York: HarperCollins, 2003.

Banks, Arthur. *A Military Atlas of the First World War.* Barnsley, South Yorkshire: Leo Cooper, 1997.

Barber, Noel. *The Sultans.* News York: Simon and Schuster, 1973.

Barnett, Corelli. *The Swordbearers.* New York: Signet, 1965.

Barrie, Alexander. *War Underground: The Tunnelers of the Great War.* Staplehurst, Kent: Spellmount, 2000.

Berenson, Edward. *The Trial of Madame Caillaux.* Berkeley: University of California Press, 1992.

Berghahn, V. R. *Germany and the Approach of War in 1914.* New York: St. Martin's Press, 1973.

Bismarck, Otto von. *The Kaiser vs. Bismarck: Suppressed Letters.* New York: Harper & Brothers, 1920.

Blond, Georges. *The Marne.* Harrisburg, Pa.: Stackpole Books, 1965.

Bonham-Carter, Victor. *The Strategy of Victory, 1914–1918.* New York: Holt, Rinehart and Winston, 1964.

Brandenburg, Erich. *From Bismarck to the World War.* London: Oxford University Press, 1933.

Bruce, Anthony. *The Last Crusade: The Palestine Campaign in the First World War.* London: John Murray, 2002.

Bruun, Geoffrey. *Clemenceau.* Cambridge, Mass.: Harvard University Press, 1943.

Buchan, John. *The Battle of the Somme.* New York: George H. Doran, 1917.

Buehr, Walter. *Firearms.* New York: Thomas Y. Crowell, 1967.

Caffrey, Kate. *Farewell, Leicester Square: The Old Contemptibles 12 August-20 November 1914.* London: Andrew Deutsch, 1980.

Cameron, James. *1914.* New York: Rinehart & Co., 1959.

Carew, Tim. *The Vanished Army: The British Expeditionary Force 1914–1915.* London: William Kimber, 1914.

Carsten, F. L. *The Origins of Prussia.* Oxford: Clarendon, 1954.

Cassels, Lavender. *The Archduke and the Assassin.* New York: Stein & Day, 1985.

Chickering, Roger. *Imperial Germany and the Great War, 1914–1918.* Cambridge: Cambridge University Press, 1999.

Churchill, Winston S. *The World Crisis, 1916–1918.* New York: Charles Scribner's Sons, 1927.

———. *The Unknown War, The Eastern Front.* New York: Scribner's, 1931.

Clark, Alan. *The Donkeys.* London: Pimlico, 1998.

Clark, Christopher M. *Kaiser Wilhelm II.* London: Longman, 2000.

Clayton, Anthony. *Paths of Glory: The French Army 1914–1918.* London: Cassell, 2003.

Coetzee, Frans, and Marilyn Shevin-Coetzee, eds. *Authority, Identity and Social History of the Great War.* Providence, R.I.: Berghahn, 1995.

Coffman, Edward M. *The War to End All Wars.* New York: Oxford University Press, 1968.

Cooper, Bryan. *The Ironclads of Cambrai.* London: Cassell, 1967.

Cowles, Virginia. *The Kaiser.* New York: Harper & Row, 1963.

Cowley, Robert, ed. *The Great War.* New York: Random House, 2003.

Craig, Gordon A. *The Politics of the Prussian Army 1640–1945.* New York: Oxford University Press, 1972.

Crankshaw, Edward. *The Shadow of the Winter Palace.* New York: Viking, 1976.

Cruttwell, C.R.M.F. *A History of the Great War 1914–1918.* 2nd ed. Chicago: Academy Chicago Publishers, 1991.

Dallas, Gregor. *At the Heart of a Tiger: Clemenceau and His World 1841–1929.* New York: Carroll & Graf, 1993.

———. *1918: War and Peace.* London: Pimlico, 2002.

Dancocks, Daniel G. *Sir Arthur Currie.* Toronto: Methuen, 1985.

Darrow, Margaret H. *French Women and the First World War.* Oxford: Berg, 2000.

David, Daniel. *The 1914 Campaign.* New York: Military Press, 1987.

Dedijer, Vladimir. *The Road to Sarajevo.* New York: Simon & Schuster, 1966.

De Groot, Gerard J. *Blighty: British Society in the Era of the Great War.* London: Longman, 1996.

Dupuy, Trevor N., Curt Johnson, and David L. Bongard. *The Harper Encyclopedia of Military Biography.* Edison, N.J.: Castle Books, 1995.

Edwards, Cecil. *John Monash.* Melbourne: State Electricity Commission of Victoria, 1970.

Eisenhower, John S. D. *Yanks.* New York: Free Press, 2001.

Eksteins, Modris. *Rites of Spring: The Great War and the Birth of the Modern Age.* New York: Doubleday, 1990.

Ellis, John. *The Social History of the Machine Gun.* Baltimore: Johns Hopkins University Press, 1975.

Enock, Arthur Guy. *This War Business.* London: Bodley Head, 1951.

Essame, H. *The Battle for Europe 1918.* New York: Charles Scribner's Sons, 1972.

Eubank, Keith. *The Summit Conferences 1919–1960.* Norman: University of Oklahoma Press, 1966.

Evans, Martin Marix. *Battles of World War I.* Marlborough, Wiltshire: Airlife, 2004.

Evans, R. J. W., and Pogge von Strandmann, eds. *The Coming of the First World War.* Oxford: Clarendon Press, 1988.

Eversley, Lord. *The Turkish Empire from 1288 to 1914.* New York: Howard Fertig, 1969.

Falls, Cyril. *The Great War, 1914–1918.* New York: Putnam's, 1959.

Farrar, L. L., Jr. *Arrogance and Anxiety: The Ambivalence of German Power, 1848–1914.* Iowa City: University of Iowa Press, 1981.

———. *Divide and Conquer: German Efforts to Conclude a Separate Peace, 1914–1918.* Boulder, Colo.: East European Quarterly, 1978.

Farrar-Hockley, Anthony. *Death of an Army.* Ware, Hertfordshire: Wordsworth Editions, 1998.

Farwell, Byron. *Over There: The United States in the Great War.* New York: W. W. Norton, 1999.

Fay, Sidney Bradshaw. *After Sarajevo: The Origins of the World War.* New York: Free Press, 1966.

Feldman, Gerald D., ed. *German Imperialism, 1914–1918.* New York: John Wiley & Sons, 1972.

Ferguson, Niall. *The Pity of War.* New York: Basic Books, 1999.

Ferrell, Robert H. *Woodrow Wilson and World War I.* New York: Harper & Row, 1985.

Ferro, Marc. *The Great War 1914–1918.* Boston: Routledge & Kegan Paul, 1982.

Fleming, Thomas. *The Illusion of Victory: America in World War I.* New York: Basic Books, 2003.

Ford, Roger. *The Grim Reaper: Machine Guns and Machine Gunners.* New York: Sarpedon, 1996.

Freidel, Frank. *Over There: The American Experience in World War I.* Short Hills, N.J.: Burford Books, 1964.

French, John Denton Pinkstone. *1914.* Boston: Houghton Mifflin, 1919.

Friedrich, Otto. *Blood and Iron.* New York: HarperCollins, 1995.

Fromkin, David. *Europe's Last Summer.* New York: Alfred A. Knopf, 2004.

Fussell, Paul. *The Great War and Modern Memory.* New York: Oxford University Press, 1975.

Geiss, Imanuel, ed. *July 1914: The Outbreak of the First World War: Selected Documents.* New York: Charles Scribner's Sons, 1967.

Gies, Joseph. *Crisis 1918.* New York: W. W. Norton, 1974.

Gilbert, Martin. *The First World War.* New York: Henry Holt, 1994.

———. *Winston S. Churchill.* Boston: Houghton Mifflin, 1971.

Gleichen, Lord Edward, ed. *Chronology of the Great War, 1914–1918.* London: Greenhill Books, 2000.

Goemans, H. E. *War and Punishment: The Causes of War Termination and the First World War.* Princeton, N.J.: Princeton University Press, 2000.

Goerlitz, Walter. *History of the German General Staff, 1657–1945.* New York: Frederick A. Praeger, 1960.

Goldberg, Harvey. *The Life of Jean Jaurès.* Madison: University of Wisconsin Press, 1968.

Goodspeed, D. J. *Ludendorff: Genius of World War I.* Boston: Houghton Mifflin, 1966.

Griffiths, Richard. *Pétain.* Garden City, N.Y.: Doubleday, 1972.

Groom, Winston. *A Storm in Flanders: The Ypres Salient, 1914–1918.* New York: Atlantic Monthly Press, 2002.

Guinn, Paul. *British Strategy and Politics, 1914–1918.* Oxford: Oxford University Press, 1965.

Haber, L. F. *The Poisonous Cloud: Chemical Warfare in the First World War.* Oxford: Clarendon, 1986.

Hall, Richard C. *The Balkan Wars 1912–1913.* London: Routledge, 2002.

Halperin, John. *Eminent Georgians.* New York: St. Martin's, 1995.

Haste, Cate. *Keep the Home Fires Burning: Propaganda in the First World War.* London: Penguin, 1977.

Hayward, James. *Myths and Legends of the First World War.* Stroud, Gloucestershire: Sutton, 2002.

Hazelhurst, Cameron. *Politicians at War, July 1914 to May 1915.* New York: Alfred A. Knopf, 1971.

Herrmann, David G. *The Arming of Europe and the Making of the First World War.* Princeton, N.J.: Princeton University Press, 1996.

Herwig, Holger H. *The First World War: Germany and Austria 1914–1918.* London: Arnold, 1997.

Heyman, Neil M. *Daily Life During World War I.* Westport, Conn: Greenwood Press, 2002.

Higgins, Trumbull. *Winston Churchill and the Dardanelles.* New York: Macmillan, 1963.

Higonnet, Margaret Randolph et al., eds. *Behind the Lines: Gender and the Two World Wars.* New Haven, Conn.: Yale University Press, 1987.

Hoehling, A. A. *The Great War at Sea.* New York: Barnes & Noble, 1965.

Horne, Alistair. *The Price of Glory: Verdun 1916.* New York: St. Martin's, 1963.

Horne, John, ed. *State, Society and Mobilization in Europe During the First World War.* Cambridge: Cambridge University Press, 1997.

Hough, Richard. *The Great War at Sea.* Oxford: Oxford University Press, 1983.

Hynes, Samuel. *A War Imagined: The First World War and English Culture.* New York: Atheneum, 1991.

Isselin, Henri. *The Battle of the Marne.* Garden City, N.J.: Doubleday, 1966.

Jackson, J. Hampden. *Clemenceau and the Third Republic.* New York: Collier, 1962.

———. *Jean Jaurès.* London: George Allen & Unwin, 1943.

James, Robert Rhodes. *Gallipoli.* New York: Macmillan, 1965.

Jannen, Jr., William. *The Lions of July.* Novato, Calif.: Presidio Press, 1997.

Jenkins, Roy. *Asquith.* New York: Chilmark, 1964.

Johnson, J. H. *Stalemate! Great Trench Warfare Battles.* London: Rigel, 2004.

Joll, James. *The Origins of the First World War.* London: Longman, 1984.

Keegan, John. *An Illustrated History of the First World War.* New York: Alfred A. Knopf, 2001.

———. *A History of Warfare.* New York: Vintage Books, 1994.

Keiger, John F. V. *France and the Origins of the First World War.* New York: St. Martin's, 1983.

Kennedy, Paul M., ed. *The War Plans of the Great Powers, 1880–1914.* Boston: Allen & Unwin, 1979.

Kent, George O. *Bismarck and His Times.* Carbondale, Ill.: Southern Illinois Press, 1978.

King, Jere Clemens, ed. The First World War: Selected Documents. London: Macmillan, 1972.

———. *Generals and Politicians.* Berkeley: University of California Press, 1951.

Kitchen, Martin. *The German Offensives of 1918.* Stroud, Gloucestershire: Tempus, 2001.

Kluck, Alexander von. *The March on Paris and the Battle of the Marne.* London: Edward Arnold, 1920.

Kohut, Thomas A. *Wilhelm II and the Germans.* New York: Oxford University Press, 1991.

Kraft, Barbara S. *The Peace Ship.* New York: Macmillan, 1978.

Lacouture, Jean. *De Gaulle: The Rebel 1890–1944.* New York: W. W. Norton, 1990.

Lafore, Laurence. *The Long Fuse.* Prospect Heights, Ill.: Waveland Press, 1971.

Lauret, René. *France and Germany.* Chicago: Henry Regnery, 1964.

Lederer, Ivo J., ed. *The Versailles Settlement.* Boston: D. C. Heath, 1960.

Leed, Eric J. *No Man's Land: Combat and Identity in World War I.* Cambridge: Cambridge University Press, 1979.

Leese, Peter. *Shell Shock: Traumatic Neurosis and the British Soldiers of the First World War.* New York: Palgrave Macmillan, 2002.

Lewis, Jon E., ed. *The Mammoth Book of Eyewitness World War I.* New York: Carroll & Graf, 2003.

Liddell Hart, B. H. *The Real War 1914–1918.* Boston: Little, Brown, 1930.

———. *Reputations. Ten Years After.* Boston: Little Brown, 1928.

Lincoln, W. Bruce. *In War's Dark Shadow.* New York: Oxford University Press, 1994.

Listowel, Judith. *A Hapsburg Tragedy.* New York: Dorset, 1986.

Lomas, David. *First Ypres 1914.* New York: St. Martin's, 1963.

Ludendorff, Erich von. *Ludendorff's Own Story.* New York: Harper & Brothers, 1919.

Lutz, Ralph Haswell, ed. *The Causes of the German Collapse in 1918.* Archon Books, 1969.

Macdonald, Lyn. *1914.* New York: Atheneum, 1988.

———. *1915, The Death of Innocence.* New York: Henry Holt, 1993.

———. *Somme.* London: Michael Joseph, 1983.

MacDonogh, Giles. *The Last Kaiser.* New York: St. Martin's, 2000.

Macdougall, A. K., ed. *War Letters of General Monash.* Sydney: Duffy & Snellgrove, 2002.

Macmillian, Margaret. *Paris 1919.* New York: Random House, 2002.

Magnus, Philip. *Kitchener.* New York: Dutton, 1968.

Mann, Golo. *The History of Germany Since 1789.* New York: Frederick A. Praeger, 1968.

Marshall, S. L. A. *The American Heritage History of World War I.* [no city given]: American Heritage, 1964.

Marwick, Arthur, ed. *Total War and Social Change.* New York: St. Martin's, 1988.

Massie, Robert K. *Castles of Steel.* New York: Random House, 2003.

———. *Nicholas and Alexandra.* New York: Atheneum, 1967.

May, Arthur. *The Passing of the Hapsburg Monarchy 1914–1918.* Philadelphia: University of Pennsylvania Press, 1966.

Mayeur, Jean-Marie, and Madeleine Reberieux. *The Third Republic from Its Origins to the Great War, 1871–1914.* Cambridge: Cambridge University Press, 1987.

McDougall, Walter A. *France's Rhineland Diplomacy, 1914–1924.* Princeton, N.J.: Princeton University Press, 1978.

Middlebrook, Martin. *The First Day on the Somme.* New York: W. W. Norton, 1972.

Miller, Steven E., Sean M. Lynn-Jones, and Stephan Van Evera, eds. *Military Strategy and the Origins of the First World War.* Princeton, N.J.: Princeton University Press, 1991.

Millis, Walter. *Road to War, America 1914–1917.* Boston: Houghton Mifflin, 1935.

Mitchell, David. *Monstrous Regiment: The Story of the Women of the First World War.* New York: Macmillan, 1965.

Mombauer, Annika. *Helmuth von Moltke and the Origins of the First World War.* Cambridge: Cambridge University Press, 2001.

Mommsen, Wolfgang J. *Imperial Germany, 1867–1918.* London: Arnold, 1990.

Moore, William. *The Thin Yellow Line.* Ware, Hertfordshire: Wordsworth, 1974.

Moorehead, Alan. *Gallipoli.* New York: Perennial Classics, 2002.

Mosier, John. *The Myth of the Great War.* New York: HarperCollins, 2001.

Muncy, Lysbeth Walker. *The Junker in the Prussian Administration under Wilhelm II, 1888–1914.* New York: Howard Fertig, 1970.

Neiberg, Michael S. *Fighting the Great War.* Cambridge: Harvard University Press, 2005.

Neillands, Robin. *Attrition: The Great War on the Western Front, 1916.* London: Robson, 2001.

Nomikos, Eugenia, and Robert C. North. *International Crisis: The Outbreak of World War I.* Montreal: McGill–Queen's University Press, 1976.

Ousby, Ian. *The Road to Verdun.* New York: Anchor, 2003.

Palmer, Alan. *The Gardeners of Salonika.* New York: Simon & Schuster, 1965.

———. *Twilight of the Hapsburgs.* New York: Grove, 1995.

———. *Victory 1918.* New York: Atlantic Monthly Press, 1998.

Palmer, Svetlana, and Sarah Wallis. *Intimate Voices from the First World War.* New York: Perennial, 2005.

Panichas, George A., ed. *Promise of Greatness: The War of 1914–1918.* New York: John Day, 1968.

Parkinson, Roger. *Tormented Warrior: Ludendorff and the Supreme Command.* New York: Stein & Day, 1979.

Paschall, Rod. *The Defeat of Imperial Germany, 1917–1918.* Chapel Hill, N.C.: Algonquin Books, 1989.

Passingham, Ian. *All the Kaiser's Men.* Stroud, Gloucestershire: Sutton, 2003.

Pedersen, P. A. *Monash as Military Commander.* Carlton, Victoria: Malbourne University Press, 1985.

Perry, Roland. *Monash: The Outsider Who Won a War.* Sydney: Random House Australia, 2004.

Philpott, William James. *Anglo-French Relations and Strategy on the Western Front, 1914–1918.* New York: St. Martin's, 1996.

Pitt, Barrie. *1918: The Last Act.* New York: Norton, 1963.

Ponsonby, Frederick, ed. *The Letters of Empress Frederick.* London: Macmillan, 1929.

Pontig, Clive. *Thirteen Days: The Road to the First World War.* London: Chatto & Windus, 2002.

Pope, Stephen, and Elizabeth-Anne Wheal. *The Macmillan Dictionary of the First World War.* London: Macmillan, 1997.

Pound, Reginald. *The Lost Generation of 1914.* New York: Coward-McCann, 1964.

Preston, Diana. *Lusitania.* New York: Walker, 2002.

Rachamimov, Alon. *POWs and the Great War: Captivity on the Eastern Front.* Oxford: Berg, 2002.

Radzinsky, Edvard. *The Last Tsar.* New York: Doubleday, 1992,

Read, James Morgan. *Atrocity Propaganda 1914–1919.* New Haven: Yale University Press, 1941.

Remak, Joachim. *Sarajevo.* New York: Criterion Books, 1959.

Renouvin, Pierre. *The Immediate Origins of the War.* New York: Howard Fertig, 1969.

Ripley, Tim. *Bayonet Battle: Bayonet Warfare in the Twentieth Century.* London: Sidgwick & Jackson, 1999.

Ritter, Gerhard. *The Sword and the Scepter; The Problem of Militarism in Germany.* Coral Gables, Fla.: University of Miami Press, 1970.

Röhl, John. *1914—Delusion or Design?* New York: St. Martin's, 1973.

Rutherford, Ward. *The Russian Army in World War I.* London: Gordon Cremonesi, 1975.

Schmitt, Bernadotte E., and Harold C. Vedeler. *The World in the Crucible, 1914–1919.* New York: Harper & Row, 1984.

Schulz, Gerhard. *Revolutions and Peace Treaties 1917–1920.* London: Methuen, 1967.

Schwink, Otto. *Ypres 1914* [An Official Account Published by Order of the German General Staff]. London: Constable & Co., 1919.

Serle, Geoffrey. *John Monash.* Melbourne: Melbourne University Press, 1982.

Seton-Watson, R. W. *Sarajevo.* London: Hutchinson, 1926.

Sharp, Alan. *The Versailles Settlement.* New York: St. Martin's, 1991.

Sheehan, James J., ed. *Imperial Germany.* New York: New Viewpoints, 1976.

Shephard, Ben. *A War of Nerves.* Cambridge, Mass.: Harvard, 2001.

Silkin, Jon. *The Penguin Book of First World War Poetry.* London: Penguin, 1996.

Simpson, Andy. *Hot Blood and Cold Steel.* London: Tom Donovan, 1993.

Sked, Alan. *The Decline and Fall of the Hapsburg Empire 1815–1918.* London: Longman, 2001.

Smithers, A. J. *Sir John Monash.* London: Leo Cooper, 1973.

Spears, Major General Sir Edward. *Liaison 1914.* New York: Stein and Day, 1968.

Steinberg, Jonathan. *Yesterday's Deterrent: Tirpitz and the Birth of the German Battle Fleet.* London: Ashgate, 1965.

Stevenson, D. *French War Aims Against Germany.* Oxford: Clarendon Press, 1982.

Stevenson, David. *Cataclysm: The First World War as Political Tragedy.* New York: Basic Books, 2004.

———. *The First World War and International Politics.* New York: Oxford University Press, 1988.

Stone, Norman. *The Eastern Front, 1914–1917.* New York: Scribner's, 1975.

The Story of the Great War. New York: P. F. Collier & Son, 1916.

Strachan, Hew. *The First World War,* vol. 1, *To Arms.* Oxford: Oxford University Press, 2001.

———, ed. *World War I, A History.* Oxford: Oxford University Press, 1998.

Sweetman, John. *Tannenberg 1914.* London: Cassell, 2002.

Swettenham, John. *To Seize the Victory: The Canadian Corps in World War I.* Toronto: Ryerson, 1965.

Taylor, A.J.P. *The First World War: An Illustrated History.* New York: Penguin, 1972.

Taylor, Edmond. *The Fall of the Dynasties.* Garden City, N.Y.: Doubleday & Co., 1963.

Terraine, John. *The Western Front 1914–1918.* Philadelphia and New York: Lippincott, 1965.

———. *To Win a War.* Garden City, N.Y.: Doubleday & Co., 1981.

Thoumin, General Richard. *The First World War.* New York: G. P. Putnam's Sons, 1964.

Tolstoy, Leo. *The Cossacks.* Boston: Houghton Mifflin, 1932.

Tschuppik, Karl. *Ludendorff: The Tragedy of a Military Mind.* Boston: Houghton Mifflin, 1932.

Tuchman, Barbara W. *The Guns of August.* New York: Macmillan, 1962.

———. *The Proud Tower.* New York: Macmillan, 1966.

———. *The Zimmermann Telegram.* New York: Macmillan, 1966.

Tucker, Spencer C. *The Great War 1914–18.* Bloomington: Indiana University Press, 1998.

———. *The European Powers in the First World War, An Encyclopedia.* New York: Garland, 1996.

Vincent, C. Paul. *The Politics of Hunger: The Allied Blockade of Germany 1915–1919.* Athens: Ohio University Press, 1985.

Ward, Candace, ed. *World War One British Poets.* Mineola, N.Y.: Dover Publications, 1997.

Weintraub, Stanley. *Silent Night.* New York: Free Press, 2000.

Welch, David. *Germany: Propaganda and Total War, 1914–1918.* New Brunswick, N.J.: Rutgers University Press, 2000.

Williamson, Samuel R., Jr. "The Origins of the War." In *World War I: A History,* edited by Hew Strachan. New York: Oxford University Press, 1998.

Winter, Denis. *Haig's Command.* New York: Viking, 1991.

Winter, Jay. *Sites of Memory, Sites of Mourning.* Cambridge: Cambridge University Press, 1995.

Winter, Jay, Geoffrey Park, and Mary R. Habeck, eds. *The Great War and the Twentieth Century.* New Haven, Conn.: Yale University Press, 2000.

Winter, Jay, and Jean-Louis Robert. *Capital Cities at War: Paris, London, Berlin 1914–1919.* Cambridge: Cambridge University Press, 1997.

Wolff, Leon. *In Flanders Fields: The 1917 Campaign.* New York: Viking, 1958.

Woodward, Sir Llewellyn. *Great Britain and the War of 1914–1918.* London: Methuen, 1967.

Zeman, Z.A.B. *The Gentlemen Negotiators: A Diplomatic History of the First World War.* New York: Macmillan, 1971.

Zuckerman, Larry. *The Rape of Belgium.* New York: New York University Press, 2004.

Index

THE WAR IN THE EAST

NORWAY

Stockholm

SWEDEN

DENMARK

North Sea

Baltic Sea

Copenhagen

Königsberg

Danzig

EAST
PRUSS

Tannenberg

Elbe

Berlin

Vistula

Amsterdam

NETHERLANDS

Oder

Posen

Lodz

POLAN

Brussels

BELGIUM

GERMANY

SILESIA

Luxembourg

Vistula

Krakow

WEST

FRANCE

Rhine

Danube

BAVARIA

Munich

Danube

Vienna

AUSTRIA-HUNGARY

Budapest

SWITZERLAND

TRENTINO

Trento

Piave

Caporetto

Milan

Vittorio
Veneto

Isonzo

Trieste

Danube

Po

Venice

ITALY

BOSNIA-
HERZEGOVINA

Sarajevo

Belgra

Rome

Adriatic Sea

MONTENEGRO

Mediterranean Sea

ALBA